SCRIBE

of

HEAVEN

The New Century Edition
of the Works of Emanuel Swedenborg

SCRIBE

of

HEAVEN

Swedenborg's Life, Work, and Impact

Essays contributed by George F. Dole, David B. Eller,
Olle Hjern, Robert H. Kirven, Jean-François Mayer,
Frank S. Rose, Jonathan S. Rose, Alice B. Skinner,
Richard Smoley, and Jane Williams-Hogan

Edited by Jonathan S. Rose, Stuart Shotwell,
and Mary Lou Bertucci

SWEDENBORG FOUNDATION
West Chester, Pennsylvania

Printed in the United States of America

ISBN (paperback) 0-87785-474-2

Excerpt from "The Tuft of Flowers" from *The Poetry of Robert Frost,* edited by Edward Connery Lathem. Copyright 1962 by Robert Frost, Copyright 1934, © 1969 by Henry Holt and Company. Reprinted by permission of Henry Holt and Company, LLC.
Permission to translate "Emanuel Swedenborg" by Jorge Luis Borges courtesy of the estate of Jorge Luis Borges.
Façade for Tomb of Sarah Morley courtesy of The Conway Library, Courtauld Institute of Art, London.
Headpiece illustration from the foreword of *The Garden behind the Moon: A Real Story of the Moon Angel* by Howard Pyle courtesy of the Delaware Art Museum, Wilmington, Delaware.
Jacob's Ladder by William Blake copyright The Trustees of the British Museum.
Photograph of Helen Keller courtesy of the American Foundation for the Blind. Used with permission of the American Foundation for the Blind, Helen Keller Archives.

Library of Congress Cataloging-in-Publication Data

Emanuel Swedenborg.
    Scribe of heaven : Swedenborg's life, work, and impact / essays contributed by George F. Dole . . . [et al.] ; edited by Jonathan S. Rose, Stuart Shotwell, and Mary Lou Bertucci.
    p. cm. — (The new century edition of the works of Emanuel Swedenborg)
    Also published as: Emanuel Swedenborg.
    "A Swedenborg bibliography": p.
    Includes bibliographical references and index.
    ISBN 0-87785-474-2 (pbk. : alk. paper)
    1. Swedenborg, Emanuel, 1688–1772.   I. Dole, George F.   II. Rose, Jonathan, 1956–   .
III. Shotwell, Stuart, 1953–   .   IV. Bertucci, Mary Lou.   V. Title.   VI. Series: Swedenborg, Emanuel, 1688–1772. Works. English. 2000
BX8748.E46 2005b
289'.4'092—dc21
[B]
                                                                00-048255
This book is printed on acid-free paper that meets the American National Standards Institute Z39.48-1992 standard.

Additional editorial assistance by Alicia L. Dole
Cover, diagrams, and map designed by Caroline Kline
Text designed by Joanna V. Hill
Index compiled by Bruce Tracy
Typeset by Alicia L. Dole

A hardcover edition of this book was published simultaneously under the title *Emanuel Swedenborg: Essays for the New Century Edition on His Life, Work, and Impact* (ISBN 0-87785-473-4).

For information contact: Swedenborg Foundation
                                320 North Church Street
                                West Chester, PA 19380 USA

Contents

Organizational Impact

An Alternative Approach to Studying Swedenborg's Impact

Bibliographies and Index

Preface

JONATHAN S. ROSE
AND STUART SHOTWELL

THIS volume is a companion to the New Century Edition of the works of Emanuel Swedenborg.[1] Although the New Century Edition translations have prefaces, introductions, and notes to provide background information and to set the works in the context both of Swedenborg's other writings and of their intellectual milieu, the editorial committee perceived a need for a companion volume that would explore Swedenborg's biography, writings, and influence more intensively. The volume has been divided into parts in accordance with this purpose: biography is treated in the section titled "Swedenborg's Life"; writings in "Theological Works"; and influence in the sections titled "Cultural Impact," "Organizational Impact," and "An Alternative Approach to Studying Swedenborg's Impact."

The first part, "Swedenborg's Life," presents an overview by Richard Smoley of Swedenborg's life and career, showing Swedenborg's constant drive to investigate scientifically the phenomena of this world. Smoley explains the turn Swedenborg's life took toward theological interests and spiritual experiences as an extension of this drive—that is, as stemming from a desire to see the deepest possible reality.

The second part, "Theological Works," contains three essays on the material Swedenborg wrote as the result of his spiritual awakening. Jonathan S. Rose's essay in this section uses a comparison between Swedenborg's theology and the plan of his garden in Stockholm as an explanatory device to survey his theological perspective and some of its many interesting features.

George F. Dole then presents some thoughts on the sequence in which Swedenborg published his theological titles. Dole explains why these volumes are of greatly varying lengths, what pressures seem to have directed and shaped each work in the series, and even why individual titles seem to be aimed at widely different audiences.

---

1. For a list of works in the New Century Edition series, see page 98 below.

Frank S. Rose follows this look at the published theological works with an analysis of the theological material Swedenborg left in unpublished form. Rose makes the observation that although these numerous manuscripts have often been seen as authorial false starts or dead ends, they were in fact critical to the development of the works actually published by Swedenborg.

After thus summarizing Swedenborg's life and work, the volume shifts its focus to studies of his impact. It turns first to examine the great number of individuals, acting outside the organized Swedenborgian groups, who were significantly influenced by Swedenborg's insights, and especially those among them who went on to found or participate in social, philosophical, or religious movements on which the label "Swedenborgian" does not fit well. Such individuals and movements are treated in the third part of the volume, "Cultural Impact."

Olle Hjern begins this section by describing how his homeland of Sweden and the surrounding countries of Scandinavia were affected by Swedenborg's writings. Hjern presents little-known and surprising evidence for the lasting resonance of Swedenborg's works in Swedish Lutheran culture, as well as in Swedish ecumenism and antislavery movements.

Jean-François Mayer then discusses the response to Swedenborg in the rest of continental Europe. From Mayer we learn how Goethe and Schelling took Swedenborg to heart, and thereby made his teachings a part of the Romantic movement. We learn that some see the architects of the French Revolution as moved by Swedenborg, although others deny any such connection. We also discover that Swedenborg's teachings may have served as the basis of the Russian Project of the Holy Alliance; that they definitely had something directly to do with the emancipation of millions of Russian serfs; that they were held in high regard by Mouravieff and the Russian nobility; and that they proved significant in the development of Dostoevsky's thought.

At the close of this section, Robert H. Kirven and David B. Eller deal with the area where Swedenborg's writings had the most visible consequences: the English-speaking world—especially Great Britain and the United States. Kirven and Eller point to the response of Blake, Emerson, Whitman, and others; and to the incorporation of Swedenborgian concepts in several nineteenth-century movements, including Shakerism, utopianism, homeopathy, and vegetarianism.

From this survey of cultural impact, the topic shifts in the fourth part of the volume to what is here called "organizational impact" (in a distinction from "cultural impact" that is admittedly somewhat artificial), meaning the development of institutions that are self-described as "Swedenborgian" or "New Church" in orientation. For although Swedenborg himself took no steps to institutionalize his theological perspective, his writings did lead directly to the founding of a number of churches, publishing houses, and other organizations.

Institutions all over the world could have been included here, but the focus has been restricted to just two regions. The first is, once more, the English-speaking world of Great Britain, the United States, and Canada. Jane Williams-Hogan and David B. Eller survey the institutional responses to Swedenborg's works in these lands—particularly the rather turbulent histories of the four major branches of the Swedenborgian church. In addition, they discuss the colleges, schools, and publishing houses that have arisen there in reaction to Swedenborg's teachings. The second region is Africa, covered in a separate essay by Jane Williams-Hogan. She highlights two stories of Swedenborgian charismatic leaders who built sizable church organizations in that continent.

The fifth part of the volume, "An Alternative Approach to Studying Swedenborg's Impact," proposes, and briefly models, such an approach. Here Alice B. Skinner turns the scholarly microscope around, making a wide-angle telescope to study impact not by citing individuals and tracing the source of their ideas, but by following ideas as they spread among individuals. The essay sketches various responses over time to three powerful Swedenborgian concepts: the reality of the spiritual world; the principle of usefulness; and Swedenborg's unique concepts of learning and knowledge.

The volume ends with a lengthy section of bibliographical material and an index. First, David B. Eller presents a compact list of "must-have" reference works—the best places for any research on Swedenborg to start and the volumes that should be considered for inclusion in any serious study collection devoted to Swedenborg.

Then follows Jonathan S. Rose's annotated bibliography of Swedenborg's works. It begins with an index to virtually all the English titles by which these works have been known and covers both the works published by Swedenborg and those left unpublished by him, as well as treating some documents no longer extant or of disputed authorship. All these works are here assigned convenient descriptive titles, many of which reflect the relationships between published and unpublished material highlighted in Frank S. Rose's essay in the second part of the volume.

The list ends with a chronology of the works, which allows readers to see the ebb and flow of Swedenborg's wide-ranging interests over time.

The volume concludes with a list of all works cited in the essays and an index to the whole.

Scope of the Volume

It must be emphasized that the present volume is far from all-inclusive. Although broad in scope, it necessarily omits much, for the simple reason that the requisite information is not readily obtainable. In the case of what is here termed cultural impact, this lack of resources makes it difficult to establish and characterize Swedenborg's effect on thinkers, artists, and writers who have not explicitly taken up his banner. In the case of those who have joined Swedenborgian organizations and thus have identified themselves as responding to his teachings, the researcher has to cope with the humble and practical consideration that these individuals were often too busy to chronicle their own labors. True, as Jean-François Mayer's essay points out, they have published out of all proportion to their small numbers;[2] but publication is just one aspect of their industry: they have been exceptional entrepreneurs, architects, artists, dreamers, and doers in every walk of life; and they have not always felt it appropriate to record actions taken in accordance with their creed that one must be useful in society.

Two examples may be given of the limitations in coverage that have resulted from this obstacle. First, the map of Swedenborgian worship communities that accompanies the essay by Jane Williams-Hogan and David B. Eller covers only the United States and Canada. Similar research in Great Britain, continental Europe, Australia, and other lands would make an extension of the map possible; but such research simply was not feasible for the editorial committee to undertake. Second, the full story of Swedenborg's influence around the world is much greater than any regional narratives might suggest. Thus the article by Jane

---

2. See pages 193–194 below. The many modern languages—thirty-five and counting—into which Swedenborg's works have been translated attest to this level of production. They are Arabic, Bulgarian, Burmese, Chinese, Czech, Danish, Dutch, English, Esperanto, Finnish, French, German, Greek, Gujarati, Hindi, Hungarian, Icelandic, Italian, Japanese, Korean, Latvian, Norwegian, Pilipino, Polish, Portuguese, Romanian, Russian, Serbo-Croatian, Sotho, Spanish, Swedish, Tamil, Welsh, Yoruba, and Zulu.

Williams-Hogan on Swedenborgian church organizations in Africa is offered as only an example of the many narratives that could be written detailing Swedenborgian influence on church movements in that region, or in Australia, Asia, or many other areas around the world.

The volume as a whole is tendered to the reader, then, as the beginning, not the end, of a path.

That said, it must be added that in many respects the volume also extends beyond the scope of previous works in the field,[3] making several unique contributions to Swedenborgian studies. The biographical treatment and the general introduction are fresh in their approach. The explanations of the purpose of Swedenborg's many works and manuscripts are more thorough-going than their predecessors. The documentation of Swedenborg's influence is the most panoramic attempt to date. The bibliography of Swedenborg's works is the most inclusive and thoroughly cross-referenced yet compiled. In short: Never have Swedenborg's life, work, and impact been documented together in so compact and usable a form.

Acknowledgments

Any work that attempts, as does the present volume, the accurate representation of over a thousand items of bibliography, countless in-text cross-references, and biographical data on hundreds of individuals, to say nothing of historical information, is promising more than the very human abilities of its writers and editors can perfectly accomplish. The authors and the editorial committee take responsibility for any errors that may remain, and will vigilantly correct in future editions any errors pointed out to them.

It is not enough, however, for the editorial committee merely to state its willingness to bear this responsibility. It should further note that the present volume could not have been published without the assistance of numerous libraries, archives, and individuals in the United States and Europe. All cannot be mentioned, but it would be remiss not to name those whose contributions were extraordinary.

---

3. Among the several that could be mentioned, the present volume builds on and augments the two volumes published in celebration of the tricentennial of Swedenborg's birth: Larsen and others 1988, and Brock and others 1988.

The major research institutions, and employees thereof, providing such assistance were the following: Carroll Odhner and Rachel O. Longstaff at the Swedenborg Library in Bryn Athyn, Pennsylvania, along with Erik E. Sandström of the Swedenborgiana Library (a collection within the Swedenborg Library), and Cynthia H. Walker and Martha McDonough of the Swedenborg Library's Archives; Michael Yockey, librarian at the Swedenborgian House of Studies at Pacific School of Religion in Berkeley, California; Maria Asp of the Kungliga Vetenskaps-akademien (the Swedish Royal Academy of Sciences) in Stockholm; the Swedenborg Society in London, England; and the Swedenborg Memorial Library at Urbana University in Urbana, Ohio.

The individuals who also deserve special notice are these: C. Alan Anderson, Derek Antrobus, Christopher Bamford, Martha Bauer, Reuben P. Bell, Maria Berggren, Hugh A. Blackmer, Kate Blackmer, Peter G. Bostock, Kate Bristow, Sarah Buteux, Lynn Clarke, Carolyn Andrews Cole, Dandridge Cole, Stephen D. Cole, James P. Cooper, Will Cooper, Kate Cuggino, Alicia L. Dole, Clark Echols, Carla Friedrich, Anders Hallengren, Willard L. D. Heinrichs, Martie Johnson, Inge Jonsson, Kristin King, Caroline Kline, Thomas L. Kline, Carol S. Lawson, John L. Odhner, John Perry, Luken Potts, Edward Rogers, Donald L. Rose, Frank S. Rose, Patrick Rose, Norman Ryder, Susan V. Simpson, Wickham Skinner, Lee Woofenden, William Ross Woofenden, Susan N. Wright, and Sewall Foster Young. Even this considerable list will leave some unnoticed.

Finally, special acknowledgment goes to Jean-François Mayer, whose initial suggestions for the structure of the volume provided a solid framework on which to build; and to the late Robert H. Kirven, a founding member of the editorial committee, whose insights helped in many ways to plan and shape our work.

SWEDENBORG'S LIFE

The Inner Journey of Emanuel Swedenborg

RICHARD SMOLEY

Outline

LIKE most great figures in history, Emanuel Swedenborg both epito-mizes his time and transcends it. The great theme of his life was also the great theme of his era, but he surpassed his era in resolving the di-chotomy between faith and science that sounded its fundamental note. This fissure was to grow wider and more apparently unbridgeable in later times; indeed, we today have not bridged it. In the end we may find that Swedenborg's solution is the only one that will succeed. He did not rec-oncile his science with his religion through some jury-rigged combina-tion of inimical worldviews, but by taking one of them—the scientific perspective—and moving further and further inward with it, until he reached, as he believed, a transcendent realm of spiritual realities. It is this constant movement inward that furnishes the key to both his life and his work.

I. Family Background

Swedenborg was born in a home that would provide him with a firm foundation for his spiritual researches. His father, Jesper Swedberg (1653–1735),[1] was a pastor of solid and simple convictions in a Sweden dominated by the Lutheran state church. Alarmed by the complacency of his fellow Swedes, which he ascribed to solifidism, the doctrine of justification by faith alone,[2] Swedberg denounced what he called "faith of the head"[3] and insisted that true Christianity must be lived out in practice. He even went so far as to praise Roman Catholics, whose care for the poor and destitute surpassed that in his own Protestant country (Trobridge 1992, 3).

---

1. Swedberg was the family surname until 1719, when the family was ennobled by Queen Ulrika Eleonora as part of her effort to fortify her position as monarch by creating a larger noble class sympathetic to her. It was common to alter the surname slightly in the process of ennoblement in token of the recipient's change in status; and at this point the Swedbergs became the Swedenborgs. Jesper Swedberg himself, however, was not ennobled and did not change his name. For the sake of convenience in this essay, I will refer to Emanuel Swedenborg throughout as "Swedenborg" and to Jesper Swedberg as "Swedberg."

2. Justification by faith alone is the doctrine that mere faith in God's mercy is sufficient to save one from eternal condemnation. In other words, the actions one performs in life (traditionally re-ferred to as "works") are not a determining factor.

3. As quoted in Trobridge 1992, 2. Translations in this essay are those of the cited source unless otherwise indicated.

Jesper Swedberg was a commanding presence. At an early point in his career, he served as chaplain to the regiment of the Horse Guards, and he would recall that when the dragoons presented themselves to him for examination in catechism, they cringed before him "as they never trembled in the face of the enemy."[4] He was also a prolific writer of hymns and sermons, attributing his indefatigable desire to write and publish to the Hebrew meaning of his given name, which is "he shall write" (Lamm 2000, 4–5). One of Swedberg's great ambitions was to prepare a cheap edition of the Bible in Swedish, an aim that came to fruition only in 1728, late in his lifetime. His energy and uprightness enabled him to rise in his profession: he was made bishop of Skara in 1702, a position he would hold until his death in 1735.

Jesper Swedberg's earnest and broadminded simplicity would leave its mark on his son, as would his unslakable thirst for writing. Another of his traits that would make itself felt in Swedenborg's character was an awareness of the immediate presence of angels and malevolent spirits; the latter, he held, could only be banished by prayer and reading of Scripture. Indeed, Swedberg himself claimed that word of his talent for exorcism had spread to England and the Netherlands (Tafel 1875, 148).

II. Childhood and Youth

Emanuel Swedenborg was born in Stockholm on January 29, 1688, the third child and second son of Swedberg and his wife, Sara Behm (1666–1696), the daughter of a wealthy mine owner. Comparatively little is known of Swedenborg's early life, but he retrospectively provides a glimpse of his youthful religious experience in a letter written in 1769:

> From my fourth to my tenth year I was constantly engaged in thought upon God, salvation, and the spiritual life. Several times I revealed things at which my father and mother wondered, saying that angels must be speaking through me. From my sixth to my twelfth year I used to delight in talking with clergymen about faith, saying that the life of faith is love, and that the love which imparts life is love [for one's] neighbor; also that God gives faith to everyone, but that those only receive it who practice that love. I knew of no other faith at that time

---

4. Lamm 2000, 4; for more on Swedberg as chaplain, see Tafel 1875, 104.

than that God is the Creator and Preserver of nature, that he imparts understanding and a good disposition to us. . . . I knew nothing at that time of that learned faith which teaches that God the Father imputes the righteousness of his Son to whomsoever, and at such times as he chooses, even to those who have not repented and have not reformed their lives. And had I heard of such a faith it would have been then, as it is now, above my comprehension.[5]

Swedenborg's diary of his spiritual experiences, written in his late middle age, suggests a link between his early and later spiritual life. He observed a close connection between rhythms of breathing and states of consciousness, and he remarks that even in his childhood he was accustomed to hold his breath in prayer and to coordinate his breathing with his heartbeat; when he did, he noticed that "his intellectual capacity would often begin to virtually disappear." Similarly, when as a mature man he was engaged in writing in a state of inspiration, he would find that his breath would almost stop.[6] It is interesting to note that regulation and cessation of breath is often associated with mystical experiences, as can be seen in the discipline of *pranayama,* or yogic breathing. One Buddhist sutra says the Buddha's breath ceased for six years as he meditated before reaching enlightenment.[7]

The young Emanuel was only eight in 1696, when a fever carried off his mother and his eldest brother. Eighteen months later Jesper Swedberg married a second time, to Sara Bergia (1666–1720), a widow who, like his first wife, held considerable property in mines. Swedenborg's stepmother took a great liking to him, and in later years the bishop would have to dissuade her from favoring Swedenborg above his siblings.

In 1699, at the age of eleven, Swedenborg matriculated at the University of Uppsala, where his father was then a professor. Although the university's ledger describes Swedenborg as "a youth of the best talent" (Sigstedt 1981, 9), early matriculation was not such an indication of precocity as it may appear: universities at the time provided something akin to secondary education. Already well versed in Latin, the common

---

5. Quoted in Trobridge 1992, 3; for a different version, see Tafel 1877, 279–280.

6. *Spiritual Experiences* (= Swedenborg 1998–2002) §3320; translated here by Jonathan S. Rose. References to Swedenborg's works, here and elsewhere in the essay and notes, are to section numbers. These were inserted by Swedenborg himself and are standard in most editions of his works.

7. On *pranayama,* see Rama and others, 1979. For the Buddhist sutra, see Bays 1983, 2:392–393 (a translation of the *Lalitavistara Sutra*).

language of European scholarship in which all his major works would be written,[8] he enrolled in the faculty of philosophy, a curriculum that included science and mathematics (Sigstedt 1981, 11). In 1702 Jesper Swedberg moved his family from Uppsala to take up his bishopric at Skara. Emanuel was left behind with his older sister Anna (1686–1766), who had married the distinguished humanist Erik Benzelius (the younger; 1675–1743), the university's librarian. Swedenborg would live with the Benzelius family for the rest of his student years. The relationship between Swedenborg and Benzelius was to become a warm one, and much of Swedenborg's early correspondence is addressed to his brother-in-law.

Indeed, many of Swedenborg's biographers have seen Benzelius as the first great influence upon Swedenborg after his father. Benzelius, like Swedenborg after him, was something of a Renaissance person. His greatest scholarly interests were in philology (he prepared editions of Philo of Alexandria and Ulfilas),[9] but he was also an ardent admirer of the "mechanical philosophy" that French philosopher René Descartes (1596–1650) had brought with him to Sweden in the last months of his life.[10] It was probably under Benzelius's influence that Swedenborg turned his attention to science and technology, which were to dominate the earlier part of his career.

In 1709 Swedenborg presented his thesis, a commentary on some maxims from Latin authors (Swedenborg [1709] 1967). Although like all students in Sweden at that time he did not earn a degree as we know it, the presentation of his thesis was to mark the end of his formal education. In that era it was customary for young men of Swedenborg's class to take an extensive tour of Europe upon completing their studies, and he was minded to go to England, at the time the world's center of scientific learning, but he was forced to delay this trip by political circumstances, including the disastrous defeat of Sweden's King Charles XII (1682–1718) by the armies of the Russian czar Peter the Great (1672–1725) at Poltava in 1709.

---

8. Latin was still widely spoken at the time; for example, all of Swedenborg's classes were conducted in it; see Helander 1993, 22–48, especially 22–28. For a country-by-country account of the diffusion of Neo-Latin, the version of Latin used in Swedenborg's era, see IJsewijn 1990, 54–327.

9. Philo (about 15 B.C.E.–about 50 C.E.), also known as Philo Judaeus, was a Jewish philosopher and writer. Ulfilas (about 311–about 382) was a bishop who translated the Gospel of Mark into the Gothic language.

10. On Cartesianism at Uppsala see Broberg 1988, 281–282, and Stroh 1911, xv–xxxvii, in which Descartes's effect on Swedenborg's scientific thinking is also discussed.

This event was to mark a turning point in the destiny of Sweden, which had been on the ascent as a European power since the reign of Gustavus Adolphus (1594–1632) in the early seventeenth century. When Swedenborg was born, his native country ruled over Finland, the Baltic states, and Pomerania. But with the accession to the throne of the fifteen-year-old Charles XII in 1698, the nation's fortunes changed. The apparent weakness of Sweden, headed by a young king and reeling from several years of famine in the 1690s, tempted neighboring powers to encroach upon its territory. Russia invaded the Baltic states. The young Charles was astonishingly successful in repelling them at Narva in Estonia in 1700. Encouraged by this victory, he went on to invade the Ukraine, but was defeated by the Russians at Poltava. He fled to Turkey, from which he was able to return only after a breakneck fourteen-day journey across Eastern Europe.

The twenty-year reign of Charles XII was marked by continuous warfare and, despite some military successes, by counterbalancing defeats that would change the course of Sweden's history—not only depriving her of her overseas territories but motivating the Swedish nobles to impose a limited monarchy upon the king's successors, inaugurating the period of Swedish history known as the Age of Freedom. These events would form a backdrop to Swedenborg's life and career, and as a member of the nobility he would find himself called upon to deal with such matters as peace, war, and national finance.

III. First Journey Abroad

In the short term, however, these events chiefly affected Swedenborg by imposing a delay upon his travels. The Danes, who were also at war with Sweden, dominated the seas, making passage to England almost impossible. Several months of enforced and unwelcome leisure led Swedenborg to apply to study as a private pupil of Christopher Polhem (1661–1751), the most respected inventor in Sweden. Although Polhem would become another great influence on Swedenborg's early life, their meeting was delayed for several years by Swedenborg's decision to take a ship leaving for England in the summer of 1710 (Sigstedt 1981, 16–18).

The journey to England offered its share of adventures: the ship was stopped en route by French privateers and mistakenly fired upon by an English patrol boat. When it docked in London, the travelers found that news of a plague in Sweden had preceded them, and the vessel was quarantined for six weeks. Swedenborg audaciously went ashore on a boat that belonged to some visiting Swedes, but was arrested and detained. He was nearly hanged for the offense. "I was saved from the rope," he wrote, "but with the reservation that no other person would thereafter escape who ventured to do the like."[11]

Once safely in London, Swedenborg plunged into the current ferment of science and technology. He frequented a circle that included such luminaries as Isaac Newton (1642–1727) and Edmond Halley (1656–1742) and lodged with artisans of various trades so as to learn their crafts. He also became friendly with John Flamsteed (1646–1719), the brilliant but cantankerous Astronomer Royal, for whom Greenwich Observatory was built. Swedenborg managed to disarm Flamsteed's suspicions and spent a great deal of time with him, observing his methods and instruments, and reporting on them to Swedish scientists in Uppsala (Tafel 1875, 218–219).

In England Swedenborg became preoccupied with the leading scientific question of the time: finding the correct longitude at sea. This was a matter that Britain, as a maritime power, regarded as of the highest importance. The Royal Society offered a large sum of money as a prize for a practical solution. With a certain youthful cockiness, Swedenborg felt he had found a viable method, which made use of the position of the moon, but in order to make it practicable, he needed exact tables of lunar movements. He tried to get them from Flamsteed but did not succeed, and he did not win the prize (Benz 2002, 38–40). The problem would be solved in 1755 only by an entirely different approach: the development of an exact chronometer, which, as Newton had indicated, would make the calculation feasible.[12] Swedenborg would try to resurrect his own theory in the 1760s, but without success.[13]

Swedenborg spent two and a half years in England before moving on to the Netherlands and France to continue his scientific investigations. He turned his mind to inventions of all sorts, and in a 1714 letter to Benzelius, he boasts of having plans for inventions including a submarine, an air gun

---

11. As quoted in Sigstedt 1981, 19; see also Tafel 1877, 3–4, and Acton 1948–1955, 768.

12. For a popular account of the search for a method of determining longitude at sea, see Sobel 1995; unfortunately, it makes no mention of Swedenborg's efforts.

13. Swedenborg published an initial version of his method in Swedish (Swedenborg 1716–1718, 4:86–89), then reprinted an edited version (Swedenborg 1718), and an expanded version in Latin (Swedenborg 1721). This latest version he reprinted in a new edition forty-five years later (Swedenborg 1766); for this edition and his correspondence on the topic at that time, see Tafel 1875, 590–597. For a review of his method, see Cole 1933, 169–178.

that could fire a thousand shots at once, and even "a universal musical instrument, whereby the most inexperienced player can produce all kinds of
melodies, these being found marked on paper and in notes" (Acton
1948–1955, 57). He sent these plans home, but on his return to Sweden at
the end of 1714, he found that his father had unfortunately mislaid them
(Acton 1948–1955, 63). They have never been recovered.

IV. Initial Projects

Relations between Swedenborg and his father showed signs of tension
during these years; money seems to have been the main cause. Writing
from England, Swedenborg had complained that his father had cut back
on his traveling funds, and when he returned to Sweden, he found himself again facing financial restrictions. In December 1715 he wrote to
Benzelius, asking him to intervene. "A single word from you to my father
on my behalf will be worth more than twenty thousand remonstrances
from me. Without making any recommendation, you can advertise him
of my project, and of my solicitude for studies, so that he will not imagine in the future that I would waste my time and, at the same time, his
money" (Acton 1948–1955, 75–76).

Overall Swedenborg's first year at home was one of frustration. He
found no professional post, and in March 1716 he wrote to Benzelius suggesting that a professorship of mechanics be established for him at Uppsala, to be funded by cuts in salaries of the current professors. Benzelius
wrote back warning him against telling anyone about this, lest he make
enemies among the faculty (Acton 1948–1955, 89–93). Other plans, ranging from the academic (creating a Swedish astronomical observatory) to
the commercial (spying some white clay, he suggested that it might become the basis of a native porcelain industry), also came to naught.

Indeed the only project that bore fruit at this time was the *Daedalus
Hyperboreus* (Northern Daedalus), a scientific journal Swedenborg had
undertaken to publish. Six issues of this periodical would appear between
1716 and 1718. The title *Daedalus*—the name of the great artificer of
Greek myth—was chosen as a compliment to Polhem, and the issues
contained a number of Polhem's articles and designs. Upon returning to
his homeland, Swedenborg had fulfilled his ambition of several years earlier and made friends with the distinguished inventor, serving for some
time as his assistant. The publication met with the approval of Charles

XII, who was extremely interested in science and technology, and in late 1716, Swedenborg, in the company of Polhem, made the monarch's acquaintance.

The restless and ambitious mind of Charles resonated with that of the young Swedenborg. The king was a mathematical genius. Taking up the contention of mathematician Blaise Pascal (1623–1662) that the decimal system was only a convention, he urged Polhem and Swedenborg to create a new system of mathematics based on the number 64. When the two scientists demurred, saying such a system would be impractical, Charles produced a paper the next day setting it out in great detail (Acton 1948–1955, 460–463). Other pursuits encouraged by the king were more concrete, including the domestic production of salt, the construction of a dry dock for the navy, and the commencement of a canal connecting Lake Väner in central Sweden to the Atlantic seaboard. Swedenborg even engineered the overland transfer of warships to help Charles in a siege in southern Norway (Sigstedt 1981, 42, 45).

Charles soon became a powerful sponsor of Swedenborg. At Polhem's behest, the king offered the young man a choice of three posts. Swedenborg chose the position of assessor extraordinary[14] at the *Bergscollegium,* or Board of Mines, not only because of his family connections to the mining industry but because it offered him the greatest chance of scientific investigation: the mining industry had the only laboratories and workshops in Sweden at that time (Benz 2002, 81).

Despite these favors, Swedenborg eventually became estranged from both the king and Polhem. Writing later in the diary of his spiritual experiences, Swedenborg mentions that the king's disposition changed "from good to anger" at the very end of their friendship.[15] The cause for this break is mysterious. The most plausible supposition is that Charles wanted Swedenborg to accompany him again as a military engineer to his Norwegian campaign, but, as Swedenborg reports in a letter of December 8, 1718, "I . . . used plots to withdraw myself" (Acton 1948–1955, 200). In any event, this campaign was to be Charles's last: he was killed by a bullet while besieging a Norwegian stronghold in November 1718.

---

14. An assessor extraordinary was essentially an associate member. In addition to participating in the development and adjudication of regulations on the Board of Mines, assessors also made extensive tours of inspection. The Board was extremely important in Sweden during that era, as mining was critical to its economic health.

15. *Spiritual Experiences* (= Swedenborg 1978b) §4704, as quoted in Acton 1948–1955, 200.

The break with Polhem is equally perplexing. We only know that in April 1719 Polhem wrote to Benzelius telling him that he had sent Swedenborg three letters, all of which were returned unopened. Professional rivalry no doubt played a part. Another cause may have been Swedenborg's ruptured engagement with one of Polhem's daughters, but this episode is so obscure that it is unclear even which girl Swedenborg was supposed to have courted. Years later, when asked if he had ever been married, Swedenborg said that Charles XII had urged Polhem to give him his daughter in marriage, but she would not have him, "as she had promised herself to another" (Tafel 1877, 437). This account suggests that the young woman in question was Maria (1698–?), Polhem's elder daughter. In a letter of September 14, 1718, to Benzelius, Swedenborg remarks that Maria was engaged to a courtier, Martin Ludwig Manderström (1691–1780). Swedenborg hints that he has arranged this engagement, adding that he thinks Emerentia (1703–1760), the younger daughter, is much prettier (Acton 1948–1955, 193). Although the language of the letter is ambiguous, some scholars believe that Swedenborg arranged Maria's betrothal so that he could marry Emerentia—Polhem, like the biblical Laban, wanting to marry off his elder daughter first (Acton 1948–1955, 193).

Much later, Polhem's son Gabriel (1700–1772) cast more light on the situation: Swedenborg preferred Emerentia, but she was so young—being only fifteen—that Polhem would not consent to her marrying at that time. He did give Swedenborg a written document promising him her hand, but Emerentia was so upset at the prospect that Gabriel stole it from Swedenborg's room. Polhem ordered that the document be returned to Swedenborg, but the suitor, struck with the girl's grief, left the household for good. Several years later, in 1726, Swedenborg made another offer of marriage, this time to Kristina Maria (or "Stina Maia") Steuch (1708–1739), daughter of the archbishop of Uppsala; but she chose another man. After that point Swedenborg apparently resigned himself to bachelorhood forever (Sigstedt 1981, 49, 105).

In 1719 Ulrika Eleonora (1688–1741), the sister of Charles XII, ascended to the throne as queen. In May of that year the Swedberg family was ennobled and given the surname by which Emanuel has come to be known—not in consequence of his own achievements, but because the queen hoped the Swedbergs and other families similarly ennobled would form a supportive faction in the nobility.

Despite his rise in status, this was a time of setbacks for Swedenborg. The death of Charles XII, his royal patron, enabled the Board of Mines to eliminate Swedenborg's salary and to keep him from being appointed as a full assessor. Although he persistently promoted his own case, he did not succeed in getting a full appointment and salary until 1724.

The year 1720 was marked by the death of Swedenborg's stepmother. She had been so devoted to him that she would have left him the whole of her estate, but Jesper Swedberg persuaded her not to disinherit the other children. Even so, her will favored Emanuel over her other family members, some of whom contested it. In the end it was determined that Emanuel would share the estate with his brother-in-law, Lars Benzelstierna (1630–1755), and both bought out the other heirs. Swedenborg also bought up the other shares of his birth mother's estate, which consisted of a fifth of an iron works owned jointly with his aunt Brita Behm (1670–1755). Although these properties would involve Swedenborg in a number of disputes and lawsuits in coming years, they provided him with financial security at a time when he had no job (Sigstedt 1981, 67–68).

The tumult of this period did not blunt Swedenborg's creativity. In a 1718 issue of *Daedalus Hyperboreus,* he published an essay titled "A Proof That Our Vital Essence Consists for the Most Part of Small Vibrations, That Is, of Tremulations." A 1719 work titled "On the Height of Water and the Great Ebb and Flow of the Primeval World" endeavored to show that in ancient times Sweden had been covered by water. Another essay from that period, discussing the motion of the earth, argued that the earth had once moved faster around the sun than it does today, accounting for such phenomena as legends of a Golden Age and the longevity of the biblical patriarchs. Yet another treatise appeared in 1721, titled *Prodromus Principiorum Rerum Naturalium* (A Precursor to Basic Principles of Nature).[16]

These works show the influence of Polhem. The treatise on vibrations posited the existence of a superfine matter that served as a medium for transmitting thoughts and sensations—an idea advocated by Polhem. The concept was not a new one; the occult philosophy of the Renaissance had also assumed the existence of such a subtle matter, known as

---

16. The traditional English short title of the first of these works, a brief paper in Swedenborg 1716–1718, 5:10–14, is *On Tremulation;* the more recent title is *Small Vibrations.* It can be found printed with a longer, posthumously published paper of the same name in Swedenborg [1717] 1976d. The traditional short titles of the rest of these works are, respectively: *Height of Water* (= Swedenborg [1719] 1992a, 17–50); *Earth's Revolution* (now *Rotation of the Earth,* = Swedenborg [1719] 1915); and *Chemistry* (now *Chemistry and Physics,* = Swedenborg [1721] 1976f, 8–179). On these works see Sigstedt 1981, 57–63.

the *anima mundi* or "soul of the world"; later occultists would call it the "astral light."[17] Unlike Descartes, who drew a rigid and nearly unbridgeable boundary between spirit and matter, Polhem and Swedenborg posited a form of emanationism, suggesting that the Divine made itself manifest in progressively more palpable forms, of which matter as we customarily know it is only the last (Lamm 2000, 37–39). Although in this period Swedenborg's interest in the inner worlds was more or less embryonic, these ideas foreshadowed crucial aspects of his later teaching, such as the doctrine of correspondences.[18]

Disappointed in love and career, Swedenborg took another trip abroad that lasted from May 1720 to July 1722. During this time he visited the Netherlands and Germany to gather information about mining (Benz 2002, 97). On his return he devoted himself to writing about mining, metallurgy, and finance: one pamphlet, dating from the summer of 1722, argued against a plan to solve Sweden's acute fiscal crisis by inflating the currency.[19] In 1724 he received his long-awaited full appointment to the Board of Mines, on which he would serve for the next twenty-five years.

Most of the rest of the 1720s would find Swedenborg occupied with his duties on this board and involved in a protracted lawsuit brought against him by his aunt Brita Behm, with whom he had difficulties over use of the iron works they jointly owned. Ironically, Swedenborg had to bring the matter before the Board of Mines, absenting himself from the proceedings as an interested party. The dispute began in 1724 and dragged on until the end of 1729, when documentation comes to a halt. Presumably after that point Swedenborg sold his interest in the property.[20]

V. First Major Works

In 1728 Swedenborg, by now settled in a house of his own in Stockholm, resumed his literary activities, which had been interrupted by

---

17. See, for example, Agrippa 1993, 1:44; also Smoley and Kinney 1999, 103–105.

18. On the doctrine of correspondences, see pages 66, 341–342, and the notice in passing on page 61 note 20 in this volume.

19. For discussion, see Sigstedt 1981, 87–88; for the pamphlet, see Swedenborg [1722] 1987. Swedenborg reissued the pamphlet nearly fifty years later, with extensive additional commentary (Swedenborg 1771). See also Tafel 1875, 471–474.

20. For documents relating to this dispute, see Acton 1948–1955, 345–438.

more commonplace duties. He began to write his three-volume *Opera Philosophica et Mineralia* (Philosophical and Metallurgical Works), which would take him five years to complete, and which he would publish in 1734 (see Sigstedt 1981, 107). The first volume, titled the *Principia Rerum Naturalium* (Basic Principles of Nature), constitutes his first major philosophical work. Along with *De Infinito* (The Infinite), also published in 1734, it provides the most comprehensive portrait of Swedenborg's philosophical thought before his visionary experiences began in earnest.[21]

In these works, three things stand out as especially noteworthy. The first is Swedenborg's effort to reason deductively, from first principles, as well as empirically, from evidence: he contends that both are equally important. This concern reflects one of the great philosophical issues of his era: the relationship between knowledge *a priori* (which explains phenomena by a system built up from one's initial intellectual principles) and knowledge *a posteriori* (which is inferred from observed phenomena). The discussion of these different types of knowledge would reach its culmination in the major work of German philosopher Immanuel Kant (1724–1804), *Critique of Pure Reason* (1781). The second is Swedenborg's concern to relate the infinite to the finite. His means of doing so is by positing the mathematical point, the juncture between the infinite and the finite, as the basis of all manifest reality: "It is comparable to the two-faced Janus, seeing in opposite directions simultaneously, each of his two faces turned toward one of the two universes."[22] He developed this idea further in *The Infinite* (Sigstedt 1981, 133–139).

The third, and perhaps most distinctive, aspect of this phase of Swedenborg's work is that he accepts the mechanistic worldview of the era, but only to a degree. In *Basic Principles of Nature* he writes: "The world is mechanical and consists of a series of finite things, which have resulted from the most varied contingencies; . . . the world can accordingly be investigated by experience and with the aid of geometry." But, as he goes on to say, "the infinite cannot be comprehended

---

21. For the Latin version of *Philosophical and Metallurgical Works,* see Swedenborg 1734. For the English translation of volume 1 (that is, *Basic Principles of Nature*) see Swedenborg [1734] 1988b = Swedenborg [1734] 1912; for a translation of volume 3, see Swedenborg [1734] 1938. (Volume 2 has never been translated into English.) For *The Infinite,* see Swedenborg [1734] 1965.

22. As quoted in Lamm 2000, 39, where the passage is incorrectly ascribed; it actually appears in *Basic Principles of Nature* (= Swedenborg [1734] 1988b), page 53. Janus was the god of gateways and beginnings in Roman mythology.

by geometry," nor can the "mental principle in the soul." Swedenborg asks, "What is this something in the soul, which is nothing mechanical, and what are the appropriate means of understanding it?"[23] Even at this comparatively early stage of his thought, he is drawn away from purely scientific investigations toward a deeper level of knowledge.

VI. Further Journeys

Like most of Swedenborg's writings, *Basic Principles of Nature* was published abroad—in this case, in Dresden and Leipzig. At this point Swedenborg settled into a pattern that would become the standard for the rest of his life. He would spend some time in his native country, then would depart for extended trips abroad, sometimes lasting three or four years, to England or the European continent, where he would publish one or more of his books. This particular journey, lasting from May 1733 to July 1734, took him to Germany and Bohemia, where he again conducted mining and geological researches.

When Swedenborg returned to his native land in 1734, he found it in political crisis. There was much agitation for war with Russia to regain the territories Sweden had lost under Charles XII. This dispute led to the rise of two political parties: the Caps, under the leadership of the great statesman Count Arvid Horn (1664–1742), so called because they opposed war and thus were accused of being ready only to rest, or of wearing nightcaps; and the Hats, so called because they claimed to be staying alert, or to be keeping their hats on for war. Swedenborg's own party affiliation is unclear. On the one hand, he was on friendly terms with Count Frederick Gyllenborg (1698–1759) and (much later) Count Carl Gustaf Tessin (1695–1770), leaders of the Hats, and in 1760 disputes over Sweden's fiscal policy would find him in the Hat camp (Sigstedt 1981, 293). On the other hand, in 1734, as a member of the House of Nobles, he drafted a memorandum opposing war on the grounds that the risks far outweighed any likely gains and that "Russia is indeed more formidable than before."[24] He would reiterate this position in 1740 (Sigstedt 1981, 300). Events would prove Swedenborg right. The Hats came to power in

---

23. As quoted in Benz 2002, 124–125. A translation in context can be found in Swedenborg [1734] 1988b, 25.

24. For a complete text of this memorandum, see Acton 1948–1955, 468–475.

1738; war would follow in 1741. Again Sweden suffered a painful defeat and had to conclude peace with Russia on humiliating terms in 1743 (Scott 1988, 246–247).

In July 1736 Swedenborg set out for another trip, which would take him to Rome via Paris, Venice, and Bologna. En route he stopped in Amsterdam, where his journal gives an interesting glimpse into his political thinking at the time: "I have considered why it was that it has pleased our Lord to bless such an uncouth and avaricious people as the Dutch with such a splendid country. . . . The principal cause seems to me to have been that it is a republic, wherein the Lord delights more than in monarchical countries." Because everyone is equal in a republic, "the only one for whom they entertain a veneration is the Lord, putting no trust in flesh" (Tafel 1877, 86). It may have been the climate of freedom here and in England that led him to spend so much of his time, and to produce so much of his work, in these nations.[25]

VII. Researches into the Realm of the Soul

In Amsterdam, a little more than a month after leaving Sweden, Swedenborg began to write his next major work, the *Oeconomia Regni Animalis* (Dynamics of the Soul's Domain).[26] The first volume, completed in 1739 and anonymously published in 1740, mainly discusses the heart and the blood, which, Swedenborg said, are "the complex of all things that exist in the world and the storehouse . . . of all that exists in the body."[27] The second volume, published in 1741, covers the brain, the nervous system, and the soul.

In this work Swedenborg describes an intricate interrelation among the blood, the cerebrospinal fluid, and the "spirituous fluid," a subtle substance that constitutes the essence of life. He also sets out a view of the structure of the human soul, which, he argues, consists of a higher, intuitive spiritual faculty called the *anima;* the familiar rational mind, or *mens;* and the so-called vegetative soul, or *animus,* which controls vital

---

25. His derogatory comments about the Dutch in 1736 can be contrasted with his positive remarks in the 1763 work *Supplements* 48 and the 1771 work *True Christianity* 801.

26. The traditional title is *Economy of the Animal Kingdom,* a misleadingly literal translation of the Latin. See Swedenborg [1740–1741] 1955.

27. *Dynamics of the Soul's Domain* (= Swedenborg [1740–1741] 1955) §3.

functions. In a portrait that echoes his later vision of the human soul as a meeting place between the contending forces of hell and heaven, he describes the *mens* as divided between the higher, heavenly impulses of the *anima,* and the coarse physical urges of the *animus.* The *mens* is thus the battleground on which the struggle of human free will is played out.[28]

Dynamics of the Soul's Domain was apparently well-received: surviving notices are mostly favorable, and a second edition appeared in 1742, this time under Swedenborg's name; a third edition would follow six years later. But Swedenborg himself was not satisfied with his conclusions. He later confessed, "[When] I published *[Dynamics of the Soul's Domain],* a work . . . treating only of the blood, the arteries of the heart, etc. . . . I made a rapid passage to the soul. . . . But on considering the matter more deeply I found that I had directed my course thither too hastily."[29] These words appear in the prologue to his next work, *Regnum Animale* (The Soul's Domain).[30] In it he resolved to remedy the deficiencies of his previous work. He planned to go through the entire human anatomical structure before attempting to penetrate to the mysteries of the soul. Two parts of this work were published at The Hague in 1744; a third part would be published later in London. But Swedenborg did not finish *The Soul's Domain* as he had projected it. And even though he wrote several other anatomical treatises during this period, including *Draft on the Reproductive Organs, The Brain,* and *Draft on the Five Senses,* he did not publish them.[31] They appeared in book form only in later centuries. *The Brain* is especially noteworthy in setting out some prescient theories about the brain's functioning, such as the idea that the higher functions of reason take place in the grey matter of the cerebrum. He also devoted considerable attention to the cerebrospinal fluid, the "dew of heaven" that has been a subject of intense interest to esotericists since at least medieval times.[32]

---

28. For a summary of Swedenborg's views on this point, see Lamm 2000, 77–84.

29. *The Soul's Domain* (= Swedenborg [1744–1745] 1960) §19.

30. The traditional title is *The Animal Kingdom,* again a transliteration of the Latin. See Swedenborg [1744–1745] 1960.

31. See respectively Swedenborg 1928 (which appears under the traditional title *The Organs of Generation*); Swedenborg 1882–1887, and Hyde 1906, entries 322–323; and Swedenborg 1976b (which appears under the traditional title *The Five Senses*). Parts of the treatise on the senses were expanded and included in Swedenborg [1744–1745] 1960, 369–593.

32. Sigstedt 1981, 170–172. On esoteric views of the cerebrospinal system, see Hall 1972, chapter 10.

VIII. Spiritual Crisis

Swedenborg's project of exploring the entirety of the human body as a vehicle for the soul was interrupted by a radical change in his life's direction. It was to mark the turning point in his life, and it would lead him to the vocation for which he would be most remembered—that of spiritual visionary and sage.

The process was a slow one. Although a devout Christian all his life, Swedenborg had not made religious issues per se the primary subject of his writing. Instead he had attempted to explore such questions as infinity and the nature of the soul primarily through scientific methods; the cleft between science and religion was not as great in his day as it is in ours. Even at this stage, his views tended toward what scholars today would consider an esoteric perspective, though some of his devoted readers might reject that classification. His notion of the *anima* as set out in *Dynamics of the Soul's Domain,* with its intuitive, higher perception of truth, illustrates this tendency.

Moreover, this transition in Swedenborg's intellectual thought appears to have been the result of his own inner experience. We have already seen how in his childhood he learned how to regulate his psychological state through breath control. While writing *Dynamics of the Soul's Domain* he again observed how his breath would spontaneously cease when he was contemplating certain matters. He also referred obliquely to researchers whose conjectures were affirmed by "a certain cheering light, and joyful confirmatory brightness, . . . a kind of mysterious radiation—I know not whence it proceeds—that darts through some sacred temple of the brain."[33] Scholars have naturally drawn from this the inference that he is speaking of his own experience.[34]

Although Swedenborg would later say that his spiritual sight had been opened only in 1745, these early experiences suggest that this shift began several years before, around 1736.[35] Possibly the death of his father the previous year turned his thoughts toward the Last Things. At any rate he began to record his dreams and spiritual experiences at this point. Unfortunately,

---

33. *Dynamics of the Soul's Domain* (Swedenborg [1740–1741] 1955) §19.

34. See Sigstedt 1981, 144; compare *Spiritual Experiences* (= Swedenborg 1998–2002) §2951.

35. See Benz 2002, 151–152; and also Woofenden 1974, 3–10, and Tafel 1877, 1082–1089. Although Swedenborg sometimes assigns the date 1745 to his spiritual transition, he occasionally gives other dates. Twice he explicitly assigns it to 1744 (*Draft on Divine Wisdom* §95, in chapter 7; Acton 1948–1955, 627) and three times to 1743 (Acton 1948–1955, 679, 682, 739). See also Tafel 1877, 1118–1127.

this part of the biographical record is missing. After his death, the portion of a travel diary that contained certain of his dreams during the period 1736–1740 was removed and retained by Swedenborg's relatives. It has never been recovered (Tafel 1877, 130).

During these years Swedenborg probably showed few, if any, outward signs of these shifts in his inner orientation: he continued to travel and work on his books as before; and later it was even reported that he had had a mistress while in Italy.[36] When he returned to Sweden in 1740, he was elected to the newly established Academy of Sciences, an organization whose founding he had urged early in his own career. He resumed work at the Board of Mines and bought a house and garden in south Stockholm in March 1743, although he would not move there until three years later (Sigstedt 1981, 163–164, 174). He left Sweden again in July 1743 to complete and oversee the publication of *The Soul's Domain* in the Netherlands.

It was on this trip that the major events of his spiritual conversion took place, a conversion that would bring about great inner upheaval and transformation. We have an intimate portrait of one phase of this process in Swedenborg's *Journal of Dreams* (= Swedenborg 2001b), which recounts his inner experiences from March to October 1744. These records, intimate and often brutally frank, were not published in his lifetime and were never meant for publication. Despite or because of this fact, they give us a tremendous amount of insight into this climactic moment in Swedenborg's life.

At this time Swedenborg made contact with the Moravian Brethren (frequently known as the Herrnhutters). Moravians were a pietistic Christian society led by Count Nikolaus von Zinzendorf (1700–1760) that emphasized a radical and personal acceptance of the suffering Christ as essential for salvation.[37] While in the Netherlands, Swedenborg attended Moravian services, and it is likely that the Moravian influence helps explain the religious fervor that Swedenborg shows in his journal of dreams for this period. In the entry for April 6–7, 1744, he writes:

> I went to sleep, and about twelve o'clock, or perhaps it was at one
> or two in the morning, such a strong shivering seized me, from my head

---

36. The accuracy of this second-hand report is much contested. For example, Tafel vigorously disputes it (see Tafel 1875, 43, 628–630; Tafel 1877, 437, with note); Sigstedt considers it but inclines to reject it (Sigstedt 1981, 478–479 note 718); and Benz accepts it (see Benz 2002, 183–184).

37. For an exhaustive view of Zinzendorf's teachings, see Deghaye 1969 or Freeman 1998. A short readable biography is Weinlick 1984. The standard treatment of the Moravian movement is Hamilton and Hamilton 1967.

to my feet, as a thunder produced by several clouds colliding, shaking me beyond description and prostrating me. And when I was prostrated in this way, I was clearly awake and saw how I was overthrown.

I wondered what this was supposed to mean, and I spoke as if awake but found that the words were put into my mouth. I said, "Oh, thou almighty Jesus Christ, who of great mercy deignest to come to so great a sinner, make me worthy of this grace!" and I clasped my hands and prayed. Then a hand emerged, which pressed my hands firmly.

In a little while, I continued my prayer, saying, "Thou hast promised to receive in grace all sinners; thou canst not otherwise than keep thy words!" In the same moment, I was sitting in his bosom and beheld him face to face, a countenance of a holy mien. All was such that I cannot describe. He was smiling at me, and I was convinced that he looked like this when he was alive. He spoke to me and asked if I have a health certificate; and to this I replied, "Lord, thou knowest better than I." He said, "Well, then, do!"—that is, as I inwardly grasped this, "Do love me" or "Do as promised." God give me grace thereto! I found it beyond my powers and woke up, shuddering. (Swedenborg 2001b, §§52–54)

Here we see classic elements of a religious conversion combined with highly personal details. As some scholars have suggested, the "health certificate" may allude to Swedenborg's first visit to England as a youth, when he was nearly hanged for violating a quarantine; here it obviously refers to spiritual health. The rest of the *Journal of Dreams* has similarly personal themes: Charles XII and Jesper Swedberg appear frequently, and strongly sexual elements are manifest as well. These elements present a theme that is fairly typical of Christian religious experience—a radical tension between impurity, often linked with sexual desire, and purity, equated with chastity. It is noteworthy that early on in this process, Swedenborg remarks that his desire for women, which had always preoccupied him intensely, has suddenly gone away (Swedenborg 2001b, §§12, 14).

Yet it is clear from the *Journal of Dreams* that Swedenborg's preoccupation with purity was not only, or even primarily, sexual. He experiences temptations to personal grandeur, which he pushes away from himself. At one point he wonders what would happen if someone were to venerate him as a holy man. "In the excitement in which I then was, I would be willing to inflict upon him every evil, even unto the extreme, rather than any such sin cleave to him" (Swedenborg 2001b, §72). At other times, he struggles between the worldly knowledge that has been his chief preoccupation up to that point and a higher, more spiritual knowledge (see, for example, Swedenborg 2001b, §§266–267).

In May 1744, Swedenborg went to London, where he lodged with a gold-watch engraver named John Paul Brockmer,[38] who was a member of the Moravian Brethren. Brockmer later was reported to have given an account of Swedenborg's behavior at this time that many have found alarming or suspect or both. The testimony came out only after Swedenborg's death, and it was publicized through a Swedish Lutheran clergyman named Aaron Mathesius (1736–1808), who was known to be prejudiced against Swedenborg, so it cannot be taken entirely at face value.[39] In it Brockmer says that Swedenborg was for the most part a quiet and unobtrusive tenant who went every Sunday to the Moravian chapel. At one point, however, Swedenborg's behavior changed. One evening he ran after Brockmer, "looked very frightful, his hair stood upright, and he foamed at the mouth. . . . At last he said he had something particular to communicate, namely, that he was the Messiah, that he was come to be crucified for the Jews, and that as he had a great impediment in his speech, Mr. Brockmer was chosen to be his mouth, to go with him next day to the synagogue." Swedenborg then told Brockmer that an angel would appear to him that night to confirm all that he said. But Brockmer saw no angel. Eventually he prevailed upon Swedenborg to see a doctor, who found other lodgings for him (Bergquist 2001, 54–57).

Brockmer's reported testimony cannot be independently corroborated—in fact, a later report describes him as denying key parts of the story—but scholar Lars Bergquist argues that it has rough parallels in Swedenborg's *Journal of Dreams*.[40] Certainly it echoes the feverish tone of that account. Debate over Brockmer's story has tended to center on whether this episode points to a mental imbalance in Swedenborg, but this may not be exactly the right question to ask. In recent years psychiatrists have come to recognize the "spiritual emergency" as a unique

---

38. Details concerning Brockmer are difficult to find. He was admitted to communion in the Moravian Society in 1743, and was still alive as late as 1788, though he had died by 1791. See Higham 1914, 36–37, with note.

39. For these accusations, see Tafel 1877, 586–590; for extensive refutation, 590–604.

40. Bergquist 2001, 57–59. For Brockmer's denial of the report ascribed to him, see Tafel 1877, 601–604.

psychological category in its own right. Although the process by which such "emergencies" occur is not well understood, they are common enough. In Christian contexts, as in Swedenborg's case, they can take the form of intense conversion experiences.[41] In traditional cultures, they can produce "shamanic crises," in which the aspirant may feel he is being attacked by spirits or even disassembled and restructured (Smoley and Kinney 1999, 159–161). However this is to be understood in purely psychological terms, it clearly points to a fundamental shift in the individual from an outward, "worldly" orientation to one that is oriented toward the unseen worlds. The individual does not remain dysfunctional, but moves on to a higher level of functionality.

Likewise, Swedenborg was far from incapacitated by these upheavals. He continued to work on *The Soul's Domain* (some of the dreams of this period reflect his attempts to figure out aspects of human anatomy; see Sigstedt 1981, 171). But as we have seen, he would never finish this work. In the prologue to *The Soul's Domain* he had rejected synthetic or *a priori* reasoning and proclaimed his adoption of analytic or *a posteriori* reasoning (Swedenborg [1744–1745] 1960, §§6–14). Now he extended *a posteriori* reasoning to knowledge that lay beyond the boundaries of material reality by applying it to the evidence of visions and revelations.

Swedenborg's mystical experiences throughout most of 1744 were concentrated on his dreams, which helps explain why he chronicled them so meticulously at this time. But in September 1744 a crucial shift occurred. While thinking about his work, he heard a voice say, "Hold your tongue or I will strike you!" He took it as a sign that he should not immerse himself in his labors so much on Sundays and in the evening. It was to be his first conscious encounter with the world of spirits.[42]

It was in the following spring that Swedenborg's orientation changed definitely and permanently: later he would say that this was the time when his spiritual eyes were opened. The incident occurred in April 1745. Swedenborg, dining alone in a private room in a London inn, sees and hears a man or an angel telling him not to eat too much. Then he sees a vapor rising from his body; it settles on the carpet and turns into worms of various types, which burn up with a loud pop. "A fiery light then appeared there and a rustling was audible," Swedenborg writes. "It felt as if

41. The classic account of such experiences can be found in James 1910, chapters 9 and 10.

42. Sigstedt 1981, 191; see Swedenborg 2001b, §242.

all the worms produced by an immoderate appetite had been expelled and burnt, and I had been purged of them."[43]

This episode would serve as a prelude to Swedenborg's decisive experience. It is curious that Swedenborg, who wrote so voluminously about his spiritual encounters, left no direct description of this one.[44] What we know of it comes from secondhand accounts given by two friends of his, which differ in some details. Swedenborg's friend Carl Robsahm (1735–1794), recounting Swedenborg's recollection of the event at the end of his life, says that on the evening of the meal at the inn, Swedenborg went home, and the "man" who had appeared to him that afternoon "said he was the Lord God, the Creator of the world, and the Redeemer," and that he had chosen Swedenborg "to explain the spiritual sense of Scripture" (Tafel 1875, 36). Another account, by his friend Gabriel Beyer (1720–1779), says Swedenborg saw the Lord "in imperial purple and majestic light." Beyer adds, "I remember that I asked him, how long this lasted; whereupon he answered, About a quarter of an hour; also, whether the strong light did not affect his eyes; when he said, No."[45]

IX. Transition to Theology

Even before these encounters, Swedenborg showed signs of his new orientation. In the fall of 1744 he had abandoned work on *The Soul's Domain* and began writing another book, titled *De Cultu et Amore Dei* (Worship and Love of God). This work, which would also remain unfinished, marks a transitional point in Swedenborg's oeuvre. It is a prose epic, half-scientific and half-poetic, that gives an account of the story of creation. It tells of a tree that produces a small egg in which the highest powers of nature have been concealed. This egg contains the embryonic Firstborn,

---

43. As quoted in Benz 2002, 195, who mistakenly ascribes it to the posthumous work *Adversaria* 2:1957, a passage that can now most easily be found under the new numbering system as §3557 in Swedenborg 1927–1951b. (On the *Adversaria* see note 47 below.) The passage Benz quotes is actually a slightly different version found in the posthumously published *Index Biblicus* (Bible Index; see Swedenborg 1859–1873); it is most readily accessible in Swedenborg 1998–2002, §397. Yet another account was given by Swedenborg's friend Carl Robsahm, to whom Swedenborg told the story years later; see Benz 2002, 194–196, and Tafel 1875, 35.

44. Swedenborg does give a reference to one incident from this episode in *The Old Testament Explained* (= Swedenborg 1927–1951b) §3557 and *Spiritual Experiences* (= Swedenborg 1998–2002) §397.

45. Quoted in Benz 2002, 196; see also Sigstedt 1981, 198–199, and Tafel 1877, 426.

Adam, who breaks through his shell and lies on the ground, his hands lifted in adoration of the Lord. During his education by angelic beings called "Wisdoms," he encounters both Christ as personified Love (§55) and the fallen Prince of This World (§81). Eventually he meets his bride, Eve, amid a choir of beings called "Understandings" (§110).

By the time of Swedenborg's decisive visions in the spring of 1745, the first two parts of *Worship and Love of God* had been issued. Since that time, some of his followers have wondered how this work is to be treated, since it appears to expound doctrines that Swedenborg would later repudiate, such as the teaching of three persons in the Trinity and the existence of a personal Devil. Swedenborg's own retrospective view of this book did not address such issues. He simply said that although it was based on truth, some egotism had intruded into it. He had been criticized for his Latin style, so he wrote this book making "a playful use of the Latin language" (Tafel 1877, 710).

In July 1745, Swedenborg returned to his native country and resumed work on the Board of Mines. In the spring of the following year, he moved into the house he had bought three years earlier, which was located in the southern part of Stockholm. All the while he immersed himself in biblical exegesis according to the new understanding awakened by his spiritual sight. He began by preparing a three-volume Bible index for his own use (Swedenborg 1859–1873), and proceeded to write some smaller works.

During this time, Swedenborg seems to have been able to maintain a connection with the newly discovered spiritual world while in ordinary human company. "I mingled with others just as before," he writes, "and no one observed the fact that there was with me such a heavenly intercourse. In the midst of company I have sometimes spoken with spirits, and with those who were around me. . . . At such times they could think no otherwise than that I was occupied with my thoughts."[46]

X. Exegesis of Scripture

He also kept up his duties with the Board of Mines, and when the post of councillor (a higher position than assessor, which was Swedenborg's title) became vacant, Swedenborg was offered the position. He not

---

46. Quoted in Sigstedt 1981, 213; the portion of her digest version cited here is based on passages that can be found in Swedenborg 1927–1951b, §§943, 3347.

only declined, but, in order to devote all his time to his spiritual studies, he petitioned the king to relieve him of his duties and give him a
pension equal to half his salary. His request was granted, and in June
1747 Swedenborg took leave of the institution he had served for over
thirty years. His intention was to devote his time to an exegesis of
Scripture. This work eventually took up three folio volumes in manuscript; nevertheless it remained unfinished, and Swedenborg never
published it. It did not appear in print until a century later, when it
was published under the title *Adversaria*. The English titles currently
used for it are *The Word Explained* or *The Old Testament Explained*.[47]

Most likely Swedenborg changed his mind about this project because
he felt it did not give a fully accurate portrayal of the unseen realities he
had begun to encounter. Although the great turning point of Swedenborg's
life and vision had come in 1744–1745, it appears that even after this time
he did not understand the full spiritual sense of the Scriptures. At least that
was his own assessment. In *The Old Testament Explained,* he often remarks
that the sense of some passage is obscure to him. In any event, its thrust is
chiefly to explain the first five books of the Bible as a prefiguration of the
coming of Christ—a form of exegesis that can be found in Christianity going back to its origins.[48]

In August 1747, however, he makes a note saying, "There was a
change of state in me into the heavenly kingdom, in an image."[49] Some
of his followers have interpreted this as meaning that at this point his intuition was fully awakened to the deepest and most spiritual sense of
Scripture. He himself pointed out that *The Old Testament Explained* contained "the interior historical sense"[50] of Genesis and Exodus, but not

---

47. For this work, see Swedenborg 1927–1951b; for biographical context, see Sigstedt 1981, 213–216.
The word *adversaria* refers to a book reserved for jotting down daily expenses or other ephemeral
notes; it was applied to *The Old Testament Explained* by the Swedenborgian scholar Johann
Friedrich Immanuel Tafel (1796–1863) when he began to publish the text in 1842, perhaps because
he was under the impression that the work consisted of notes or material collected for one of
Swedenborg's later works, *Secrets of Heaven*.

48. The apostles themselves read the books of the Hebrew Scriptures in the light of Christ's time
on earth; see, for example, Acts 1:20, referring back to Psalms 109:8; and Hebrews 5:5, 6, referring
back to Psalms 110:4.

49. Translation by Jonathan S. Rose. The original note appears on the first page of Swedenborg's
handwritten manuscript of his Bible index (Swedenborg 1859–1873) of Isaiah and Genesis. For
further information, see Tafel 1877, 839–840, and Acton 1927, 127 (with note 3).

50. Swedenborg distinguishes among the various senses of the Bible in *The Old Testament Explained* (= Swedenborg 1927–1951b) §§505, 5392–5398, and many other places.

the deepest, spiritual sense. His magnum opus, *Arcana Coelestia* (Secrets of Heaven), begun in December 1748, sets out his version of this spiritual sense. No longer do the stories of the Pentateuch merely serve as types for the coming Christian Church, but they apply to the inner life of the individual. The creation account of Genesis, for example, is seen in *Secrets of Heaven* 6–52 as a description of the regeneration of a human being: it begins in a dark state that is "without form and void" (Genesis 1:2) and reaches its conclusion—the fulfillment of spiritual potentiality—in the creation of a human being, "the image and likeness of God" (Genesis 1:26–27).

Hidden meanings in Scripture—even several hidden meanings, each nested inside the other—have been a recurrent theme in the Christian tradition from its beginnings. The earliest examples of allegorical exegesis of Scripture appear in Philo of Alexandria, a Jewish philosopher who lived at the time of Christ. Following Philo's lead, the church father Origen (about 185 to about 254) taught that there were three senses of Scripture, corresponding to the spirit, soul, and body (the tripartite structure of the human being as understood in early Christianity; see Origen 1966, 4:1:11). In medieval times this was expanded to four different levels of meaning (expounded, for example, by Dante [1265–1321] in his *Letter to Can Grande;* see Dante 1964). The four-part structure was also adopted by the Jewish Kabbalists, who equated them with the four worlds of Kabbalistic teaching: the physical, psychological, spiritual, and divine. These ideas were in turn reabsorbed into esoteric Christianity.[51] Swedenborg, too, saw three levels of meaning in Scripture besides the literal (Lamm 2000, 225).

These considerations lead to what may be the most vexed issue in Swedenborgian scholarship: How did Swedenborg's ideas relate to the esoteric and mystical currents of his era, as well as to broader trends in philosophical and theological thought?

Swedenborg himself stressed that his teachings were not influenced by human thought. He denied reading works of systematic theology both before and after his conversion, insisted on his total unfamiliarity with the works of the mystic Jacob Boehme (1575–1624), and condemned the Pietist mystic Johann Konrad Dippel (1678–1734).[52] On the other

---

51. See Smoley 2002, 3–5, 18–20; also Benz 2002, 280.

52. For Swedenborg's denial that he had studied either formal theology or Boehme's works, see Acton 1948–1955, 630, and also 623. For Swedenborg's rejection of Dippel, see *Spiritual Experiences* (= Swedenborg 1998–2002) §§3485–3487, 3890–3891, 5962, 5995.

hand, he must have had at least some familiarity with Philo's works—of which, as we have seen, Benzelius had prepared an edition—and his own library contained a number of works on esoteric topics such as magic, alchemy, and occultism.[53]

As often happens, the most sensible conclusion seems to lie in a middle ground. It is unlikely that Swedenborg's exegesis had no connection with esoteric interpretations of the Bible prior to his own; on the other hand, that does not mean it was derivative of them. Swedenborg certainly had some ideas of the esoteric currents of his time; he is just as likely to have known something of the Kabbalah as a philosopher today would be to know something of Zen.[54] On the other hand, Swedenborg was nothing if not a mystic and a visionary, and as his biographer Martin Lamm points out, "The history of mysticism teaches us that it is neither by their reading nor through personal influences that the great mystics generally realize their mission. On a closer look, one finds that the beginning of their mystical commitment is more often related to a personal experience that they considered to be divine revelation" (Lamm 2000, 59). Swedenborg certainly regarded his understanding of the internal sense of the Word as being revealed by the Lord. He did not think it had arisen out of his study of Philo or of Hermetic and Kabbalistic literature. On this point, I suggest, we must take him at his word.

The first volume of *Secrets of Heaven* was published anonymously in London in the summer of 1749; it sold at a cost of six shillings unbound. The printer makes much of the book's low price, attributing it to "the generous author's absolute command, . . . for he lacks neither purse nor spirit to carry out his laudable undertaking" (Tafel 1877, 497). And it is undoubtedly true that Swedenborg underwrote much of the cost of printing—or at any rate someone did. After a thorough examination of Swedenborg's accounts, Frans G. Lindh, a Swedish New Church scholar, advanced the hypothesis that some unknown patron secretly sponsored

---

53. On these books, see Lamm 2000, 57. On Hermetic philosophy, which formed the basis for alchemy, Swedenborg is reported to have declared, "I consider it to be true, and one of the great wonders of God, but I advise no one to work in this subject" (Tafel 1875, 62); but see the rejection of this report in Tafel 1875, 650–653.

54. Swedenborg's mentor Benzelius is known to have worked with Johan Kemper, a converted Jew and scholar of the Kabbalah who taught at Uppsala from 1697 until his death in 1714 or 1716 (Schuchard 1988, 363). For general information on Kemper (in German), see Schoeps 1965, 60–67; for a translation of the Schoeps material, see Dole 1990, 10–17.

the publication of Swedenborg's writings, but Bergquist suggests that the matter requires further research.[55]

XI. A Life in Two Worlds

In the years between 1749 and 1756, Swedenborg lived in obscurity, writing *Secrets of Heaven,* which was published in London in eight quarto volumes, one volume coming out more or less each year. During this time, he settled into the life that he would lead for the remainder of his days. For his first years on his Stockholm property, which covered about an acre, he lived in a small country house he shared with the gardener, the gardener's wife, and their three daughters. In 1752 he constructed a garden house for his own use. A simple and austere building, it contained a parlor, a bedroom, an orangerie or conservatory, and a study in which Swedenborg did his writing. In later years, Swedenborg's friend Robsahm would observe that the house "was no doubt comfortable for him, but not for anyone else."[56] The bedroom was never heated; Swedenborg slept under three or four English woolen blankets when it was cold. He kept no books here except his Hebrew and Greek Bibles and the indices to them that he had prepared. The study also contained a small stove on which he brewed his coffee, which he drank, heavily sugared, in large amounts throughout the day. Both the orangerie and the garden contained a wide range of plants, many of them exotic to Sweden. Swedenborg's records indicate that he planted chamomile, artichokes, and lemons, and that he ordered a variety of rare seeds and plants from the New World, including corn, watermelons, mulberries, dogwood, and beech (Sigstedt 1981, 238–239).

And yet as Swedenborg advanced into old age, the physical world seemed to recede from him, and he lived half among humans, half among spirits. Sometimes his trances left him impervious to the physical world. One of Swedenborg's friends, the Danish general Christian Tuxen (1713–about 1792), once found him in such a state, his head in his hands and his elbows resting on a table. Swedenborg replied when Tuxen spoke to him, but it took him some time to tune his attention back to earthly reality (Tafel 1877, 434). Although he sometimes spoke aloud when conversing

---

55. Bergquist discusses Lindh's researches in a comment on the text in Swedenborg 2001b, 322–323; his bibliography cites Lindh 1927–1930.

56. Quoted in Benz 2002, 221; see Tafel 1875, 31–32.

with spirits, usually the conversations were conducted in silence. It is clear
from his descriptions of these encounters that they took place in the realm
of the mind—that is, he did not hear them with his physical ears or see
them with his physical eyes. In fact he insists that this is impossible: "We
cannot possibly see [heavenly sights] with our physical eyes, but as soon as
the Lord opens our inner eyes—the eyes of our spirit—similar sights can
immediately present themselves to view."[57]

Swedenborg attributed human impulses to the influence of spirits either benign or evil. "We cannot think or form an intent on our own;
everything comes as an outside influence. What is good and true flows in
from the Lord by way of heaven and so by way of the angels present with
us. What is evil and false flows in from hell and so by way of the evil spirits present with us."[58] He himself blamed spirits for making a meal taste
bad as a punishment for gluttony (Swedenborg 1998–2002, §618) and
even said that they could give sugar the taste of salt: "A person's taste is
thus changed in accordance with the fantasies of spirits."[59]

These experiences may be best understood by recalling that Swedenborg
viewed his journey as an inward one: it was not merely a matter of ascent to
the heavens but of moving deeper within his own being. Thus he might well
have perceived common impulses, emotions, and sensations as external to
himself rather than identifying with them, as people ordinarily do. And as
the anecdotes above suggest, at this deep inner level, one's feelings and attitudes toward something—such as food—are even more tightly interwoven
with sensory experience than usual.

These considerations raise questions about human cognition and
identity that remain unresolved to this day. As the Swedenborgian psychologist Wilson Van Dusen suggests, Swedenborg's spirit theory often
serves to explain mental disorders such as schizophrenia as well as conventional theories do (Van Dusen 2004, 135–156). What the ordinary person
experiences as simply part of the mind's ongoing commentary can, under
certain circumstances, seem to be due to external suggestion. Shamans,
too, have experiences of spirits and other unseen agencies. In these areas
the line between sanity and insanity is an easy one to step over. Most spiritual traditions warn against becoming too immersed in alternate realities,
lest one become unhinged. The countermeasure generally recommended is

---

57. *Secrets of Heaven* 1532; translation by Lisa Hyatt Cooper.

58. *Secrets of Heaven* 5846; translation by Lisa Hyatt Cooper.

59. *Spiritual Experiences* (= Swedenborg 1998–2002) §645.

to keep a solid footing in earthly reality, as Swedenborg himself did. "The old man talks most reasonably on all other subjects," admitted the Swedish historian Johan Hinric Lidén (1741–1793), who regarded Swedenborg somewhat disparagingly.[60]

In any event Swedenborg felt the presence of alternate realities so vividly that he often believed he encountered friends and acquaintances who had died. Their fates frequently display a Dantesque sense of justice. We learn from the diary of spiritual experiences that Swedenborg's old mentor Polhem, who died in 1751 at the age of ninety, "had thoroughly convinced himself, while he was alive in the physical world, that there is no God, that nature is all there is, and that the life force in people and animals is something mechanical." Unable to free himself from these conceits in the other world, Polhem condemns himself to making mechanical "birds, mice, cats, and even human babies."[61] Charles XII, "more than all other people, was inwardly embroiled in self-love—in his life and his religious philosophy he had saturated himself with that love." In the afterlife he "wanted not only to conquer hell and become the most powerful devil but also to conquer heaven and place his throne above the Divine."[62]

Benzelius, who died in 1743, fares better. His "outer self was full of pride, but his inner self was good. . . . In the world, he had seen himself as better than everyone else. He had despised all others in comparison with himself, except for one person who had a better memory than he did—he had seen all learning and wisdom as a function of memory." This excessive preoccupation with brain power caused him difficulties in the next life. A "thick bony skin" around his cerebrum had to be broken, which caused him great pain. "Then he was brought back to his inner self, which was good, and then he was like a little child."[63]

XII. A New Theology

The eighth and final volume of *Secrets of Heaven* appeared in 1756. It takes Swedenborg's scriptural commentary to the end of Exodus. Although there is some evidence that he intended to offer a spiritual commentary

---

60. As quoted in Lamm 2000, 199; see Tafel 1877, 701–703.

61. *Spiritual Experiences* (= Swedenborg 1978b) §4722; translated here by Jonathan S. Rose.

62. *Spiritual Experiences* (= Swedenborg 1978b) §4750; translated here by Jonathan S. Rose.

63. *Spiritual Experiences* (= Swedenborg 1978b) §4749; translated here by Jonathan S. Rose.

on the whole Bible, he never undertook this effort; the only biblical book that would merit this close attention afterward was the Revelation of John. In 1758 Swedenborg again appeared in London with manuscripts to publish: *White Horse,* a collection of extracts from *Secrets of Heaven* on the nature of the Bible; *Other Planets,* a visionary account of beings from other worlds; *Last Judgment; New Jerusalem,* an exposition of the key teachings of the New Church that Swedenborg saw as his mission to proclaim; and *Heaven and Hell,* a meticulous account of the many dimensions of the afterlife.

Heaven and Hell would become Swedenborg's most popular work. The reasons are clear: the human fascination with the afterlife is universal, and there is a tremendous appetite for any work that claims to cast some light on this darkest of topics. Moreover, *Heaven and Hell* presents a succinct digest of many of the key elements of Swedenborg's theology, including his teaching that heaven has the structure of a human being (the *maximus homo* or universal human; see *Heaven and Hell* 59–67); the doctrine of heavenly marriage, "the union of two people into one mind" that may occur in the afterlife;[64] and the idea that the earth is a proving ground for the human soul, which after death gravitates strictly toward whatever its ruling passion (a concept sometimes translated "love" or "dominant love") was in life and thus tends toward heaven or toward hell (§§476–477), after an interval in the intermediate world of spirits (§§421–431).

It is this idea that we move of our own accord toward heaven or hell that represents a key advance in Swedenborg's teaching, for, unlike conventional Christianity, he stresses that heaven is not a reward, nor is hell a punishment. Rather each place is a suitable home for those disposed toward it. In ancient Egyptian art the trial of the soul after death is frequently represented as a weighing of the heart in the scales of good and evil by the gods. Swedenborg's view is similar, except that it is the human heart itself that delivers the verdict. Another comparable perspective appears in *The Tibetan Book of the Dead,* where the soul in the *bardo* or intermediate realm is led by its desire to choose its next incarnation (Thurman 1994). Swedenborg's doctrine differs from traditional Buddhist thought, however, inasmuch as it holds that we can only pass through life once. He rejects reincarnation (*Heaven and Hell* 256), an idea known in the West since at least the time of Plato.

---

64. *Heaven and Hell* 367; translation by George F. Dole.

Last Judgment, published in the same year, makes another revelation that is more startling than any of these. According to this work, the Last Judgment does not entail the physical return of Christ to earth. Instead the term refers to an actual event that took place in the spiritual world (*Last Judgment* 45). Up to Swedenborg's time, this dimension was dominated by religious tyrants who used superstition and spiritual materialism to dominate weaker and more credulous souls. In Swedenborg's vision, these evil spirits were cast down and the souls that were held in bondage to them were released into heaven, where they could be instructed in truth. The souls of those who had belonged to Christian churches did not escape this judgment, which was visited first upon the Catholics, and later upon the Protestants; the fate of the latter is described in a treatise titled *Continuatio de Ultimo Judicio: Et de Mundo Spirituali* (Supplements on the Last Judgment and the Spiritual World; 1763).[65]

In Swedenborg's Last Judgment, the earth is not dissolved nor the moon turned to blood; the event takes place in dimensions unseen to the physical eye. But Swedenborg says he was permitted to see this event with his spiritual vision. "I was allowed to see all these things with my own eyes so that I could testify to them. This Last Judgment started in early 1757 and was completed by the end of that year."[66]

This Last Judgment does not affect the physical world (which remains largely unchanged), nor did it radically change Swedenborg's life, at least in the short term. On the other hand, he saw his own mission very much in the light of this process. This housecleaning in the spirit world made it possible for human beings on earth to see spiritual truths more directly and more "inwardly." It also created the possibility of a new church that would accept and incorporate these insights. Swedenborg saw it as his mission to promulgate them.

XIII. Fame for Spiritual Encounters

Coincidentally or not, the period following the year 1757 marked another major change in Swedenborg's destiny. Unlike the spiritual crisis of

---

65. The short title is *Supplements;* the traditional English title is *Continuation Concerning the Last Judgment.* Because of the limitation of this latter title, the supplement on the spiritual world (§§32–90) has often been overlooked.

66. *Last Judgment* 45; translation by Jonathan S. Rose.

1744–1745, it did not alter his vision or his theology, but it did impel him to go public with them.

a. The Stockholm Fire

Swedenborg returned to his native country from England in July 1759. En route home he stopped in the Swedish city of Göteborg, where he dined at the house of a prominent merchant. At six o'clock Swedenborg left the room and returned in great agitation. He said that a fire had broken out in south Stockholm and was spreading rapidly; a house belonging to a friend had already burned down and his own house was in danger.

At eight o'clock, Swedenborg went out again and returned, saying, "Thank God! The fire is extinguished the third door from my house!" Two days later messengers arrived from Stockholm confirming Swedenborg's report down to the smallest detail (Sigstedt 1981, 269–270).

News of this incident caused a sensation in the capital and marked the beginning of the last phase of Swedenborg's career, one in which he became the object of public attention not only in Sweden but throughout the continent of Europe. Count Tessin, the leader of the Hat party and a former prime minister, was motivated to make his acquaintance, chiefly out of curiosity. He evidently found Swedenborg's vision convincing—though he expressed reservations about Swedenborg's theology. Concerning *Heaven and Hell,* he observed, "Throughout the entire work one recognizes Bishop Swedberg's son, who is dreaming with far greater profundity than the father. . . . All this may be read with the same credence that one gives to Mohammed's Alcoran [the Qur'an]."[67] Tessin's polite amusement probably represents a widespread attitude toward the visionary among the higher ranks of Swedish society. All the same, to this day many people find the story of the Stockholm fire to be the strongest objective evidence supporting Swedenborg's claim of spiritual sight.

b. Madame de Marteville's Receipt

The incident of the Stockholm fire was, however, only the beginning of Swedenborg's proofs of interior vision. Another famous anecdote involves

---

67. Tessin, as quoted in Sigstedt 1981, 275; she cites the entry for July 4, 1760, in the manuscript of Tessin's diary (2:890–891) at his estate of Åkerö, Sweden, most accessible in Tessin 1760.

the wife of the Dutch ambassador, one Louis de Marteville (1701–1760). The account is given in twelve different versions in twelve sources (Tafel 1877, 643–646), but the gist is as follows.

At some time after de Marteville's death, a goldsmith presented his widow, Marie Louisa Ammon de Marteville,[68] with a bill for twenty-five thousand guilders for a silver service her husband had bought. Madame de Marteville was thrown into a panic. She was sure her husband had paid the goldsmith, but could not find the receipt. She was advised to pay Swedenborg a visit and ask for his help. He offered to try, and a few days later encountered the dead ambassador in the spirit world. De Marteville assured Swedenborg that he would go and look for the receipt. Several days later, the ambassador appeared to his wife in a dream and explained that she should look behind a drawer in his desk. "My child, you are worried about the receipt. Just pull out the drawer of my desk all the way. [At some time when the drawer was being pulled out], the receipt was probably pushed back, and is lying behind it." Madame de Marteville looked in this spot, and not only found the receipt but a hairpin set with diamonds that she believed was lost.

When Swedenborg paid a call on her the following day, he said he had tried to meet with the ambassador, but the latter refused, simply saying he had to tell his wife something, and that after doing so he would be going on to a more exalted part of heaven.[69]

c. Queen Lovisa Ulrika's Secret

A third demonstration of Swedenborg's powers involved still more exalted company—Lovisa Ulrika (1720–1782), the sour and imperious queen of Sweden. In the autumn of 1761, Swedenborg was presented at court, and the queen asked him if it was true that he could communicate with the dead. Swedenborg said he could.

The queen then took Swedenborg aside and gave him a question to put to her brother, Augustus Wilhelm, Prince of Prussia (1722–1758), who had died a few years earlier. He agreed to do this and returned to

---

68. The dates of birth and death of Madame de Marteville are not readily available. Some idea of her lifespan can be deduced from the fact that her husband was ambassador to Stockholm from 1752 until his death in 1760 at the age of fifty-nine (Tafel 1875, 653; see also Tafel 1877, 1229). She seems to have died by 1790, as she is described in the past tense in a document published in that year (see Tafel 1875, 653–654).

69. This is the composite version of the account given by Sigstedt 1981, 277–278.

court three weeks later. He was presented to Lovisa Ulrika while she was playing cards. The queen told him he could deliver his message in front of the whole company, but Swedenborg demurred, saying he could tell it to her only in private.

The queen and Swedenborg withdrew to another apartment with a courtier in attendance. When Swedenborg disclosed his message, the queen turned pale and took a few steps backward, exclaiming, "That is something which no one else could have told [me] but my brother!"

Although Swedenborg was pressed on many sides to disclose the secret of the message, he never did. One account says he repeated to the queen the exact words of her last conversation with her brother, but even this is not certain. Possibly Swedenborg felt he had to keep the matter secret because the queen and her brother were Prussians, and Sweden was at war with Prussia at the time. Lovisa Ulrika was already a suspect figure to her adopted nation. She did not conceal her pleasure at Prussia's triumphs in the war and Sweden's reversals. Moreover, in 1755 she had been implicated in an abortive plot to overthrow the Swedish constitution and replace it with an absolute monarchy.[70]

XIV. The Man in His Times

These three anecdotes are not the only pieces of evidence attesting to Swedenborg's paranormal powers, but they are both the most famous and the best documented, and they made his reputation as a visionary. From this time on, he no longer worked anonymously but spoke openly of his experiences and received visitors from all over Europe. He also began to accumulate followers and opponents.

Nonetheless Swedenborg did not neglect his more conventional duties. At this time Sweden was in a financial crisis brought about by the war with Prussia, in which Sweden had yet again fared badly. The nation's leaders had adopted a familiar yet ruinous means of dealing with this problem: issuing a virtually worthless paper currency. Swedenborg wrote a lengthy paper on the matter, which was presented to the Swedish Diet in November 1760 (Acton 1948–1955, 537–544). He argued against the current fiscal policy and incidentally proposed state regulation of the sale of liquor, which he believed had brought great harm in Sweden. The

---

70. The account given here follows that of Sigstedt 1981, 278–280, 289–291. The many versions of the incident are gathered in Tafel 1877, 647–673, 675–679.

next year, he delivered an address defending Sweden's limited monarchy against absolutism.[71] He did not read these addresses himself but simply presented them as reports. A slight stutter, to which he had been prone all his life, made him shy of public speaking.

In these matters, Swedenborg demonstrated his wisdom and clear-sightedness, proving that his encounters with the invisible worlds had not unhinged him mentally. What is perhaps most striking about his political statements is that he makes his arguments in purely conventional terms—the only kind his colleagues would have understood and appreciated. Had he inserted claims of religious authority into these papers, he would have undermined his position, and he clearly knew this.

As Swedenborg became more renowned for his visions and teachings about the spirit world, people naturally became curious about him. It is from this era that we have the most vivid descriptions of Swedenborg personally. He was a man of medium height, with clear blue eyes. In demeanor he was universally polite and good-humored, and reluctant to speak about his mystical experiences unless he was directly asked or he believed the person was genuinely interested. To overcome his stutter, he spoke slowly and deliberately, which gave dignity and weight to his speech. His dress was simple: Robsahm reports that he wore a fur coat of reindeer skins in the winter and a dressing gown in summer. When he went out, he wore a black velvet suit in the style of the day, though he was prone to missing small details of his dress and might be found at a stylish dinner with mismatched shoe buckles (Tafel 1875, 33–34).

Swedenborg spent much time alone, communing with the spirits and writing, but he generally accepted dinner invitations when they were offered, and was regarded as pleasant and urbane company. At home he ate and drank very little apart from enormous quantities of coffee; a roll soaked in milk was his principal meal. But when he dined out as a guest, he would eat what was served, and was not averse to drinking wine, which, like his coffee, he preferred heavily sugared. Despite the peculiarities of his diet, he generally enjoyed excellent health throughout his life, and attributed the minor ailments he had to attacks from evil spirits. He kept to his own schedule, sleeping and waking as he liked regardless of the hour. He did not require his servants to adjust to the eccentricities of his timetable; consequently they found that he required almost no attention at all (Benz 2002, 221–230).

---

71. See Tafel 1875, 538–542, and for another version, Acton 1948–1955, 591–595.

During his travels abroad, he kept as much as possible to the same manner of life. Johann Christian Cuno (1708–1796), a friend of Swedenborg's in Amsterdam, asked his landlady there whether she had to do much for her tenant. "'Almost nothing,' was her answer. 'My maid has nothing to do with him other than lighting the fire on the hearth in the mornings. He goes to bed every evening as the clock strikes seven and gets up the next morning at eight o'clock. . . . I really wish he would spend the rest of his life with us. My children will miss him most, for he never goes out without bringing them something to nibble.'"[72]

When at home in Stockholm, Swedenborg, normally reclusive, began to receive visitors: clergymen interested in his teachings, nobles wanting him to communicate with dead relatives, even children. A neighbor's daughter asked him on several occasions to show her an angel, and Swedenborg finally yielded to her request: he led her to a curtain, which he pulled aside to reveal the little girl's own image reflected in a mirror (Tafel 1877, 724–725).

XV. Reality and Knowledge

Another visitor, an Englishman named Green,[73] came bearing a letter from one Immanuel Kant asking for Swedenborg's views on the nature of reality. Swedenborg did not reply directly to Kant. This was perhaps a tactical mistake, because Kant would publish a book in 1766 titled *Dreams of a Spirit Seer* mocking and deriding Swedenborg and permanently damaging his reputation in learned circles. But Swedenborg had told Green that he was about to publish a book that would answer Kant's questions (Tafel 1877, 627). The work he had in mind was probably *Divine Love and Wisdom,* published in 1763 (although some say it is the small treatise *Soul-Body Interaction,* which appeared in 1769).

And yet the message of *Divine Love and Wisdom* suggests that Kant's objections were not merely due to an imagined slight or even to Swedenborg's claims of mystical knowledge. The essence of Swedenborg's teaching is strikingly different from Kant's. Kant stressed the ultimate unknowability

---

72. As quoted in Benz 2002, 229; see Tafel 1877, 446.

73. Despite the assertions of Tafel 1877, 1222–1225, the identity of "the Englishman Green" is unknown. See Kant [1766] 2002, 184–185 note 11.

of reality in itself. He contended that we experience the world only through categories of experience such as time, space, and causality, and that these are essentially impenetrable; human understanding cannot go past them.

For Swedenborg, on the other hand, reality *is* ultimately knowable; it is the result of "a constant inflow from the spiritual world into the earthly world."[74] Knowledge of any kind is made possible only by an emanation of power from the Lord, and although the human orientation toward the material world ordinarily blocks our understanding of higher realities, there is nothing that intrinsically prevents us from elevating ourselves to those levels. We are impeded not so much by the limits of our minds as by the limits we place on love: "The reason we do not become rational to the highest degree we are capable of is that our love, which is a matter of our intent, cannot be raised up in the same way as our wisdom, which is a matter of our discernment. The love that is a matter of intent is raised only by abstaining from evils as sins and then by those good actions of thoughtfulness that are acts of service, acts that we are then performing from the Lord."[75]

Although these ideas may sound unusual, they resonate with an ancient teaching that true wisdom cannot be isolated as a mere intellectual phenomenon. The wise individual must also be a good individual. This is the essence of the moral theory of Plato (427–347 B.C.E.), as expounded, for example, in *The Republic;* it also explains why Aristotle (384–322 B.C.E.) insisted that moral philosophy could only be taught to those who have good moral training to begin with (Aristotle *Nichomachean Ethics* 1096b).

Furthermore, Swedenborg distinguishes between this true wisdom, which must be linked to morality, and mere intellectual attainment. This distinction was well on its way to being lost in the eighteenth century, and in our own era it is generally disregarded: good character is seen as irrelevant to the acquisition of true knowledge.

XVI. Later Works

The year 1763 saw the publication of several works besides *Divine Love and Wisdom. Supplements* (mentioned above) is a discussion of the fate of

---

74. *Divine Love and Wisdom* 337; George F. Dole's translation.

75. *Divine Love and Wisdom* 258; George F. Dole's translation.

the Protestant sects in the Last Judgment that had taken place six years earlier in the spirit world. The great Dragon mentioned in Revelation 12 represents those Protestants who observed the outward forms of religion without amending their lives in accordance with it (§16). The Last Judgment, as portrayed by Swedenborg, was harsh not only on the Lutherans (§§14–31) but on his old associates the Moravian Brethren (§§86–90). Members of that sect did not forgive him for his reports on the fate of their predecessors. Swedenborg's followers claim that this was why he was later maligned by his one-time landlord, the Moravian Brockmer (Sigstedt 1981, 311).

The other four books published in 1763 were *The Lord, Sacred Scripture, Life,* and *Faith.* The preface to *The Lord* speaks of "the doctrine of the New Jerusalem, that is, the doctrine of the new church, which the Lord is to set up today, since the old church has come to an end."[76] This idea was to form a central theme of the last phase of Swedenborg's teaching. Since the Last Judgment had purged the spirit world of its corruption, there was now the possibility—and a need—for a new church on earth that would encourage a deeper understanding of spiritual truths as well as greater freedom in exploring them. Swedenborg did not want to start a new sect; rather he hoped that his ideas would percolate into the established denominations and transform them slowly and peacefully (Lamm 2000, 325–326). It was only after his death that his disciples created a new denomination to promulgate his teachings.[77]

In 1764 Swedenborg began writing a commentary on the Revelation of John called *Revelation Unveiled.* This was a distinctly new examination of a topic Swedenborg had treated in an earlier text, *Revelation Explained,* begun in the late 1750s but never completed.[78] *Revelation Unveiled* resembles *Secrets of Heaven* in that it is a detailed exposition of the inner meaning of a portion of the Bible, and again this meaning has to do with spiritual truths. The Book of Revelation, according to Swedenborg, does not allude to empires and kingdoms, as conventional explanations both in his and in our day assert, but to spiritual dimensions (§1). The whore of Babylon is the Church of Rome (§631); the Dragon is those who advocate Trinitarianism

---

76. The translation is mine.

77. For a brief history (limited to Great Britain, the United States, and Canada) of the Swedenborgian movement after Swedenborg's death, see pages 245–310 below.

78. The traditional titles of *Revelation Explained* (= Swedenborg 1994–1997a) and *Revelation Unveiled* are, respectively, *Apocalypse Explained* and *Apocalypse Revealed.*

and solifidism (§537); and the woman clothed with the new sun is the new church whose coming Swedenborg proclaims (§434:2). The description of the New Jerusalem in Revelation 21 refers to the state of the church after the Last Judgment (§§876–925). *Revelation Unveiled* marks an important innovation in Swedenborg's writings: the insertion into the text of relatively free-standing accounts of "memorable occurrences," specifically so called. These are Swedenborg's own experiences in the spiritual world. Previously he had recorded them in his journal *Spiritual Experiences* and woven them into his theological expositions. He no longer kept the journal after 1765 (Sigstedt 1981, 316–317).

XVII. A Following

By the mid-1760s Swedenborg had begun to attract a following both in his own country and abroad. The German clergyman Friedrich Christoph Oetinger (1702–1782) was one of the earliest advocates of Swedenborg's teachings. In 1765 he published a volume titled *Swedenborgs und anderer irdische und himmlische Philosophie* (The Earthly and Heavenly Philosophy of Swedenborg and Others), in which he asserted that "God [has made] use of an eminent philosopher in order to communicate to us heavenly information."[79] But pressure from the Lutheran establishment in Germany forced Oetinger to back away from his position, and he ended by taking a skeptical view of Swedenborg's works (Sigstedt 1981, 335–340).

Two of Swedenborg's countrymen would prove more loyal. En route to the Netherlands on another journey in the summer of 1765, Swedenborg stopped in Göteborg. He was invited to a dinner party at the house of Johan Rosén (1726–1773), a poet, editor, and secondary-school teacher. Also present was Gabriel Beyer, another teacher. Beyer had read some of Swedenborg's books and found them incomprehensible. He asked Swedenborg for a fuller account of his teaching. Swedenborg agreed to provide it. Dining with Beyer and Rosén the next day, he gave an eloquent presentation of his ideas. The two men asked him for a written summary of them, which Swedenborg delivered the day after that. As he handed it to the two men, tears ran down his face. Turning to Beyer, he said, "My friend, from this day the Lord has introduced

---

79. Quoted in Tafel 1877, 1028.

you into the society of angels, and you are now surrounded by them"
(Tafel 1877, 700).

In the years from 1766 to 1768, Swedenborg composed another major
work, *Marriage Love*. Addressing the nature of love both on earth and in
heaven, Swedenborg takes issue with much of the Christian tradition,
which has tended to portray sexuality as a sordid necessity, far inferior to
chastity. Swedenborg, on the other hand, contends that only true marriages are genuinely chaste. He goes so far as to say, "Chastity cannot be
attributed to people who have renounced marriage by vowing perpetual
celibacy unless some true love of marriage remains alive within them."[80]
He also says that marriages continue in heaven, although if the partners
are not compatible at a deep level, they will eventually separate and find
new mates (*Marriage Love* 45, 49).

This teaching may have struck a personal note. Swedenborgian oral
tradition (not documented in his own writings or journals) says that
Swedenborg himself felt that the spouse who awaited him in the next
world was Elisabet Stierncrona Gyllenborg (1714–1769), the wife of his
friend Count Frederick Gyllenborg. She was the author of a devotional
work, anonymously published, titled *Marie bäste del* (The Best Part of
Mary; 1756–1760), and the copy she presented to Swedenborg still exists
(Sigstedt 1981, 245).[81] It is evident why Swedenborg thought this devout
lady would ultimately find herself incompatible with her husband. In
his journal *Spiritual Experiences,* Swedenborg describes Gyllenborg as
situated in "the hell of those who are cunning, and act clandestinely,
and with deliberation, caution, and [excessive reliance on human]
prudence."[82]

In the spring of 1768 Swedenborg took yet another trip to the
Netherlands, this time to publish *Marriage Love*. The book appeared
in September of that year; it has the distinction of being the first of
Swedenborg's theological works to bear his name on the title page; all
of his previous writings on this subject had appeared anonymously
(Sigstedt 1981, 362). During this time he also worked on his last book,
True Christianity. In the spring of 1769 he went to Paris, intending to

---

80. *Marriage Love* 155; translation by George F. Dole.

81. For the story, see Sigstedt 1981, 245; for the book itself, see [Gyllenborg] 1756–1760; for a
painting of Elisabet Stierncrona, see Kirven and Larsen 1988, 44.

82. *Spiritual Experiences* (= Swedenborg 1978b) §5161. Human prudence is often negatively contrasted with divine providence in Swedenborg's works; see *Divine Providence* 191.

publish it there, but it would not pass the strict French censorship. The censor advised him to resort to a subterfuge: having it printed in Paris but listing the place of publication as Amsterdam. Swedenborg demurred. He revised the book and had it published in Amsterdam, where it appeared in the summer of 1771 (Sigstedt 1981, 376, 415).

By this time Swedenborg's spiritual teachings had spread widely enough to arouse strong allegiances and oppositions. In his trip to Amsterdam in 1768–1769, he made the acquaintance of a merchant named Johann Christian Cuno, who always maintained a high regard for Swedenborg personally, though he had difficulties with many of his ideas. This was no doubt due in part to the weight of learned opinion, which often found Swedenborg's views at odds with conventional doctrines (Sigstedt 1981, 366–373). Later in 1769, on a trip to London, Swedenborg made the acquaintance of some men who would form the nucleus of the Swedenborgian movement in England, notably a Quaker named William Cookworthy (1705–1780), and Thomas Hartley (1708–1784), a clergyman of the Church of England. They were instrumental in issuing some of the first editions of Swedenborg's works in English: Cookworthy published a translation of *Life* in 1772, and later underwrote publication of an English version of *Heaven and Hell*.[83] For Hartley, who asked him for some account of himself as a means of countering critics, Swedenborg wrote a small autobiographical sketch that serves as an interesting source document for the seer's own view of his background and work.[84]

XVIII. Challenged by the Consistory

Before Swedenborg went back to his native land in the fall of 1769, his English friends told him they could find a home for him in their country if a hostile clergy made life difficult for him in Sweden. Swedenborg dismissed their concerns; he was, he said, on intimate terms with the bishops and nobility; consequently, "I have not the least fear of the persecution of

---

83. Sigstedt 1981, 378–379, suggests that the translation of *Life* was published in 1770, but Hyde 1906, entry 1859, prefers 1772. For these translations, see respectively Swedenborg [1763] 1772 and Swedenborg [1758] 1778.

84. For Hartley's letter and Swedenborg's reply, see Acton 1948–1955, 673–680.

which you are somewhat apprehensive."[85] In a sense, Swedenborg was right: he was far too well-connected to be the object of any direct harassment. It was his disciples Beyer and Rosén who had to bear the brunt of official opposition.

Beyer and Rosén had stepped beyond the limits of safety that hitherto had been drawn around Swedenborg's works, for he wrote in Latin and most discussions and reviews of his ideas appeared in that language, guaranteeing that they would remain in the domain of the educated public. But Rosén had published a translation of a German review of *Revelation Unveiled* (Ernesti 1768, 97–109), and Beyer had published a book based on Swedenborg's teachings called *New Attempts at Explaining the Texts for Sundays and Holidays* ([Beyer] 1767; traditionally referred to as *Household Sermons*). Both of these were published in Swedish as opposed to Latin, and they caused a turmoil in the Göteborg Consistory.[86] Olof A. Ekebom (1716–1784), dean of the Consistory, contended that Swedenborg's teachings were opposed to those of the Lutheran Church and smacked of Socinianism, and wrote up his opinion in the spring of 1769.[87] Swedenborg, writing from Amsterdam, where he was staying at the time, indignantly repudiated Ekebom's accusations.

The matter was referred to the national House of the Clergy,[88] which ruled that Beyer and Rosén would have to report to the king himself about the errors and heresies of Swedenborgianism. The two

---

85. Quoted in Acton 1948–1955, 679.

86. Under Swedish church law, the consistory was a committee of senior Lutheran clergy with supervisory powers over pastors and teachers in its diocese, operating under the immediate oversight of the local bishop. It had no authority to censor outside its own jurisdiction, though this limitation did not usually undercut the state church's effectiveness in quashing unorthodox teachings. Eventually the Göteborg Consistory referred its protests of Swedenborgianism to higher ecclesiastical bodies.

87. Acton 1948–1955, 664. The term *Socinianism* refers to the teachings of the Italian theologian Faustus Socinus (also known as Fausto Sozzini; 1539–1604) and his uncle Laelius Socinus (Lelio Sozzini; 1525–1562), who denied that Jesus was divine. By the term, Ekebom probably meant heresy in general; otherwise the accusation would have been particularly ill-informed, as Swedenborg spoke disparagingly of Socinianism many times in his theological career, both before and after 1769 (see *Secrets of Heaven* 5432, 6865, 7233, 8521, 8993, 9300, 9424; *Heaven and Hell* 3, 83; *Divine Providence* 231, 256, 257, 262; *Revelation Unveiled*, preface and §571; *True Christianity* 94, 159, 339, 378, 380, 450, 795). For the other charges Ekebom leveled at Swedenborg, see Acton 1948–1955, 661–665.

88. The House of Clergy was one of the four divisions of the Diet, or Swedish national parliament. The others were the House of Nobles, of which Swedenborg was a member; the House of Burghers; and the House of Peasants.

men defended themselves ably, and Swedenborg wrote letters to aid them. But in the end the Royal Council stripped Beyer of his post as teacher of theology and sacred languages and ordered Rosén, who taught Latin, to keep Swedenborgian doctrines out of his lectures. An indignant Swedenborg wrote to the king, asking why he himself had not been informed of the proceedings when it was his doctrines that were in question (Acton 1948–1955, 721–726).

Swedenborg's own actions, along with the aid of influential friends, helped to blunt the harshness of the judgment against Beyer and Rosén. By December 1771, the Royal Council had tired of the case and referred it to an appeals court. Here it dragged on for another three years before it was referred to scholars at Uppsala University for a ruling. In the meantime Rosén died. In February 1779 Beyer was allowed to resume teaching, but he, too, died shortly thereafter.

Swedenborg himself remained above legal action, but he and his ideas were subjected to widespread mockery, and there was a movement afoot at one point to have him declared insane. When Swedenborg heard the news, "going straightway into his garden, [he] fell upon his knees and prayed to the Lord, asking Him what he should do. He received the comforting assurance that no evil would befall him" (Tafel 1875, 47). At another point a young man came to Swedenborg's house to make an assassination attempt, which failed when he caught his coat on the nail of a fence, causing his sword to fall out. Panicking, the man ran away.[89] The controversy even led Swedenborg's gardener and his wife to doubt the wisdom and goodness of their master on the grounds that he did not go to church.

"My friends," Swedenborg replied, "look back upon the years you have daily seen me before your eyes, and then decide for yourselves whether I am a Christian or not. I submit myself to your judgment. Do what you deem to be right."

The next day they stood before him and said they could find no fault in him.[90]

XIX. *True Christianity*

While these controversies were raging, Swedenborg, now in his early eighties, was finishing *True Christianity*, a defense of his doctrine against

89. Tafel 1875, 59–60, quoting the account of Pernety 1782, §12.

90. Tafel 1877, 729–734, translates this story from Wetterbergh 1848, 2:457–467. See the shorter version in Sigstedt 1981, 397–399.

the imputation of heresy implicit in the attack on Beyer and Rosén. The essence of its message can be found, perhaps, in an account of a memorable occurrence in the spiritual world, in which Swedenborg reports:

> A magnificent temple appeared to me. It was square in form and its roof was in the shape of a crown; . . . its door was made of a pearly substance. . . . Later, when I came closer to the temple, I saw an inscription over the door: "Now permission is granted"; which meant that now permission is granted to explore the mysteries of faith intellectually. . . . In the new church . . . permission has been granted to explore with the intellect, and delve deeply into, all the mysterious teachings of the church, and also to check those teachings against the Word.[91]

This idea lies at the center of *True Christianity* and of Swedenborg's thought as well. Reason is no longer to be at odds with faith, nor faith with experience; but rather they are all to be integrated into a seamless garment woven of love and understanding. For Swedenborg himself, this integration took place as the result of the opening of his spiritual sight and his entry into the kingdom of heaven through visions; for others, he indicated, it would come through a study of his works, which were the result of direct revelation from the Lord. An individual's responses to these works would be dictated by his or her own capacity for divine illumination (Sigstedt 1981, 430).

The heresy trial at Göteborg suggests why Swedenborg did not attempt to publish his works in his native country. The censorship imposed by the Lutheran establishment was far too rigid; as we have seen, even the attitude of the Catholic censors in France was more indulgent. Consequently, when *True Christianity* was finished, Swedenborg made another journey abroad to publish it. In July 1770, he embarked for the Netherlands, but this time he seemed to sense that the journey would be his last. When his friend Robsahm asked him if they would meet again, Swedenborg replied, "Whether I shall return again, I do not know, but of this I can assure you, for the Lord has promised it to me, that I shall not die before I have received from the press this work which is now ready to be printed, *Vera Religio Christiana* [True Christianity]."[92] And although he refused to write a will, he did arrange to leave his property in trustworthy hands and settled his servants with a comfortable pension.

---

91. *True Christianity* 508; translation by Jonathan S. Rose.

92. Sigstedt 1981, 412. Though she cites Tafel 1875, 38–39, as her source, the inversion of the normal word order of the Latin title *Vera Christiana Religio* is not found there, but in Tafel 1875, 71.

XX. Final Voyage

Most of *True Christianity* was published in Amsterdam, but Swedenborg decided to have the supplement, called *Coronis* (Coda),[93] printed in London, where he went in August 1771. There he conferred with disciples like Hartley and the physician Husband Messiter,[94] who were occupied with English translations of his works. During this time Messiter borrowed the manuscript of *Coronis* and unfortunately lost it. Before it disappeared, however, half of it was copied, and this half at least was later published posthumously (Swedenborg 1996j).

In December 1771 Swedenborg suffered a stroke, which incapacitated him for several weeks, and, to his great discomfiture, temporarily removed his spiritual sight. It was soon restored, but Swedenborg remained partially paralyzed, and he began to tell his friends he was not long for this world. One particularly striking anecdote involves John Wesley (1703–1791), the founder of Methodism. In February 1772, Swedenborg sent a letter to Wesley saying, "Sir—I have been informed in the world of spirits that you have a strong desire to converse with me. I shall be happy to see you, if you will favor me with a visit."

Wesley was astonished, because although it was true that he wanted to meet Swedenborg, he had not told anyone about it. He wrote back saying that he could not meet with him now, as he was about to embark on a six-month trip, but would be happy to meet him on his return.

Swedenborg replied to Wesley that this would be impossible, as he, Swedenborg, was going to depart for the world of spirits on the twenty-ninth of the following month (Tafel 1877, 564–566).

The prophecy proved true. On the afternoon of March 29, 1772, Swedenborg lay in bed, attended by his landlady and her housemaid. It was a Sunday, and he heard the church bells ring. He asked the ladies what time it was.

"Five o'clock," he was told.

"That is good," Swedenborg replied. "I thank you. God bless you!" And he died, at the age of eighty-four.

---

93. The traditional English title, *Crown,* is a mistranslation, as the Latin word *coronis* means an appendix. A more accurate indicator of its form and content is *Sketch for "Coda to True Christianity."* For more on the history of this manuscript, see pages 118–119 with note 7 below.

94. Considering the notable role Messiter played in the last days of Swedenborg's life, precise biographical facts about him are very difficult to obtain. Even his first name is variously given—as Husband, as Henry, or as the mere abbreviation H., as if the full name were unknown to the writer. For further information, see Tafel 1875, 601; Tafel 1877, 534–535.

On his work table lay a piece of paper with the following words on it: "An invitation to the new church, so that people may come and meet the Lord. . . . From now on, they are not to be called Evangelicals or the Reformed, still less Lutherans or Calvinists, but Christians."[95]

Swedenborg was buried in the graveyard of the Swedish Church in London. His remains were exhumed in 1908, however, and returned to be buried at Uppsala Cathedral, where they rest to this day.

XXI. Assessment

The story of Swedenborg's influence extends beyond the limits of this essay, but although at one point he estimated that he could count some fifty people who accepted his teachings (Tafel 1877, 440), soon his followers would assemble themselves into a new denomination. His legacy extends much further than the New Church, of course, and can be seen in the work of such seminal figures as William Blake (1757–1827), Honoré de Balzac (1799–1850), and Charles Baudelaire (1821–1867). To take only one example, the entire Symbolist movement in nineteenth-century art was inspired by Baudelaire's sonnet "Correspondences"—a poem that was in turn inspired by Swedenborg's teachings (Starkie 1958, 225–233).

And yet Swedenborg's most profound legacy is one that remains largely untapped. More than most, his life has an architectonic structure to it. On the one hand, it encompasses an ascent from an investigation of the mineral kingdom to one of the plant and animal realms. When Swedenborg began the age-old quest for the link between the soul and the body, he had to go past reason and rise into the unseen dimensions of the spirit. On the other hand, Swedenborg's journey was also one toward the interior of the self and of the universe. He started at the outward surface of things—with minerals and technology—and went inward to explore human anatomy before reaching the inmost essence of things, which is spiritual and invisible.

Over two centuries after his death, the issues that concerned Swedenborg still concern us. We have taken technology in directions that probably even his capacious mind could not have dreamed of. And our thirst for the knowledge of ultimate realities remains as powerful as ever. But unlike

---

95. Outline for *Invitation to the New Church*, items [9] and [10]; translation by Jonathan S. Rose. See Sigstedt 1981, 433.

Swedenborg, we have not, as a civilization, managed to find a satisfying link between these two realms. Investigations of the interface between matter and mind in some ways seem even more mechanistic than they were in his day, while explorations of analogies between, for example, submolecular physics and the teachings of Zen and the Tao seem interesting though premature. I do not know how our civilization will integrate its understanding of these two dimensions of objective reality, nor whether such an integration will take place in my lifetime. And yet I feel confident that when such a unification takes place, it will be due at least in part to the influence of Swedenborg.

THEOLOGICAL WORKS

Swedenborg's Garden of Theology

An Introduction to Swedenborg's Published Theological Works

JONATHAN S. ROSE

Outline

IN the 1740s, in the heart of the Enlightenment and in the middle of his life, a European scientist by the name of Emanuel Swedenborg underwent a spiritual crisis and personal transformation. He had been abroad for several years on one of his many journeys, but now returned home to his native Sweden, where he had some property near Stockholm—an unassuming plot of land, about 1.2 acres (about .5 hectares) on Södermalm, an island just south of the city.[1] This property was destined to become a showcase garden.

Sometime over the following decade, Swedenborg had contractors enclose the entire plot with a high board fence. A second fence divided the eastern third of the land, which held the main buildings, from the rest, which was to be dedicated to plantings. A pathway east to west and another south to north divided the rectangular garden into four equal areas. These quadrants, although their plantings no doubt changed over time, seem generally to have been dedicated each to a different type of vegetation: trees valued for their edible fruit, trees valued for other reasons, smaller plants valued for their fruits and vegetables, and smaller plants valued for their flowers.

Within his garden's large-scale order and symmetry Swedenborg put many strange and wonderful things. The gate into the garden was a massive, highly ornate, baroque French archway, very much out of place among the simple Swedish buildings and fences. The vegetation ranged from the ordinary—such as carrots, spinach, and cucumbers—to the foreign and exotic, such as blue roses; shaped boxwoods from Holland; dogwoods, mulberries, and sweet corn from Pennsylvania; and roses and melons from Africa. In one spot was a large suspended cage for exotic birds; in another a door in the fence seemed as if it must lead to a second garden, but instead opened onto a set of mirrors reflecting the real garden behind the viewer. Toward the southwest corner by the rose gardens Swedenborg had his workers construct a virtually inescapable maze formed of boards, intended for the amusement of his many visitors.[2]

---

1. Swedenborg bought the property in 1743, about the same time his spiritual eyes began to open, to use his phrase. He had never owned a home before. Though he had inherited a share in the Starbo iron works and other mining properties, during his adult life he had generally lived in rented quarters, an arrangement made simpler by his lifelong bachelorhood.

2. For descriptions of the garden, see Dole and Kirven 1992, 43–45; Hjern 1988b, 325–330; Sigstedt 1981, 237–246, 312, 491–493; Tafel 1875, 32–33, 55–56, 390–392. The first three of these four sources provide drawings that reconstruct what Swedenborg's garden may have looked like in its heyday. The

Equally noteworthy was the pretty and diminutive summerhouse with a full view of the garden. It held little more than a writing desk. Here, in this modest house, Swedenborg often labored over the theological works for which he is now best known.

These theological volumes were the product of more than two decades of labor. They comprised eighteen separate and quite distinctive works in twenty-five quarto volumes totaling about three and a half million words—researched, composed, published, and (for the most part) distributed by Swedenborg himself.[3]

In a number of ways Swedenborg's theological works resemble his garden. Viewed in general terms, they display symmetry and balance, method and sequence. Their approach is varied, their scope comprehensive. In them one senses the author's intelligent yet humble reverence for the peace that order brings. As Swedenborg's garden had large-scale symmetry both east to west and south to north, his theology shows horizontal symmetries of love and wisdom, will and intellect, good and truth, goodwill and faith; and vertical symmetries of the Lord and humankind, heaven and hell, heaven and earth, spirit and body, and inner and outer levels of the mind. Although twenty-two years passed between publication of the first and the last title, the theology of the eighteen works is extremely coherent and consistent. Viewed more narrowly, however, Swedenborg's published theological works—again, like his garden—contain many elements that excite bafflement, wonder, or delight.

This essay is an invitation to the reader to enter the garden of Swedenborg's works, and to look at them from both the long and the close perspective.

---

drawings should be treated, however, with some caution. They are based on eyewitness accounts, but follow them somewhat loosely. Furthermore, the accounts reflect the state of the property over a wide range of dates: 1752, 1921, 1867, and 1772, respectively. Though the description of the plants and buildings in this essay is based on these eyewitness testimonies, given the nature of that evidence and the ephemerality of garden stock, certainty about what the garden looked like at a given time is unobtainable now. As a further aside, it may be worth noting that Swedenborg records having seen a garden in the spiritual world in which different types of vegetation grew at the various points of the compass; see *True Christianity* 78:1. (It is customary to refer to passages in Swedenborg's works by section numbers rather than page numbers, as the former are uniform in all editions.) And finally, readers may be intrigued to know that in *True Christianity* 112 Swedenborg recounts a spiritual experience that occurred in his own garden.

3. The eighteen theological works published by Swedenborg (see appendix, page 98) stand in contrast to works on theology that he did not publish or in most cases even complete. See note 88 below and the essay on the posthumously published theological works on pages 117–148 of this volume.

I. The Gateway: Swedenborg's Claim

> I realize many will claim that no one can talk to spirits and angels as
> long as bodily life continues, or that I am hallucinating, or that I have
> circulated such stories in order to play on people's credulity, and so on.
> But none of this worries me; I have seen, I have heard, I have felt.[4]

The gateway to Swedenborg's theological garden lies in understanding
his unique claim to spiritual experience. The first chapter of the first of
his published theological works closes with a bold claim of his direct experience of the spiritual realm: *Vidi, audivi, sensi,* "I have seen, I have
heard, I have felt." His phrase is a conscious echo of Julius Caesar's terse
encapsulation of a great victory: *Veni, vidi, vici,* "I came, I saw, I conquered." Unlike Caesar, though, Swedenborg is proclaiming conquest
not of a foe, but of the uncertainties that vitiate so much human experience of the spiritual realm. He asserts that another world exists: he has
seen it, heard it, felt it.

Swedenborg had ample credentials in European society and in his
scientific career. He was born the son of a high-ranking Lutheran cleric
and educated at Uppsala, the most prestigious university in seventeenth-
century Scandinavia. He held a seat in the Swedish House of Nobles as
head of his family, which was ennobled in 1719. He undertook extensive
research in various fields, ranging from earth science to anatomy, and he
earned an international reputation as a scientist. With this noteworthy
career behind him, and conscious of his status in European society, when
he turned to theology after his spiritual crisis he could not help being
acutely aware of his lack of credentials as a theologian.[5] Thus the importance of his claim: it constitutes his authority to share the spiritual insights he felt compelled (even in fact divinely commanded) to publish to
humankind.

He is of course not alone in claiming experience of this other world.
It has many names: paradise, eternity, the world beyond the grave, the

---

4. *Secrets of Heaven* 68; translation by Lisa Hyatt Cooper.

5. In an account of a memorable occurrence in the spiritual world, Swedenborg reports that an
adversary described him as someone "out of the herd of the laity. He has no gown, no cap, no laurel"
(*True Christianity* 137:2). These items are all trappings of advanced priestly and academic status.
For a discussion of Swedenborg's accounts of memorable occurrences, see pages 94–95 below.
(This and all other translations in this essay are my own, unless further ascription is given in the
notes or bibliography.)

Hereafter, the spirit world. Many have reportedly journeyed there in meditation, in near-death or other transcendental experiences, or in dreams. Most such reported experiences are not bodily. Travelers to this realm usually leave the body inactive behind them, and even report seeing the physical self from a distance. To the skeptical, claims of such nonbodily experiences certainly seem enough to strain belief; but Swedenborg claimed even more. He asserted that from his mid-fifties through the rest of his life he lived and functioned in both the material and the spiritual world at once.[6] He could maintain an awareness of another world with all his senses, carrying on conversations with its inhabitants, beholding its nature and structure, while nevertheless pursuing a wide range of activities in this world, from publishing to gardening, from socializing to being active in politics.[7]

Some critics have indeed labeled him mentally ill or insane for his claim. Contemporary reports, however, attest that he was intelligent, clear-headed, reliable, and kind. There is abundant documentary evidence that he was physically, politically, and intellectually active until his death at eighty-four. If this was insanity, it was an illness strangely beneficial.[8]

There is also independent evidence, reported by multiple witnesses, that supports Swedenborg's claim to be in contact with angels and spirits, although as proof it is not incontestable. Three incidents in particular caused a stir in his lifetime, drawing the attention and commentary even of the philosopher Immanuel Kant (1724–1804), who discussed them in a letter to an acquaintance (Kant [1766] 2002, 67–72). In brief they are as follows: (1) While on a visit to Göteborg, Swedenborg clairvoyantly saw and accurately reported details of a fire simultaneously raging three hundred miles away in Stockholm. (2) He helped a widow find a receipt for a

---

6. Swedenborg was born in 1688 and died in 1772. He reports that he began having spiritual experiences in 1743 and by 1745 was in daily contact with the other world. He claims a number of times that from then on he lived in both worlds at once: see *Secrets of Heaven* Genesis 16 preface:3, 9439; *Heaven and Hell* 577:3; *Marriage Love* 1; *True Christianity* 157, 281, 695:2, 851. Nevertheless he occasionally mentions leaving his body and returning, and at one point he records a spirit's astonishment at seeing Swedenborg passing in and out of visibility as he moves himself back and forth between an earthly and a spiritual state (*Marriage Love* 326). In §157 of his last work, *True Christianity*, he seems to nod to this discrepancy when he asserts that for twenty-six years he has been "in my spirit and my body at the same time, and only sometimes out of my body."

7. A striking instance of interaction between the two worlds can be seen in *Marriage Love* 329, in which some boys in the spiritual world follow Swedenborg home to his lodgings in the material world and comment on an insect that crawls across the page on which he is writing.

8. On the question of Swedenborg's sanity, see *[The Madness Hypothesis]* 1998.

substantial sum that a silversmith claimed her husband had never paid, though only the deceased husband could have known its location. (3) In response to a challenge, he confounded Queen Lovisa Ulrika of Sweden (1720–1782) by telling her a family secret that she declared no living person could have revealed to him.[9]

Although he himself did not record these incidents, he attested to their accuracy, maintaining they were evidence that he was in contact with angels and spirits (Acton 1948–1955, 749–750). Both at the time and since, people have found these and several other independently recorded anecdotes (see Sigstedt 1981, 281–286) convincing testimonies to the veracity of Swedenborg's larger claim.

II. The Layout of the Garden of Swedenborg's Theological Works

Once through the gateway, the visitor confronts the overall layout of the garden of the eighteen works. In this theological garden, Swedenborg presents a Christian message, but one that is distinct from other forms of Christianity. Its core teachings, terms, and phrases recur consistently throughout, surrounded by an unending variety of illustrative and experiential material. If he had used his spiritual experiences alone as the foundation of his theology, the structure would stand on something relatively unprovable, requiring a leap of faith on the reader's part. However, he makes extensive use of objective foundations as well, including logic, established empirical knowledge, and Scripture (which as a devout Christian he considers an objectively sound authority). He employs deductive argumentation, draws analogies to physical and social realities, quotes the Bible, and recounts and comments on his spiritual experiences to support a comprehensive theology whose layout can be summarized as follows.

a. God and Humanity, and the Humanity of God

In Swedenborg's theology, there is one God, who is generally called "the Lord" (Latin *Dominus,* a title rather than a name, meaning "the one in

---

9. For documentation and discussion of these three anecdotes, see pages 34–36 above, as well as Tafel 1877, 613–666, and Sigstedt 1981, 269–281. To these more notable events might be added a fourth: he accurately predicted the date of his death (Tafel 1877, 546, 567).

charge"). The Lord is human, and therefore all creation to a greater or lesser degree reflects humanity.[10] To be human is to possess heart and mind, or in other words, will or volition and intellect or discernment. The will or volition is the faculty that enables human beings to experience purposefulness, values, intent, love, and emotion, while the intellect or discernment enables the experience of wisdom, intelligence, reflection, and thought. The human body is "merely an obedient servant" (*True Christianity* 397), doing what the will intends and saying what the intellect thinks. To be human, then, is to have a spirit or mind composed of will and intellect that lives in the spiritual world, and a body composed of flesh and blood that lives in the material world or physical realm. The spirit possesses feeling, thought, and awareness; it also enlivens the body's sensation, speech, and movement.

Love is the essence and source of human life. There are four overarching categories of love: love for the Lord, love for our neighbor, love for the world, and love for ourselves. The former two are good loves. The latter two are good unless they predominate over the former, in which case they become evil (*Divine Love and Wisdom* 396). Love for the Lord is the highest of the two good loves, and is opposite to love for ourselves, the lowest love. Each of these loves has derivative feelings or desires, like the branches of a tree, and attendant thoughts and knowledge. Everyone is in essence his or her own ruling love, a love unique to that individual. Nonetheless, all human loves can be grouped under the four overarching loves.

Perfect humanity characterizes the Lord. The Lord's essence is pure love and pure wisdom, an infinite love that intends the salvation of every human being, and an infinite wisdom that sees what laws and structure the universe must have to achieve this intent.[11] The object of the Lord's love, the overall purpose in creating and sustaining the universe, is to populate a heaven with human beings whom the Lord loves and who

---

10. Although the identification of Jesus (after the process of glorification) with God is central to Swedenborg's theology, as is the related concept of God's humanity, Swedenborg seems stringently to avoid any indication of masculine or feminine gender in God. He consistently uses the neutral term *homo,* "a human," rather than a gendered term for God's humanity; and where he uses adjectives in the role of nouns as terms for God, such as "the Infinite," "the Divine," "the Divine Human," and "the Human," he casts them as neuter rather than feminine or masculine.

11. Swedenborg clarifies that divine love and divine wisdom are utterly united. We ourselves divide them into two in our thinking, just as we generally conceive of the sun's light and heat as two different things when in fact they are the same energy (*True Christianity* 41).

love the Lord freely in return.[12] Central to the Lord's plan then is human spiritual freedom, meaning the individual's ability to choose between good and evil loves, and between true and false thoughts. Until their choice of heaven or hell is complete, human beings remain in a balance between good and evil, and between truth and falsity, so that their choice will be free and deliberate.

In the beginning God created two worlds, the spiritual and the physical. The spiritual world is more real than the physical world. Composed of spiritual substance, it shares nothing in common with physical reality. Yet although these two worlds are discrete, the human mind senses and perceives them as being similar.[13] Human beings living in the physical world form a necessary bridge between the two worlds, having minds in the spiritual world and bodies in the physical world. From creation human beings were intended to live consciously in both worlds at once, sensing spiritual reality with the senses of their spirit and physical reality with the senses of their body (*Secrets of Heaven* 69).

Because the Lord is human, heaven reflects humanity, and does so at multiple levels. The whole of heaven reflects a single human form, and yet each of its two kingdoms and three heavens is by itself a complete human form. On even smaller scales, each community in heaven is in the human form, as is each angel.[14] On whatever level, then, and on however wide or narrow a scope, there is wholeness and humanity.[15] As the ancients implied with their concept of a human being as a microcosm, each individual has a whole heaven and a whole world within.[16] Swedenborg

---

12. See especially *Divine Providence* 27–45, 323–324, and *True Christianity* 66–67; see also *Secrets of Heaven* 6698, 9237, 9441; *Heaven and Hell* 417; *Last Judgment* 13; *Other Planets* 112; *Divine Providence* 202:1; *Marriage Love* 68.

13. Swedenborg indicates that many people in the spiritual world do not realize they have died (*True Christianity* 80:4, 160:3, 7). Others are amazed after death to find themselves in a world so much like the one they left (*Marriage Love* 182:7).

14. See *Heaven and Hell* 51–77. Swedenborg even goes so far as to say that everything that is good and true is in the human form (*Heaven and Hell* 460). By "human form" in all these instances, Swedenborg is not referring to the physical shape of a human body but rather to the complex functional interaction of components, both mental and physical, that comprise a human being.

15. This concept anticipates the phenomena of fractals and holograms, large and small fragments of which contain an image of the whole. See Dole 1988a, 374–381; Talbot 1988, 443–448.

16. *Secrets of Heaven* 4523:2, 5115:1, 6013, 6057, 9278:3; *Heaven and Hell* 30, 57; *New Jerusalem* 47; *Divine Love and Wisdom* 251, 319, 320, 323; *True Christianity* 604.

at times suggests a parallel relationship between the mind and heart and the male and female human, although the relationship is highly complex.[17] Nevertheless he presents each gender as fully human, because each has will and intellect. In one presentation, the essential distinction between female and male is that will or volition predominates in women and intellect or discernment in men (*Heaven and Hell* 369), which gives the genders different abilities and forms of wisdom (*Marriage Love* 168, 174–176). Although Swedenborg's work on marriage implies that every cell of the female is female and every cell of the male is male (*Marriage Love* 33), his works generally emphasize the differences between male and female much less than their similarities, in that his theology is usually expressed in universal terms and concerns both sexes equally.[18]

b. The Meaning of Heaven and Hell

In the spiritual world the Lord's humanity is but rarely experienced with the senses.[19] Instead angels usually see the Lord as a sun far above heaven whose love and truth shower the spiritual world much the way the heat and light of our sun shower the earth.[20] The spiritual world comprises

---

17. Swedenborg's work on marriage presents men as inwardly being forms of love but outwardly forms of wisdom, and women as inwardly forms of wisdom but outwardly forms of love (*Marriage Love* 32). In briefer treatments elsewhere in the same work, women are generally related to volition and love, while men are related to intellect and wisdom (*Marriage Love* 33, 91, 160, 187, 218:2, 296:1). In another title, though, the association is reversed: women are related to wisdom and men to love (*True Christianity* 37:3, 41:3). One passage suggests that in the so-called heavenly kingdom of heaven, love corresponds to the male and wisdom corresponds to the female; in the so-called spiritual kingdom of heaven, however, the opposite obtains: love corresponds to the female and wisdom corresponds to the male (*Secrets of Heaven* 8994:4).

18. Only in his work on marriage are the sexes treated separately in any sustained way. The generic Latin term *homo*, "human being," occurs approximately 28,300 times in the published theological works—far more than the approximately 6,100 combined instances of gendered terms such as *vir*, "man" or "husband"; *femina*, "woman"; *mulier*, "woman"; and *uxor*, "wife."

19. In heaven the Lord is sometimes experienced directly in the human form (*Heaven and Hell* 121). More often he appears in heaven or on earth by filling an angel with his presence and sphere. See *Secrets of Heaven* 1925:3–4; *Divine Providence* 96:6; *Revelation Unveiled* 465.

20. One difference is that our sun is but one of many stars, while the Lord is the only sun of the spiritual world. Another difference is that our sun is "pure fire" while the sun of heaven is pure love (*Revelation Unveiled* 468). The relationship between the two suns is an example of what Swedenborg calls correspondence—a relationship of causality and therefore similarity between something spiritual and something physical. For a lengthy treatment of the spiritual sun, see *Divine Love and Wisdom* 83–172.

heaven and hell, with the so-called world of spirits between the two.[21] People who have turned toward God and their neighbor have become a heaven, so to speak, during life in this world, and will live in heaven after death. People who have turned toward themselves and the world to the exclusion of God and their neighbor have become a hell here, and will live in hell after death. The world of spirits, with heaven above and hell below, is a temporary home to all those who have died but are not yet in either heaven or hell. The world of spirits is also a temporary home to the human mind while the body remains alive in the physical world, although people on earth are generally unaware of the world of spirits because their spiritual senses are usually closed.

Heaven and hell are separate and opposite. Although inhabitants of hell are free to visit heaven, without special protection they find they cannot breathe properly there and suffer severe distress until they return home. Neither can angels breathe in hell unless they are granted special protection. All inhabitants of heaven (called angels), all inhabitants of the world of spirits (called spirits, angelic spirits, and evil spirits), and all inhabitants of hell (called satans, devils, demons, and evil spirits) were once human beings living in the physical world, whether on this earth or on some other planet. There is but one universal human race.

The human mind has three levels: a lowest or earthly plane, a middle or spiritual plane, and a highest or heavenly plane. At birth these levels are neither open nor closed. As a person grows and makes choices, these levels open or close. The three levels of the mind answer to three levels of willingness to follow the Lord.[22] To follow the Lord, but with no more than bodily obedience, opens our minds at the lowest level and prepares us for life in the lowest heaven; to follow with intelligence as well opens our minds at the middle level and prepares us to live in the middle heaven; and to follow with love opens our minds at the highest level and prepares us to live in the highest heaven (see *Secrets of Heaven* 9594). The amount of openness is something we choose and allow ourselves. To turn away from the Lord and heaven toward an exclusive focus on ourselves and the world closes our minds to heavenly influence from above and

---

21. "Heaven" and "hell" are widely used terms with a long history. "The world of spirits" is less well known. It names the area (as well as the state) between heaven and hell to which most spirits first proceed after death (*Heaven and Hell* 421–422).

22. Swedenborg writes that willingness to follow the Lord is a form of innocence; not the innocence of childhood, but a wise innocence like that of the angels. See *Heaven and Hell* 276–283.

opens them to hellish influence from below, again to different levels depending on the depth and intensity of our participation in evil. The higher levels of the mind close, and the spirit becomes merely earthly; or worse yet, sense-oriented; or worst of all, flesh-oriented.

c. Inflow and the Individual

The Lord is present in time and space, but is not subject to their limitations. Omnipresent, the Lord flows directly into heaven; into the world of spirits; into hell; into the human mind; and into animals, plants, and inanimate objects, in the same way on the largest and smallest imaginable scales.[23] At the same time there is also a hierarchy of inflow. Good and truth from the Lord cascade through the higher and lower heavens, passing through angelic spirits in the world of spirits into the higher levels of the human mind; while evil and falsity, which are simply twisted echoes of that same inflowing life from above, then rise up from the lower to the higher hells, passing through evil spirits in the world of spirits into the lower levels of the human mind. While we are alive in this world, then, all our thoughts and perceptions, whether true or false, and all our emotions, values, and desires, whether good or evil, flow in from God through various parts of the other world.[24]

Swedenborg sees the universe as responding to the direct and indirect inflow of the Lord's life in an unlimited variety of ways. He draws an analogy to sunlight, which flows out as one thing but seems to change according to its reception, occasioning beautiful colors and aromas when it shines on flowers, for example, but disgusting colors and odors when it shines on excrement (*Heaven and Hell* 569; *Divine Love and Wisdom* 348). Like all things in nature, human beings are vessels formed to receive life rather than life-forms in their own right. Unlike flowers and excrement, human beings have a range of choices in their response to the life that inflows from the Lord. Swedenborg urges us to welcome the good that flows in and reject the evil, by attributing the former to the Lord and sending the latter back to hell:

> If we believed the way things really are, that everything good comes
> from [the Lord] and everything evil from hell, then we would not take

---

23. See *Divine Love and Wisdom* 77–82.

24. This inflow creates the balance between good and evil in which we are kept until we finally choose heaven or hell; see *Heaven and Hell* 589–600.

credit for the good within us or blame for the evil. Whenever we thought or did anything good, we would focus on the Lord, and any evil that flowed in we would throw back into the hell it came from. But since we do not believe in any inflow from heaven or from hell and therefore believe that everything we think and intend is in us and from us, we make the evil our own and defile the good with our feeling that we deserve it.[25]

By design, we cannot escape the appearance that we live on our own. What Swedenborg calls our sense of autonomy is a gift from the Lord that makes reciprocation and salvation possible. Therefore the intellectual belief and recognition that good and evil flow in will be repeatedly undermined by the experience of being alive, of apparently possessing in ourselves feelings, thoughts, and sensations.

To progress spiritually, then, requires both a recognition and an action. We need to recognize intellectually that everything good and evil flows in, and yet we need to act with all our apparent power and life to stop doing what is evil and start doing what is good. To acknowledge the Lord and not to take action is to remain where we began; to take action and not to acknowledge the Lord is to overinflate one's self.

Our seemingly autonomous action and the recognition of our debt to the Lord appear in a five-point summary of what to believe and how to live:

1. There is one God; the divine trinity exists within him; and he is the Lord God the Savior Jesus Christ.
2. Believing in him is a faith that saves.
3. We must not do things that are evil—they belong to the Devil and come from the Devil.[26]
4. We must do things that are good—they belong to God and come from God.

---

25. *Heaven and Hell* 302; translation by George F. Dole. Compare *Divine Providence* 320. See also *Secrets of Heaven* 4151 and 4206, the latter of which adds that angels are more able to help those who take this objective stance. Swedenborg reports that "thousands of times" he has identified and rebuked the evil spirits who have directed a flow of evil and falsity into his mind, telling them to take it back and not to inflict it on him anymore (*Divine Providence* 290; see also *Secrets of Heaven* 6191). To spirits questioning this practice of Swedenborg's and claiming that he has no life of his own as a result, he replies that he was not alive before he began it (*Revelation Explained* [= Swedenborg 1994–1997a] §1147:3).

26. As discussed further below, by the term "the Devil," Swedenborg means hell in general.

5. We must do these things as if we did them ourselves, but we must believe that they come from the Lord working with us and through us.[27]

III. The Population of the Garden

Just as Swedenborg's garden comprised a wide variety of both common and exotic plants, his theological garden encompasses the varied spiritual forms taken by the human race in the past. According to Swedenborg, at any time throughout human history on this planet only one of the many existing religions carried the primary responsibility for connecting heaven and earth. His theology is unusual in that it teaches that a variety of religions is necessary because only multiple religions can provide important diversity (*Divine Providence* 326:10) and lead a variety of peoples to salvation.[28] Yet for the sake of heaven's connection to earth, there has been at any given time a single monotheistic religion at the spiritual center, so to speak. Although different religions with different forms of revelation have played this central role at different times in history, Swedenborg calls them all *ecclesiae* or "churches" (even though that term originally had a strictly Christian connotation),[29] and refers to each church's revelation as "the Word."[30]

---

27. *True Christianity* 3. These five points first appear in *Marriage Love* 82:1, and are discussed at some length there. They appear again in *Survey* 43 and 117, with an explanation at §44. Swedenborg's concept of apparent self-life leads to a unique picture of what happens to the self in the course of spiritual progress. He emphasizes the uniqueness of all individuals even before they regenerate, or undergo a process of spiritual rebirth (*Heaven and Hell* 486; *Divine Love and Wisdom* 318; *Marriage Love* 186:2). As people then regenerate, rather than losing self and merging with the Divine, the closer they get to the Lord the more distinctly they feel like themselves and feel free (*Divine Providence* 42–44). Although heaven consists of countless communities, the best angels of all live on their own (*Heaven and Hell* 50), perhaps because they have become increasingly differentiated from others as they have drawn closer to the Lord.

28. *Heaven and Hell* 318–319; *Divine Providence* 253–254, 325–326, 330:5, 6.

29. Throughout this essay I have used the term "church" in Swedenborg's special sense as the spiritually central religion of its time. Many readers of Swedenborg feel that as humanness is universal on scales both large and small, the qualities of each of the churches discussed below reflect aspects of the individual; thus ecclesiastical history can also be taken personally.

30. *Last Judgment* 46 and notes; *Divine Providence* 328; *True Christianity* 760, 762, 786. The term "the Word" also applies to the Bible, or such parts of it as Swedenborg recognizes as spiritually relevant; for further discussion see notes 46 and 51 below.

a. The Early Churches

In the beginning there was a Golden Age, called the earliest or most ancient church. Human beings responded to the Lord with their hearts and allowed the Lord to open their minds at the highest or heavenly level. As a result there was open communication between those living on earth and those in heaven. People saw the Lord as the only source of humanity and by contrast would not call themselves human. The will and intellect were so united that whatever people loved they thought about and did. There was no loop of objectivity in the intellect to second-guess the desires of the heart. And at first no such objectivity was needed, because what their hearts desired was good. Marriages were strong and deeply spiritual in earliest times (*Marriage Love* 75). By means of what Swedenborg calls correspondences, that is, the living embodiment of something spiritual in something earthly, people saw heavenly qualities reflected in the trees, plants, and animals around them, as well as in each other and in the events of their lives. Having no spoken or written language, and needing none, they received direct revelation and guidance from God through the mirror of nature, through dreams and visions, and through their contact with angels.

In time, however, the human race fell. People turned away from the Lord and heaven to set their primary focus on themselves and the world. No longer wanting to be receivers and containers of life from God, people wished to be life-forms in themselves. This development, symbolized by the Flood in Genesis, caused evil desires and twisted thinking to inundate their minds, to the point that they passed beyond salvability. They "drowned" in their inability to separate thought from desire. Although they retained the indestructible quality known as the *likeness* of God, meaning life, awareness, creative power, and immortality, they were no longer in the *image* of God, no longer godly. Life became a spiritual death. That age, then, passed from the light side to the dark side of living from the heart.

The Lord restored freedom and the possibility of salvation to the human race by making the intellect separable from the will. The intellect gained the ability to rise at times above the tide of evil in the will so that it could see what is true and what would be good. The sight of truth could then redirect thoughts and behavior toward a new will, a second nature that was loving and heavenly.

The alteration of the human mind began the Silver Age, which Swedenborg calls the early or ancient church, a collection of diverse religious groups widely spread around the eastern Mediterranean Sea.[31] People then were centered in the intellect rather than the heart and needed written revelation to communicate with heaven. Their revelation, the ancient or early Word, now lost, contained profoundly allegorical tales and obscure prophecies of the Messiah to come. They imbibed it intellectually, which led to a communication with heaven, but a poorer one than the Golden Age had enjoyed. Swedenborg labels them spiritual rather than heavenly. In time, just as the earliest people had fallen from their golden state, the people of the Silver Age lapsed into worshiping idols and using their knowledge of correspondences to do evil, in some cases in the form of black magic.

To ensure protection from evil the Lord then took away spiritual knowledge altogether, providing instead written instructions in the books of Moses[32] for rituals and practices that would link heaven and earth obliquely. Conscious contact of the mind or heart with heaven was lost. The Copper and Iron ages—the Hebrew and the Israelite and Jewish churches respectively[33]—were neither heavenly nor spiritual; Swedenborg labels them earthly, and even sense-oriented and flesh-oriented. As marriage and religion go hand in hand, the marriages of that time were not spiritual either (*Marriage Love* 78). Those people following the Lord did so no more than bodily, obeying instructions written in Scripture.[34]

b. The Christian Church

In time people rebelled against even this lowest form of adherence, making it necessary for the ancient prophecies to be fulfilled. God

---

31. The ancient church extended across "Assyria, Mesopotamia, Syria, Ethiopia, Arabia, Libya, Egypt, Philistia as far as Tyre and Sidon, and the whole land of Canaan on both the far and the near sides of the Jordan" (*Secrets of Heaven* 1238:2; translation by Lisa Hyatt Cooper). To this list *Sacred Scripture* 21 adds Chaldea and Nineveh. Elements of this early religion later affected Greece and Rome (*Sacred Scripture* 117; see also *Secrets of Heaven* 2762, 9011, 10177:10; *Sacred Scripture* 26).

32. "The books of Moses" was the term Swedenborg and others of his time applied to the Pentateuch in the Bible (Genesis, Exodus, Leviticus, Numbers, and Deuteronomy).

33. See *Divine Providence* 328:2–3. In Swedenborg's terminology, the "Hebrew" church or nation refers to the descendants of Abraham; later this group split into two, and was known as "Judah," or the "Jewish" nation or church; and "Israel," or the "Israelite" nation or church (see 1 Kings 11:30–37).

34. These generalities echo Swedenborg's sweeping statements. He does not clarify whether this spiritual bankruptcy applied to the apparently good and noble characters depicted in Scripture from these times—for example, Josiah (2 Kings 23:1–25; 2 Chronicles 34–35); and Elizabeth, Zacharias, Mary, Joseph, Anna, and Simeon (see Luke 1–3)—or whether such figures were exceptions allowed by the existence of free will.

("Jehovah,"[35] "the Father," or "the Divine") conceived in Mary's womb the child Jesus (the "Son" or "the Human"), whose soul was divine but whose lower mind was riddled with accumulated hereditary evil. Though God had always been *spiritually* human, in Jesus God became *physically* human.[36] Referring to Jesus, Swedenborg gives the following as "the faith of the new heaven and the new church in universal form":

> The Lord from eternity, who is Jehovah, came into the world to gain control over the hells and to glorify his own human nature; without this, not one mortal could have been saved; those who believe in him are saved. (*True Christianity* 2)

While alive on earth, Jesus underwent something parallel to the process of repentance, reformation, and regeneration that everyone must go through to be united to God and heaven. For ordinary human beings, the process involves examining oneself, recognizing and acknowledging evil of act or even of thought and desire, praying for help, and beginning a new life. Doing so leads at times to battles between good in our higher or inner self and evil in our lower or outer self, which are called crises or temptations and occasion great pain but also enhance spiritual freedom of choice. If we fight against the evil habit or inclination with apparent autonomy, yet acknowledge the Lord's power and our own true helplessness,

---

35. Following a Christian practice of his times, Swedenborg often used "Jehovah" as a rendering of the tetragrammaton, יהוה *(yhvh),* "YHWH," the four-letter name of God in Hebrew Scriptures. A complex set of circumstances gave rise to the name "Jehovah." The Hebrew alphabet originally consisted only of consonants. It was not until the eighth century of the Common Era that a complete system of diacritical marks for vowel notation was developed. When for any reason the consonantal text was held not to be suitable for reading as it stood, the vowels of an approved reading would be added to the consonants that stood in the text, whether the number of syllables in the two words matched or not. Since the sanctity of the name of God, YHWH, was felt to preclude its being pronounced, the word אֲדֹנָי *(Ǎdōnāi),* "Lord," was regularly substituted, and to indicate this, vowels closely resembling those of the name Adonai were added to YHWH: YeHoWaH. This combination of consonants and vowels was transliterated into Latin as "Jehovah." (Some English Bibles since then have adopted the name "Jehovah," while others have rendered the term as "LORD," so capitalized.) The currently accepted scholarly reconstruction of the original pronunciation of the name is "Yahweh": see *Theological Dictionary of the Old Testament* under "YHWH." As others have done, Swedenborg relates the name YHWH or Jehovah to the concept of being or "is-ness"; see his 1771 work *True Christianity* 19:1, as well as 9:2–3.

36. For a brief overview of Swedenborg's teachings on God, with copious biblical support, see *The Lord.* See also *New Jerusalem* 280–310; these sections form a chapter on the topic that includes abundant further references to *Secrets of Heaven.* For a more extensive treatment, see the first three chapters of *True Christianity* (1–188).

the Lord pushes the evil to the periphery and clears a larger channel for love to flow through. Numerous battles over a lifetime bring us from a selfish, hellish state to a loving, heavenly one.

Jesus' battles were comparable, though on an infinite scale, and though divinity rather than heavenliness was the desired outcome. From early childhood he was under continual attack by every devil and satan in hell. Over the course of his life on earth he conquered all the hells and brought them under his dominion, restored freedom to heaven and the world of spirits, and glorified his human nature, which means that he made it divine.[37] His suffering and dying on the cross completed the process of glorification. The unknowable Divine had become picturable and knowable in Jesus Christ.

Although states of apparently separate consciousness in Jesus cause the appearance of a Duality or Trinity of persons in the New Testament (such as when, for example, he calls on, prays to, or even feels forsaken by his "Father"), there was never more than one person of God. There is a Trinity in the Lord, but a Trinity like that of the spirit, the body, and the actions of an individual (*The Lord* 46). One person includes the three aspects known as Father, Son, and Holy Spirit.[38]

One of the reasons Jesus came to earth was to begin a new church. Like the churches that preceded, Christianity was characterized by initial purity and clarity. According to Swedenborg, early Christians focused on worshiping the Lord, repenting of evil, and loving others. However, by the time of the Nicene Council in 325 that purity and clarity were already lost, as evil and falsity took hold of the Christian church. Roman Catholicism fell into believing in a Trinity of persons, adoring Mary and the saints, and withholding Scripture and the wine of communion from the laity. In Swedenborg's view, though, Catholicism's great error was to attribute to the pope and the ecclesiastical hierarchy the power to open and shut heaven, which belongs to the Lord alone.

According to Swedenborg, the Protestant Reformation led to a new church that corrected many of Catholicism's errors. The greater study of Scripture increased the amount of spiritual light in the world (see *True Christianity* 270). The Protestant or Reformed churches, however, fell

---

37. Swedenborg refers to this as the Lord's process of glorification or transformation. See note 49 below.

38. Swedenborg summarized this most briefly as follows: "There is one God; the divine trinity exists within him; and he is the Lord God the Savior Jesus Christ" (*True Christianity* 3).

into the error of seeing Jesus' divine and human natures as separate and asserting the possibility of justification by faith alone. Swedenborg briefly but repeatedly charges that the Reformed church split God into three and the Lord into two, and separated faith from love and goodwill.[39] Protestantism's study of the Bible brought no correction to the doctrine of the Trinity; and its doctrine of salvation by faith alone induced complete spiritual darkness.

Swedenborg says that every church follows a certain pattern: it rises, it falls, and it comes to an end in a Last Judgment. The end of the first church was symbolized by the Flood (Genesis 7 and 8). The other pre-Christian churches came to their Last Judgment at the time of Christ's coming. The Book of Revelation in its spiritual meaning predicts the Last Judgment on Catholicism and Protestantism as churches, and also the coming of a new church symbolized by the New Jerusalem. These Last Judgments were spiritual rather than physical. They all occurred in the spiritual world and affected its inhabitants, although they also had an impact on the mental condition and spiritual freedom of people still alive in the physical world, because the mind is spiritual. The long-standing expectation of a Last Judgment on earth, a cataclysmic change in the political and physical arenas of this world, is the result of Christianity taking Scripture too literally, after its heart and life had turned away from God.[40] The Last Judgment predicted in Matthew and in the Book of Revelation took place in the spiritual world when the Christian calendar read 1757.[41]

c. The New Church

Swedenborg presents himself, then, as writing at a dramatic and even crucial point in human spiritual history. He claims to have witnessed the Last Judgment on the Catholic and Protestant churches. The entire sequence of the ages had been enacted, from Golden, Silver, Copper, and Iron, to Iron Mixed with Clay (see Daniel 2:31–35; Ovid *Metamorphoses* 1:89–150).

---

39. *Revelation Unveiled* 263, 294:6, 481, 537, 550; *Survey* 88.

40. Swedenborg frequently criticizes contemporary belief in an eventual Judgment Day when human beings will all rise from their tombs. *Marriage Love* 29 concludes that from this belief "it then follows that nothing would be more regrettable than to be born human" (translation by George F. Dole). Swedenborg writes that such ludicrous ideas undermine more important beliefs in the Lord and the Word (*Heaven and Hell* 312).

41. For Swedenborg's teachings on and experiences of the Last Judgment, see especially *Last Judgment* and the first part of *Supplements*. More details are given throughout *Revelation Unveiled*.

Although the solstice of divine absence had passed with the birth of Christ seventeen hundred years earlier, and ever since then a greater light had become available to the world, nevertheless a winter of evil and falsity had increased to the point that at Swedenborg's day "a total damnation stood at the door and threatened" (*True Christianity* 3, 121, 579). Swedenborg reports that during his own lifetime the most recent church, Protestantism, had become spiritually defunct (see *True Christianity* 760–762). As its leaders and followers died, many of them were bringing unrepentant lives and twisted impressions of Scripture and theology into the world of spirits, from which they influenced those still on earth. Hell was on the verge of winning the struggle for every human soul.

By his own testimony, Swedenborg was given consciousness of the spiritual world to witness the Last Judgment and to facilitate the Lord's Second Coming[42] and the establishment of a new church. Many of the eighteen titles of Swedenborg's published theological works present them as teachings for this new church, the new Jerusalem.[43] Swedenborg predicted that the new church would be slow in taking hold on earth, and would be small at first, because false views of Christ would stand in the way.[44] He also predicted, however, that the Lord would eventually restore a spiritual form of monogamy like that of the ancient church, and draw the new church into a closer relationship with himself and a greater affiliation with angels than any previous church had enjoyed.[45]

---

42. For the way in which Swedenborg's works relate to the Second Coming, see *True Christianity* 779 and its context.

43. See appendix, page 98, for a list of these eighteen titles in their short form. Ten of the eighteen, in their full form, refer to the New Jerusalem or the Book of Revelation (whose last two chapters foretell the New Jerusalem). For complete details concerning these ten titles, see the entries referenced by the numbers P102–P104, P107–P110, P114, P119, and P126 in the list on pages 385–519 in this volume.

44. In contrast to many millenarians of his age, Swedenborg maintained that the Last Judgment would have virtually no immediate political or social effect on earth (*Last Judgment* 73). Although he implies that the new church will last forever (*True Christianity* 791), he predicts that at first it will grow slowly (*Revelation Unveiled* 546–547), that the spiritual meaning of the Word will not be recognized for "a long time" (*Sacred Scripture* 25), and that "a time, times, and half a time" (a reference to Daniel 12:7 and Revelation 12:14) will pass before these teachings will be well received on earth (*Marriage Love* 533).

45. On the restoration of spiritual monogamy in the new church, see *Marriage Love* 81:5 and 43. On the new church's predicted oneness with the Lord, see *Revelation Unveiled* 882–883 and *Heaven and Hell* 304. On the new church's affiliation and communication with heaven, see *Revelation Unveiled* 176–177; also see *Secrets of Heaven* 68, 1276, 1771, 1880:4, 2737, 2759:2, 2760:2, 2851:2, 5344, 5700, 5726, 8367, 8512–8513, 8694:2, 8971:1, 9594, 9709, 10156:4; *Heaven and Hell* 304; *New Jerusalem* 43–44; *True Christianity* 401:7–8, 719, 846:2.

d. Swedenborg's Theology vs. Other Forms of Christianity

Swedenborg presents his theology as essentially Christian, and in fact more truly Christian than either Protestantism or Catholicism, as suggested by the title of his last published work, *True Christianity*. Although he suggests a new direction for Christianity, his theology has much in common with mainstream denominations: He believes in the sacraments of baptism and communion, the latter of which he calls the Holy Supper. He subscribes to the divine inspiration of the Word (Christian Scripture).[46] He supports the existence of heaven and hell, angels and devils, and the salvation or condemnation of the individual after death. He urges repentance and the shunning of evils as sins against God. He speaks of faith and goodwill, and recommends good works. He believes in the Father, the Son, and the Holy Spirit, and in the divinity of Jesus Christ. Yet in the main both Protestants and Catholics differentiate Swedenborg's theology from their own, as does Swedenborg himself.

His claimed otherworldly experience gives him a radically different perspective on Scripture that occasions much of his departure from mainstream Christianity. Many passages in Scripture are not to be taken literally, and if taken literally are not intelligible or coherent.[47] The Word is holy because it has multiple layers of sacred meaning. Its inner spiritual meaning is revealed only to those who read it in a heartfelt search for the truth itself or for knowledge of how they might help themselves or others

---

46. When not using the term "the Word" in the specialized sense described above, Swedenborg generally employs it to refer to the combination of the Hebrew Scriptures (which like his contemporaries he calls the Old Testament), and the four Gospels and the Book of Revelation (which he calls the New Testament). However, he excludes from the Word a number of books generally recognized as Christian Scripture (see note 51 below).

47. For the unintelligibility of the literal meaning of many biblical passages, see *Sacred Scripture* 15. For a discussion of incoherence, see *Secrets of Heaven* 6377:4: "The very connection shows that there is more in the words than appears on the literal level. There is coherence in the inner meaning but not in the outer meaning. Take for example the statement that 'the threshing-floor and the winepress will not feed them,' that 'the new wine will deceive them,' and that 'Ephraim will return into Egypt, and they will eat what is unclean in Assyria' [Hosea 9:2–3]. Without a deeper meaning, what could Ephraim's 'return into Egypt' or their 'eating what is unclean in Assyria' mean?" See also *Secrets of Heaven* 3228: "Anyone can see that material like this does supply the religious history of that era but provides little for a person's spiritual life—and yet it is our spiritual life that the Word exists for. What difference does it make knowing who Abraham's sons by Keturah were [Genesis 25:2–4], or who Ishmael's were [Genesis 25:13–15]? Does it matter that Esau became worn out hunting and asked for lentil soup, or that Jacob cleverly took the opportunity to exchange it for the birthright [Genesis 25:29–34]?" (Translations by Lisa Hyatt Cooper.)

become more angelic. As will soon be shown, Swedenborg's understanding of certain biblical passages is very different from that of some Roman Catholics and Protestants, specifically the mention of the keys of the kingdom that are given to Peter (Matthew 16:19), and the promised opportunity to rest from labors after death (Revelation 14:13). Although Swedenborg uses many volumes to lay out the inner meaning of Genesis, Exodus, and the Book of Revelation verse by verse,[48] he asserts that there are only three topics in Scripture: the church, heaven, and the Lord (*Sacred Scripture* 16, 17:4). These topics parallel three inner layers of meaning: the internal historical meaning, depicting human spiritual history; the regenerative meaning, portraying the rebirth of the individual; and the supreme meaning, relating Jesus' process of glorification[49] or becoming divine. Scripture is not, he emphasizes, concerned with worldly events.[50]

Upsetting to some mainstream Christians is Swedenborg's creation of a different canon of Scripture through the identification of certain books in the Bible as exclusively constituting the Word because they have a spiritual meaning throughout. At the same time, he holds other books of the Bible to be intermittently spiritual or to lack an inner meaning

---

48. *Secrets of Heaven,* an exposition of Genesis and Exodus, filled eight thick quarto volumes in the first edition, and *Revelation Unveiled,* an exposition of the Book of Revelation, filled a ninth. Yet Swedenborg presents these books as revealing only a fraction of the inner meaning (*Secrets of Heaven* 64).

49. The terms "glorify" and "glorification" are easy to misunderstand, because they each have two different meanings: to *deem* glorious or ascribe glory to, and to *render* glorious or actually transform. It is the latter meaning in which Swedenborg usually uses "glorify" and "glorification" in relation to Jesus' human nature. Swedenborg specifically defines it as rendering divine or uniting with the Divine (see *True Christianity* 2:2; see also 97, 105, 110:4, 114, 126, 128, 130:2, 154:6). Swedenborg apparently derives this usage from the Gospel of John. Although generally in the Bible the word "glorify" means to praise or extol (the first meaning just given) and Swedenborg occasionally uses the word in this sense (see *True Christianity* 16:1, 117), the Gospel of John often uses "glorify" in the second sense given just above. For example, to say that the Holy Spirit had not yet come into existence because Jesus was not glorified yet (John 7:39) clearly does not mean that Jesus was not praised yet; it means that he was not yet completely transformed or rendered fully divine. For this latter usage, in addition to John 7:39 see John 12:16, 23; 13:31–32; 17:1, 5; Acts 3:13; Hebrews 5:5.

50. See Swedenborg's assertion in his preface to *Revelation Unveiled* that the Book of Revelation has nothing to do with earthly kingdoms and empires. What he means by a spiritual or inner meaning is deeper than ordinary allegory: alchemical readings he describes as worldly rather than spiritual, since those doing such readings seek gold rather than the Lord (*Sacred Scripture* 23). The "meaning that shines forth from the Word's literal sense when one examines and unfolds it to confirm some dogma of the church" is more literal than spiritual; the inner meaning is deeper still (*Sacred Scripture* 5).

altogether, and therefore as not constituting the Word, although they are nonetheless "useful books for the church."[51]

Also disturbing to many Christians is Swedenborg's disavowal of three persons in the Godhead. He believes, as mentioned before, in a Trinity of aspects, but not of persons, in God. Jesus was the one only God, born in human form on earth. Swedenborg presents this view of God as the central tenet of the new church. His disavowal of a Trinity of persons leads to a reframing of many other Christian concepts: Redemption was not achieved through a sacrifice on the Cross, but through a restoration of spiritual freedom as the result of a reorganization of the heavens and the hells. Christ's merit is not something we can borrow like a cloak at the hour of our death, but a power we can call on as we expend effort to improve ourselves spiritually. The Lord saves all who have indicated by the way they live that they truly desire to be saved, but he will not intercede in any extraordinary way for those who have chosen to be evil at heart.

The concept of the angry God and Jesus' sacrifice to appease him Swedenborg rejects out of hand. God was not angry, nor did the Son come into the world to satisfy the Father's rage. The Father did not look at the Son bleeding on the Cross and change his mind about condemning the human race. The Son does not now literally sit at the right hand of a separately existing God the Father, whose rage he appeased, and send out a separately existing Holy Spirit. Swedenborg portrays these concepts of God as ludicrous and damaging; none of them would be consonant with pure love and mercy.

---

51. *Revelation Explained* (= Swedenborg 1994–1997a) §815:2. Books in the Protestant Old Testament that Swedenborg does not consider to be the Word are Ruth, 1 and 2 Chronicles, Ezra, Nehemiah, Esther, Job, Proverbs, Ecclesiastes, and the Song of Solomon. Of the New Testament, he does not consider the Acts or any of the Epistles to be the Word, only the four Gospels and the Book of Revelation (*Secrets of Heaven* 10325; *New Jerusalem* 266). In a work written at the same time as the published theological works but left in manuscript form, he writes, "I wish to cite here passages that mention 'faith' and 'believing,' but only passages from the Gospels, not from the Letters of the Apostles. The reason for my doing so is that the Gospels contain the sayings of the Lord himself, all of which have a hidden spiritual meaning, through which direct communication with heaven is possible. There is no comparable meaning within the writings of the Apostles" (*Revelation Explained* [= Swedenborg 1994–1997a] §815:2). Swedenborg did not restore any books removed from the Catholic Bible by the Protestants, nor did he bring into his canon any other apocryphal works. He does make use, however, of what he characterizes as non-canonical works, especially Job and the works of Paul. Such quoting is heaviest in *True Christianity*. He also quotes Christian creeds and other ecclesiastical documents.

Swedenborg rejects the vicarship of the pope and the intercession of Mary and the saints. The Lord alone has divine authority and leads the church; he alone is the gate to the fold of heaven. Peter, to whom Jesus gave the keys, means not the disciple himself but the faith in the Lord he symbolically represents. Swedenborg also rejects monastic approaches to spiritual life, insisting that the only way to a full, useful, and joyful life in heaven is through a full, useful, and joyful life in this world, including its politics, business, and social and family life.

Swedenborg rejects the doctrine of original sin. Adam and Eve's actions did not curse the human race. (The biblical Adam and Eve were not individuals but figures standing for the people of the earliest church.) Swedenborg's theology includes only two types of evil: hereditary and actual. Hereditary evil takes the form of inclinations or tendencies toward evil passed genetically from one generation to the next. Actual evil is evil that we actually commit. Hereditary evil is not at all damning, because it cannot be helped. Actual evil becomes sinful and damning only if we do it knowingly and deliberately and we never repent.

Although some branches of Christianity have many sacraments, Swedenborg recognizes but two: baptism and the Holy Supper.[52] Their point and efficacy are spiritual and symbolic rather than physical. Swedenborg characterizes these two sacraments as gates at either end of a large field. We go through the gate of baptism to enter the church, and through the gate of the Holy Supper to enter heaven while still on earth (*True Christianity* 721).

Baptism is appropriate not only for infants but for adults as well. It does not grant or guarantee salvation, but it attests that we are part of the church. The water and the sign of the cross symbolize being cleansed and saved by learning truth about the Lord and undergoing spiritual crises. The Holy Supper affords partnership with heaven to those who approach in the right frame of heart and mind. And even if the heart and mind are not in the right place, the Holy Supper still affords the Lord's presence. Both the bread and the wine are to be taken, as they symbolize the love for the Lord and the faith in the Lord necessary for salvation.

---

52. Short chapters on each sacrament appear in *New Jerusalem* (202–222) and longer chapters in *True Christianity* (667–752). See also the account by Swedenborg of a discussion that took place in the spiritual world in *Revelation Unveiled* 224:11–13. Although Swedenborg does mention the need for worship and ritual observance, his works present it as a secondary aspect of religious life; primary is the individual's repentance and useful service to others.

There is no condemnation, Swedenborg teaches, of children who die, whether baptized or not. All people who die before reaching adulthood go to heaven.[53] Although all human beings have hereditary inclinations toward evil, children who die have not yet had a chance to commit purposeful, adult, actual evil, and so nothing impedes their salvation. They have free choice, but all freely choose to go to heaven.

Swedenborg dismisses the notion of a single Devil who started out as an angel of light, and then fell, taking a crew of others with him. Swedenborg uses the terms *the devil* and *satan* instead to denote hell in the aggregate. He also uses the plural to denote inhabitants of different parts of hell, devils being those who love evil, and satans those who think and believe falsely (*Heaven and Hell* 311, 544).

The notion of predestination to hell Swedenborg greets with a special expression of horror and distaste.[54] The only true form of predestination, he says, is God's intention that everyone should go to heaven, although the individual is free to thwart that intention. False is the notion that the chosen few or the elect have foreordained places in heaven, while the rest of humanity is simply condemned without recourse, as it goes against the concept of a God who is pure love and mercy (*Survey* 66).

Although Swedenborg agrees with the Christian notion that there is no time and space in heaven, he adds a qualification: there is an *appearance* of space and time in the spiritual world, and that appearance is real because it is fixed and constant, anchored not to physical motion but to the states of mind of those who live there (*True Christianity* 29). To the apocryphal Scholastic quibble about how many angels can dance on the head of a pin, Swedenborg might reply that the same number of angels could dance on the head of a spiritual pin as physical bodies could dance on a physical pin—that is, none.

Swedenborg says that the eternal "rest from labors" promised in Revelation 14:13 does not mean that angels are perpetually idle. In fact he

---

53. See *Heaven and Hell* 329 and the ensuing chapter (§§330–345). Here as elsewhere Swedenborg paints with broad strokes. He does not specify a minimum age of death by which people have made a choice of heaven or hell. At one point Swedenborg writes that infants make up "a third part of heaven" (*Heaven and Hell* 4). Given the number of young children who die, it would make sense to interpret this phrase as "one third of heaven" rather than as "a third distinct heaven," but the Latin is as ambiguous as its English translation.

54. He applies many adjectives to the notion of predestination to hell: it is "insane" (*True Christianity* 56, 487:5), "cruel" (*Divine Providence* 330:8; *True Christianity* 486:3, 487:5), "hurtful" (*Survey* 66:3; *True Christianity* 486:3), "monstrous" (*True Christianity* 488), "grotesque" (*Survey* 64), and "detestable" (*Survey* 66:3; *True Christianity* 485, 628, 634).

maintains quite the opposite. "Labors" in that passage refers not to useful activity but to the spiritual effort in "being tested"—effort that comes to an end as we become ready for heaven (*Revelation Unveiled* 640). Idleness is no blessing; the very joy of heaven comes from useful activity. All angels have jobs, positions, and functions. Although marriage love is the central love of heaven, angels' marriages are nourished and made more delightful by their useful activity. The life of heaven as Swedenborg portrays it is a full and concrete life. Unlike traditional Christian images of genderless angels endlessly playing harps in praise of God, Swedenborg's angels are female and male; they have stimulating marriages and jobs; they have homes, streets, and gardens, and lives more useful and varied than our own.[55]

e. Swedenborg's Theology vs. Other Modern Religious Perspectives

Swedenborg's views variously embrace and challenge not only mainstream Christianity, but other modern religious perspectives as well. Wouter Hanegraaff (1998, 424–429) has pointed out Swedenborg's "highly significant and widely influential" contribution to the amorphous spiritual movement commonly known as the New Age. There is much for the New Age and other modern religious perspectives to love in Swedenborg's theology: the existence of spirits and the possibility (however dangerous) of human interaction with them; the notion of correspondence between the spiritual world and the physical world; the focus on the human anatomy, including the notion of body memory (the storing of life events in physical parts of the body); the idea of inflow; Swedenborg's use of gardens for spiritual connection; and his recognition of the energy or auras around rocks and plants and human beings.[56]

---

55. For Swedenborg's idea of usefulness as crucial to heavenly happiness, see the accounts of memorable occurrences in the spiritual realm at the beginning of *Marriage Love* (1–26). See also the chapter in *Heaven and Hell* on the work that angels do (§§387–394).

56. On the potential dangers of interacting with spirits, see *Heaven and Hell* 249 and 292. On the possibility of such interaction, see notes 6, 7, and 25 above. On correspondences, see *Heaven and Hell* 87–115. On correspondences as they relate to the human form, see *Secrets of Heaven* 2987–3003, 3213–3277, 3337–3352, 3472–3485, 3624–3649, 3741–3750, 3883–3896, 4039–4055, 4218–4228, 4318–4331, 4403–4421, 4523–4534, 4622–4634, 4652–4660, 4791–4806, 4931–4953, 5050–5062, 5171–5190, 5377–5396, 5552–5573, 5711–5727, and Worcester 1987. On memories stored in body parts, see *Heaven and Hell* 463. On inflow, also called influx, see *Soul-Body Interaction* and Potts 1888–1902, 3:637–671 (under "Influx"). For Swedenborg's use of gardens for spiritual connection, see *Heaven and Hell* 109. For the energy or auras around human beings, animals, plants, metals, stones, and soils see *Divine Love and Wisdom* 292–293 and *Marriage Love* 171 and 224.

Swedenborg's views on reincarnation, however, and the eternity of the individual's stay in hell, as well as his perspective on animals and nature, distance him from the New Age. His system leaves no room for reincarnation. The individual remains the individual. She or he has one life that begins in time and never ends. That life begins when we are born on this planet. Our body breathes and lives, and eventually dies; our spirit then awakens in the spiritual world, undergoes a process of reduction to our own inner essence, and finally finds a home in heaven or hell where we remain to all eternity. Swedenborg makes no mention of people shifting from one heaven to another, or transferring in any permanent way from hell to heaven, or coming back to earth, or being aware of the details of their upcoming lives on earth.[57] Swedenborg writes that the notion of reincarnation resulted from occasional leaks from spirits' memories into human memories, making people think they had had previous lives.[58]

Swedenborg's view of hell in specific may endear him to few modern readers. Seen in heaven's light, hell is a miserable, polluted place, largely barren of vegetation, in constant political turmoil, where excruciating pain is the only remaining form of social control and restraint. The newcomer's first few hours are pleasant enough, while he or she is being sized up by those already there. After that, life consists in enslaving and being enslaved, working for food and shelter in cavernous workhouses, and indulging in lust and avarice after hours, while the agony of deserved punishment gradually reduces the desire to attack the Lord and angels to a smoldering coal, never quite extinguished and certainly never replaced by goodness. There is no parole. Hell itself is eternal, and so is the individual's stay in it.[59]

Nevertheless, even in his description of hell Swedenborg conveys the Lord's love. To dwell in hell is the individual's choice, freely made. The Lord could not and would not take that away, or transplant someone to a

---

57. Swedenborg calls the idea that the soul of one person could pass into another an "absurd notion" (*True Christianity* 171). He implies rejection of other such beliefs in *True Christianity* 79:6 and *Heaven and Hell* 183. (For one classical myth of reincarnation in the Western tradition, in which the souls choose the lives they will lead when next born, see Plato *Republic* 10.617–620.)

58. See *Heaven and Hell* 256. Swedenborg explains that this phenomenon is rare. The usual order of things is that the spirits who are with us use and experience our memory as their own, and not the reverse (*Heaven and Hell* 256, 298).

59. For Swedenborg's teachings on hell, see especially *Heaven and Hell* 536–588. On the relative pleasantness of one's first few hours in hell, see *Heaven and Hell* 574.

heaven they would find repellent and even physically intolerable. Hell is governed entirely by the Lord and is magnificently arranged and sorted in three dimensions according to varieties of evil. There is no literal fire or gnashing of teeth. Heaven's light only occasionally intrudes and shows the reality of their situation; most of the time they are spared. In their own light, the devils look human to each other and their world looks normal and even pleasing. They are allowed to indulge their evil fantasies and sexual desires as long as they do not hurt others beyond what those others deserve. The Lord's love for the inhabitants of hell allows them a godless, unreal world whose only major frustration, but a significant one, is the limit set on their cruelty and revenge.

Another teaching that may rankle some modern readers is that human beings go to heaven and have eternal life, but animals do not. Animals do not have a human soul, and only the human soul lives forever. A human being is not simply an ape with extraordinary language skills and social problems. Animals are born already knowing everything they need to know. Human infants know almost nothing, not even enough to prevent them from putting harmful objects in their mouths (*Marriage Love* 133). What humans have that animals lack is the quality of being completely empty at birth, which allows them to be filled without end. An animal, which will never be much more than it was at birth, is unable to depart from the order of its life. People can and do depart from the order of their lives, but in return they can also achieve eternal bliss and endless growth in heaven. Therefore, Swedenborg says, animals' perfection at birth becomes their imperfection, while humans' imperfection at birth becomes their perfection (*True Christianity* 48:9).

Swedenborg explains that there are plants and animals on earth that were not originally part of creation (*Divine Love and Wisdom* 339). Corresponding to human evil loves and false thoughts, they came into being after creation as the human race fell. Still, their harmfulness and savagery is confined, he writes, to the need to protect and nourish themselves. Human savagery is much worse. Swedenborg holds that humane qualities, although acquirable in the course of life through religion and spirituality, are not native to the human race.

Swedenborg's attitude to nature, like that of his contemporaries, is also out of step with some modern views. Although he sees heavenly wonders in bees and silkworms, when it comes to vegetation his writings, like his property, treasure cultivation. Heaven is not like a wilderness but like a garden. Hell is sand and rock, or at its most vegetative, mere brambles and briars, nature gone to seed.[60] Repentance of the mind parallels tilling of the soil.[61] Nature is not heavenly when left to itself but becomes heavenly through work and cultivation.[62]

IV. Problematic Content

Swedenborg's theological garden contains views that, like the taste of unfamiliar fruit, some readers might find offensive or incredible, whatever their background. Three controversial areas concern his statements about women, about Jews, and about human beings on other planets.

Some have seen a bias against women in Swedenborg's writings. *Marriage Love,* for example, seems to lay out a double standard in which virginity is a vital attribute of brides (*Marriage Love* 503, 504:2), but a merely preferable attribute of bridegrooms, expected of only "a few" (*Marriage Love* 459:1, 460:5). In the main, though, Swedenborg's treatment of men and women is remarkably balanced, particularly if one takes into account the largely male readership of the time. He is an adamant proponent of monogamy and of equality in marriage. He asserts that domination by either the husband or the wife completely destroys the love in a marriage (*Heaven and Hell* 380). Women are capable of domination—they are if anything a stronger rather than a weaker sex; by nature they possess the power and skill to subject their husbands to "the yoke of

---

60. "Around individuals in hell, and generally in the deserts there, there appear flying creatures of the night such as bats, screech owls, and other owls. There are also wolves, leopards, tigers, rats, and mice. There are poisonous snakes of all kinds, as well as dragons and crocodiles. Where there is any vegetation, brambles, stinging nettles, thorns, thistles, and certain poisonous plants spring up. Alternately, the vegetation disappears and you see only stones in piles and swamps where frogs croak" (*True Christianity* 78:5).

61. "The human mind is like soil whose quality depends on the way it is tilled" (*Heaven and Hell* 356:3; translation by George F. Dole). "Before repentance we are like a wilderness where there are terrifying wild beasts, dragons, screech owls, vipers, and snakes whose bite causes unstoppable bleeding, and in the thickets there are howling birds of night, and there satyrs dance. But when these creatures have been cast out by our work and effort, that wilderness can be plowed and made ready for planting, and sown first with oats, beans, and flax, and afterward with barley and wheat" (*True Christianity* 531; see also 614). Compare the account of a memorable occurrence in the spiritual realm at *Marriage Love* 521–522, in which an area in the woods where satyrs play is later cultivated to become a field.

62. Many of the decorative ornaments in Swedenborg's first editions feature gardening and cultivation, most notably the first ornament at the beginning of *Secrets of Heaven* (Rose 1998b, 295–296, 306).

their authority" if they wish (*Marriage Love* 292). They also possess an extrasensory perception unknown to men (*Marriage Love* 155b:4).

One central teaching, however, favors fathers genetically over mothers. Swedenborg maintains that our soul comes from our father alone (*True Christianity* 103). Our mother contributes our body and our lower mind, but our soul and inner life is exclusively from our father.[63] Unlike other challenging but merely illustrative statements Swedenborg makes,[64] this concept is integral to the heart of his theology. Jesus was divine, because his Father was divine; Jesus' soul was the life itself that created the universe. All that Jesus inherited from Mary were the lower aspects of human nature that he put off in the process of glorification, including the flesh and hereditary inclinations to every form of evil. Although that process was indescribably intense and took over three decades, success was possible because Jesus inherited his soul and life exclusively from his "father," meaning God himself. This, explains Swedenborg, is why Jesus never acknowledged Mary as his mother, and why Mary, speaking to Swedenborg once in the spiritual world, said that although she gave birth to Jesus, ever since he became fully divine she has not wanted people to view him as her son (*True Christianity* 102).

As for Jews, Swedenborg writes more than a dozen hard statements about those of Old Testament times, saying that they utterly lacked interest

---

63. Swedenborg extends the father's influence even to such apparently bodily characteristics as race when he asserts that black fathers have black children by white mothers and vice versa (*Divine Providence* 277:3). *Divine Providence* 330:1 gives a somewhat different perspective: it asserts that life comes from the Lord as heavenly Father, while earthly fathers merely supply the body, the "clothing of life." In a note on *Divine Love and Wisdom* 269 (see Swedenborg 2003, 282 note 146), Gregory Johnson gives historical background to the idea that the soul comes from the father: "The view that in conception the father contributes the spiritual or formal element of the offspring while the mother contributes only the material element dates back at least as far as Aristotle (*Generation of Animals* 1:20–22). See also Lacus Curtius Pliny (Pliny the Elder, 23/24–79 C.E.) *Natural History* 7:15. This view was widely accepted until the late Renaissance and continued to be a live option in debates about generation well into the eighteenth century."

64. In merely illustrating rather than laying a foundation for his theology, Swedenborg here and there mentions scientific beliefs that current science generally sees as unfounded or unscientific. For example, he believes in the existence of the ether, a light-conducting atmosphere more rarified than air (as for example at *Divine Love and Wisdom* 158; *True Christianity* 30:2); he assumes the action of spontaneous generation, or abiogenesis, a process by which under certain conditions animals are formed spontaneously out of inert matter (*Divine Love and Wisdom* 342); he accepts the notion that all plants are male and the ground is female (*True Christianity* 585), despite the contemporaneous elucidations on the two sexes in plants by Carolus Linnaeus (1707–1778), Swedenborg's famous cousin-in-law (Bergquist 1997, 23–39; Hübener 1988, 449–456; *Secrets of Heaven* 9441; *Heaven and Hell* 417; *Other Planets* 126; *Marriage Love* 29, 39, 182; *True Christianity* 693:5).

in things spiritual and as a result were idolatrous, cruel, contemptuous, vengeful, and unforgiving.[65] The Jews of his own day he also criticizes over a dozen times, characterizing them as adulterous, avaricious, and still closed to spiritual truth.[66] Nevertheless he mentions exceptions: "better" Jews, Jews who are open to spiritual instruction in the other world, and Jews who live in mutual love without contempt;[67] and he says that when Jews are mentioned in Scripture they have the highest of connotations: they mean all who live in the goodness of love.[68] It is important to note, in the light of intervening history, that there is in Swedenborg's works no advocacy of violence against Jews or will for their destruction. On the contrary, his remarks concerning them are immovably imbedded in a clear context of love and respect for all humankind (*True Christianity* 406–407), which accords with his own practice in life.

Comments of this kind were common in a place and time marked by prolonged, intense religious warfare; they were made in a spirit of zeal for what the observers saw as the truth. But unlike the anti-Jewish remarks of many of his contemporaries, Swedenborg's comments are clearly not part of a prejudice in favor of contemporary Christianity, the learned, the clergy, and Western Europe. That is, he does not single Jews out for notice. He makes sweeping, often negative, characterizations of other world religions, especially Catholicism, and of various European nationalities. He often asserts that the learned compare poorly with the simple, the clergy compare poorly with the laity, Christians compare poorly with non-Christians, Europeans compare poorly with Africans and the Chinese, and the inhabitants of Earth compare poorly with the inhabitants of other planets.

Life on other planets is the third area that some might find problematic. Swedenborg maintains that there is life on every planetlike body, including the moon that orbits our earth. He asserts that to believe anything else would be to underestimate the divine love. Given the Lord's primary

---

65. To the best of my knowledge, an exhaustive list of such references in Swedenborg's published theological works is as follows: *Secrets of Heaven* 908:3, 3147:10, 4750:6, 4818:2, 4825, 4832, 4865, 6561:2, 8301:5, 8588:4, 9391:19, 9942:14, 9960:18, 9962, 10033:6.

66. Again, to the best of my knowledge, an exhaustive list of such references in Swedenborg's published theological works is as follows: *Secrets of Heaven* 302, 788:2, 1094:2, 1850:4, 3479:3, 3881:10, 4750:6, 4865, 4911, 6963:2, 7051, 8301:6; *Supplements* 82; *Divine Providence* 182; *True Christianity* 521, 801.

67. *Secrets of Heaven* 941, *Supplements* 80, and *Secrets of Heaven* 3479:3 respectively.

68. *Divine Providence* 260; *Revelation Unveiled* 96, 182.

goal of a heaven from the human race, why else, he argues, would planets exist except to support human beings and ultimately populate heaven?[69] He reports his conversations with spirits from other planets, and passes on from them sociological and political information about life on their planets. In his work *Other Planets* he reports interactions with spirits from Mercury, Venus, Mars, Jupiter, Saturn, and our moon, as well as five other planets from outside our solar system. In all of his discussion of other planets, Swedenborg's central point is clear: he aims to show that the worship of the Lord is not simply an Earth-centered religion. Jesus Christ is God of the entire universe. God chose to be born on this earth because, unlike other planets, the Earth has sustained written languages and global commerce for thousands of years. God was also born here because this earth is spiritually the lowest and outermost planet, and by coming from the highest to the lowest point he would bridge all points in between (see *Other Planets* 122).

V. Unusual Specimens and the Doorway to the Mirror Garden

Many readers have noted the large-scale features of Swedenborg's theological garden just summarized. These features are hard to miss because Swedenborg frequently repeats his main points. However, like the specimens of exotic flora, the strange and wonderful little buildings, and the maze in Swedenborg's garden, his published theological works incorporate many striking and noteworthy small-scale features that have rarely received notice.

a. The Unique and Intriguing

When strolling through Swedenborg's individual sections, one frequently comes upon unusual concepts of few words but extensive implications, like a single imported flower in Swedenborg's garden that stands for an otherwise unrepresented continent. For example, just once Swedenborg mentions gorgeous temples on another planet woven and pruned into shape out of whole groves of still living trees, with prisms between the leaves splashing colored sunlight inside (*Other Planets* 151).

Elsewhere, in a discussion of the four directions in heaven Swedenborg briefly mentions spiritual gravity (*Heaven and Hell* 142). He points out

---

69. See *Secrets of Heaven* 9237; *Heaven and Hell* 417; *Last Judgment* 13.

that gravity gives all who live on earth a common center, to which the lowest parts of their bodies are closest. Heaven, he says, has a spiritual gravity that affects all its inhabitants, but the front of the body and the face are closest to the common center there, the Lord. In three and a half million words this intriguing concept of spiritual gravity occurs but once.

Likewise at the end of a chapter on heavenly language that maintains there is one universal language in heaven, Swedenborg appends a brief but provocative list of other heavenly languages, including languages of facial expressions, images, bodily movements, shared feelings and thoughts, and perhaps most intriguingly, thunder (*Heaven and Hell* 244).

In another part of Swedenborg's theological garden one comes upon a single mention of atmospheric and rainbow heavens:

> There is a heaven containing atmospheres of various colors, in which the whole air flashes as if with gold, silver, pearls, precious stones, flowers in tiny forms, and countless other substances. There is also a rainbow heaven, containing the most beautiful rainbows, great and small, varied with the most vivid colors.[70]

Although Swedenborg wrote this early in his theological period and later produced an entire work on heaven, he never mentions these particular heavens again.

A strange and fascinating structure in the garden of Swedenborg's theology is his own persona in the spiritual world as portrayed in his accounts of memorable occurrences (narratives of his experiences in the spiritual realm).[71] He does not draw attention to the role he plays in the other world, or its contrast with his role in this world; yet phrases now and then depict him as a preacher and teacher in the spiritual world, widely traveled, famous to some, notorious to others, having extraordinary powers and protection from evil.[72]

---

70. *Secrets of Heaven* 4528:3; translation by Lisa Hyatt Cooper.

71. For a thorough collection of passages on Swedenborg's persona in all his theological works, both published and unpublished, see Potts 1888–1902, 6:114–158 (under "Swedenborg").

72. Swedenborg travels to all ages and levels of heaven, including areas for spirits from other planets; to all areas of the world of spirits, including its region closest to hell, known as the lower earth; and to areas of hell. He teaches angels (*True Christianity* 76; *Marriage Love* 444). Spirits identify him as one who has been preaching repentance in the other world, whose message is so unwelcome to the evil that when he fell sick and lay apparently dead they felt joy and relief (*Revelation Unveiled* 531). He stretches out his hands and as a result evil creatures attack people

b. Humor in Swedenborg

Here and there, in an orchard of Swedenborgian seriousness, one encounters slender shoots of subtle humor. At times it occurs in similes. For example, Swedenborg writes that the effort to link genuine kindness and goodwill to a belief in three gods is "like a carriage with horses that are attached to it only by the reins in the driver's hands; when the horses start to run they pull the driver from his seat, leaving the carriage behind" (*True Christianity* 451). Another passage similarly verging on slapstick warns that we should not affirm things in Scripture that are not genuinely true. To do so would cause heaven to turn from us, just as a person would turn away if spattered by a bursting balloon full of gall (*True Christianity* 258). In one passage he sees a group of spirits whose manner of speech is like "a heap of filthy garbage overflowing its container. The intellectual element of it was presented as the backside of a horse whose forequarters could not be seen" (*Secrets of Heaven* 1644:2).

Shoots of humor occur especially in the areas of the textual garden called accounts of memorable occurrences. He reports having so challenged a spirit on his belief in faith alone that the spirit picked up a lighted candlestick to throw at him. The flame went out, however, and in the ensuing darkness the spirit hit his companion in the forehead instead, and Swedenborg laughed (*Revelation Unveiled* 484:6). During a discussion of promiscuity at another point, Swedenborg conjectures to satyrlike spirits that Circe, the sorceress of Greek myth, must have turned the wandering hero Ulysses' men not into pigs, as the legend holds, but into adulterers. The satyr-spirits find this idea and other jests of Swedenborg's raucously amusing (*Marriage Love* 521:4).

It is hard not to see humor in Swedenborg's depiction of people who think heaven will consist of eternally glorifying God. On day two of a three-day locked-in-church compulsory worship service, an angel suggests that Swedenborg "see how they are glorifying God." Swedenborg discovers that most are sleeping, and the rest are either yawning or wild-eyed, oppressed at heart and weary in spirit. They finally overcome their

---

threatening him (*Marriage Love* 79:10). He is asked to do miracles and tell the future, and refuses not because he is unable but because it would not induce belief (*Marriage Love* 535). He interacts with devils without being harmed, even using them to conduct spiritual experiments (*Marriage Love* 444:6–7). He repeatedly expresses surprise at the level of protection from malicious spirits granted him by the Lord (*Secrets of Heaven* 59:2, 699, 5863, 7479), and even derives benefit from his interaction with such spirits (*Secrets of Heaven* 968, 7479).

guards, break open the doors that confine them, and escape (*Marriage Love* 9:2).

Similarly, the people who think heaven consists of spending all eternity in paradisal gardens enjoying bucolic delights find a hellish monotony when these desires materialize. After three days of quaffing freshly squeezed juices, weaving garlands, singing melodies, and playing with water fountains, their ennui is so great that a number wander in circles begging for the way out, only to be told by some prankster that they are in the very middle of heaven, in the center of its delights, where they may stay forever (*Marriage Love* 8:1–3).

Some of the humor in Swedenborg's Latin is difficult to translate. For instance, in a speech to other national groups English spirits attribute sexual potency to physical strength and good health. At the end they follow a complex sentence one hundred nine words long with a one-word pun, "Vale," which means both "goodbye" and "be strong."[73]

c. Asymmetries in the Garden

From time to time in Swedenborg's published theological works one finds something especially significant that appears to be out of place, like the sunflowers he planted among the many types of roses in the rose garden (Dole and Kirven 1992, 45). For example, Swedenborg devotes a small volume to the topic of Scripture, yet in it he does not tackle the subject of the canon of Scripture or define "the Word" other than to say it is divine truth (*Sacred Scripture* 1). To find the list of books of the Bible that he considers to be the Word, one needs to read instead the work on Genesis and Exodus or the survey of teachings of the New Jerusalem.[74] Likewise, Swedenborg's book on hell, *Heaven and Hell,* includes no mention of cavernous workhouses; yet in a work expounding the Book of Revelation, Swedenborg describes cavernous workhouses in detail and asserts that all of hell consists of nothing but such workhouses (*Revelation Unveiled* 153).

Then there are elements that remind the reader of the mirrored "doorway" off to one side that reflected his garden; it allowed people to

---

73. *Marriage Love* 107; for a more complete discussion of this passage see Rose 1994a, 58–63.

74. *Secrets of Heaven* 10325; *New Jerusalem* 266. See note 51 above for the books that Swedenborg excludes.

glimpse the illusion of another full garden.[75] Likewise there are elements in Swedenborg's theology mentioned in pairs that imply a balance, but one element takes up far less space than the other. Balancing, as he often does, the designations "heavenly" (or celestial) and "spiritual," Swedenborg points to the existence of a complete layer of meaning running throughout Scripture called the heavenly meaning, and another complete layer called the spiritual meaning. They are equally extensive, so to speak, although the heavenly meaning is higher and more profound than the spiritual. Yet the heavenly meaning takes up far less space in Swedenborg's texts. He devotes over five thousand quarto pages to unfolding the spiritual meaning, while the heavenly meaning he acknowledges but briefly a few times, rarely articulating what it is.[76] Only once does he justify this seeming imbalance, explaining that the heavenly meaning is difficult to explain "because it does not relate to the thoughts of our intellect as much as to the emotions of our will" (*Sacred Scripture* 19). The heavenly meaning is a vast area reflected in a small, mysterious mirror.[77]

Swedenborg repeatedly indicates that there is a great deal he cannot say.[78] He finds it impossible to convey some aspects of his spiritual experiences. The limitations of human language and the transcendent nature of heavenly experience thwart his efforts at verbalization.

Swedenborg also omits material for reasons other than inexpressibility, presumably (although he does not say so directly) to leave room for the reader's participation. For example, his explanations of the inner meaning of the Word seem more like a rudimentary algebra by which the

---

75. Swedenborg told people that he found the reflected garden much more beautiful than the real one (Tafel 1875, 33, 56).

76. The heavenly meaning of a passage is given in *Secrets of Heaven* 2157, 4735, 5331, 10265, 10624; and in the chapter in *True Christianity* on the Ten Commandments (§§282–331). The heavenly meaning is acknowledged or discussed in *Secrets of Heaven* 9407:4; *Divine Love and Wisdom* 221; *True Christianity* 248; and here and there in *Sacred Scripture*.

77. For a threefold example of the same phenomenon, Swedenborg mentions that Christianity has three branches: the "Greek" church (probably meaning Eastern Orthodox Christianity); the Roman Catholic church; and the Protestant or Reformed church (*True Christianity* 760). He discusses Protestantism and Catholicism at great length and in much detail, but makes only two brief statements about the "Greek" church—that it long ago separated from Roman Catholicism (*Survey* 18), and that it believes the Holy Spirit is sent directly by God (*True Christianity* 153, 647:3).

78. For a collection of such indications from one work alone, *Heaven and Hell*, see King 1999b, 344–359, 392–410.

reader might eventually solve an equation than like the solution itself, as for instance his treatment of the following passage in Matthew:

> The lamp of the body is the eye. If your eye is simple, your whole body will be full of light; but if your eye is evil, your whole body will be full of darkness. If then the light that is in you is darkness, how great a darkness! (Matthew 6:22–23)

At five points in his published theological works Swedenborg discusses this passage. In four of them he gives the inner meaning of the eye and of no other element;[79] in the fifth he also explains one other element, the darkness.[80] He could have explained much more, however, as he does in four *unpublished* explanations of the same verses.[81] Swedenborg's incomplete exposition in the published works seems less like the garden itself than like a doorway to an otherwise invisible garden.

Another asymmetry in the garden of Swedenborg's theology concerns its practicality. Swedenborg categorically opposes faith alone and emphasizes that to bring salvation, belief has to be accompanied by action. "All religion has to do with life, and the life of religion is to do good" (*Life* 1). Without the work of repentance, and actions of love, goodwill, and useful service, we cannot reach heaven. Yet although he emphasizes life, in many areas there is little specific instruction on how to live. More than 150 times, for example, Swedenborg mentions meditating or meditation. Many of the accounts of memorable occurrences begin with a reference to Swedenborg meditating.[82] Yet Swedenborg does not define or describe what meditation is, nor does he offer advice on how to go about it. Likewise he gives the inner meaning of countless passages in Scripture, and strongly encourages readers to explore Scripture for themselves, but does not give thorough expositions nor lay out a detailed methodology for finding the inner meaning.[83]

---

79. *Secrets of Heaven* 2701:2, 2973:5, 9548:7; *Revelation Unveiled* 48.

80. *Secrets of Heaven* 9051:2.

81. *Revelation Explained* (= Swedenborg 1994–1997a) §§152:11, 274:3, 313:15, 1081:4. Although he indicates that the meaning of the eye is a key, he elaborates well beyond it: he expounds the lamp, the simplicity, the wholeness of the body, the greatness of the darkness; delves into the original Greek; and even explains what the left and right eyes would have meant if they had been mentioned.

82. *Revelation Unveiled* 926, 961; *Marriage Love* 42, 43, 75, 132, 137, 155b, 208, 261, 263, 267, 316, 380, 415, 444, 461, 483; *Survey* 119; *True Christianity* 25, 76, 78, 112, 508, 662.

83. Swedenborg's works contain a wealth of information on expounding Scripture, but a scattered wealth. Pendleton 1915 and other resources have brought these ingredients together.

In the area of repentance, though, he does give practical advice. A whole chapter in *True Christianity* gives an organized presentation with steps to follow and illustrative examples. It may be that the practical advice lacking in other areas is offered in this one because the individual needs to go through repentance to establish a partnership with the Lord. Once that partnership is forged, the Lord will lead the individual and supply things that Swedenborg's text cannot provide, as the following strikingly direct passage suggests:

> My friend, abstain from what is evil, do what is good, and believe in the Lord with your whole heart and your whole soul, and the Lord will love you, and give you love with which to act and faith with which to believe. Then with love you will do what is good, and with trust and confidence you will believe; and if you persevere, you will come into the reciprocal and perpetual partnership [with the Lord] that is salvation itself and eternal life. (*True Christianity* 484)

VI. The Style of Swedenborg's Published Theological Works

The style of Swedenborg's works is similar to their content, and both resemble the garden on the grounds where they were written. In the main, Swedenborg's theological prose style is simple and unadorned; yet small-scale features exhibit a variety of dramatic and poetical colors: descriptive accounts of extraordinary experiences, dialogs in a variety of voices, poetic diction, similes, and subtle allusions to many disciplines and areas of life. The transitions into poeticisms are often abrupt, as Swedenborg rarely forges explicit connections between them and the cognitive flow of the text. A chapter soberly explaining the inner meaning of Revelation 9 is immediately followed by the recounting of a spiritual experience in which children give expensive gifts to two-headed tortoises who rise out of the ocean to lick the children's hands (*Revelation Unveiled* 463).

In his theological works Swedenborg incorporated more and more poetical features as he went along. The first work *(Secrets of Heaven)* has few; the last work *(True Christianity)*, many. The overall effect is that of a coherent, interesting talk increasingly punctuated by a silent showing of seemingly unrelated yet colorful visuals. As the presence of such dramatic and poetical features in a theological text seems unusual, a brief account of the history of Swedenborg's Latin styles may be useful.

a. Neo-Latin and Swedenborg's Earlier Writings

Swedenborg engaged in writing and publishing over his entire lifetime, from age twelve to age eighty-three. Before his spiritual crisis he wrote volumes in one of two distinct styles: the explanatory or the poetical. (These terms are discussed more fully below.) Although a work in the explanatory style might include an occasional poetical passage,[84] or a work in the poetical style might include footnotes in the explanatory style *(Worship and Love of God),* a given volume was generally in one style or the other, not both. In his theological volumes, however, we find both of these styles within the same binding, although they remain distinct. By the time of his last publication *(True Christianity)* the poetical style had become as prominent as the explanatory.

Swedenborg used the Neo-Latin language as the vehicle for the eighteen theological works he published between 1749 and 1771. There have been three great ages of literary Latin: classical Latin, medieval Latin, and Neo-Latin. Throughout the history of Latin there was also a spoken language of the common people, which has been difficult to reach through written texts.[85] Classical Latin as it has been handed down is a relatively artificial language of writing and oratory that developed alongside ancient Roman culture. Medieval Latin was born in the hands of the first Latin translators of the Greek New Testament, people of the lower classes who cast the New Testament in a simpler Latin, presumably something like the spoken language. Medieval Latin was later spoken in churches and in the classrooms of the early universities. From the Renaissance onward, as classical Latin was rediscovered and rewoven with the spoken Medieval Latin of church and classroom, and as scientific developments forced the creation of much new Latin vocabulary, Neo-Latin came into being.

When Swedenborg first encountered Neo-Latin in the late seventeenth century, it was enjoying its golden age in Sweden (1680–1720). Swedenborg grew up hearing professors lecture, orators declaim, and poets hold forth at the University of Uppsala in a high form of the dialect (Helander 1995, 18).

---

84. For example, Swedenborg gives a number of quotations from poets in *Basic Principles of Nature* 1:387–390 (= Swedenborg [1734] 1988b, 2:251–257).

85. A few surviving sources, most notably the comedies of Titus Maccius Plautus (254?–184 B.C.E.) and Terence (Publius Terentius Afer, about 185–159? B.C.E.), give valuable impressions of what the spoken language may have been like.

By his mid-twenties Swedenborg had mastered the art of Neo-Latin poetry sufficiently to publish a volume of his own poems that came out in two editions, and two highly poetical prose works full of mythological and literary allusions to Greek and Latin classics.[86]

Later, in his thirties, forties, and fifties, as he turned to writing on mineralogy, philosophy, and anatomy, Swedenborg cultivated a straightforward and humble, almost conversational, explanatory style, with a large but accessible vocabulary. In the preface to his 1734 work, *The Infinite,* he gives his reasons:

> Here you see Philosophy reasoning about the Infinite and the soul, using perfectly familiar words and a humble style; that is, without terms hunted up from her metaphysical stockroom. This is to prevent anything unfamiliar or elevated in the words from holding the mind back or distracting it by making it ponder on the terms themselves. In discussing an elevated topic, one must make every effort to avoid the least word that might pose an obstacle. For this reason I wanted Philosophy to present herself as simply as possible, in the terms people use when speaking with friends.[87]

In 1745, not long after his spiritual experiences began, he set this simple style aside to philosophize in complex and poetical prose in *Worship and Love of God,* a work that was partly published but never completed even in draft. After devoting the next four years to biblical research, he began publishing his set of eighteen theological titles.[88]

---

86. The volume of poetry is *Heliconian Pastimes* (= Swedenborg [1707–1740] 1995b); the poetical prose works are *Joyous Accolade* (= Swedenborg [1714 or 1715] 1985) and *Northern Muse* (= Swedenborg [1715] 1988a).

87. *The Infinite,* preface; translation by Stuart Shotwell. For a Latin version of this work, see Swedenborg [1734] 1886. For a complete translation, see Swedenborg [1734] 1965.

88. Although never distributed as a "set" in Swedenborg's time, these eighteen titles can be considered a set inasmuch as their content is distinctive among Swedenborg's voluminous life works and they heavily cross-reference one other. In the first sixty pages of *Revelation Unveiled,* for example, there are fifty-four references to eleven of the thirteen previous titles. Swedenborg does not present *Worship and Love of God* as part of this set. When he lists the titles of his theological works, *Worship and Love of God* is not mentioned (see the last page of the first edition of *Marriage Love* [Swedenborg 1768, 328], and Acton 1948–1955, 744–745); and none of the eighteen theological titles refers back to it. It stands alone as a unique transitional work, written shortly after Swedenborg's spiritual awakening, and showing both the scientific and the philosophical interests that had dominated the previous decades, as well as presaging the theological interests that would dominate his writing in the decades to come.

b. Swedenborg's Theological Latin Styles

For his theological works Swedenborg crafted a Latin style that was even simpler than the explanatory scientific Latin he had written before. Latin readers both in his day and in ours have noted the remarkable simplicity and straightforwardness of his theological writing.[89] His style was extraordinarily simple compared with that of his contemporaries.[90] Yet Swedenborg was one of the best educated people in Europe at the time. Elements of both the style and the content of his published theological works reflect his panoramic interests: biblical and ecclesiastical studies, liturgy and rubric, as well as study of world religions contemporary and ancient; philosophy; geometry, calculus, and other forms of mathematics; anatomy, astronomy, botany, chemistry, metallurgy, and other sciences; classical literature and mythology, oratory, poetry, narrative, simile, dialog, drama, music, art, and sculpture; sports; education, history, geography, agriculture, economics, politics, law, business, trade, and travel; and the domestic world of marriage, home, and family. Like his garden, then, Swedenborg's theological Neo-Latin shows an overarching order and simplicity, while specific features exhibit a variety and diversity that verge on the global.

As we approach Swedenborg's theological Neo-Latin more closely we first see the two distinct Latin styles of prose mentioned above: an explanatory style and a poetical one. By the ancient table of *genera dicendi* (types of speaking) established by classical orators, the *explanatory style* would be a low or simple style, designed to inform (*Ad C. Herennium* 4:8–11). Most of its nouns come from a short list of heavily

---

89. Contemporary testimony comes from the Amsterdam merchant J. C. Cuno (1708–1796), who knew Swedenborg late in the latter's life: "One dare not accuse Swedenborg of lack of clearness, else one would do him great injustice. He writes very simply, clearly, and understandably; indeed his relations [that is, accounts of memorable occurrences] are so circumstantial and frequently so picturesque that one could paint his narratives" (Cuno 1947, 5). More recent testimony comes from the Neo-Latin scholar Jozef IJsewijn: "Somewhere between . . . strictly scientific Latin and literary prose we find some remarkable works of a very peculiar character, namely Swedenborg's natural, theosophical, and moral writings written in a straightforward modern Latin" (IJsewijn 1990, 279).

90. When Neo-Latinist scholars Margaret Benner and Emin Tengstrom give "examples of varying styles" of Swedish Neo-Latin between 1611 and 1716, they start at a low level with two texts written for "young people" (Benner and Tengstrom 1977, 98–99); yet even these seem more elevated than Swedenborg's explanatory style.

repeated abstract words that are linked to and defined by each other. The following example is quite typical:

> Since the truth of our perceptions depends on our intent for good, "servants" means people who are intent on seeing things truly because they want to do good. It also means people who are filled with wisdom because they are moved by love, since wisdom is concerned with what is true and love is concerned with what is good. It also means people who see things in the light of their faith because they care, since faith too is concerned with what is true and caring is concerned with what is good.[91]

Most of the verbs in the explanatory style are forms of the verb *to be* or abstract verbs in the passive voice, generally in the present tense. The clauses are logically subordinated and heavily nested,[92] and the sentences often follow a deductive path from a premise to a conclusion.

Swedenborg's explanatory style during the theological period is the simplest he ever wrote. Latinist Alvar Erikson has documented some of the changes in Swedenborg's syntax and vocabulary that attended his shift toward an even simpler and more conversational prose. Most notably, Swedenborg uses a nonclassical construction for expressing what grammarians call indirect discourse.[93] His explanatory Latin follows a simple, rather Germanic, word order rather than the convoluted word order of classical literary Latin. It does not stray, however, into Latin that is colloquial or incorrect. It avoids the many barbarous Latin forms then in circulation. His explanatory style is quite straightforward and unadorned.

The *poetical style* is markedly different. Although Swedenborg always uses prose to express his theology, and much of it is written in an explanatory style that is wholly prosaic, at times he uses a poetical style of prose corresponding to the middle style of the *genera dicendi,* designed to engage the imagination. The poetical style employs a large vocabulary of concrete nouns. Its verbs, too, are concrete; they are usually active in voice, in either past or present tense, and their clauses are linked side

---

91. *Revelation Unveiled* 3; translation by George F. Dole.

92. Swedenborg's clause structures are discussed in the main text of Rose 1998a and graphically illustrated in its Appendix 2.

93. To specify more precisely for interested Latinists: In expressing indirect discourse he moves away from the more literary method that uses accusative and infinitive toward the more conversational method that uses the conjunction *quod* with subjunctive verbs. For further details, see Erikson 1973.

by side with coordinate conjunctions. The following is a simile in *True Christianity*.

> They could also be compared to people who weave a life raft out of rushes and reeds, using tar to glue it together; and they set out onto the great expanse of the ocean, but out there the tar glue dissolves; and suffocated by the briny water, they are swallowed up and buried in its depths. (*True Christianity* 342:3)

For much of Swedenborg's theological period the poetical style rarely occurs, but it increases dramatically in frequency toward the end.

The most voluminous form that the poetical style takes toward the end of Swedenborg's theological period is the category of text that Swedenborg labels *memorabilia*—the accounts of memorable occurrences, traditionally known as memorable relations, which have already been mentioned above. These lengthy narratives of specific spiritual experiences recounted in the past tense often include extensive dialog with spirits and angels. There is a great variety among the voices that Swedenborg quotes: some sound simple; others hold forth in the highest form of elocution anywhere in Swedenborg's published theology (*Marriage Love* 111). In accounts of memorable occurrences Swedenborg will even at times depart from standard prose vocabulary to use a pointedly poetical diction.[94]

In Swedenborg's first editions, an account of a memorable occurrence or a set of memorable occurrences is usually typographically separated from the main text by large asterisks (Rose 1998b, 298, 339). At the beginning of each account Swedenborg labels it a *memorabile* in small capitals, and where there is more than one, gives an ordinal designation also in small capitals: THE FIFTH MEMORABLE OCCURRENCE. There is rarely any explicit connection with the preceding text or with other accounts of memorable occurrences when they occur together.

When an account of a memorable occurrence first appears (marked out as such) at the end of *Divine Providence* (1764), the thirteenth of the eighteen titles, Swedenborg asks the reader's forgiveness for including it to fill up the rest of the page.[95] From then on, however, they appear in every work. In his next work, *Revelation Unveiled* (1766), accounts of memorable occurrences appear at the end of every chapter. In two cover

---

94. For a discussion of these various styles see Rose 1994a, 49–64.

95. *Divine Providence* 340:6–7. In four cases, material that is later repeated as a memorable occurrence first appears without that label in earlier works: *Sacred Scripture* 26, 90, 102; *Faith* 42.

letters that Swedenborg sent out with *Revelation Unveiled* he draws the addressees' attention to these accounts, and suggests that they be read first (Acton 1948–1955, 610, 612). Swedenborg also arranged for a hand-bill in England promoting *Revelation Unveiled* that advertised its accounts of memorable occurrences, giving the section reference for each one (Hyde 1906, entry 2195). Accounts of memorable occurrences are even more prominent in the next work in sequence, *Marriage Love* (1768). It begins with over twenty quarto pages of them, and has on average two after each brief chapter. Some accounts of memorable occurrences appear in *Soul-Body Interaction* (1769) and in *Survey* (1769); and many grace the last work of the set, *True Christianity* (1771).

Another poetical form, the complex simile, blossoms even later than the accounts of memorable occurrences. Swedenborg uses similes with a formulaic introduction to compare theological abstractions to earthly realities, although he often includes intriguing, apparently superfluous, details (Rose 1994b, 871). Like accounts of memorable occurrences, similes at times display poetical diction (Rose 1994a, 62–64); unlike accounts of memorable occurrences, they are not set apart from the main text but occur within it. Although complex similes crop up sporadically in earlier works (see for example *Sacred Scripture* 33 and *Divine Providence* 199:2, 211:2), they occur in unique and sudden abundance in *True Christianity*, Swedenborg's last and crowning theological work. Swedenborg incorporates over four hundred of them into this book (Rose 1994b, 871), often using two or three, and in one extreme passage (*True Christianity* 348) fourteen of them in a row, to illustrate a single teaching. Although the simple explanatory style predominates in the other seventeen titles, and although *True Christianity*'s explanatory articulation is so strong that Swedenborg uses the work's table of contents as an example of truths that come together to form structures that are like fascicles of nerves (§351:1), nevertheless the lengthy accounts of memorable occurrences after chapters and the abundant complex similes and other forms of imagery within chapters make *True Christianity* word for word about half explanatory, half poetical.

c. The Labyrinthine Maze of Swedenborg's Theological Style

In Swedenborg's garden there was also a labyrinthine maze.[96] When tracing Swedenborg's thoughts through his sentences, we find ourselves at

---

96. On the popularity of garden labyrinths in Europe in the 1600s and 1700s, see Kern 2000, 247–265.

times in a labyrinth. Swedenborg even suggests that he crafted his Latin theological style for protection of the truth.

The reason behind this is evidently that all things sacred are carefully protected. For example, Swedenborg writes that access to the heaven of the earliest people is heavily guarded. Once, struck with an ardent desire to see it, he journeyed there with an angel guide through a dark forest full of intersecting and misleading pathways (*Marriage Love* 75). Responding to their prayers and approving the usefulness of their mission, the Lord granted Swedenborg and his guide the ability to see the occasional olive trees laden with grape vines that marked the true path through the maze.

Likewise, Swedenborg asserts, the treasures in the heart of the Word are not open to the approach of all. A heart and mind turned toward the Lord are necessary for finding our way through the many statements and implications, the many layers of meaning. Although at its center the Word contains a Garden of Eden with food and living water, those who have not found the right viewing angle see only a forest, and those who come from the wrong angle see sand without even grass growing on it (*Sacred Scripture* 96).

In his own writings Swedenborg may have sought to produce something as labyrinthine and self-protecting as the Word and the earliest heaven. A rough note to himself written less than two years before his death suggests that he crafted his prose to have an ambiguous effect: to shine for believers, but to seem dull and worthless to nonbelievers:

> 3 Make a list of the books that have been written by the Lord through me from the beginning up to the present time.
>
> 4 They have been written in such a way that they shine before the very eyes of those who believe in the Lord and the new revelation; but they are darkness and of no importance for those who deny those things, and who, for various external reasons, are not inclined to accept them.
>
> Experiences proving that this is the style of writing within them: 1 From the Dutch censors of books who had assembled in the spiritual world; one of them when he had read them, said that they were of the highest merit, above every other book with the exception of the Word; but another said that he saw nothing in them but matters of a trivial kind, mere fantasies, and thus that they were to be rejected as being of no importance. 2 Likewise in England the books which have been sent to the universities, for the clergy have rejected them; 3 and by those in Göteborg, Beyer, Rosén, and others; some have indeed seen those

books as mighty works of God, some nothing but trickery, and others nothing whatsoever. (Swedenborg 1975a, 193)

Because of the specific Latin style he used, then, Swedenborg can make the assertion that ends *Heaven and Hell:*

> What I have been saying in this book about heaven, the world of spirits, and hell, will be obscure to people who find no delight in knowing about spiritual truths; but it will be clear to people who do have this delight, especially to people involved in an affection for truth for its own sake—that is, people who love truth because it is true.[97]

Presumably the same applies to all of Swedenborg's theological works.

VII. Swedenborg's Invitation

In the fall of 1767, three children who had come to Stockholm for their father's funeral took refuge from a sudden downpour in a covered area by the sidewalk. It happened to be part of the fence around Swedenborg's garden. The children were startled when an elderly gentleman came out in the pouring rain toward them. He invited them in to warmth and shelter, and they accepted. They apologized, asking forgiveness for being on his property, and explained the unfortunate reason for their visit to Stockholm. He replied, "That I know already; for your father has just been with me and told me that you were coming" (Sigstedt 1981, 334).

Just as Swedenborg leaves the responsibility for salvation to the individual, so he gives his readers the responsibility for what they find. Some visitors to the garden of Swedenborg's theology are there out of curiosity, and may find beauty and order. Some who feel spiritually orphaned may also find shelter and warmth.

---

97. *Heaven and Hell* 603; translation by George F. Dole. See also *Marriage Love* 533, in which mysteries like the ones revealed by Swedenborg shine like a star in the spiritual world, but become dark as they are let down into the material world.

Appendix

Theological Works Published by Emanuel Swedenborg

The following list shows the titles adopted in the New Century Edition for the eighteen theological works[1] published by Emanuel Swedenborg, under their respective dates of publication. The numbers bearing a letter prefix correspond to the reference numbers in the annotated bibliography of Swedenborg's complete works on pages 385–519 in this volume; entries there give complete publication data, including original Latin titles, literal translations of the Latin titles, and traditional English titles.

1749–1756
Secrets of Heaven (P85–P96, P100)

1758
Heaven and Hell (P101)
New Jerusalem (P102)
Last Judgment (P103)
White Horse (P104)
Other Planets (P105)

1763
The Lord (P107)
Sacred Scripture (P108)
Life (P109)
Faith (P110)
Supplements (P111)
Divine Love and Wisdom (P112)

1764
Divine Providence (P113)

1766
Revelation Unveiled (P114)

1768
Marriage Love (P118)

1769
Survey (P119)
Soul-Body Interaction (P120)

1771
True Christianity (P126)

---

1. On the special status of the unfinished prose poem *Worship and Love of God* (published 1745; P81–P82 and U113–U114), see note 88 on page 91 above.

Swedenborg's Modes of Presentation, 1745–1771

GEORGE F. DOLE

Outline

Phase 1. Focus on Exegesis: *Secrets of Heaven*

Phase 2. Timely Topics: The 1758 Works

Phase 3. An Exegetical Cul-de-Sac: *Revelation Explained*

Phase 4. Theological and Philosophical Foundations: The 1763–1764 Works

Phase 5. Return to Exegesis: *Revelation Unveiled*

Phase 6. A Work on Morals: *Marriage Love*

Phase 7. Addressing a Lutheran Orthodoxy: *True Christianity*

Conclusion

IT is impressive testimony to the basic consistency of the message of Emanuel Swedenborg's theological works that little attention has been paid to ways in which the various works differ from each other.[1] As early as 1770, a Swedish follower of Swedenborg, Gabriel Beyer (1720–1779), noted that Swedenborg used three categories of presentation in these works: (1) exegesis specifically of the Bible; (2) explanation of other theological topics; and (3) descriptions of his experiences in the spiritual world (Tafel 1877, 331). However, neither Beyer nor other scholars seem to have asked why the different modes were used at different times.[2] Swedenborg

---

1. This essay has appeared in two earlier forms: in published form as Dole 1988b, and in oral form at the Symposium on Science and Spirituality at Tarrytown, New York, August 24–27, 1988. Another view of some of the issues discussed here can be found in Koke 1995 and Koke 1998.

2. A rare glimpse of Swedenborg's authorial process is found in *The Old Testament Explained* (= Swedenborg 1927–1951b). In this manuscript, published only posthumously, he interspersed paragraphs telling of his spiritual experiences, distinguishing them from the exegetical material by indenting them. At §475 he remarked, "As for what is written about myself, I cannot yet be sure of enough of it to swear to it by God, since I cannot be sure that the particular words are appropriate and precise enough to be absolutely right. So they need revision at some other time, God willing, so that I can seem to myself to be telling the exact truth." (It is customary to refer to passages in Swedenborg's works by section numbers rather than page numbers. All translations in this essay are mine unless ascribed specifically to R. L. Tafel or Lisa Hyatt Cooper.)

himself rarely gave reasons,[3] but there is enough indirect evidence to support a plausible reconstruction.

Phase 1
Focus on Exegesis: *Secrets of Heaven*

Swedenborg's "conversations with spirits" began in April 1745.[4] At about this time, he began to publish a remarkable work, *Worship and Love of God.* Highly imaginative, poetic, and using Swedenborg's full command of literary Latin, it is a kind of mythic hymn to the centrality of divine love in the creation of true humanity. He published only two parts of this, however, and turned to more scholarly business.[5]

It was also in 1745 that he began keeping, in Latin, the account that its first editor titled *The Spiritual Diary,* and its most recent editor has

---

3. Throughout *Secrets of Heaven,* Swedenborg prefixed and appended to each chapter of Scripture interpretation some material of a different nature, primarily drawn from his spiritual experiences. He offers the following rationale for this at the beginning of the second chapter: "The Lord in his divine mercy has given me the opportunity to learn the inner meaning of the Word, which contains deeply hidden secrets that no one has ever been aware of before. No one *can* become aware of them without learning how things stand in the other life, since almost all of the Word's inner meaning looks, speaks, and points to that life. For these reasons, I have been granted the privilege of disclosing what I have heard and seen over the past several years of interaction with spirits and angels" (*Secrets of Heaven* 67; translation by Lisa Hyatt Cooper). This may reasonably be associated with his frequent arguments against what he saw as the commonly held notion that spirit was something insubstantial or ethereal. See, for example, *Secrets of Heaven* 5084:6, 5222, and 6400:3, and *Heaven and Hell* 74, 77, 170, and 183.

4. The clearest testimony to this is found in *The Old Testament Explained* 1003: "I can solemnly swear that for the space of eight months now I have by the pure mercy and grace of the Messiah been having the same kind of conversation with people in heaven as with my friends on earth . . . namely from the middle of April 1745 to January 29, 1746." The April event marked the culmination of a process of some years. For a careful and detailed reconstruction of this process, see especially Acton 1927.

5. In response to an inquiry, the secretary of the (Swedenborgian) society *Pro Fide et Charitate,* Gustaf Billberg (1772–1844), communicated the following information on this work from Christian Johansén (about 1746–1813), one of the earliest Swedish followers of Swedenborg: "Dr. E——m has told me that you wish to know our opinion respecting the truth of the work *De Cultu et Amore Dei* [On the Worship and Love of God]. I am able to tell you on the authority of Christian Johansén, who interrogated Swedenborg himself on this subject, that he obtained from him the following answer: 'It was certainly founded on truth, but that somewhat of egotism had introduced itself into it, as he had made a playful use in it of the Latin language, on account of his having been ridiculed for the simplicity of his Latin style in later years. For this reason he did not regard it as *equal* to his other works'" (Tafel 1877, 710).

argued should be called *Spiritual Experiences*.⁶ While this is often in the form of hasty jottings, there is evidence that its publication had not been ruled out. Beginning early in the manuscript, we find such "addresses to the reader" as "To relate all the cases of experience would be prolix" (*Spiritual Experiences* [= Swedenborg 1983–1997] §153); and there is also the fact that Latin was Swedenborg's language for publication, while Swedish was the language he used in his personal diaries. The manuscript is far from ready for publication, however. He eventually indexed the diary and drew on it quite freely for the material in the third of Beyer's categories.

He did a great deal that was very directly related to the first of these categories. He plunged into the study of Hebrew and Greek and went to the considerable labor of compiling his own Bible index.⁷ He drafted a substantial commentary on parts of Genesis, Exodus, Joshua, Judges, Ruth, 1 and 2 Samuel, 1 and 2 Kings, 1 and 2 Chronicles, Leviticus, Numbers, and Deuteronomy, which he left unpublished.⁸ When he resumed publishing in 1749, it was with *Arcana Coelestia* (Secrets of Heaven), a series of eight volumes "making known the spiritual contents of Scripture" by proceeding verse by verse through Genesis and Exodus; and there are clear indications that he originally intended to continue this commentary from Genesis through all of the Scriptures.⁹ Most notable among these indications are the mentions within the text itself of the intent to deal with later books of the Bible.¹⁰ Further, the printer's advertisement for an English translation of the second volume begins, "This Work is intended to be

---

6. For a manuscript facsimile, see Swedenborg 1901–1905; for the printed Latin edition, see Swedenborg 1844–1846; for a critical Latin edition see Swedenborg 1983–1997. A British effort to replace the complete nineteenth-century translation reprinted as Swedenborg 1978b stalled after volume 1 (Swedenborg 1962b). An American effort (Swedenborg 1998–2002), by J. Durban Odhner (1924–2002), was still incomplete at the time of the translator's death, but the final volumes are forthcoming from other hands. On the title of the work, see Odhner 1998, ii–v.

7. This has been published in facsimile as Swedenborg 1916c and in an edited Latin version as Swedenborg 1859–1873.

8. This has been published in a facsimile as Swedenborg 1916b; in an edited Latin version as Swedenborg 1847–1854; and in an English translation as Swedenborg 1927–1951b.

9. This lends credence to a late (1782) report of Swedenborg's friend Carl Robsahm (1735–1794) recounting Swedenborg's statement that during the April 1745 experience the Lord charged him specifically "to make known the spiritual contents of Scripture." For the original text of the Robsahm account, see Hallengren 1989, 37. For the full text in English, see Sigstedt 1981, 198.

10. At *Secrets of Heaven* 66, Swedenborg anticipates dealing with material in Joshua, Judges, Samuel, and Kings. He states thereafter that he will, "with the Lord's divine mercy," deal with later

such an exposition of the whole Bible, as was never attempted in any language before,"[11] a statement that may well reflect the author's knowledge and consent.

We may well see in this biblical focus a reflection of Swedenborg's Lutheran background. While the battle cry of orthodox Lutheranism may have been *sola fide*, "faith alone," its charter was *sola Scriptura*, "Scripture alone." Martin Luther (1483–1546) refused to argue with the philosophers on their grounds, insisting that Christian faith must be based solely on the Bible. Even the creeds developed subsequently by the church were authoritative only because they were in perfect agreement with the revealed Word of God.[12]

The thought that there was deeper meaning in Scripture was by no means new.[13] The notion of multiple levels of meaning in Scripture can be traced back at least to Philo Judaeus (about 15 B.C.E.–50 C.E.), and stories of the even older Delphic oracle testify to a venerable and deep-rooted suspicion of literal interpretations of divine messages in Western culture. In eighteenth-century Protestantism, though, there was an equally strong mistrust of efforts to "allegorize," accompanied by a concerted effort to base theology on the literal text. For example, the eminent Lutheran biblical scholar and champion of literalism, Johann August Ernesti (1707–1781), wrote a scathing critique of *Secrets of Heaven*.[14]

Bible books as follows: in the first volume of *Secrets of Heaven* (published in 1749) he anticipates treating Numbers (see *Secrets of Heaven* 296), Leviticus (§643:4), Deuteronomy (§730:4), Jonah (§1188:2), Deuteronomy, Joshua, and Judges (§1444:4), Joshua and Judges (§1616:1), and 1 Samuel (§1672); in the second volume (published in 1750) he anticipates treating Numbers (§2280:7); in the third volume (published in 1751) Elijah and Elisha (§2762:2); in the fourth volume (published in 1752) material in Numbers and Leviticus (§4434:10). Of particular interest is a mention in the eighth and last volume (published in 1756) of his expectation to deal with material in Revelation (§10400:2), which was realized in *Revelation Unveiled* (see further discussion below). These references may not be taken as unequivocal promises of seriatim treatment of the books mentioned, but they are fully compatible with such an expectation. Also intriguing is a note at §9362 in volume 7 (published in 1754) that he would be including interchapter material on the inhabitants of other planets "right up to the end of the Book of Exodus" *(usque ad finem Libri Exodi)*. There is no hint at this point that this will mark the end of this particular exegetical project.

11. Lewis [1750] 1790, 396; quoted in Hindmarsh 1861, 2; also accessible in Academy Collection 6:756.

12. For a fuller treatment, see Dole 1988c.

13. Swedenborg states that the inner meaning has been "unknown until the present time" in *Sacred Scripture* 4 and 20 and *Revelation Unveiled* 1, and gives explanations for this ignorance in *Divine Providence* 264 and *True Christianity* 206. For historical discussion of the question of deeper meaning in Scripture see, for example, Childs 1977.

14. The original review was published in Ernesti 1760, 515–527. For a transcript and translation see Academy Collection 6:811.

In addition to being on principle hostile to any reading of inner meaning in the Bible, Ernesti seems to have been unable to find an orderly system in Swedenborg's work. It should be noted, though, that Swedenborg left as little ground as possible for such a charge. He indexed the work as he proceeded and used this index for careful cross-referencing throughout as a demonstration that the meanings assigned to various features of the Scriptures were constant.[15] In the days before computers such indexing required immense labor and discipline. Thus the evidence of the manuscripts decisively dispels any image of "the mystic" simply pouring out a stream of consciousness.

Though far from unorganized, *Secrets of Heaven* does almost immediately present the reader with an organizational duality. At the close of its second chapter, Swedenborg appends a narrative account of his experience of dying; and as the volume proceeds, he will continue to place both after and before each chapter segments of serial description of the spiritual world—the so-called interchapter material. He states his reason for doing so in *Secrets of Heaven* 67: the spiritual meanings of the Word will not be intelligible unless his readers realize what the spiritual world is like. These interchapter presentations not only continue throughout the remaining volumes, they expand to include sections explaining theological matters, as opposed to Biblical topics or experiential topics (descriptions of the spiritual world). Even the coverage of strictly experiential topics broadens to cover a number of different subjects, one of which in particular deserves special note. Following the first chapter of Exodus, he begins a serial presentation of his experiences with spirits from other planets, and from then until the end of the work each chapter is preceded by material on the doctrine of charity and followed by material on extraterrestrials. He would later revise this latter material slightly and publish it as a separate booklet.[16]

Ultimately, the experiential material and the non-Biblical expository material take center stage. In the Bible the closing chapters of Exodus, 36–40, describe the construction of the tabernacle in almost exactly the same words as are used in the divine instructions given in chapters 25–30 (though not in the same sequence). After presenting the text of chapter 36, Swedenborg simply states that this material has been treated in chapter

---

15. The index has been published in facsimile as Swedenborg 1916d; in an edited Latin version as Swedenborg 1890; and in an English translation as Swedenborg 1909.

16. See Swedenborg's 1758 work *Other Planets*. For a compilation of material from these interchapter texts on yet another topic, that of the universal human, see Swedenborg 1984a.

26 and picks up the thread of his discussion of other theological themes. He does the same for the remaining chapters of Exodus, with the result that the exegetical task is completely laid aside.

The work itself closes without epilogue. The citation of the closing chapter of Exodus is followed by this statement:

> These images too I pass over without further explanation, because once again they duplicate material that has already been described and explained—except at the end of the chapter. There the text says that after Moses finished the work, the cloud covered the tent and Jehovah's glory filled the dwelling place; that the cloud would stay over the tent by day, and fire would stay in it by night; and that the children of Israel traveled whenever the cloud rose. The symbolism here is evident from many earlier discussions of cloud, Jehovah's glory, fire, and travels.[17]

This rather abrupt treatment of a passage of considerable potential import may indicate that other matters were calling for his attention.

Phase 2
Timely Topics: The 1758 Works

It would be two years before Swedenborg's next works were published, and they mark a striking change of approach. The five works that appeared in 1758 are far shorter—one little more than a pamphlet; and in apparent deviation from his initial direction, none is exegetical. The shortest, *White Horse,* is essentially a collection of references to passages in *Secrets of Heaven* on the nature of Scripture. *New Jerusalem* is a systematic overview of the theology in the form of a preface, an introduction, and twenty-three very brief topical chapters. Much of the material in these chapters is drawn from *Secrets of Heaven,* and each chapter is followed by copious but brief references to that work.[18] *Other Planets* is a very slightly revised edition of the material on extraterrestrials from the last three volumes of *Secrets of Heaven,* mentioned above. *Heaven and Hell,* the longest

---

17. *Secrets of Heaven* 10832; translation by Lisa Hyatt Cooper.

18. Still extant are the volumes of *Secrets of Heaven* marked with the annotations Swedenborg very probably made while composing *New Jerusalem* (the Mennander Set). Volumes 1 through 6 are in the library of the Swedenborgian House of Studies at the Pacific School of Religion in Berkeley, California; volumes 7 and 8 are in the library of the Swedenborg Society in London. For more on their history, see Woofenden 2002, 305, 312.

of the 1758 works, is an overview of the spiritual world as Swedenborg had experienced it, and is generously annotated with references to *Secrets of Heaven*. *Last Judgment* describes events in the spiritual world as Swedenborg reports having experienced them in 1757.

Two of these works mention the reason for their publication. Sections 8 and 9 of *New Jerusalem* depict a Christian church that has "moved away from the good that comes from love for the Lord," and urges the need to recognize that "the whole of Sacred Scripture is nothing but a teaching of love and charity." *Heaven and Hell* is even more explicit, describing a growing denial of spiritual reality fostered by the growth of materialistic philosophy and science, and seeking "to prevent this negative attitude . . . from . . . corrupting people of simple heart and simple faith" (*Heaven and Hell* 1).

While it is highly unlikely that these "people of simple heart and simple faith" would be able to read Latin (many of them would not have been able to read at all), *Heaven and Hell* was under the circumstances admirably suited to the task it set for itself. The topic of the afterlife was of wide public interest, far more so than was biblical exegesis. The Latin was extraordinarily simple, the chapters were short, and the stories and images were memorable. The picture they drew of the spiritual world would reach beyond the immediate readership and have its impact on popular thought.[19] It is probably no coincidence that over the centuries, *Heaven and Hell* has consistently outsold Swedenborg's other works by a considerable margin. It has also been translated into Arabic, Danish, Dutch, French, German, Hindi, Icelandic, Italian, Japanese, Polish, Russian, Spanish, Swedish, and Welsh.

The copious references to *Secrets of Heaven* in all the 1758 works, possible only because of the laboriously compiled index to that work, give unmistakable evidence of the hope that readers attracted by this popular literature would be drawn to the more demanding (and for the Lutheran, more central) subject of the meaning of the Bible. In an earlier effort to reach out to a wider readership, Swedenborg had sponsored an English translation of the second volume of *Secrets of Heaven,* and in so doing he not only had invested thought and funds in its distribution, but had underwritten a significant amount of the cost of its publication.

The fifth work published in 1758 is of a different nature from the other four. *Last Judgment* claims to be a description of exactly that—

---

19. For an engaging view of heaven and hell in the history of thought, including Swedenborg's impact, see McDannell and Lang 2001.

a judgment that involved the reordering of a spiritual world that had fallen into radical disarray. Swedenborg gives clear indications in *Secrets of Heaven*[20] that he sees the Christian church as a dying institution and that momentous events are at hand, including the beginning of a new church (identified in §8988:4 with "the New Jerusalem"), but as late as 1751 he writes that the Coming of the Lord "takes place every time the gospel is preached, every time someone thinks about something holy,"[21] with no apparent suspicion that an epochal Coming is at hand.

We must assume that his experience of the event referred to as the Last Judgment had a significant impact on Swedenborg, but it is hard to discern just what that impact was. To see the apocalyptic texts fulfilled with no noticeable earthly upheavals, as he reports he did, must have reinforced his conviction of the folly of biblical literalism, and it must also have intensified his sense of the urgency of his mission. It is understandable that he would respond by making his work much more accessible and inviting; and life after death, the planets, and the Last Judgment were all subjects of widespread interest.

Phase 3
An Exegetical Cul-de-Sac: *Revelation Explained*

In the 1758 works, Swedenborg had by no means abandoned his focus on Scripture. While those works were not in themselves exegetical, each refers the reader back to *Secrets of Heaven;* and as soon as they were published, he turned back to exegesis. It is immediately evident, however, that he had abandoned any thought of writing a commentary on "the whole Bible." Now, having published a commentary on its first two books, he turned to the last, the Book of Revelation, and began writing *Revelation Explained.*

This is the only work of Swedenborg's for which we have both a rough draft and a "fair copy"—the latter being the copy written for submission to the printer, and therefore executed with particular care. While the first draft was written in narrow columns with occasionally cavalier penmanship and is replete with words, phrases, and whole paragraphs crossed out or supplemented by interlinear and marginal additions, the fair copy is written in a very legible hand with very few corrections, uses the full width of each page, and includes notations of the typefaces to be

---

20. See, for example, *Secrets of Heaven* 2243:7, 3898:3, 4057, and 4333:3.

21. *Secrets of Heaven* 3900:9; translation by Lisa Hyatt Cooper.

used. Normally, this copy would be discarded, probably by the printer, once the process of publication was completed; but this manuscript was never sent to the printer. When Swedenborg was about halfway through commenting on the nineteenth chapter (of the twenty-two in Revelation), he laid the work aside. The fair copy, incidentally, stops only a couple of paragraphs short of the first draft, suggesting that the decision to give up the project was both abrupt and definite.

There have been various opinions about his reasons for this decision (Woofenden 2002, 90–91). My own is based on the form of the work and its contrast with its published successor, *Revelation Unveiled* (1766). *Revelation Explained* is vast and sprawling. Probably because he had decided not to treat the Bible in its entirety, Swedenborg was generous with cross references to parallel passages. In commenting on "and a third of the ships were destroyed" in Revelation 8:9, for example, he wrote what amounts to approximately twelve pages in English translation, citing and interpreting passages about ships from Ezekiel, Isaiah, 1 Kings, Psalms, Daniel, Job, Genesis, Judges, Matthew, Mark, Luke, and John.

Gradually, though, the focus of the work shifted. In chapters 12 and 13, he inserted an exposition of doctrine clearly related to the biblical text under examination, treating it as part of the exegesis, as necessary digression. In chapter 15 he explicitly took off from this digression, and the doctrinal material at that point loses all connection with the exegesis and is given its own title. Thereafter, most of the numbered sections have two parts, the first being a treatment of some part of the biblical text and the second a "continuation" on this or on a subsequent doctrinal theme, often at greater length than the exegetical portion. The disproportion grows somewhat erratically, but by the time Swedenborg has reached the nineteenth chapter, there is almost four times as much text on general theological topics as there is Biblical exegesis. The work has changed character, and is less a biblical commentary with doctrinal digressions than a doctrinal treatise with exegetical digressions. This shift occurs as he approaches the climax of the Book of Revelation and of the Christian Bible, the vision of the Holy City.

Phase 4
Theological and Philosophical Foundations:
The 1763–1764 Works

It is estimated that Swedenborg laid *Revelation Explained* aside in 1759. In 1763 he published no fewer than six books: *The Lord, Sacred Scripture,*

Life, and *Faith* (often collectively called *The Four Doctrines*); *Supplements;* and *Divine Love and Wisdom.* In 1764 he published *Divine Providence.* Much of this 1763–1764 material is clearly foreshadowed in the "continuations" in *Revelation Explained.*

Now, however, we learn of a new dimension to the shift of focus. Swedenborg's preface to the first of the 1763 works, *The Lord,* reads in part as follows:

> Some years ago the following five small works were published:
>> *Heaven and Hell*
>> *The Teachings of the New Jerusalem*
>> *Last Judgment*
>> *White Horse*
>> *The Planets and Other Earths in the Universe*
> In these works many things were set forth that had been unknown before.
> Now, by command of the Lord, who has been revealed to me, the following are to be published:
>> *Teachings for the New Jerusalem on the Lord*
>> *Teachings for the New Jerusalem on Sacred Scripture*
>> *Teachings about Life for the New Jerusalem; Drawn from the Ten Commandments*
>> *Teachings for the New Jerusalem on Faith*
>> *Supplements on the Last Judgment*
>> *Angelic Wisdom about Divine Providence*
>> *Angelic Wisdom about Divine Omnipotence, Omnipresence, Omniscience, Infinity, and Eternity*
>> *Angelic Wisdom about Divine Love and Wisdom*
>> *Angelic Wisdom about Life*

While Swedenborg would eventually publish only seven of these nine works, he would in fact cover all the topics involved. It is worth particular note that one of these works, *The Lord,* quotes Scripture copiously in support of its teaching and that in sharp contrast to this there is very little biblical material in *Divine Love and Wisdom.* Swedenborg was well aware that good Lutherans (the audience of *The Lord*) would not be impressed with philosophical reasoning and that good philosophers (the audience of *Divine Love and Wisdom*) would not be impressed with biblical proofs. For Swedenborg, though, philosophy was not an end in itself; and *Divine Providence* moves purposefully from the metaphysical to the pragmatic with its concern to show how the sorry state of humanity can be understood in the light of the beauty of divine love and wisdom.

At this point, we may perhaps begin to see an evolving strategy. If we put the nature of *Revelation Explained* together with the command to publish the nine books listed in *The Lord,* then the "continuations" of the earlier, exegetically based books can be seen as the first signs of a movement toward fulfilling this new command. They suggest that Swedenborg found himself directed toward the second of Beyer's categories, focusing on theological topics rather than on exegesis.[22]

It is particularly significant in this context that while Swedenborg seems to have heard the command quite explicitly, in the form of nine specific titles, he did not feel bound to follow it to the letter. When Gabriel Beyer asked him about one of the commanded works that had not been published, he replied as follows:

> About the promised treatise on infinity, omnipotence, and omnipresence. Answer: There are many things on these subjects interspersed throughout *Angelic Wisdom concerning Divine Providence* 46 to 54, and 157; also in *Angelic Wisdom concerning Divine Love and Wisdom* 4, 17, 19, 21, 44, 69, 72, 76, 106, 156, 318; and in *Revelation Unveiled* 961; these subjects will be further treated of in *Secrets of Angelic Wisdom concerning Marriage Love;* for to write a separate treatise on these Divine attributes, without the assistance of something to support them, would cause too great an elevation of the thoughts; wherefore these subjects have been treated in a series of other things which fall within the understanding.[23]

It may also be worth mentioning that in listing the works already published, Swedenborg did not mention *Secrets of Heaven*—a substantial omission, since at that time it represented nearly 90 percent of his published theology. We could ask for no clearer indication that he regarded the 1763–1764 works as being in the same "special category" as the 1758 works, that is, as distinct from the explicit task of biblical exegesis.

---

22. For Swedenborg's explanation of these continuations, see note 3 above.

23. Here Swedenborg uses the full names of the books usually referred to simply as *Divine Providence, Divine Love and Wisdom,* and *Marriage Love.* The translation of the letter is from Tafel 1877, 261, with modernization of internal citations and a correction of the full title of *Marriage Love* based on examination of the original manuscript of the letter. (Tafel's text reads "these subjects will be further treated of in the arcana of Angelic Wisdom concerning Conjugial Love." In the manuscript of the letter, however, the word *Arcana* ["Secrets"] is clearly part of the title: not only is it capitalized, but the whole phrase is a Latin insert in a Swedish text.)

Phase 5
Return to Exegesis: *Revelation Unveiled*

Once *Divine Providence* was published, Swedenborg felt both free and commissioned to return to exegesis of the Book of Revelation in *Revelation Unveiled.* The freedom from the need to cover the topics previously commanded of him is witnessed by his single-minded and efficient exegesis: the twenty-two chapters are covered in a single volume and the work is exceptionally well disciplined. A pattern of presentation is set in the first chapter and followed very evenly throughout, and his cross-referencing is done with exceptional care. Generally speaking, in previous works he had given specific section numbers as cross-references only when pointing *back* to material on previous pages; the overwhelming majority of his references ahead were not specific.[24] Now, though, we find a reference *ahead* to §944 as early as §8, and this level of specificity is maintained with considerable consistency throughout. This could be accomplished only by the labor of inserting the numbers in the fair copy after completion of the first draft, with the aid of his carefully prepared index.

The commission for this work was apparently quite specific. At the close of an (undated) account of an experience in the spiritual world recorded in *Marriage Love* 522 he wrote, "Then I heard a voice from heaven saying, 'Go to your room and close the door. Get down to the work you started on the Book of Revelation. Carry it to completion within two years.'" *Revelation Unveiled* was in fact published in 1766, two years after the publication of the work previous to it, *Divine Providence.*

Phase 6
A Work on Morals: *Marriage Love*

On April 8, 1766, Swedenborg sent eight copies of *Revelation Unveiled* to Beyer. The next day, he received a letter from Beyer including the following request. "Another wish I have besides—to see the subject of marriage fully treated of, which among those who have delicate feelings, awakens embarrassing questions of conscience, and by most people is not well understood, and still less properly explained."[25]

---

24. There are occasional forward references by section number in *Secrets of Heaven*. Some point ahead only a short distance (for example, §3969:4 refers to §3971; §3981 refers to §§3982 and 3986), but some anticipate material quite far ahead (§2395 refers to §2447; §2356 refers to §2576).

25. Translation adapted from Tafel 1877, 238.

This had long been a subject of particular interest to Swedenborg. There are abundant references to it in *Secrets of Heaven,* including a brief excursus in §§10167–10175. While it was not among the works listed in *The Lord* as commanded, there are promises of a work on marriage in *Life* 74 and 77, published in the same year. If, however, he was working on it at the time of Beyer's request, it is strange that he made no mention of it in his prompt reply (Tafel 1877, 240–241), especially since he did respond specifically to another question about the standing of the Epistles among the other books of the Bible. A year later he was certainly at work on it, since the letter to Beyer already quoted at length above mentions it as a projected publication, although not under its final title.

The work itself, *Marriage Love* (1768), has unusual features. It was the first of his theological works to bear his name on its title page, even though the secret of his authorship had been out for at least eight years, during which seven works were published. He himself described it as not a theological work but mostly a book of morals,[26] and no other work keeps such an insistent focus, in its nonexperiential sections, on human behavior and circumstances. This attention to particular societal conditions[27] may be reflected in Swedenborg's identification of himself as "a Swede" on the title page.[28] No other work has such a high proportion of experiential narrative to theological exposition. The beginning of the full title itself, *Delights of Wisdom in,* promises pleasures to the reader, albeit pleasures of the mind, in contrast to the phrases used at the beginnings of other full titles, which suggest that a learning experience is in store (*A Disclosure of Secrets of, Teachings for the New Jerusalem on, Angelic Wisdom about*). In keeping with this more inviting approach, the work opens not with the usual theological rationale but with an extended narrative account of people shortly after death discovering the absurdity of their previous images of heaven.

---

26. Tafel 1877, 306. In stating that the book was not "theological," Swedenborg was presumably referring to the fact that it did not concern matters that were included in orthodox Lutheran theology and therefore could not technically be subjected to tests for heresy. Furthermore, Swedenborg added to *Marriage Love* a list titled "Theological Books Previously Published by Me." It is quite possible that the specification "theological" was intended to distinguish them from *Marriage Love.* No such designation was used in the parallel list in *The Lord.*

27. Swedenborg calls attention to this in §295:2 with the statement that "this chapter [on engagements and weddings] will contain frequent references to commonly accepted practices."

28. He identified himself as "a Swede" on the title page of *Soul-Body Interaction* as well; while on the title page of *True Christianity* he referred to himself as "a servant of the Lord Jesus Christ."

Phase 7
Addressing a Lutheran Orthodoxy: *True Christianity*

The list of theological works at the close of *Marriage Love* promises a presentation of the doctrine of the New Jerusalem "in fullness" within two years. The task was appropriate both to Swedenborg's advanced years and to his circumstances. Since the time his authorship had become known, criticism of his theology had begun to be addressed directly to him, and there were the beginnings of institutional opposition. Now this opposition was beginning to affect some of his few followers, and in the fall of 1768 two of them, Gabriel Beyer and Johan Rosén (1726–1773), found themselves formally accused of heresy.

It may come as no surprise, then, to find Swedenborg suddenly occupied with the study of standard Christian doctrine. His working manuscripts, for example, deal with such subjects as justification and good works, Calvin, and the remission of sins.[29] His unpublished manuscript *Bible Concordance for "True Christianity"* gives evidence of a careful study of Acts and the Epistles. While he would have been thoroughly familiar with these books because of his Lutheran upbringing, he had come to regard them as noncanonical[30] and had paid them only slight attention in his published theological works.

In 1769, he published two very different, relatively brief, books. *Soul-Body Interaction* was addressed directly to what was then a particularly intense philosophical debate on the subject of its title. It is concerned with the structure of creation, refers to Scripture only in passing, and does not touch on such theological subjects as salvation, incarnation, or eternal life.

The focus of *Survey of Teachings for the New Church,* in contrast, is intensely theological. *Survey* presents itself immediately as a kind of stopgap work. "I have taken it into my mind to bring to light the teaching of this church in its fullness, as a whole. However, since this is a work that will take some years, I have thought it wise to publish a preliminary sketch so that readers may gain some general notion about this church

---

29. The term *justification* in Christian theology is a translation of a Greek word that has been taken to mean either the process of becoming righteous or the event of acquittal from guilt. Good works are good actions. John Calvin (1509–1564) was the founder of the Reformed branch of Protestant Christianity. The remission of sins is a divinely sanctioned release from the guilt or penalty consequent upon sin.

30. See *Secrets of Heaven* 10325, *White Horse* 16, and *New Jerusalem* 266; and also Tafel 1877, 240–241.

and its teaching."³¹ In fact, the contents of the work belie its title. Far from surveying the teachings of the new church, §§2–15 present careful summaries of orthodox Catholic and Protestant doctrine, §§17–113 deliver a scathing critique of these tenets, and the closing passages §§114–115 and 118–120 consist of several accounts of memorable occurrences previously published in *Revelation Unveiled*. The only presentation of the teaching of the new church is found in §§16 and 116–117. The former passage begins "There now follows a summary of the teaching of the new church," promises a future presentation in three parts, and then lists chapter titles for each part. Swedenborg gives the first two parts, however, no further attention, specifically focusing on the third as containing the information important for his readers to have now; it is intended to "point out the disagreements between the dogmas of the present church and those of the new church," and is immediately taken up in §§17–113. In §§116 and 117 he makes brief statements of "the faith of the new heaven and the new church" in its universal and in its particular form respectively, but that is all.

Comparison of the projected contents described in *Survey* to the actual chapter titles of the full treatment of the subject in the subsequent work *True Christianity* (1771) is highly instructive. To sum up such a comparison briefly, the beginning and end of the book are substantially redesigned, and the middle is at minimum thoroughly reorganized.³² The separate treatment of the three Persons of the Trinity mirrors standard Lutheran practice with two intriguing differences. The usual format of a

---

31. *Survey* 1. It is interesting to see that Swedenborg presents this as his own decision, with no mention of divine mandate or guidance.

32. The proposed first chapter, on "the Lord God the Savior and the Divine Trinity in him," is divided into three chapters in the later and far larger work: one on God the Creator, one on the Lord the Redeemer, and one on the Holy Spirit and the operation of the Divine—a division for which there is no precedent in Swedenborg's previous works. The next three chapters in the list given in *Survey*, on love, faith, and life, are reorganized and presented in *True Christianity* in two chapters with numerous subdivisions. Where *Survey* calls for a chapter on reformation and regeneration followed by one on freedom, *True Christianity* has a chapter on freedom followed by one on repentance, and then by one on reformation and regeneration. A chapter on imputation (see note 34 below) is inserted before the proposed chapters on baptism and the Holy Supper; and the three chapters that were to conclude the first part, chapters on heaven and hell, our state after death, and eternal life, are omitted. Finally, the four proposed chapters of the second part, on the Conclusion of the Age, the Coming of the Lord, the Last Judgment, and the new heaven and the new church, are combined into a single chapter, in which less attention is given to the Last Judgment than the prospectus in *Survey* would lead one to expect.

Lutheran systematic theology called for a first chapter on the Trinity; then chapters on the Father, the Son, and the Holy Spirit; and then a chapter on the unity of God. Swedenborg obviated two of the customary Lutheran chapters by beginning his chapter on God the Creator with a section on the unity of God and by closing his chapter on the Holy Spirit with a section on the Trinity.

The standard treatment by which Swedenborg was influenced in *True Christianity* led him to begin the book with a chapter on God the Creator. We may contrast this sequence of presentation with that used in *New Jerusalem* in 1758. There Swedenborg started by exploring the relationship of the fundamental meanings of "good" and "true" as the necessary basis for understanding what was to come. He then presented chapters on human nature, the good life, the sacraments, life after death, the church, and the Bible, and dealt with the Lord as a topic only in the next to last chapter. It is at least arguable that this approach, treating the understanding of Divinity as a goal to be reached rather than as a starting point, follows more naturally from the theology itself than does the more dogmatic Lutheran schema imposed on it in *True Christianity.*

A similar accommodation to Lutheran practice may be seen in the omission of the proposed chapter on the spiritual world. This was certainly a central topic of the new theology (as was suggested in the statement in *Secrets of Heaven* 67 that the deeper meanings of the Word cannot be intelligible unless readers realize what the spiritual world is like),[33] but it was a subject not included in the creeds or in orthodox Lutheran theology. Imputation, however, was, and although its role in Swedenborgian theology is essentially negative, it is given a full chapter in the finished work.[34]

When we add to these facts the sudden attention to Acts and the Epistles, and note also that the attention paid to creedal statements increases noticeably, the pattern is quite clear. This is a summary addressed especially to a Lutheran readership, intending to show on the basis of authorities accepted by Lutherans that this theology is not heretical. In a letter to Beyer dated April 12, 1770, Swedenborg referred to support for his theology adduced from the Formula of Concord and printed in the minutes of the Göteborg trial proceedings. He added,

---

33. The passage is quoted in note 3 above.

34. In Christian theology, the word *imputation* is associated with the doctrine that the merits of Christ are transferred to those who believe in him.

"This doctrine they there call *Swedenborgianism;* but for my part I call it *Genuine Christianity*" (Tafel 1877, 354). The resemblance between this statement and the title *True Christianity* can hardly be coincidental.

In short, the work seems best understood not simply as a final summary of his theology but also as a proposal for the complete rethinking of traditional Lutheran theology. In a way, it tries to set traditional Christian beliefs in the universalizing context of *Divine Love and Wisdom*, and it is of particular interest that the first chapter argues on Scriptural grounds for a number of the same propositions that are presented on rational and experiential grounds in the earlier work. *True Christianity* is, I believe, Swedenborg's demonstration that the encounter with the transcendent requires a radical reconsideration of orthodox concepts, not necessarily contradicting them verbally, but seeing new meaning in familiar words.

Conclusion

To summarize the shifts in writing strategy seen in Swedenborg's theological works: We see him first as a person profoundly committed to a Lutheran view of the exclusive centrality of Scripture. We find him encountering meaning in quite unexpected forms, particularly in direct, intense, and enlightening spiritual experience. We find a distinct tension at this level, issuing in a creative uncertainty as to the best means of fulfilling his mission. This uncertainty is resolved by a kind of alternation between exegetical, experiential, and topical presentation; and in this alternation we can see the interactive effects of a series of divine mandates as he received and understood them, a deep and relentless sense of urgency, and his own best judgment—or what he himself would have called "prudence."[35]

---

35. See *Divine Providence* 210:2; *Secrets of Heaven* 5121:3.

Swedenborg's Manuscripts

FRANK S. ROSE

Outline

IN addition to his published work, Swedenborg left behind thousands of pages of handwritten material. What is this material like, and how does it relate to the published work? Consider the fate of just three of Emanuel Swedenborg's manuscripts in the last nineteen months of his life.

The first, *True Christianity,* was completed on June 19, 1770 (see *True Christianity* 791).[1] Swedenborg, at age eighty-two, immediately began making

---

1. As is common in Swedenborgian studies, text citations to Swedenborg's works refer not to page numbers but to Swedenborg's section numbers, which are uniform in all editions. Titles of Swedenborg's works used in this essay agree with those in the list of Swedenborg's works on pages 385–519 of this volume. For the full bibliographic information referenced by the author-date citations here, see the reference list on pages 521–558. Unless otherwise specified here, translations are those of the sources cited.

plans to leave Stockholm and travel abroad to have the book printed. About the middle of July he packed up the manuscript for it—his final major theological work—and took leave of his homeland for the last time.

He traveled by ship; and on shipboard he drafted some reports of experiences in the spiritual world to add to the book. Unfortunately, he left this second manuscript on the ship by mistake. The captain of the ship eventually gave it to a minister in Sweden, and it reappeared only after Swedenborg's death.[2]

Meanwhile, Swedenborg proceeded to Amsterdam, where he stayed for a year, seeing *True Christianity* through the press. Printing was finished by the summer of 1771.

With printed copies of this work now in hand, Swedenborg set sail for England. On arriving in London he went directly to his favorite lodgings, the home of a barber and wig maker, Richard Shearsmith (about 1731–about 1815). Swedenborg was welcomed, established himself there, and immediately continued working again. His focus now was on drafting an appendix to *True Christianity* that he had promised his readers in the volume.[3]

Just before Christmas, Swedenborg had a stroke and was somewhat paralyzed. It took him a month to recover. One day his personal physician, Husband Messiter,[4] came to his house to visit. We learn what happened next from a note on the subject written by an early follower of Swedenborg, Charles Augustus Tulk (1786–1849):

> E. S. was absent; but the Doctor being known to Shearsmith, he admitted him to go upstairs into his apartment. On the tables in the

---

2. On this event, see Tafel 1875, 62 note (though the year 1769 is erroneously given for the voyage), Tafel 1875, 724 note 146 (where the year 1771 is erroneously given), and also Tafel 1877, 758–775.

3. For this promise, see *True Christianity* 15, 177, 343, 627, 758. Whether Swedenborg intended this appended material to be a single title or more than one is moot. Acton 1957, 372–378, argues convincingly that it was intended as a single work, which he reconstructs from various sources; yet in a letter of August 1771 to the Landgrave of Hesse-Darmstadt (1719–1790), Swedenborg himself speaks of two small works, soon to be printed, on the promised topics, and mentions two other projected works as well; the relevant portion of the letter is quoted below on pages 145–146. Tradition since then has treated the manuscript material that survives as four separate titles: *Coronis* (= Swedenborg 1996j, 7–106 = Swedenborg 1931), *Consummation of the Age* (= Swedenborg 1996h), *Invitation to the New Church* (= Swedenborg 1996m), and *Sketch of an Ecclesiastical History of the New Church* (= Swedenborg 1975a).

4. On Messiter, see note 94 on page 47 above.

room lay this Manuscript [draft materials for the planned appendix to *True Christianity*], which the Doctor took up and put in his pocket, probably with the intention to read and to return it. This, however, he omitted to do. On Swedenborg's return home, missing the Manuscript, he was much displeased with Shearsmith for admitting any one into his apartment contrary to his orders, when absent.[5]

It is clear that Swedenborg attached considerable importance to the material he was adding to his last book, since in one of the surviving drafts of the appendix we read, "Unless the present work be added to the preceding *[True Christianity],* the church cannot be healed."[6] Now, however, the precious manuscript was gone.

Sometime later Messiter returned for another visit. Swedenborg inquired about the manuscript, and Messiter was obliged to admit that he had lost it. This answer evidently was very disturbing to Swedenborg, and according to his landlord, he never wrote another word. He passed from this world a short time later, on March 29, 1772.

However, the wayward manuscript did not entirely vanish; half of it was at some point copied by another follower of Swedenborg, August Nordenskjöld (1754–1792). It was later printed,[7] and on one of the flyleaves of a printed copy Charles Augustus Tulk wrote his account of the manuscript's misadventures.

That, briefly, is the story of some of the last of Swedenborg's manuscripts: one was published by the author, but two were lost and only later recovered, at least in part. How many similar volumes have disappeared completely, we do not know, but about forty do survive, most of them found in his home after his death. Since everything Swedenborg wrote has been of great interest to his followers, these volumes have been preserved, copied, and translated, and sections of them have been published individually. They have often been called "the posthumous theological works," since they were published by others after Swedenborg's death; but as this essay seeks to show, most of them are not finished "works" at

---

5. Academy Documents 1491.13. The punctuation is here modernized in part. A very different account of this incident is given in Hindmarsh 1793, 55 note, as quoted in Hyde 1906, entry 2920.

6. See *Invitation to the New Church* (= Swedenborg 1996m, 119–150) §25.

7. This is the *Draft for "Coda to True Christianity,"* traditionally known as *Coronis* (= Swedenborg 1996j, 7–106 = Swedenborg 1931).

all. Rather they can best be understood as Swedenborg's research and draft material for the theological works that he did publish.[8] In what follows I will first review briefly the historical origins of the difficulties encountered in categorizing the manuscripts, then show how despite these difficulties they can be divided into different categories, and finally indicate how they fit into the sequence of the published works. I limit my discussion to the theological manuscripts, as opposed to those on scientific, political, and other topics.

I. Historical Difficulties

Since Swedenborg did not make a will, it was left to his heirs to dispose of his property after his death. When they went into his home, they found over a hundred items—volumes or bundles of papers—written by him. Some were printed works, and others were handwritten manuscripts. They went through them with apparent care, labeling each as well as they could. In the end they had a complete list of the volumes and their contents, divided into three categories that they designated A, B, and C. Category A was intended to comprise the theological works (although in fact the heirs placed some philosophical works in this group). Category B consisted exclusively of philosophical works; though it should be observed that in the eighteenth century, the term "philosophical" included what we would call scientific works today. Category C consisted of letters and documents. The heirs made no attempt to arrange them in any kind of order within the categories. This first list of Swedenborg's works was drawn up on October 27, 1772 (Tafel 1877, 779–786).

There have been many subsequent attempts to list all of Swedenborg's writings, and no two lists are alike. For example, ten years after the first list was drawn up by the heirs, Abbé Antoine-Joseph Pernety (1716–1796), a

---

8. Swedenborg's unpublished manuscripts are not *mere* research and draft material, however; they are themselves worthy and rewarding objects of study. They provide fascinating behind-the-scenes glimpses of both the spiritual and publishing processes Swedenborg went through, and they supplement and in places even clarify points made in his published works. A number of people view them as being on a par with his published theological works.

follower of Swedenborg, published a second.[9] Three years later yet another list appeared, published by Bénédict Chastanier (about 1728–1806), another early follower.[10] In 1787 Johan Björnstjerna (1729–1797) drew up an official list for the Swedish Royal Academy of Sciences (Tafel 1877, 794–797). Some time between 1784 and 1796, August Nordenskjöld paid to have the manuscripts rebound in codices, with numbers pasted on the backs to indicate codex 1, codex 2, and so on, up to codex 114, and another official catalog was made.[11] As part of his six-volume work, *The Swedenborg Concordance,* John Faulkner Potts (1866–1923) made yet another list of Swedenborg's books, totaling forty-five titles in all.[12] Of the works Potts listed, eighteen were published by Swedenborg himself, and the remaining twenty-seven were in manuscript form when he died.

Even given our current command of the surviving documents, it is still difficult to make a list of the manuscripts of Swedenborg. The exact nature of some can be confusing: many of them are mere fragments or, though more substantial, were never completed, such as the manuscript left behind on the ship or the one taken by Messiter. To some manuscripts Swedenborg never gave titles at all. Subsequent scholars have invented titles for these nameless manuscripts, and sometimes different scholars have chosen different titles. The manuscripts overlap in subject matter enough that it is not always clear to which manuscript a title in a list refers. In a few cases an invented title represents a number of manuscript fragments grouped together by a translator.[13] Some traditional titles are in Latin—a phenomenon that can be seen in Potts's list, which gives Latin titles for eight works for the simple reason that they had not been translated into English when Potts wrote

---

9. R. L. Tafel maintains that this was really August Nordenskjöld's list (Tafel 1877, 787).

10. See Tafel 1877, 792–794, where again Tafel maintains that this list was compiled by Nordenskjöld.

11. For the catalog, see Tafel 1877, 798–800. The catalog was prepared by the secretary of the Academy, J. C. Wilcke (1732–1796). Some of the codex volumes were numbered twice: codex 63 is the same as codex 110, and codex 95 is the same as codex 111. It seems necessary to add, in an age unfamiliar with such terms, that a codex (plural "codices") is simply a bound volume, especially of handwritten material.

12. Potts 1888–1902, 1:xii–xv. Potts (1:xii note) implies that his list is based on still another list, one compiled by R. L. Tafel (Tafel 1877, 884–1023).

13. For example, *God, Providence, and Creation* (= Swedenborg 1896) is a title invented by the translator, John C. Ager (1835–1913), for material taken from the last volume of *Revelation Explained* (= Swedenborg 1994–1997a).

his concordance.[14] These Latin titles do not always correspond to later titles given the works in English.

Other circumstances increase the divergence among the lists. A group of followers of Swedenborg in Sweden and England requested permission to borrow the manuscripts from the Royal Academy of Sciences in Stockholm, which had become the home of the manuscripts. The Academy released many of them, and some were taken to England as early as 1783. There Swedenborgians eagerly began the work of transcribing Swedenborg's often difficult handwriting to establish the Latin text, and later translated their transcripts into English and other languages.[15] As key people died, the manuscripts that had been taken to England were passed from hand to hand, and eventually the ownership was not clear. The Swedenborg Society[16] gained possession of most of the manuscripts in 1841, and after inquiring of the Royal Academy in Sweden about their status, determined that the Academy was the rightful owner. To the Academy it then returned them, after an interval of almost sixty years. During that time it was virtually impossible to formulate a definitive list of what Swedenborg had left behind. What was worse, some items were lost.[17]

This confused interval was only one factor impeding the emergence of the manuscripts into the light of scholarly scrutiny. Most of the

---

14. The Latin titles are (with their current English equivalents): *Adversaria* (*The Old Testament Explained* = Swedenborg 1927–1951b), *De Athanasii Symbolo* (*Commentary on the Athanasian Creed* = Swedenborg 1994–1997b, 6:571–634), *Coronis* (*Draft for "Coda to True Christianity"* = Swedenborg 1996j, 7–106), *Diarium Minus* (part of Swedenborg's diary *Spiritual Experiences* = Swedenborg 1998–2002, 3:411–505), *De Conjugio* (*Second Sketch for "Marriage Love"* = Swedenborg 1996p, 357–396), *De Domino* (*Draft of "The Lord"* = Swedenborg 1994–1997c, 635–647), *De Justificatione* (*Brief Index of Catholic Teachings* = Swedenborg 1996n, 539–549), *De Verbo* (*Draft of "Sacred Scripture"* = Swedenborg 1996f, 325–396), *Sciagraphia Doctrinae Novae Ecclesiae* (*Summary of New Church Teachings* = Swedenborg 1996v, 561–567). As of this writing, more than a hundred years after Potts's concordance was published, the computerized search engine of English-language versions of Swedenborg's writings known as NewSearch still uses Latin titles for these works.

15. This work could not have been undertaken in Sweden, since on January 2, 1770, the Swedish king issued a decree against "reviews or translations of Swedenborg's works, or of other similar writings, which contain anything conflicting with our pure doctrine." See Tafel 1877, 318–320; Acton 1948–1955, 703.

16. Originally the London Printing Society, the Swedenborg Society was founded in London in 1810 to promote the diffusion of the works of Emanuel Swedenborg.

17. The story of the borrowed manuscripts is told in documents collected in Tafel 1877, 802–834. Although some manuscripts were lost, Tafel maintains that in fact "the Swedenborg MSS. which were missing from the Academy of Sciences in 1841 are . . . all satisfactorily accounted for," insofar as copies had been published of the two manuscripts that were still missing when he wrote his account (Tafel 1877, 834).

scholars involved were fully employed in other careers, and their work was often sporadic. As a result, decades were required to copy, translate, and print the material. Even when Potts completed his concordance—some 130 years after Swedenborg's death—all the unpublished material had still not been printed or even identified. Furthermore, since Potts's time other manuscripts have emerged.[18] Now instead of the forty-five titles he listed, the total is more like seventy-eight.

Clearly, these historical facts work against a definitive presentation of the manuscripts and their place in Swedenborg's total output. It is not difficult, however, to categorize them.

II. Categories

The manuscripts vary considerably in size and quality. Some of them are very large, extending to several bound volumes. These are *The Old Testament Explained* (= Swedenborg 1927–1951b), *Spiritual Experiences* (= Swedenborg 1998–2002), *Revelation Explained* (= Swedenborg 1994–1997a), and the six Bible indexes (= Swedenborg 1859–1873). Other manuscripts are much smaller. The longest of this shorter group, *Draft of "Supplements,"*[19] is less than two hundred pages in English translation; the shortest is less than a page in length. The categories I propose cut across these physical classes. The four main categories are as follows.

a. Research Material

This category includes Swedenborg's journal, *Spiritual Experiences* (formerly known as *Spiritual Diary*), his various indexes to the Bible, and indexes to Christian theology and to his own works. It also includes marginal notes in his copy of the Latin translation of the Scriptures by Sebastian Schmidt, or Schmidius (1617–1696). Much of this research material has never been published in translation. Some has been published but is currently out of print.[20]

---

18. For an example of manuscripts rediscovered in the twentieth century, see Acton 1922, 568–578.

19. Traditionally referred to as *Last Judgment (Posthumous)* (= Swedenborg 1996o, 397–556).

20. For *Spiritual Experiences,* see Swedenborg 1998–2002; for the Schmidt Bible, see Schmidt 1696; for the marginalia, see Schmidt and Swedenborg 1872 and Swedenborg 1917; the latter three sources are currently out of print. The most notable examples of research material that have never been published in translation are the Bible indexes (in Latin in Swedenborg 1859–1873).

b. Draft Materials for Works Later Published by Swedenborg

In this category are the manuscripts normally thought of as Swedenborg's posthumous works. But as has been pointed out, to anyone actually inspecting the manuscripts, or at least their photolithographic reproductions, it is obvious that most of them are not finished works at all. These "works" are sometimes scattered over the page. Some lack headings. Most do not have the section numbers characteristic of Swedenborg's published works. In some cases the sentences are incomplete. For the most part it is clear that they were written in preparation for other works, and it is more accurate to call them "draft materials" than "works" or "posthumous works." The traditional titles have often disguised the relationship between draft and published work. For example, the work traditionally titled *De Domino* (About the Lord) was written in preparation for the published work *The Lord.* Thus its current title, *Draft of "The Lord"* (= Swedenborg 1994–1997c, 6:639–647). Similarly, the work traditionally titled *De Verbo* (About the Word)[21] was written in preparation for the published work *Sacred Scripture,* and is here referred to as *Draft of "Sacred Scripture"* (= Swedenborg 1996f, 325–384).

c. Tracts

Swedenborg wrote a number of small tracts. Each one is just a few pages long. Some of them were actually printed during Swedenborg's lifetime.[22] Many of them were included with letters Swedenborg sent out to some of his friends. The main theological tracts are:

> *Answers to Three Questions* (written 1767; = Swedenborg 1996c, 573–574)
> *Answer to a Friend* (= Swedenborg [1769] 1996b, 1–4)
> *Draft Supplement to "White Horse"* (written 1769; = Swedenborg 1996d, 419–423).
> *The Word's Earthly and Spiritual Meanings* (= Swedenborg [1770] 1996r, 577–579)

---

21. The term "the Word" was used by Swedenborg for the books of the Bible that he considered to possess an inner sense.

22. These are *Answer to a Friend* (= Swedenborg [1769] 1996b, 1–4), *The Word's Earthly and Spiritual Meanings* (= Swedenborg [1770] 1996r, 577–579), and *Reply to Ernesti* (= Swedenborg [1771] 1975d, 197–199). The published work *Soul-Body Interaction* may also be viewed as a tract. It was printed and circulated privately. See Tafel 1877, 1009–1011.

Answers to Nine Questions (written 1771; = Swedenborg 1997b, 126–132)

Reply to Ernesti (= Swedenborg [1771] 1975d, 198–199)

d. Theological Portions of Swedenborg's Letters

About forty of the extant letters written by Swedenborg contain theological material. There is only one in the period up to 1766 (dated August 11, 1760), and a few in the years 1766–1768. Most of them were written in the last three years of his life. Apparently Swedenborg did not keep the letters he received, or copies of those he wrote. The letters that have survived come from the estates of those who received them.

Because the categories of the tracts and letters are well understood, this essay will not deal further with them. Instead, it will focus on the first two of these categories: research and draft materials. In the next section, I will consider the relationship between the manuscripts Swedenborg was working on during each of the periods when he was in Sweden and the published works that resulted.

III. The Chronology of the Manuscripts

At first glance the categories of Swedenborg's manuscripts I have just sketched out may be bewildering. The function of the manuscripts becomes clearer, however, if one considers their connection to the books that he did actually publish; then a consistent pattern can be seen in Swedenborg's career as a theological writer. He began a given major work by amassing research material. Then he developed draft materials or outlines. Using this preparatory material, he went on to write and publish the major work at which he had been aiming. Sometimes he produced an index of this work for his own purposes. Finally, in some cases he wrote certain smaller works derived from the larger one. This pattern is repeated five times during his theological career.

During the last twenty-seven years of his life, Swedenborg went abroad at least six times, in every case to publish one or more books. Altogether he spent more than nine of those years outside of Sweden. Each of the five distinct periods of Swedenborg's theological career involves an interval of writing in Sweden and ends in a trip abroad. (On some of those trips he continued to edit the text in preparation for the printer.)

The five periods are as follows (with approximate totals of years and months in parentheses):

> Period 1: April 1745–July 1759 (fourteen years, three months). In Sweden from August 1745 to July 1747 (about one year, eleven months) and again from May or June 1750 to May or June 1758 (about eight years)
>
> Period 2: August 1759–March 1764 (four years, eight months). In Sweden from July 1759 to May or June 1763 (about three years, eleven months)[23]
>
> Period 3: April 1764–September 1766 (two years, six months). In Sweden from August 1764 to July 1765 (about eleven months)
>
> Period 4: September 1766–October 1768 (two years, one month). In Sweden from September 1766 to May 1768 (about one year, eight months)
>
> Period 5: October 1768–March 1772 (three years, six months). In Sweden from October 1769 to July 1770 (about ten months)

The generalization holds true that whatever material Swedenborg used to prepare a book for printing while he was traveling was thrown away after the final version had been printed. The preparatory material written at home in Sweden, however, has survived, and it is this material that makes up the writings that Swedenborg's heirs collected and cataloged before handing them over to the Royal Academy of Sciences.

One manuscript, *Spiritual Experiences* (= Swedenborg 1998–2002), does not exactly fit into this pattern; it is a journal Swedenborg wrote over a twenty-year period.[24] The rest, however, can be placed in one of these five periods, with some overlap.

---

23. Although there is hearsay reported by John Henry Jung-Stilling (1740–1817) in 1809 that Swedenborg was in Amsterdam on July 17, 1762 (see Tafel 1877, 490), Swedenborg's confirmed presence in Stockholm a month earlier on June 16 and three weeks later on August 5 makes this unlikely, since Swedenborg rarely traveled for less than a year, and the journey from Stockholm to the Netherlands took about a month each way.

24. On one of his trips he took a bound blank volume to continue writing down the same kind of material he recorded in *Spiritual Experiences*. In this book, which was smaller than the books he had used in Sweden, he resumed the numbering of his paragraphs where he had left off in the other volumes. Yet when he returned home and began writing in a large volume again, he picked up the numbering where he had left off there, thus creating double ranges of paragraph numbers. In order to distinguish the material in the smaller volume, it was traditionally given the name *Spiritual Diary Minor* (= Swedenborg 1998–2002, 3:411–505); editors have added the letter *a* its section numbers.

a. Period 1: April 1745–July 1759

Period 1 includes by far the most material of the five periods. During this time Swedenborg wrote over five thousand pages of preparatory material, mostly in the form of indexes, Bible commentary, and journal entries, plus two complete copies of the eight-volume work *Secrets of Heaven* (a total of about twelve thousand pages). *Secrets of Heaven* was the major work of this period; he published it serially between 1749 and 1756. These manuscripts leading up to *Secrets of Heaven* deserve a closer look, as do the drafts of the major work itself and the derivative works that followed.

***Passages on the Coming Messiah* (1745)** Swedenborg's life took a dramatic turn when he was in his mid-fifties. In the span of a few years, he went from being a thoroughly trained and highly regarded scientist and philosopher, to being a theologian without credentials or following. Though he was technically an amateur in this new field, it should be noted that he was the son of a bishop, that he had been a deeply religious man all his life, and that he had prayed and read the Bible daily, though he was not much of a churchgoer. This change of career began as early as 1743. Over the following two years he had a series of dreams and other experiences that led him to question whether he should continue his writing on anatomy and philosophy. Then, while staying in London in April 1745, he had a vision of Jesus Christ. The result was a sense of clarity that his life needed to go in a new direction. He had recently published three parts of the scientific study *Dynamics of the Soul's Domain* (= Swedenborg [1740–1741] 1955), as well as two parts of the quasi-scientific prose poem *Worship and Love of God*. After the Christ-vision he determined that he had to abandon his worldly studies to write on spiritual matters.[25]

He began with an intensive study of the Bible. He immediately purchased a Latin translation and began reading it closely, starting with the Prophets, looking for any passages that seemed relevant to the theme of the Coming of the Lord. The work that resulted from this research, *Passages on the Coming Messiah* (= Swedenborg 1949), is a kind of biblical index, the first of eight indexes to the Bible Swedenborg made in his lifetime. Since concordances were available (his new Bible even had one at the back), one cannot help wondering why he went to so much trouble to make a new index. The answer seems to be that he was looking not only for relevant passages, but for enlightenment and guidance, and felt

---

25. It should be noted that he reprinted various of his scientific works later in life, and issued at least one new such work, *Inlaying Marble* (= Tafel 1875, 586–590).

he received these in the process of gathering particular passages that resonated with him.[26] Therefore *Passages on the Coming Messiah* was not simply an index; it was written as the fruit of spiritual discipline, during which he meant to open himself up to hearing the Lord speak to him through the pages of Scripture. Having completed this little work, he set out for his homeland.

Bible Index and *Notes on the Creation Story* (1745–1747) On his return to Stockholm, Swedenborg moved into the house on Hornsgatan Street that he had purchased two years before. There he began another Bible index. This one was an alphabetical index of words in the books from Joshua to 2 Kings, as well as Deuteronomy.[27] He also wrote a small treatise on the first two chapters of Genesis, *Notes on the Creation Story* (= Swedenborg 1927–1951a).

He recognized now that some of his previous work had in large part been motivated by a search for personal fame. He decided that the only goal that would suit his study of the Word was a sincere search for the kingdom of God. On the first leaf of his small treatise on the history of Creation he wrote out a verse of Scripture that summarizes the spirit in which he undertook this new and vital phase of his life: "First seek God's kingdom and its justice and you will gain all. . . ."[28]

This little book served as a bridge between his earlier scientific work, in which he sought to trace the origins of the planet and its many life forms from a scientific and philosophic point of view, and the theological view of the Creation story as told in Genesis. After discussing the first chapter of Genesis, he writes:

> The origin of the earth, and also paradise, the garden, and the birth of Adam, have been dealt with in the first part of my treatise *On the Worship and Love of God*, but under the guidance of the understanding, or according to the thread of reason. Since, however, no trust is to be placed in human intelligence unless it be inspired by God, it is to the interest of truth that we compare what has been set forth in the above-mentioned

---

26. Van Dusen 1975, 316–319; see also Rich 1956, 63–76.

27. Earlier scholars were not aware that Swedenborg included Deuteronomy in this index. See Rose 2002, 303–304.

28. Matthew 6:33; translation by Lisa Hyatt Cooper. Swedenborg here added the words "the things that are recounted" to explain the word "all,"—that is, things to eat, drink, and wear, as mentioned in Matthew 6:25, 31. He also placed this text on the back of the title page of *Secrets of Heaven*.

little work with what is revealed in the Sacred Volume. . . . With this end in view, I have deemed it well to premise a very brief commentary on the first chapters of Genesis. . . . When I had made a diligent comparison with these chapters, I was amazed at the agreement.[29]

***The Old Testament Explained* (1745–1748)** The little work *Notes on the Creation Story* covered only a portion of the first three chapters of Genesis; but between it and Swedenborg's other studies of the Bible, the ground had been prepared for a major book. It was a work that would occupy him for the next two years and would cover much of Old Testament Scripture in a total of four volumes (eight in English translation). Swedenborg began it on a Sunday, and records the date along with a prayer: "November 17, 1745: Began here to write. Lord Jesus Christ, lead me to and upon the way on which Thou wouldest have me walk" (quoted in Acton 1927, 122).

Commencing with Genesis chapter 1, he continued verse by verse through the Bible, commenting on its meaning. Rather than restricting himself to one Bible translation, he used two—the first by Sébastien Castellion (1515–1563), whose rendering of 1551 was more a paraphrase than a true translation, and the second by Sebastian Schmidt, whose 1696 version was much more literal. By the time he reached the study of Genesis 24, he had ceased citing Castellion's translation.[30]

The book is in two parts. The first consists of three manuscript volumes devoted to the first two books of the Bible, Genesis and Exodus; briefer attention is given to other parts of the Bible up to 2 Kings, and it also includes a very short treatment of 1 Chronicles. The second part, in the fourth volume, is devoted mostly to the two great prophets Isaiah and Jeremiah. He does not treat the Psalms or the Minor Prophets. In the only complete translation (Swedenborg 1927–1951b), the two parts are combined under the title *The Word of the Old Testament Explained,* usually called just *The Word Explained;* in the current discussion they are given the common title *The Old Testament Explained.*

***Spiritual Experiences* (1745 or 1746–1765)** As noted above, Swedenborg had begun to have apparently paranormal dreams and experiences in

---

29. *Notes on the Creation Story* (= Swedenborg 1927–1951a) §§9–10. *Worship and Love of God* was an unfinished prose poem about Creation and Adam and Eve that Swedenborg published in 1745.

30. The reason he abandoned Castellion can be seen in *The Old Testament Explained* (= Swedenborg 1927–1951b) §2073.

1743. While he was writing *The Old Testament Explained* these experiences continued and increased until, according to his reports, he finally came to a full consciousness of spirits and angels, and could converse with them on a daily basis. He had long been in the habit of writing journals, especially in his travels around Europe. Now he was writing a journal of his spiritual experiences. He initially recorded these experiences in *The Old Testament Explained,* indenting them for easy reference.[31] He also wrote some of them in the last of his Bible indexes. At some point, probably in 1747, he began a separate volume for them, which modern scholarship has titled *Spiritual Experiences.*[32] The first 148 numbered sections are missing, but their contents can be reconstructed by reference to Swedenborg's own index. The first section we have (§149) is dated October 9, 1747.

Of all the manuscript material, *Spiritual Experiences* may well be the most fascinating. The language is not polished in the least. In many cases the sentences are incomplete and the handwriting extremely difficult to read. Yet the incidents are described with an immediacy and freshness that are lost when Swedenborg recounts them in the more formal settings of the published works, where they serve to illustrate his theological exposition.

As Swedenborg transferred the material to *Secrets of Heaven* or some other work intended for publication, he drew a line through the original version in *Spiritual Experiences* as a reminder to himself that he had used it. Some experiences were never transferred in this way: Swedenborg apparently felt the need for divine guidance in determining which of his spiritual experiences to recount in a printed work. For example, in one of the indented paragraphs of *The Old Testament Explained,* he writes: "As to whether these words are to be inserted, see when the time for printing arrives whether it is permitted."[33] In other places he mentions limitations that have been set on what he is allowed to write about certain things.[34]

These works show a common marker of one aspect of his understanding of theology in these early years. In all of the theological works

---

31. See Swedenborg 1927–1951b, §317, for the first memorable occurrence in *The Old Testament Explained;* see Odhner 1998, vi, for a reproduction of one of the manuscript pages with such an indented entry. The indented paragraphs have been included in the most recent translation of *Spiritual Experiences* (= Swedenborg 1998–2002), discussed below.

32. On the title, see Odhner 1998, ii–v.

33. *The Old Testament Explained* (= Swedenborg 1927–1951b) §1511; though the translation here is by J. Durban Odhner in *Spiritual Experiences* (= Swedenborg 1998–2002) §[22a].

34. *Spiritual Experiences* (= Swedenborg 1998–2002) §§2271, 2393, 2697, 2749, 2984, 3358, 3447, 5040.

up to this time, the name he used for Christ was "God Messiah." He ended this practice on January 23, 1748, when he abruptly shifted to the more traditional term, "The Lord," the term that he used until the end of his life. Very early in his major published work *Secrets of Heaven* he explains what he means by this term:

> From this point on, the term *Lord* is used in only one way: to refer to the Savior of the world, Jesus Christ; and the name "Lord" is used without any additions.[35]

Secrets of Heaven **(1748–1756)** Swedenborg's life during this time was very full. It included devotional reading of the Bible, compiling several Bible indexes, making marginal notes in his Latin Bible, recording his spiritual experiences, studying Hebrew, and filling one volume after another with Bible commentary. Until 1747 he also continued in his roles as an active member of the Board of Mines and the Swedish House of Nobles. By the summer of 1747, however, he had determined that it would be necessary to resign his position on the Board of Mines, even though he had been offered the position of councillor at twice his current salary.[36] No sooner had he retired than he set out for the Netherlands.

About the time he arrived in Amsterdam, he made a note in his manuscript: "1747, August 7, old style. There was a change of state in me into the heavenly kingdom in an image."[37] This note suggests that he had experienced a profound change in his spiritual status on that day. It is intriguing that he did not begin publishing theological material until after this change had taken place.

A year later Swedenborg continued on to England,[38] where he began to write the first of his major published theological works, *Secrets of Heaven*. As has been mentioned, before undertaking the writing of this book, he had completed over five thousand pages of preparatory material. The Bible indexes were vital to his treatment of Genesis and Exodus, and some of his previous manuscripts were preliminary attempts to explain the same Bible

---

35. *Secrets of Heaven* 14; translation by Lisa Hyatt Cooper.

36. On Swedenborg's resignation, see Acton 1927, 126. On the position of councillor, see Lindqvist 1984, 97.

37. Acton 1927, 127, with translation modified by Jonathan S. Rose; see also Tafel 1877, 839–840.

38. We know from a note he jotted on the flyleaf of a codex containing *Spiritual Experiences* that on November 23, 1748, he took up six months' lodging in London (Tafel 1875, 386).

books. His journal *Spiritual Experiences* contains material that he edited and copied into *Secrets of Heaven.* Also vital to his effort were the marginal notes in his copy of Schmidt's translation of the Bible. It might be noted in passing that scholars after Swedenborg's time were especially slow to publish this particular preparatory material, either in Latin or translation. It was only in the 1920s that a full English translation of *The Old Testament Explained* (Swedenborg 1927–1951b) began to appear in English translation, and publication of the full work took over twenty years.

After seeing the first volume of *Secrets of Heaven* through the press and spending almost a year in Aix-la-Chapelle (Aachen, Germany, a popular spa), where he wrote volume 2, Swedenborg returned to Stockholm in 1750. For the next six years he worked on the *Secrets of Heaven* project in his modest home in Stockholm, writing the work down in great folio volumes. In the warm weather he sometimes wrote in a little summer house at the far end of his beautiful garden. In the winter he donned his reindeer fur coat, sharpened his quill pen, and wrote in his study in the main house.[39]

Indexes to *Secrets of Heaven* and *Spiritual Experiences* (1748–1756) During this eight-year period, Swedenborg was working on four separate projects simultaneously. In addition to writing *Secrets of Heaven* and continuing to make entries in his *Spiritual Experiences,* he was also working on two indexes, one for each work. The *Spiritual Experiences* index[40] enabled him to locate passages that he wanted to copy into the *Secrets of Heaven* volume. The *Secrets of Heaven* index (= Swedenborg 1909 = Swedenborg 2004) enabled him to cross-reference his work, and to refer back to it when writing later works.[41] He apparently began keeping the index when the work became too lengthy for his memory to retain the detailed cross-references he intended it should have. Thereafter,

---

39. There is one other small fragment from this period, a draft essay on miracles originally intended as one of the topical essays that appear at the beginning and end of chapters in *Secrets of Heaven.* Instead Swedenborg included an essay on freedom. This material on miracles is found in the original handwritten copy of *Secrets of Heaven,* codex 80, leaves 23–26. See Acton 1942, 396. The work itself can be found in Swedenborg 1942, 400–411, and Swedenborg 1947. The chapter on freedom that Swedenborg included instead can be found in *Secrets of Heaven* 2870–2893.

40. As of this writing, a translation of the index is forthcoming from the General Church of the New Jerusalem, Bryn Athyn, Pa. The most recent Latin edition is Swedenborg 1983–1997, volumes 5 and 6.

41. For example, the many cross-references to *Secrets of Heaven* in Swedenborg's footnotes in *Heaven and Hell* were made possible by this index.

when he wrote about a new topic in the text of *Secrets of Heaven,* he would make an entry in the index, so that when that same subject came up again, he could immediately refer readers back to earlier material on the same theme.[42] Altogether *Secrets of Heaven* came to eight volumes in Latin (at least ten in English translation). Swedenborg continued to have the work published in London while living in Sweden. Because he was so far away from the printer, he could not easily see the volumes through the press. The printer made mistakes, and from time to time Swedenborg would send a page of corrections.

Besides the first printed edition we also have his own handwritten copy—known as the "autograph," the term generally used for any manuscript in an author's own hand. This autograph is complete except for volume 1. When working in Sweden, Swedenborg apparently wrote out two complete manuscripts of each volume, one to keep and the other to send to the printer in London (Johnson 1949, 1). The printers routinely discarded the manuscripts after they were typeset, or reused the paper in some fashion, and therefore none of the printer's copies have survived; but the autograph of volumes 2–8 was found among Swedenborg's papers after his death.

Derivative Works As he was finishing the publishing of *Secrets of Heaven,* Swedenborg began working on smaller books, largely adapted from *Secrets of Heaven.* In May or June 1758 he set off for England with five manuscripts to publish. As they all appeared in 1758, we do not know the order in which he wrote them, though internal cross-references do suggest certain possibilities (Dole 2000, 1 note 1). We do know, however, that virtually every time he referred to them, he did so in this order: *Heaven and Hell, New Jerusalem, Last Judgment, White Horse, Other Planets.*[43]

Heaven and Hell was a fresh treatment of aspects of the next world, with copious references in footnotes to guide readers who wanted the full account in *Secrets of Heaven. New Jerusalem* was copied from material that appeared at the conclusion of chapters in *Secrets of Heaven,* and it

---

42. There is extant not only a first draft of the index of *Secrets of Heaven,* but a fair copy. Recopying the text was necessary because the first draft would have been difficult to work with: in it Swedenborg underestimated the amount of space he needed for a number of the longer entries, so he continued them on blank pages at the end of the book.

43. An exception occurs in *Spiritual Experiences* 5946, in which these books are said to have been given to Africans (apparently in the spiritual world) in the order *Heaven and Hell, Last Judgment, Other Planets, White Horse,* and *New Jerusalem.*

too had cross-references to the larger work. *Last Judgment* was adapted from *Spiritual Experiences*. *White Horse* was adapted from *Secrets of Heaven*. *Other Planets* (traditionally known as *Earths in the Universe*), was again material copied from the end of chapters in *Secrets of Heaven*.

To recapitulate: This period, 1745–1759, includes all the material written from the time of Swedenborg's Christ-vision in April 1745, through the publication of his longest theological work, *Secrets of Heaven*, right up to the year 1758, when he returned to London to publish the five works drawn largely from *Secrets of Heaven* and from *Spiritual Experiences*, and ending in July 1759, when he returned home. The unpublished material that is clearly preparatory work consists of his indexes to the Bible and his journal of spiritual experiences. A major part of this first period consists of the years 1745–1747 and 1750–1758, which total the longest interval Swedenborg spent in Stockholm during his career as a writer of theology. Period 1 is also summarized in the chart on the facing page.

b. Period 2: August 1759–March 1764

Another large group of the draft materials written by Swedenborg during his theological career—that is, those that can be seen as preparation for any of the published works—dates from the second period, a five-year interval spent in Stockholm. This second period includes *Revelation Explained* (= Swedenborg 1994–1997a) and many manuscripts written in preparation for works published in the Netherlands in 1763 and 1764. These published works were *The Lord, Sacred Scripture, Life, Faith, Supplements,* and the closely linked pair *Divine Love and Wisdom* and *Divine Providence*.[44]

After his publishing trip of 1758, Swedenborg stopped in Göteborg, in southern Sweden, on his way back to Stockholm. On the evening of his arrival, July 19, 1759, he attended a dinner party at the house of a local merchant. He did not enjoy it, however. Throughout the gathering he had a clairvoyant vision of a fire that had broken out in Stockholm, three hundred miles away, which was burning in a district that included his house (Tafel 1877, 628–632). When the other dinner guests noticed his agitation, he told them what was taking place. Fortunately, as he reported with relief to the assembly, the fire stopped several houses away from his. Messengers who arrived several days later confirmed his account of the fire, and

---

44. Some of the manuscripts written during this period were also used for *Revelation Unveiled,* which was published in 1766.

PERIOD 1 (APRIL 1745–JULY 1759)

RESEARCH MATERIALS
(JOURNAL ENTRIES, INDEXES)

Passages on the Coming Messiah
(Messiah About to Come)

Bible Indexes

Spiritual Experiences

Index to *Spiritual Experiences*

Marginal Notes in the Bible

DRAFT MATERIALS/OUTLINES

Notes on the Creation Story
(History of Creation)

The Old Testament Explained
(The Word Explained)

Draft Essay on Miracles

MAJOR PUBLISHED WORK

Secrets of Heaven *(Arcana Coelestia; 1749–1756)*

DERIVATIVE PUBLISHED WORKS

Heaven and Hell (1758)

New Jerusalem (1758)

Last Judgment (1758)

White Horse (1758)

Other Planets
(Earths in the Universe; 1758)

DERIVATIVE UNPUBLISHED WORK

Index to *Secrets of Heaven*

Arrows show the approximate flow of Swedenborg's work, from research and draft materials to published books. The listing of works is not exhaustive, and chronological order is only roughly suggested here. The relationships among the works have necessarily been simplified. Major works are shown in larger type sizes. Published material is followed by a publication date. Traditional titles are shown (in parentheses) in some cases.
Black indicates manuscripts; red indicates published works.

news spread very rapidly about Swedenborg's paranormal powers. This event marked a turning point in Swedenborg's life. Up until that time he had published his theological works anonymously, but his anonymity came to an end with the publicity attending the fire and his clairvoyant experience describing it. Though it would be another nine years before he actually specified that his name should appear on a printed edition *(Marriage Love),* his authorship of the published theological works became known, and reactions to them soon began to reach him.

After the events at Göteborg, Swedenborg went on to Stockholm, where he arrived on August 21, 1759. For the next four years he continued his routine of research and writing. His next major project was a verse-by-verse explanation of the spiritual meaning of the last book of the Bible, the Book of Revelation; he gave his work the title *Revelation Explained* (= Swedenborg 1994–1997a). We do not know when he started this project; it may have been as early as 1757. The place and date of intended publication are given on the title page of the manuscript as London, 1759.

The first chapter of the book is a fairly straightforward explanation of each verse. In the second chapter, when Swedenborg came across a key word, instead of simply giving its meaning in the Book of Revelation, he used his Bible indexes to research other places where the word is used, giving the spiritual meaning of those other Bible verses as well. For example when he came to Revelation 2:12, with its reference to a "two-edged sword," he not only explained the meaning in its context in Revelation, he went on to explain thirty-three other Bible verses containing the word "sword," in many cases giving their spiritual, or inner, meaning (*Revelation Explained* [= Swedenborg 1994–1997a] §131).

By the time he reached Revelation chapter 6, over 90 percent of the text was devoted to explaining passages in other parts of the Bible. This makes *Revelation Explained* a rich source of exegetical material, but very difficult to follow. We can see his attitude changing a little in chapter 6, where he discontinued the notes to the printer in the margins of the text. It seems that even at that point he was starting to have doubts about publishing the work, though he continued to write explanations of the next thirteen chapters.

In the explanation of Revelation chapter 12, he began to introduce articles on various subjects, some of them divided into sections. This continued in chapter 13; almost half of the text there is devoted to essays on subjects like faith, good works, and love. When he came to chapter 15, these articles now occurred in a series, continued from one section number to the next, beginning with an essay on the Ten Commandments. He also added short articles or essays on other subjects. Initially the essays were in some way connected with the portion of the Bible under consideration, but later the subjects were quite different from the Bible material in question. At this point (chapter 15) he set the material apart with the heading "Continuation." Whereas in *Secrets of Heaven* he had placed this type of independent essay at the beginning and end of every chapter, in *Revelation Explained* he included essays much more frequently: by the end of the book he was including them with every numbered paragraph or section. There is a wealth of new material here on the laws of providence, the life of animals and plants, infinity and eternity, and so on. Much of this material was later expanded into published works. By the nineteenth chapter (out of twenty-two), the essays had become the main focus. When he reached Revelation 19:10, however, he abruptly stopped writing.

Despite his apparent doubts about publishing *Revelation Explained,* Swedenborg did not fully give up the idea until the moment he ceased working on the book. This is clear from the fact that as he was writing the volume, he made two versions, a first draft and a second "fair copy" intended for the printer. He continued to update the fair copy with the latest sections he had composed until nearly the very end of his work: when he stopped writing, the fair copy lacked only the three final numbered sections of the first draft. So there can be no question that he was intending to publish the book.

Scholars have advanced many theories as to why he did not publish this, his second-longest theological work. Some think it was because the work was getting too long. Perhaps it is because the essay material had grown in importance and he wanted to publish it in separate volumes before attempting to finish the explanation of the Book of Revelation. He may also have decided that it would be too expensive to print in its projected entirety.[45]

During the period from 1759 to 1763, Swedenborg was also working on other material in addition to *Revelation Explained.* He continued to

---

45. His reluctance is all the more striking when one considers that in the case of *Secrets of Heaven* he was so confident of his course that he was willing to publish it not only as each volume was complete, but even fascicle by fascicle, at least while he was composing the second volume. (A fascicle is a bundle of pages that makes up a portion of a larger book; it is issued for sale individually. In this case, Swedenborg's treatment of each chapter of Genesis 16–21 formed its own fascicle.)

work on his index to *Spiritual Experiences* and continued to use that index and his index to *Secrets of Heaven* in writing new works. In some cases there is a clear connection between the new manuscripts and a later published work. For example, the unpublished *Draft of "Sacred Scripture"* (= Swedenborg 1996f, 325–384) covers much of the same material as the published *Sacred Scripture,* but is only half as long, and has fragmentary passages. In rewriting the draft, Swedenborg rearranged the chapters, omitting some and adding others, while expanding some of the items. Other manuscripts directly related to books that were published in 1763 are: *Draft of "The Lord,"* traditionally known as *De Domino* (On the Lord; = Swedenborg 1994–1997c, 635–647); *Commentary on the Athanasian Creed* (= Swedenborg 1994–1997b, 6:571–634), which was also a draft in preparation for *The Lord; Draft of "Life,"* traditionally known as *Precepts of the Decalogue* (= Swedenborg 1996t); and *Draft of "Supplements,"* traditionally treated in parts known by such names as *Last Judgment (Posthumous)* (= Swedenborg 1996o, 397–515), *The Spiritual World* (= Swedenborg 1996o, 515–556), and *Argument Concerning the Judgment* (= Swedenborg 1996e, 557–563).[46]

The last manuscript from this period is *Draft on the Inner Meaning of Prophets and Psalms* (= Swedenborg 1996w), a work that Swedenborg wrote out in a fair hand as if he intended it for publication, but ultimately left unpublished. This work, traditionally called *Prophets and Psalms,* is similar to *Passages on the Coming Messiah,* in that Swedenborg was again going to the Scriptures seeking an understanding of their meaning, especially as it related to the Coming of the Lord. He started by making a numbered list of seventeen different themes; he then distinguished verses dealing with each theme by placing the corresponding number in the margin next to brief summaries of their inner meanings. Using this system, he identified a thread of spiritual meaning in the Prophets, Major and Minor, and also in the Book of Psalms. In his later writings he referred indirectly to *Draft on the Inner Meaning of Prophets and Psalms* a number of times.[47]

The Seven Works Published in 1763 and 1764 Many of the doctrinal themes of the seven books Swedenborg published in 1763 and 1764 were initially developed in essays in *Revelation Explained.* For example, the

---

46. *Last Judgment (Posthumous), The Spiritual World,* and *Argument Concerning the Judgment* are often treated as one work and printed together.

47. *The Lord* 2, 3; *True Christianity* 113, 272; *Draft of "Sacred Scripture"* (= Swedenborg 1996f) §25; *Sacred Scripture* 97; *Revelation Unveiled* 43, 239, 709, 859.

themes of the Lord, charity, divine love and wisdom, and marriage are all treated in that work. Some of these topics were further developed in later manuscripts, such as those on the subject of marriage. By the spring of 1763 Swedenborg had final manuscripts ready for the printers in the Netherlands, for which place he set sail on May 29, according to one account. The first four books published were *The Lord, Sacred Scripture, Life,* and *Faith.* As Swedenborg once referred to them as "the four doctrines" (*Revelation Unveiled* 668), others since have used this phrase as a collective title for them. Swedenborg also published a follow-up work on the Last Judgment that is now titled *Supplements.* This included a continuation of his treatment of the Last Judgment and some additional material on the spiritual world that is a supplement to *Heaven and Hell.* Finally, he published two books that function as companion pieces to one another, *Divine Love and Wisdom* [48] and *Divine Providence.* The chart on page 140 summarizes this period.

The sheer number of manuscripts that survive from this second period allows us to deduce their relationship with published works. Fewer survive from the remaining three periods.

c. Period 3: April 1764–September 1766

The main activities Swedenborg undertook in the third period were a complete recasting of the long manuscript *Revelation Explained* (rewritten as *Revelation Unveiled*) and the compilation of an index to this new version. He began his rewrite on his return to Sweden in August 1764. He used the same references to other parts of the Bible that he had used in *Revelation Explained,* though not always in the same order.[49] This time he explained the inner meaning of the supporting passages he quoted only if they came from the Book of Revelation. This reduced the work to a much more manageable size. He also prefaced the volume with summaries of Roman Catholic and Reformed doctrines. As a new feature he appended stories of his experiences in the spiritual world to each chapter; they are referred to as "memorable occurrences" or (traditionally) "memorable relations." He continued to include these stories in all his works for the rest of his life.

---

48. Of this work we have two fragmentary drafts (= Swedenborg 1994–1997a, 6:413–452, and Swedenborg 1994–1997a, 6:453–537).

49. Dating from the preparatory period for this work is the five-page manuscript *Summaries Explaining the Book of Revelation* (= Swedenborg 1975e, 86–97).

DRAFT MATERIALS/OUTLINES

Revelation Explained (Apocalypse Explained)

Draft on the Inner Meaning of Prophets and Psalms

Commentary on the Athanasian Creed

Draft of "The Lord" (De Domino)

Draft of "Sacred Scripture" (De Verbo)

Draft of "Life"
(Precepts of the Decalogue)

Draft of "Supplements"
(Last Judgment [Posthumous])

Draft on Divine Love

Draft on Divine Wisdom

RESEARCH MATERIALS
(JOURNAL ENTRIES, INDEXES)

Bible Indexes

Spiritual Experiences

Index to *Spiritual Experiences*

Index to *Secrets of Heaven*

MAJOR PUBLISHED WORKS

The Lord (1763)

Sacred Scripture (1763)

Life (1763)

Faith (1763)

Divine Love and Wisdom (1763)

Divine Providence (1764)

DERIVATIVE PUBLISHED WORK

Supplements (Continuation Concerning the Last Judgment; 1763)

Arrows show the approximate flow of Swedenborg's work, from research and draft materials to published books. The listing of works is not exhaustive, and chronological order is only roughly suggested here; furthermore, some works shown without dates stem from years before this period. The relationships among the works have necessarily been simplified. Major works are shown in larger type sizes. Published material is followed by a publication date. Traditional titles are shown (in parentheses) in some cases.

Black indicates manuscripts; red indicates published works.

By the summer of 1765, *Revelation Unveiled* was finished, and he took it to the Netherlands for printing. By April 8, 1766, printing was complete. At some point in this process he also made an index, first in a rough form and then in a fair copy, to enable him to insert cross-references in the final version. He gave this index hard use: *Revelation Unveiled* contains more internal cross-references than any of his other works.

During this third period, Swedenborg's stay in Stockholm was about as long as his time abroad. While at home he prepared manuscripts for the printer and attended to his duties as a member of the House of Nobles and to personal matters. Much of his time abroad was spent overseeing printing in Amsterdam. The chart on page 142 summarizes the period.

d. Period 4: September 1766–October 1768

On returning from the Netherlands after the printing of *Revelation Unveiled,* Swedenborg began writing with greater focus on one of his favorite subjects, marriage. The last entry in *Spiritual Experiences,* one of the longest, is on the subject of marriage. He had also written a good deal about marriage in *Secrets of Heaven* and *Heaven and Hell.* In addition, he had included material on marriage toward the end of *Revelation Explained.* Now he set himself the task of writing a separate book on the subject.

In the manuscript volumes, we find what appear to be two indexes (= Swedenborg 1996l, 397–497) to a work on marriage that is sometimes referred to as *The Missing Work on Marriage* or the *Missing Treatise.* However, although certain of Swedenborg's manuscripts have been lost, as has been described already, there is no supporting evidence for the theory that Swedenborg wrote a major book on marriage, compiled two indexes to it, and then lost it. It seems much more likely that the indexes are part of his preparatory material for his published work on marriage, *Marriage Love* (1768).

It is not clear whether the indexes refer to a draft that was actually written out in full or to a rough plan for the book. If it was just a plan, Swedenborg went to the length of assigning chapters, chapter headings, and section numbers (over two thousand of them). It is quite possible, however, that this was the very manner in which Swedenborg planned his books.

The first index covers the whole of the work, while the second gives a more detailed description of the first few chapters. From these materials it is possible for us to reconstruct the draft or plan to which it refers,[50]

---

50. See Acton 1956 for such a reconstruction.

PERIOD 3 (APRIL 1764–SEPTEMBER 1766)

RESEARCH MATERIALS
(JOURNAL ENTRIES, INDEXES)

DRAFT MATERIALS/OUTLINES

Bible Indexes

Spiritual Experiences

Index to *Spiritual Experiences*

Index to *Secrets of Heaven*

Revelation Explained
(Apocalypse Explained)

Summaries Explaining
the Book of Revelation

MAJOR PUBLISHED WORK

Revelation Unveiled (*Apocalypse Revealed;* 1766)

DERIVATIVE UNPUBLISHED WORK

Index to *Revelation Unveiled*

Arrows show the approximate flow of Swedenborg's work, from research and draft materials to published books. The listing of works is not exhaustive, and chronological order is only roughly suggested here; furthermore, some works shown without dates stem from years before this period. The relationships among the works have necessarily been simplified. Major works are shown in larger type sizes. Published material is followed by a publication date. Traditional titles are shown (in parentheses) in some cases.
Black indicates manuscripts; red indicates published works.

and we find that it is substantially the same as the work that Swedenborg published under the title *Marriage Love* in 1768. We can see that the original plan called for twenty-two chapters in part 1 and eleven chapters in part 2. In *Marriage Love*, Swedenborg retained eleven of the twenty-two headings called for in part 1, combined a few, added some others, and dropped some. In part 2 he retained almost the same chapters, in the same order, but made two interesting changes. He moved the chapter on jealousy to part 1, and added a chapter on "imputation," or the issue of assigning credit or blame, reminding readers that they could not judge the internal state of married couples.

In addition to the two indexes to the supposed *Missing Work on Marriage*, another manuscript from this time can be considered preparatory material to *Marriage Love*. Traditionally called *De Conjugio* (On Marriage; = Swedenborg 1996p, 357–396), it is here referred to as *Second Sketch for "Marriage Love."*[51] This nineteen-page draft was probably written in 1767.

In May of 1768 Swedenborg went back to the Netherlands and had *Marriage Love* printed, taking the dramatic step of putting his name on the title page, the first theological work to include it. His output during this fourth period is summarized in the chart on page 144.

e. Period 5: October 1768–March 1772

The fifth period includes the last interval that Swedenborg spent in Stockholm (less than a year). After publishing *Marriage Love*, Swedenborg turned his attention to crafting *True Christianity*, a work that is at once a major restatement of much of his theology and a defense of that theology to the Christian world, especially to Lutherans. *True Christianity* took on this specifically contra-Lutheran perspective because in the very closing years of Swedenborg's life, two of his followers, Gabriel Beyer (1720–1779) and Johan Rosén (1726–1773), were under attack by elements of the Lutheran state church in Sweden, and various accusations were made against Swedenborg as well.

It can be said that the manuscripts that date from this period were generally composed in preparation for this final work and for an appendix to it. (Much of the appendix material was lost in the manner described at

---

51. For the *First Sketch for "Marriage Love,"* a one-page draft traditionally called *Articles on Marriage*, or *De Conjugio I* (On Marriage I), see Swedenborg 1975c, 100–101.

**RESEARCH MATERIALS
(JOURNAL ENTRIES, INDEXES)**

DRAFT MATERIALS/OUTLINES

Bible Indexes

Spiritual Experiences

Index to *Spiritual Experiences*

Index to *Secrets of Heaven*

Indexes to Lost Sketches
for *Marriage Love*

*First Sketch for "Marriage Love"
(De Conjugio I)*

*Second Sketch for "Marriage Love"
(De Conjugio II)*

MAJOR PUBLISHED WORK

Marriage Love (*Conjugial Love;* 1768)

Arrows show the approximate flow of Swedenborg's work, from research and draft materials to published books. The listing of works is not exhaustive, and chronological order is only roughly suggested here; furthermore, some works shown without dates stem from years before this period. The relationships among the works have necessarily been simplified. Major works are shown in larger type sizes. Published material is followed by a publication date. Traditional titles are shown (in parentheses) in some cases.

Black indicates manuscripts; red indicates published works.

the beginning of this essay.) The lone exception to this pattern is a short book, more of a pamphlet, published in 1769. This is *Soul-Body Interaction,* on the means by which the soul acts in the body. It is also distinctive for being the only publication Swedenborg put through the press in London in the last fifteen years of his life.

The manuscripts preparatory to *True Christianity* include *Summary of New Church Teachings* (= Swedenborg 1996v, 561–567); *Notes on a Conversation with Calvin* (= Swedenborg 1996i, 551–556); and *Outline about God the Savior* (= Swedenborg 1996k, 557–560). These draft materials led first to *Survey,* a small book published by Swedenborg himself in 1769. *Survey* in turn was clearly composed in preparation for *True Christianity.*[52] Swedenborg also made one more Bible index, this time including the Acts and the Epistles. The work has been given the Latin title *Dicta Probantia* (Supporting Passages), and the English title *Bible Concordance for "True Christianity"* (= Swedenborg 1962a = Swedenborg 1996u, 235–347). He also produced two indexes, one of Lutheran and the other of Roman Catholic theology; the first of these can be titled *Index to "The Book of Concord" for "True Christianity"* (= Swedenborg 1975b, 57–73); the second, *Brief Index of Catholic Teachings* (= Swedenborg 1996n, 539–549).

When the preparatory material had been gathered, the writing of *True Christianity* proceeded apace. When it was complete in 1770, Swedenborg journeyed to Amsterdam and stayed there to see the work through the press. As has been mentioned, he noted several times in the book that he anticipated an appendix volume that would make it complete. By August 1771, he was planning to publish four small works, as we learn from a letter to Ludwig IX, the Landgrave of Hesse-Darmstadt (1719–1790):

> I am now on the point of departing for England, where, the Lord favoring, I intend to give to the light, that is, to publish, four small works, namely:
>
> I. Concerning the Consummation of the Age, and the Abomination of Desolation predicted by the Lord in *Daniel* and in *Matthew.*
> II. An Invitation to the New Church, addressed to the whole Christian world; and therein much concerning the Lord's Advent, and an Exhortation that they receive Him worthily.
> III. On the Human Mind.

---

52. The opening paragraph explains that his intention is "to bring to light the whole and complete teaching of the church," but since that would be a work of many years, he is setting out the general principles in outline form (*Survey* 1; translation by Jonathan S. Rose).

IV. Egyptian Hieroglyphics laid bare by Correspondences.
When these works are printed, I will forward copies [from England].⁵³

The first two works listed have similar topics to the promised appendix to *True Christianity*. In fact, copies of drafts of these works, or at least of manuscripts on the same topics, have survived, which we might title *Outlines for "End of the Age"* (= Swedenborg 1996h) and *Draft Invitation to the New Church* (= Swedenborg 1996m); but the works on the human mind and on Egyptian hieroglyphics were apparently never undertaken.

The manuscript Swedenborg left on the ship on his last voyage from Sweden should be mentioned again, as it falls in this period. As noted above, it was eventually returned to Stockholm, and since it contained material that was included in the published text of *True Christianity*, his followers after his death perceived that it was connected to that work and published it under the title *Additions to True Christian Religion*.⁵⁴ However, this is not what it was at all. It was simply a draft of some of Swedenborg's memorable occurrences in the spiritual world intended for *True Christianity*, all but a few pages of which appeared in the final form of the book despite the loss of the manuscript on the ship. As for the manuscript that was borrowed by Husband Messiter (traditionally called *Coronis, or Appendix to True Christianity* [= Swedenborg 1996j, 7–106 = Swedenborg 1931]), fortunately it was at least partially copied before it was lost. For a summary of Swedenborg's works in this period, which are too numerous to describe in detail here, see the chart on the facing page.⁵⁵

IV. Conclusion

It is not impossible that Swedenborg wrote other manuscripts, now lost or destroyed, of which we know nothing. Some of these putative manuscripts may someday be discovered. We do not, however, have any reason to suspect major gaps in the manuscript record after 1745. What is even more important is that we can be satisfied that we have all of the material that

53. Letter of August 24, 1771, as translated by Acton 1948–1955, 755–756. For a reconstruction of the appendix volume to *True Christianity*, see Acton 1957, 372–378.

54. See Swedenborg 1996a, and also Tafel 1877, 758–773. *True Christian Religion* is the traditional title of *True Christianity*.

55. For further bibliographic information on the works mentioned in chart 5, consult the relevant entries on pages 402–509 below by using the index on pages 395–402.

DRAFT MATERIALS/OUTLINES

Notes on Conversations with Angels

Sketch on Goodwill (Charity)

Notes on a Conversation with Calvin

Outline about God the Savior

*Summary of New Church Teachings
(Specimen and Sketch of the
New Church)*

*Sketch for "True Christianity"
(Canons of the New Church)*

*Draft Memorable Occurrences
for "True Christianity"*

*Sketch for a History of the New Church
(Sketch of an Ecclesiastical History
of the New Church)*

**RESEARCH MATERIALS
(JOURNAL ENTRIES, INDEXES)**

Bible Indexes

Spiritual Experiences

Index to *Spiritual Experiences*

Index to *Secrets of Heaven*

*Bible Concordance for "True
Christianity" (Dicta Probantia)*

Index to *The Book of Concord*

Brief Index of Catholic Teachings

PUBLISHED WORKS

Soul-Body Interaction (*Intercourse between the Soul and Body;* 1769)

Survey (*Brief Exposition;* 1769)

True Christianity (*True Christian Religion;* 1771)

DERIVATIVE UNPUBLISHED WORKS

Sketch and Draft for *Coda to True Christianity (Coronis)*

Sketch and Outlines for *End of the Age (Consummation of the Age)*

Draft Invitation to the New Church

Arrows show the approximate flow of Swedenborg's work, from research and draft materials to
published books. The listing of works is not exhaustive, and chronological order is only roughly
suggested here; furthermore, some works shown without dates stem from years before this period.
The relationships among the works have necessarily been simplified. Major works are shown in
larger type sizes. Published material is followed by a publication date. Traditional titles are shown
(in parentheses) in some cases.
Black indicates manuscripts; red indicates published works.

Swedenborg completed with the intention of publishing. These eighteen published books must be our main resource in studying his theology.

That is not to deny that there is much to be learned from Swedenborg's unpublished theological manuscripts; it is only to suggest that they are to be used with caution. The originals of some of them have been lost, leaving us to rely on imperfect copies. In the autograph versions many pages are almost indecipherable. Furthermore, some contain ideas that Swedenborg omitted from the published works, possibly because he felt led to do so.

On the positive side, the manuscripts represent a valuable source of information about how Swedenborg worked and the mode of his inspiration. We see how his largest work, *Secrets of Heaven,* was written after several initial attempts that he did not publish. We can follow his journal entries in *Spiritual Experiences* as they are modified and incorporated into other works. We can see how in some cases he made several different outlines of a work before settling on its final structure. By sorting the manuscript material into different categories and then tracing its chronology, we can see how he arrived at the final published works.

Anyone who works with the manuscripts of Swedenborg soon perceives that much research remains to be done on them. It is my hope, however, that until that effort is undertaken this essay may help to clarify what these manuscripts are and how they fit into the larger picture of Swedenborg's published works.[56]

---

56. For further study of Swedenborg's manuscripts and their relationship to Swedenborg's published works, see especially Hyatt [1978?]; Swedenborg 1917; Kingslake 1986; Odhner 1943; Regamey 1935 (see especially the *Tableau Synoptique* at the back, a sixteen-page chart of Swedenborg's manuscripts); Rose 1964; Rose and Rose 1970; and Swedenborg Society 1968, which contains an excellent chart of Swedenborg's published and unpublished works.

CULTURAL
IMPACT

The Influence of Emanuel Swedenborg
in Scandinavia

OLLE HJERN

Outline

I. Theology and Philosophy
   a. The Spread of Swedenborgianism
   b. The Effects of Swedenborgian Doctrines
   c. Publishing and Philanthropy

II. Arts and Letters
   a. The Romantic Period
   b. Strindberg
   c. Ekelund

III. Denmark and Norway

IV. Swedenborgian Influence in Recent Times

BEGINNING in the years of his youth, Emanuel Swedenborg sought recognition on that international stage where the boisterous drama of the Enlightenment was in progress. He offered the scientific works of his early period to Europe as a whole; and when his interest shifted to theology, he continued to reach out to readers beyond the borders of his native country.[1] It is a testimony to the success of his efforts that he influenced thinkers far beyond Sweden, and that in recounting his influence today we must discuss intellectual trends not only in Europe but in points far beyond that continent.

Yet despite his international orientation, he left his mark on Sweden and the larger Scandinavian community as well. Here, however, it has often been said that his influence was primarily that of a writer influencing other artists of the written word. As I hope to show in this brief sketch,

---

1. For a discussion of the development of Swedenborg's life work from scientific to theological themes, see above, pages 10–29.

151

that influence on the writers of Scandinavia was real and persists to this day, but it is not the only impact Swedenborg had on the region. Accordingly, I will begin my observations by looking at his effect on theology and philosophy. Though Sweden is the primary focus of my attention in this essay, I will make some digressions to other Nordic nations.

I. Theology and Philosophy

One obvious reason that the artistic influence of Swedenborg in Scandinavia appears greater than his theological influence is that in his day a rigid censorship by the Lutheran state church existed in Sweden for all books of theology. It was easier to get approval for works of a Swedenborgian bent than for the works of Swedenborg himself. Even as early as 1766 the consistory of the Göteborg diocese approved a book of sermons that is undeniably Swedenborgian, written by Swedenborg's close friend Gabriel Beyer (1720–1779).[2] Some of the Göteborg clergy immediately and strenuously opposed this authorization with legal action, but a considerable group of laypeople in the city supported Swedenborg and those who were friendly to him.[3] As Göteborg was the center for the activities of the Swedish East India Company, the presence of a strong Swedenborg faction there encouraged the wider dissemination of Swedenborgian ideas.

a. The Spread of Swedenborgianism

Despite the ban of the state church, Swedenborg's writings gradually became available. That he wrote in Latin was both an impediment and an aid to the spread of his work: it restricted his audience to the educated and it relieved official anxiety that his writings would corrupt "simple folk."[4] His appeal was extended by several early translations made by Carl Fredrik Nordenskjöld (1756–1828), Jonas Pehrson Odhner (1744–1830), Christian Johansén (about 1746–1813), and others, printed in Copenhagen

---

2. See [Beyer] 1767.

3. For a discussion of the so-called Göteborg trial, see above, pages 43–45. Further sources are: Lenhammar 1966, 43–112; Sundelin 1886, 58–115; Berg 1891, 58–145, and separately paginated appendix 1–306; [Kahl] 1847–1864; and Acton 1948–1955, which covers this topic intermittently on pages 690–736.

4. People of simple heart and faith were, in fact, the audience Swedenborg intended for his 1758 work *Heaven and Hell;* see §1 there.

or circulated in handwritten form throughout western Sweden and Finland (at that time a part of Sweden).[5]

These early days were times of great contradiction. The estate of the clergy in the Swedish diet resisted Swedenborg's message, fearing a schism in the Lutheran Church of Sweden; while the king, Gustav III (1746–1792), actually supported the printing of Swedenborg's works in Denmark, as did his brother, Charles (1748–1818), both as prince and later as King Charles XIII. Charles, in fact, attended at least one meeting of the *Exegetiska och Philantropiska Sällskapet* (Exegetical and Philanthropical Society), a Swedenborgian printing organization founded in 1786 after a gathering of Swedenborgians took place at Varnhem. This society counted some 150 of Sweden's elite among its members, including Baron Leonhard Gyllenhaal (1752–1840) and Count Claes Ekeblad (1742–1808). Although it was short-lived, becoming entangled in shady projects in animal magnetism[6] and gold making, it was followed by another, more sound society that upheld the scholarship and spiritual interests of Swedenborg, *Pro Fide et Charitate* (On Behalf of Faith and Charity).

Meanwhile, in Göteborg the vigorous opposition of the orthodox Lutheran circle soon overwhelmed the Swedenborgian element. Though as the second city of the nation Göteborg has in a sense remained a nexus of Swedenborgian activity within Sweden, the main focus of the Swedenborgian movement shifted to the neighboring diocese, Skara. Swedenborg had of course a historical connection with this region, having lived there when young with his father, Jesper Swedberg, the bishop of the diocese.[7] Even during Swedenborg's lifetime "Swedenborgianism" was much discussed in Skara; there, as in Göteborg, one main point of dispute was Swedenborg's rejection of three separate persons in the Trinity, and in connection with that his further denial of the idea that Christ effected vicarious atonement for human sin.[8] Swedenborg himself viewed this anti-Trinitarian doctrine

---

5. For these early translations, see the following: for Nordenskjöld, Swedenborg [1758] 1787; for Odhner, Hyde 1906, entry 1934; for Johansén, see Hyde 1906, entries 1511, 2472. For other references to these translations, see Lenhammar 1966; New Church Collection; Falck-Odhner Correspondence; and Odhner Translation Manuscript.

6. On animal magnetism, see below, page 180 note 22.

7. On the names Swedberg and Swedenborg, see above, page 4 note 1.

8. For Swedenborg's view of the unity of God, see page 74 above and *True Christianity* 5–17; for his view of vicarious atonement, see *The Lord* 18. (It is customary to refer to passages in Swedenborg's works by section numbers rather than page numbers, as the former are uniform in all editions.)

not as his invention but as a fundamental fact of proper Christian belief. Concerning the discussions of this topic at Göteborg, he wrote: "There they call this Swedenborgianism, but I for my part [call it] true Christianity."[9] All the same, he never called for or supported the founding of a separate church to foster this change in doctrinal outlook, particularly not in his own name.

A large number of the clergy in Skara became open to Swedenborg's view of the Trinity, although they remained within the Church of Sweden. Arvid Ferelius (1725–1793), who had been Swedenborg's pastor during his final days in London, returned to Sweden an ardent believer and proselytizer; his three sons-in-law eventually became members of the half-secret *Pro Fide et Charitate*.[10] The dean of Skara, Anders Knös (1721–1799), in time acknowledged that he was a disciple of Swedenborg, and the unofficial movement grew to include bishops and professors of theology.[11]

Political changes in 1809 brought increased freedom of the press, and it thereafter became easier to print and distribute within Sweden works deviating from orthodox Lutheran doctrine. The new freedom soon bore rich fruit through one of the sons of Dean Knös, Gustav (1773–1828), who was a professor of what were then called oriental languages at the University of Uppsala and a mystic in the Swedenborgian tradition. His book *Samtal med mig sjelf om werlden, Menniskan och Gud* (Talks with Myself Concerning the World, Humankind, and God; 1827) stoutly defended Swedenborg's theology, while simultaneously repulsing proposals for the establishment of separate New Church institutions—which in any case was still strictly forbidden.[12]

A later exemplar of the initial Swedenborgian movement in Sweden was Achatius Kahl (1794–1888), a scholar of Swedenborg connected with the University of Lund; he wrote a seminal work in four parts titled *Nya Kyrkan och dess inflytande på Theologiens Studium i Sverige* (The New Church and Its Influence on the Study of Theology in Sweden; 1847–1864), in which he documented the role of Dean Knös and others.

---

9. Letter to Gabriel Beyer, April 12, 1770; see Acton 1948–1955, 709. Translations in this essay are those of the author, unless the source cited is in English.

10. On Ferelius, see Lenhammar 1966, 272, and Ekman 1924, 14.

11. On Anders Knös, see Lenhammar 1966, 114; Sundelin 1886, 172; and Josefson 1937, 100 and the following pages.

12. On the Uppsala Knös family in general, see Horn 1921 and Mansén 1993.

b. The Effects of Swedenborgian Doctrines

The activities of the Swedenborgian movement were in many ways successful. Swedenborg's teachings concerning the Lord, the Trinity, redemption, and the spiritual world were widely spread within the Swedish clergy. It would be difficult to ascertain exactly how many members of this body could be counted as holding Swedenborgian beliefs during the early 1800s. In particular, a common rejection of the idea of vicarious atonement produced a cohesive group of dissenters from the theology of the state church. All the same, most Swedenborgian ministers maintained a diplomatic stance toward their more orthodox counterparts, and so were generally tolerated. There was, however, one important exception: the Reverend Johan Tybeck (1752–1831), a zealous and provocative exponent who dispersed numerous pamphlets throughout the country, including some aimed at the less educated class. Though defrocked in 1819, he continued his activities until his death with an unbroken zeal, supported by Swedenborgians both within Sweden and abroad (Lenhammar 1966, 235–255; [Kahl] 1847–1864, 3:106–144). So powerful was the ultimate effect of this entire discussion that Bishop Esajas Tegnér (1782–1831) declared vicarious atonement "a butcher doctrine, a blasphemy against both God and reason" (Tegnér [1827] 1921, 401). To this day it is rare to find Swedish clergy who actively espouse this particular teaching.

As we look back on those times, we can see that the hymnals and catechisms also became a field in which Swedenborgians could find expression. Johan Olof Wallin (1779–1839) was the editor of the state church hymnbook of 1819, in use until 1939; it reverberates with Christian Platonism and Swedenborgianism. Arvid August Afzelius (1785–1871) composed a hymn to the Creator that has outlived the hymnals of his day, "Dig skall min själ sitt offer bära" ("My Soul Gives Sacrifice to You"; Wallin 1819, number 28). This work dates from the time when Afzelius was a member of *Pro Fide et Charitate* in Stockholm; if his testimony is to be believed, New Church services were held by the organization in the very early years.[13] Bishop Jakob A. Lindblom (1746–1819) proposed a catechism in 1810 that maintained that the Father, Son, and Holy Spirit were different forms of revelation of the one eternal God ([Kahl]

---

13. Afzelius became a great folklorist and a cataloguer of folk traditions; together with Erik Gustaf Geijer (see below), he published a highly regarded work on old Swedish folk songs (Afzelius and Geijer 1814–1816). See also Afzelius 1901 and Hjern 1964, 102 and following.

1847–1864, 4:88). A somewhat later catechism, by the Skara bishop Sven Lundblad (1776–1837), was entirely Swedenborgian (Lundblad 1825).

Similar ideas appeared in the study by Erik Gustaf Geijer (1783–1847) titled *Thorild: Tillika en philosophisk eller ophilosophisk bekännelse* (Thorild: Also, a Philosophical or Unphilosophical Confession; 1820). Because of this work Geijer was actually prosecuted for heresy on the grounds that its account of the Trinity and the atonement of Christ was contrary to the teachings of the state church. According to Geijer, Christ's atonement was a reconciliation between God and humanity, a restoration of the broken bond between them, as made by God himself in his human form; and furthermore, God continues in his human aspect to fight evil on our behalf. In Geijer's view, Christ was divine love and wisdom in human form, a revelation of the ideal human, the true higher personality that can be realized in each human being—and in this world, not by necessity in the next. In his *Svenska folkets historia* (History of the Swedish People; 1832),[14] he claims that Swedenborg represents the true religiosity of the Swedish people in modern times, as did St. Bridget in medieval times.[15]

c. Publishing and Philanthropy

Despite the abiding interest in Swedenborgian theology, no separate New Church society could be formed in Sweden until 1866 (Goerwitz 1894, 270). Furthermore, such societies have remained small in Scandinavia as a whole, though they have often had an influence larger than their size might suggest, serving as the nuclei of major publishing initiatives.

An example of this publishing effort, albeit an idiosyncratic one, is the Swedenborgian bookseller and publisher Per Götrek (1798–1876). This "first Communist in Sweden" distributed both Swedenborgian tracts (Götrek 1854) and the *Communist Manifesto*. Odd though he may be, he represents the hunger for justice and social welfare that Swedenborg often inspired in his Swedish followers.

It should be observed that the early restriction against forming independent church societies did not stop Swedes from putting their Swedenborgian principles to use in organizations that were at least nominally secular. The Norrköping Association, founded in 1779, was one of the earliest Swedenborgian organizations in the nation; its goal was to create

---

14. Reprinted in Geijer 1873.

15. See Geijer 1873, 244. On his work in general, see [Kahl] 1847–1864, 4:43, 56, 58, 91, 92.

new societies in Africa based upon equal rights for all, without permitting slavery or participation in the slave trade.

In general, the Swedenborgians of Sweden were confirmed abolitionists and organized themselves to implement their beliefs. In 1787, the naturalist Anders Sparrman (1748–1820) and Carl Bernhard Wadström (1746–1799), one of the founding members of the Exegetic and Philanthropic Society, visited Mezurado (present-day Monrovia, Liberia) and began to propagate the idea of the district serving as a haven for liberated slaves. Under the leadership of Wadström, and in conjunction with August Nordenskjöld (1754–1792) and English abolitionists, Swedenborgians actually did found a colony at Sierra Leone in West Africa.[16] Though it held much promise, it survived only for a brief time. Others worked without the benefit of such organizations; for example, Governor Salomon Maurits von Rajalin (1757–1825), an acknowledged Swedenborgian, tried unsuccessfully to end reliance on the slavery system in the Swedish West Indian colony of St. Barthélemy.[17]

Swedenborgian theology supported women, too, in philanthropic endeavor. Frederika Bremer (1801–1865) found two aspects of Swedenborg's writings particularly influential: his emphasis on the importance of being of use to one's neighbor, and his insistence that women should be free of domination by men.[18] She traveled to America, most likely drawn to Swedenborgian contacts in New England; later the same interest took her to London. In America she studied social relationships, focusing on slavery and the preparation for the emigration of liberated slaves to Liberia in West Africa.[19]

Although, strictly speaking, ecumenicism may not be considered a component of philanthropy, it springs from the same source. Swedenborgians have contributed to striking advances in ecumenicism, following their leader's belief that the particular form of worship is not important, so long as the worshipper has the intention to live morally and do

---

16. On Njordenskjöld, see Häll 1995, 19–226; on Wadström, see Wadström 1790, 70–73, 126–132, and Dahlgren 1915.

17. For general background, see Skytte 1986.

18. On the concept of use in Swedenborg, see below, pages 358–359. On the avoidance of domination in marriage, see above, pages 80–81; and for one possible example out of many passages that could be offered, see *Marriage Love* 248.

19. On Bremer, see Bergquist 1995, 85–107, and Hallengren 1998b, 34–37.

good.[20] The World's Parliament of Religions of 1893, initiated by Swedenborgians in Chicago, had immediate consequences in Sweden.[21] On the initiative of New Church minister Albert Björck (1856–1938), a close collaboration began among Björck, the Jewish rabbi Gottlieb Klein (1852–1914), the liberal Christian scholar S. A. (Samuel Andreas) Fries (1867–1914), and the young minister and student of religions Nathan Söderblom (1836–1931). The result was a congress that took place in Stockholm in 1897 (Björck 1898). Björck and Söderblom, who were close friends, formed an organization that can be said to have been the beginning of the movement for a religious dialog and ecumenicism as a whole within Sweden.

II. Arts and Letters

I turn now to Swedenborg's influence on arts and letters, though of course these fields overlap with philosophy and theology. The end of the 1700s, less than three decades after the passing of Swedenborg, marks the beginning of the romantic era.

a. The Romantic Period

During this time the irrational, the emotional, and the experience of beauty found a new meaning in human thought. Those following this new trend eagerly seized on Swedenborg's idea that all of nature was a "representative theater" of the spiritual world[22] and a testimony of the divine love and wisdom of the Creator. His work *Marriage Love,* with its teaching that neither spouse should dominate, and its promise of a higher form of marriage in the other world—a virtual melding of two souls into one angel—held immense appeal to men and women trying to redefine love between the sexes. It is easy to trace the influence of Swedenborg during this period because Swedish poets and philosophers of the romantic era were generally quite ready to acknowledge their sources.

One of the first Swedish romantics to incorporate Swedenborg's works into the romantic vision was Thomas Thorild (1759–1808), a brilliant

---

20. On Swedenborg's view of religions other than the Christian faith, see page 65 with note 28, as well as note 102 on page 304.

21. On the parliament in general, see pages 303–305 in this volume and Block 1984, 366–369.

22. See, among many other passages, *Secrets of Heaven* 3000, 3483:4, 3518:2.

philosopher and a disciple of Gabriel Beyer at Göteborg. During a stay in England, he had extensive contact with Robert Hindmarsh (1759–1835) and the New Church society then forming in London.[23] At Thorild's request, Hindmarsh published his small work, *True Heavenly Religion Restored* (1790), in which Thorild describes the wonderful beauty of both the earthly and the spiritual world, as revealed by Emanuel Swedenborg.

Another testimony to the sway Swedenborg held over the romantic imagination appears in the work of the two leading literary critics of the early 1800s, Lorenzo Hammarsköld (1785–1827) and P.D.A. (Per Daniel Amadeus) Atterbom (1790–1855). In literary magazines they proclaimed Plotinus (205–270) and Swedenborg the spiritual leaders of the new era.[24] Hammarsköld's 1821 work *Historiska anteckningar rörande fortgången och utvecklingen af det Philosophiska Studium i Sverige* (Historical Notes Concerning the Progress and Development of the Study of Philosophy in Sweden; 229–246), demonstrates the part Swedenborg had come to play in Swedish philosophical enquiry and integrates his thought into the older models of Plato (427–347 B.C.E.) and Plotinus.[25] Atterbom, a professor at Uppsala University, published *Svenska siare och skalder* (Swedish Seers and Poets; 1862–1863), a massive work in which Swedenborg holds a central place. Atterbom focused in particular on *Worship and Love of God, Heaven and Hell,* and *Marriage Love,* surprising even Swedenborgians familiar with these works by his exposition of the beauty and wonder to be found in them.

Carl Jonas Love Almqvist (1793–1866) was, particularly in his younger years, almost the perfect type of the romantic. A poet and novelist, he embraced Swedenborgian thought early, in part because of his attachment to his grandfather, Carl Christofferson Gjörwell (1731–1811), who had met Swedenborg and written an account of him (Tafel 1877, 402–405). After his graduation from Uppsala University, he soon became the president of *Pro Fide et Charitate,* which at the time was involved in publishing Swedenborg's works in Swedish translation, in particular *Secrets of Heaven.* The records of his speeches at the meetings of *Pro Fide* show him absorbed with applying elements of divine revelation in the Bible to the journey of the human soul toward regeneration.[26]

---

23. For a discussion of Hindmarsh, see below, pages 255–263.

24. Nilsson 1916, 115–118; Atterbom 1814, columns 290–295.

25. On the influence of Swedenborg on Swedish philosophy, see Kylén 1910, 142–151.

26. Almqvist's talks in the *Pro Fide et Charitate* meetings can be found in Almqvist 1926, 37–84.

In his works in general we are constantly confronted with the importance of maintaining a relationship with the spiritual world and the necessity for being useful here so that we can be useful as well in the next life.

Almqvist's favorite among Swedenborg's works seems to have been *Marriage Love*. Almqvist often emphasized that the inner bonds that knit a couple together are far more important than any external rites; and although this is not a Swedenborgian idea in itself, it is consonant with Swedenborg's belief that one's true intention is what really matters, not the superficial practices that often paper over bad intentions. Many New Church members then opposed, and many of them now would still oppose, Almqvist's radical views of marriage; but it should be noted that Almqvist was most concerned to stress that there can be no good marriage without perfect equality between woman and man. What is more, he advocated the same equality in social and professional fields.

Education, too, deeply interested him. As an active teacher and the author of a large number of school textbooks, he could be regarded as one of the framers of the Swedish system of elementary education.

Almqvist suffered an unfortunate reversal in 1851 when he was accused of fraud and the attempted murder of a moneylender and fled from Sweden, though it seems most likely that he was in fact innocent.[27] In Philadelphia, Pennsylvania, he found a group of New Church followers where he evidently felt at home, returning to Europe only in 1865, shortly before his death.

In the same circle of romantics as Almqvist was Bernhard von Beskow (1796–1868), the secretary of the Swedish Academy and the author of a fine though slim biography of Swedenborg. He maintained that "even if we, together with the followers of this seer, claim that there is nothing imaginary in Swedenborg's spiritual world, nevertheless it is highly poetical, just as is Plato" (von Beskow 1860, 61). He emphasized this poetical aspect in his correspondence with the great Finnish writer Johan Ludvig Runeberg (1840–1877), who was deeply influenced by Swedenborg and his ideas concerning the spiritual world (Hjern 1963a, 107). Von Beskow's credentials as a romantic are impeccable; he was probably the only Swedish intellectual who was personally acquainted with Johann Wolfgang von Goethe (1749–1832), Friedrich Schlegel (1772–1829), and most prominent German writers of the time.

---

27. On this controversy and Almqvist in general, see Bergquist 1993, 44–46; Hjern 1988a, 88–89, and 1999a, 42–45; Lysell 1999, 4–10; and Wirmark 1999, 27–34.

b. Strindberg

From our perspective, Swedish letters in the latter decades of the 1800s is dominated by August Strindberg (1849–1912). It is arguable that he has done as much as anyone to make Swedenborg's name known both within Sweden and beyond it. Though he doubtless knew of Swedenborg's works during his intermittent studies at the University of Uppsala, he did not study them intensively until his stay in Paris in the 1890s. Here the Swedenborgian novel *Seraphita* by Honoré de Balzac (1799–1850) had become something of a cult phenomenon in literary circles (Balzac [1835] 1970); intrigued, Strindberg soon found translations of Swedenborg in French by Antoine-Joseph Pernety (1716–1796), as well as *Abrégé des Ouvrages d'Ém. Swédenborg* (Abridged Presentation of Emanuel Swedenborg's Works), an old anthology by Jean François D'Aillant de la Touche (1744?–1827?) that was actually Balzac's main source.[28] He also had some contact with a New Church congregation at Rue Thouin in Paris (Hjern 1963b, 12).

To Strindberg, who at that point was wandering in a kind of personal underworld, Swedenborg was a guide as compassionate and knowledgeable as the fictitious Vergil in Dante's *Inferno*, who guided the poet through the circles of hell. Under the immediate influence of his first view into Swedenborg's theology, Strindberg wrote his own *Inferno* (1897), followed by the book *Legender* (Legends; 1898). In these autobiographical pieces, Swedenborg is mentioned on nearly every page. Strindberg wrote the former work in France and the latter after his return to Sweden, where he was able to gain access to many more Swedenborgian texts.

Reading Swedenborg brought Strindberg a tremendous liberation from depression. He had been harassed by visions and by what Swedenborg describes as infestations of evil spirits; now that Strindberg had a spiritual explanation for these experiences, they were no longer threatening to him. However, it should be noted that his understanding of Swedenborg was quite idiosyncratic. Upon the publication of Strindberg's works on Swedenborg, the Stockholm New Church minister Albert Björck (whose ecumenical activities have been mentioned above) took Strindberg to task in a booklet titled *Swedenborg, Strindberg och det ondas problem* (Swedenborg, Strindberg, and the Problem of Evil; 1900). Björck criticized Strindberg's understanding of Swedenborg and suggested that the dramatist would gain immeasurably by a better comprehension of the theologian's message.

---

28. For Pernety's translations, see Hyde 1906, entries 1108, 1109 (with further reference to 3349), 1110, 1111, 2078, and 2079. For the translation of D'Aillant de la Touche, see Swedenborg 1788.

Over the years that followed his homecoming in Sweden, Strindberg turned again and again to Swedenborg's theological writings as explicative of human psychology and as the only compelling description of the spiritual world. He repeatedly echoed Swedenborg's summons to us to repent our egoistic and materialistic existence, making that theme a hidden motif in his many dramas. *Dödsdansen* (The Dance of Death) is a prime example (Strindberg 1901). In this play a couple cannot live together in harmony, and yet cannot achieve a separation from one another; they suffer from *odium conjugiale,* marriage hatred, a concept utilized as early as Swedenborg's 1742 work *Rational Psychology,* and dealt with indirectly in *Marriage Love* (1768), from his theological period.[29] Strindberg also studied Swedenborg's diaries,[30] in both Latin and Swedish, where he found political notions that supported him in his animosity to dictatorship; these views were welcomed in the socialist circles in which Strindberg moved in his later years.

Ultimately Strindberg worked with his erstwhile critic, Björck, to publish the voluminous *En blå bok* (A Blue Book; 1907–1912), which is replete with Strindberg's thinking on Swedenborgian correspondences,[31] as well as with references to Swedenborg's writings. Strindberg acknowledged his debt with an opening inscription that read: "To Emanuel Swedenborg, the teacher and leader, this book is dedicated by the disciple."[32]

c. Ekelund

The Swedish writer who took Swedenborg's message most to heart, perhaps, is Vilhelm Ekelund (1880–1949). Unfortunately, he is not well known outside Sweden. Though a poet, he primarily wrote books of philosophical aphorisms; he was both a mystic and a philosopher at once. His purpose is to lead us as readers to self-reflection and to encourage us to open our minds to an influx from a higher power, or, to put it another way, to understand through self-examination a sublime governance within ourselves. He supports our movement toward a new understanding of divine revelation,

---

29. See *Draft of a Rational Psychology* (= Swedenborg 2001a) §208. For an example of *odium* between partners in the work *Marriage Love,* see §292.

30. See pages 129–131 above for a discussion of Swedenborg's diaries of his spiritual experiences (= Swedenborg 1998–2002).

31. For more on correspondences, see pages 66 and 341–342 in this volume.

32. Strindberg 1907–1912, title page of volume 1. On Swedenborg's influence on Strindberg in general, see Stockenström 1988, 137–158; and on *A Blue Book* in particular, 138–139. Other relevant studies include Stockenström 1972, Lamm 1936, and Berendsohn 1948.

wherever we may find it. Although he constantly refers to Swedenborg in most of his works, one of his most remarkable is *På hafsstranden* (On the Seashore; 1922), in which the chapter on Swedenborg's experiences is of perennial interest.[33]

III. Denmark and Norway

Swedenborg has exerted an influence on Scandinavian countries outside Sweden as well, though this influence is little studied or appreciated. The early Danish role in the republication of Swedenborg's works has been noted already. Denmark was also a hotbed for proselytizers who wished to start New Church societies in Sweden in the 1800s. However, the first "Scandinavian" New Church society was formed not on Swedish soil, but in the Danish colony of St. Thomas, in the West Indies, in 1848 (Hallengren 1994b, 128–142).

Aside from their ecclesiastical interest in Swedenborg, the Danes have absorbed him, if indirectly, into their literature. The Danish writer Meir Goldschmidt (1819–1887), now best known for his controversy with the philosopher Søren Kierkegaard (1813–1855),[34] reflects Swedenborg's influence, as does Kierkegaard himself—or at least some scholars suggest as much (Bohlin 1925, 50–59, and Rubow 1952). Goldschmidt often speculated about the origin of religion, and in 1862 he played on this in a dramatic piece titled *Swedenborgs ungdom* (Swedenborg's Youth). Johannes Jørgensen (1866–1956) wrote his early works under the influence of Swedenborgian symbolism (Jørgensen 1916, 80). The romantic poet and dramatist Ernst von der Recke (1848–1933) was a member of the New Church. Under the rubric of Danish students we should also include the many prominent New Church followers in Greenland. At Thule, for example, in the northern part of the region, the minister Gudmund Boolsen (1927–) began translating the works of Swedenborg into Danish in the early 1960s.[35]

---

33. On Ekelund and Swedenborg, see Andersson 1999, 33–37; Hjern 1999b, 197–200; and Bergquist 1999a, 209–222.

34. For the classic description of this controversy by a biographer sympathetic to Kierkegaard, see Lowrie 1938, 347–363. For an account in primary sources, see Kirmmse 1996, 65–88.

35. See Swedenborg [1758] 1971 (a translation of *Heaven and Hell*); [1758] 1978a *(Other Planets)*; 1983–1995 *(Spiritual Experiences)*; [1758] 1995c *(Last Judgment)*; [1768] 1995d *(Marriage Love)*; [1763] 1998a *(Divine Love and Wisdom)*; and [1763] 1998b *(Life* and *Faith)*.

In the 1900s, an important circle of Swedenborgian discussion was formed by students in Oslo, Norway, although the initial impetus for this gathering was the reading of the romantic poet and writer Henrik Wergeland (1808–1845). Norway is the original home of the man who can be considered the first truly Scandinavian New Church minister, Adolf Theodor Boyesen (1823–1916). Cosmopolitan, to say the least, he was trained in the United States and ordained in Britain by Jonathan Bayley (1810–1886) in 1871 as a missionary to Denmark. From 1876 on he worked permanently in Stockholm, becoming a diligent translator into the Scandinavian languages.[36]

IV. Swedenborgian Influence in Recent Times

The further histories of Swedenborgian influence in the separate Scandinavian nations did not coalesce until 1978, when the Scandinavian Swedenborg Society was founded. The Society has published a number of new translations; and as part of that renewed interest, scholarship on the topic has increased. In the latter part of the twentieth century, scholars at the universities of Uppsala, Lund, and Stockholm contributed many papers, dissertations, and book-length studies on Swedenborg. The dissertation by Inge Jonsson, *Swedenborgs skapelsedrama De Cultu et Amore Dei* (Swedenborg's Drama of Creation "On the Worship and Love of God"; 1961); and that by Harry Lenhammar, *Tolerans och bekännelsetvång: Studier i den svenska swedenborgianismen 1765–1795* (Tolerance and Doctrinal Unity: A Study in Swedish Swedenborgianism 1765–1795; 1966), are fine exemplars of the work of the later 1900s; they blazed a new path for their traditional disciplines. Jonsson contributed a postscript to balance my own introduction when Martin Lamm's seminal 1915 biography *Swedenborg: En studie över hans utveckling till mystiker och andeskådare* (Swedenborg: A Study of His Development into Mystic and Visionary; 1987) was republished.

Recent works have brought Swedenborg studies into the new millennium, many of them outside the umbrella of the Swedenborgian organizations. One striking instance is the massive new biography by Lars Bergquist, *Swedenborgs hemlighet: Om Ordets betyldese, änglarnas liv och*

---

36. For examples, see Swedenborg [1771] 1903 (*True Christianity;* Swedish); and the following entries in Hyde 1906 (all in Danish): 983 (*Other Planets*), 1103 (*Heaven and Hell*), 1199 (*Last Judgment*), 1275 and 1276 (*New Jerusalem*), 1768 (*The Lord*), 2024 (*Supplements*), 2077 (*Divine Love and Wisdom*), and 2799 and 2800 (both *True Christianity*).

tjänsten hos Gud (The Secret of Swedenborg: The Meaning of the Word, the Life of the Angels, and Life [or Service] with God; 1999b); another is the volume by a leading Swedish literary critic, Olof Lagercranz, *Dikten om livet på den andra sidan; En bok om Emanuel Swedenborg* (Poem about Life on the Other Side: A Book about Swedenborg; 1996). The latter was issued in Swedish and German, and mostly recently (2002) in English in the United States. Its unheralded appearance on the scene was a surprise to Swedish New Church members, and it went on to achieve a certain popularity. In fact, it can be said to have been more widely read and reviewed than any other single book about Swedenborg in Sweden.

The arts, too, continue to explore Swedenborgian themes. The great Swedish modernist poet Gunnar Ekelöf (1907–1968) owes much to Swedenborg, especially in his poem *En Mölna-Elegi* (A Molna Elegy; 1960). Scandinavian art has always been intrigued by the idea that spirituality suffuses the material world, from the painters of "emblematic" art in Swedenborg's time, to the impressionists and symbolists of the 1800s, on to moderns such as Jewish artist Ernst Josephson (1851–1906), whose work is in this sense Swedenborgian. Thus, too, Oskar Bergman (1879–1963), a great proponent of Swedenborg's writings, often claimed that he painted the spiritual world by painting the physical world as realistically as possible.

As for theater, the plays of Almqvist and Strindberg have already been mentioned; they occasionally undergo revivals. The dramas of Erik Johan Stagnelius (1793–1823) also bear the impress of Swedenborg's experiences.[37] As of this writing, Ingmar Bergman, the director of film and stage, is exploring Strindberg, and is reported to be a daily and devoted reader of Swedenborg.[38]

To summarize this long and fruitful engagement with the thought of Swedenborg in Sweden and Scandinavia as a whole, we could return to the suggestion that the history of Swedenborg's influence in the region is a story of one great writer acting upon others. Clearly, however, Swedenborg's effect is greater than this. He has been a catalyst not only for artists, but for philosophers and those pondering the meaning of their religion and their place on earth. In this respect there is no particular Swedish or Scandinavian model of Swedenborgian influence, but rather a parallel to the catalyzing effect one sees in other cultures, both in Europe and beyond.

---

37. On Stagnelius in general, see Böök 1919; and Lysell 1993, especially after page 439.

38. Personal communication with the author by a member of Bergman's theater troupe. See also Sundgren 1998, 24, 27, 29–31.

Swedenborg and Continental Europe

JEAN-FRANÇOIS MAYER

Outline

IN researching Swedenborg's influence and legacy in Sweden or in the English-speaking world, one works with accessible and familiar sources. In Sweden, he belongs to the history of the nation: his achievements as a scientist and his activities as a public figure in his fatherland are widely known, even if his theological works stirred some negative reaction during his lifetime and for some years after his death. In Britain, where he published many of his theological works, organized groups of his followers have enjoyed the longest continuous existence. Not only have such groups also spread rapidly from Britain to the other side of the Atlantic Ocean, but ultimately they created an established and respected Swedenborgian milieu throughout the English-speaking Western world.

The situation in continental Europe is quite different: varied languages as well as varied religious and cultural histories render the impact of Swedenborg's work and ideas uneven, and thus more difficult to gauge. Not that others have not attempted to do so: in those few countries where small numbers of dedicated readers of Swedenborg's writings organized themselves, they carefully monitored their world for any indications of Swedenborgian influence. For example, in French-speaking Switzerland, an "Evidence Society" operated for several decades, along the pattern of the American association with the same name,[1] and collected any reference to Swedenborg its members could find in French books or media reports. In Germany a few scholars, especially the renowned historian of religions Ernst Benz (1907–1978) and a gifted New Church minister,[2] Friedemann Horn (1921–1999), investigated the spread of Swedenborgian ideas in the German-speaking world. Thus there are leads in assessing Swedenborg's influence in these areas.

When it comes to other European language areas, however, it is difficult to weigh his impact. The scarcity of available translations of his works in several languages might lead one to suspect at first glance that Swedenborg simply did not have any influence in some places,[3] but unexpected evidence may emerge on closer examination. It is always problematic to trace the history of ideas, except where there are acknowledged borrowings. But an exploration of the influence of Swedenborg in continental Europe (leaving aside Scandinavia) nevertheless shows that his work has had an impact on people in many places and sometimes left traces in the work of illustrious thinkers and artists. This exploration also reveals that active dissemination efforts and financial support from Swedenborgians in the English-speaking world have in several cases played an important role in making the writings of Swedenborg, if not widely familiar, at least available in

---

1. On the New Church Evidence Society in the United States, see Block 1984, 359–361.

2. The new church is the name given by Swedenborg to the order of things that was to arise after the Last Judgment, which according to his report took place in 1757. The term was taken up by followers who organized after his death in 1772; they applied it to their own ecclesiastical organizations. See below, page 246 note 2.

3. The languages into which Swedenborg's works have been translated show a pattern that is not surprising. All or most of his theological works have been published (although they are not necessarily still in print) in the major European languages, such as German, French, and Italian, as well as in several other languages in those areas where small but active groups of readers (or dedicated translators) existed. Worth noting is the relative lack of translations into Spanish, despite its prominent rank.

other language zones. One must also investigate the activities of Swedenborgians themselves to get a full and accurate picture of his impact.

I. Interest in Swedenborg in Europe during His Lifetime

In the letter to the Archbishop of Paris that opens his presentation of
Swedenborg's theological works, Bénédict Chastanier (about
1728–1806) claimed that people all over Europe as well as in the
Americas were discussing Swedenborg ([Chastanier] 1786, 5). While
such an assertion probably is a little too generous, reflecting the fervor Chastanier shared with a number of Swedenborg's early readers,
it is true that his writings had attracted attention beyond Britain and
Sweden. Certainly, well-educated people at that time were able to
read them, because they had been published in Latin, which was then
the common language of scholarship. But there is other evidence of
readers of Swedenborg on the Continent, even if the names of most
of them will forever remain unknown to us: a German translation of
Other Planets was published in Leipzig in 1770 (Swedenborg [1758]
1770), with three subsequent editions in 1771.[4] The fact that the book
went into reprint demonstrates that there was a curiosity about the
more exotic aspect of Swedenborg's works, at least.

Such curiosity, however, did not always denote an inclination for
Swedenborg's theology, as can be seen from the exchange of correspondence in 1771 between Swedenborg and the Landgrave of Hesse-
Darmstadt, Duke Ludwig IX (1719–1790). The duke's interest clearly
centered on hearing about the fate of some deceased acquaintances,
not on serious theological matters.[5]

Though the name of Swedenborg had become recognized by this period, it was not always seen in the best light. The Swedish seer had attracted the attention of a German philosopher, and no less a philosopher
than Immanuel Kant (1724–1804); though in the mid-1760s, when Kant
wrote on Swedenborg, he had yet to reach the fame he possessed later. As
appears from a letter presumably written in 1763 (Benz 1947, 235–271),
Kant had first heard of Swedenborg around that time, after he received a

4. For bibliographic information on the editions of this translation, see Hyde 1906, entries
989–992.

5. On this correspondence, see Acton 1948–1955, 736–742.

letter from a young woman who inquired his opinion regarding some strange stories about Swedenborg's clairvoyance. Kant did his best to investigate and to obtain accurate reports from correspondents in Sweden; through one of them he even sent a letter to Swedenborg, but no reply is known to have been made. He also acquired a set of Swedenborg's massive exegetical work, *Secrets of Heaven*. Kant took Swedenborg seriously,[6] and concerns arising from his reading of Swedenborg played a role in the development of his philosophical thought, even if his ultimate public judgment was a severe one, as can be seen from the book he published in 1766, *Träume eines Geistersehers* (Dreams of a Spirit-Seer). In it he wrote that *Secrets of Heaven* was "full of non-sense," and classified Swedenborg as a *Schwärmer,* a dreamer or fanatic.[7] Whether or not Kant's criticism is ambiguous, and whatever the underlying reasons for his sarcastic comments may have been (see Florschütz 1992), his judgments had long-term consequences for the image of Swedenborg, at least insofar as German academic circles are concerned: according to Benz, *Dreams of a Spirit Seer* was no less than an intellectual "death sentence" pronounced on Swedenborg (Benz 1979, 122). Subsequent advocates of Swedenborg's writings would take great care to justify their hero against Kant's criticisms: the anonymous editor of a 1786 German edition of *Survey* devoted a fifty-page introduction to a refutation of the description of Swedenborg as a fanatic ("Prüfungsversuch" 1786). On the other hand, Robert H. Kirven has rightly remarked that Kant's comments served to make Swedenborg's clairvoyant abilities widely talked-of in Europe: "The stories of the Queen's Secret, of the Lost Receipt, and of the Stockholm Fire . . . were first told to a broad audience by Kant" (Kirven 1988, 109). Even among Kant's friends in Riga and Koenigsberg, there were indications of curiosity about Swedenborg's writings two decades after Kant's *Dreams of a Spirit-Seer:* ironically, the publisher of that very book made repeated but unsuccessful attempts in 1786 and 1787 to obtain a set of *Secrets of Heaven* in order to publish it (Benz 1947, 271–280).

Other readers in German-speaking areas during Swedenborg's lifetime were more receptive. Prominent among them was the Swabian

---

6. Apparently more seriously than the *Dreams of a Spirit-Seer* would seem to indicate, as it appears from textual evidence (Johnson 1996–1997). However, this is an issue that will no doubt continue to give rise to debate among scholars.

7. Kant [1766] 1902, 360. Throughout this essay, the translations of quotations from sources other than English are my own, unless a translated source is specified.

Protestant prelate, Friedrich Christoph Oetinger (1702–1782). A man of wide knowledge, familiar with the mystical or esoteric trends of his time as well as with early Christian authors, Oetinger could not fail to notice Swedenborg's works. Actually, Swedenborg's name was already familiar to him, as Oetinger had read some of the Swede's scientific publications.

Deeply impressed by Swedenborg, Oetinger considered him an authentic prophet and seer, though he never became an unconditional adherent of Swedenborgian doctrines, and at times expressed disagreement with Swedenborg's views, at one point writing to him: "I wish that you yourself would acknowledge that your explanations of Scripture are not quite as worthy of belief as your visions and revelations from heaven" (Acton 1948–1955, 640). Indeed, Oetinger was mostly interested in what Swedenborg had seen and heard in the spiritual world; accordingly, he took accounts of memorable occurrences[8] in the spiritual world from the first volume of *Secrets of Heaven* (leaving the exegesis aside) and incorporated them in a book he published, *Swedenborgs und anderer irdische und himmlische Philosophie* (Earthly and Heavenly Philosophy of Swedenborg and Others; [1765] 1855). The publication of Oetinger's book irritated the Consistory in Stuttgart, and their disapproval led the authorities of Württemberg to confiscate the book. "You will hardly believe how much I have to suffer on your account," Oetinger wrote to Swedenborg in 1766 (Acton 1948–1955, 624).

Though Oetinger disagreed with Swedenborg on several points, he continued to defend him in spite of the adversity he himself suffered by doing so. In a long text written in his own justification in 1767,[9] he argued that time would tell what was not true in Swedenborg's teachings, as had been the case with the apostles of old, who had expected Christ to return while they were still on earth. To his way of thinking, controversial issues were subordinate; Swedenborg's explanations concerning life after death seemed to be perfectly consistent with the original Christian teachings. Not even the deep disagreement expressed by Oetinger about the content of *True Christianity* (1771), which contradicted many of his own beliefs, could produce a break between the two men; their long-held plan to meet was ultimately forestalled only by Swedenborg's death.

---

8. For a discussion of Swedenborg's accounts of memorable occurrences, see pages 94–95 above.

9. See Oetinger 1767, reprinted in Benz 1947, 291–308.

Oetinger's *Earthly and Heavenly Philosophy* was republished several times and remained for many years an important source of information about Swedenborg for German-speaking readers.[10]

Swedenborg intended his visit to Oetinger as a stopping point on his way to Zürich, where he planned to meet the Reformed minister Johann Kaspar Lavater (1741–1801). Lavater was to gain fame not long afterward for his work in physiognomy,[11] a field influenced not only by general Christian principles, but quite likely by the theological works of Swedenborg, with which Lavater was familiar (Benz 1979, 207–267).

The Protestant minister and educator Johann Friedrich Oberlin (1740–1826) also owned several volumes by Swedenborg; he seems to have first read *Heaven and Hell* around 1783. He studied Swedenborg's treatises with great care; his own sermons reflect a similar blend of rationalism and mysticism; and his life was a model of the Swedenborgian teaching that we are meant to be of use to others.[12] Even though—like Oetinger and most readers in continental Europe during that period—he did consider some passages "risky reasonings," he was pleased to discover in them "admirable lights" for which, he said, he did not know how to thank God enough.[13] He felt that Swedenborg had received part of his doctrines from the Lord, even if he had been unknowingly misled by

---

10. For bibliographic information on these editions, see Hyde 1906, entries 876–881 and 3149.

11. Lavater's four-volume study of the relation between facial features and character appeared between 1775 and 1778 under the title *Physiognomische Fragmente zur Beförderung der Menschenkenntnis und Menschenliebe* (Physiognomic Fragments Intended for the Advancement of the Knowledge and Love of Humankind). Goethe (see page 179 below in this essay) is known to have assisted Lavater in its composition. The connection between the spiritual and the facial fascinated Swedenborg's age. He himself recognized that the human face could mask ill intentions, but believed that in general "Our face molds itself in the image of our deeper qualities, in order to let what is inside us show on the outside and therefore to let what belongs to the spiritual world come to view in the physical world." (See *Secrets of Heaven* 9306; translation here by Lisa Hyatt Cooper. It is customary to refer to passages in Swedenborg by section numbers rather than page numbers.)

12. Oberlin, a Lutheran minister, devoted his life to improving the lives of his parishioners in the Vosges region of France. His philanthropic innovations included a system of free education, communal road-building, a local bank, the establishment of factories for workers trained at his expense, an agricultural information collective, and the distribution of modern farming implements at cost. He was progressive in spiritual as well as material matters: his communion services were interdenominational. Widely admired in his day, he gave his name to a town and progressive college in the United States. Statements on the importance of being of use to others are ubiquitous in Swedenborg; for examples, see *Secrets of Heaven* 1097:2, 1103:2, 7038.

13. Quoted in Sjödén 1985, 61, from comments by Oberlin on *Heaven and Hell;* no further reference given.

spirits on other points, especially those that contradicted the literal meaning of the Scriptures (Sjödén 1985, 59–62).

While Swedenborg's effect on Kant, Oetinger, Lavater, and Oberlin is clear to us, he may also have had in his own lifetime or shortly thereafter an influence on other European thinkers that is more difficult to document. His books did not sell in huge numbers, but he made up for slow sales by actively distributing his texts to individuals or to learned societies he thought might be interested, not only in Britain and Sweden, but also in France and other places in Europe—thus sowing the garden of European thought in an unpredictable fashion. This deliberate but irregular distribution yields both pleasant surprises and disappointments for the historian of ideas.

II. Eclectic Swedenborgianism on the Eve of the French Revolution

In Britain, the years following the death of Swedenborg saw the emergence of the first congregations of a church based on his teachings as well as of societies, promoted both by "separatist" and "nonseparatist" Swedenborgians,[14] that were determined to translate, publish, and distribute Swedenborg's works as widely as possible. These organized groups, both the religious societies and the publishing societies, tended to promote a Swedenborgian orthodoxy; otherwise such groups would not have been able to remain united and survive as long as they have. Early Swedenborgianism developed in a quite different atmosphere on the Continent, without real attempts to create congregations at that time (for there was no setting on the Continent comparable to the nonconformist milieu in Britain).[15] "French and German interest in Swedenborg had arisen mostly among speculative Freemasons and students of the occult," some of whom also visited Britain, but "sober English readers were rather bewildered by these foreign visitors" (Lineham 1988, 113).

A man who sat on both sides of the fence, so to speak, has already been mentioned: Bénédict Chastanier (Sjödén 1985, 36–41). A French surgeon

---

14. For discussion of separatist and nonseparatist elements in church Swedenborgianism, see pages 255–263 below.

15. For a brief discussion of nonconformism in Britain and its effect on church Swedenborgianism, see pages 253–254 below.

resident in London beginning in 1774, he was among the first people to attempt to organize a Swedenborgian society in Britain. In addition, he published (in London) French translations of some of Swedenborg's works[16] and four issues of what has sometimes been described as the first Swedenborgian periodical, the *Journal Novi-Jérusalémite* (New Jerusalemite Journal), which for the most part actually contained translations of Swedenborg's writings. He had originally hoped to be able to publish it on a monthly basis. The *Journal* was dedicated to those "lovers of truth who have already tasted it in the theological writings of Swedenborg" as well as to "all the Freemasons," a group to which Chastanier openly admitted belonging. He explained to them that Swedenborg would open an inner understanding of those symbols that they knew only externally (Chastanier 1787, i–xvii). Chastanier's goal was to provide translations of Swedenborg's works not only in French, but also in all the languages spoken in countries that did not have a free press. However, it was only logical to give priority to French, since it was at that time "the most universal of all languages" (Chastanier 1787, ii).

Another French citizen was to win even more notice, even if he would always be looked upon with suspicion by mainstream Swedenborgians: Antoine-Joseph Pernety (1716–1796), a Benedictine priest, who in 1767 became the librarian of Frederick II of Prussia (1712–1786). Two books that he published in 1758 reveal his growing interest in alchemy.[17] While in Berlin he also became interested in physiognomy, like Lavater. It was in Berlin as well that Pernety discovered the works of Swedenborg—probably shortly before 1779; and there he published a French translation of *Heaven and Hell* (Swedenborg [1758] 1782). But Pernety was not satisfied just to read Swedenborg and to follow his doctrines: along with a small group around him, he claimed to be able to receive heavenly instructions from the "Holy Word."[18] In September 1779, this source of information confirmed that everything contained in Swedenborg's *Marriage Love* was true. Pernety left Berlin in 1783 and settled in southern France, where the group pursued its activities, attracting some dubious figures along with honest

---

16. For bibliographic information on Chastanier's translations, see the index entry listing instances of his name in Hyde's bibliography (Hyde 1906, page 725).

17. See Pernety 1758a and Pernety 1758b.

18. A complete transcript of the manuscript of the replies received by the group from the "Holy Word" has been published in a recent scholarly book on Pernety and his group, Meillassoux-Le Cerf 1992, 333–448.

adherents. It still survived as a peaceful and forgotten circle for a few years after Pernety's death.

In the maelstrom of ideas during the decades preceding the French Revolution, several occult and masonic groups took an interest in Swedenborg (Le Forestier 1987, 701–703). Not all of these groups really knew his works: he was, rather, one of those mysterious figures who seemed to belong in any creditable gallery of initiates.

Ranging as they did from Oetinger to Pernety, adherents of eighteenth-century continental European Swedenborgianism were definitely an eclectic crew. It has been said, with good reason, that "true Swedenborgians would come later" (Viatte 1969, 103).

The frequent invocations of the name of Swedenborg in this period had consequences for the history of ideas, and not only in those circles keen to incorporate any kind of reference to the Swedish philosopher in their literature. When the French Revolution broke out and upset Europe, there were authors who looked for the hidden causes behind such a cataclysm. Eager conspiracy theorists identified Illuminati as the source of, and the driving force behind, the turmoil. They soon came to list Swedenborg among the instigators of those sinister developments. In his multivolume *Mémoires pour servir à l'histoire du Jacobinisme* (Memoirs of Jacobinism), first published in French in London in 1797–1798, the famous Jesuit author Augustin de Barruel (1741–1820) devoted about thirty pages to Swedenborg (Barruel 1798, 110–143). According to Barruel, the Illuminati had drawn their principles from Swedenborg; Barruel equated the New Jerusalem with the French Revolution.[19] Barruel's memoirs still have a readership today; but a balanced assessment cannot give credence to Swedenborg's alleged influence on the ideas that led to the French Revolution. It is true that Swedenborg expected mighty changes in the internal conditions of the world, though not the external (see *Last Judgment* 73), but he was not the only one in his own times to do so, and to infer from his expectation that he laid one of the ideological foundations of the French Revolution would constitute a gross misstatement of his real influence. In addition, among the multitude who anticipated change, there were differing views as to what shape it would take, or what ideology it would follow. For example, Chastanier (1787, viii) criticized the "very dangerous works" by Voltaire (1694–1778) and the "false and erroneous

---

19. On the significance of the New Jerusalem as a symbol, see page 248 with note 6 below.

sophisms" of Jean-Jacques Rousseau (1712–1778). Since these two authors clearly did exercise an influence on the intellectual developments that led to the French Revolution, it is salutary to observe that a leading Swedenborgian and Freemason could express deep disagreements with their views even before that event.

III. The Age of the Great Translators

By the early nineteenth century, the original Latin editions of Swedenborg's works had become quite scarce. English-speaking Swedenborgians invested much energy in making English translations as well as collateral works available. But the lack of translations into other languages was glaring, and had to be remedied if Swedenborg's influence was to spread. Beginning in 1786, Jean Pierre Moët (1721–1806 or 1807), royal librarian at Versailles, had translated most of Swedenborg's theological writings; but they remained unpublished until a wealthy and dedicated Swedenborgian from Britain, John Augustus Tulk (about 1751–1845), bought the French translations from Moët's widow and printed a dozen of those volumes at his own expense.[20] However, this was to be only a beginning: during the nineteenth century, highly dedicated and able individuals in three European countries undertook translations of Swedenborg's works. In doing so, they became important channels for Swedenborg's influence in continental Europe.

A general pattern must also be mentioned here: while publication of Swedenborgian literature in English was self-supporting, the help given by English-speaking Swedenborgians to publications on the Continent proved to be vital—except for those few treatises which, like *Heaven and Hell*, might have sold well anyway. As early as 1818, the still nascent Swedenborg Society[21] in London was deliberating how it could help the publication of Swedenborg's works in languages other than English.

a. Germany

In the 1820s, there were only a few small Swedenborgian groups in the German-speaking part of Switzerland, and they had little contact with

---

20. For bibliographic information on Moët's translations, see the index entry listing his many works in Hyde's bibliography (Hyde 1906, page 731).

21. On the Swedenborg Society, see pages 250–251 below.

other believers. There were also some isolated readers in Germany. About this time, however, Johann Friedrich Immanuel Tafel (1796–1863) became active (Dress 1979). The son and grandson of Protestant ministers in Württemberg, he was a student at the University of Tübingen, where he decided in 1819 to study theology. He had already discovered some of Swedenborg's works as a teenager (beginning with *Other Planets*); his student years allowed him to become more familiar with the rest. In 1821, after completing his theological training, he came in contact with some other German readers of Swedenborg, and they convinced him of the pressing need to translate those works into German. The first volumes were printed in 1823 and 1824, although Tafel had found by that time only 110 subscribers and had to borrow money from his aunt in order to go to press ("Miscellaneous Intelligence" 1824, 245). After publishing a prospectus for raising subscriptions, Tafel also sent a copy of it to the authorities of Württemberg and to the Consistory in order to explain the reasons for his undertaking: he declared that he "had no intention to originate a party that should separate [itself] from the Established Church of the Kingdom." The recipients came to the conclusion that he could not enter into the Lutheran ministry, and he finally found a position as a librarian at the university, a post in which he could continue his translating ("Miscellaneous Intelligence" 1825, 693–697). Tafel received the support of some people who had been readers of Swedenborg's works for many years—for example, the industrialist Peter Eberhard Müllensiefen (1766–1847), who had discovered Swedenborg's writings as early as 1782. Tafel married Müllensiefen's daughter, and the Müllensiefen family went on to play an important role in German Swedenborgianism during most of the nineteenth century (Groth 1995).

Tafel's contribution was amazing and served the cause of Swedenborg well beyond German-speaking countries. In addition to his translations, he published a number of Latin editions of Swedenborg, as well as some important, previously unpublished texts; after his death the Swedenborg Society bought the remaining copies of the Latin volumes for continued distribution. Tafel also wrote several books in defense of Swedenborg and his doctrines, along with philosophical works of his own.

A major question for readers of Swedenborg on the Continent in Tafel's time and afterward was whether they should adopt a separatist or nonseparatist policy. People like Tafel were cautious: they knew that a clear departure from the established church might not necessarily be beneficial, "the number of receivers [adherents] being everywhere too small to be collected into societies with adequate external forms." He consoled himself by remarking that "non-separation has also its good, as it opens channels of influence which would not exist in a state of separation" (Tafel 1847).

Tafel and his friends paid keen attention to any indication of new trends and movements that might demonstrate the influence of a new spirit in the age, hoping that their times might become ready for those truths they held dear to come into being, or at least might prove receptive to the views propagated in Swedenborgian publications. When a "German Catholic" movement emerged in early 1845 around people like the former Roman Catholic priest Johannes Ronge (1813–1887), it rapidly found a receptive audience among liberal Catholics, culminating with a gathering of the representatives of some 250 local groups in 1847; German "free Catholic" congregations were even founded among emigrants in the United States. Tafel closely followed those developments: in May 1845, he explained to an American correspondent that the new German Catholic movement had a very general confession of faith and left "individual congregations at liberty to make what additions they [might] think proper": in one of those congregations, the articles of faith "agree[d] entirely with those of the New Church" (Tafel 1845). Tafel wrote an address to the German Catholics and also distributed among them translations of sermons written by English Swedenborgians. Those materials were said to have been received "with applause" ("Miscellanea—Germany" 1846, 107). But after its initial success the German Catholic movement very soon declined, and what was left of it became part of religious liberal and rationalist circles.

The political developments in 1848 at last allowed German Swedenborgians the chance to organize themselves: the Union of the New Church in Germany and Switzerland was formed that same year, and at the beginning gathered about a hundred members. But Swedenborgianism as an institutionalized body never developed strongly in Germany.

However, Swedenborg's influence there was by no means to be limited to small organized groups. When Tafel passed away, he had published a total of thirty thousand printed volumes: those in German continued to be distributed through the agency of a member of the Müllensiefen family, and unfinished translations were completed. If earlier translations are added into the total, probably tens of thousands of volumes of Swedenborg in German were circulating from the late eighteenth century through the nineteenth. Such publishing efforts continued into the twentieth century, in particular through the efforts of the Swedenborg Verlag publishing house in Zürich, which printed new translations by Friedemann Horn.

Those many volumes have affected uncounted and unknown individuals, as well as a few more visible figures. Among the most illustrious of the visible was Johann Wolfgang von Goethe (1749–1832). A giant figure in German intellectual history, Goethe developed an outlook of his own and cannot be categorized under "one religious, literary, or philosophical school" (Heinrichs 1979, 179). Yet this does not mean that there were no influences on Goethe's thought—and Swedenborg indisputably attracted his interest. It is possible, but not certain, that Goethe first heard about Swedenborg from the German writer Johann Heinrich Jung-Stilling (1740–1817), whom he met in 1770. In any event, Goethe read some texts of Swedenborg in the years immediately after 1770, and was also in touch with Lavater.

There are few explicit references to Swedenborg in Goethe's works. As a result, some scholars remain undecided about the full extent of Swedenborg's influence: typical of this group is Michael Heinrichs, who believes it would be mere conjecture to go beyond the statement that "Goethe knew Swedenborg" (Heinrichs 1979, 205). However, especially in considering such works as *Faust,* other scholars are convinced that there are unmistakable Swedenborgian elements: Friedemann Horn goes so far as to say that some passages are "pure Swedenborg" (Horn 1999, 190–195). While the young Goethe sometimes mentions Swedenborg's name, it may be that the older Goethe prefers to avoid any specific reference to it in order not to compromise his career (Kirven 1988, 105–106).

In any case, Swedenborg's influence in nineteenth-century Germany went beyond Goethe. Benz was of the opinion that Swedenborg's views on marriage and love exercised a deep influence on German Romanticism (Benz 1969, 423). As will become apparent below, this influence on the Romantic movement was not limited to Germany. The case of Friedrich Schelling (1775–1854) has been well studied, and despite the fact that "there is no single passage in the works of Schelling published during his lifetime that explicitly indicates that the author was engaged with Swedenborg" (Horn 1997, 27), one of his posthumous works cites Swedenborg (without explicitly using his name), and research conducted by Benz and Horn has conclusively demonstrated that he was influenced by Swedenborg.

Not all of the thinkers and writers who immersed themselves in Swedenborg's works reached the same conclusions about him. The

German poet Heinrich Heine (1797–1856) expressed respect for Swedenborg and deemed his reports on the spiritual world to be "credible," inasmuch as our current and future existence form a whole and cannot be divided (Horn 1999, 201). But Christoph Martin Wieland (1733–1813) refused to believe that Swedenborg had enjoyed communication with the spiritual world (Heinrichs 1979, 221–222).

Swedenborg's influence went beyond the intellectual and literary realm. Nineteenth-century Germany provides a good example of how the reading of Swedenborg encouraged social action. Gustav Werner (1809–1887) came in contact with Tafel and other Swedenborgians as a theology student in Tübingen. His growing interest in Swedenborg brought him into conflict with his family as well as with his theology professors. The development of his social thought continued in Strasbourg, where he lived from 1832 to 1834, as there he came in contact with the circle of some friends of Oberlin. Though he became a Lutheran curate in 1834 and remained in that position for several years, he was always suspect because of his Swedenborgian leanings. Yet Werner ultimately left behind an impressive body of social reforms. He began by focusing on care of orphans, extended his assistance to handicapped persons, and finally created a network of institutions with dedicated volunteers—several of whom happened to be highly sympathetic to Swedenborg (Zwink 1988, 405–424; Zwink 1993, 18–25).

b. France

Swedenborgianism in nineteenth-century France, like that movement in Germany, emerged in a milieu where interest in the theory of animal magnetism was running high.[22] This simultaneity is part of a pattern evident during this period: people who were generally sympathetic toward new and unusual ideas were therefore more open to Swedenborg; and conversely, some Swedenborgians themselves, looking for trends indicative of the new worldview they expected to be "permeating" current

---

22. Austrian physician Franz Anton Mesmer (1734–1815) identified animal magnetism as a kind of invisible fluid emanating from the stars and permeating the universe. According to his theory, this fluid was supposed to enable occult transmissions from one individual to another. The effect of Mesmer's ideas was particularly strong in France, where he reestablished his practice after having been driven out of his native land in 1778. Though animal magnetism was debunked in the 1780s by a commission of scientists that included American inventor Benjamin Franklin (1706–1790) and French chemist Antoine-Laurent Lavoisier (1743–1794), the theory remained popular for decades. It was eventually superseded by the more respectable fields of hypnotism and psychotherapy.

thought, sometimes saw parallels to Swedenborg in the theories prevalent in their times.[23]

Captain Jean-Jacques Bernard (1791–1828) took part in the military campaigns of Napoleon in Russia, Saxony, and France. Investigation into animal magnetism marked the beginning of his interest in spiritual matters, which broadened during the late 1810s, when he became acquainted with the ideas of Louis-Claude de Saint-Martin (1743–1803).[24] After discovering Swedenborg through Saint-Martin, he became an eager follower of the doctrines of the New Jerusalem and undertook to share them with others—including some of his fellow officers—as well to get in touch with other readers across the country. He was instrumental in initiating small groups of readers of Swedenborg's writings in various places. Among those whom his efforts brought to Swedenborg's following was a promising young author from Nantes, Edouard Richer (1792–1834), who despite his premature death left an extensive body of work promoting Swedenborg. French literary scholar Auguste Viatte (1901–1993) saw in Richer the first clear influence of Swedenborgianism on French literature (Viatte 1931, 439–443).

A French counterpart of Tafel soon appeared on the scene: Jean-François-Étienne Le Boys des Guays (1794–1864). Born in a family of magistrates, he too became a judge, after participating as a young man in some of the final military campaigns of Napoleon. In the early 1830s, he became interested in animal magnetism. During a trip to Paris in connection with that field, he was given *Heaven and Hell* and some other works by Swedenborg on loan. He was entirely won over

---

23. Certain nineteenth-century Swedenborgians advanced the "permeation theory" to explain why New Church beliefs had not been openly adopted worldwide. According to the permeation theory, "the whole world is being gradually permeated by the new truths. . . . Though the world has not accepted the Writings of Swedenborg nevertheless its teachings have influenced its thought far more than it is aware" (Block 1984, 357). As one adherent of the theory observed, "the growth and influence of the visible New Church cannot be measured by the progress of its technical institutions," adding that there were many outside its ranks who had been "more or less favorably impressed with the doctrines of Swedenborg" (Holcombe 1881, 334–335). Another writer perceived Christian churches as "animated by a different spirit from what ruled them a century ago," and made the claim that "Christians think and feel very differently now from [the way] they did formerly" ("B." 1888, 574). Faced with the modest size of their congregations, not a few Swedenborgians found comfort in this theory.

24. Louis-Claude de Saint-Martin, a philosopher, was influenced by the Jewish mystic Martinez de Pasqually (1727–1774) and the German mystic Jacob Boehme (1575–1624) as well as by Swedenborg. He was a leading proponent of Illuminism, a movement against rationalism and materialism.

by Swedenborg's doctrines and after a few years gave up not only his experiments in animal magnetism but his career in jurisprudence to devote his entire efforts to the dissemination of Swedenborg, supported by wealth acquired through marriage. In 1837 he opened a public place of worship at his home in the town of Saint-Amand, in the department of Cher. In 1838 he launched a periodical, *La Nouvelle Jérusalem* (The New Jerusalem), writing most of it himself. This journal continued until 1848, when its publication was interrupted owing to a lack of funds and contributors. More important than these activities, however, were his continual efforts to carefully and faithfully translate the theological writings of Swedenborg, at a pace of ten pages a day. In fact, Le Boys des Guays translated more of Swedenborg than Tafel (who never completed the translation of *Secrets of Heaven*), and probably more than any other translator before or since. Except for a few titles that have been translated more recently, the translations by Le Boys des Guays remain in use in France today.

The attempt by Le Boys des Guays to establish Swedenborgian worship at Saint-Amand (Brody de Lamotte 1938, 133–173) can serve as an example of the progress of institutionalized Swedenborgianism in France in general. The Saint-Amand society had begun under promising auspices, and there was even a project to build a temple of the New Church there in 1840. As many as fifty of the faithful attended services during the lifetime of Le Boys des Guays, but thereafter it ceased to grow. A hundred years after its founding, its congregation had dwindled to only three members. Even in a large center like Paris, organized Swedenborgianism has never achieved a stable presence in France, despite some periods of relative success—including the period between 1883 and 1910, when there was a temple of the New Church located in the capital. As was the case nearly everywhere in continental Europe, the major achievement of Swedenborg's followers lay not in the establishment of a lasting organized institutional presence in France, but in making available Swedenborg's writings in translations and other publications. Through these, in turn, Swedenborg has clearly left his mark on French letters, though his influence cannot always be directly measured.

In a survey of this impact on French literature, Honoré de Balzac (1799–1850) is the first author of note who comes to mind. Actually, Balzac may never have read any book by Swedenborg in its entirety, but he was familiar with *Abrégé des Ouvrages d'Ém. Swédenborg* (Abridged Presentation of Emanuel Swedenborg's Works), composed of extracts from various treatises (Swedenborg 1788). Even if Balzac sometimes seems to express ambivalent feelings toward Swedenborg in letters to correspondents, it is significant that his public statements were uttered in a very different tone from those found in Kant. In his novel *Seraphita,* for example, a number of pages are devoted to a positive summation of Swedenborg's life and teachings (Balzac [1832–1835] 1900, 54–80). In the novel *Louis Lambert,* he wrote that Swedenborg incorporates all the best principles from the various religions while making Christianity acceptable for the rational mind: "Swedenborg will perhaps be the Buddha of the North" (Balzac [1832–1835] 1900, 268).

Balzac is something of an embarrassment to "orthodox" Swedenborgians: they take pride in the fact that this literary giant showed interest in Swedenborg, but they feel that he did not really understand Swedenborg and tended to make him into a kind of proto-spiritualist (Sjödén 1966, 41–42). French Swedenborgians complained that in *Seraphita* Balzac had "clothed Swedenborg with the dreams of his [Balzac's] imagination" (F. P. 1841, 39). Unorthodox though Balzac's appropriation may be, it is far more explicit and sympathetic than that of any other major French author. This was not lost on a certain French Swedenborgian who wrote that though it was true that Balzac had misunderstood Swedenborg, he had, on the other hand, also "succeeded in causing the name of Swedenborg to reach with favour the ears of people who, otherwise, might never have heard it" ("Miscellaneous Information: France" 1836, 215). Through Balzac, Swedenborg's influence reached even beyond the French-speaking world: for example, the Austrian-born musical composer Arnold Schönberg (1874–1951) discovered Swedenborg when reading *Seraphita* (Wörner and Horn 1994, 244).[25]

Several other well-known nineteenth-century French authors mention Swedenborg. Gérard de Nerval (1808–1855) was one of them. He felt especially attracted to Swedenborg's accounts of memorable occurrences in the spiritual world. Alphonse de Lamartine (1790–1869) writes in one of his books of the "sublime and obscure Swedenborg" (Lamartine 1847). The name of Swedenborg occasionally appears in some works by Théophile Gautier (1811–1872). According to some scholars, Charles Baudelaire (1821–1867) may have read some of Swedenborg's works themselves, not just the *Abrégé,* or abbreviated version

---

25. Swedenborg's work impressed a famous pupil of Schönberg's: composer Anton von Webern (1883–1945), who wrote to Schönberg in 1913: "I am now reading Swedenborg. . . . I had expected something colossal, but it is even more" (Adam 1986, 241).

(Blin 1939, 64–67). His sonnet "Correspondences," describing the human being "among forests of symbols," is familiar to any student of French letters.[26] Swedenborg was known to other writers of the symbolist school of literature besides Baudelaire, and to writers of other schools; the complete list would include famous as well as forgotten names.

c. Italy, Portugal, and Spain

Swedenborg's impact in Italy has been studied less than his influence in Germany and France. The dissemination of Swedenborg's writings began later in Italy than it had in those two countries. There were regular meetings in Florence and Rome, but they included only English-speaking expatriates. However, the journal of the British Swedenborgians, the *New Jerusalem Messenger,* announced in 1869 that an Italian translation of *New Jerusalem* was going through the press under the auspices of the Swedenborg Society in London ([Ford] 1869, 25). The author of that translation was Loreto Scocia (1836–1902), who had first been a political activist, then a Methodist minister. He was a professor of languages in Lausanne, Switzerland, when he began to read the writings of Swedenborg in French in 1868. His efforts during the subsequent years would make about ten of Swedenborg's books available to an Italian-speaking audience. In addition, in 1871 he launched a periodical, *La Nuova Epoca* (The New Era), and gave public lectures on the message of Swedenborg, first in Turin and then in Florence. Dedicated subscribers to *La Nuova Epoca* lived in various places across Italy. However, the most ardent followers of Swedenborg's doctrines could be found not in Scocia's own northern Italy, but in Sicily and the vicinity of Naples.

Since Scocia's day, there have always been readers of Swedenborg in Italy, some of them even gathering in congregations; and the occasional academic book dealing with Swedenborg has appeared there from time to time.[27] But he remains a "Prophet of the North": his impact in southern European countries has been limited, in terms of institutional church activities as well as intellectual influence.

This observation is relevant to Portugal as well, although it was reported that there were readers in Lisbon in 1789 (Hindmarsh 1861, 162). In Spain, Jean-Jacques Bernard (mentioned above) had been able to

---

26. On the principle of correspondence in Swedenborg, see pages 66 and 341–342 in this volume.

27. For an example, see Crasta 1999.

awake the interest of some toward Swedenborg, including a Spanish priest who accepted Swedenborg's works, attended New Church meetings, and gave money to Le Boys des Guays in order to support his publishing activities. This work, however, was not enough to produce any major Swedenborgian influence in that country: a few books were translated in the early 1910s *(Heaven and Hell, New Jerusalem, True Christianity),* but this was thanks to the efforts of a foreign Swedenborgian settled in Spain and to the support of a foreign Swedenborg printing society.[28]

IV. Turning East

Swedenborg had a stronger impact on some minds in central and eastern European countries than in southern Europe.[29] It is true that there were never such extensive translations into eastern European languages as in some western European tongues. But this lack of translations had a reduced effect because members of the intellectual elites in the eastern countries were accustomed to speak and read one or several western European languages.

a. Russia

Given the strong orientation of Russian nobility and intellectuals toward European culture from the nineteenth century, it is not surprising to find early indications of interest in the intriguing works of Swedenborg. If the memoirs of Swedenborg's friend and follower Carl Robsahm (1735–1794) are accurate (Hallengren 1998a, 79–88), the chaplain to the Russian legation in Stockholm "read Swedenborg's books with the greatest delight" and was moved to tears of joy on hearing from Swedenborg's own lips that the late Empress Elizabeth (1709–1762) was in a very happy state in the spiritual world ([Odhner] 1904b, 269). It is also reported that there was a group of readers in Moscow as early as 1783. Another such group apparently existed in St. Petersburg at the beginning of the nineteenth century (Hallengren 1998a, 73). A few names of eager, but apparently isolated, Russian readers of Swedenborg appear in the early decades of the nineteenth

---

28. Specifically, the Swedenborg Society. See Swedenborg [1758] 1910c (a translation of *New Jerusalem*); [1758] 1911a *(Heaven and Hell);* [1771] 1911b *(True Christianity).*

29. For a general discussion of Swedenborg's influence in Slavic nations, see Čiževskij 1956, 269–290, translated in Čiževskij [1956] 2002, 1–30.

century, and a Russian imperial counselor translated *Divine Love and Wisdom* into Russian; it was published many years later, in 1864, in Germany.[30]

It is an interesting problem in political history to consider the extent to which Swedenborgian ideas may have played a role in the project of the Holy Alliance, devised in 1815 by Emperor Alexander I of Russia (1777–1825) and ratified along with him by Emperor Francis I of Austria (1768–1835) and King Frederick William III of Prussia (1770–1840). Although the Holy Alliance was drawn up by the czar himself, it is widely accepted that he was at that time under the influence of Baroness Krüdener (1764–1824). Krüdener was acquainted with most of the mystical and theosophical figures in southern Germany and Switzerland at that time. Her discussions with Swedenborgians Jung-Stilling and Oberlin had made a lasting impression on her, and she herself read Swedenborg.

But familiarity with Swedenborg does not necessarily entail being a follower of his doctrines; and like many other readers of Swedenborg, Krüdener selected elements of his thinking that appealed to her. The Holy Alliance reflected a set of ideals and aspirations that were in general circulation at that time, and were not exclusive to Swedenborgian doctrine. All the same, Swedenborgians definitely welcomed it, and they were not the only ones to see it as the fulfillment of cherished hopes and expectations. It was, as one of them commented, a matter of great rejoicing "to behold the monarchs of Europe proclaiming their acknowledgement of the principles of the New Jerusalem, now descending from God out of heaven" ("The Holy League" 1817, 58–61). The pillar of the nascent New Church in Britain, Robert Hindmarsh (1759–1835), wrote *Remarks on the Holy League*[31] and in 1816 sent it along with a letter to the three crowned heads who had become parties to the treaty. Only the King of Prussia acknowledged receipt, and Hindmarsh remarked with barely concealed disappointment: "It is probable my feeble efforts to make known the truth to such high and distinguished personages were altogether unavailing, and perhaps deemed unworthy of notice" (Hindmarsh 1861, 252).

But there were Russian minds more ready for Swedenborg's message: probably the most famous was General Alexander Mouravieff (1792–1863). He had discovered in a bookshop in Moscow a copy of Moët's 1821 French

---

30. For full bibliographic data, see Hyde 1906, entry 2092.

31. For the text of the remarks in this pamphlet, "or at least the substance of them," see Hindmarsh 1861, 229–237. For further discussion of Hindmarsh, see pages 255–263 below.

translation of Swedenborg's treatise *Life* (Swedenborg [1763] 1821). It capti-
vated him so completely that he undertook to read all the works available
in Latin or in French. Though Swedenborg's writings could be found in
Russia, it would not have been feasible to publish them there at that
time: the authorities were suspicious of unorthodox teachings, which
were perceived as potentially subversive not only of the traditional faith,
but of civil order as well. A system of censorship was being enforced, and
it was quite unlikely that the printing of books like Swedenborg's would
have been allowed. Yet Mouravieff found an unusual way to spread the
newly discovered doctrines:

> He maintained two amanuenses or secretaries, constantly writing copies
> of the smaller works; and these he presented, as he saw opportunity, to
> his friends. . . . A considerable number of the Russian nobility, as well
> as a large portion of his own family—one of the most distinguished in
> the empire—came by this means to delight in the truths of the New
> Jerusalem. (Bayley 1884, 203)

No wonder travelers from abroad who visited the Russian readers of
Swedenborg a few years after Mouravieff's death observed that "the persons who have received the doctrines of the New Church in Russia are
nearly all in high positions, being nearly all nobles" (Bayley 1867, 36). For
them, Swedenborgianism did not preclude adherence to the religious practices of the established church: even during his final illness, Mouravieff received the Holy Sacrament three times.

Mouravieff belongs to the gallery of heroes of Swedenborgianism,
since he played a role in the emancipation of serfs in Russia, which finally became an accomplished fact in 1861. While it would probably be
inaccurate to claim that Mouravieff's efforts toward the abolition of serfdom were solely due to his reading of Swedenborg—his humanitarian
ideals evidently predated his first acquaintance with Swedenborg's
works—it is nevertheless obvious that those doctrines only reinforced
his aspirations and were his spiritual nourishment for many years. Humanitarian ideals and practical involvement with them are central to
Swedenborg's doctrines.

The first Russian translations of Swedenborg's works, printed in Germany, became available in the 1860s. This development was connected
with the interest in spiritualism in Russia at that time, which paralleled
the spiritualist movements in other countries. The first translation of
Heaven and Hell, however, was made by Alexander Aksakov (1823–1903),

who actually discovered Swedenborg before becoming interested in spiritualism. In addition to his translation of *Heaven and Hell,* he published translations of spiritualist works by European writers, often at his own expense (Carlson 1993, 24).

As in the West, writers and artists in Russia took especial interest in Swedenborg's works. Among those who were influenced by Swedenborg was Feodor Dostoevsky (1821–1881), who owned Aksakov's translations of and commentaries on Swedenborg in his library (Milosz 1988, 160). Swedenborg's influence on Dostoevsky has been analyzed by Nobel prize laureate Czeslaw Milosz, who believes it "more than likely" that Dostoevsky read Swedenborg at the time he was writing *Crime and Punishment* (Milosz 1988, 164). It has also been suggested from time to time that a Swedenborgian influence can be detected in Father Zosima in *The Brothers Karamazov,* but this seems questionable: the Russian tradition and the spiritual context of the nineteenth century supply all that is needed to account for Father Zosima's discourses. Milosz acknowledges that it is not possible to determine with certainty what Dostoevsky may have borrowed from Swedenborg. So once again we confront the irritating problem we have already encountered with respect to Goethe and others: we know that these authors were—to a greater or lesser extent—familiar with Swedenborg; we have good reason to think that Swedenborg's doctrines had an influence on them; but in the absence of an explicit reference, tracing the genealogy of ideas is a difficult venture.

At least when we come to the philosopher Vladimir Soloviev (1853–1900), we can be sure that he conducted an in-depth study of Swedenborg, since he wrote a long article on him in the Russian *Brockhaus-Ephron Encyclopedia,* published in St. Petersburg in 1900. In the very first lines of his article, Soloviev describes Swedenborg as the most remarkable theosopher of the modern age after Jacob Boehme (1575–1624). He considers his work to represent a "unique and original theosophical system."[32]

At the end of his article, Soloviev mentions as an example of a Russian Swedenborgian "the well-known writer, V. I. Dal'" (Soloviev 1900). The erudite Swedish Swedenborg scholar, Anders Hallengren, rediscovered in the archives of the Swedenborg Society in London a manuscript on the Apocalypse by Vladimir I. Dal' (1801–1872): it appears to be derived from Swedenborg's works on the Book of Revelation (Hallengren

---

32. Soloviev 1900, under "Swedenborg." For an English translation of the article, see Solovyov [1900] 2001, 39–73.

1998a, 76–77). Such examples as those of Soloviev and Dal' indicate that there were in Russia thinkers and people of letters who were not satisfied with a superficial knowledge of Swedenborg, but immersed themselves deeply and seriously in his writings, coming to a remarkable understanding of his message.

b. Poland

A nineteenth-century French Swedenborgian reported that General Maciej Rybinski (1784–1874), one of the heroes of the Polish insurrection in 1830–1831, had participated in Swedenborgian meetings in Paris over a period of many years and had even translated some books into Polish (Chevrier 1879, 81). But the publication of Swedenborg's works in that language would only begin in the 1870s, when a Pole who was living in Russia, F. J. Toustanovsky (?–1872), left as a legacy a translation of some of the volumes in Polish, as well as a significant amount of money entrusted to the Swedenborg Society to provide for their publication and for the publication of other books in Polish about Swedenborg and his teachings ("Polnische Ausgabe" 1874, 238). However, little came of that generous legacy. It apparently proved difficult to find competent collaborators fluent in Polish and motivated to make Swedenborg more widely recognized in that language. In later years, there was also simply a lack of demand for books in Polish. Despite the fact that the income had been meant to be used "exclusively" for printing books in Polish, it was finally decided in 1937 that it could be used for other purposes as well, and from 1955 on it helped to finance the Latin edition of *Secrets of Heaven*.

But as early as the beginning of the 1800s the most important Polish Romantic poets were already being influenced by Swedenborg, although they obviously did not read his works in their mother tongue. Juliusz Słowacki (1809–1849) is said to have discovered Swedenborg first as a teenager; although he was not able to understand very much of what he was reading at that young age, in a later poem he described those early experiences with nostalgia. Swedenborg's influence is reported to be most obvious in his last productions, but is traceable in the earlier poems as well: for instance, in *Kordian* (1834), the hero refers to the angelic destiny of human beings and exclaims: "For one angel, two terrestrial souls are needed!"[33]

---

33. My translation from the French version in Słowacki [1834] 1996, 69 (act 1, line 423). Compare, for example, *Marriage Love* 52, where Swedenborg makes the statement that married partners in heaven are not two but one angel.

The greatest Polish poet, Adam Mickiewicz (1789–1855), is reported to have become fascinated by Swedenborg as early as age fifteen, although this cannot be proved with absolute certainty (Borowy 1999, 153). Among members of the secret patriotic student organization "The Philomates," with which he became involved in 1815, it was indeed quite common to find enthusiastic young readers of the works of Swedenborg, of the mystic poet of the Counter-Reformation Angelus Silesius (1624–1677), and of the French visionary philosopher Louis-Claude de Saint-Martin.[34] Mickiewicz "considered Boehme, together with Saint-Martin and Swedenborg, about whom he had, however, some serious reservations, as the three prophets of modern times" (Weintraub 1954, 267). He ranked Boehme at the top, and Swedenborg in second place, since he considered the latter not as deep and clear as the former; he apparently felt uncomfortable with some of Swedenborg's visions (Kallenbach 1926, 228). There seems to be a wide agreement among experts on Mickiewicz that, although the general framework and background of his work is Polish and Catholic, the prologue to the third part of his major work *Dziady* (Forefathers' Eve; 1822–1831), in which angels and evil spirits are competing in order to influence the thoughts of the prisoner, reflects Swedenborgian influences; and the same can be said about scene 2 (titled "Improvisation") in the same act.[35] In any case, at whatever the time at which Mickiewicz first acquired a direct knowledge of Swedenborg, he quoted a passage from Swedenborg during a course he gave in Paris in 1843.

This presence of Swedenborgian concepts in the creative work of the major Polish poets can be seen as one more indication of the popularity of Swedenborg's works across Europe during the Romantic period. After all, Rybinski, Mickiewicz, and Słowacki spent a long part of their lives in exile in Western Europe, longing for the freedom of their country. The influence of Swedenborg in their works shows us, as in a mirror, what was happening in the wider European intellectual world. But the fact that some of them became familiar with Swedenborg at a young age, while still living in Eastern Europe, gives a significant indication of the way in which Swedenborg's views spread across Europe, even to those places where his works had not been translated into local languages. Ironically, some anti-Swedenborgian writings may have contributed to that fame in places where Swedenborg's works were not directly available:

---

34. See Szymanis 1992, 29.

35. The famous literary critic Stanisław Pigoń (1885–1968) devoted an entire article to the question of Swedenborg's influence on the third part of *Dziady;* see Pigoń 1922, 141–162.

Barruel's *Memoirs of Jacobinism* had been translated and published in Polish as early as 1812 by Karol Surowiecki (1750–1824) under the title *Historja Jakobinizmu* (Pigoń 1922, 141–142, 145–146).

c. Bohemia and Other Areas of Central and Eastern Europe

Swedenborg was in Prague twice in 1733, years before the period in which he wrote his theological works. It was not until long after his death that they became available in the local language of what is today a part of the Czech Republic. When Jaroslav I. Janecek (1870–1953) discovered the writings of Swedenborg at the beginning of the twentieth century, no single volume of Swedenborg had yet been published in Czech.[36]

Janecek came to Swedenborg after a long journey as a spiritual seeker that touched on spiritualism, Quakerism, and the French attempt at a restoration of a Gnostic church. He undertook to translate several of Swedenborg's works into Czech, doing for his country the service that Tafel, Moët and Le Boys des Guays, and Scocia had done for theirs, although he had to pass over the larger works, including *Secrets of Heaven* and *Revelation Unveiled*.[37] The first Swedenborgian church service was held in Prague in 1909; and a periodical, *Novy Jeruzalém* (New Jerusalem), was launched in 1911; it continued until 1939.

There were also occasional Swedenborgian activities in other central and south-eastern European countries. With the support of the Swedenborg Society, some books were published in Hungarian as well as in Serbo-Croatian. Toward the end of the Communist regimes in the late twentieth century, and since their collapse, some titles were republished in those languages as well as in Polish and in Russian.[38] However,

---

36. Information in this section is based partly on an English translation of Janecek's memoirs (Janecek 1949–1950).

37. For a few examples of Janecek's published translations, see Wainscot 1967, entries 999/4 *(Other Planets)*, 1159/3 (extracts from *Heaven and Hell*), 1209/3 *(Last Judgment)*, 1304/2 *(New Jerusalem)*, 1355/2 *(White Horse)*, 1932/9 *(Life)*, 1987/1 and 1987/1a *(Faith)*.

38. Full bibliographic details of these works are extremely difficult to obtain. However, the following translations can be noted as examples: *Divine Love and Wisdom* and *Divine Providence* (1986), in a Hungarian translation; *Heaven and Hell* (1989), in a Serbo-Croat translation by Risto Rundo; *Heaven and Hell* (1992), in a revision of an 1880 Polish translation (see Hyde 1906, entry 1130); *Heaven and Hell* (1993), in a reprint of an 1863 Russian translation by A. N. Aksakov (see Hyde 1906, entries 1131 and 3452); *Divine Love and Wisdom, Divine Providence,* and *Marriage Love* (during the 1990s), in Russian translations by V. A. Maliavin. Several works have been available in Latvian since at least the 1920s, most of them translated by one R. Grava (for example, Swedenborg 1921, a translation of *Heaven and Hell*); there is new translation activity ongoing in Latvia as of this writing.

as of this writing, none of those countries has access to a complete translation of Swedenborg's theological writings in its local language.

V. A General Evaluation

While the existence of Swedenborgian church societies is not in itself a sufficient indicator of the extent of Swedenborg's influence on the Continent, it does, however, provide leads regarding the penetration of his writings into that region. Shortly before World War II, there were organized worship groups in Austria, Czechoslovakia, Denmark, France, Germany, Italy, Latvia, the Netherlands, Sweden, and Switzerland, not to mention the United Kingdom, plus other active groups at a smaller scale or interested individuals in about ten other European countries. The war led to the cessation of activities in several countries for many years. In any case, most of the smaller groups organized for worship or other activities would not have been able to continue without support from the English-speaking world. In addition, even in a country like Switzerland, where there were small but well-organized and stable groups, with their own church buildings, persevering efforts to give Swedenborgian teachings a higher profile did not result in the growth of the groups; or if so, the growth was only temporary (Mayer 1984).

One could conclude that organized Swedenborgianism has never taken off in continental Europe. But this is probably not the right way to state the matter. The perspectives opened by the writings of Swedenborg are not necessarily conducive to the creation of organized congregations, at least in the continental European context. One can be a deeply convinced Swedenborgian without feeling inwardly compelled to become a member of a Swedenborgian group. In its essence, Swedenborgianism is not a sect, even if some of its segments have adopted sectlike organizational features. Sociologist Ernst Troeltsch (1865–1923) distinguished among three ideal-types of religious behavior: churchly, sectarian, and mystical. The churchly type has all-embracing claims; it requires a dominant, mainstream institution. The sectarian type requires a group of voluntary believers, the gathering of the elect, all fully involved in the life of the group, in which a high degree of conformity to its ideals and lifestyles is the norm. The mystical type of religious behavior forms a sharp contrast to the other two types: in this case, it does not matter so much if one belongs to a movement or not; much more than external actions or group structures, what matters is the inner state of the believer, which means that the adherent of mysticism is not inclined to build an organization; or if so, the mystic may then adopt some features of sectarian behavior. "Emphasis is placed on ideas and not on worship."[39] Individualism is a keyword of the mystical type. Beyond any doubt, Swedenborg's message and Swedenborgianism itself exhibit features associated with the mystical type of religious groups.[40] When those dynamics are better understood, the limited success of organized Swedenborgianism in terms of statistics no longer seems so strange and certainly cannot be taken as an adequate measure of Swedenborg's influence.

VI. The "Silent Missionaries"

However, it is not possible to describe Swedenborg's impact properly without giving adequate coverage to the efforts of Swedenborgian groups to focus attention on Swedenborg. On June 5, 1886, the London *Times* made the following comment regarding the then latest catalog of the British Museum: "It will probably astonish most people to learn that the most energetic and active propagandists of modern religious sects are the Swedenborgians. The catalog shows that there are four times more publications devoted to Swedenborg than to any other forms of belief."[41] A book published at the time of the World's Parliament of Religions in Chicago in 1893 (in which American Swedenborgians played a key organizational role) includes—after a description of the state of the organized New Church on each continent—a chapter titled "The Silent Missionaries":

> Silent to the ear, yet appealing to the thought by means of printed characters, the literature of the New Church has won, and will increasingly win, triumphs of the most worthy kind. (Mercer 1894, 201)

For Swedenborgians, following the pattern of Troeltsch's mystical type of religious groups, spreading ideas is what really counts. And books have

39. The quotation is from Hamilton 1995, 195. In this discussion I have also built on Séguy 1980, 100–141, a text that supplies further details on Troeltsch's distinction between these three types of religious associations.

40. Swedenborgians have often disliked the description of Swedenborg as a mystic, and many of them would probably not describe themselves as "mystical." In order to avoid any misunderstanding, it should be emphasized here that "mystical" is used in the sociological sense, which is not the same as the popular sense of the word.

41. Quoted in Griffith 1960, 30.

always been the best channels for fulfilling this mission. In September 1856, when Le Boys des Guays and his wife visited fellow readers of Swedenborg in Neuchâtel, Switzerland, they had the opportunity to meet the curator of the public library, who, when offered a complete set of Swedenborg's works in French (in fifty-two volumes), accepted them gratefully. Le Boys des Guays repeated this offer in Geneva. His success there as well encouraged him to send a letter to the main libraries in France and abroad, which brought him eighty-four positive replies and made Swedenborg's writings available in most French (as well as French-speaking Swiss and Belgian) cities of any importance (Le Boys des Guays 1865, 332–338). These very volumes can still be found today in many of them.

If the publication of Swedenborg's works had been undertaken only by commercial publishers, it is highly unlikely that complete translations of his theological writings would be available today in any language of continental Europe. It is striking to see that a considerable number of publications in various European languages were to a large extent paid for by English-speaking Swedenborgians, beginning with the Swedenborg Society. It may well have been one of the wisest investments possible: books are not only silent missionaries, but long-lasting ones too. In the twenty-first century people will read Swedenborg with delight thanks to the nineteenth-century efforts to make those works available. Only in the English-speaking world is it possible at this point to prepare entirely new and modernized translations. It cannot be ruled out, however, that the perspectives opened by new technologies will make translations available even in languages for which there is relatively little numerical demand—provided the like of a Tafel or a Le Boys des Guays appears in the Cyber Age.

Selected Examples of Swedenborg's Influence in Great Britain and the United States

ROBERT H. KIRVEN AND DAVID B. ELLER

Outline

I. Early Reactions
  a. Prominent Attacks
  b. The English Romantics

II. The Antislavery Movement

III. Transcendentalism and Beyond
  a. From Reed to Whitman
  b. The James Family

IV. Approaching the Mainstream

V. Spiritualism

VI. Utopian Socialism

VII. Homeopathy

VIII. New Thought

IX. Vegetarianism

X. Conclusion

THERE can be little doubt that the theological works of Emanuel Swedenborg (1688–1772) have had a significant impact on cultural and social life in the English-speaking world. Exact measurement of this influence, however, is an impossible task. Ideas evolve from person to person, from generation to generation. Moreover, subtle shifts have taken place over time in the values and ideas that shape the intellectual foundations of Western society. In this post-postmodern era, interest in formal theological ideas has obviously lost ground. Yet the fact remains that over time Swedenborg's works have been widely studied and discussed in religious, philosophical, and scientific circles in Great Britain and the United States, and the evident vitality and power of Swedenborgian ideas have enriched intellectual life in those countries. This essay will offer instances of the influence of Swedenborg's ideas on literary and social history, with an emphasis on movements for social reform.[1] Some of the individuals discussed here were devoted Swedenborgians who forged social theories from Swedenborg's philosophy, while others were casual readers who selectively adapted his concepts to their work.

I. Early Reactions

The detectable spread of Swedenborg's influence began immediately upon the publication of his Latin first editions. In Britain particularly, his impact gathered force rapidly, as some of his works were available to readers of English even during his lifetime; and within twenty years of his death in 1772, all of the major and many of the lesser theological works had been translated into English. Some were translated by Thomas Hartley (1708–1784), a nonresident Anglican pastor of Winwick, who was personally acquainted with Swedenborg; most of the remainder were translated by John Clowes (1743–1831), an Anglican pastor in Manchester. The first publishing house devoted to printing works by Swedenborg, the Manchester Printing Society, was formed in 1782, a mere decade after his death. In the United States, Francis Bailey (1744–1817) began printing Swedenborg's 1771 work *True Christianity*[2] as early as 1789 (Eller 1999, 3–4).

These early readers did not limit their reaction to Swedenborg's works to translating and publishing; many became involved in the formation of a Swedenborgian congregation or body of congregations. The foremost example here is certainly Robert Hindmarsh (1759–1835), son of

---

1. Swedenborg's impact on the fine arts, music, architecture—to say nothing of his broader impact in countries besides Britain and the United States—is beyond the scope of this essay; thus it should be read in conjunction with the treatment of other aspects of his influence, and of influence in other nations, to be found in the other essays in this volume. Furthermore, readers should note two studies on Swedenborg's influence that were produced as part of the tricentennial of his year of birth: Brock and others 1988; and Larsen and others 1988. Also significant for the early nineteenth century is Silver 1983.

2. Bailey published this text under its traditional title, *True Christian Religion*. See Swedenborg [1771] 1789–1792.

a Wesleyan preacher and teacher, who was a leader in starting a church organization based on Swedenborgian principles.[3]

a. Prominent Attacks

Some readers, of course, were influenced only in the negative. There is no way of knowing how many of these reacted by simply ignoring Swedenborg, but at least four prominent figures attacked him in print.

Joseph Priestley (1733–1804), the English clergyman and chemist best known for his 1774 discovery of "dephlogisticated air," or oxygen, published a booklet titled *Letters to the Members of the New Jerusalem Church, Formed by Baron Swedenborg*,[4] in Birmingham in 1791. Priestley had heard at least one Swedenborgian sermon and had met with a few leading Swedenborgian clergy members, and it appears he had read some of the literature they gave him. His attacks provoked the publication of at least three retorting pamphlets (Kirven 1965, 141–149). A Unitarian who sympathized with separatist movements (that is, groups separating from the Church of England), Priestley praised the "eminent good sense, and good conduct" of Swedenborgians he had met, comparing them to the founders of Christianity itself (Priestley [1791] 1989, iii, xiii). But he also questioned Swedenborg's testimony about his spiritual experiences, calling them "very much like inventions, and fictions"—and thus challenging Swedenborg's entire theological outlook (Priestley [1791] 1989, 60).

Without the same preliminary bow to Swedenborg's followers, a certain minister, G. Beaumont,[5] published *The Anti-Swedenborg* in London in 1824, declaring the Swede to be "a learned man . . . [of good] moral character, . . . piety and sincerity," but questioning his sanity (Beaumont 1824, 6). Quoting Swedenborg's *Heaven and Hell* 249,[6] he

---

3. For details concerning these individuals and the founding of the Swedenborgian church in England, see Kirven 1965, 109–157, and the essay on organizational Swedenborgianism in this volume. Although dated, an indispensable starting point for studying the spread of Swedenborgianism in England is Hindmarsh 1861.

4. Priestley [1791] 1989. Two points are worth noting in regard to this title. First, Swedenborg was not a baron in the medieval sense, though some British writers, followers of Swedenborg as well as opponents, prefixed this title to his name as an indicator of his noble status in Sweden. (The third tier of nobility in England, that of barons, parallels the third tier in Sweden, which is without title.) Second, Swedenborg did not found a church.

5. Biographical data on Beaumont was not available to the authors.

6. It is customary to refer to passages in Swedenborg's works by section numbers rather than page numbers, as the former are uniform in all editions.

ignored Swedenborg's distinctions there between his own life and "en-thusiasm and delusion," claiming that the passage indicted Swedenborg for the same errors Swedenborg himself described.[7]

In addition, two British literati well known at the time, Robert Southey (1774–1843) and Thomas De Quincey (1785–1859), publicly and specifically attacked Swedenborg. In his *Letters from England: by Don Manuel Alvarez Espriella,* Southey described Swedenborg and Swedenborgian theology in unflattering terms, calling the former a madman and the latter a mythology (Southey [1807] 1951, 387, 381). But these comments are not as hostile as they appear out of context. *Letters from England* rests on a complex premise: it purports to be a translation of actual letters written by a Spanish Catholic, who would be expected by Southey's English readers to condemn anything but Catholic beliefs. The persona of Espriella allows Southey to present a clever exposé not only of English but of Spanish foibles, and he makes several other religious groups, including the Church of England, the object of his wit as well. In fact, one reviewer complained that the writer—obviously an Englishman—was "unfortunately too much addicted" to "attempts at wit,"[8] and Southey's gibes should be read with that criticism in mind: in the hopes that the book would earn him some cash much-needed at the time, he strove with transparently conscious purpose to make it as titillating as possible. He had, however, studied Swedenborg's works (Simmons 1951, xx note 25), probably relying on the rather rugged literal translations available at the time,[9] and his description of the theology shows his research was thorough, if skeptical. He also dispatched his brother to visit a Swedenborgian chapel and report to him on what he found.[10] The staunchly Catholic Espriella thus reports in turn that

---

7. Beaumont 1824, 8–9. Beaumont is here using "enthusiasm" in the sense of a mistaken belief that one has been personally and directly enlightened by God.

8. Review of *Letters from England* 1808, 370–390, cited in Simmons 1951, xxiii.

9. Espriella repeats Swedenborg's report (in *Heaven and Hell* 258) that in heaven "they have books both written and printed," adding that though Swedenborg was able to read them, he "could seldom, he says, pick out any meaning; from which I concluded that he has successfully copied their style" (Southey [1807] 1951, 387).

10. Simmons 1951, xx. The editor of *Letters from England* concludes that the focus on anatomical features in Swedenborg's theology, as reported by Southey, indicates the influence of Southey's brother, a medical doctor (Southey [1807] 1951, 383 note 5). It is not clear whether the editor is aware of the prominence of these features in Swedenborg's works themselves.

the chapel is "singularly handsome," the congregation "respectable," the service "decorous," and even the singing "remarkably good"; but concludes that he has "never in any other heretical meeting heard heresy so loudly insisted upon" (Southey [1807] 1951, 380).

For his part, De Quincey translated for publication in a popular magazine (De Quincey 1824, 489–492) the most anti-Swedenborgian excerpts of the influential diatribe *Träume eines Geistersehers* (Dreams of a Spirit-Seer, 1766) by the German philosopher Immanuel Kant (1724–1804). Kant had written his pamphlet with carefully crafted ambiguity and humor so that he could dissociate himself from similarities he suspected readers might notice between Swedenborg's system and his own.[11] Out of this ambiguous context, the attack took on particular vehemence.

In addition, De Quincey wrote a piece thirteen years later for *Tait's Magazine* in which he spoke dismissively of the Swedenborgian minister and translator John Clowes. Clowes, rector of St. John's parish in Manchester, was a friend whose scholarship he admired—except for the fact that Clowes translated and espoused Swedenborg. He disapproved of Clowe's conversion in terms that were almost paradigmatic among those who had read Swedenborg under the influence of Kant:

> Already, on the bare mention of that word [Swedenborgianism], a presumption arises against any man, that, writing much (or writing at all) for a body of doctrines so apparently crazy as those of Mr Swedenborg, a man must have bid adieu to all good sense and manliness of mind. Indeed, this is so much of a settled case, that even to have written *against* Mr Swedenborg would be generally viewed as a suspicious act, requiring explanation, and not very easily admitting of it.[12]

b. The English Romantics

By contrast, two great British poets—William Blake (1757–1827) and Samuel Taylor Coleridge (1772–1834)—were influenced affirmatively and

---

11. On Kant's book, see Kirven 1965, 57, 108; Kirven 1988, 103–120; and especially Kant [1766] 2002, a translation with notes.

12. De Quincey 1837, 65. For more details on these authors and their attacks, see Kirven 1965, 141–149, on Priestley; 196–198, on Beaumont; and 204–206, on Southey and De Quincey. On De Quincey specifically, see Sugden 1910, 70–82.

significantly by Swedenborg's theology. When the first General Conference of Swedenborgians from throughout England was convened in
1789, the signatures of "W[illiam] Blake" and his wife "C[atherine] Blake"
(1762?–1831) appeared below the following statement:

> We whose Names are hereunto subscribed, do each of us approve of
> the Theological Writings of Emanuel Swedenborg, believing that the
> Doctrines contained therein are genuine Truths, revealed from
> Heaven, and that the New Jerusalem Church ought to be established,
> distinct and separate from the Old Church. ("Minute Book" 1885, xx)

This endorsement, however, did not represent Blake's final opinion of
Swedenborg and his teachings: the name of neither William Blake nor
his wife appears in any further records of the British Conference of the
New Church[13] or its societies, and his work issued in the following year,
The Marriage of Heaven and Hell, generally opposed the establishment
of any church at all. Here Blake claimed that "Swedenborg has not written one new truth: . . . he has written all the old falsehoods" (Blake
[1825–1827] 1927, 3).

Blake's detailed acquaintance with Swedenborgian theology is documented by his marginal notes in two of Swedenborg's works, *Divine Love
and Wisdom* and *Divine Providence* (Blake 1907, 109–115; Blake 1966,
viii). References to Swedenborgian ideas, both explicit and implicit, may
suggest that Blake was familiar with more of Swedenborg's thought than
he could have found in those two books, but it is not clear how much he
knew about Swedenborg, whether from reading in Swedenborg's works
or attending New Church meetings. It also seems evident that his *Marriage of Heaven and Hell* did not represent Blake's ultimate opinion of
Swedenborg. Scholars such as J. G. Davies, Jacques Roos, Helen C.
White, Kathleen Raine, Raymond Deck, and others have highlighted
Swedenborg's influence on Blake's thought.[14] If indeed Blake did reject
Swedenborg as a theologian, he appears to have retained an ontology and
epistemology very similar to Swedenborg's, regarding him—borrowing a
biblical image—as a Sampson, someone with unusual power who had
been shorn of his strength by the institutional church.

Samuel Taylor Coleridge wrote little if anything publicly about
Swedenborg. However, he carefully annotated the margins of eight of

---

13. On the use of the term *New Church* to designate Swedenborgian religious organizations, see
page 248 below, along with page 246 note 2.

14. See Davies 1966, 32–33; Roos 1951, 22, 58; White 1964, 31; Raine 1979; and Deck 1978.

the theological works, and he appears to have incorporated many Swedenborgian ideas into his personal worldview. Certainly some of his verse reflects a familiarity with Swedenborg's description of "correspondences," which in a poetic sense may be understood as spiritual truths shining through to the material world.[15]

In the mid-nineteenth century, Robert Browning (1812–1889) and Elizabeth Barrett Browning (1806–1861) stand as prominent examples of English writers utilizing Swedenborgian concepts and imagery. Neither of them made any known public profession of their Swedenborgianism, probably because in post-Kantian Britain writers depending on public support for their livelihood were unlikely to make such statements. Gail Kienitz, however, has detailed the Swedenborgian influences in much of Robert Browning's highly popular theological writing and lecturing (Kienitz 1991). From the early 1840s, Barrett Browning was an ardent reader of Swedenborg (Garrett 2000, 98 note 4). Kienitz cites this explicit admission from one of Barrett Browning's letters:

> Let us examine the charges against me. *1st the tendency of my poetry,* (and of Robert's!!!) is to Swedenborgianism. Well—I have heard that before, & always consider it an immense compliment to my poetry. There's great truth in Swedenborg.[16]

The optimism of Robert Browning's poetry—tenaciously maintained, though not without its nuances—may be traceable in part to such influence. As for Barrett Browning, her Swedenborgianism led her to use her poetic voice to attack numerous social ills—for example, the slavery still flourishing in the United States at the time, child labor, and political oppression in Italy.[17] In one poem the voice of an angel strikingly like those who conversed with Swedenborg tells her:

> Some women weep and curse, I say
> (And no one marvels), night and day.

---

15. See Edmisten 1954. Edmisten's dissertation includes a transcript of Coleridge's notes, providing detailed documentation of the poet's understanding of Swedenborg. For more on the concept of correspondences, see pages 66 and 341–342 in this volume.

16. Kienitz 1991, 15, quoting a letter of January 10, 1854, in Browning and Browning 1958, 207.

17. For her comment on slavery, see "Runaway Slave at Pilgrim's Point" (Browning 1900, 192–195) and "A Curse for a Nation" (423–424); for her comment on child labor, see "The Cry of the Children" (156); for her political interests, see *Casa Guidi Windows* (224–253). On the connection between Barrett Browning's religious thought and her role as a social reformer, see Lewis 1998.

And thou shalt take their part to-night,
  Weep and write.
    (Browning 1900, 423)

To write, under angelic injunction, against the ills committed by human against human, even though she wept as she did so, was in large part what Barrett Browning saw as her task on earth.

II. The Antislavery Movement

One of the earliest demonstrable influences of Swedenborg in the American colonies and later in the early decades of the nineteenth century was part of the larger antislavery movement, a reform effort that gained religious motivation and theoretical support from Swedenborg's theology. Earlier, in Sweden, philanthropist Carl Bernhard Wadström (1746–1799) had noticed Swedenborg's favorable references to spirits who had lived in Africa, and Wadström found in those references a radical challenge to the widespread practice of enslaving Africans.[18] With the assistance of British Swedenborgians and others, he organized a colony intended for freed Africans on the coast of Sierra Leone. The colony failed, and most of the settlers were killed when it was attacked by French privateers in 1795 (Block 1984, 54–55).

Even after this setback, British Swedenborgians continued to be active in antislavery activities. One example of this commitment is Thomas Goyder (1786–1849), a prominent minister of the New Church, who in 1833 delivered a stirring antislavery sermon to his parish at Waterloo Road in London. Later the sermon was issued in pamphlet form as *Christianity and Colonial Slavery Contrasted* (Goyder 1833). In the sermon, he argued that chattel slavery and Swedenborg's teaching were totally incompatible, and he concluded by asking his parishioners to sign a petition to Parliament asking for the immediate end to slavery within the British Empire.[19]

---

18. For representative statements concerning Africans in Swedenborg's theological works, see *Spiritual Experiences* [= Swedenborg 1889] §4777, *Secrets of Heaven* 2604, *Heaven and Hell* 326, *Last Judgment* 118, *Supplements* 75–77, and *True Christianity* 837–839.

19. One hundred and ninety-two people signed the petition. For an appraisal of Goyder's antislavery influence on American Swedenborgians, see Hawley 1936, 187–190. A biographical sketch of Goyder may be found in his obituary, [R. A.] 1849, 474–476. Although the British outlawed the slave trade in 1807, slavery itself remained legal in British colonial possessions until it was phased out between 1834 and 1838.

In America, the Swedenborgian perspective entered the antislavery debate through a work by Lydia Maria Francis Child (1802–1880), *An Appeal in Favor of That Class of Americans Called Africans* (1833). First acquainted with Swedenborg's works when she was an eighteen-year-old schoolteacher in Gardiner, Maine, Child enlarged her knowledge of Swedenborg over the next decade, joining a Swedenborgian congregation in Boston shortly after her marriage in 1828. Although her earlier writing had been about home and family issues, her *Appeal* placed her in the ranks of the abolitionists, and its publication created a furor in Boston literary circles.[20]

Like Wadström and Goyder, Child based at least part of her opposition to the South's "peculiar institution" on ideas she found in Swedenborg's theology. The two most prominent of these were the uniquely spiritual nature and moral inclination Swedenborg ascribed to souls in the spiritual world who had lived in Africa, and his repeated assertions that Africans were more receptive of heavenly doctrine than others on this earth.[21] At least by implication, Africans were thus important to humanity's hopes for spiritual rebirth. Although Swedenborg said little about slavery as such, he regarded a desire to control or dominate another human being as the most grievous of sins.[22] Child believed that this attitude was not only applicable to but decisive on the slavery question, yet she found herself at odds on this point with her friends in the Swedenborgian church (at least in Boston) and separated herself from the congregation (Karcher 1994, 200; Kellow 1991).

Robert Carter (1728–1804) of Virginia, and later of Baltimore, was one of a group of wealthy colonial landowners who became readers of Swedenborg. "Councillor" Carter, as he was called in his day, was a

---

20. The *Appeal* argued against African colonization for freed slaves and was critical of racial segregation. A recent and balanced biography of Child is Karcher 1994; see especially pages 183–192. A recent dissertation argues that Child's reading of Swedenborg influenced her writings throughout her long career, even after she officially left the Boston congregation in 1828; see Anders 2002. The most thorough discussion of Swedenborgians in the American antislavery movement can be found in Swank 1970, 323–350.

21. See the passages cited in note 18 above.

22. See, for example, *True Christianity* 405:2–3. A representative passage on the evil of domination (*Secrets of Heaven* 1749:3) reads as follows: "The power exerted by evil and falsity is entirely contrary to the power exerted by goodness and truth. The power exerted by evil and falsity is the desire to enslave everyone; the power exerted by goodness and truth is the desire to free everyone." (Lisa Hyatt Cooper translated this and all other passages from *Secrets of Heaven* in this essay.)

member of the Baltimore Abolition Society and probably the first American reader of Swedenborg to implement those theological principles in the specific act of emancipating slaves.[23]

The arguments from Swedenborg that appealed to Child, and to her readers among the Boston and New York intelligentsia, were theoretical, even metaphysical. Carter, however, was a slaveowner whose slaves accounted for much of his wealth. Typical of the gentry of his time, he had inherited from his grandfather (Robert "King" Carter [1663–1732]) a town house in Richmond, a plantation of sixty thousand acres called Nomini Hall (with a library reputed to hold over 1,450 volumes of French and English classics), and six hundred slaves. As befit a gentleman of his position and interests, he journeyed to England to have his portrait painted by Sir Joshua Reynolds (1723–1792). Yet he appears to have been a religious seeker. He had grown up—and lived to the age of forty-nine—persuaded by the Deism that was popular among such leading Virginia gentry as Thomas Jefferson (1743–1826). During a period of religious awakening in 1778, he had been converted by a Baptist preacher, and thirteen years later embraced Swedenborg's theology.

In 1790 Carter borrowed and read one of Swedenborg's smaller works, *A Treatise on Influx* (now known as *Soul-Body Interaction*), wrote soon thereafter to Philadelphia to order his own copy of *True Christianity,* and began a correspondence with Swedenborgians there. The following year, he emancipated the 455 slaves he owned at that time—some immediately and some on a schedule as they reached certain ages. That action, however laudable from an ethical or theological viewpoint, also forced him to divest himself of several plantations and a good deal of livestock. Having depleted his resources, Carter found that he had "neither the Funds nor the strength of Body" for the program of Swedenborgian publication and "propagation" that he had planned to conduct in Virginia's Westmoreland County.[24] A parallel for Carter's story can be seen in that of a fellow Swedenborgian Virginian, Thomas Fairfax II (about 1765–about 1849), who also emancipated his slaves after training

---

23. On Carter, see Block 1984, 83–86, and Levy 2002, 188–212. For a biography, see Morton 1969.

24. See [Hinckley] 1892, 250, and Odhner 1904a, 152. The quotation is from Carter's letter of April 6, 1801, to John Hargrove in the Robert Carter Collection. It should be noted that Carter's biographer, Louis Morton, concludes that he sold his estate and freed his slaves for economic rather than religious reasons (Morton 1969, 260 and following).

them in trades by which they could support themselves.[25] It may be an exaggeration to suggest that these men died without financial means. However, manumission of their slaves did amount to a voluntary divestiture of a large part of their personal wealth and the adoption of an extremely different style and manner of living than that which they had known before and which the neighboring gentry continued to enjoy.

Another parallel can be seen in the case of James Glen (1750?–1814),[26] an early member of the group that was to become the first Swedenborgian congregation in the world (Great East Cheap, London, 1787). As a wealthy plantation owner from Demerara (a Dutch colony later to become part of British Guiana, the present Guyana), Glen set sail from Britain in 1784 to introduce Swedenborg's teachings to the Americas. He delivered a series of lectures on Swedenborg in Philadelphia, New York, and Boston, but without apparent results. In his later years, Glen retired to Guyana, where his missionary zeal led to the establishment of a Swedenborgian congregation. But Glen, too, was a slaveowner in the British colony; and the same Swedenborgian principles that had goaded Carter and Fairfax afflicted his conscience as well. Eventually he too freed his slaves, and—at least partly as a result—died too poor to provide himself with adequate food and shelter toward the end of his life.[27]

Within the New Church in the nineteenth century, however, efforts to end slavery were controversial, as has already been indicated in the case of Lydia Maria Child. From the early days of the Republic, a precedent had developed against the New Church's becoming involved in political matters, although individual members were free to act on their convictions. With regard to the antislavery movement, the key question eventually was framed in these terms: Was slavery a *sin* (which must be

---

25. Fairfax, who resided near Mt. Vernon, should not be confused with an older relative, Thomas Fairfax (about 1690–about 1781), sixth baron of Cameron (England), who migrated to Virginia in 1746. This previous Thomas Fairfax was also a reader of Swedenborg, perhaps the first such reader in America; see Silver 1920, 291. See Block 1984, 433 note 33, for Lord Fairfax's role in introducing George Washington (1732–1799) to Swedenborg's works. However, the account in Block 1984, 83, should be consulted with caution, as her description of the Fairfax lineage is in error.

26. Glen's story is told in Hindmarsh 1861, 10–17, 28.

27. In a lengthy letter printed under the title "On the Negro Character," Glen later questioned his previous optimism about the possibility of converting African slaves to Christianity as well as granting them freedom without careful preparation (Glen 1813, 338–341). For more on Glen, see "Obituary [for James Glen]" 1815, 445–446.

stopped immediately) or an *evil* (which might be eliminated more gradually)? One of those taking the latter view was Richard de Charms (1796–
1864), pastor of New Church societies in Cincinnati and Philadelphia. In
1850 he issued *Discourse on the True Nature of Slavery and Freedom,* which
found widespread distribution both inside and outside of the New
Church.[28] De Charms argued that slavery was a hereditary evil but not
heinously sinful. It could be eradicated only over time, with great prudence, care, and patience.

III. Transcendentalism and Beyond

Like Lydia Maria Child, many involved in New England antislavery efforts
were also part of the Transcendentalist movement, an American intellectual
reform effort that viewed the world through a mystical lens and also subordinated fact to feeling. Although not a Transcendentalist himself, Sampson
Reed (1800–1880) was the Swedenborgian link to this body of ideas.

a. From Reed to Whitman

It was not uncommon for college students in the nineteenth century to
see themselves as on the way to distinction and also as studying in the
company of greatness soon to be recognized. In Reed's case, such a self-
image had some objective validity. He was a leading student at Harvard
Divinity School, and his friends—ministry student Ralph Waldo Emerson
(1803–1882), and law student Theophilus Parsons (1797–1882)—would
indeed later be seen as "great." The somewhat aggressive brilliance of his
roommate, Thomas Worcester (1795–1878), would change the world in a
more limited way—but would change Reed's life dramatically. In 1815
Worcester found several volumes of Emanuel Swedenborg's theological
works in a kind of purgatorial storage room of the divinity school (to
which they had been consigned by some unknown librarian) and gathered a circle of students to explore them. The members of this group, including Reed and Parsons, became convinced and committed disciples of
what they called the "Heavenly Doctrines," or, in the phrase used at the
time, they became "receivers of the heavenly doctrines," accepting the

---

28. See de Charms 1850a. This pamphlet of forty pages was based on a sermon de Charms had
given in Washington, D.C. It was reprinted the following year as *Some Views of Freedom and Slavery in the Light of the New Jerusalem* (de Charms 1851).

revelatory nature of Swedenborg's writings. Most became members of New Church religious societies.[29]

Parsons remained a supporter while independently forging his eminent career in law and teaching at Harvard's School of Law. Worcester soon became the founding, and controversial, pastor of the first Swedenborgian church in Boston in 1818. Reed went on to graduate, receiving his divinity school baccalaureate degree in 1821. However, he found himself barred from clerical employment with the Unitarians because of his Swedenborgian convictions and unable to secure employment with the New Church because its numbers were too small at that time to support any minister besides Worcester. Thus Reed settled for an apprenticeship with a Boston pharmacist and a career as a druggist.

Reed's friend Emerson, who was in the audience at Reed's baccalaureate address, was so impressed by the speech, and by a subsequent book of Reed's,[30] that he became a supporter of Swedenborgianism (although never a member of any New Church organization) and thus a prominent part of the channel by which Swedenborgian ideas flowed into Transcendentalism.[31] After publicly repudiating the Transcendentalists (including Emerson) in 1838 for their counter-Swedenborgian tendency to reduce spiritual phenomena to an aspect of material experience, Reed himself remained active as a writer only in Swedenborgian publications.

Reed's major contribution to American literature, his slender 1826 volume, *Observations on the Growth of the Mind,* can be described as a study on aesthetics (Shaw 1992, vii). It can also be called a survey of the human condition (in potential, but not yet full realization) in the dawning historical epoch that Swedenborg calls the "new church"—although Reed avoids Swedenborgian terminology as studiously as he avoids the adjective "Swedenborgian." Without naming Swedenborg, Reed refers to his theology in impersonal terms, such as any romantic might use to avoid appearing arrogant about self-generated ideas; for example:

> There is a philosophy of mind, founded not on the aspect it presents in
> any part or in any period of the world, but on its immutable relations

---

29. For documentation on Worcester, Parsons, and Reed, see Block 1984, 102–104, 106; and Shaw 1992, ii–xii. Reed's *Biography of Thomas Worcester* (Reed 1880) is a New Church classic.

30. *Observations on the Growth of the Mind,* originally published in Boston in 1826 and reprinted in Reed 1992, 17–49. See the discussion below.

31. Transcendentalism was also influenced by British Swedenborgians. See Cameron 1984.

to its first cause; a philosophy equally applicable to man, before or after he has passed the valley of the shadow of death; not dependent on time or place, but immortal as its subject. (Reed 1992, 19)

Using memory, time, and the natural sciences for illustration, and frequently alluding to the dawning of a new age, he writes: "The light of this new philosophy has begun to beam faintly on the world" (Reed 1992, 19). And again, "The world is beginning to be changed from what it was" (42). Throughout *Observations on the Growth of the Mind,* Reed summarizes the Swedenborgian worldview, paying particular attention to Swedenborg's concept of the correspondence between spiritual and physical reality. "There is a language, not of words, but of things," he writes (33), asserting that "fiction in poetry must fall with theory in science, for they depend equally on the words of creation" (32). Reed follows the growth of an individual mind through the stages of life to explain, in effect, why the new revelation is so slowly being recognized and acknowledged (46–49).

Emerson's opinion of Reed's *Growth of the Mind* was straightforward: "Can anything be more greatly, more wisely writ? . . . Has any looked so shrewdly into the subtle and concealed connection of man and nature, of earth and heaven?"[32] This favorable opinion was seconded by his use of Reed's ideas—especially in his 1844 essay "The Poet," which in turn had such a striking resonance in the poetry of Walt Whitman (1819–1892).[33]

Whitman was a great admirer of Ralph Waldo Emerson, and Emerson in turn was perhaps the first notable figure to express admiration for Whitman in the public press. Literary historian Anders Hallengren describes how, just before the publication of *Leaves of Grass,* an encouraging message arrived from Concord. Emerson saluted Whitman's collection of poems as "the most extraordinary piece of wit and wisdom that an American has yet contributed" and greeted the young writer "at the beginning of a great career." Whitman quoted that letter in the second edition (1856) where he also paid tribute to Emerson, his "Master."[34] Hallengren also notes that both Emerson and Whitman translated Swedenborg's teachings about correspondences, the relationship between spiritual and

---

32. This passage, from Emerson's letter to his aunt Mary Moody Emerson (1774–1863), is quoted in Shaw 1992, viii–ix, from Hotson 1929a, 130–131.

33. For the essay "The Poet," see Emerson 1959–1972, 347–365; and for interpretation, Shaw 1992, ix. For more on the relationship between Emerson and Reed, see Hotson 1929b, 249–277; and Hallengren 1994a, throughout.

34. Hallengren 1991, 3–4. A later version of the essay quoted here appears in Hallengren 1998a, 89–104.

physical reality, into their notion of "hieroglyphics," and he highlights Emerson's foreshadowing of Whitman's title: "All things are symbols. We say of man that he is grass."[35]

Emerson offered Swedenborg-influenced content, and Whitman picked it up, particularly from the essays Emerson developed from his lectures, and especially from *Nature, Addresses, and Lectures* (Emerson [1849] 1884) and "Swedenborg, or the Mystic" in *Representative Men* (Emerson 1850).[36] However, Whitman had also been reading Swedenborg on his own. He attended Swedenborgian meetings and study groups in New York (Kaplan 1980, 231–232), and he wrote an essay, "Who Was Swedenborg?" for the June 15, 1858, issue of the Brooklyn *Daily Times*.[37] Both men imported ideas from Swedenborg's teachings on correspondences into their own vocabulary about nature, but Whitman's use of the concept was extensive and detailed (see Hallengren 1992).

Perhaps the most decisive insight of Hallengren's study of Swedenborg and Whitman is his discovery that a study of correspondences as used by Swedenborg significantly illuminates a reading of Whitman, in the same manner that translating a translation back into the original language sometimes provides clarifying insights. For example, Whitman's famous title for his great collection of poetry, *Leaves of Grass*, presents an enigma that has always resisted explanation. Some light is shed on the question by Emerson's statement that "we say of man that he is grass," noted above. However, using a Swedenborgian dictionary of correspondences[38] as an interpretive key, Hallengren is able to probe more deeply

---

35. Hallengren 1998a, 96, 97–98, quoting Emerson 1959–1972, 361. On hieroglyphics, see Hallengren 1998a, 97–100. The term "hieroglyphics" here refers not to ancient Egyptian writing, but to something with a hidden or secret meaning. Swedenborg wrote, but never published, a brief manuscript on this topic, *Draft of a Hieroglyphic Key* (Swedenborg 1984b, 157–194).

36. It should be noted that Emerson had reservations about many aspects of Swedenborg's theology. Hotson 1929a offers several explanations for Emerson's criticisms. He observes that early versions of "Swedenborg, or the Mystic" were more affirmative, expressing Emerson's fundamental attitude; but Emerson's competition as a Bostonian on the lecture circuit with George Bush of New York City—whose praises of Swedenborg were a main staple of his talks—provoked an increasingly negative tone in Emerson's presentations over the years. See also Bush's *Reply to Ralph Waldo Emerson on Swedenborg* (Bush 1857b). For more on George Bush, see below.

37. Research to date has not located an extant copy; the article is excerpted in Whitman 1921, 2:16–18.

38. Several lexica of important terms and statements from Swedenborg have been collected over the centuries. The major English efforts are Hindmarsh 1794, Nicholson [1800] 1931, and Sechrist 1973. Unfortunately, these dictionary compilations have been misread as works by Swedenborg himself, an error that has resulted in an oversimplification of his system of correspondences.

and provide another perspective, identifying the leaves of grass as the "truths of what is alive in man" (Hallengren 1991, 18)—an interpretation that well describes the contents of the poems.[39] A clear implication is that much of the often obscure symbolism of Whitman's image-filled poetry can be made more understandable by applying Swedenborg's teachings about correspondences to it.

In addition to Emerson, and later Whitman, many of the influential leaders of the Transcendentalist movement are known to have read Swedenborg, although his full impact on their spiritual worldview can only be guessed. In general, they believed that his understanding of spiritual reality supported their own idealist philosophy. Of these figures, Bronson Alcott (1799–1888), the poet and educator, shows the most easily documentable influence. Indeed, his *Conversations with Children on the Gospels* (1836–1837) can be understood as an application of Reed's theory on the growth of the mind in a practical setting. Another of his works, "Orphic Sayings," was taken in part from Swedenborg's *True Christianity* and *Heaven and Hell* (Silver 1983, 101–102). Discussions on Swedenborg were also a feature of the intellectual life at Alcott's short-lived utopian communal experiment known as "Fruitlands" at Harvard, Massachusetts, in 1843.[40]

Other Transcendentalists, including Margaret Fuller (1810–1850), Theodore Parker (1810–1860), and Henry David Thoreau (1817–1862), engaged in discussions about Swedenborg's cosmology, although he is not specifically referenced in their works. To cite but one example, Thoreau's use of images from nature (the "pond," the "loon") in *Walden, or Life in the Woods* (1854) demonstrates a Swedenborgian understanding of correspondences, and his analogy between "macrocosm" and "microcosm" is strikingly similar to Swedenborg's treatment of analogy in *Heaven and Hell* (Harding 1974).

b. The James Family

Another of Emerson's friends was the elder Henry James (1811–1882), the most prolific writer on Swedenborgian topics in nineteenth-century

---

39. In the later version of his essay, Hallengren restates his interpretation; see Hallengren 1998a, 97–98. Hallengren's most recent discussion of Whitman (Hallengren 2004, 45–59) appeared too late to be available to the authors of this essay.

40. See Dahlstrand 1982 for a complete biography of Alcott. The Alcott name is perhaps best known today through his daughter, writer Louisa May Alcott (1832–1888). The grounds of the Fruitlands community are now a museum open to the public.

America. James became acquainted with Swedenborg around 1840 and began a correspondence with the British Swedenborgian James John Garth Wilkinson (1812–1899), whose work he had encountered in a London periodical, the *Monthly Magazine*.[41] However, his active interest in, and actual reading of, Swedenborg's works began in 1844 during a period of intense depression while traveling in England. Physicians suggested rest, fresh air, and the water cure, and a friend at one of the cure establishments advised him to read Swedenborg. In describing how he felt upon beginning to read *Divine Love and Wisdom* and *Divine Providence,* James can only compare himself to a fever patient "suddenly transported where the free airs of heaven blow . . . and the sound of running waters refreshes."[42] After that dramatic discovery, James was cured of his depression and went on to acquire most of Swedenborg's theological works. These he studied so assiduously that he even carried them on his travels in a trunk purchased specifically for this purpose, arraying them on the mantelpiece of hotel rooms in which he stayed.[43]

James scholar Paul Jerome Croce identifies James's intellectual starting point as Swedenborg's assertion that "nature is spirit clothed in matter."[44] From that basis, James used Swedenborg's theology as the foundation for a philosophical system that he saw as combining science and religion. He published this system in a series of substantial books written in extraordinarily dense prose. The difficulty of reading these books was crisply characterized by one of James's friends, the literary critic William Dean Howells (1837–1920), in a review of James's *The Secret of Swedenborg* (1869). There

---

41. See Hoover 1988, 265. Later, when James was editing the Brook Farm journal the *Harbinger,* he published a monthly letter from Wilkinson. Wilkinson also corresponded with Emerson.

42. Quoted in Grattan 1932, 52, who cites the source only as "one of [James's] theological books, written thirty-five years later" (Grattan 1932, 46). See also Croce 1995, 53–54, who describes how a friend told James he was suffering from what Swedenborg called "vastation," a spiritual process that removes both various evils that afflict the external component of the personality, and beliefs that are accepted as truths by the individual but are in fact untrue. The term is similar in force to the current expression "a shattering experience."

43. The trunk and its contents are now in the archives of the Swedenborgian House of Studies in Berkeley, California. It was donated in 1963 to the school's predecessor, the Swedenborg School of Religion, by members of the James family.

44. Croce 1988, 257. Variations of the cited statement appear in many contexts throughout Swedenborg's theological works. In reference to human beings, for example, see *Secrets of Heaven* 69 and *Heaven and Hell* 433; in reference to all creation, see *Divine Love and Wisdom* 173–281 (chapter 3), especially §§222–229.

Howells commented that whatever the secret was, Mr. James certainly had kept it (James 1920, 12).

The titles of James's books, on the other hand, though lengthy and hardly transparent, do eventually suggest their meaning. For example, *Society the Redeemed Form of Man, and the Earnest of God's Omnipotence in Human Nature* (1879) refers to James's development of Swedenborg's idea that an individual is a microcosm of society, which in turn mirrors heaven and ultimately reflects God. His *The Church of Christ Not an Ecclesiasticism: A Letter of Remonstrance to a Member of the* Soi Disant *New Church* ([1854] 1983)[45] demonstrates that he had rejected the institutionalized New Church with the same passion with which he embraced Swedenborg's teachings themselves, making James a forerunner of many "nonchurch" Swedenborgians today. The titles he chose for two other books, *Substance and Shadow, or Morality and Religion in Their Relation to Life: An Essay Upon the Physics of Creation* (1863) and *The Secret of Swedenborg: Being an Elucidation of His Doctrine of the Divine Natural Humanity* (1869) can perhaps be left as an exercise for the reader.

Studies of Henry James, Sr., cite passages scattered throughout his works when summarizing any one of his ideas, thus unintentionally but eloquently testifying to the complexity of his thought and style.[46] Croce has noted that "Henry James contributed to his own obscurity because he wrote with more passion than clarity," and notes that "his cosmic subject matter is inherently elusive" (Croce 1988, 251). Nevertheless, the elder Henry James was widely known and read in his day, much more so than his sons, novelist Henry (1843–1916) and philosopher William (1842–1910), although their reputations have largely eclipsed his, as Dwight Hoover notes.[47] The elder James's writings—and his friendships, which he formed throughout the circle of New England transcendentalists and the other intelligentsia of the Boston area—made him a major factor in

---

45. The subtitle of this book appears in various forms not only in the different editions, but within the book itself. The subtitle used on the title page of the first edition is *Letter to a Sectarian;* in the preface it is *Letter of Remonstrance to a Member of the* Soi-Disant *New Church;* on the part-title page before the text it is *Letter to a Member of the* Soi-Disant *New Church;* and by the first page of the text itself, it has become merely *Letter of Remonstrance Etc. Etc.*

46. See, for example, Grattan 1932, volume 1; and Hoover 1969.

47. Hoover 1988, 263. A major biographical study that removes James, Sr., from the shadow of his children is Habegger 1994.

Swedenborg's prominence in American thought during the late nineteenth century.

Studies of William James up to the 1960s ask why he, though a son of Henry James, Sr., says so little about Swedenborg in his *Varieties of Religious Experience* (James 1902). *Varieties* was, after all, an exhaustive study of a subject area in which not only Swedenborg's work but his life experiences as well as could have been expected to have a prominent place.[48] Subsequent scholars pursue the question with careful reading of the works of father and son, finding valuable insights into their relationship and its effects on William James's attitude toward Swedenborg.[49] William James came to maturity not only under the influence of his father, but also of his teachers. It is worth noting that these included the noted zoologist Louis Agassiz (1807–1873); professor of medicine and American man of letters Wendell Holmes, Sr. (1809–1894); the father of American pragmatism, Charles Sanders Peirce (1839–1914); and two scientists of great prominence at the time, chemist and educator Charles Eliot (1834–1926) and the natural historian Jeffries Wyman (1814–1874). Among these, Holmes and Peirce especially were close friends of the elder Henry James, and frequent guests at his table, where, of course, William also dined (Croce 1996b, 8; Taylor 1988, 155–176).

These high-powered and conflicting intellectual influences on James's view of the debate between science and faith, augmented by others less well known today, led to the development of mutually incompatible convictions underlying William James's early writing. He wrote in 1897 that he enjoyed the challenge of this kind of conflict: "Certainty is the root of despair. The inevitable stales, while doubt and hope are sisters" (James 1978, 189). His position between these opposites almost certainly contributed to his near-suicidal depression in 1870, shortly after receiving his M.D. from Harvard Medical School (Taylor 1988, 160). However, a struggle toward their resolution may be said to characterize the development of his thought. Seeking coherence between science and religion, he began by reacting against his father and assuming that science was supreme, but ended by working toward a

---

48. See, for example, Young 1951, as well as his predecessors Grattan 1932 and Perry 1935.

49. See Hoover 1969 and Hoover 1988, 263–276. See also Croce 1996b and Taylor 1988, 155–176. A previously unpublished letter by William James discovered by Gregory R. Johnson in 2002 sheds fresh light on this question; see Johnson 2003, 61–67.

synthesis of the science of Agassiz and Eliot on the one hand, and religion as a loosely defined psychological phenomenon on the other.[50]

Incomplete as it was, this harmony was still in the unforeseeable future. When he was writing *Varieties of Religious Experience,* the dueling loyalties he owed to his father, his teachers, and his own ambiguity were too troubling for him to discuss Swedenborg, much less to reach a final personal conclusion about him. William James cannot be ignored in a study of Swedenborg's influence in America, but the nature of that influence remains a matter of speculation and interpretation.

IV. Approaching the Mainstream

Another public figure with an intellect no less keen than that of William James, although focused in a different direction, was John Bigelow (1817–1911). Bigelow, a prominent New York attorney, journalist, and author, as well as minister to France for President Abraham Lincoln (1809–1865), may have been the most widely known author writing on Swedenborgian subjects in the United States in the latter half of the nineteenth century. Admitted to the New York bar in 1839, he soon embraced politics and reform, gaining prominence for his improvements at Sing Sing prison during his appointment as inspector there. Later he served on the board of inspectors of the army and naval academies at West Point and Annapolis.

Politically active with the Free Soil Party, Bigelow gained the friendship of Martin Van Buren (1782–1862). Other notable associates included the Democratic presidential candidate in the controversial 1876 election, Samuel J. Tilden (1814–1886), whose biography by Bigelow (1895) was later a best-seller; and newspaper editor and poet William Cullen Bryant (1794–1878). Bryant's invitation to Bigelow to join him in owning and editing the *New York Evening Post* in 1848 led him into a distinguished newspaper career. Bigelow became one of the nation's best-known journalists during the turbulent period in which the *Post* was instrumental in the formation of the Republican Party and the election of Lincoln. Lincoln sent him to Paris, first as consul in 1861 (with special responsibilities related to

---

50. For a more nuanced interpretation, see Croce 1996b, 14–24.

the French press), and from 1863 to 1866 as envoy extraordinary and minister plenipotentiary. He was also a major force in the creation of the New York Public Library (founded in 1895).[51]

Bigelow discovered the theological writings of Emanuel Swedenborg while returning to New York from a trip to the West Indies in 1854, where he had viewed the progress of freed slaves. At St. Thomas he happened to stay in the same hotel as a local court official of Danish descent, Niels Andreas Vibe Kierulff (1796–1874).[52] During a conversation Bigelow struck up with Kierulff in the hotel dining room, Kierulff introduced him to Swedenborg's exegesis of the inner sense or spiritual meaning of Genesis. Bigelow was intrigued and subsequently became absorbed in reading Swedenborg's *Secrets of Heaven,* as well as other works. During the passage home, his study of the books supplied by Kierulff was so intense that he could not eat or sleep. He wrote:

> It would not be possible to convey to anyone, who had not a similar experience, the effect [Swedenborg's books] produced upon me, the almost insane appetite with which I devoured them, the complete revolution that they wrought in all my opinions about spiritual matters, especially the Bible. Though, like the blind man in the gospel, I as yet only saw men as trees walking, before I reached home I had acquired a thorough conviction that "these were not the words of him who hath a devil," and that Swedenborg was "a scribe instructed unto the Kingdom of Heaven." It seemed that every line I read removed some difficulty, cleared up some doubt, illuminated some mystery, revealed some spiritual wealth in the Word of which I had no conception.[53]

The poet Henry Van Dyke (1852–1933), in a memorial address, said of this time in Bigelow's life:

> It was during his journalistic period that three good fortunes came to Mr. Bigelow; first, the beginning of his happy domestic life, by his marriage with Miss Jane Poultney in 1850; second, the commencement of his life as an author in 1852, with a volume called "Jamaica in 1850;

---

51. For details of his impressive public life, see Clapp 1947.

52. For additional details on Kierulff and Swedenborgianism in the West Indies, see Hallengren 1998a, 43–60.

53. Bigelow [1893] 1979, 22. He quotes John 10:21 and Matthew 13:52.

or the Effect of Fifty Years of Freedom on a Slave Colony"; and third, the recovery of his faith in the Bible, through an acquaintance in 1853[54] with the works of that wondrous interpreter, Emanuel Swedenborg. (Van Dyke 1924, xvi–xvii)

In addition to his numerous works on political subjects, Bigelow wrote a series of books on Swedenborgian topics. *The Bible That Was Lost and Is Found* ([1893] 1979), which tells the story of his rediscovery of his Christian faith, is perhaps his best-known religious work. Other titles include *Resist Beginnings, or The Blinding Influences of Sin* (1880), *The Mystery of Sleep* (1924), *The Useful Life: A Crown to the Simple Life as Taught by Emanuel Swedenborg* (1905), *The Proprium* (1907), and *Toleration* (1927). All explain and apply significant Swedenborgian teachings and were circulated beyond New Church membership.

Another eminent Swedenborgian journalist was Clarence W. Barron (1855–1928), who worked in Boston, Philadelphia, and New York. A financial editor and a man of decidedly practical bent, Barron founded news bureaus in Boston and Philadelphia before he took over ownership and publication of the *Wall Street Journal* in 1901 and started a financial newspaper, *Barron's National Business and Financial Weekly,* in 1921. As an active member of the Boston New Church, Barron brought his businesslike approach to his religion and applied market research techniques to his enthusiasm for evangelism. Surveying a national sampling of eight hundred Swedenborgians active in the General Convention[55] in 1906, he found that a quarter of the members were raised by Swedenborgian parents, and of those who were not, 42.5 percent were converted by conversation with a friend, 45 percent by reading (that is, 19.5 percent by reading Swedenborg, 19.5 percent by reading church literature, 6 percent by other reading), and only 7.5 percent by an address by a minister or missionary.[56] Apparently he saw no means of dramatically improving the results of personal evangelism, so he seized on publishing as the proven evangelistic technique, and in 1927 he contributed seventy thousand dollars to the

---

54. The correct date is 1854.

55. The General Convention of the New Jerusalem is one of the national organizations of Swedenborgian churches that developed in the United States in the nineteenth century. For the history of these organizations, see the essay on institutionalized Swedenborgianism on pages 245–310 in this volume.

56. See Block 1984, 361, who cites Barron 1906, 234–235. Five percent were unclassified.

church for publicity and publication.[57] He also tried to increase the effectiveness of the church's publication efforts by writing an article for *New Church Review,* "Reading Swedenborg—A Help for Every Man and Woman" (Barron 1924), and later reprinting the article as a pamphlet.

Another publishing effort was more for his own convenience than in service of evangelistic ideals. Barron was accustomed to carting his set of Swedenborg's theological works with him when he traveled. The elder Henry James had dedicated a travel trunk to his Swedenborg, but Barron found a solution that suited his character. He engaged the Riverside Press of Cambridge, Massachusetts, to produce a more compact and portable set of the works by printing them on "India" or "Bible" paper. When the Riverside printers objected to making ready their presses to print only one copy of each volume, Barron agreed to an edition of thirty copies, each numbered on the verso of the title page. In this edition, the number of volumes was reduced from thirty-two volumes to eleven, and from just under four feet of bookshelf (or hotel-room mantelpiece) to fourteen inches—a set that could be carried in a small Pullman case rather than a trunk.[58]

Barron, in his commitment to Swedenborgianism, is just one example of the many successful business and professional people who were attracted to the New Church in the late nineteenth and early twentieth centuries. The number of such people in the New Church was out of all proportion to the modest membership figures of its organizations. Numerous Swedenborgians had distinguished careers in business, law, and government. Boston publisher Timothy H. Carter (1798–1894); Chicago financier Jonathan Young Scammon (1812–1890); industrialist John Pitcairn (1841–1916), founder of Pittsburgh Plate Glass; Charles C. Bonney (1831–1903), a prominent Chicago attorney and the convener of the 1893 World's Parliament of Religions; noted architect and city planner Daniel H. Burnham (1846–1912); and philanthropist Margaretta Lammot DuPont (1808–1903) were but a few of the men and women who used their wealth and influence on behalf of Swedenborgianism in the United States.[59]

---

57. See Block 1984, 361, citing Murray 1927, 130.

58. Barron's set was a reprint of the Rotch Edition of Swedenborg's published theological works. Set 1 was kept in the office of the president of the Swedenborg School of Religion prior to the school's relocation in 2000; set 24 is in the library of Robert H. Kirven, having been purchased from the estate of Waldo Peebles, late professor of German at Boston University and a younger contemporary of Barron in the Boston Church of the New Jerusalem. Other sets are in church and private libraries.

59. On Pitcairn, see Gladish 1989; on Bonney, see Dole 1993; on Burnham, see Hines 1974.

V. Spiritualism

The origin of American Spiritualism, as a socio-religious movement, is popularly dated to 1848 and the occurrence of the "Rochester Rappings" reported in that city; or to a slightly earlier event, the publication of Andrew Jackson Davis's controversial work *Principles of Nature* in 1847 (Tyler 1962, 82–84). But there was also a decidedly Swedenborgian flavor to this movement, as recent scholarship has recognized.[60]

The story of George Bush (1796–1859) is a good example.[61] A Swedenborgian and professor of Asian languages at New York University, Bush began giving public lectures on Swedenborg in 1845 and was offered the leadership of the New York New Church in 1848. However, his anticlerical convictions precluded his ordination, and in 1857 he published a book opposing the clergy.[62] Despite his failure to gain support for his anticlerical ideas, Bush remained an active leader in the New Church and in 1852 assumed the leadership of the members of the Brooklyn New Church with an agreement "not to engage among them as a pastor or minister in the normal acceptation of the term."[63]

Bush had his struggles with Swedenborg as well as with the institutional New Church. He rejected *Heaven and Hell* at his first reading, suspecting it was influenced more by Swedenborg's expectations of life after death than by actual revelation. Furthermore, his training as a philologist made him suspicious of Swedenborg's methods of interpreting the Bible. After further reading, however, he was eventually convinced on both counts. He later contributed to the conversion of journalist John Bigelow, mentioned above (Block 1984, 297).

Bush had long been interested in Mesmerism (Block 1984, 133–134). Franz Anton Mesmer (1734–1815), a German physician, had developed this theory, also known as "animal magnetism"; its practice involved a trance state later associated with hypnotism. Many Swedenborgians and others

---

60. For example, see Swank 1970, 240–277, who offers an entire chapter on the interaction between Spiritualism and the New Church.

61. As his name suggests, Bush was an ancestor of United States presidents George Bush and George W. Bush.

62. See his book *Priesthood and Clergy Unknown to Christianity: or The Church a Community of Co-equal Brethren* (Bush 1857a). It is just one example of the anticlericalism that has appeared at various times and places in the history of the New Church in the United States, particularly in the Midwest.

63. Quoted from an unnamed source in Block 1894, 298. Bush also assumed a leading role in opposition to the growing movement toward a single national organization of Swedenborgian churches.

naturally linked Mesmer's hypnotic state with the growing Spiritualist phenomenon of communication with spirits. This connection led Bush to his involvement with the "Poughkeepsie seer," Andrew Jackson Davis (1826–1910),[64] and clairvoyant Thomas Lake Harris (1823–1906). Indeed, Bush's endorsement was largely responsible for the wide public acceptance of Davis's *Principles of Nature* (described below), and Bush was a central figure in the controversy within the Swedenborgian Church that erupted over Davis's writings and Spiritualism in general (Block 1984, 133–137).

Animal magnetism had been controversial in American Swedenborgian circles since 1794, when founders of the Baltimore Society of the New Church exchanged heated letters on the subject (Block 1984, 88–89). The Swedenborgian congregation in New York became divided in 1844 over Spiritualism—or "Pseudo-Spiritualism," as it was called in the course of sermons by Philadelphia minister Richard de Charms, who bluntly denounced it.[65] In 1845 the *New Jerusalem Magazine* published a series of articles by Benjamin F. Barrett (1808–1892), then of New York, on the dangers of (and precautions to be taken against) "open intercourse with the spiritual world."[66] Neither de Charms's sermons nor Barrett's articles settled the controversy, however.

Andrew Jackson Davis drew Swedenborgians even more deeply into the controversial subject of Spiritualism. Davis was a cobbler in Poughkeepsie, New York, who was able to enter a trance state in which he gave lectures on various topics that were unknown to him in his waking life. These trance-lectures attracted the attention of many, including Edgar Allan Poe (1809–1849); Bush's friend, Thomas Lake Harris; and ultimately Bush himself (Ellwood 1991, 4). At some point, either before or after meeting Bush, Davis communicated with a spirit he subsequently identified as Swedenborg.[67] He later went on to publish a book (1847), which is indebted to Swedenborg for the concepts of graduated spiritual worlds, spiritual marriage, and the teaching that "like attracts

---

64. For a brief account of Davis, see Campbell 1998.

65. Block 1984, 99. De Charms's lectures were later published as *Three Sermons Presented to the New York Society of the New Jerusalem Against the Pseudo-Spiritualism of Modern Times* (de Charms 1853).

66. For the original article, see Barrett 1845, 13–28, 50–64, 89–104. For responses, see "Open Intercourse" 1846a, 280, and "Open Intercourse" 1846b, 364.

67. Ellwood 1991, 9–12, quotes and examines Davis's account of this meeting at length. It is given in detail also in Davis 1857, 242–244, 248.

like"—ultimately derived from Swedenborg's concept of correspondences (Ellwood 1991, 1–2).

Historian Bret E. Carroll observes:

> [Spiritualists'] references to Swedenborg indicate that they looked pri-
> marily to him as an example of using contact with spirits to glimpse
> cosmic order. As an inspirational religious practitioner and the source
> of their spirit-centered worldview, the Swedish Seer was regarded by
> Spiritualists as a forerunner of their religion and became for them a
> cultural icon. This is why they, like Andrew Jackson Davis, so often
> sought communication with his spirit. This, too, is why they consid-
> ered Davis "the youthful Swedenborg of our day" and dubbed him the
> "Poughkeepsie Seer." (Carroll 1997, 22)

Both Carroll (1997, 17–34) and J. Stillson Judah (1967) have documented
the intellectual connections between Swedenborg and the Spiritualists
and related movements, demonstrating that in varying ways all of them
incorporated teachings from Swedenborg's theological works in the fundamental suppositions of their systems.

Bush was so convinced of the authenticity of Davis's mediumship that
he wrote a testimonial on his revelations, including it in his work *Mesmer
and Swedenborg* (1847) as an appendix. Though Bush was not completely
convinced that the spirit Davis had met was Swedenborg, he did maintain
that, while in a trance, Davis could lecture on subjects he had never studied (astronomy, geology, and physics, among others) and could quote
Swedenborg by the page, as well as speak in Latin, Greek, and Hebrew.
These facts, he thought, were incontestable proof of Davis's claims.[68]

Bush's endorsement was partially responsible for the public acceptance
of Davis's exposition of his worldview, *Principles of Nature*. However, studying the contents of Davis's book when it appeared forced Bush later to acknowledge publicly that not only was Davis's use of Swedenborg's teaching
highly selective, but "in the theological department it [was] absolutely *de-
structive*" (Bush 1860, 227–228). In response to Bush's retraction, the *New
Jerusalem Magazine* went even further: "We feel gratified that Professor
Bush . . . does not hesitate to declare that book [Davis's *Principles*] to be
wholly unworthy of any confidence whatever. . . . [Davis] must have been,
some of the time at least, under the influence of spirits from beneath."[69]

---

68. Bush 1847, 169–218; see also Block's discussion of this appendix (Block 1984, 135–136).

69. "Professor Bush and Mesmerism" 1848, 509–555. The expression "spirits from beneath" of
course refers to evil spirits, as opposed to good.

For Swedenborgians, the controversy over communication with spirits involved more than a merely intellectual matter, or a dispute between high-profile public figures such as Bush and Davis. In many locations, from Maryland to Boston, New York to Michigan, Spiritualism wreaked havoc in New Church circles. Part of the problem was that in their reading of Swedenborg, members of the New Church found grounds for taking a stand on either side of the issue. This ambiguity led many of them into crisis not only in their own mind and spirit, but also in their interaction with the organized church (Block 1984, 132–143). Although Swedenborg had issued ample warnings against contacting the dead, at least some of his statements on this matter have seemed to some to be obscure or ambiguous, especially in the context of his practice of cooperating when spirits contacted him. For example, he wrote in *True Christianity* 475 that there is a spiritual influence on all of life:

> Our mind is our spirit, which lives after death. Our spirit has constant association with others in the [spiritual] world who are like us. Through the material body that surrounds it, our spirit is also among people in the physical world. . . . If we were deprived of all interaction with spirits, we would die instantly.[70]

On the other hand, in *Revelation Explained* 1182:4–5, Swedenborg cautioned:

> Many people believe that the Lord can teach us through spirits talking to us, but people who believe this and try it do not realize that with it comes a danger to their souls. . . . The moment spirits start to talk with us they shift from their spiritual state to our earthly one. . . . The result is that the spirits who are talking with us are convinced of the very same principles as we, whether they are true or false, . . . and by uniting their feelings with ours they powerfully validate our own feelings. . . . We do not know the quality of our feelings, whether they are good or bad.[71]

Other aspects of Davis's system, as described both in his 1847 *Principles of Nature* and in his 1857 autobiography, were unlikely to leave Swedenborgians any doubts that he had stepped beyond the bounds of spiritual truth. Swedenborg's teaching on "spiritual marriage" will serve

---

70. Translation by Jonathan S. Rose.

71. Translation by George F. Dole.

as an illustration.[72] Swedenborg promises that "the Lord provides compatible partners to those who desire true marriage love. If this does not happen on earth, it does in heaven."[73] He offers many statements concerning the purity and fidelity of genuine marital love, including the following from *Marriage Love* 143:

> True marriage love is chastity itself, because: (1) It is from the Lord and corresponds to the marriage of the Lord and the church. (2) It derives from the marriage of what is good and what is true. (3) It is spiritual, to the extent that the marriage partners are spiritual. (4) It is the fundamental love, supreme among all loves—heavenly and spiritual. (5) It is the true seedbed of the human race, and therefore of the angelic heaven. (6) Therefore, it also exists with angels of heaven (although they produce spiritual offspring—love and wisdom). (7) Its function is therefore preeminent among the purposes of creation.

It is difficult to reconcile Davis's earthly teachings and practice on spiritual marriage, although they were clearly borrowed from Swedenborg, with the lofty description of marriage just quoted. When Davis used his version as a persuasive tool in proposing marriage to his second wife, it appeared to Swedenborgians as little more than deceit and trickery; and when he used it in declaring their divorce, it seemed to them little more than a screen for his libido.

Davis's friend Thomas Lake Harris seemed to appreciate Davis's approach, and further adapted the notion of spiritual marriage. For him, as for Swedenborg, each person has a spiritual counterpart in the heavenly realms. And like Swedenborg, Harris also thought that each individual's counterpart must be sought through the human form of someone of the opposite sex. Perhaps in response to Swedenborg's assertion that true marriage love was rare in the eighteenth century (*Marriage Love* 58), Harris maintained that in practice the earthly search for one's mate almost never led to one's spiritual spouse. In some of his communal experiments (see below), Harris reportedly kept mistresses (although claiming to be celibate), and he provided the married men of his communes with numerous reasons for keeping concubines. As one observer wrote, "The practical result of this theory [spiritual marriage] is 'free love' or experimenting with 'affinities,' which has prevailed among the

---

72. The Latin phrase Swedenborg often used for this concept was *amor vere conjugialis*—here translated "true marriage love." See note 78 on page 289 below.

73. *Marriage Love* 229. All translations from *Marriage Love* used in this essay are those of George F. Dole.

Spiritualists."74 Free love was, in fact, a much-discussed topic in various re-form circles during the nineteenth century.75 It goes almost without saying, however, that such an interpretation of love (in or outside of marriage) is counter to Swedenborg's intent. Although Swedenborg does approve of ex-tramarital relationships in certain extreme circumstances, as when one partner is in a coma or is riddled with deadly contagion (*Marriage Love* 470), he speaks strongly for the sanctity of the marriage relationship.

The connection between Swedenborgianism and Spiritualism out-side the United States can only be touched on here. In Great Britain more than in the United States, the mid-1800s was an age of religious un-certainty, and the Spiritualist movement, though small, became popular among the working classes, in intellectual and literary circles, and among wealthy elites. To some extent, those engaged in séances or psychic re-search saw the march of science as a threat to the spiritual values of Christianity. It is not surprising that the most well-known Swedenbor-gian spiritualist, though trained as a physician, became critical of medical practices. This was James John Garth Wilkinson, mentioned earlier as a correspondent of Henry James, Sr. He took issue with the excessive use of drugs as well as the practice of vaccination, and over time abandoned traditional medicine for homeopathy (discussed below). Wilkinson also dabbled in Mesmerism, had an interest in the socialism of Charles Fourier (also to be discussed below), and translated several volumes of Swedenborg's scientific works. His belief in the spiritual world was broadened by contacts with a circle of friends that included writers William Howitt (1792–1879) and Mary Botham Howitt (1799–1888), as well as other middle-class intellectuals. James Wilkinson's contribution to British spiritualism included editing an issue of the *Spiritual Herald,* a short-lived periodical published by Swedenborgian spiritualists in 1856.

74. Noyes [1870] 1961, 592–593. Although Noyes was an astute observer of communal life in the nineteenth century, his implied disapproval is somewhat ironic. His own community at Oneida, New York, practiced "complex marriage," an arrangement whereby all men in the community were married to all the women. For Swedenborg's description of open marriage, with implied censure, see *Marriage Love* 376.

75. One fascinating example of how free love was combined with various medical and social re-forms was the short-lived Memnonia Institute at Yellow Springs, Ohio. Founded in 1856 by Thomas Low Nichols (1815–1901) and Mary Gove Nichols (1810–1884), Memnonia was a "water cure" establishment that also involved free love, Spiritualism, and communalism. The Nichols were married by a Swedenborgian minister in New York, and some Swedenborgian ideas, particularly on Spiritualism and spiritual marriage, may have influenced their reform work. Both dramatically converted to Catholicism in 1857; see Gleason 1961, 283–307. On Thomas Low Nichols, see Silver-Isenstadt 2003, 186–205; for a recent biography of Mary Gove Nichols, see Silver-Isenstadt 2002.

He also published a volume of poems, *Improvisations from the Spirit,* written in the style of William Blake (Wilkinson 1857).[76]

In Continental Europe, particularly in the artists' colony established in Florence by expatriate Britons and Americans, table rappings and floating objects were all the rage in the mid-1800s. Elizabeth Barrett Browning (see above) was especially taken with the Spiritualist fad—although for her it amounted to something of a religion, to the dismay of Robert Browning. Barrett Browning subscribed to Spiritualist publications (Lewis 1998, 140) and at one point had her servant attempt automatic writing (Forster 1988, 289). In Swedenborg's writings and in Spiritualistic experiments, the valetudinarian poetess found much comfort and assurance of a continuing life after death, including an eternal life with her beloved husband.[77] Linda M. Lewis has also argued that Swedenborg's identification of heaven with spiritual love and of hell with self-love meshed with Barrett Browning's own religious beliefs (Lewis 1998, 141).

Among the friends and frequent guests at Barrett Browning's séances were several American Swedenborgians: sculptor Hiram Powers (1805–1873), artist William Page (1811–1885), and art critic and collector James Jackson Jarvis (1818–1888). Powers, who had been acquainted with Swedenborg's writings since his youth in Cincinnati, Ohio, and who (along with his entire family) was to be baptized into the Swedenborgian Church while living in Florence, reciprocated the Brownings' hospitality with séances of his own. He saw the appearance of ghostly hands, the floating faces, the moanings, and the levitated objects as confirmation of Swedenborg's experiences in the world beyond death (Reynolds 1977a, 117). As it was for Barrett Browning, to Powers this proof was as much a joyful confirmation of spiritual existence and a foundation for artistic endeavor as it was a social occasion and a thrilling adventure.

VI. Utopian Socialism

Thomas Lake Harris's role as a communal leader is part of the larger story of utopian communalism in early nineteenth-century America.

---

76. See Oppenheim 1985, 232–235, and Podmore 1902, 2:23.

77. The best short study of Elizabeth Barrett Browning's Swedenborgianism is Gladish 1965, 506–513, 559–570.

Several of these utopian experiments were either directly or indirectly influenced by Swedenborg's teachings. Arthur Bestor has described this era in American history as teeming with "patent office models of the good society" (Bestor 1970, 230–231). Much of the experimentation was brought on by the social upheaval of the Industrial Revolution and the stimulus of the French Revolution. Other Christian communal influences stemmed from the legacy of radical and millenarian sects, such as the Ephrata community in colonial Pennsylvania and the Harmony Society of George Rapp (1757–1847) in Pennsylvania and Indiana. Such groups found a fertile home for their ideas on American soil.

As a young Universalist pastor in New York City in the 1840s, Harris had absorbed some Swedenborgian ideas, perhaps from George Bush as well as from his own reading. After a short stay at a community he co-founded in 1850 near Mountain Cove in what is now West Virginia, Harris returned to New York City, where he established a congregation, the Church of the Good Shepherd, based on Swedenborgian doctrines and Spiritualist practices. Over the next few years, he published several volumes, some of which Swedenborgian leaders found little short of scandalous. Among them was *The Arcana of Christianity* (Harris [1858–1867] 1976), sporting a title adapted from *Arcana Coelestia,* the Latin title of Swedenborg's *Secrets of Heaven.* It was issued by a "New Church Publishing Association" that, despite appearances, had no connection with the organized New Church.

Bush and others in the American New Church were probably relieved when Harris departed for England in 1859—only to be chagrined when he was warmly received by some Swedenborgians there. Among his acquaintances was James John Garth Wilkinson. Wilkinson was a Spiritualist, homeopathic physician, and translator of several of Swedenborg's scientific works.[78] He introduced Harris to Laurence Oliphant (1829–1888), a well-known novelist and Spiritualist, and to his mother, Lady Maria Oliphant (about 1811–1881), both of whom played a major role in Harris's later communal experiences in New York state. These began when Harris organized a group under the name "Brotherhood of the New Life" in 1861. In 1867 the group moved from its home near Wassaic, New York, across the state to

---

78. Although not a member of the New Jerusalem Church, Wilkinson was nevertheless one of the most important British admirers of Swedenborg of his day. His *Emanuel Swedenborg: A Biography* (first full edition 1849) was highly influential. It is possible that he introduced Robert Browning to Swedenborg's works (Morris 1915, 162). For biographical information, see Wilkinson 1911; for other references in this essay, see pages 211 and 223–224.

Brocton ("Salem-on-Erie"); and in 1875 Harris and several of his followers relocated to Santa Rosa, California. Here they established the commercially successful Fountain Grove Community. Harris's views continued to grow more ethereal, however, and eventually stories about free love and other practices in the community led to its dissolution.[79]

Spiritualism and Swedenborgianism are also associated with one of America's oldest and most successful communal groups, the Shakers, or the United Society of Believers, founded in Britain by "Mother" Ann Lee (1736–1784). A tiny group of believers immigrated to New York in 1774 and grew to several thousand members in eighteen flourishing communal villages by the mid-nineteenth century. Clarke Garrett has amply shown that both early Shakerism and Swedenborgianism in Britain are products of the same popular religiosity, with equivalent beliefs in visitant angels and a regenerate spirituality developing within the individual (Garrett 1987, 146–147.) According to later interpreters, Mother Ann considered Swedenborg "her John the Baptist,"[80] and a few Swedenborgians saw striking parallels between their theology and that of the Shakers concerning the "spiritual body, the nature of life after death, [and] the laws of the spiritual world."[81]

Still, few readers of Swedenborg joined the Shakers; most likely the celibacy required of converts was a deterrent.[82] Swedenborgians were, however, involved in several communities based as much on social planning and utopian socialism as on their religious faith. The first of these

---

79. Schneider and Lawton 1942, 276–279, 262–268. Following the dissolution, Harris married his secretary, and the couple lived in New York until his death in 1906. Besides Schneider and Lawton 1942, which is the best treatment of Harris, see also the brief assessment in Block 1984, 140–142.

80. Evans 1869, 59–60. Ann Lee was illiterate, so it is unlikely that she was personally familiar with any of Swedenborg's works.

81. See, for example, the essay "A Few Words about Shakerism and the Shakers" ([W.B.H.] 1848, 573), from which this quotation is taken. Major portions of this essay were taken from *A Summary View of the Millennial Church, or The United Society of Believers* ([Green and Wells], 1848). This second, revised edition contains several extracts from the writings of Swedenborgian George Bush. For general background on the Shakers, see Stein 1992.

82. One frequent Swedenborgian visitor to Shaker communities was Harriot Hunt (1805–1875), a physician and feminist reformer who was welcomed among the Shakers because of her special ability to work with women patients using natural remedies. Other incidental facts suggest close links between the Swedenborgians and the Shakers: Hunt reports meeting an unnamed Swedenborgian minister and his wife at the Canterbury village in New Hampshire in 1853, and the minister's wife had sisters in office there. See Hunt 1856, 275.

was associated with Robert Owen (1771–1858), a wealthy Scots mill owner turned social reformer. He visited the United States during 1825 and 1826 with plans for a model community based on common owner-ship of property and moral reform through education. The site selected for this bold experiment in social planning was New Harmony, Indiana, a town purchased from the Harmony Society.[83]

These ideas attracted the attention of Swedenborgian pastor Manning B. Roche (?–1842) in Philadelphia, and several members of the New Church society in Cincinnati (Block 1984, 80–82). Roche's plan to begin an Owenite colony (involving members of his congregation and another nearby) came to nothing, but Owen's Cincinnati supporters, led by Daniel Roe,[84] a lay preacher, attorney, and member of the Cincinnati society, was more successful. Roe visited New Harmony with Owen in 1825 for a first-hand look. A constitution was drawn up modeled on New Harmony, ad-vertisements for members were taken out in Cincinnati newspapers, and 720 acres were secured to the north of Cincinnati in Greene County at Yel-low Springs. This venture, which probably did not include more than a hundred members, survived only a few months. The first families arrived in the summer of 1825. They used a former inn located on the property and constructed a large communal log building. For a few months, a commu-nal system of ownership and labor worked adequately. By winter, however, the new moral order without class distinctions envisioned by Owen proved difficult to bring about, and the colony collapsed financially. It is unlikely that many Cincinnati Swedenborgians took part in the experiment; Roe returned home disappointed, severed his ties with New Church, and moved to Dayton.[85] The New Harmony experiment failed the following year, and Owenism as a utopian socialist movement was dead.

A revival of socialist utopian thought swept the country a few years later under the name "Fourierism" or "Associationism." Charles Fourier (1772–1837), a French social theorist, proposed organizing society into co-operative and self-sufficient "phalanxes," each large enough to provide for the economic and social needs of all the residents. An integral part of his

83. In addition to Bestor 1970, a helpful source on Owen is Harrison 1969.

84. Further biographical data on Roe was not available to the authors.

85. Block 1984, 118–120; Bestor 1970, 210–212. The only known contemporary account of the colony is an untitled newspaper report published in Noyes [1870] 1961, 59–65. The site of the communal dwelling at Yellow Springs is now Glen Helen, a nature preserve owned by Antioch University.

plan was that all human activity was to be organized according to the principle of "passionate attraction," in which an individual's interests, rather than background, and passion, rather than reason, were developed and utilized to meet all personal and social needs. In the United States, the foremost advocates of Fourier's ideas were two journalists affiliated with the *New York Tribune,* Horace Greeley (1811–1872) and Albert Brisbane (1809–1890), both of whom had close ties with members of the New Church, not only in Britain but in the United States. Brisbane's interpretation of key aspects of Fourier's thought appeared in the book *Social Destiny of Man* (1840), which enjoyed enormous popularity.[86]

The famous Brook Farm community, in West Roxbury, Massachusetts, had begun under Transcendentalist inspiration; but in 1844 it changed its orientation to a Fourierist phalanx and began planning for an ambitious program of industrialization. As Fourierism swept the country in the 1840s, many saw a resemblance between the social philosophy of the French theorist and Swedenborg. As Transcendentalists, those associated with Brook Farm were already familiar with Swedenborg, but now they felt a new urgency of belief.[87] The founder of the community, George Ripley (1802–1880), wrote in 1845:

> We study [Swedenborg] continually for the light he sheds on many problems of human destiny, and more especially for the remarkable correspondence, as of inner with outer, which his revelations present with the discourses of Fourier concerning social organization, or the outward forms of life. The one is the great poet and high-priest, the other the great economist, as it were, of the Harmonic Order, which all things are preparing. (Ripley 1845, 92–94)

While there were no official ties between Brook Farm and the New Jerusalem Church, a close examination of the community's publication, the *Harbinger,*[88] reveals a keen interest in Swedenborg, and several articles

---

86. Reprinted as Brisbane 1968. The core of Fourier's vision, from a Swedenborgian perspective, may also be found in Gladish 1983. The most accessible treatment of Fourier, however, is Beecher and Bienvenu 1983.

87. Swedenborg's influence on Brook Farm is discussed in Gladish 1983, 8–18; and Swank 1970, 360–362.

88. The *Harbinger* was published by the Brook Farm Phalanx from 1841 until 1844. Publication was then taken over by the American Union of Associationists, New York and Boston, and continued from 1845 through 1849.

in its pages may have been written as a thinly veiled appeal to the New Church to embrace Fourier's social theories.[89] The first volume of the *Harbinger,* for example, contained an essay by Otis Clapp (1806–1886) titled "The Family Sphere." It was originally read at a meeting of Boston New Church members invested in Fourier Associationism. Clapp writes:

> We are therefore, Fourierists, so far as we can find materials in his system adapted to our wants; and we consider ourselves responsible for those parts of his system only which we after careful examination find it to our advantage to adopt. . . . Objections are often made to Associationism on the ground that the family sphere will be destroyed . . . I hold . . . most unqualifiedly to the inviolability of the domestic sphere. (Clapp 1845, 70)

By "domestic sphere" Clapp of course meant marriage and family life. In the end, it was precisely the issues of sexual freedom and free love associated with Fourierism (as well as Spiritualism) that prevented the Boston group from making more concrete plans toward forming a phalanx. Not surprisingly, two phalanxes with direct links to the New Church were short-lived. The first of these was at the tiny community of Le Raysville in Bradford County, Pennsylvania, a short distance east of the Susquehanna and south of the New York state line. The local leader was Lemuel Belding,[90] a physician and New Church minister, who gave his farm to the joint-stock enterprise in 1844. The group numbered about forty men, women, and children, and controlled perhaps 1,500 acres. Associated with Belding was another Swedenborgian minister, Solyman Brown (1790–1876), a dentist from Darby, New York, who also served as a teacher and preached for the community as well. The community, most of which was made up of members of the New Church, lasted between eight and twelve months; it ended in a controversy over equity in the enterprise. Brown moved back to New York and went on to become a pioneer in dentistry education in New York. Belding, however, was stripped of his New Church ordination a few years later, although the reasons for

---

89. See the fine study by Delano (1983). The first issue of the *Harbinger* carried an essay by Benjamin F. Barrett (see above) of the New Church in New York. Several of the articles on Swedenborgian topics were penned by Henry James, Sr. (see above). Brook Farm resident Charles A. Dana (1819–1897), later to gain fame as a newspaper editor, reviewed several Swedenborgian books for the periodical.

90. Further biographical data on Belding was not available to the authors.

this are far from clear. By the late 1850s, Le Raysville had disappeared from the General Convention's roster of New Church societies.[91]

The Canton Phalanx in central Illinois was founded in the spring of 1845 by John Randolph (died 1845), who at the time was also the lay leader of the Canton New Jerusalem Society and president of the infant Illinois Association of the New Church. Like Belding, he donated his farm to the project; it was a few miles west of Canton and consisted of about four hundred acres. In addition to the main residence of the Randolph family, the property included several log cabins and a large mill, which was immediately moved. It was augmented by a communal kitchen and dining area, a washhouse, and dormitory space for single men. Board shanties were provided for the other residents. The patchwork building took on the distinctive shape of a bird, and thus came to be called by that name. Approximately twelve families were involved in this utopian experiment; they also conducted a neighborhood school. Adversity struck in the fall of 1845 with the death of Randolph, and without his leadership the communal ties quickly dissolved. The farm reverted to the Randolph family, the nonresident stockholders were paid off through the sale of bricks that had been fired in order to build the main "phalansterie," and miscellaneous communal property was divided. This misadventure dealt a crushing blow to the Canton New Church society.[92]

While the Le Raysville and Canton phalanxes were being created in 1844 and 1845, New Church periodicals were reluctant to give a full hearing to Fourierist apologists. The one exception was the *Retina,* published in Hamilton, Ohio, in 1844–1845 by W. C. Howells (1807?–1894), father of the writer William Dean Howells (mentioned above as a friend of Henry James, Sr.).[93] For a short period, there was some interest in establishing an "industrial school community" in Pennsylvania along Fourierist principles and under New Church auspices, but these plans were vigorously opposed by others within the denomination (Swank 1970, 365–367). The problem, as noted previously by Otis Clapp, was clearly the antimarriage teaching of Fourier, which the public understood as an advocacy of free love. As the

---

91. The most complete information on the Le Raysville Phalanx is the A. J. MacDonald Collection at Yale University. Portions were published in Noyes [1870] 1961, 259–264. See also Gladish 1983, 41–48.

92. A brief description of the Canton experiment is [Hibbard] 1884, 81; see also Block 1984, 153–154; and Odhner 1904a, 509.

93. Gladish 1983, 37. A complete run of this rare periodical is included in the Special Collections of the Swedenborg Memorial Library, Urbana University, Urbana, Ohio.

above discussion of Thomas Lake Harris has indicated, Swedenborgians were extremely sensitive on this point and concerned to uphold the church's teachings on monogamy and the eternal spiritual affinity of married couples.

In many respects, New Church involvement with Fourier came to a climax—after the demise of the Brook Farm, Le Raysville, and Canton phalanxes—with the publication in 1848 of *The True Organization of the New Church,* by Charles Julius Hempel (1811–1879).[94] A native of Prussia, Hempel practiced homeopathic medicine first in New York and later in Philadelphia. He dedicated his book to adherents of Fourier and Swedenborg, and continued, "The doctrines of these two men can not remain separate. Their union constitutes the union of Science and Religion" (Hempel 1848, 13). He argued that God's plan was to restore harmony to the universe, which could be done by reducing human-made chaos to order and peace. Swedenborg provided the spiritual insights necessary for this task, while Fourier provided the mechanism for the realization of love in all social relationships. Reaction to Hempel's book in the New Church press was swift and scathing. A review in the *New Jerusalem Magazine* roundly condemned it as a book full of falsehoods and perversions of Swedenborg's doctrines ([Reed] 1848, 298–304). Other vocal opponents included the well-known Swedenborgian minister Benjamin F. Barrett.[95] In the end, Hempel's efforts met with no success. By the late 1840s, most of the dozens of communities founded under Fourierist influence had failed, and public interest in utopian socialist experimentation was rapidly drawing to a close.

Among the most intriguing of the Swedenborgian communalist organizations in the nineteenth century was one that had only indirect links with Fourierist thought. This community was the Jasper Colony;[96] it was located in Iowa County, Iowa, and was active between 1851 and 1853. Its leader was Herman H. Diekhöner (1796–1867), about whom surprisingly little is known. A native of Prussia, he was a reader of Swedenborg and socialist utopian literature when he immigrated in the early 1840s.

---

94. This work (Hempel 1848) was published anonymously, but its authorship was deducible at the time; a few years earlier, Hempel had published a glowing depiction of Associationism titled "The Phalanx" in the Swedenborgian periodical *Newchurchman* (Hempel 1843, 369–370).

95. See Gladish 1983, 95–101; Swank 1970, 370–374; "Editorial Items" 1848, 186–187; [Barrett] 1848, 529–543, 596–610; and [Hempel] 1848–1849, 69, 85–86, 100–101, 108–109.

96. In German the name was *Jaspis;* it stems from Revelation 21:19, in which jasper is the first foundation stone of the heavenly New Jerusalem.

He eventually settled in St. Louis and opened a cobbler shop. He soon attracted a following of German-speaking Swedenborgians and served as their unsalaried lay pastor, but he apparently had little contact with a struggling New Church society organized in St. Louis in 1842. Several factors, including a dislike for slavery and a cholera epidemic that hit St. Louis in 1848, prompted his group to seek relocation to newly opened prairie lands in Iowa (Smith 1955, 237–238; Hawley 1935, 10–13).

The Jasper community acquired between 1,500 and 2,000 acres some four miles south of the small town of Norway. The settlers lived communally in a log dwelling and farmed cooperatively; all property was held in the name of elected trustees. The land was fertile, and their farming efforts prospered, although hard currency was in short supply and some who had specialized trades resented turning over outside income to the community. In the end, the lure of private ownership proved too powerful to resist, and in early 1853, the colonists voted to dissolve the communal organization. Disillusioned, Diekhöner returned to St. Louis, where he formed another German Swedenborgian church in 1854. The Iowa settlers also continued to meet for worship and several years later formally organized a New Church congregation (Hawley 1935, 19–21).

VII. Homeopathy

Several of the Swedenborgians interested in Fourierism were also involved in homeopathy, including James John Garth Wilkinson and Charles Hempel. Otis Clapp, the Boston druggist and printer, prepared homeopathic remedies. One of the best known homeopathic pharmaceutical firms, Boericke and Tafel in Philadelphia, was founded by Swedenborgians.[97] Though well known in the eighteenth century, and enjoying an upsurge of interest as of this writing, this medical tradition is still so obscure today that it needs a working definition in a study of this kind. A medical practice totally unlike the European tradition, homeopathy works on the principles of "infinitesimals" and the theory that "like cures like." Specifically, homeopaths believe that disease and its symptoms can be cured by miniscule doses of a substance that produces symptoms similar to disease in a healthy person.

---

97. The Swedenborgian influence on homeopathy in the United States has been explored as part of lengthy studies by Taylor 1995, 80–81; Swank 1970, 381–412; Silver 1983, 223–229; in *Arcana* 2001 (volume 6, number 1); and in three specific, shorter essays by Peebles 1988, 468–472; Whitmont 1988, 473–474; and Moskowitz 1988, 475–476.

The American homeopathic movement has been linked traditionally, though informally, with Swedenborgianism from the earliest days of the older homeopathic movement in Great Britain. The connection has appeared self-evident both to homeopaths and to Swedenborgians. Ann Jerome Croce tells the story of a Boston Swedenborgian group that distributed T-shirts with lettering that read on the front, "Here comes a Swedenborgian," and on the back, "There goes a homeopath" (Croce 1996a, 1). The implied assumption of kinship between the two movements has persisted, despite the absence of any evidence that the founder of homeopathy—German medical doctor Samuel Hahnemann (1765–1843)—ever read Swedenborg or came into contact with Swedenborgian thought.[98]

It is known, however, that homeopathy was brought to America by an American-born Swedenborgian of Danish descent, Hans Burch Gram (1786–1840), when he returned to the United States in 1825 after training in Europe. Furthermore, the Hahnemann Medical College, which moved from Allentown, Pennsylvania, to Philadelphia, was founded in part by the Swedenborgian Constantine Hering (1800–1880). Other connections were described in a notice printed in *New Church Life* after a ceremony to mark the opening of the college:

> The intimate relation existing between Homeopathy and the New Church was illustrated at the recent dedication of the Hahnemann College in Philadelphia. Several New Churchmen are trustees of this Institution. Before the dedication the Pennsylvania State Society held its meeting with a New Church physician in the chair. The meeting was opened with prayer by a New Church minister. This was the first prayer offered in the building. The first bureau that reported was under the chairmanship of another New Church physician. On the walls of the room where the meeting was held hung the portraits of three deceased physicians, two of whom were New Churchmen, and the third a reader for a number of years. The building was dedicated by the Vice-President

---

98. Croce 1996a, 4–5. Croce argues that Hahnemann would have rejected Swedenborg for excessive emphasis on the spiritual at the expense of the material, which Hahnemann claimed to be his primary focus. However, Swedenborg maintains a strong materialism as well, finding what is earthly or material to be the basis, container, and support of what is spiritual; see, among other passages, *Secrets of Heaven* 8408:1, along with *True Christianity* 112:5: "Our soul's life is the life in our body. It is something the soul and the body share" (translation by Jonathan S. Rose). For more on Hahnemann, see Bradford 1895. Hahnemann's classic *Organon [of Homeopathic Medicine]* has gone through numerous editions and printings; among the most recent is Hahnemann [1836] 1982. One early attempt to connect Swedenborg and Hahnemann is de Charms 1850b.

of the College, a New Churchman, and during the exercises another New Church physician presented a portrait of Hahnemann to the College. ("News Gleanings" 1886, 175)

Undoubtedly the most influential nineteenth-century American homeopathic physician was James Tyler Kent (1849–1916), who was introduced to Swedenborg's teachings by his wife shortly before he wrote his major contributions to homeopathic theory (Peebles 1988, 470–471; see also Croce 1996a, 8–9).[99] Croce points to some of Kent's subtle amendments to Hahnemann's homeopathic theory, highlighting the Swedenborgian principles behind them. For example, Swedenborg's conviction that "human beings are spirits clothed in bodies"[100] pointed the way to experimental confirmation that the effectiveness, or "potency," of a remedy was in direct proportion to its dilution. More dilute remedies had smaller amounts of the effective matter in them and, therefore, were more spiritual, acting on more interior aspects of the patient (Croce 1996a, 9). Although not intuitively obvious, the theory behind "high-potency remedies" dominates much of homeopathic practice today.

VIII. New Thought

Homeopathy, however, was only one approach to the idea of healing through spiritual principals. Another was New Thought, a loosely defined movement that taught that health could be achieved through "right thinking." It can be traced to the Maine clockmaker Phineas P. Quimby (1802–1866).[101] To Quimby and his followers, illnesses seemed

---

99. Treuherz 2001, 24, suggests that Kent became a Swedenborgian in Philadelphia when he was dean of the Philadelphia Post Graduate School of School of Homeopathy between 1888 and 1899.

100. See page 211, with note 44 above.

101. Anderson and Whitehouse 1995, 19, consider Swedenborg to be a possible source of influence on Quimby's thinking, but state that Quimby himself did not acknowledge Swedenborg's views. It is worth noting, however, that the "Declaration of Principles" of the International New Thought Alliance reveals parallels with Swedenborgian theology. For example, one principle states: "We affirm that we are invisible spiritual dwellers within human bodies continuing and unfolding as spiritual beings beyond the change called physical death," a belief certainly consonant with if not limited to Swedenborgian theology. Another reads: "We affirm that the universe is the body of God, spiritual in essence, governed by God through laws which are spiritual in reality even when material in appearance," a notion that closely parallels Swedenborg's idea of the Universal Human. The principles are quoted in Anderson and Whitehouse 1995, 5.

the result of wrong beliefs, which could be "caught" as well as "cured." His converts—all of whom were healed—include Mary Baker Eddy (1821–1910),[102] the founder of Christian Science, and Warren Felt Evans (1817–1889), a Methodist-turned-Swedenborgian minister who also became prominent in mental healing ("mind cure") circles (Parker 1973, 3–4, 48). Evans based his medical practices on Swedenborg's teaching about correspondences, specifically that part of it that holds that the external, or physical condition, of each person corresponds to his or her internal state. Through personal hygiene, the physical body could be "purified," making it a proper "vessel" for the "influx" of spiritual truth. In books such as *The New Age and Its Messenger* (1864) and *The Mental-Cure* (1869), Evans expounded on this theme, insisting that the theory of correspondences was an exact science.[103]

Other converts of Quimby's included Julius Dresser (1838–1893) and Annetta Seabury Dresser (1843–1935).[104] In the late 1890s, after the death of her husband, Annetta Dresser converted to Swedenborgianism. One of their three surviving sons, Horatio Dresser (1866–1954), became a popular writer of inspirational self-help books and works related to New Thought and Swedenborgianism, including many articles in Swedenborgian periodicals.[105] He studied at Harvard University under teachers who included William James and Josiah Royce (1855–1916), and was ordained a Swedenborgian minister in 1919 (as his brother, Jean Paul Dresser [1877–1935], had been ten years earlier). Although he withdrew from the roll of ordained ministers and from church membership from 1929 to 1942, Horatio Dresser continued to write on Swedenborgian subjects, returning to the church and the ministry for the last years of his life. His biographer, C. Alan Anderson, notes that it is perhaps impossible to determine the full extent of Dresser's attachment to Swedenborg's teachings. At different times, for different readers, he expressed different

---

102. References to her vary in the contemporary literature. Baker was her birth surname, and Glover, Patterson, and Eddy were the married names she took from her respective husbands.

103. It is worth recording that *The New Age and Its Messenger* was issued by a Swedenborgian publisher, T. H. Carter & Company. For more on Evans see Sanchez Walsh 1997. For more on the history of mental healing in general, see Podmore 1963.

104. The Dressers' major contributions to the literature of New Thought can be found respectively in Dresser 1899 and Dresser 1895.

105. See Anderson 1996. The most complete study of Horatio Dresser is Anderson 1993.

viewpoints. His thought on mental healing and Swedenborg undoubtedly evolved over time. Yet his attachment to Swedenborg's teachings is fundamental, as Anderson shows in quoting Dresser's assessment of them:

> The main truth of which Swedenborg insists . . . as I understand it is that God is the one sufficiency. . . . That is to say, we have no life or selfhood apart from God, who individuates himself in us, gives us our being, and is the source of all truth, the ground of all law and universality.[106]

Two of Dresser's most important works were *A History of the New Thought Movement* (1919) and *The Quimby Manuscripts* (1921). The former work offers unqualified praise for Quimby but is highly critical of Evans's interpretation of Swedenborg. In the latter, Dresser suggests that Mary Baker Eddy's foundational work *Science and Health* (Glover 1875) was little more than a revised draft of papers written by Quimby, with a pinch of Swedenborg thrown in for good measure.[107] It is clear that at one time Eddy and Quimby had a close personal relationship, but she later distanced herself from him. Historian Gail Parker concludes: "It is difficult to compare Quimby's writings with those of Mrs. Baker and still doubt that she lusted after his ideas, whatever she thought of the person."[108]

The New Thought movement has had a continuing impact on the society of the United States, feeding the affirmative attitudes and determination of a "can-do" society. However, it has undergone so much permutation that the term "New Thought" has been virtually eradicated from the twenty-first century lexicon, replaced by labels such as "positive" or "affirmative" thinking (Anderson and Whitehouse 1995, 66). Social evangelists such as Norman Vincent Peale (1898–1993) and Robert Schuller (1926–) have to some degree reconceptualized the essence of New Thought, as have many of the movements that have sprung up under the amorphous rubric of the New Age.[109]

---

106. Quoted in Anderson 1993, 9, from Dresser 1911, 6.

107. The subtitle of *The Quimby Manuscripts* is *Showing the Discovery of Spiritual Healing and the Origin of Christian Science*. For this work, see Dresser [1921] 1961.

108. Parker 1973, 124. For a recent and more balanced interpretation of Eddy's relationship with Quimby, see Gill 1998, 334–336.

109. Anderson and Whitehouse 1995, 66–84, discuss the similarities and differences in New Thought and the New Age movement.

IX. Vegetarianism

Just as Swedenborgian theology played a role in the antislavery movement, though Swedenborg himself did not directly condemn the institution, so too his theology was a contributing factor in the growth of vegetarianism, despite the lack of any precise statement by him in its favor. Historian Colin Spencer notes that Swedenborg "had little to say about the human relationship with animals, but what he did say on meat-eating was highly significant. He saw meat-eating as the most vivid symbol of our fall from grace and the source of all evil."[110] Swedenborgians, taking up this cue, were instrumental in the vegetarian movements of the 1800s in both Britain and the United States.[111]

William Cowherd (1736–1816), a minister of the Church of England, left the national church to join the growing Church of the New Jerusalem. In 1793 he was invited to be the first minister of the New Jerusalem Temple in Manchester; however, in 1800 he left his congregation and started his own Swedenborg chapel in nearby Salford. Cowherd believed in Swedenborgian regeneration, a steady, life-long process of moral and spiritual renewal, and felt that eating meat obstructed the spirit's emergence into a new and cleaner life (Spencer 1993, 253). He preached "the doctrine of abstention from the flesh of animals as food, and total abstinence from all intoxicating liquors, as religious duties" (Maintenance Committee 1922, 20). After nine years, Cowherd's preaching proved too radical for the

---

110. Spencer 1993, 253. Perhaps the most explicit treatment of this topic can be found in the passage where Swedenborg explains the inner meaning of the Bible verse "Only flesh in its soul [you must not eat], its blood you must not eat" (Genesis 9:4, translated by Lisa Hyatt Cooper):

> Regarded in itself, eating meat is a profane custom, since people of the very earliest times never ate the flesh of any animal or bird but only grains (particularly wheat bread), fruit, vegetables, different kinds of milk, and milk products (such as butter). Butchering living creatures and eating the flesh was heinous, in their eyes, and characteristic of wild beasts. . . . But when time passed and people turned as savage as wild animals and in fact more savage, for the first time they started to butcher animals and eat the meat. In view of the fact that people were like this, the practice was also tolerated, as it still is today. To the extent that people follow it in good conscience, it is permissible, because everything we consider true and consequently allowable forms our conscience. For this reason, no one these days is ever condemned for eating meat. (*Secrets of Heaven* 1002)

111. There were, of course, practicing vegetarians long before the 1800s. In addition to Spencer 1993, see Dombrowski 1984 for a general history of the movement.

members of his Swedenborgian congregation, and most abandoned him (Spencer 1993, 254).

Yet the loss of his congregation did not deter Cowherd; he built another chapel, which he called "the Bible-Christian Church." Its Swedenborgian roots—including a belief in the government of divine love and wisdom, a rejection of the doctrine of the resumption of the material body after death in the Last Judgment, and the acceptance of Swedenborg's revelation about the Second Coming—can be clearly see in its statement of principles (Maintenance Committee 1922, 30–34).

Among Cowherd's parishioners in the Bible-Christian Church was Joseph Brotherton (1783–1857), who had also been a member of Cowherd's Swedenborgian congregation (Antrobus 1997, 17). Brotherton succeeded Cowherd as pastor of the Bible-Christian Church in 1816, and in 1847 he presided over the meeting that led to the creation of the Vegetarian Society. Another member of the Bible-Christian Church, James Simpson (?–1859) was elected the society's first president. The Bible-Christians continued in the vanguard of the vegetarian cause in Britain under the leadership of James Clark (1830–1905), who served as pastor for fifty years beginning in 1858 (Antrobus 1997, 96).

British and American vegetarians were closely connected throughout the nineteenth century. In 1817 another Bible-Christian by the name of James Clarke (1778–1826) left Britain and sailed for the United States along with William Metcalfe (1788–1862) and thirty-nine other members of the Bible-Christian Church, where Metcalfe and he intended to establish a church in Philadelphia. Though Clarke soon succumbed to a fever, Metcalfe went on to foster vegetarianism in the United States.[112]

At first, Metcalfe and his congregation were not readily accepted in Philadelphia, and they were particularly unpopular in the religious press; but the group persevered. Metcalfe was especially active in spreading the word of temperance and vegetarianism. The Bible-Christian congregation also advocated pacifism, at least until the Civil War. In 1821 Metcalfe privately published an essay titled *Bible Testimony on Abstinence from the Flesh of Animals,* which he distributed at no cost. He published several newspapers, all of which were unprofitable: *The Independent Democrat* (1832), *The Morning Star* (1838–1841), and *The Temperance Advocate* (1832–1835).[113]

---

112. On Clarke, see page 295 below, with note 89 there.

113. For summaries of his views, see Metcalfe 1872, especially the reprint of his 1821 essay mentioned here, "Bible Testimony on Abstinence from the Flesh of Animals as Food" (Metcalfe 1872, 151–183).

Although these efforts were financial failures, they did attract attention—in particular, that of two influential Americans: Sylvester Graham (1794–1851) and William Alcott (1798–1851).[114]

Metcalfe kept in touch with his English colleagues, and, after the Vegetarian Society was formed in Britain, he wrote to Graham, Alcott, and others concerning the need to establish a comparable American society. In May 1850, an American Vegetarian Convention assembled in Clinton Hall in New York. Metcalfe was elected president of the convention, which passed the constitution and by-laws of the American Vegetarian Society. The first president was Alcott; Metcalfe was elected the corresponding secretary. Later that year, Metcalfe published (edited, printed, folded, and mailed) the first issue of *The American Vegetarian and Health Journal,* but this too was short-lived, ceasing publication in 1854. In 1859 Metcalfe succeeded Alcott as president, a post he held until his death in 1862.

X. Conclusion

Swedenborg's theological works are voluminous, and despite the manifold doctrinal repetitions they contain, they are incredibly rich. Their influence on their readership is accordingly broad and deep. They speak of the correspondence of the spiritual and material world, a concept that in the past two centuries has intrigued writers and artists no less than spiritual seekers. Their focus on an equal and spiritual form of marriage has promoted equality in the home and in the voting booth. Their picture of the universe as a chain of ordered being stretching from the smallest to the largest of things has appealed to scientists no less than to poets. Such a list might be continued at length.

Out of this wealth of influences, however, there is one theme of Swedenborg's works that had an impact on virtually all of the individuals and movements described in this essay: his often-stated insistence that what makes people most human is their willingness to turn

---

114. Though Graham is best remembered today for the whole-grain cracker to which he gave his name, he was a leading health reformer during the nineteenth century. He also was a mentor to Mary Gove Nichols (see note 75 above). William Alcott was cousin to Bronson Alcott, mentioned above, whom he introduced to vegetarianism.

away from the limitations of self—to love one another, and to show that love by serving society. A clear illustration of these values of usefulness and love for one's neighbor can be seen in the career of Helen Keller (1880–1968), probably the best-known Swedenborgian of her generation, if not of the twentieth century. Her fame stems in large part from her work as a blind and deaf person on behalf of others similarly sense-impaired.

Keller's religious orientation can be documented from her conversation and correspondence, her public statements on the topic, and her writing—especially her 1927 book, *My Religion*, reissued (in augmented form) in 1994 and again in 2000 as *Light in My Darkness*. She may have been affected by Swedenborgian ideas even earlier than her own account indicates, however. Apart from her friends and her teacher, her first religious instructor was Phillips Brooks (1835–1893), the well-known preacher and first rector of Trinity Church in Copley Square in Boston's Back Bay. There is some evidence that his theology was Swedenborgian, even though he chose to be ordained in the Episcopal church in the belief that his service would be wider there.[115] However, Keller's account of their interaction does nothing to undermine or support this suggestion (Keller 2000, 9–10).

In 1893, at age sixteen, Keller made the acquaintance of John Hitz (1828–1908), the Swiss consul-general in Washington. Hitz, hearing-impaired himself, had worked with Alexander Graham Bell (1847–1922) on the *Volta Review*, a magazine for the deaf. He corresponded with Keller, met with her as often as possible, and selected and copied much reading material into Braille for her. One day he gave her a copy of Swedenborg's *Heaven and Hell*. In *Light in My Darkness* Keller describes her discovery of Swedenborg through this Braille volume, recounts the joy she felt at her first reading of it, and summarizes Swedenborg's theology with eloquent explanations of how the theological system—and especially the vivid and detailed descriptions of heaven, hell, and the world of spirits—brought spiritual light into the darkness of her life. She found one particularly compelling aspect of life after death to be its

---

115. The source of this information about Brooks is a personal communication to Robert H. Kirven from Antony Regamey (1899–1976), pastor of the Boston Church of the New Jerusalem and a teacher at the New Church Theological School. Regamey asserted that he had heard this from Brooks and from mutual acquaintances. Brooks consistently avoided calling himself an Episcopal priest, preferring the generic designation "preacher of the Word of God."

focus on the essential meaning of humanness, people's usefulness to one another:

> By focusing on their God-given talent, men and women who are becoming angels rise continually to nobler tasks. . . . In heaven we shall find the beauty and strength of men and women, selfless love between the sexes, the frolic of children, the joys of companionship, and the vital power of touch exquisitely soothing and eloquent. So, in the light of Swedenborg's teachings, heavenly life is a truly human life, and there are all kinds of service—domestic, civil, social, and inspirational—to be performed and enjoyed. (Keller 2000, 89)

Further reading of Swedenborg throughout Keller's life increased her faith in his descriptions of spiritual life and in his theology. It also persuaded her to undertake a life of service:

> Swedenborg says that "the perfection of [humankind] is the love of use," or service to others (*Divine Love and Wisdom,* paragraph 237). Our halting attempts to act are mere stammering suggestions of the greatness of service that we intend. We will to do more than we can ever do, and it is what we *will* that is in essence ourselves. The dearest of all consolations that Swedenborg's message brings me is that in the next world our narrow field of work shall grow limitlessly broad and luminous. . . . The greatest workers for the race—scientists, poets, and artists who possess all their faculties—are at times shaken with a mighty cry of the soul, a longing more fully to bring forth the energy, the fire, and the richness of imagination and human impulse that overburden them. What wonder, then, that we with our limited senses and more humble powers should crave wider range and scope of usefulness? (Keller 2000, 106, 107)

Under this influence, Keller became an advocate for people impaired in sight and hearing, traveling throughout the world six times over during her lifetime to promote their education and full engagement in society. In one eleven-year span alone (1946–1957) she made seven voyages, taking her message to thirty-five nations on five continents. During one of these years, at age seventy-five, she made a forty-thousand-mile tour through Asia that lasted five months. Improved conditions for the blind and deaf can be shown to be a direct result of her work in many nations that she visited. At home, too, she promoted humane values through constant writing, not only of books but of numerous articles published in popular magazines. She spoke against racism, poverty, capital punishment, and nuclear war, and defended women's suffrage and the rights of workers. It was typical of her zeal that she considered her visits to soldiers blinded or otherwise disabled in World War II to be one of the most profound experiences of her life.[116]

Though Keller is one of the clearest examples of Swedenborg's influence, the same words that stirred her to her task also moved other actors, great and small, on the stage of British and American culture in the nineteenth and twentieth centuries. The passion of Elizabeth Barrett Browning in her search for social justice, of the abolitionists in working for the freedom of slaves, of Sampson Reed envisioning a larger use for science and poetry, of the utopian socialists, of homeopathic doctors or New Thought healers experimenting with a new way to cure human ills—all stems in large part from the Swedenborgian vision that human life is, in its essence, service to others, not an exercise in self-advancement. Certainly the many players on the stage had their petty motives as well, their egotisms, their vanities, and their failings, and their very human squabbles and failures may seem at times to have cast obstacles in the way of their success. Nevertheless, it can still be said that under Swedenborg's influence they were all "shaken with a mighty cry of the soul, a longing more fully to bring forth the energy, the fire, and the richness of imagination and human impulse" in the service of others.

116. For a recent life of Keller, see Herrmann 1998. Other sources include Keller 2003; Brooks 1956; and Harrity and Martin 1962.

ORGANIZATIONAL IMPACT

Swedenborgian Churches and Related Institutions in Great Britain, the United States, and Canada

JANE WILLIAMS-HOGAN
AND DAVID B. ELLER

Outline

I. Publishing Ventures

II. Church Organizations
    a. Beginnings in Great Britain
    b. The General Conference

III. The New Church Comes to America
    a. Early Societies
    b. The West and Canada
    c. Ethnic Churches

IV. The General Convention
    a. Forms of Worship
    b. Ministry and Other Activities
    c. Stresses in the National Organization
    d. Membership Trends

V. The General Church
    a. Origins of the Schism
    b. Achieving Equilibrium
    c. The Battle over *Marriage Love*
    d. Growth of the Church

VI. The Lord's New Church Which Is Nova Hierosolyma

VII. Other Church Groups
    a. The Bible-Christian Church
    b. The St. Thomas Christians

VIII. Schools and Colleges
    a. The Waltham New Church School
    b. Urbana University

c. Swedenborgian House of Studies

d. The Academy Theological School and Bryn Athyn College

IX. Building Community

a. The World's Parliament of Religions

b. Movements in Art and Science

c. Assemblies, Retreats, and Spiritual Growth Centers

X. Conclusion

FOLLOWING his remarkable career as a mining engineer, scientist, civil servant, and theological writer, Emanuel Swedenborg died a bachelor in relative obscurity at his rented lodgings in London, England, in 1772. A communicant Lutheran, he was interred in a burial vault under the floor of the altar of the Swedish Lutheran Church, on Princes Square. More than 130 years later, however, Swedenborg's casket was removed with great ceremony to a place of honor in a side chapel of Uppsala's cathedral, the final resting place of Sweden's monarchs and illustrious citizens. The shift in his burial place testifies to the change in the world's appreciation of his work, a change wrought by his followers and readers over many years.

By his own account, Swedenborg viewed himself as a "servant of the Lord Jesus Christ,"[1] who in his latter years had been permitted a deeper insight into the meaning of the Christian Scriptures and a visible glimpse into the workings of heaven and hell. While Swedenborg claimed to have seen the creation of a "new church" in the spiritual world,[2] he took no steps to organize an earthly counterpart. Although thousands of individuals across the years have gained spiritual wisdom and satisfaction from

---

1. See the title page of his 1771 work *True Christianity*. For the sake of simplicity, the modern titles of Swedenborg's works are used throughout this essay; see the list on page 98 above. For the traditional titles, see the index and list on pages 395–509 below. Full bibliographic data on any older editions of Swedenborg's works mentioned here but not represented in the list of works cited in this volume can be found in Hyde 1906, supplemented by Wainscot 1967.

2. Generally speaking, Swedenborg referred to any widespread spiritual revitalization as the formation of a "new church." More specifically, the term refers to an era of God-human relations that will acknowledge and worship the one true God; hold God's revealed Scriptures as holy; love spiritual truth; and reject faith separated from love for one's neighbor. According to Swedenborg, the most recent new church was initiated in 1757; see *Last Judgment* 45. (As is common in Swedenborgian studies, text citations of Swedenborg's works refer not to page numbers but to Swedenborg's section numbers, which are uniform in all editions.)

devotionally reading his theological works and many of them have organized into worshiping communities, Swedenborg should not be regarded as the "founder" or "reformer" of a religion, in the manner of Martin Luther (1483–1546), John Calvin (1509–1564), or John Wesley (1703–1791), Swedenborg's contemporary. He did not give public lectures on his spiritual experiences, revise the Christian liturgy, or start a theological school. Rather, he was content to do as he believed God had instructed him: to publish his books with the confidence that their spiritual message would find a ready audience within the existing church, and beyond.[3] He believed that readers of his books would use the message they contained to create a truly new kind of Christianity.

Swedenborg's works did gradually find a wide audience. For more than two hundred years, numerous individuals have accepted some portion of his theological insights yet have remained (or have found a home) in other faith traditions. Swedenborg's beliefs have served as leaven for Roman Catholics, Anglicans/Episcopalians, Lutherans, Methodists, Friends (Quakers), Unitarians, Mennonites, and even Latter-Day Saints (Mormons) and Christian Scientists, to name a few. His influence within Christianity, particularly his descriptions of heaven, hell, spiritual growth, and the soul after death, is beyond measure.

This essay explores movements and institutions that developed a unique Swedenborgian identity, that is, movements grounded in Swedenborg's theological works and the spiritual worldview they present. Unfortunately, limitations of space restrict the scope of this essay to the major developments in Great Britain, Canada, and the United States. Though a similar pattern of institutionalization followed in Africa, Australia, New Zealand, and other lands, it cannot be examined here.[4]

Perhaps it is natural to think of church groups as the primary means by which Swedenborg's teachings took on an organizational form. Numerically, Swedenborgian churches have been a tiny part of the Christian

---

3. In his last published work (*True Christianity* 779) Swedenborg wrote: "Since the Lord could not manifest himself in person . . . and yet he foretold that he was going to come and establish a new church, the New Jerusalem, it follows that he would do this through some person who had both the intellectual capacity to receive the teachings of this church and the ability to publish those teachings in print" (translation by Jonathan S. Rose).

4. For discussion of the development of Swedenborgian institutions in certain regions of Africa, see pages 317–335 below.

family; in the year 2003 their membership numbered perhaps 35,000 worldwide, not including 15,000 readers and associates.[5] Within the Swedenborgian tradition, there are distinct denominational families and differing forms of institutional organization. Swedenborgianism, as a body of ideas, has demonstrated an amazing variety in its patterns of worship, educational enterprises, publishing ventures, missionary activities, and the patterns through which Swedenborgians have sought to reshape (or perhaps give back to) society. Again, a full study of these developments would require volumes. It is hoped that the highlights offered here will stimulate further scholarly interest, study, research, and writing about ways in which ideals from Swedenborg's works have led to institutional and organizational forms.

A word concerning terminology may be helpful. The terms "Swedenborgian Church" and "New Church" are used here to refer to a broad movement based on Swedenborg's teachings. Unless the context suggests otherwise, they do not mean a specific denomination, legal entity, or group. Organized congregations (frequently known as "societies") were given such names as the "Church of the New Jerusalem" or "New Jerusalem Church," in a direct reference to the holy city, the new Jerusalem, descending from the heavens as described in Revelation 21:10–27.[6] Historically, members of these churches have accepted the divine or revelatory nature of Swedenborg's works (which some have referred to collectively as "the Writings"), have described themselves as "receivers of the heavenly doctrines," and have believed that Swedenborg's works would gradually lead to a new form of Christianity that would truly reflect the New Jerusalem. They have spoken of their movement as the "New" Church (to distinguish it from the "old" Christian churches), and referred to its adherents as Swedenborgians or as New Church men and women. Yet virtually all branches of the organized New Church would agree that Swedenborg's spiritual vision of a New Church that would replace the varieties of Christianity with which he was familiar should not be equated with any specific earthly body or organization.

---

5. For background on this estimate, see Williams-Hogan 2003, 90–97.

6. See *Secrets of Heaven* 3858:2, 4434:2, and especially 8988:4, which says, in explaining the Revelation passage: "The new, holy Jerusalem symbolizes the Lord's new church" (translation by Lisa Hyatt Cooper).

I. Publishing Ventures

While Christian movements have often depended on a charismatic personality, or employed emotional mass evangelism techniques, Swedenborgians have overwhelmingly preferred pen and press to share their faith. Although New Church teachings may be based on revelation, adherents have insisted that their faith is entirely rational, reflecting the divine pattern of an orderly universe. An individual comes to accept truths or insights from Swedenborg, not (or only rarely) through a conversion experience, but by reading what Swedenborg wrote, followed by study and reflection. Swedenborgian Christianity can be described as a "charisma of the book" (Williams-Hogan 1997, 2). It follows that all manner of publishing and distribution activities—translation work, tracts and pamphlets, periodicals and newsletters, reading rooms and reading circles, book-agent programs, books about Swedenborg or Swedenborgian thought, even records, film, and video productions—have been the main instruments in the spread of Swedenborg's ideas. His many theological works, as well as various excerpts and abstracts from them, have been reprinted numerous times in dozens of languages.

Even before Swedenborg's death, a tiny group of dedicated readers in England began the daunting task of translating his Neo-Latin books into English so that they could reach a larger audience. John Marchant[7] was commissioned by Swedenborg to translate the second volume of *Secrets of Heaven* (1750) and *Survey* (1769). Thomas Hartley (1708–1784), a clergyman in the Church of England, and William Cookworthy (1705–1780),[8] a leader in the Society of Friends, collaborated in translating *Soul-Body Interaction* (1770), and later *Heaven and Hell* (1778). John Clowes (1743–1831) in Manchester and Robert Hindmarsh (1759–1835)[9] in London became convinced of Swedenborg's revelations and undertook the translation of several titles. Hindmarsh was later instrumental in organizing the first Swedenborgian churches, described below. Clowes, who was also involved with the spread of the New

---

7. Marchant was an English writer and compiler of the mid-eighteenth century who wrote on current events and literary themes such as the Bible and *Paradise Lost*. His dates of birth and death were not available to the authors, though erroneously specified in Hyde 1906, page 731. In some cases his name is given as Merchant.

8. For a biography of Cookworthy, see Compton 1895.

9. For a biography of Hindmarsh, see Odhner 1895.

Church, deserves special recognition for his ten-volume translation of the massive *Secrets of Heaven,* on which most subsequent English editions have been based. He devoted a considerable amount of his time to this project over twenty years (1783–1803).

In both Britain and the United States, Swedenborgian publishing enterprises were closely linked in time with the organization of communities of worship. Indeed, one of the very first Swedenborgian organizations was the Manchester Printing Society, formed in 1782, only ten years after Swedenborg's death (Hindmarsh 1861, 7, 15–17, 143–157). Two years later, the Theosophical Society was organized in London, under Hindmarsh's leadership, for the purpose of promoting Swedenborg's teachings through translating and publishing. The oldest continuously operating Swedenborgian publishing organization in the world is the Swedenborg Society (originally the London Printing Society), founded in Great Britain in 1810 with John Augustus Tulk (about 1751–1845) as its chair. Located in the heart of London, the Society operated as a charitable, membership-based organization, dedicated to the translation, printing, and distribution of Swedenborg's theological writings. In 1862 the Society also took over the inventory and functions of the Swedenborg Association (founded in 1844) for printing Swedenborg's scientific and philosophical works (Griffith 1960, 3–5, 23).

Following early translation and printing work, one of the Society's important projects was commissioning R. L. Tafel (1831–1893) to travel to Sweden in 1869 and arrange to have photolithographs made of Swedenborg's original manuscripts; these photolithographs filled ten oversized volumes (Photolithographs 1869–1970). This effort also led to the publication of Tafel's monumental *Documents Concerning the Life and Character of Emanuel Swedenborg* (1875–1877). A similar project headed by Alfred Stroh (1878–1922) took place between 1901 and 1916 (jointly sponsored by the Society and other Swedenborgian publishers).[10] This research resulted in eighteen oversized volumes of manuscript phototypes (Phototypes 1901–1916).[11] Other major reference works produced by the Society

10. Other financial partners included the British General Conference, the Academy of the New Church, the American Swedenborg Printing and Publishing Society (now the Swedenborg Foundation), the Rotch Fund, and the General Convention of the New Church in America. Copies of the set were presented to major academic libraries in the United States and Europe (Eby 1926, 47–57).

11. The Photolithographs and Phototypes should be distinguished from a third manuscript reproduction series in twenty-one volumes, the Photostats (1926–1930), undertaken by Alfred Acton (see page 306 below) in the United States. For further information, see the list of works cited in this volume under these three entries (Photolithographs, Photostats, and Phototypes).

include the *Swedenborg Concordance* (1888–1902), compiled by John F. Potts (1866–1923), and *A Bibliography of the Works of Emanuel Swedenborg* (1906), compiled by James Hyde (1861–1910).[12] For its centennial celebration in 1910, the Society sponsored a major international gathering, the Swedenborg Congress of July 4–9, which gave public recognition in Britain to Swedenborg's achievements in science and philosophy, as well as in theology. More than nine hundred people attended the congress, which included daily sessions, special evening events, and a gala garden party.[13]

Until the mid-twentieth century, most Swedenborg Society editions were revisions of eighteenth-century translations. Renewed interest in translation work following World War II led to several new publications. John E. Elliott, of the British New Church clergy, completed a new edition of *Secrets of Heaven* (1983–1999), the first totally new translation since that by John Clowes. The distinguished Oxford classical scholar John Chadwick (1920–1997) also produced in rapid succession a series of new Swedenborg Society translations of *True Christianity* (1988), *New Jerusalem* (1990), *Last Judgment* (1992), *Marriage Love* (1996), and *Other Planets* (1997).[14]

The Society has an extensive library, begun in 1824, and maintains offices at 20–21 Bloomsbury Way in London. By the time of its 150th anniversary in 1960, the Society had printed and distributed almost two million copies of Swedenborg's works in thirty different languages, including Danish, Icelandic, Polish, Arabic, Dutch, Italian, and Hindi, to cite a few (Griffith 1960, 65).

On the other side of the Atlantic, the cities of Philadelphia, Boston, Cincinnati, New York, and later Chicago, Bryn Athyn (Pennsylvania), and San Francisco have all been centers for Swedenborgian book, tract, and periodical publishing. As was the case in Britain, publishing began in the same era as the organized churches. The first American publisher of Swedenborg was Francis Bailey (1744–1817), a printer who resided in Lancaster and Philadelphia.[15] He brought out both John Clowes's *A Summary View of the*

---

12. On these works, see Griffith 1960, 23, 26, 28.

13. For addresses from the full program, see Swedenborg Society 1910.

14. These volumes appeared respectively as *True Christian Religion* [1771] 1988c; *The New Jerusalem and Heaven's Teaching for It* [1758] 1990; *The Last Judgment* [1758] 1992b; *Conjugial Love* [1768] 1996g; and *The Worlds in Space* [1758] 1997d.

15. Bailey was official printer to the Commonwealth of Pennsylvania and the United States Congress. A historical marker at 14 West King Street in downtown Lancaster marks the spot where he operated a printing business between 1773 and 1780.

Heavenly Doctrines in 1787 and the first volume of *True Christianity* in 1789
(Block 1984, 75). In the Boston area, William Hill (1762–1804), an Angli-
can priest, paid for the publication of the first American edition of *Divine
Love and Wisdom* (1794).

Most publishing ventures in the early nineteenth century were
linked to local societies, at least informally. One of the most ambitious
of these was the Boston New Church Printing Society, which was active
from 1834 to the mid-1840s (Eller 1999, 5). It brought out one of the first
American printings of *Heaven and Hell* (1837) and several volumes of
Secrets of Heaven (1837–1840).

The largest and oldest continuously operating United States publisher of Swedenborg's works is the Swedenborg Foundation, founded
in New York in 1849 as the American Swedenborg Printing and Publishing Association. It was modeled organizationally after both the
Swedenborg Society in London and the American Bible Society, whose
offices were also in New York. The name was changed in 1920 when
the charter purposes were enlarged to include Swedenborg's scientific
writings and work about Swedenborg or his ideas (often termed "collateral literature"). Since its inception, the Foundation has been a
membership organization, composed primarily of New Church women
and men committed to publishing and distributing Swedenborg's works
in inexpensive editions. For more than 140 years, the Foundation
maintained a book room and publishing offices in midtown Manhat-
tan. Largely as a result of financial considerations, however, the Foundation relocated to West Chester, in the greater suburban Philadelphia
area, in 1993.

Two complete editions of Swedenborg's theological works published
by the Swedenborg Foundation enjoyed wide distribution, the Octavo
Edition in the nineteenth century and the Standard Edition (which also
included many of Swedenborg's previously unpublished and posthumous
works, as well as miscellaneous items) in the twentieth century. As is the
case with the Swedenborg Society, a major focus of the Foundation's activities has been the distribution of Swedenborgian literature. Thousands
of books and pamphlets have been supplied to public and academic libraries, book rooms, ministers of various denominations, and contacts
overseas through a network of volunteer book agents (Eller 1999, 22–30,
45–46). Unlike the Swedenborg Society, however, the Foundation has
published relatively little in languages other than English. Rather, it has
branched out into producing popular books and videos for the general

religious book market that explore Swedenborgian concepts or themes. One of its foremost titles in this field is Helen Keller's *My Religion*[16] and it has also offered books on topics such as angels, the near-death experience, and spiritual growth, among others. Its journal *Chrysalis,* issued quarterly from 1985 to 1994 and as an annual reader since 1995, seeks to address Swedenborgian themes of spiritual exploration in fresh and creative ways.

Two of the most ambitious projects of the Foundation were part of a year-long celebration in 1988 of the three-hundredth anniversary of Swedenborg's birth. The first of these was a major international conference, the Symposium on Science and Spirituality, held in August of that year in Tarrytown, New York. It included presentations by thinkers noted for exploring the unity between scientific thought and spirituality, including Larry Dossey, John L. Hitchcock, Robert McDermott, Raymond Moody, and Renee Weber, among others.[17] The second project, and the Foundation's single most ambitious publishing venture to that time, was the release of *Emanuel Swedenborg: A Continuing Vision,* edited by Robin Larsen and others, also in 1988. This commemorative, oversized volume contained numerous essays on Swedenborg's continuing legacy, a fresh biography, poetry, and more than four hundred illustrations.

II. Church Organizations

The determined publication effort of Swedenborgians is intertwined with the growth of their church organizations. The Swedenborgian church movement began in the late 1700s in England, a land where legal religious toleration had been secured after a century of bitter struggle. Swedenborgian groups that started on the European continent, where religious freedom was more fragile and dissenting traditions less well accepted, faced a more difficult challenge. This fact had

---

16. The original edition of Keller's book was issued in New York by Doubleday, Page in 1927; it was reprinted several times through the 1970s by the Swedenborg Foundation and other firms. In 1994 the Swedenborg Foundation reissued it in an expanded and revised edition as *Light in My Darkness,* edited by Ray Silverman. A second edition was published in 2000.

17. See *Science and Spirituality* 1989 for selected symposium proceedings.

two important results in the subsequent development of the New Church. The first is that virtually every branch of the Swedenborgian Church outside Europe may be traced back to British roots. Five major New Church bodies in particular have grown from these roots, one headquartered in the United Kingdom, three in the United States, and one in Africa. These are the General Conference of the New Church (British Conference) formed in 1789; the General Convention of the New Jerusalem, founded in Philadelphia in 1817;[18] the General Church of the New Jerusalem, founded in 1897 in Bryn Athyn, Pennsylvania;[19] the Lord's New Church Which Is Nova Hierosolyma,[20] founded in 1937, also in Bryn Athyn; and the New Church of Southern Africa founded in 1911 by David Mooki (1876–1927), originally called the New Church of Africa.

The New Church's emergence from the seedbed of English religious liberty has, secondly, shaped both worship and polity to the present. Because dissenting groups were permitted outside the Church of England and allowed to evangelize, they found it possible to develop distinctive patterns of church life, as long as they did not disturb public order. Some dissenting groups such as the English Methodists retained Anglican features, while others such as the Quakers and Baptists retained relatively little. Swedenborgian churches have at times reflected both orientations. For example, the early development of a Swedenborgian liturgical order of worship stems directly from its Anglican heritage. At the same time, the congregationalist and anticlerical stance of many in the General Convention during the nineteenth century reflects a dissenting or nonconformist, even sectarian, worldview.[21]

---

18. Incorporated in 1861 as the General Convention of the New Jerusalem in the United States of America, this body adopted the name the Swedenborgian Church of North America in 1989. (The name indicates only the inclusion of Canada; there are no Convention-sponsored churches in Mexico.) Within the New Church community, it is commonly referred to as the "General Convention" or, simply, "Convention."

19. The forerunner of this group is the Academy movement, discussed below. Within the New Church community it is commonly known as the "General Church."

20. "Nova Hierosolyma" is Latin for "the New Jerusalem" and refers to Swedenborg's identification of the New Church with the New Jerusalem, as mentioned above. Within the New Church community, this group is generally referred to simply as "the Lord's New Church."

21. The classic "church" vs. "sect" typology was developed by German sociologist Ernst Troeltsch (1865–1923); see Troeltsch 1960, and pages 192–193 above. For a description of English church life following the Act of Toleration (1688), see Collinson 1982.

a. Beginnings in Great Britain

Given the length of time required to translate and print books on the scale of Swedenborg's works, it is little short of remarkable that by 1783, just eleven years after Swedenborg's death, there were several hundred individuals in Europe who were not only reading his writings devotionally but holding public worship services inspired by them (Hindmarsh 1861, 200). Undoubtedly, much of this virtually instantaneous growth may be attributed to the freshness and power of Swedenborg's ideas. In London, Robert Hindmarsh began to organize some readers into a worshiping community. First he began a reading group in his home in Clerkenwell in 1783, then as noted above, organized a publishing venture and discussion group called the Theosophical Society (Odhner 1895, 10–16).

At its peak in 1787, the Theosophical Society had approximately one hundred members. Translation and publication were its public functions, but its members met together privately to read and discuss various aspects of Swedenborg's theology. They also worshipped together for a time under the leadership of Jacob Duché (1738–1798),[22] a reader of Swedenborg and chaplain at the Asylum for Female Orphans in St. George's Field. In July of 1787, Hindmarsh's group held its first public worship service. One of its number, James Hindmarsh (1731–1812), young Robert's father and a former Methodist preacher, was chosen by lot to officiate. He administered holy communion and baptized five candidates into the New Church. A meeting place was secured in a rented chapel in Great East Cheap, London, and a liturgy developed for regular worship. Legal recognition as a dissenting church was soon secured, and the organized New Jerusalem Church was born (Hindmarsh 1861, 50–63). Eventually it became known as the British Conference.

However, London was not the only locus of interest in the teachings of Swedenborg. According to Hindmarsh: "The Church was now spreading itself in many towns and villages where heretofore the doctrines had been unknown, and in several places public worship was instituted as soon as rooms or meeting-houses could be engaged for that purpose" (Hindmarsh 1861, 200). He reported that Radcliffe, in Lancashire, England, was one

---

22. An Episcopalian priest, Duché had offered prayers at the First Continental Congress in 1775 in Philadelphia but emigrated to London after deciding that he could not support the American Revolution. For more information on Duché, including an account by John Adams (1735–1826) of the prayers he offered, see Reed 1880, 1.

such place.[23] Here the first reading of Swedenborg's writings proved such a profound spiritual experience for some that they developed a desire to worship the Lord as disclosed in those works. The memoirs of John Clowes (1874) offer a glimpse of this phenomenon.

Clowes, a resident of Manchester, was an Anglican cleric—the rector of Saint John's parish—who became the spiritual shepherd of Lancashire's fledgling Swedenborgian societies in the last quarter of the eighteenth century. He had ordered a copy of Swedenborg's *True Christianity* from London in 1773, but only leafed through it upon its arrival and then put it on a shelf. He picked it up again later in the year, and the words *Divinum Humanum* ("divine human") caught his attention.[24] Nonetheless, he closed the book, and as it happened, departed on a fortnight's journey. Several days later, he woke early in the morning in a state of inexpressible tranquility and peace. He ascribed this inner harmony to the concept of *Divinum Humanum.* The next morning he had a similar but even deeper experience of peace. As he wrote later, "The effect was no other than the excitement of a strong and almost irresistible desire to return home immediately, in order to enter upon a serious and attentive perusal of the neglected volume" (Clowes 1874, 5). Following his prompting, he returned home and began a systematic examination of *True Christianity.* According to his memoirs, its impact on his mind was inestimable. He wrote that reading *True Christianity* resolved for him "all difficulties and doubts . . . respecting the Sacred Scriptures" (Clowes 1874, 36). Clowes, however, never left the Church of England. He was perhaps the foremost representative of the nonseparatist approach to Swedenborg—the acceptance of Swedenborgian teachings without membership in a distinctive and independent New Church organization.

Imbued with a spirit of confidence that comes from committed action, those who had separated and taken steps to establish the New

---

23. Prior to the founding of the General Conference in 1789, there were seven Swedenborgian societies in the Lancashire region of England, with a total membership in the hundreds. By 1784, the Radcliffe society had a Sunday school that accommodated two hundred children, and by 1790, approximately fifty families made up the membership. These groups were run by lay leaders and were tutored in their understanding of Swedenborgian Christianity by John Clowes (see below); they sprang up in the villages surrounding Manchester during the takeoff phase of industrialization. Samuel Compton (1753–1827), inventor of the spinning mule, was the leader of the Bolton society (founded 1781); James Hargreaves (1720–1778), inventor of the spinning jenny, was a member at Bolton. See Williams-Hogan 1985, 520–550, and generally Dakeyne 1888.

24. The "divine human" is an important concept in Swedenborgian theology, referring to Jesus *after* his "glorification" (the process by which his human nature became divine; see *Secrets of Heaven* 4735:2; and also John 7:39; 12:16, 23; 13:31–32).

Church soon wanted to share their enterprise with others. On December 7, 1788, they sent out a "circular letter" announcing the formation of the New Church and their reasons for separating from the Church of England. In the letter, they also articulated forty-two principles that they felt mandated their separation and invited all interested readers of Swedenborg's writings to gather with them for a General Conference in April 1789. The purpose of the assembly was to determine "the most effectual means of promoting the establishment of the New Church, distinct from the Old" (Hindmarsh 1861, 80). These principles, which were to be voted on at the conference, were designed to provide the doctrinal basis for the new organization that they hoped would emerge.

Somewhere between seventy and eighty men and women gathered at the chapel in East Cheap in London on Easter Monday, April 13, 1789.[25] They were more than likely inspired by the previous day's Easter celebration, with its joyful message of eternal life. After five days, they had achieved unanimity for thirty-two of the proposed resolutions, among which were the following:

I. That the Theological Writings of the Hon. Emanuel Swedenborg are perfectly consistent with the Holy Word [the Bible]; that they also contain the Heavenly Doctrines of the New Church, which he was enabled by the Lord to draw from the Holy Word, while under the Inspiration and Illumination of his Holy Spirit.

XII. That a complete and total Separation from the Old Church is warranted.

XIII. That the Doctrinals of the Old and the New Church are in full opposition to each other.

XXII. [That] all who [desire] to become members of the New Jerusalem Church . . . be baptized in the Faith of that Church.

XXIII. That the Holy Supper in the New Church is the most sacred and solemn of all Worship; but that it ought not to be received in the Old Church.

XXV. That the Second Advent of the Lord, which is a coming in the internal sense of his Holy Word, has already commenced, and ought to be announced to the world.

XXVII. That men of every religion are saved, provided they have lived a life of charity.

---

25. Although there were some elderly individuals in attendance, many of those who gathered were young people in their twenties and thirties; see Duckworth 1998, 53.

XXX. That it be recommended to all the readers and lovers of the Theological Works of Emanuel Swedenborg to form themselves into Societies distinct from the Old Church, and to meet together as often
as convenient.[26]

The final resolution stipulated that the congregants would meet in the
next year, again in the month of April. Those in attendance signed these
resolutions.[27] In this remarkable meeting, which focused on the articulation of the basic principles of faith, the organized New Church was begun.

The next two conferences, in 1790 and 1791, focused on elaborating
the means through which the new faith could be embodied. The second
conference set about developing a catechism for the young, a hymn
book, a distinctive prayer book, and a liturgy for worship.[28] Most of
these published worship materials, however, were patterned after those
used in the Church of England. Two additional clergymen were ordained
during this conference, Manoah Sibly (1757–1840) and Joseph Wright
(?–1811).[29] Following these developments, the third conference took up
such matters as the dedication of church buildings, new vestments for
the clergy, and a new and unique way to date the calendar from the New
Church perspective.[30] Clergy were to wear vestments consisting of a purple cassock, a white linen surplice, and a golden cord girdle (Duckworth
1998, 64). The fabric and color of these vestments were chosen in accordance with Swedenborg's descriptions of clothing in heaven.[31]

---

26. The resolutions as given here are condensed from Hindmarsh 1861, 101–104.

27. Among those who signed the circular and who attended the first conference were the noted
English poet and artist William Blake (1757–1827), and his wife Catherine Sophia Boucher Blake
(1762?–1831). For a theory about why the Blakes soon ended their participation in the fledging
movement, see Dole 2003, 6–7.

28. The powerful preacher and writer Joseph Proud (mentioned below) composed the hymns; he
later went on to write several hundred more for the New Church, some of which remain in use.

29. See Duckworth 1998, 64.

30. In this unique reckoning, the year reported by Swedenborg as that in which the Last Judgment
had taken place (1757) marks the spiritual commencement of the New Church and thus becomes
year 1. According to this system, the year 1791 in ordinary reckoning is designated as the year 35. It
is difficult to determine whether these New Church reformers were inspired to formulate this system completely on their own, or whether the new dating system employed in revolutionary
France was their inspiration; see Duckworth 1998, 64.

31. On purple and linen clothing in heaven, see *Marriage Love* 15, 74:4, 266; and *True Christianity* 537.
On the inner meaning of purple as described by Swedenborg, see Potts 1888–1902 under "crimson."

The first notes of discord emerged during the 1791 conference. Some of the participants tried to make a distinction between nonvoting and voting members based on an individual's rebaptism into the New Church. The nonvoting (not rebaptized) attendees would be classified as visitors, who would sit in the gallery and observe. To counter this proposal, another faction suggested that any distinction between the clergy and the laity be abandoned. Neither proposal passed, but these issues would resurface more sharply during the next two years. The underlying question among the participants in the General Conference was the growing attachment to opposing models of church governance: one model in which the polity of the church was congregational (democratic and locally focused), and another in which it was more episcopal in orientation (hierarchical and centralized). The question of governance casts a long shadow over subsequent New Church development, not only in Britain but in the United States and Canada (Williams-Hogan 1985, 607–614).

The sympathies of the majority began to coalesce around the congregational model. This became apparent during the fourth conference in 1792, even though this gathering approved Hindmarsh's concept of a ministry with a threefold order ("high priests," or bishops who would be ordaining ministers; "priests," or teaching ministers; and "licentiates," those who were preparing for ordination; see Hindmarsh 1861, 141, 238). The two sets of minutes recorded for this conference provide evidence of the growing tension over the question of church government. The Great East Cheap Society was also sharply divided over this matter. It was resolved when the majority, favoring congregational self-government, withdrew from the society and formed a separate group under the leadership of Manoah Sibly.

The Fifth General Conference was convened in 1793 in two locations, London and Birmingham. The two sides were no longer in dialog on the question of governance. Only five people attended the conference in London, including Robert Hindmarsh and James Hindmarsh. They concluded by proposing an episcopal organization, a creed for the New Church, and a rite of ordination (Hindmarsh 1861, 155–157).[32] Representatives at the majority conference, held in Birmingham, affirmed the congregational model. The right of societies to elect their ministers was also agreed upon, as was the proposal that all societies annually elect a president who would be invested with the authority to govern the society. The previous conference decision on the necessity of rebaptism for entry into the New

---

32. In his history of the early New Church, Robert Hindmarsh included a report on the London gathering and omitted discussion of the Birmingham conference (see Hindmarsh 1861, 156–157).

Church was revoked. Instead, rebaptism was made a "matter of conscience" and left to the "discretion of every person" (General Conference 1885, xxxiii). As articulated by the majority, the vision of the organized New Church was one of "numerous societies, which for their mutual strength and support of the common cause, must conform to certain *general rules* of fraternal union and ecclesiastical order" (General Conference 1885, 95).

With this split began a brief period at the end of the eighteenth century in which the General Conference no longer held annual meetings. Numerous factors contributed to this situation. In addition to issues of church government and the nature of the ministry, a third problem centered on the character of Swedenborg's works themselves. Although many participants of the infant church found Swedenborgian teachings congenial, they had not resolved the issue of the authority of those teachings—whether they were divinely authored, divinely inspired, or the product of strictly human thought. The indefatigable Hindmarsh, however, had long made up his mind on these questions. He held that the teachings of the New Church were divinely revealed. Furthermore, in his view, Swedenborg's works supported episcopal principles of church government; therefore the New Church ought to follow that pattern. Others, such as Joseph Proud of Birmingham (1745–1826), a former Baptist preacher, while holding similar views concerning the inspired nature of Swedenborg's teachings, was not convinced that the New Church required hierarchical church government. Still other early leaders who formed the majority party may have come from nonconformist backgrounds or may simply have had negative experiences with episcopacy in the Church of England. In any event, congregationalism became the early principle of New Church organization.

Following the 1793 London and Birmingham meetings, a united General Conference floundered. Nearly a generation would pass before a successful formula for the national organization was developed. The absence of such a national conference, however, did not stop the growth of the church or the spread of Swedenborgian ideas. Twenty-three new societies sprang up in Lancashire between the First General Conference of 1789 and the Eighth General Conference held in Manchester in 1815. The important work of translating Swedenborg also continued. As has already been mentioned, Clowes in 1803 completed his work on *Secrets of Heaven,* after decades of labor. In somewhat belated celebration of this enormous achievement, the Manchester Printing Society convened a

meeting at Hawkstone, in Shropshire, in July 1806. This, in turn, initiated the annual gathering of New Church nonseparatists that continued
over the next three generations.[33] At this meeting, those in the assembly
affirmed the criteria for being regarded as part of the New Church. They
affirmed their belief that members were

> All . . . who believe in the sole Divinity of the LORD JESUS CHRIST and
> in the internal and spiritual sense of his HOLY WORD, as revealed to his
> servant E. Swedenborg, and who live a Life according to [the Ten
> Commandments] . . . ; and that everyone ought to be left at perfect lib-
> erty to use his own external Forms of Worship, whether in the Estab-
> lishment [the Church of England] or out of it, and thus be judged
> from his Life and Conversation,[34] rather than from Ceremonies and
> Observances. (*Hawkstone Inn* 1806, 1)

Those attending the meeting hoped that this definition would be
universally adopted by the members of the various New Church societies. Although such an adoption did not occur, the meeting may well
have stimulated an attempt to reestablish the General Conference on the
part of the separatists. By 1807, three congregations had developed in
London, and in that year they called a conference for the societies of the
New Jerusalem church, perhaps in an attempt to make one organization
out of the separate and independent societies that professed a Swedenborgian faith. They were able to approach the issues of organization in a
fresh manner, since few who attended had been present during the events
of the early 1790s. At the conference they passed several resolutions.
Among them was one that affirmed their separation and their distinctiveness as a religious body; another in which they affirmed the original
method of ordination as the proper way to commence the church anew;
and a third that affirmed an ordained priesthood for the sake of orderly
worship (General Conference 1885, 101–104).

---

33. For a discussion of these meetings, see Williams-Hogan 1985, 591–594. In the beginning and
until the General Conference successfully reconvened in 1815, these meetings were attended by
separatists as well as nonseparatists. John Clowes, who, as has been mentioned, remained a priest
in the Church of England, endorsed the annual gatherings at Hawkstone. These meetings ended
in 1861, thirty years after Clowes's death, a casualty of the failure to recruit a new generation of
Anglicans simultaneously interested in the teachings of Swedenborg and membership in the
Church of England.

34. The word "conversation" here may be used in its archaic sense "behavior toward others."

In the following year, 1808, another conference was held, this time in Birmingham. Attendance was better than it had been in 1807. After reaffirming the work of the previous year, the participants focused on developing a uniform liturgy. While they greatly favored a uniform order of worship, the conference felt it could only recommend and not actually endorse a liturgy, since they were uncertain of their own authority. They also had a strong desire to develop a plan that would unite both separatists and nonseparatist factions "together as Brethren, into one general body, for the more [effectual promotion of] the Establishment, Growth, and Prosperity of the New Church" (General Conference 1885, 120).

Those who gathered at Hawkstone that same year responded affirmatively to the Birmingham proposals, and a period of cooperation between the separatists and nonseparatists followed. However, differences still remained—specifically, the emphasis of the separatists on doctrine and external aspects of worship and the focus of the nonseparatists on inner worship, as manifested in the life and acts of the individual. Both sides found support for their principles in Swedenborg's theological works. One example of cooperation between these two factions, however, was the formation of the London Printing Society (later the Swedenborg Society, discussed above) in 1810 (Griffith 1960, 65).

b. The General Conference

A profound desire for order and an inescapable need for regulation were the dominant factors that brought the conference of 1815 into existence. At this point in the history of the British New Church, it was clear to those who longed to see the church grow and develop that it needed a more defined organizational structure. "The ministry needed to be ordered and so did the congregations and the church services, 'since it is from order alone, that the church can obtain a permanent establishment amongst us.'"[35]

To work at creating order, thirteen different societies sent representatives to a conference in Manchester. Six other societies sent letters of support. An estimate of the overall membership of General Conference societies at this time is approximately one thousand.[36] Robert

---

35. Lineham 1978, 342, quoting London Conference 1815, 13.

36. This estimate is based on figures from the minutes of the conference in 1816, in which specific numbers are given for ten different societies. The number attending worship services may have been two or three times as many. See General Conference 1885, 5–9.

Hindmarsh, now of Salford, Lancashire, was elected president, and Richard Jones (1771–1833) of Manchester, also a minister, was elected secretary. The primary focus of the conference was the development of suitable regulations for the orderly development of the ministry. A proposal for a threefold order in the ministry was unanimously approved, as were several resolutions detailing the necessary qualifications for the ministers of the New Church.[37] A candidate for the ministry was required to have been baptized into the New Church, to have received the sacrament of the Lord's Supper, to be of exemplary character and life, to have full acknowledgment of the divine inspiration of Scripture, and to be acquainted with the teachings of the New Jerusalem as revealed in Swedenborg's theological works. The candidate also had to become competent in Hebrew, Greek, and Latin, if not so already (General Conference 1885, 8–10).[38]

Two other important concerns of this conference were the establishment of a missionary ministry and the development of Sunday schools wherever possible. These propositions, too, were unanimously endorsed, in the spirit of harmony that characterized the conference. One can imagine the deep satisfaction that Hindmarsh must have felt at the close of this gathering. The vision for which he had labored for over twenty years had at last been realized, at least in part. While compromises might be required in the future, they would take place within an organization dedicated to the well-being and promotion of a distinctive and separate New Church body. By the time the 1815 conference concluded, the New Church in Great Britain possessed a theology focused on the religious writings of Swedenborg and had created an institutional structure suited to its needs.

By 1815 New Church societies had also been formed in Scotland, beginning at Alloa in 1798 and followed by Edinburgh in 1807 and Glasgow in 1813. Organizationally, these groups are part of the story of the growth

---

37. Although the General Conference endorsed a threefold order of the ministry, implementation of that resolution was continually postponed until 1821, when it was allowed to fade away, and both the resolution and its postponement ceased receiving mention in the minutes. Eventually, the General Conference settled on two degrees for clergy, of which "ordaining ministers" constituted the second, or higher, degree.

38. Prior to 1865, when the New Church College for ministry training was established in London, education for the clergy was characterized by private study and tutorials with senior ministers. It should also be noted that an unwritten requirement in the British New Church at that time was that the candidate be male; this was true in all Christian denominations in the early nineteenth century, except for radical sects.

and development of the General Conference. A Scottish association of
the New Church, which also included churches at Paisley and Dun-
fermline, took organized form in 1874 (Gill and Laidlaw [2000], 17).

Throughout the nineteenth century and into the early twentieth century, the New Church in Great Britain grew and prospered. Controversial
issues, such as the degree to which the New Church might support socialist interests or the Academy movement (discussed below), arose and were
settled. In 1840 there were fifty-four societies with a membership of 2,490
in the General Conference. By 1901, this had increased to seventy-three
societies and just over 6,300 members. Several day schools as well as Sunday schools were also in operation, teaching over seven thousand children
(General Conference 1902, 123). The twentieth century, however, witnessed a dramatic reversal of these trends. By 2000, the membership was
down to just over 1,300 served by thirteen ministers and two assistants in
thirty societies (General Conference, 1999–2000, 66–67).

These trends may be partly explained by the fact that overall church
attendance in Europe and the United Kingdom declined sharply following World War II. Another persistent challenge to the Conference that
undoubtedly hindered development has been a shortage of clergy. A theological college for training clergy was established in 1865, but it was
never able to produce enough graduates to alter the relatively low ratio of
clergy to societies. In a consolidation effort, the school has left London,
its home for over a century, and moved to Lancashire, the heartland of
Conference membership. Ordination of women has also been permitted.
Since many societies have not had stable or resident ministers, another
reason for decline may be that doctrinal development, worship, and congregational life were essentially in the hands of the laity. In withdrawn,
sectarian movements, formally trained ministers are often unnecessary.
But in the case of the New Church, its theology and liturgy have encouraged reliance on a well-educated clergy. Significant lay leadership has
meant that Conference churches in the twentieth century placed less emphasis on the doctrinal uniqueness of the New Church and more on a
Christian message that employs Swedenborg's teachings.

Still, the British General Conference looks to the future and divine
guidance. As one writer observed, summing up the waning of the Swedenborgian Church in London:

> This [decline] does not mean that the real New Church has been im-
> peded or restricted in any way, or its influence and presence lessened
> in any way in the hearts and minds of people. That could not be,

given the promise of the Lord in His Second Advent. What it does mean is that the organization of the Church has changed, and is still continuing to change, and that this is inevitable, and should be seen as something positive and good, and not as negative and detrimental. Movement and change are signs of life. The outward organization is certain to change, and there are many signs today that the change has been beneficent. (Duckworth 1998, 127)

III. The New Church Comes to America

It is customary to trace the beginnings of the New Church in America to the arrival of James Glen (1750?–1814) in Philadelphia in the early summer of 1784. Glen advertised in the press a public lecture on Swedenborg, which attracted a small but enthusiastic audience. Several of those in attendance became important in the organization of the American church, among them Francis Bailey, the printer and soon-to-be Swedenborgian publisher already mentioned. Glen departed for Boston, but a box of Swedenborg's books from Robert Hindmarsh arrived at Bailey's residence shortly thereafter. This led to a reading circle in Bailey's home, which soon began meeting on a regular basis.

a. Early Societies

By 1811, these Philadelphia readers had organized themselves into a church conducting public worship. This was followed in 1816 by the construction of a Swedenborgian house of worship (called a "temple" and based on a description by Swedenborg),[39] the cost of which was born almost exclusively by William Schlatter (1784–1827), a Philadelphia shipping merchant (Block 1984, 75–77). A tireless promoter of the New Church, Schlatter distributed thousands of free copies of Swedenborg's works by packing them in bales of dry goods that were being shipped all over the country.

Elsewhere in Pennsylvania, the New Church also found ready adherents. John Young (1762–1840), for example, who was a youthful attorney when he heard Glen lecture, later became a prominent judge in western

---

39. See *True Christianity* 508. An engraving of the building, which could seat up to three hundred people and later housed the Academy of Natural Sciences, may be found in Childs 1827–1830, B2.

Pennsylvania. He resided near Greensburg and played an important role in the spread of Swedenborgian ideas west of the Alleghenies. A congregation of German-speaking adherents formed in Lancaster in the 1790s, the first of several German-speaking congregations that flourished in the first half of the nineteenth century. One society was formed at Germantown (today part of Philadelphia) in 1792 and another at Frankford, in north Philadelphia; the latter was comprised of converts from the Free Will Baptist movement, who continued their practice of immersion baptism (Block 1984, 76, 78–79).

The original congregation in Philadelphia was agitated by the arrival in 1817 of a group calling themselves Bible-Christians, who came from Salford, near Manchester, England. This latter congregation combined Swedenborgian theology with vegetarianism, temperance, and religious pacifism, practices that alarmed the more orthodox Philadelphia group. (The Bible-Christians will be discussed further below.) Philadelphia was also a major center of activity for the Society of Friends in America. It is not surprising that numerous contacts developed between Quakers and Swedenborgians in Philadelphia, and that over the years some Quaker families affiliated with the New Church. Another significant early convert was Manning B. Roche (?–1842), an Episcopal priest who accepted the teachings of the New Church in 1822 and soon afterwards founded the Second New Jerusalem Church Society in the Southwark section of the city. But despite promising beginnings and ready leadership—that of Maskell Carll (1783–1856)—the First Philadelphia Society was reduced to a state of near collapse by 1824, in part because of the financial troubles of its principal members (Block 1984, 80, 82).

Although Philadelphia was the first city to have an ongoing group of Swedenborg readers, the city with the first organized Swedenborgian church was Baltimore. This organization took place under the leadership of James Wilmer (1750–1814), a former Episcopalian priest, in 1792. Like the First Philadelphia Society, the small Baltimore group faced numerous struggles. Its numbers were small, the members of modest means, and growth was slow. Somewhat disillusioned, Wilmer resigned within two years. The church group was subsequently reorganized in an openly anticlerical fashion by Robert Carter III (1728–1804), formerly of Virginia. Carter had previously arranged for the church to publish the first American liturgy of the New Church, a reprint of the British liturgy, substituting only a prayer for the president in the place of the British prayer for the king, and including a prayer for the establishment of the New Church in the United States (Odhner 1904a, 170). Although not ordained, Carter conducted worship and administered the sacraments. His correspondence also reveals some of the controversies the infant society experienced, among them the first mention of the "animal magnetism" controversy. This hypothetical phenomenon, also known as mesmerism and later as hypnosis, was believed by some early readers of Swedenborg, in various countries, to be a means of confirming the truth of Swedenborg's teachings. Mesmerism was to create chaos in the New Church in New York, New England, Michigan, and elsewhere in the 1840s (Block 1984, 131; Silver 1920, 160–163).

The most important early minister of the Baltimore Society was John Hargrove (1750–1839). A native of Ireland, Hargrove immigrated to America in 1769 and was ordained by Francis Asbury (1745–1816) into the ministry of the Methodist Church in 1795. He converted to the New Church in 1798 and was ordained by the Baltimore church that same year. From that ceremony descends nearly the entire line of Swedenborgian ministers in the United States. Hargrove proved to be one of the most important early leaders of the church in America. Shortly before 1800, he reorganized a new congregation out of a dissatisfied group from Carter's church. They built the first New Church Temple in America, dedicated in 1800 (Odhner 1904a, 195). He issued the first, if short-lived, American New Church serial publication, *The Temple of Truth,* and under his leadership the Baltimore Society prospered, forty families joining the church in a year.

Until 1812, Hargrove was the only New Church minister on this side of the Atlantic, but he nevertheless made an effort to engage the nation's political leaders in the New Church. He sent a copy of *True Christianity* to President George Washington (1732–1799) in 1793 and another in 1801 to President Thomas Jefferson (1743–1826). Both presidents responded graciously. Perhaps because of this gesture, he was also invited to preach before Jefferson and the Congress in the Capital Rotunda in 1802 and again in 1804 (Block 1984, 92; Odhner 1904a, 172, 200).

Many of the early New Church members in Baltimore were German. They organized a separate congregation, probably sometime after Hargrove's death, and built their own building in 1857. The German Swedenborgians here also published a short-lived periodical, *Der Bote der Neuen Kirche* (Messenger of the New Church; Block 1984, 92–93).

Carter's involvement with the New Church before he settled in Baltimore is illustrative of Swedenborgianism in the Southern states. Here the story is rather one of individuals than of reading circles and organized societies, in part because of the great distances between plantations and towns, though societies existed at one time during the nineteenth century in cities such as Charleston and New Orleans. Carter, or "Councillor" Carter, as he was known in his day, was master of the Nomini Hall[40] plantation in Virginia when he converted to the New Church sometime around 1790. Under the stimulus of his new faith he began to free his slaves and sell his estates (Block 1984, 82–86). His wealth greatly diminished, Carter moved to Baltimore in 1794.[41] Worthy of mention as well were those who were perhaps the first documented readers of Swedenborg in America before the arrival of James Glen, the British lord and colonist of Virginia, Thomas Fairfax (about 1690–about 1781), and his relative, Thomas Fairfax II (about 1765–about 1849).[42]

Further north, the first New Church services in New York City were led by Joseph Russell[43] of the Great East Cheap Society in London. He had gone to Nova Scotia in 1791 and founded a society in Halifax, but by 1793 had relocated to New York, where he gathered about him other New Church families from England. These efforts, however, were short-lived. In 1795 William Hill (1762–1804), one of the Church of England clergy led by John Clowes into nonseparatist Swedenborgianism, preached in the city, but his efforts were also without success, and he returned to England the following year (Block 1984, 93–94).

Edward Riley (?–1830), still another English New Church figure, began to hold services in his home in New York City in 1805; they were attended mostly by his relatives. By 1811 the group was holding services in a school building on James Street. One of its members was Samuel Woodworth (1785–1842), the poet and author who penned the well-known poem "The Old Oaken Bucket."[44] Woodworth published the *Halcyon Luminary* in 1812, the first American New Church periodical to reach a wide circulation, but its subscriptions fell off sharply during the War of 1812, after only two years of publication. He later became editor

---

40. The spelling of this name varies widely; the current spelling is adopted here.

41. The basic interpretative study of Carter is Morton 1969.

42. The Fairfax family evidently continued its interest in Swedenborg. The papers of a later Thomas Fairfax (1830–1900) at the archives of the University of Virginia contain the family's correspondence (1800–1840) with John Hargrove of Baltimore regarding the Swedenborgian Church.

43. Further biographical data on Joseph Russell was not available to the authors.

44. A brief sketch may be found in *American National Biography* 1999, 23:840.

of *The New-Jerusalem Missionary,* a monthly church publication. In 1816 an association was formed in the city for the "Dissemination of the Doctrines of the New Jerusalem Church" with Nathaniel Holley (1771–1861), a schoolteacher, as president; Samuel Woodworth as vice-president; and James Chesterman (about 1778–1854), proprietor of a bookstore, as treasurer (Odhner 1904a, 250).

The leader of the group, however, was Charles Doughty (1784–1844). A successful attorney of Quaker background, he served as its secretary and lay preacher. A house of worship was built in 1821 on Pearl Street, but the society was soon torn by controversy. Doughty was removed from the society by a team of ordaining ministers in 1838, and the dwindling membership was forced to relinquish its new temple. The society next experienced a disruptive episode of Spiritualism (the "New Era movement") in 1844. This faction was led by Silas Jones,[45] but it also included Samuel Worcester (1793–1844), formerly of Boston, who claimed "ordination as high priest by the spirit of Swedenborg" (Block 1984, 99), and his son Samuel H. Worcester (1824–1891), both New Church clergymen. The Worcesters later renounced Spiritualistic practices, and the society was in a relatively peaceful state when Chesterman bequeathed it property on Thirty-fifth Street. A new church building was erected there in 1858 (Block 1984, 98–99), and it continues as the home of the New York New Church today.

Other early societies in New York include one on Long Island at Baiting Hollow (1831). There were also a few early societies upstate at Danby (1817), Spencer, and Plattekill (Newburgh). These were led by Louis Beers (1768–1849) a former Universalist clergyman and physician who accepted Swedenborgian teachings in 1814 and was ordained in 1816. He also formed a society at Ithaca (Odhner 1904a, 556–557).

The American New Church found a strong home in New England, but the dissemination of Swedenborgian ideas in the heartland of Puritan Calvinism was neither quick nor without controversy. Boston, which became a prominent intellectual center of the New Church, was slow to see the establishment of churches. Both James Glen and William Hill lectured there, in the 1780s and 1790s respectively, but the results of their efforts were mixed, with no lasting effect. The New Church did not establish a foothold until 1816, when the Worcester family became

---

45. Aside from the fact that Jones was ordained in 1850, further biographical data was not available to the authors.

active in it. Samuel was the first of his family to accept Swedenborg, but his younger brother Thomas (1795–1878) became the first pastor and a leading figure in the Boston New Church.[46] A circle of twelve members, meeting in the home of Margaret Hiller Prescott (1775–1841), was organized by Samuel Worcester (Silver 1920, 72). The Boston Society was formally established in 1818; Maskell Carll of the Philadelphia Society was the first to officiate (Odhner 1904a, 264).

The Boston Society grew very slowly, but what it lacked in missionary activity, it made up for in intellectual rigor, with an intensity that bordered on exclusiveness. In the decades before the Civil War, the Boston Society was known for its grammar school, publishing activities, liturgical music, and its worship, as well as for its controversial minister, Thomas Worcester. The problem of providing a pastoral salary for Worcester and financial stability for the society loomed large at first, but a solution was found in 1822, when the society instituted the practice of tithing, an idea not well received in Philadelphia. Perhaps Worcester's most remarkable innovation, also dating from the 1820s, was his theory on the relation of a pastor to the parish. Essentially, he taught that the minister is "married" to the parish for life and that he could not preach or serve any other society without committing spiritual adultery. Philadelphia and other New Church centers quickly labeled this the "Boston principle" or the "Boston heresy" and were hostile to it (Block 1984, 105–109).

For a number of years, the Boston Society lived a nomadic existence, holding its meetings in various halls of the city—Boylston Hall, Pantheon Hall, the lecture hall of the Boston Athenaeum, and finally its own hall in Phillips Place (1832), built for its use by Timothy Harrington Carter (1798–1894).[47] A native of England, Carter was the founder of the Old Corner Bookstore,[48] and like Francis Bailey was also a successful printer and publisher; he joined the New Church in 1821. The church

---

46. For a fascinating biography, see Reed 1880. For the story of how Thomas Worcester obtained his first copy of one of Swedenborg's works, see Reed 1880, 17–18, and pages 206 and 342 in this volume.

47. For more on Carter, see Ticknor 1969, 15–17.

48. Now on Boston's Freedom Trail of historic sites, the building that housed the Old Corner Bookstore was over a century old when Carter's firm of booksellers first occupied it in 1828. Nine other publishing firms conducted business there in subsequent years, including Ticknor & Fields and E. P. Dutton. *The Scarlet Letter* and other classics of American literature were published on the site, and it was also the early home of *The Atlantic Monthly Magazine*.

building on Bowdoin Street, with seating for one thousand, was dedicated in 1845 (Silver 1920, 95, 78A; Odhner 1904a, 510).[49]

In the meantime, the New Church was also spreading in other parts of New England. In Maine, the cities of Bath and Gardiner had organized societies by 1820, and Yarmouth and Portland by 1824. In Massachusetts, the towns of Abington, Bridgewater, and North Bridgewater (Brockton) had societies in the early 1820s. In 1818 Maskell Carll of Philadelphia spoke in the Town Hall of Providence, Rhode Island, before an audience of nearly one thousand, among whom were the student body of Brown University and some clergy of the town. A congregation was not organized in Providence, however, until 1839 (Block 1984, 110–111).

b. The West and Canada

In the Ohio Valley, across the Alleghenies from the New Church centers developing at Baltimore, Philadelphia, New York, Boston, and beyond, establishing New Church societies in the nineteenth century posed special difficulties. Urban centers, as well as ordained clergy, were few and far between. Bibles, books, and other reading materials were in short supply. In addition, American popular religion in the aftermath of the Second Great Awakening (1804 and following) in the West frequently took on a more urgent, if not evangelical, approach than was customary along the Atlantic Coast. These factors would have an impact on the growth of the New Church.

Mention has been made of the preference early New Church leaders had for printing and publishing as a primary means of spreading Swedenborgian teachings. This tradition continued in the West. The first society organized in Ohio, at Cincinnati in 1811, soon embarked on an ambitious publishing program.[50] Years later, after the New Church was established in Chicago (1849), the Western New Church Union, organized in 1885, turned out books and periodicals for New Church consumption and operated well into the twentieth century ([Williams] 1906, 325–332).

The story of the popular American folk hero "Johnny Appleseed" Chapman (1774–1845) also suggests something of the way in which

---

49. The site is still owned by the church to this day, though the original building has been replaced by smaller church quarters and an apartment complex.

50. A brief overview of the Cincinnati society is [Hobart] 1911.

Swedenborgian ideas were spread.[51] Although much of his life is lost in legend, it is known that Chapman was born in Boston and surfaced on the Ohio frontier shortly after 1800. He is best known, of course, for his interest in planting apple orchards, friendship with Native Americans, love of animals, and picturesque dress (including bare feet and a cooking pot as a hat). Less well known is that he was a lay preacher of Swedenborgian ideas, who in 1822 sent a report of his activities to the General Convention meeting in Philadelphia.[52] Chapman organized no churches, had no regularly appointed circuits as did Methodist itinerant preachers, and did not administer any sacraments. Yet for decades, wherever he traveled, "Appleseed John" would leave pages from *Secrets of Heaven* and other books in pioneer homes where he lodged, perhaps returning again to collect the pages and leave other passages. In this way, a family might have the opportunity to read an entire Swedenborg book. According to one description,

> On entering a log cabin he would throw himself down on the floor, open his precious package of books, ask the people if they would have some "news right fresh from Heaven," and then proceed to read aloud the strange Gospel to the astonished family around the hearthstone, or else expound the glorious truths with a glow of enthusiasm such as to affect even those who looked upon him as half-witted or a heretic. . . .
> In this manner he undoubtedly did much to prepare the ground for the numerous New Church which at one time flourished in Ohio. (Odhner 1904a, 533–534)

Other new adherents in the West were not reluctant to present Swedenborgian Christianity in a more aggressive fashion than their colleagues had employed in Philadelphia, Baltimore, or Boston. Hundreds if not thousands of Swedenborgian sermons were preached at towns throughout the Ohio Valley in the early decades of the nineteenth century. Although his name has been lost from New Church history, a convert from the Baptist ministry reported the enthusiastic response to his preaching of Swedenborgian Christianity in Kentucky and Ohio. The year is about 1814:

> I . . . preached in Lexington Court-house three days, twice in each day, where two-thirds of the inhabitants crowded to hear me, and I baptized

---

51. The standard study of Chapman is Price 1967. For a bibliography, see Price 1944 and Jones 2000, 114–119.

52. An excerpt from this report is printed in Jones 2000, xiii–ix.

many. At Frankford, Paris, Washington, and Russellville, I met with the same success. At Louisville the Sheriff was a Catholic, and refused me admission to the Court-house; I therefore preached in the street, and all the town came to hear me. I baptized six adults, and fourteen children. But the spirit of [the] war [of 1812] dampened my prospects, so that I returned to Ohio, where I preached in Chillicothe and Cincinnati with my usual success. Then I visited my [former] flock . . . [and] found that the seed brought forth fruit in many, so that I baptized eleven adults and twenty-seven children. I preached under a tree at the same hour that a meeting was held in the Meeting-house, and I was crowded, but the Meeting-house was empty. ("Miscellaneous Intelligence" 1817, 188–189)

Illustrative of the work of pioneer Swedenborgian ministers in the West are John R. Hibbard (1815–1894) and George Field (1810–1884). Hibbard, a "boy preacher" when converted, went on to become the long-time pastor of the Chicago Society. A native of England, Field was already a lay preacher when he immigrated to New York in his twenties. A teacher by profession, he moved to southern Michigan in 1838, where he resided until his death. For nearly fifty years, he was a tireless apologist for the New Church. He preached in at least six states and Canada, held debates with other clergy, penned numerous doctrinal letters and essays, organized churches, served on various New Church committees, and administered over five hundred baptisms. Field was also elected chaplain to the Michigan State Senate in 1847.[53]

The 1840s seemed an especially promising beginning to the New Church in Michigan. Various Swedenborgians held important offices, such as Lucius Lyon (1800–1851), assistant surveyor general of the United States (1850–1851), with responsibilities for the (Old) Northwest territory, and member of the United States Congress (1843–1845).[54] Abiel Silver (1797–1881) was a territorial judge, land commissioner, and former Episcopalian, who became a New Church minister and leading missionary pastor (Block 1984, 125–126).[55]

---

53. His memoirs are in Field 1879; see also "George Field" 1884, 60.

54. For a biography of Lyon, see Shirigian 1961.

55. For a somewhat sentimental biography, see Silver 1920, 129–216. An accident in 1836 forced the amputation of Silver's arm. Because he still continued to feel the arm's presence, however, he became convinced of the reality of spiritual world described by Swedenborg in *Heaven and Hell*; see Silver 1920, 154–155.

Numerous societies were formed in the Trans-Mississippi West and along the Pacific coast during the latter half of the nineteenth century. Numerically, however, the strength of the New Church remained in Ohio, Pennsylvania, and the northeast states. By 1890, membership had peaked at approximately seven thousand in 154 societies with 119 ordained ministers (Block 1984, 173). In general, the western churches were also located in urban areas, such as St. Louis (1842) and San Francisco (1895). In Canada, the earliest societies were also in cities. A short-lived group emerged in Halifax in 1791, and a more stable church in Toronto around 1830 and in Berlin, now Kitchener, around 1840 (Block 1984, 175).

c. Ethnic Churches

An unusual exception to the growth pattern just described can be seen in the significant number of rural Mennonites who converted to the New Church. Two such congregations were formed in Kansas, one at Pawnee Rock (1888) and one at Pretty Prairie (1901). In Canada, a society was formed in Manitoba at Gretna (1900), two in Saskatchewan in the Rosthern-Hague area (1898, 1901), and another at Herbert (1915). Small societies were also formed in Alberta at Didsbury (1903) and in British Columbia at Renata (1910?). These Mennonite settlers were ethnic Germans who had relocated from the Ukraine (Russia) to the United States and Canada, beginning in the 1870s. Swedenborgian ideas entered the Russian Mennonite settlements through the unlikely route of revivalism and a new Mennonite denomination organized by John Holdeman (1832–1900).[56] The reasons for Mennonite acceptance of New Church teachings, however, may have had as much to do with their dissatisfaction with the fractured Mennonite community in the United States and Canada as it did with the teachings of Swedenborg (Ens and Doell 1992, 103, 105–107, 111). Russian Mennonite Swedenborgians retained their use of German until about World War I.

Another German-speaking society unique to the New Church movement in the West was the Jasper Colony in Iowa. This consisted

---

56. Holdeman founded a new group, the "Church of God in Christ, Mennonite," in 1859. In an attempt to gain new adherents, he visited numerous isolated communities of Russian Mennonite immigrants in the 1880s. One of his assistants, Marcus Seiler, was sent to Manitoba in 1881 to address the problem of Swedenborgian influences there but was himself converted to the New Church; see Hiebert 1973, 204–205, 535–536. (Further biographical data on Seiler was not available to the authors.)

of Swedenborgians from St. Louis who formed a communal church in Iowa County in 1851 led by Herman H. Diekhöner (1796–1867), a cobbler and unordained minister.[57] Although the colony built a communal log dwelling, was financially successful, and controlled about one thousand acres, it dissolved its socialist organization in 1853, and the disillusioned Diekhöner returned to St. Louis. The German pioneers who remained, however, formed the first New Church society in Iowa, south of Norway in Iowa County (Hawley 1935, 10, 15, 19–20). German-speaking societies, such as those in Canada, Iowa, St. Louis, Chicago, and Brooklyn, as well as earlier groups formed in Philadelphia, Lancaster (Pennsylvania), and Baltimore, formed a significant minority in the New Church in the nineteenth century.

African-Americans formed another minority group for which the New Church had at least limited appeal, although much of this story belongs to the twentieth century. White New Church leaders were aware of Swedenborg's appreciation for the spirituality of Africans,[58] and some of them sought a way for black participation in the New Church. However, prevailing racial and segregationist attitudes of the day precluded the idea of integrated churches. Black churches were formed in the early twentieth century and served by ordained pastors in places such as Chicago, Philadelphia, and Harlem. These groups were considered "missions" and thus not counted as societies in official lists from the period. The first such society, the African Church of the New Jerusalem, was located in Washington, D.C. It was organized about 1892 largely through the efforts of Civil War veteran and brigadier general Reuben Delavan Mussey (1833–1892) and his wife Ellen Spencer Mussey (1850–1936), both members of the Washington New Church.[59] The pastor of the African church was Peter Louis (?–about 1900), formerly a minister with

---

57. Biographical information on Diekhöner varies considerably. His last name is given as Diekhöner, Deikhoener, and Dickhörner, and his given names as Herman H., Hermann Henry, Henry, and even Wilhelm.

58. For references to passages in which Swedenborg mentions the spirituality of Africans, see page 202 note 18 above.

59. As a colonel during the Civil War, Mussey had commanded a black regiment when it was formed in Kentucky in 1864 (Hundredth U.S. Colored Infantry). He and his wife were frequent visitors to the Washington African Methodist congregation; see Mussey 1932. Ellen Spencer Mussey was also an extremely noteworthy Swedenborgian: a lawyer and suffragist, she founded the Washington College of Law and helped found the American Red Cross. For brief sketches of her career, see pages 359–360 in this volume and Poole 1999, 93–101.

the African Methodist Episcopal Church, who contacted Mussey to inquire about Swedenborgian beliefs and ultimately was ordained in 1893. Although a building was constructed, it could not be maintained. Gradually, the mission work faltered, and the church closed it doors about 1910.[60]

One remarkable African-American convert was James E. Thomas (1874?–1925), who served for a time as Louis's assistant in Washington. He attended the New Church Theological School (see below), graduated, and was ordained in 1900. In an era of racial segregation and discrimination, Thomas faced numerous obstacles in presenting the message of the New Church, not the least significant of which was the failure of the General Convention's Board of Missions to provide him adequate financial support. He was thus forced to work at other occupations. After doing missionary work in Alabama between 1904 and 1908, he returned to Washington; but by 1912, he joined the ministry of the African Methodist Episcopal Church in an effort to support his family (Smith 1903; General Convention 1902–1912).

Another African-American Swedenborgian minister was Samuel O. Weems (1891–1975), who began mission work in the North Cambridge (Massachusetts) community in 1915 while a student at the New Church Theological School. Ordained in 1916, Weems worked with the support of white congregations in the area to organize the North Cambridge Community Church. A church building was completed in 1930 but the Depression and other difficulties prevented the congregation from becoming self-supporting. Although the church reorganized in 1939 as a New Church society, the trustees lacked confidence in Weems's continued work as pastor and forced his removal in 1940. By 1947, efforts to revitalize the congregation failed, and the church closed. Weems, a vegetarian and advocate of physical education, was not given another pastorate, although he continued to write on a variety of religious subjects. He subsequently worked as a mechanic for the Boston and Maine Railroad and later for the Portsmouth (New Hampshire) shipyard. Most of his large family eventually joined the African Methodist Episcopal Church, although a granddaughter, Gladys A. Wheaton, was ordained a New Church minister in 1980.[61] In addition to North Cambridge and Washington, there were African-American missions in Philadelphia, Chicago, and Harlem in the first half of the twentieth century.

---

60. See [C.F.K.] 1892, 26; "Church News" 1896, 250; Smith 1903.

61. For Weems's story, see Buteux 1998.

Besides these African-American mission efforts, settlement houses were another means by which the General Convention sought to reach out to America's minorities and urban poor in the early twentieth century. Patterned after the famed Hull House in Chicago founded by Jane Addams (1860–1935), settlement houses offered various kinds of social services, such as vocational classes, boys' and girls' clubs, as well as recreational and cultural activities. Two early New Church settlement houses, which also held Sunday schools and worship services, were located in New York City (Kennedy House) and in Lynn, Massachusetts. Both were started about 1907; the Lynn house was supported by the Boston society well into the 1940s. The church's Young People's League frequently supplied needed volunteers.[62]

IV. The General Convention

Swedenborgian congregations were active in Baltimore, Philadelphia, New York, Boston, Cincinnati, and elsewhere by the mid-1810s, and they developed an interest in associating. The First Philadelphia Society formally issued a call in 1817 for a gathering of all "receivers of the heavenly doctrines" to discuss matters of general concern to the church. Thus the first General Convention was held in Philadelphia with John Hargrove of Baltimore as president. At this point, there was perhaps a total of 360 members in twelve or more organized societies in nine states. The convention decided to meet annually, thus laying the foundation for a permanent denominational structure. Other key issues discussed were support for missionary activities, and standards and training for ordination to the ministry (General Convention 1888, 2–3).

A correspondence committee and a publication committee were also formed, and letters and reports from the United States and abroad were read and were subsequently published in the journal of the proceedings. Two of the reports were from Great Britain. One was from the Ninth General Conference held in Manchester in 1816, and the other from the annual Hawkstone meeting organized by John Clowes. These communications were gratefully received by the American New Church, providing as they did both inspiration and support for the infant movement.

---

62. On Kennedy House, see Ager 1907, 130–132. On the Lynn house, see Reed 1908, 143; Reed 1909, 131; "New-Church Settlement House" 1906, 346; Whitman 1922, 116. There are frequent minor reports on the Lynn house in the *New-Church Messenger* in the early years of the 1900s.

The War of 1812 had made exchanges between the United States and Britain problematic. When the hostilities were over in 1815, communication had resumed on a regular basis and has continued to the present. Paradoxically, it was in this postwar period of renewed contact that both the General Conference in Britain and the General Convention in the United States assumed their distinct structures and achieved separate but permanent organizations.

a. Forms of Worship

One of the most important early efforts of the Convention was to create a uniform liturgy. In principle, most Swedenborgians believed that there should be a distinctive form of worship that separated them from the "Old Church," but that also included rituals such as baptism, communion, and ordination. Putting these rituals into practice, however, was problematic. In Great Britain this task proved nearly impossible because of the varied background of the early members. Some favored a more formal, high-church ritual patterned after the Church of England. Others, from Baptist or Methodist backgrounds, followed a much less structured service. Even though Joseph Proud had developed a liturgy, ultimately the problem was solved by allowing each society the freedom to develop its own order of worship (Block 1984, 183).

In America, uniformity was also difficult to achieve. Baltimore published its liturgy in 1792, based on the 1789 British Conference model. Both the Philadelphia Society and the Convention issued liturgies in 1822, the latter based on the British order of worship developed by Proud.[63] Tilly B. Hayward (1797–1878), a minister in the Boston Society, developed the first uniquely New Church order of service, the *Book of Public Worship,* in 1829. In an attempt to distance itself from the old church and its hymnody, Hayward substituted scriptural chants and retained only baptism as a sacramental rite. Throughout the nineteenth century, many societies, particularly in the western United States, also developed their own patterns of worship. Convention liturgies, issued in 1836, 1854, and 1857, combined chants and scriptural choruses with many features found in an Episcopalian service, but they were not uniformly used (Block 1984, 185–186). The liturgy was again revised in the 1890s by an earnest student of worship, the former president of Urbana College, Frank Sewall (1837–1915). The results were *The*

---

63. Copies of these 1822 liturgies were not available to the authors for corroboration, but they are attested in Block 1984, 184–185.

Book of Public Worship (1907, 1910a, 1913) and a hymnal, *The Magnificat* (1910b), both of which incorporated a hundred years of effort to infuse New Church teachings into a satisfactory ritual form (Block 1984, 183–184, 381–384). A thoroughly revised *Book of Worship* with orders of service, chants, sacramental liturgies, and hymns for all occasions was issued in 1950.

Ideally, however, worship flows from beliefs, and the convention of 1822 was decisive in this regard. A committee had been appointed earlier to review the best means of distributing and promoting the knowledge of the doctrines of the New Jerusalem. Prior to making its proposal, the committee prepared what could be called a statement of faith. This is the first such statement of New Church principles by the Convention; it can be summed up as follows:

> The Lord and Savior Jesus Christ [is] the only God of heaven and earth. Successful missionary work depends upon the Lord, yet it is the duty of the members of his church, as his instruments, to promote the good of the neighbor by every means possible. Knowledge of the Lord, in his Divine Humanity, is the fundamental principle of all true religion, and all who have acquired this heavenly knowledge are desirous of communicating it to others in order for the Lord's kingdom to come. Since faith, charity, and good works make one [form a unity], every member of the New Church ought to practice the divine precepts of charity, good works, and love to one another.[64]

The report proposed that the members of the New Church ought to read the works of Swedenborg and recommend them "to others who may be disposed to receive spiritual instruction" because the committee itself was

> fully convinced of the divine mission of the herald of the New Church, Emanuel Swedenborg, who was specially commissioned and enlightened to publish the glad tidings of salvation, and expound the internal sense of the Holy Word, and thus prepare the way for the second advent of the Lord, in the power and the glory of that Word. (General Convention 1888, 58)

The committee also asserted that members of the New Church ought to have family worship and read a portion of Swedenborg's works daily. The committee was convinced that missionary endeavors would be in

---

64. This summary has been condensed from the text in General Convention 1888, 58, with slight changes in punctuation.

vain without a sincere commitment to the genuine amendment of their own life and conversation[65] on the part of those involved in that work. Missionaries thus devoted to the New Church way of life could be of great use in the propagation of the doctrines throughout the various regions of the nation. A quarterly New Church publication would also serve this function (General Convention 1888, 59). Despite these recommendations of the committee, the New Church would later have bitter struggles over the exact nature and authority of Swedenborg's religious works.

b. Ministry and Other Activities

Another important issue for the General Convention in the nineteenth century was the question of preparation for the ministry. The fifth convention adopted several guidelines to clarify the process. For example, candidates had to be nominated by a specified number of male members acquainted with their religious and moral development. Candidacy was terminated if a licentiate denied any doctrines of the New Church, or if he behaved contrary to divine commandments. Finally, the ministers of the societies at Philadelphia, New York, and Boston were requested to examine candidates and hear trial sermons before ordination (General Convention 1888, 60). This system operated more or less successfully until the opening of a theological school to prepare ministers in 1867.

There was also a question concerning the degrees or levels of ministry. In the tradition of Robert Hindmarsh, some called for three levels of ministry, of which the highest would be that of bishop. In 1830 a report was presented on the "respective duties of the three orders of the clergy." However, the committee also recognized that the church was not yet up to the task of fully defining these offices (General Convention 1888, 105). While a handful of clergy was ordained and functioned in the third degree as "ordaining ministers," the office was abolished in 1849 (Block 1984, 208). This rejection of what some perceived as the power of clergy over the laity in control of the emerging national organization also reflects a democratic bias that had been part of the American New Church since its earliest days. This attitude was most pronounced in the Midwest, where titles such as "Reverend" were thought to convey a spirit of self-love and thus were dropped from records and publications. The Michigan Association went a step further and renounced the ordaining of ministers in 1850 (Block 1984, 127; Field 1879, 195–197).

---

65. See note 34 above on the possible meaning of "conversation."

The office of ordaining minister could be seen as symbolizing an episcopal form of national church government, and the early rejection of such an office was in keeping with the spirit of the times. From the beginning, the General Convention was patterned according to democratic and congregational principles of polity. When the first convention met in 1817, it reflected local societies that were already operating under these same principles. At the first convention, John Hargrove was unanimously elected president and Condy Raguet (1784–1842) was appointed secretary. The next year, the position of vice-president was created and was filled by Maskell Carll (General Convention 1888, 3, 23). Throughout most of the nineteenth century, the General Convention operated as a loosely structured organization that included almost all the Swedenborgian churches in the United States, and after 1871, in Canada as well. While there have been many changes in the operation of the General Convention over the years, it has retained a similar structure until the present day—that is, a representative assembly of local societies with an elected president and vice-president.

As the new General Convention grew in size and financial stability, it took on various programmatic activities associated with other American denominations, such as organized mission work and Sunday schools. It also became particularly energetic in publishing books, tracts, and the works of Swedenborg. The formation of the Lydia Rotch Legacy (1863) and the Iungerich Fund (1873) financially supported the printing and distribution of thousands of volumes of Swedenborgian material. Currently the Convention press operates under the name J. Appleseed & Co. The denominational magazine, which dates from the mid-1800s and is now published ten times per year, is *The Messenger.*

c. Stresses in the National Organization

It was not long after the founding of General Convention that delegates from Boston and elsewhere in New England gained a dominating influence in the decisions of the organization. To cite but one example, in 1853 the Convention purchased the *New Jerusalem Magazine,* the leading monthly magazine of the Church, begun as a private effort in 1827, as its official publication. However, there was no change in the editorial staff—Caleb Reed (1797–1854), Theophilus Parsons (1797–1882), and Sampson Reed (1800–1880)—all of whom were prominent figures in the Boston New Church. Though the powerful Boston and New England influence operating on the General Convention did lend it some cohesion, with the controversial pastor Thomas Worcester at its head it was hardly a unified or monolithic organization. From the very beginning, there were divergent views on worship, the nature of the ministry, the interpretation of Swedenborg's works, rebaptism, and other issues. Virtually every attempt to require some degree of conformity to principles or practices governing all the churches was met with hostility, resistance, or threats of withdrawal by local societies or pastors.

Among the first challenges was the organization of a Western Convention in 1830 encompassing societies in Ohio, Michigan, and points west. Originally the Western Convention was to deal with matters of local or regional importance and was to send delegates periodically to the gathering of the national body meeting in the East. The Western Convention was also decidedly anticlerical and independent in spirit, and more accepting of evangelical approaches to spreading Swedenborgian teachings. In 1838 the General Convention adopted a Rule of Order that required all member societies to have (1) a constitution or its equivalent, (2) a leader, (3) a secretary, and (4) a roster of members. Critics called this regulation the "squeezing rule," and the Western Convention protested. It declared itself "coordinate" (that is, equal) to the General Convention rather than "subordinate" to it (Block 1984, 196–197). Two years later, a group based in Pennsylvania and led by Richard de Charms (1796–1864),[66] then pastor in Philadelphia, created the Central Convention with the same coordinate status. The primary motivation for forming the Central Convention was an attempt to check the influence of Worcester and the Boston group (Gladish 1988, 55–59). Thus in the 1840s it appeared that the General Convention itself might be reduced from a national organization to a regional one limited to New York and New England. However, both the Western and Central associations rejoined the General Convention in 1849–1850, with compromises on both sides. From that point on, a fragile national denominational structure existed throughout most of the remaining nineteenth century (Block 1984, 198–204).

d. Membership Trends

The twentieth century witnessed a significant decline in the membership of the General Convention. By 1930, it had dropped from its 1890 peak of just over 7,000 members to 5,800. By the end of 1999, it had dropped still further to just over 2,100 members (1,531 considered active), in some

---

66. An excellent if brief biography is Gladish 1988.

forty churches, served by thirty-six active clergy ("Swedenborgian Church" 2000, 116).

Numerous attempts have been offered to explain this decline, none totally satisfactory. One might argue that the nineteenth century was the Age of Swedenborg, as evidenced not only by church membership, but by interest in Swedenborg on the part of numerous writers, artists, and intellectuals, including Ralph Waldo Emerson (1803–1882), Walt Whitman (1819–1892), George Inness (1825–1894), and Henry James, Sr. (1811–1882). In the twentieth century, both the General Convention and American society changed. Culturally, strong loyalty to religious institutions declined. Faith become a private and personal matter that many saw as something that could not be embodied in an organized church. Paralleling these trends, the General Convention also became more ecumenical and universal. One significant departure from its past, reflective of the times, was approval for the ordination of women clergy in 1975. The first to receive ordination was Dorothea Harvey, a professor at Urbana University.[67] Rather than focusing on doctrine, or education, or ritual, Convention energies in recent decades have centered primarily on personal spiritual growth.[68]

V. The General Church

The most significant and divisive development in the General Convention during the late nineteenth century was the Academy movement, which ultimately resulted in a schism in 1890. The architects of the Academy movement were Richard de Charms; his younger protégé, William H. Benade (1816–1905);[69] and James Parke Stuart (1810–1882). De Charms, a graduate of Yale University, studied New Church doctrine in London with the noted General Conference leader Samuel Noble (1820–1853).

a. Origins of the Schism

From Noble, de Charms acquired Robert Hindmarsh's views on the priesthood and the divine authority of Swedenborg's religious writings.

---

67. *Journal of the Swedenborgian Church* listed sixteen women in its roll of ministers in 2000 ("Roll of Ministers" 2000, 14–26).

68. For an analysis of these trends from 1932 through 1984, see Kirven 1984, 407–420.

69. For a careful study of Benade's life that stresses his role as a New Church reformer and founder of the Academy movement, see Gladish 1984.

As a young pastor in Cincinnati in the 1830s, de Charms started a periodical for the Western Convention titled *The Precursor* and published articles that would later reflect the doctrinal basis of the Academy movement. A sampling includes "The Authority of the Doctrine," "On the Priesthood of the New Church," "The State of the Christian World, and the Distinctiveness of the New Church," and "The Need for New Church Education" (Block 1984, 195–196).

Benade, raised and educated in Pennsylvania as a Moravian, was baptized in March 1845 by de Charms into the New Church and licensed to preach the very same day. Stuart, who had studied at Princeton University, had been a Presbyterian minister before his conversion in 1847. He met Benade the same year, and the two men developed a close and lasting friendship. Benade, Stuart, and others with similar views originally called themselves "the Harmony" ([Odhner] 1976, 11, 17–19). While the intensity of the controversy at the end of the nineteenth century has distorted some of the issues, it seems clear that the Harmony group was particularly concerned about New Church education, specifically the training for the clergy, and the divine authority of Swedenborg's works. Tied to these controversies was a debate over the "boundaries of association," which involved the right of clergy to establish new societies outside their immediate home area.

In this campaign, Benade and Stuart were fighting against what they perceived to be too much democracy and too little doctrine in the church. Like de Charms, they took particular exception to Thomas Worcester's outlook and leadership. During the early days of Worcester's ministry in the 1830s, he had been an advocate of New Church education, of the "Boston heresy" (which tied a congregation to its pastor; see above), of episcopal government (Smith 1952–1953, 384–385), and of the uniform application of the General Convention's Rule of Order, adopted in 1830. But over time, Worcester softened many of his views, including his belief in the importance of New Church education. He even suggested that Swedenborg did not merit any special title such as revelator or seer. As his brother Samuel Worcester wrote, "We read them [Swedenborg's works] for instruction, and not for authority; hence we talk of what we have learned, and not of what he says."[70]

Also coming to the fore of leadership in the General Convention was a younger generation of more progressive clergy such as Benjamin F.

---

70. From a letter of Samuel Worcester to Daniel Lammot on February 25, 1822, published as Worcester 1843, 105–108, and cited in Gladish 1984, 38. Gladish notes that Samuel Worcester is apparently also speaking for his brother Thomas.

Barrett (1808–1892)[71] of New York and later Chauncey Giles (1813–1893)[72] of Philadelphia. Leaders such as these argued that the most fruitful posture for the church was one of openness rather than exclusiveness. This faction worked to protect the religious freedom of individuals and local societies, while also making Convention meetings more representative. For example, closed communion (that is, communion open only to New Church members) was abandoned, and the General Convention in 1845 decided that its actions should be understood as recommendations rather than binding rules (Block 1984, 202, 295–296, 307–308).

Benade and the Harmony group found such openness and the seemingly casual regard for Swedenborg's writings distressing. They insisted that Swedenborg's works were not merely inspired but an infallible, authoritative, divine testament, the very means of the Lord's Second Coming (Gladish 1984, 309–310). Equally distressing was the anticlericalism prominent in some areas of the denomination. While most Swedenborgians accepted the idea of a divinely instituted ministry, to some the terms *priest* and *priesthood* were problematic, if not offensive. They connoted pride, pomp, and a hierarchical authority of ministers over the laity. Although Swedenborg spoke of a priesthood and described its functions,[73] acceptance of it was difficult for some Protestant sensibilities. Yet in the mid-1870s Benade was attempting to have the General Convention adopt a more episcopal form of government, by stripping the laity of its authority and creating an ecclesiastical council with pastors and a presiding bishop (Block 1984, 211). His report encouraging these measures, while accepted, was never implemented.

Benade used the term "Academy" for the first time in a letter to Stuart in 1859 (Gladish 1984, 99). He saw it initially as an intellectual community whose members would foster the development of the New Church by making its foundational ideals more readily accessible. The Harmony group believed that such an Academy would be a resource through which the New Church would be instructed in its own unique truths and apply them to other fields of study. It was not until twenty years later, however, that the Academy became an organization. In 1874

---

71. For an autobiography, edited by Barrett's daughter, see Barrett 1908.

72. For a biography based on his diary and letters, see Carter 1920.

73. See, for example, *Secrets of Heaven* 10794–10798; *Revelation Explained* (= Swedenborg 1994–1997a) §§444a:2–3, 444c:14; and *Charity* (= Swedenborg 1995a) §160.

John Pitcairn (1841–1916),[74] a wealthy Pittsburgh industrialist, donated five hundred dollars toward the theological training of priests along Academy principles. At Benade's urging, a preliminary meeting was held the following year during the General Convention gathering in New York. This led to a more formal organization during the convention in Philadelphia in June 1876 (Gladish 1984, 231–235). The Academy was formally chartered by the Commonwealth of Pennsylvania in early November 1877,[75] and the first classes of the Theological School opened that fall in Philadelphia. The subsequent story of the Academy schools is treated below.

Another issue championed by Benade that strained relations with the General Convention was that of geographical boundaries for the regional grouping of societies. While leaders in the General Convention were not pleased with the formation of the Academy, rules were adapted to accommodate it. These adjustments had the effect of giving greater freedom to state associations, which had been part of the Convention organization since the mid-1830s. In 1883 the General Convention adopted a resolution with far-reaching consequences. It acknowledged the spiritual character of the Church and stated that all relationships between individuals, associations, and the General Convention were spiritual in nature. Therefore, societies should be granted freedom of social and spiritual association. In addition, it held, "geographical boundaries should not be so rigidly applied as to interfere with the freedom of any Society to choose, from doctrinal, or other internal considerations, to affiliate itself with any Association with which it can act" (Block 1984, 216).

Benade undoubtedly saw this as an opportunity to recreate de Charms's earlier Central Convention. The new organization could serve as a basis for the reform of Convention and bring with it an opportunity to implement a more episcopal form of polity. Under his leadership, the Pennsylvania Association took this opportunity to reorganize as the "General Church of Pennsylvania," with Benade as its "general

---

74. Biographies of Pitcairn include Childs 1999 and Gladish 1989.

75. Academy founders were Benade, Stuart, Pitcairn, Walter C. Childs (1835–1934), John R. Hibbard (mentioned above), Samuel M. Warren (1822–1908), Nathaniel C. Burnham (1813–1891), R. L. Tafel (mentioned above), Louis E. Tafel (1840–1909), Francis E. Boericke (1826–1901), and Franklin Ballou (1845–1903); see [Odhner] 1976, 22–25. "Charter Day," celebrated in October, would later become the Academy's principle commemorative anniversary.

pastor," essentially a bishop. It was comprised of seven societies with just under four hundred members. Within a few years, however, the Concordia Society (Kansas), the First German Society of Brooklyn, and the Immanuel New Church (Glenview, Illinois, near Chicago), resigned their regional affiliations under Academy influence and affiliated with the Pennsylvania body, while still remaining within the Convention (Block 1984, 218).[76] A split between the General Convention and the General Church of Pennsylvania seemed inevitable.

These events deeply disturbed members of the General Convention, but it was Benade's act in 1888 of ordaining William Frederic Pendleton (1845–1927) into the third degree of the ministry that ultimately led to the complete separation of the two bodies. Benade's action was not sanctioned by General Convention's constitution. This breach, and his statement that by his act a "'priesthood of the Academy' was established," all but declared the independence of the General Church (Gladish 1984, 401). For two years, recriminations and resolutions flew back and forth, and each group was convinced of the lack of charity of the other—an especially significant breach of church teachings among Swedenborgians. In 1890, as all the issues between the two bodies still hung unresolved, the General Convention refused to accept a report from the General Church of Pennsylvania that in its view was "disrespectful" towards the Convention. Neither side backed down (Gladish 1984, 425). This disagreement, though couched in procedural terms, was a sign that an era had come to a close. In November 1890, members of the General Church of Pennsylvania made the breach within the church official by withdrawing from General Convention by a three-fourths vote of the membership ([Odhner] 1976, 29).

b. Achieving Equilibrium

The General Church of Pennsylvania soon changed its name to the General Church of the Advent of the Lord, and an independent denomination

---

76. Benade's Moravian heritage may be evident in these moves. Since its early days in seventeenth-century Europe, the Moravian model had included both bishops for administrative purposes and strong, locally led communities engaged in missionary work. Moreover, as organized by Nikolaus von Zinzendorf (1700–1760), Moravians were to be "little churches within the church" (*ecclesiolae in ecclesia*) in Germany's state Lutheran church. Zinzendorf's idea was that small, scattered, but disciplined groups of believers would serve to renew the spiritual growth of the whole. The similarity with Benade's Pennsylvania organization is striking. See Weinlick 1984, 87–88, 190–193.

was born. It was not long, however, before Benade, the chancellor of the Academy and bishop of the church, lost his base of power. Always strong-willed, he became increasingly autocratic following a stroke in 1889. Matters came to a head in 1897 when Pendleton resigned as bishop from the fledgling church. His resignation was quickly followed by the resignations of many of the young priests, the leading members of the Academy board, and others in the Philadelphia Society. The shepherdless flock then petitioned Pendleton to begin the work afresh, which he agreed to do (Gladish 1984, 512–548). The reorganized group took the name General Church of the New Jerusalem.

Under Bishop Pendleton, clear distinctions were made between the functions of the General Church and the Academy, distinctions that had been blurred in Benade's era. The journal *New Church Life,* begun in 1881 as a student paper to give a wider audience to Academy principles, took on the role of a General Church magazine. Pendleton also established the principle that the leadership should take into account the counsel of the laity, which was applied to the governance of both the church and the Academy. Moreover, he avoided assuming the kind of personal authority that Benade asserted. Rather, Pendleton developed "twelve definitions" that served as the basis of common doctrinal understanding for the General Church, among them:

- The Writings, as the Second Coming of the Lord, contain the essential Word; the Church acknowledges no other authority.
- The former Christian Church is dead, except with those who accept the New Church, which is therefore to be distinguished from it.
- The priesthood, as agent for the establishment of the Church, must be placed under no external bonds.
- Baptism introduces man to the New Church on earth and consociates him [brings him to friendly association] with it in the other world.
- Baptism and the Holy Supper are the essentials of worship; the sacramental wine is the "pure fermented juice of the grape."
- The heavenly principle of unanimity should be applied to the Church. Doubt should be occasion for delay so that a common understanding may be reached.
- The true field of evangelization is with the children of New Church parents; schools are needed that children may be kept in the church sphere until they can think for themselves. ([Odhner] 1976, 34)

c. The Battle over *Marriage Love*

Some in the General Convention, such as Frank Sewall, saw Benade's departure as an opportunity for the schism of 1890 to be healed. Unfortunately, a raging controversy between Convention and General Church leaders over the interpretation of Swedenborg's work *Marriage Love* (1768) crushed all hope for easing tensions and soured relations between the two churches for decades. Swedenborg wrote that under certain very limited circumstances a married man might take a mistress without spiritually condemning himself (*Marriage Love* 468–476). Across the years, controversy over these passages caused havoc in the New Church, beginning with the very first society in England.[77] More liberal interpretations, found within Convention, suggested that Swedenborg should not be taken literally on this point, or that this particular work was not a divine revelation. From this viewpoint, Swedenborg's teaching on "conjugial love"[78] was an embarrassment and a hindrance to evangelism. Academy priests, who were charged with the education of New Church youth, took the opposite view. They considered any doubt about the revelatory nature of *Marriage Love* equivalent to blasphemy. Consequently, the possibility of a married man having a mistress—even if it was only a remote possibility—was within the doctrine of "permissions," or those things tolerated by God in order to preserve human freedom of action, though not necessarily desired by God (Block 1984, 219–223).

The controversy might have remained at the level of a civil, albeit spirited, discussion among Swedenborgian clergy and scholars had it not been for the will of Frederick Kramph (1811–1858). Kramph was a German immigrant and successful merchant and tailor in Lancaster, Pennsylvania, who converted to the New Church in 1836.[79] His will provided that his estate, held by seven trustees, was to support a (then nonexistent) New Jerusalem university in Philadelphia. After Kramph's widow died in 1902, there was little doubt among the trustees that the Academy

---

77. See Odhner 1895, 25–31. For a fuller background, see Academy of the New Church 1910, 3–76.

78. The spelling "conjugial," unique to Swedenborgian texts, is based on Swedenborg's use of the Latin adjective *conjugialis,* "of or pertaining to marriage," rather than the more common form *conjugalis.* (The latter gave English its ordinary form, "conjugal.") Some scholars believe Swedenborg distinguishes between conjugial and conjugal love in *Marriage Love* 203, but the reading of the text is in dispute.

79. Kramph introduced Benade to Swedenborg's works in 1843; his congregation in Lancaster was part of de Charms's short-lived Central Convention (Gladish 1984, 22–23; [Odhner] 1976, 41).

was entitled to the money. However, by the time the estate, totaling about $37,000, was settled in 1907, a minority of the trustees had had a change of heart and decided to contest the Academy's claim. One line of attack was an assertion that the Academy's unqualified acceptance of the "conjugial love" doctrine led to immorality and vice. From that point on, the case became a contest of charges and countercharges, sensationalized in public newspaper headlines and in virtual editorial warfare in the pages of *The New-Church Messenger* and *New Church Life*. The first trial awarded the money to the Kramph heirs with a stinging indictment of the entire New Church for teachings contrary to Pennsylvania law. On appeal, the trial judge repeated Kant's statement that Swedenborg's *Secrets of Heaven* were "eight quarto folios of pure nonsense"[80] and suggested that Swedenborgian teachings were against the foundations of American society. Ultimately the case found its way to the Commonwealth Supreme Court, which, in 1909, reversed the lower court judgment. The General Church position and the Academy were vindicated and found to meet the requirements of the will.[81]

d. Growth of the Church

In 1897, before the Kramph case had begun, the Academy had moved to a rural community outside Philadelphia, which they named Bryn Athyn. The spot had become the spiritual center of General Church life, a place in which its distinctive institutions could be developed in salutary isolation from the "old church."[82] One such institution—for many the centerpiece of the General Church and the heart of Bryn Athyn—is the majestic Bryn Athyn Cathedral, which combines both Gothic and Romanesque features. The philanthropist John Pitcairn provided for its construction and engaged a firm for this purpose in 1912.[83] Numerous artisans, using traditional craft-guild techniques, worked in stone, wood, and metal to fashion the structure. The gently sloping hills and

---

80. As quoted in Block 1984, 252. For the views of the German philosopher Immanuel Kant (1724–1804), see pages 38–39 and 169–170 above. For the original quotation, see Kant 2002, 49.

81. Block 1984, 247–254. Thorough background on the trial and its complete proceedings, as well as the story from the Academy's perspective, are presented in Academy of the New Church 1910.

82. For a study of the communal and social values integral to the creation of Bryn Athyn, see Meyers 1983.

83. The story of the cathedral's construction is told in Glenn 1971.

beautifully landscaped grounds around it provide a setting that is both tranquil and inspiring. Although John Pitcairn died in 1916, by 1919 his son Raymond Pitcairn (1885–1966) had brought the work to completion (Block 1984, 283–287).

In addition to education and community building, another area in which the General Church exerted considerable energy was worship. The first General Church liturgy was published in 1908 and revised in 1921 (General Church 1908; General Church 1922). Under Bishop Pendleton's guidance, the new liturgy contained twelve "General Offices," or orders of service. The first six were called "Offices of Humiliation." They contained confession of sin and include the Ten Commandments, which were read by the minister with the congregation kneeling. To these was appended a responsive prayer by the congregation. The next five offices were the "Offices of Glorification." They focused on "adoration and praise" and were arranged as responsive (antiphonal) chants. This was followed in the liturgy by readings from the Psalms and Prophets, the Law, and the Gospel (Pendleton 1957, 154–155). In addition to readings from the Old and New Testaments, a third reading (lesson) from Swedenborg was also introduced. Congregational music, in both hymns and chants, was also made an integral part of the service.

Since 1921 significant changes have taken place in the General Church worship service: there are fewer and shorter offices, and many congregations have stopped using the liturgy altogether, relying instead on songbooks or a simplified order of worship that varies from week to week. The music employed in the services has also undergone modernization: antiphons are no longer featured, the use of chants has been sharply cut back, contemporary music has been added. In quotations from Scripture, language from the New King James Version has been adopted. In short, changes in worship in the General Church reflect contemporary trends in many other Christian churches throughout the world.[84]

Because of the orientation of the General Church toward education, the General Church in the United States, Canada, and elsewhere took on the task of creating schools and residential communities wherever possible. One of the most successful and longest-lived of these communities outside Bryn Athyn is in Glenview, Illinois. Early leaders believed that the church would grow not only as doctrines and ritual were refined but as

---

84. Information on recent changes in worship was supplied by John Odhner in a personal communication of August 18, 2003.

the New Church embraced a comprehensive way of life as well. This approach remained the focus of the General Church for several generations.

Growth was slow but steady. In 1900 the General Church had 560 members. The total membership had increased to just over 2,000 by 1930, of which approximately half resided in Bryn Athyn. By the year 2003, the membership had increased to 4,810 worldwide.[85] Undoubtedly, factors contributing to this steady growth and the stability of the church organizationally include a strong system of education, generous financial backing by its members, and more recently, new efforts at evangelism.

VI. The Lord's New Church Which Is Nova Hierosolyma

The 1930s saw another doctrinal and organizational crisis confronting the General Church. The result was that approximately 138 individuals, both clergy and lay members, resigned in 1937 to establish their own organization, the Lord's New Church Which Is Nova Hierosolyma (Block 1984, 404).[86]

In 1930 Ernst Pfeiffer (1890–1979), a General Church minister, founded the periodical *De Hemelsche Leer* (The Heavenly Teaching) in the Netherlands. In this journal he argued that it is necessary to extend the belief that Swedenborg's theological works are an integral part of Scripture to the idea that the works themselves must also contain a divine inner meaning. Pfeiffer explicitly stated that "the Writings of Emanuel Swedenborg are the Third Testament of the Word of the Lord" and that Swedenborg's teaching about Scripture must therefore "be applied to all three Testaments alike" (The Lord's New Church 1985, 2). By this Pfeiffer meant that the "internal sense" (the inner meaning) that Swedenborg described in the Old and New Testaments can be found in the writings of Swedenborg themselves. Readers can enter into that sense only by means

---

85. Membership figures do not include baptized minors and young adults who participate in the life of the church but who have not signed the membership roles of the society where they reside. If those groups were included, the totals would be 11,680 members and baptized minors, or 15,422 members, baptized, and associated individuals. These statistics were generated by the General Church–Academy of the New Church Data Management Department, August 18, 2003, at the request of the authors.

86. For the most accessible account of the origin and theology of this group—written by someone who participated in its development—see Pitcairn 1967.

of spiritual rebirth. By labeling Swedenborg's theological works a "Third Testament," however, Pfeiffer appeared to elevate them above the Old and New Testaments, just as in Christian teaching the New Testament is elevated above the Old. For him, it was precisely this third testament that unfolds in meaning to individuals experiencing spiritual transformation, a renewal achieved as a divine gift (Block 1984, 404).

While the leadership of the General Church at that time acknowledged that there were interior truths in the writings of Swedenborg that could be perceived in particular during the process of spiritual transformation and that these perceptions "would be of comfort if they could be clearly labeled," they insisted that they could not be so identified. Furthermore, they believed that doctrines for the church were to be derived through the application of the human mind, "based on the 'clear and open teaching' of the Writings [of Swedenborg] as they can be discovered and affirmed in the arena of sense experience" ([Odhner] 1976, 54).

These issues came to a head in 1937 when George de Charms (1889–1989) was named bishop of the General Church. Although the newly appointed bishop made a determination that the doctrine of the "Hague Position" was incompatible with General Church thought, he was willing to let the matter cool before taking any action. This was not acceptable to Pfeiffer, who wished to form a separate jurisdiction within the church for the observance of his beliefs.[87] De Charms did not feel that this was conducive to sound order in the church and therefore asked Pfeiffer to resign. When Pfeiffer did so, others joined him, including a group in Natal, South Africa, twelve years later ([Odhner] 1976, 54).

Although international in scope, the group has remained even smaller than other Swedenborgian bodies, with a membership of approximately one thousand by the year 2000. A sense of governance and order were also slow to evolve. The first official statement on polity, a provisional "Plan of Order," was not issued until 1947. Initially, the Lord's New Church recognized no distinction between priests and the laity, since everyone could enter into the proper understanding of the Word. An international, democratically operated council to govern the church was created by several members, including Pfeiffer and Theodore Pitcairn

---

87. Pfeiffer's suggested course of action—forming his own jurisdiction within a larger body—sounds very much like the "church within the church" approach of Benade when he reorganized the Pennsylvania Association into the General Church of Pennsylvania in 1883. It is possible that Benade's actions were still very fresh in the minds of the General Church clergy and that they suspected what the outcome would be if such an organization were permitted.

(1893–1973), who provided much of the financial backing for the new group. This Plan of Order document was revised in 1956, creating an "International Interior Council," and again in 1967, when an episcopal form of government was formalized (The Lord's New Church 1985, 15–29, 32). Philip N. Odhner (1908–1998) served as bishop from that time until his resignation in 1986. The post remained vacant thereafter, however, until 2000, when an acting bishop was named. In the United States, the oldest and most robust society is located at Bryn Athyn, Pennsylvania. Newer societies have also formed in Charleston, South Carolina, and elsewhere. In the late 1990s the church was shaken by a lawsuit between members of the congregation contesting control of the church assets; a court decision upheld the interests of the majority.

VII. Other Church Groups

This survey of church organizations would not be complete without reference to other church bodies that have been based in part on Swedenborg's teachings. These groups were not a part of the denominational families described above, yet came to include Swedenborgian thought in their church life in various ways. Two such organizations will serve to illustrate the variety of groups that have adopted at least a part of Swedenborg's theological teachings as part of their beliefs.[88]

a. The Bible-Christian Church

The earliest of these other groups was the Bible-Christian Church, organized in Salford, England, in 1809. From the teachings of this church derives the misconception held by some that Swedenborgians are doctrinally vegetarians. The founding minister was William Cowherd (1736–1816) of Christ Church Chapel in King Street. Cowherd, a former Anglican cleric, had come under the Swedenborgian influence of John Clowes in Manchester, but left the Church of England in 1793 to act as pastor to a Swedenborgian parish. Following a disagreement with Clowes and other New Church leaders he relocated to nearby Salford in

---

88. Omitted from discussion here is Brotherhood of the New Life, a spiritualist communal organization led by Thomas Lake Harris (1823–1906). He formed churches partly shaped by Swedenborgian teachings in New York City; New Orleans, Louisiana; Amenia and Brocton, New York; and Santa Rosa, California. A brief mention of Harris and his ideas is made on pages 222–223 above.

1808. His movement, which embraced a mixture of Swedenborgian theology, vegetarianism, temperance, and Christian pacifism, flourished for several decades. It maintained chapels in the Manchester area at Ancoats, Hulme, and Stockport, and possibly other sites as well (Greenall 2000, 28–60). Cowherd's successor at Salford was Joseph Brotherton (1783–1857); Brotherton was followed by James Clark (1830–1905). Both were well-known British vegetarians. In fact, Bible-Christians were deeply involved in the founding of the British Vegetarian Society (1847) and the International Vegetarian Union (1908). The Bible-Christian Church continued as an organized group at Cross Lane until 1930, when it merged with a local Unitarian group.

Two ministers that Cowherd trained and ordained brought Biblical vegetarianism and their version of Swedenborgian teachings to America. They were William Metcalfe (1788–1862) and James Clarke (1778–1826), not to be confused with James Clark.[89] They led a group of about forty Bible-Christians to Philadelphia in 1817. This congregation built its own church building in 1823, prospered, and by the Civil War had a membership of about one hundred. Although they gradually lost touch with their Swedenborgian roots, Bible-Christians became known for their opposition to war, the death penalty, and slavery (Block 1984, 80). Metcalfe, who supported himself as teacher and journalist, was an outspoken proponent of a vegetarian diet and was a central figure in the American Vegetarian Society (founded in 1851). His sermon "Bible Testimony on Abstinence from the Flesh of Animals" was published as a tract and widely circulated (Metcalfe 1872, 151–183). In 1852 Metcalfe also completed training as a homeopathic physician, becoming one of the large number of Swedenborgians associated with homeopathic medicine. One of the last pastors before the demise of the congregation in the early twentieth century was Henry S. Clubb (1827–1921), also a journalist and for many years president of the American Vegetarian Society (Maintenance Committee 1922, 76, 82).

b. The St. Thomas Christians

In an altogether different spirit than the vegetarianism of the Bible-Christians is the status accorded Swedenborg within the St. Thomas

---

89. To complicate matters, the James Clarke who went to the United States also had a son by the same name. This son traveled with his father to America and remained there.

Christian Church in America. This church represents a mystical Orthodox heritage whose lineage (spiritual if not historical) may be traced
back to the apostle Thomas (?–about 53). According to tradition,
Thomas spread Christianity to the western coast of India, in the region
of Malabar. Following his martyrdom (near Madras), the churches he
established there developed independently from Christianity as it advanced in Egypt and the Middle East, as well as in Europe. At one time
this group was allied with the Monophysite Syrian Orthodox patriarch
of Antioch. Following immigration to the United States, however,
some adherents separated from the Syrian Orthodox Church (which
observed the Malabar Rite) and formed an independent body. The patriarch and presiding bishop of this group, Mar Timotheus Josephus
Narsai Vredenburgh, whose see is in Santa Cruz, California, was conse-
crated to this office in 1963.

The St. Thomas Christians numbered perhaps two thousand in 1983
when Patriarch Mar Josephus Narsai elevated Swedenborg to the status of
sainthood (as "Saint Emanuel"). A feast day is celebrated in Swedenborg's
honor on March 29. Part of the liturgy for that ceremony reads: "Saint
Emanuel, you have opened the Book of Ages. . . . You have dreamed
great wonders. . . . You have shown us the mind of Christ" (Gutfeldt
1994, 147). According to Swedenborgian psychologist Wilson Van
Dusen, the St. Thomas Christians seem "to combine an ancient liturgical
tradition with a modern liberality and a personal search." The St.
Thomas Christians canonized Swedenborg, suggests Van Dusen, "because he so well enunciated their own position" (Van Dusen 1994, 149).[90]

VIII. Schools and Colleges

From the earliest days of the organized Swedenborgian Church in both
Great Britain and the United States, education has been a topic of intense interest.[91] How should the New Church best educate its youth
regarding Swedenborg's teachings? Was there, or should there be, a distinguishing form of New Church education? Who should be admitted
as students? What subjects should be taught? As might be expected,
opposing viewpoints developed. In Britain, educational ventures were

---

90. For more on the St. Thomas Christians, see Aerthayil 2001.

91. The most comprehensive study of New Church education is Gladish 1968–1973. Other important works are Pendleton 1957 and Hite 1939.

focused in urban day schools that were open to the public. Dozens of such schools, such as the New Jerusalem Free School in London (1822–1853) or the Peter Street School in Manchester (1827–1871), served thousands of students, offering classes in reading, writing, arithmetic, and religious instruction by New Church teachers. The day schools were operated as public charities, but they also provided an opportunity for evangelization (Gladish 1968–1973, 1:v, 43).

In the United States, early church schools were much more modest, usually involving only a handful of students. They were also directed toward the children of New Church parents in an effort to ground them in the beliefs of the new Christianity. Among the earliest and most successful of such schools was the coeducational Boston School (1836–1843), affiliated with the Boston New Church. Its principal was Edmund A. Beaman (1811–1908). The school in Cincinnati (1840–1843) was led by Milo Williams (1804–1888), who later played a significant role in founding Urbana University. The Philadelphia school (1857–1861) was headed by William H. Benade, later a founder of the Academy movement. Several other less successful schools were attempted in Maine (Bath and Portland) as well as Massachusetts (Abington, Bridgewater, and Yarmouth), among other places. While societies in the General Convention gave a high priority to educational ventures before the Civil War, that interest waned in the late nineteenth century, and with it came a diminishment in emphasis on education for membership or doctrinal understanding (Gladish 1968–1973, 2:28, 40–47; 3:21–22, 131–133).

a. The Waltham New Church School

In New England, the continuing interest in a Swedenborgian educational program for youth led to the opening of the Waltham New Church School, Waltham, Massachusetts, in 1860. Unlike earlier, short-lived educational ventures, however, this school was a project of individual Swedenborgians, not a local society or pastor. Although many of its early faculty were New Church men and women, the school stressed personal development and creative expression rather than Swedenborgian beliefs. After its incorporation in 1858 as the Waltham New Church Institute of Education, the head of the school for many years was Benjamin Worcester (1824–1911), who shaped the school's early character and curriculum.[92] It

---

92. For more on Worcester and his leadership of the school, see Mason 1911, 366, and Silver 1920, 112–114.

was originally operated as a coeducational institution, but in 1912 it became an all-girls preparatory boarding school, the Waltham School for Girls (Worcester 1923, 139–140). The name changed again in 1937 to the Chapel Hill School ("Waltham School" 1960, 175).

The area including the campus and the adjacent Waltham New Church, in which the first classes were held, became known as "Piety Corner," and well into the twentieth century many New Church families from New England and beyond sent their children to be educated there (Block 1984, 181–182; Silver 1920, 112–114).[93] One of its well-known students in its coeducational phase was John Whitehead (1880–1930), who became a much-loved pastor, educator, and translator.

b. Urbana University

The idea of higher education, or a New Church university, that might help prepare some of its students for theological studies and the ministry was also much discussed. The oldest New Church–inspired educational institution is Urbana University, located in Urbana, Ohio, and founded in 1850.[94] John H. James (1800–1881),[95] who owned property in Urbana, was persuaded by James Parke Stuart that the time had come to undertake a distinctly New Church university. Milo Williams was also important in its development.[96] With land donated to the General Convention by James and funds partly raised by Convention, a building (Bailey Hall) was erected,[97] and classes began in 1853 with just under a hundred students—fifty-nine men and thirty-nine women (Higgins 1977, 26). Urbana thus became only the second coeducational school in Ohio, after Oberlin College. Williams was asked to be president, but

---

93. Chauncy Hall (founded 1818), a boy's preparatory school in Boston, merged with the Chapel Hill School on the Waltham campus in 1971 to become the Chapel Hill–Chauncy Hall School. The school has lost most of its Swedenborgian connections, although several New Church members served as trustees well into the last decades of the twentieth century.

94. Helpful histories of the institution include Higgins 1977 and Weisenberger [1950].

95. For an excellent study of James, see Smith and Smith 1953. James was an energetic man of wide and varied interests—agriculture, politics, law, banking, railroads, writing—who eventually joined the New Church.

96. For a sketch of Williams's life, see Murdoch 1945.

97. James had married Abigail Bailey (1800–1863), the youngest daughter of the Francis Bailey mentioned above, the first American printer of Swedenborg.

declined, preferring the title of dean; Chauncey Giles, then pastor of the Cincinnati Society, was appointed the nonresident president; and Stuart was secretary for the faculty of four.

Williams and Stuart, however, had somewhat different visions for New Church education, so from the start the school was wracked with internal division. Stuart, who became a leader in the Academy movement, was a graduate of Illinois College and had studied Calvinist theology at Yale, but left the ministry of the Presbyterian Church for the New Church in the 1840s. He advocated a curriculum infused with New Church teachings. Williams, a school teacher in Cincinnati, Dayton, and Springfield, interpreted Swedenborg's teaching on "uses"[98] to mean that education must develop morals, yet be practical. His view, shared by James, was that the university should explore all of human knowledge and offer a well-rounded liberal arts program, using field experiences when practical. From the beginning, enrollment was open to students from outside the New Church (Higgins 1977, 22–35).

During the Civil War, the school virtually shut down, but it experienced a new beginning in the 1870s under the strong presidency of Frank Sewall, an energetic Ohio pastor who has already been mentioned above.[99] Chronically under-enrolled and short of operating funds, the college languished again until the 1920s. In that era, a distinguished alumnus, T. Coleman DuPont (1864?–1930), then a senator from Delaware, provided a substantial endowment of $150,000, which helped to secure the school's future (Higgins 1977, 89–90).

Beginning in the late 1920s, the school operated as a junior college, but by the mid-1950s even its modest costs were greatly exceeding revenues.[100] In 1956 the trustees were on the verge of converting the college into a nonprofit research foundation. However, a resurgence then

---

98. On the concept of use in Swedenborg, see pages 358–363 in this volume.

99. In addition to being an artist, musician, and translator, Sewall was a significant force in nineteenth-century Swedenborgian scholarship, and his training fitted him for that role. After graduating from Bowdoin College in Maine in 1858, he studied theology at Tübingen, Paris, and Berlin. While in Europe he made the acquaintance of the great Swedenborgian scholars Jean-François-Étienne Le Boys Des Guays (1794–1864) in France and Johann Friedrich Immanuel Tafel (1796–1863) in Germany. He is further mentioned below as one of the founders of the Swedenborg Scientific Association.

100. At one point in the 1950s its enrollment of seven students made it literally the smallest college in the United States (Higgins 1977, 134, citing Gauvey 1958, 273–275).

began under the leadership of Carolyn Blackmer (1899–1972), an innovative New Church educator who would go on to become a professor of philosophy at Urbana. Blackmer and several other dedicated reformers, returning to the principles of Swedenborgian philosophy, refocused the curriculum to stimulate creative thinking and self-responsibility (Higgins 1977, 134). Prospective students rose to the challenge.

By 1968 enrollment had increased to 631 and the college was again offering four full years of courses (Higgins 1977, 143). With financial backing from New Church members throughout North America, the college opened its new Swedenborg Memorial Library. In 1975, on the school's 125th anniversary, Urbana received full accreditation as a four-year college (Higgins 1977, 160). In a reorganizational effort again strongly supported by the church constituency, it has since become Urbana University. Though the last Swedenborgian president resigned in 1956, Swedenborgians have continued to serve as trustees, and the university maintains a cordial if informal relationship to the denomination.

In 2000 Urbana enrolled about 1,200 students in several areas of study, including two graduate programs. The university hosts an annual Swedenborgian lecture and offers occasional courses on Swedenborgian topics. The Swedenborg Memorial Library has a collection of rare Swedenborgian books and periodicals. In addition, the Johnny Appleseed Education Center and Museum, created in 1999, promotes the ideals by which Johnny Appleseed lived.

c. Swedenborgian House of Studies

With Urbana and Waltham in operation before the Civil War, perhaps it was natural that voices in the General Convention would call for the establishment of a theological school as well. The course to establishing such a school, however, was indeed difficult, and the issue was debated for years. Immediately following the Civil War, the Convention appointed a committee that would, again, explore the need for training of future ministers. It was chaired by James Parke Stuart, formerly of Urbana and a supporter of the Academy movement, who recommended establishing a "school for priests" in New York; this school was to be headed by William H. Benade (Block 1984, 210). In 1866 the General Convention met in Boston. The delegates received a memorial from a young ministry candidate who asked that a regular course of doctrinal and biblical instruction be created immediately, in a convenient location (by which was meant Boston, not New York or Philadelphia) for him

and five other Massachusetts men. With the backing of the Committee
on Ecclesiastical Affairs, chaired by Benade, another committee to consider a divinity school was appointed. The following year, this committee reported that it had taken prompt action. The new school began in
July 1867, with six students and a course of lectures (by fourteen instruc-
tors), held in the Waltham, Massachusetts, New Church building.

Although several Academy supporters were among the first lecturers,
none was appointed to the permanent faculty, and the school was soon
reorganized under the presidency of Boston's controversial pastor,
Thomas Worcester. It was incorporated as the New Church Theological
School in 1881. Throughout its history, the school struggled for financial
stability, stable enrollments, and a curriculum balanced between preparation for professional ministry and the study of Swedenborg. The Theological School also experienced its share of significant divisions among its
students, faculty, and governing boards. Still, academic standards remained high, and it graduated a steady stream of capable New Church
leaders and pastors.[101]

For most of the twentieth century, the school was located in Cambridge, adjacent to the Harvard University campus. Its striking stone
chapel, built in 1901, continues to be the home of the Cambridge New
Church. In what was incidentally its centennial year, 1965–1966, the
school relocated its campus to nearby Newton, Massachusetts, and reorganized as the Swedenborg School of Religion. Its Master of Arts curriculum was approved by the state of Massachusetts, and students who
desired an accredited Master of Divinity degree could take further study
at nearby Andover Newton Theological School. Its scholarly journal,
Studia Swedenborgiana, was launched during this era. Enrollment was
seldom greater than twelve students. In 2000, after a thorough self-
study, the school was reorganized yet again, and the number of full-time
faculty was reduced. Renamed the Swedenborgian House of Studies, the
school moved with its library to the campus of the Pacific School of Religion in Berkeley, California (Lawrence 2001, iv–vi). These changes allowed Swedenborgian studies and the school's students to be integrated
into the Pacific School of Religion's well-respected Master of Divinity
program, but at the cost of a departure from the New England theological heritage that shaped its first 130 years.

---

101. A careful study of the school is Gladish 1991.

d. The Academy Theological School and Bryn Athyn College

As might be expected, backers of the Academy movement in the 1860s were upset with the creation of a theological school in Waltham dominated by New Englanders. Their response came in 1876 with the organization of the Academy of the New Church for the training of ministers under Benade's leadership (see above). Two Urbana students who did not wish to attend the lectures in Waltham followed the lead of the Massachusetts men in requesting training for the ministry. The Academy movement became a reality with the granting of its charter and the opening of the Theological School in 1877. The first classes were held in Philadelphia at the Cherry Street New Church, a congregation for which Benade had served as pastor several years earlier. The first faculty, headed by James Parke Stuart as vice chancellor, quickly discovered that the students needed additional undergraduate work, so collegiate courses were offered as well ([Odhner] 1976, 25).

From these modest beginnings, the Academy soon expanded with a boys' school (1881) and girls' school (1884). In 1896–1897, several years after the legal separation of the General Church from the General Convention, the Academy schools moved to Bryn Athyn, Pennsylvania. The theological school was placed under the direct supervision of the bishop of the General Church at that time (Acton 1926, 17–43), and it has remained so to the present. The theological school, whose curriculum focuses primarily on the study of Swedenborg's theological works, is housed in Pendleton Hall on the Bryn Athyn College of the New Church campus (see below), and grants a Master of Divinity degree. The school's peak enrollment occurred during the 1970s, when fourteen students were in training for the ministry. More recently, a graduate program was initiated that admitted women students, although women are not eligible for ordination in the General Church.

The Academy of the New Church College, renamed in 1997 the Bryn Athyn College of the New Church, was formally organized in 1914 with its own dean, Reginald Brown (1877–1937). Under the guidance of N. D. Pendleton (1865–1937), George de Charms, and Willard D. Pendleton (1908–1998) the college by the 1950s had matured into a stable institution, faithful to its charter purposes, and was much stronger than Urbana in terms of enrollment, academic program, and endowment ([Odhner] 1976, 43–64). The college offers a full range of liberal arts studies and in recent years has admitted non–New Church youth. Enrollment in 2000 was approximately 150 in the college, compared to 280 in the secondary schools (*The Academy Journal 1999–2000*, 58–63). Its 113-acre campus, set in suburban Montgomery County, Pennsylvania, is adjacent to one of the prominent architectural features of the Bryn Athyn community, the Bryn Athyn Cathedral (described above) and includes another, the Glencairn Museum. The museum, which is the former home of philanthropists and art collectors Raymond Pitcairn and Mildred Pitcairn (1886–1979), was donated to the Academy by them. It houses a priceless collection of art and architectural exhibits from various historical eras depicting the history of religion. The Academy charter also provided for a Swedenborg library. A new facility, which opened in 1988, contains one of the best collections of Swedenborgian materials in the world.

As mentioned above, the Academy movement also promoted elementary schools outside of Philadelphia that offered a distinctly New Church curriculum. The earliest efforts, dating to 1888, were in Glenview, Illinois, and Pittsburgh, Pennsylvania. Similar schools were also opened in Berlin (now Kitchener), Ontario; in Toronto, Ontario; and in Bryn Athyn. By 1896, however, the Academy assigned responsibility for these schools to the local parish in which they were located. The largest of the parish elementary schools is in Bryn Athyn. Outside of the Boys School and Girls School in Bryn Athyn, Glenview has offered a curriculum at the elementary level, as have schools in Kempton, Pennsylvania, and Mitchellville, Maryland, as well as in countries that lie outside the scope of this essay.

IX. Building Community

For much of their history, most American Swedenborgian churches have had little to do with other religious traditions, Christian or otherwise. Part of this stemmed from the belief widely held among Swedenborgians that the New Church was indeed a new Christianity and therefore superseded other faiths. Contact with other churches was not important, or at worst, harmful. On the other hand, both mainstream Protestant groups and Roman Catholics considered the tenets of the New Church to be outside general Christian orthodoxy. In the United States, at least, members of the New Church were often viewed with suspicion or reproach by their non-Swedenborgian neighbors, and stories of social ostracism are legion. These circumstances helped foster a sense of New Church distinctiveness.

a. The World's Parliament of Religions

Despite this isolationist background, it was a Swedenborgian attorney, Charles Carroll Bonney (1831–1903) who brought about the World's

Parliament of Religions. This unique event was held at the Art Institute in Chicago in 1893, in connection with the famed Chicago Exposition (World's Fair). Bonney joined the New Church in Peoria, Illinois, as a teenager, and there learned "the fundamental [Swedenborgian] truths that made a World's Parliament of Religions possible."[102] Later, as a prominent Chicago attorney, he came into contact with ministers from several churches and learned to appreciate the distinctive beliefs and practices of each. He wrote: "Thus I came to feel kindly, not only towards the various religious denominations of Christendom, but also in regard to the different religions of the world. . . . While thinking about the nature and proper characteristics of this great undertaking [the World's Fair], there came to my mind the idea of a comprehensive and well-organized Intellectual and Moral Exposition of the Progress of Mankind" (Dole 1993, 24–25).

As his ideas were shared and took concrete form, Bonney subsequently chaired the Committee of Organization, delivering the opening and concluding addresses of the Parliament. Another prominent Chicago Swedenborgian, the chief architect of the Chicago Exhibition, Daniel H. Burnham (1846–1912),[103] chaired a separate session on architecture. Included in the Parliament was a congress on the New Church, held on September 13, 1893, and chaired by Chicago pastor Lewis P. Mercer (1847–1906); it also included a women's program, chaired by Arianna E. Scammon (1848–1898).[104] The Parliament itself lasted for seventeen days and was a tremendous success, exposing some New Church delegates to an unanticipated spirit of cooperation, friendliness, and vitality in the "old Church" (Mercer 1894, 29–66). Although plans for a permanent World Parliament of Religions did not materialize, the Federal Council (1917) and later National Council of Churches (1946) were formed in

---

102. Dole 1993, 1–2, 21. For example, in *Secrets of Heaven* 3241 Swedenborg observes: "Although there are many variations and differences in matters of religious teaching—many directions in which it develops—nevertheless all these variations and differences form a single religious culture if people acknowledge thoughtfulness toward others to be the essence of such a culture" (translation by Stuart Shotwell).

103. See Hines 1974 for a full-scale biography. Burnham was the grandson of Holland Weeks (1768–1843), a clergyman who founded the Detroit New Church.

104. Scammon was a daughter of Jonathan Young Scammon (1812–1890), an attorney and founder of the New Church in Chicago, and one of the most influential businessmen in Chicago in the decades following the Civil War. Biographical information on both may be found in [Williams] 1906, 18–38; the World Parliament is discussed in [Williams] 1906, 346–359.

America, both stressing cooperation and unity among Christian denominations. General Convention churches joined at the local and state level, and the church as a whole debated the question of membership in the National Council in 1959 and 1960, officially joining in 1967. A second Parliament of the World's Religions was held in Chicago in 1993 (celebrating the one-hundredth anniversary of the original event); most branches of the New Church sent representatives.

A significant example of cooperation among Swedenborgian churches themselves was the Swedenborg World Assembly held in 1970. Though it took place in London, the assembly had been proposed by the General Convention in America, and attracted members from all bodies of the New Church worldwide. It included opportunities for worship, a tour of Swedenborg's London, and sessions on New Church education, worship, prayer, spiritual healing, mission work, and publications (London Committee for the World Assembly [1972]).

b. Movements in Art and Science

Part program for spiritual growth through creative expression and part continuing education, the Urbana Movement was the innovation of Alice Archer Sewall James (1870–1955), eldest daughter of Frank Sewall. A painter, poet, and playwright, James had been a member of the Urbana College faculty before she formally launched the program in 1933. The movement continued in various forms into the 1940s, primarily in Urbana, Ohio. Courses based on Swedenborgian teachings were offered in painting, dance, literature, music, languages, art history, and related topics; the classes met in rented rooms or homes and were open to anyone who wanted to learn. The movement had a constitution and officers; it also met monthly for worship and issued an annual report. No set fee was charged for courses (three terms a year), and students paid what they could afford (James Archives; Skinner 2001, 198–207).

James saw the movement as an attempt to recapture "the Real, the Inner Urbana University," which she believed had departed from its original New Church mission of developing each student's interest and spiritual nature.[105] Family circumstances, however, led her to spend 1934 in

105. The quoted phrase is from Founders 1933, 1; see Skinner 2001, 209 (an unpublished typescript study of James). James had been a student at the Girls School, and her husband, John H. James (mentioned above), was a longtime trustee. In 1932 she was barred from offering her courses in Lyceum Hall by the school's president (and her brother-in-law) Russell Eaton (active 1905–1945), who believed she was mentally unstable.

Detroit and the 1942–1943 academic year teaching at the Waltham School in Massachusetts. After she returned to Urbana (at age seventy-three), she continued to take on students in painting; but by 1947, community support for the movement had waned (Skinner 2001, 230–242).

A totally different type of organization, which its members thought would further education in its fullest sense, also began in Urbana with James's father, Frank Sewall. While not a religious body or New Church agency, the Swedenborg Scientific Association has been concerned with the translation, publication, and exploration of Swedenborg's philosophical and scientific works. Although various New Church presses had issued some of these works, they were generally neglected. The first meeting of those interested in forming the association took place in 1898 in the offices of the Swedenborg Foundation in New York City. Thirty-seven individuals attended and officially formed the association (Doering 1932, 83–84). Sewall served as the first president from 1898 until his death in 1915.

In addition to publishing a periodical, *The New Philosophy,* the association has undertaken efforts to collect, preserve, translate, and edit several of Swedenborg's scientific works. One of most energetic scholars to undertake translating and editing work for the society was Alfred Acton (1867–1956) of the Academy of the New Church. Among his many ambitious projects were the translation and serial publication of one of Swedenborg's unpublished manuscripts on physiology, *Draft on the Fiber* (published as *The Fibre;* see Swedenborg 1976a). Initially, *The New Philosophy* was published in Urbana, and then Boston, but after 1910 its editorial office moved to Bryn Athyn, Pennsylvania, where it has since remained.

c. Assemblies, Retreats, and Spiritual Growth Centers

Yet another institutionalization of Swedenborgian life can be seen in the numerous New Church summer retreat or camping programs. Both the General Convention and General Church have operated summer retreat assemblies or camps in the twentieth century: Split Mountain on the Pacific Coast (General Convention) and Laurel in Pennsylvania, Sunrise in New Jersey, Maple Leaf in Canada, and Winding Waters in Oregon (all General Church), among others. Frank S. Rose pioneered the General Church camps, beginning with the British Academy Summer School in the late 1960s. Intended primarily for youth and young adults, Rose's summer camps featured doctrinal instruction, small-group work, and experimental or creative worship, along with traditional summer outdoor recreational activities. Initially held at various locations throughout

Britain, the camps found a permanent home at Purley Chase, a country estate near Atherstone, in Warwickshire.

Two summer programs oriented toward family camping developed with their own organizational form independent of denominational ties, one in the Midwest and one in New England. The Almont Assembly, north of Detroit, is the oldest Swedenborgian summer camping program. It was originally modeled after the popular Chautauqua (New York) movement of the late-nineteenth century, which blended elements of a camp meeting, lyceum, and summer resort. Summer school programs in Michigan began in 1887 at a New Church summer resort, "Weller's Grove," led by Henry Weller (?–1868), the first minister of the La Porte, Indiana, New Church. In the 1890s, doctrinal instruction was provided by Eugene J. E. Schreck (1859–1951), who in 1900 conducted the first session at the Almont location. His original idea was to provide an opportunity for doctrinal instruction for children and youth who lived some distance from the Almont New Church and who could not regularly attend Sunday School. Two-week sessions became the norm beginning in 1920, after which permanent facilities were constructed. In addition to various recreational activities, the Almont Assembly has included regular periods for worship as well as lectures on Swedenborgian topics and discussion groups (Block 1984, 374).

The Fryeburg New Church Assembly, Fryeburg, Maine, began largely through the efforts of John Whitehead, who had been a long-time resident of Fryeburg, and Louis A. Dole (1885–1964), who became pastor of the New Church society there in the fall of 1920. Patterned after the family camping program at Almont, the first meetings were held in the summer of 1921. By 1928, the two-week assembly meetings had grown in popularity and attendance to the point that steps were taken to incorporate and purchase property for a permanent site. While the purpose of the assembly has been to provide instruction on New Church teachings in a relaxed camp setting, its social values and the strong family ties it fosters have endeared it to three generations.[106]

The church-sponsored summer camps as well as the programs at Almont and Fryeburg are intended primarily for those interested in learning more about or deepening their Swedenborgian beliefs. A unique form of community outreach that uses a natural, scenic setting to communicate Swedenborgian concepts is the famed Wayfarers Chapel at Rancho Palos

---

106. For more on the Fryeburg camp, see Wheaton and Briggs 1980.

Verdes, California. In many ways, the chapel was a dream of Elizabeth Trufant Sewall Schellenberg (1879–1966), a daughter of Frank Sewall, and Paul Sperry (1879–1954). Recalling the famed California missions, which according to tradition were built about a day's travel apart, Schellenberg proposed a chapel overlooking the Pacific Ocean where wayfarers could stop, rest, sense the wonder of nature, and refresh their spirits (Diaconoff 1966, 76). Property for the chapel and grounds was acquired through the generosity of Narcissa Cox Vanderlip (1879–1966) of New York. The stunning glass and timber-beam structure, dedicated in 1951, was designed by the noted architect Lloyd Wright (1890–1978), son of Frank Lloyd Wright (1867–1959).

The chapel site, which attracts up to a half-million visitors a year, was designed as a testimony to the correspondence between the spiritual and physical realms, a key concept in Swedenborgian thought. The visitor looking forward from the back of the chapel sees the Lord's Prayer inscribed on the chancel steps. At the front is a waterfall and lush foliage. Outside the glass walls is a grove of redwood and pine trees, and the view extends to the Pacific and beyond. Given the beautiful and tranquil setting, it is not surprising that the primary program at the chapel is a wedding ministry staffed by Swedenborgian clergy. A new visitor's center and administrative center were completed in 1999, designed by Eric Lloyd Wright, son of the chapel architect.[107]

Another outreach program set in a rustic environment is the Temenos Conference and Retreat Center, in West Chester, Pennsylvania. Temenos, which means "sacred place," began as the dream of Ernest O. Martin, a former president of the General Convention and minister at the Wayfarers Chapel, who was installed as the pastor of the First Philadelphia Society in 1984. The congregation had experienced declining membership for several years and struggled to maintain a large, aging church facility in downtown Philadelphia. A feasibility study, conducted by Martin, showed promise for a spiritual growth center in the greater Philadelphia area, and the congregation saw relocating and reshaping their outreach program as a way to bring about revitalization. Approximately fifty-three acres of woodlands and meadows were purchased in 1986 (with funds from the General Convention) near the village of Marshallton in Chester County. The centerpiece for the

107. For more on Wayfarers Chapel, see the fifteen short articles on the topic featured in [Wayfarers] 1974, 98–112.

property was a colonial-era fieldstone farmhouse (dating from the 1730s) along Broad Run Creek (Martin 1986, 199–202).

A modern home, dubbed Sky Meadow, was soon built on the property; it doubled as a residence for the pastor and as a retreat center (Martin 1987, 114–115). The congregation remodeled the farmhouse for use as a chapel, while a variety of spiritual growth programs were brought under the aegis of the center, including yoga, reiki, meditation, art and music therapy, and religious ritual, among others. A modern and spacious retreat house, also designed by Eric Lloyd Wright, was completed in 1998.[108]

X. Conclusion

This overview of the history and institutionalization of Swedenborgian thought and worship in Britain, the United States, and Canada speaks to the continuing energy and vision of believers in the new Christianity, but also to the incredible difficulty of establishing a church without the presence of a single charismatic leader. Such a leader through his or her vision and direction reduces the ideational and structural options possible for the following generations to implement in good faith. While the New Church has had an abundance of capable leaders, it has not been able to avoid some of the ambiguities that would have been removed by the directives of a charismatic founder.

Considered from the point of view of religious history and sociology, it is this very lack of a charismatic founder that makes the survival and continued growth of the New Church in its various forms such a remarkable achievement. Otherwise it would be merely one more small church.

Yet because of the ambiguities inherent in it, members of the organized New Church continue to struggle with questions that have been with the movement since its very beginning. One immediate question is the matter of the authority of Swedenborg's works. Some hear in Swedenborg's words God speaking directly to them; some hear the teachings of a human theologian or revelator interpreting his experience of the divine. Even within the individual believer this question is not always resolved. Members of the New Church must also confront the

---

108. Several congregations affiliated with the General Convention have experimented with various models for centers for spiritual growth. Other than Temenos, one of the most long-lived is the Swedenborgian spiritual growth center at DeLand, Florida, the Chrysalis Center for the New Wisdom Culture. This site includes a converted farm house, guest cottage, and orange grove (Martin 1985, 13).

challenges presented by those who see no divine authority in the theological works, and who reject those works on that basis.

Another persistent question is whether to separate from other institutions or to remain within them. Robert Hindmarsh sought to form a New Church because he believed that the forms of worship found in the old church—the confession of beliefs that ran counter to Swedenborgian tenets, for example—could not adequately provide for the salvation of souls. John Clowes, on the other hand, by remaining within the Church of England, insisted that the revelation of Swedenborg could be promoted and preserved even within the existing forms of the church. Like other movements that initially tried to work within established churches (such as Moravianism and Methodism), Swedenborgianism did eventually form its own new organization, and at least in a historical and sociological sense, Hindmarsh's vision won out; but readers of Swedenborg today are still faced with the choice between joining an established Swedenborgian church or keeping their Swedenborgianism alive and well, though perhaps not outwardly visible, in the heart of another religious organization.

A third question that continues to confront Swedenborgians is simply what kind of organization to form or to join. For example, some devote their energies to supporting Swedenborgian publishing organizations and seldom attend church. Others bring their Swedenborgian faith to small reading groups or spiritual growth sessions. Some are dedicated churchgoers; some avidly seek the growth of the churches but remain aloof from them.

A fourth question is what form the church organizations should take—should they be episcopal or congregational, centralized or local, national or international? Modern New Church groups show every sign of wrestling with these issues on an ongoing basis.

And finally, New Church groups today must decide whether being different and offering a clear alternative is sufficient to attract new members or whether they should adapt the church to the existing audience of spiritual seekers. So far the New Church as a whole seems to be exploring answers to this issue on a broad continuum.

Though these questions have parallels in other denominations, the unique origins of Swedenborgianism cause them to take a distinctive form in the New Church. Indeed, given that commitment to spiritual freedom is the hallmark of Swedenborgian Christianity, each succeeding generation of New Church members will continue the church's engagement with these questions.

New Church (Swedenborgian) Societies in the United States and Canada, 1790–2003

THE following list includes New Church societies or gatherings in the United States and Canada that sponsored public worship for at least ten consecutive years between 1790 and 2003, or were in operation in 2003. The three main branches are listed in the order in which they were formed: The Swedenborgian Church of North America, The General Church of the New Jerusalem, and The Lord's New Church Which Is Nova Hierosolyma.

The list was compiled from information provided by the three main branches indicated, combined with further data from independent research. Both the list and the accompanying map representation (page 313) had to be limited in scope to the United States and Canada because of the general difficulty of obtaining reliable historical data about international New Church activities. Even for this relatively restricted area, the data should not be considered exhaustive or definitive, as the records on which it is based are in some respects obscure.

In cases in which the affiliation of a given society may have changed, or may be unclear for any reason, it is listed under all of the branches in question, as long as it has met the test of having sponsored public worship for each branch for at least ten consecutive years. Some societies moved from their original site to a suburban location; the latter is indicated in parentheses.

THE SWEDENBORGIAN CHURCH OF NORTH AMERICA

Alabama
Fairhope

Alberta
Calgary
Edmonton

Arkansas
Hackett
Hot Springs
Winslow

British Columbia
Kelowna
Vancouver

California
Alameda
Berkeley
El Cerrito
Los Angeles
Oakland
Palos Verdes
Riverside
San Diego
San Francisco

Colorado
Boulder
Denver

Connecticut
New Haven
Norfolk
Stratford

Delaware
Wilmington

District of Columbia
Washington

Florida
Deland
Fort Myers Beach
Jacksonville
St. Petersburg
Tampa

Georgia
Atlanta
Savannah

Illinois
Canton
Chicago
Des Plaines
Henry
Joliet
Peoria
Pittsfield
Pontiac
Quincy
Rockford
Springfield

Indiana
Elkhart
Goshen
Indianapolis
La Porte
Richmond

Iowa
Des Moines
Fort Madison
Lenox
Norway

Kansas
Montezuma
Pawnee Rock
Pretty Prairie
Topeka

Kentucky
Louisville

Louisiana
New Orleans
Shreveport

Maine
Bangor
Bath
Fryeburg
Gardiner
Hallowell
Portland

Manitoba
Winnipeg

Maryland
Baltimore
Easton
Preston

Massachusetts
Abington
Boston
Bridgewater
Brockton
Brookline
Cambridge
Fall River
Foxborough
Lawrence
Lowell
Middleborough Center
Newton
Springfield
Taunton
Waltham
Yarmouthport

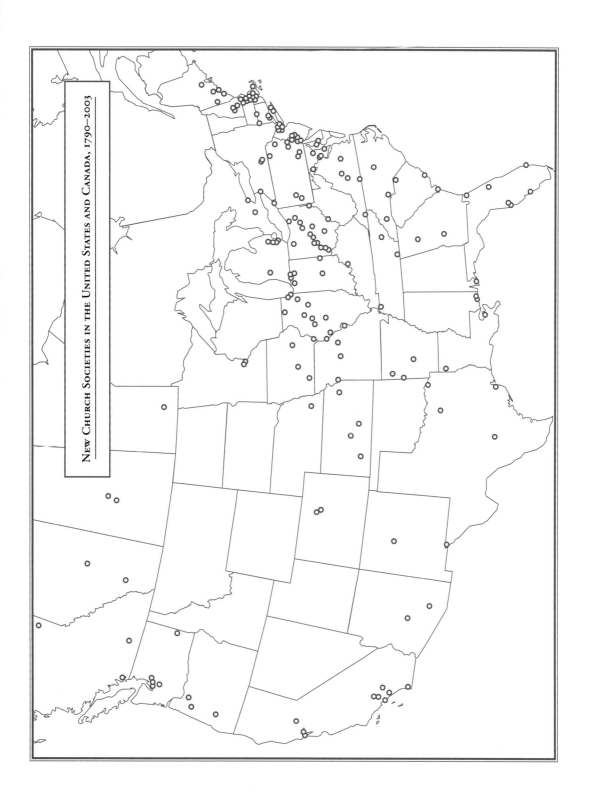

New Church Societies in the United States and Canada, 1790–2003

Michigan
Almont
Detroit
Edwardsburg
Grand Rapids
Niles
Royal Oak

Minnesota
Minneapolis
St. Paul

Mississippi
Biloxi
Gulfport

Missouri
Boonville
Kansas City
St. Louis
Wellsville

Nebraska
Lincoln

New Hampshire
Concord
Contoocook
Manchester

New Jersey
Hoboken
Newark
Orange
Paterson

New York
Bayside
Brooklyn
Buffalo
Greenport
Ithaca
New York City
Riverhead
South Danby

Ohio
Akron
Bowling Green
Cheshire
Chillicothe
Cincinnati
Cleveland
Dayton
Glendale
Lakewood
Lebanon
Lucas
Newark
Plain City
Pomeroy
Springfield
Urbana
Wooster
Wyoming

Ontario
Kitchener

Oregon
Ballston
Fair Oaks
Portland

Pennsylvania
Allentown
Frankford
Lancaster
Le Raysville
Philadelphia
Pittsburgh
Upper Darby
West Chester

Rhode Island
Pawtucket
Providence

Saskatchewan
Rosthern
Saskatoon

South Carolina
Cash Depot
Charleston

Tennessee
Chattanooga
Knoxville
Union City

Texas
Clarksville
Dallas/Fort Worth
El Paso
Galveston
San Antonio

Virginia
Abingdon
Danville
Lynchburg
Richmond
Warminster

Washington
Pine City
Redmond
Seattle

West Virginia
Shepherdstown
Wheeling

THE GENERAL CHURCH OF THE NEW JERUSALEM

Alberta
Calgary

Arizona
Phoenix (Scottsdale)
Tucson

British Columbia
Dawson Creek

California
El Toro
La Crescenta–Montrose
Sacramento
San Diego
San Francisco

Colorado
Boulder (Lafayette)

Connecticut
Shelton

District of Columbia
Washington

Florida
Lake Helen
Miami (Boynton Beach)

Georgia
Americus
Atlanta (Alpharetta)

Illinois
Chicago
Glenview

Indiana
Indianapolis
Richmond

Maine
Bath

Maryland
Baltimore
Bethesda
Mitchellville

Massachusetts
Boston

Michigan
Rochester

Minnesota
St. Paul/Minneapolis

New Jersey
Ridgewood

New Mexico
Albuquerque

North Carolina
Charlotte
Raleigh/Durham

Ohio
Cincinnati
Cleveland
Middleport

Ontario
Kitchener
Toronto (Etobicoke)

Oregon
Portland

Pennsylvania
Bryn Athyn
Elizabethtown
Erie
Freeport (Sarver)
Harleysville
Ivyland
Lenhartsville (Kempton)
Philadelphia
Pittsburgh
Wallenpaupack

Texas
Dallas/Fort Worth

Washington
Seattle (Edmonds)

The Lord's New Church Which Is Nova Hierosolyma

New York
Yonkers

North Carolina
Asheville

Pennsylvania
Philadelphia (located in Bryn Athyn)

South Carolina
Charleston

Washington
Lynwood
Puyallup

Compiled with the assistance of Martha Bauer, Hugh A. Blackmer, Kate Blackmer, Peter G. Bostock, Dandridge Cole, Stephen D. Cole, James P. Cooper, Lisa Hyatt Cooper, Kate Cuggino, George F. Dole, Clark Echols, Martie Johnson, Thomas L. Kline, John L. Odhner, Frank S. Rose, Patrick Rose, Susan V. Simpson, Alice B. Skinner, Wickham Skinner, and Cynthia H. Walker.

Examples of Internationalization

The New Church in Africa

JANE WILLIAMS-HOGAN

Outline

I. South Africa
 a. David Mooki
 b. Obed Mooki
 c. The Ethiopian Catholic Church in Zion
 d. The New Church in Southern Africa

II. Nigeria
 a. Africanus Mensah
 b. Rapid Growth in Nigeria
 c. Problems with Polygamy

III. Conclusion

FROM their first publication, the religious teachings of Emanuel Swedenborg (1688–1772) have had an international audience. Swedenborg was compelled to publish all of his theological works outside his Swedish homeland, not only to avail himself of two major foreign printing centers, Amsterdam and London, but to avoid stringent censorship in his home country. His works came to Sweden only as imports, of which he was the chief supplier; a role that caused him difficulties, though this distribution was carried out privately.[1] For public distribution

---

1. For example, in 1769 he sent home to Sweden a box of books containing fifty copies of his 1768 work *Marriage Love.* Upon his own arrival in Sweden he learned that the books had been confiscated (Sigstedt 1981, 393). During his lifetime his books were not readily available in Sweden. Abortive attempts were made to start a journal and publish some of his religious writings in Stockholm in the decades immediately following his death, when there was somewhat greater freedom of the press under Gustav III (1746–1792). On the general Swedish reception of Swedenborg's teachings to this day, see pages 151–165 above.

he depended on his printers in Holland and England, who both advertised and sold his books, and he himself sent copies to various church of-
ficials and other learned individuals throughout Europe.

Although not quantitatively large, this international distribution of
his teachings proved surprisingly wide.[2] By the time the first New Church[3]
organization, the General Conference, had come into being in Britain in
1787, Swedenborg's religious writings were being read not only in England, but in France, Germany, Holland, Denmark, Sweden, and Russia,
as well as in North and South America. Copies were on the first ship carrying convicts banished to Botany Bay, and so arrived in Australia in 1788
(Robinson 1980, 97, citing Hindmarsh 1861, 49).

It would be a labor beyond the scope of this paper to detail the expansion of the organized New Church throughout the world. Instead I
have chosen to focus on two specific regions on one continent, Africa.
The individuals who were initially responsible for its growth there,
though they seem extraordinary, are in fact typical of those who spread
New Church ideas beyond Europe, and I offer them as examples of leadership in the world-wide expansion of the church.

In further justification for this focus on individuals, I should note
that though I have just said that the dissemination of Swedenborgian
ideas was surprisingly rapid, in some sense this swift dissemination
should not surprise us. Swedenborg's ideas traveled by book, the preemi-
nent means of spreading information and by far the most important factor in the development and internationalization of the New Church. But
books are not the only factor. A book works on its audience one mind at
a time. There are many instances in the history of the New Church in
which an individual has read a single work by Swedenborg, adopted his
teachings, and plunged wholeheartedly into the establishment of a New
Church organization, whether as a central figure or as a more modest
participant, whether the organization was a local society or a national
conference. It is to such individuals, then, as well to publication efforts,
that the rapidity of New Church expansion is owed. Examples in the

---

2. The print run of the first volume of Swedenborg's 1758 work *Heaven and Hell* was probably
typical; it amounted to only one thousand copies (Hyde 1906, entry 1002).

3. In this essay, the term *New Church* refers to a broad ecclesiastical movement based on Swedenborg's
teachings. For more information on this term and on the specific church groups mentioned in this
essay, see the essay on pages 245–310.

West are the Swede Gabriel Beyer (1720–1779), the Britons John Clowes (1743–1831) and Robert Hindmarsh (1759–1835), and the American Francis Bailey (1744–1817)—all prominent figures in the history of the New Church.[4] In Africa, the primary examples are David Mooki (1876–1927), the founder of the New Church in Southern Africa, who discovered Swedenborg's teachings in 1909 in Krugersdorp, South Africa; and Africanus Mensah (1875–1942), whose discovery came in 1915 in Egwanga, Gold Coast (now Ghana), and who later founded the New Church in Nigeria.[5]

I. South Africa

The history of the New Church reveals an interest in overseas development from the beginning. In fact, four foreigners—an American, a Jamaican,[6] and two Swedes—were among those who signed the minutes of the first

---

4. For more on Beyer, see pages 41–45 above; on Clowes and Hindmarsh, see pages 255–263 above; on Bailey, see pages 251–252 with note 15 above.

5. For discussion of adult adoption of New Church teachings, see my forthcoming paper "Charisma of the Book: Weber's Concept Modernized," extending my previous work on this topic (Williams-Hogan 1997), and incorporating the results of my interviews in June 2000 with people from the United States, Canada, Sweden, Ghana, and Jamaica who discovered the works of Emanuel Swedenborg in their adult life. I analyze these conversions in terms of the inherent charisma of the theological works. It is striking that Swedenborg described a similar power in the inner sense of the Christian sacred texts (the Word); see *Secrets of Heaven* 3954 (here in translation by Lisa Hyatt Cooper):

> This is what happens with the Word's inner sense: The literal message rises up to heaven, where it enters an environment in which everyone thinks from the Lord, and about the Lord, and about the things that are the Lord's. In the end, it is perceived by angels in just these terms. The inner meaning, after all, is the angels' form of the Word; the literal meaning simply serves as a platform or a medium for thinking about the inner meaning. The literal message cannot reach the angels because in most places it deals with worldly matters, earthly affairs, and bodily concerns. Angels cannot think about these, because they focus on heavenly and spiritual concerns and so remain far above such things. That is why we were given a Word that can serve humans and angels simultaneously. In this aspect it differs from any other kind of writing.

(As is common in Swedenborgian studies, text citations of Swedenborg's works refer not to page numbers but to Swedenborg's section numbers, which are uniform in all editions.)

6. Hallengren 1998a, 49, identifies up to eight of the delegates at this initial meeting as Jamaicans.

annual meeting of a British New Church ecclesiastical organization, the General Conference, in April 1789. In 1826 the annual meeting adopted Rules for the Secretary for Foreign Correspondence that stipulated that the secretary was to obtain the most accurate information possible concerning interest in the New Church overseas and to submit reports of developments annually. In 1874, a Foreign and Colonial Missions Committee was organized to handle foreign correspondence and to appeal for aid when it was deemed necessary.

During the 1800s the main work of the secretary and the committee focused on keeping up foreign correspondence and providing financial support for New Church ministers in Europe. The committee also authorized the ordination of a number of ministers to serve either in their own country or in various missions. This work continued into the 1900s. The result of this effort in the British colonies and in the independent nations that arose from them was the development of New Church organizations in Australia, New Zealand, Nigeria, and South Africa.

In South Africa, however, the narrative of the institutionalized New Church in the region begins, strictly speaking, not with missionary activity, but with the formation by British immigrants of their own General Conference society in Durban in 1880. General Conference activity continued in South Africa into the twentieth century. In addition, two New Church organizations based in the United States, the General Church of the New Jerusalem and the Lord's New Church, established branches in South Africa in 1914 and 1937, respectively. In fact, it may be true that nowhere on earth is the New Church thriving as much as in South Africa.[7] Even if one confines one's focus to South Africa, it is not feasible to discuss the activities of all the different New Church groups there; thus the focus in this section on the work of David W. Mooki and his son, Obed S. D. Mooki (about 1919–1990).[8]

---

7. If the New Church in South Africa is compared with its counterpart in the United States and Canada, the South African church appears the stronger in terms of numbers: it has as many as twenty-five thousand members, as opposed to the approximately fifteen thousand individuals affiliated with the New Church in the two northernmost nations of North America, including all three major organizations incorporated in the United States: the Swedenborgian Church of North America (usually referred to as General Convention), the General Church, and the Lord's New Church. However, in terms of material organization and educational opportunities, the churches in the United States and Canada are stronger. For example, the American groups maintain not just one but three theological schools among them.

8. The information in this section is based mainly on Evans [1994?].

a. David Mooki

David Mooki was born in South Africa in 1876. By 1909 he was a minister of the African Holy Catholic Church. It was in that year that he found a copy of Swedenborg's 1771 work *True Christianity* in a pile of secondhand books in an old furniture shop in Krugersdorp. The title (*True Christian Religion* in that edition) caught his attention; he picked it up and read a few pages. His interest was piqued rather than satisfied, and he decided he must have the book. He bought it, took it home, and soon had read its 816 pages from cover to cover (Evans [1994?], 13).

When he closed the book he was convinced that the Lord had made his Second Coming on earth as Swedenborg maintained. He was also impressed by statements in the text and in a supplement to it that emphasized Swedenborg's belief that Africans had a special genius for discerning spiritual truth.[9] Given the nature of the book, it was evident that an organization calling itself the New Church existed somewhere in the world; Mooki felt he could not rest until he had found it. He also determined that he wanted to center his life on the sharing of these new truths with his fellow Africans (Evans [1994?], 13).

When David Mooki brought *True Christianity* to the notice of his congregation, many others in the African Holy Catholic Church accepted its teachings. It became the authority to which they referred in all matters of doctrine. They continued in this way—as Swedenborgians within a non-Swedenborgian organization—until the bishop of the African Holy Catholic Church became determined to join another, non-Swedenborgian religious movement in the United States. This neither Mooki nor his followers wanted to do, and a difference arose between the parties. When the bishop persisted in his plans, the New Church element of the African Holy Catholic Church elected to withdraw and form its own church. Calling a conference, David Mooki and his converts formed the New Church of Africa on January 25, 1911.

For the next five years they worshipped independently, although David Mooki continued his attempts to locate an existing New Church organization with which they could form an alliance. The matter became pressing because under race restrictions Africans were not permitted to

9. In *True Christianity* 837 Swedenborg remarks that Africans surpass others in interior judgment; in §838 he adds that they have a clearer perception of spiritual matters than others because their powers of reasoning about inner things are superior; and in §839 that they excel in inner vision. In §840 he declares that a revelation has been made among them that is spreading through the interior of the continent. See also page 202 note 18 above.

register with the white authorities as a completely independent black church; in their unaffiliated state they were viewed with suspicion. Mooki's persistence eventually led him to write care of the Manchester Book Depot, the book distribution office of the General Conference in Britain, requesting his church's admission into an organized branch of the New Church.

The General Conference at first responded only by sending books, though it also made inquiries concerning David Mooki's group among New Church circles in South Africa. These produced no information, and no official personal contact was made between the General Conference and the New Church of Africa until 1917. At that time James F. Buss (1857–1934), a minister who had served the Durban society of the General Conference from 1903 to 1907, was returning from Britain to South Africa. Having previously been a member of the overseas missions committee for several years, he was commissioned by that body to contact David Mooki upon his arrival in South Africa.

The meeting took place at the Victoria Hotel in Johannesburg. Buss was greatly impressed by Mooki, whose intelligence and sincerity commanded respect. A report was sent to the missions committee recommending that the New Church of Africa be brought under the committee's direction, and in 1919 an arrangement to do so was made. Buss spent thirteen months instructing the ministers and leaders in Mooki's movement in "the way of the New Church" (Evans [1994?], 25). In adopting them in this fashion, under the protection of the General Conference, Buss was able "'to secure for their Mission such status, privileges and exemptions as are granted under the Government of the Union of South Africa to duly accredited Christian Missions.'"[10]

On January 23, 1921, David Mooki was ordained by the General Conference of the New Church. Two weeks later nine other ministers were ordained into the New Church. These new ministers served congregations from as far north in South Africa as Tamposstad, and as far south as Liphiring in Basutoland. In this new mission there were about one hundred congregations and two thousand members.[11]

---

10. Evans [1994?], 25, quoting Buss 1924; see Buss 1927, 23.

11. It should be emphasized that these figures are only approximate; no precise statistics were available even at the time. See Evans [1994?], 31. Buss 1927, 26–27, reports that when he visited the mission it had 1,500 adults and junior members. In 1927 a review of only forty societies of the one hundred established at that time showed they had 1,546 adult members and 503 junior members, for a total of 2,049.

With the establishment of the mission—that is, with the formal affiliation between the New Church of Africa and the General Conference—
Buss's work was finished. On his return to Britain, E. John Pulsford
(1878–1952), a General Conference representative, was sent to the mission.
He arrived in 1924 and remained there until 1928.[12] The focus of his work
was to train the mission ministers to serve their very scattered flock. To
this end he traveled a great deal overseeing the work of the mission.

This was difficult work, given the very rough nature of the roads in
South Africa at that time, the distances that had to be covered, and the
trials of living in a world defined by strict patterns of racial segregation.
Although two ministers of different races might share a common faith,
when traveling together they could not share a seat on a train or in any
other means of public conveyance. These difficulties and other human
indignities threatened the connection between the General Conference
and the African members of the mission as South Africa went from a policy of simple segregation toward one of active apartheid. The records
seem to indicate, however, that the ministers of both races always managed to rise above these restrictions and work together in a common
spirit to further the establishment of the New Church.

Perhaps the greatest challenge came with the death of David Mooki
in 1927, during the tenure of the first superintendent. He was only fifty-
one years old and left a wife and four children, by whom he was sorely
missed; they faced severe economic hardship after his passing. "His"
church felt his loss deeply as well, as it now had to confront the future
without his personal strength and vision. The mission superintendent,
Pulsford, was able to provide some assistance to the Mooki family, and
particularly to Obed, the youngest, then eight years of age. Furthermore,
upon his return to Britain, Pulsford saw to it that some additional financial help was given to the children through a church orphans' fund. As
for the church as a whole, its recently acquired status as a mission helped
to ensure its survival and ultimately allowed it to grow in spite of the loss
of its founder.

New Church minister and historian Brian Kingslake (1907–1995)
gives some insight into the issues facing the mission in 1930, a few years
after Mooki's death:

> The Mission now numbers about 4000, and has more societies than
> we have in England. It spreads over a vast area, comprising practically

12. Evans [1994?], 5a, 27, 31, gives slightly varying dates for E. John Pulsford's superintendency of
the mission, but his approximate tenure seems to have been 1924–1928.

the whole of South Africa. Financially, of course, it is unhealthy—and really it is remarkable how the ministers exist on the few shillings a month they receive from their poverty-stricken societies.

Another weakness is the common tendency of all loosely constructed organizations to become unwieldy and split into pieces. Mr. Johnson[13] is doing wonderful work to bind it together, with but slender support. . . . I should scarcely think there is another mission our size in Africa without quite a body of ministers in control and a substantial income from home. . . .

The problem will be on the road to solution when there is enough money for the Mooki Memorial College. Here will be an organic centre, from which African ministers can issue forth, . . . full of the wonder of the Doctrines of the Church, binding the Mission together into a firm and healthy unit.[14]

b. Obed Mooki

The David Mooki Memorial College was established in 1933, in Orlando.[15] Mooki's son, Obed, began his theological training there with Superintendent Johnson in 1934, when he was fifteen years of age. He went on to take his junior certificate under the direction of the next superintendent of the mission, Edwin Fieldhouse.[16] On completion of the certificate, he took some time to secure a teacher's diploma from the Department of Education in the Transvaal before returning to finish his theological education; he was ordained in 1940 (Evans [1994?], 56).

At the time of his ordination, the mission had 122 recognized societies and 19 unofficial groups. In 1940 alone, 3 new societies were added. These societies and groups were served by only twenty-three ordained

---

13. Philip Johnson was superintendent from 1929 to 1935.

14. Quoted in Evans [1994?], 46; she does not cite her source, but it was probably a report sent by Kingslake to the General Conference in Great Britain. Kingslake served as the superintendent of the New Church Mission in South Africa from 1950 to 1962 and also as the principal of the David Mooki Memorial College for African ministers (see below).

15. Orlando lies outside Johannesburg; it is one of the South Western Townships, also known as Soweto.

16. Edwin Fieldhouse (died 1962) was superintendent from 1935–1950. He is remembered for the tremendous energy he exerted in strengthening the mission—increasing the number of its physical structures, enlarging its membership, and promoting its spiritual growth.

ministers, though they had eighty-two lay preachers and seven proba-
tioners to assist them in their work. During this same year, the superintendent traveled over seventeen thousand miles and organized twelve
district conferences (Evans [1994?], 54).

Even prior to his ordination, Obed Mooki was employed by the mission as its secretary, so it was only natural that after his ordination he
should take on these duties full time. As David Mooki's son, he had
known all the superintendents of the mission who had come from the
British General Conference. He was linguistically gifted, speaking
Afrikaans, English, Sechwana, Sesuto, Xosa, Zula, and some Nyanja
(Evans [1994?], 88). Given the variety of African groups that were part of
the mission, Obed Mooki's skills made a vital contribution to the work
of the college, where the students often arrived speaking only their
mother tongue. The same skills also helped immeasurably in uniting the
far-flung societies of the mission, with their tremendous varieties of peoples and locations, as Obed Mooki generally traveled with the superintendent and served as his interpreter.

Obed Mooki served the mission in these capacities from 1936 until
1969. From 1936 through 1950 he worked closely with Fieldhouse. During the early 1940s he also served as chaplain to the African National
Congress. However, he became disillusioned by what he believed to be its
neglect of the spiritual dimension and left the organization in 1947.[17]

In 1950 Brian Kingslake became superintendent of the mission. He
had his work cut out for him: by that time there were 4,128 adult
members of the mission and 1,094 junior members in 130 societies and
other groups. To serve this large mission church there were 25 ordained
ministers, 3 evangelists, 105 lay preachers, and 82 lay preachers on pro-
bation. The mission owned fifteen church buildings, and three more
were under construction. There were four day schools and seven Sunday schools (Evans [1994?], 84). Much of Kingslake's work during the
1950s was intended to democratize the organization and prepare it for
eventual independence; in this effort he worked closely with Obed
Mooki. Mooki had become so central to the mission that he was the
natural choice to be deputy-superintendent during Kingslake's absence
in 1956.

---

17. This part of Obed Mooki's story is particularly fascinating and moving. See Evans [1994?],
65–74, for a full discussion of his involvement with the African National Congress.

c. The Ethiopian Catholic Church in Zion

If the decade of the 1950s had been a busy time in the mission, the early 1960s brought even more change. The South African government's ever-shifting policy toward black South Africans led to its decision in 1960 that all unregistered black churches in urban areas must be closed down. One of the requirements for registration was that the candidate church have a theological school. This did not present a problem for the New Church mission, which did have one; but another black church that did not, the Ethiopian Catholic Church in Zion, found its existence threatened. The Ethiopian Catholic Church petitioned the New Church mission to consider the amalgamation of its tens of thousands of members. It was a missionary's dream come true, and Kingslake wrote to the Overseas Mission Committee in Britain exclaiming, "Imagine the Mission suddenly acquiring 30,000 new members" (Evans [1994?], 126). Of great importance too were the Ethiopian Catholic Church's premises, including no fewer than forty good brick buildings (Evans [1994?], 126).

As exciting as this prospect of instant growth might be, the most important considerations were doctrinal and functional. Would the amalgamation work spiritually and organizationally? As it happened, the Ethiopian Catholic Church in Zion had been founded by a friend of David Mooki's, Samuel James Brander,[18] who had almost joined David Mooki's movement in 1915. He had lost interest in doing so at that time as it became clear that David Mooki would join with a European-based organization. Now, almost fifty years later, Brander's original intention might well become a reality.

Amalgamation was not straightforward. However, on one central issue, maintaining the integrity of New Church doctrine, there were soon positive developments. At an exploratory meeting considering amalgamation, held in January 1960 and attended both by spiritual leaders and by lawyers for the two sides, a summary of the New Church teachings about Christ ("the doctrine of the Lord") was presented to an audience of eleven ministers of the Ethiopian Catholic Church in Zion.[19] Their initial reaction was positive, and they wanted to learn more.

With this encouragement, Kingslake attacked the second major issue, organization, by devising a plan of amalgamation. Initially the mission

---

18. Further biographical information on Brander was not available to the author.

19. For more on the New Church doctrine of the Lord, see pages 58–61 above.

would be divided into two sections, the Ethiopian section and the General Conference section, and it would be administered as such. The ministers of the Ethiopian Catholic Church in Zion would be instructed in New Church doctrine, examined in it, and then reordained into the ministry of the New Church. At that point they would enter the General Conference section of the mission. The process would take place over a number of years, the goal being the eventual closure of the Ethiopian section (Evans [1994?], 132).

Not only would the two groups in Africa have to assent to this plan, but the Overseas Mission Committee would also have to endorse it. As negotiations proceeded in Johannesburg, reports were periodically sent via express to Britain. Amalgamation could not occur until all the parties were in agreement, and yet a deadline set by the South African government was looming. At first the parties had six months, but then this interval was shortened by the government so that all the initial negotiations had to take place within about six weeks. One local authority was set to seize an Ethiopian Church building on February 29, 1960; however, approval arrived from Britain on February 18, preventing seizure with only a few days to spare (Evans [1994?], 134). After this initial agreement, negotiations continued throughout 1960 to work out the complete arrangements. Amalgamation was supposed to be finalized in April 1961, but the whole process actually took somewhat longer.

Several unexpected events radically altered the tenor of the amalgamation. First the government reversed its policy, removing the external pressure for merger. When some 650 delegates attended a ten-day conference on the union of the two churches, the archbishop of the Ethiopian Catholic Church in Zion stayed away (Evans [1994?], 137). Then, a short time later, he wrote a letter to Kingslake withdrawing his petition to amalgamate the two churches.

Many members of his church, however, disagreed with him, and opted to continue with the amalgamation process. For Kingslake and the others who had worked to share the vision of the New Church, it was a thrilling moment. They viewed the decision of those who had decided to proceed with amalgamation as now clearly based on a conscious appreciation of New Church doctrine and on a deliberated conviction, rather than on pragmatic considerations (Evans [1994?], 137).

Even though the archbishop persisted, bringing lawsuits whose resolution took several years, in the end he failed to halt the amalgamation. After the merger was finalized, the statistical profile of the church founded by David Mooki in South Africa was significantly altered. It now had 114 ministers, twenty-five thousand members, thirty-nine churches, and fifteen manses.[20]

d. The New Church in Southern Africa

In 1968, as a preliminary step to granting the General Conference mission in South Africa full autonomy, Obed Mooki was appointed general superintendent. This move toward independence was precipitated by two factors: the internal strength of the church itself, and a new policy of the South African government, which was withdrawing from the British Commonwealth and was determined that the mission churches within South Africa should also sever ties with overseas organizations.

In 1970 the mission of the New Church became completely independent, assuming the title "The New Church in Southern Africa." It was governed by an elected Conference Council of South Africa, of which Obed Mooki was the first president (Evans [1994?], 153). Mooki continued in this capacity until his death in 1990 (Evans [1994?], 167).

Throughout the period of troubles in South Africa, the New Church in Southern Africa survived and prospered, even though the needs of the church for more ministers and adequate buildings persisted. The last membership figures for the New Church in Southern Africa given by church historian Jean Evans date from 1988; they indicate a total membership of 24,800.[21]

Since 1988 the organization has undergone significant changes brought on by the death of Mooki in 1990 and that of his wife, Eulalia, a few years later. While the organization continues, things have not been easy without their leadership. Soon after Mooki's death a split occurred within the New Church of Southern Africa that had not been resolved by the summer of 2000. According to President Paul Kanene, his group, which is based at the founding headquarters in Orlando, has about fifteen thousand members and the splinter group has about five thousand.[22]

---

20. For these figures, see Evans [1994?], 139. As always, membership figures present some difficulties. It is clear that as amalgamation proceeded, individuals and groups returned to the Ethiopian Catholic Church in Zion. Evans [1994?], 135, quotes Kingslake as stating that the actual membership gain was about fifteen thousand.

21. See Evans [1994?], 154.

22. Personal interview with the author, August 2000.

In the fall of 2000, twenty-five theological students were scheduled to train for several weeks in Orlando. This pattern of short sessions over a period of several years constitutes the current system of theological training in the church; it takes into account the need of the students to have full-time jobs outside the ministry. The theological school buildings constructed in the 1920s are in disrepair, but the church has built a new school with dormitory space sufficient for the projected student population. The library facilities remain inadequate: the old library is in desperate need of conservation and the new library houses no books.

However, despite the difficulties facing the organization, at the turn of the century Mooki's vision had survived and was unfolding in the new millennium. It is on such a note that Jean Evans concludes her book, citing Mooki's dream for the future: "My wish is that the College will be built and that young men will come forward for training—that they will then go North, East, West, and South to spread the teachings—we need not only Tswana, but Basothos to go to Lesotho, Pedis to go into the Northern Transvaal, Zulus and Swazis as well. I believe the teachings of the New Church are for the new age, and I believe as Swedenborg said, that the Africans understand the Writings and it is time that they were extended" (Evans [1994?], 170).

II. Nigeria

The burden David Mooki foresaw for his college—to spread throughout Africa—no longer must be carried by "his" church exclusively. Today there are strong New Church groups in Kenya, Ghana, and Nigeria bringing life to Swedenborg's understanding of the special genius of the African and to Mooki's faith in that genius. Nigeria in particular offers an interesting parallel to the development of the New Church in South Africa.

a. Africanus Mensah

The story of the New Church in Nigeria begins with the birth of Africanus Mensah, in Mount Pleasant, Gold Coast, in 1875.[23] Educated in a Wesleyan school, Mensah entered government service in the post office at the age of twenty. He then transferred to the telegraph service and took part in

---

23. This section is based on Kingslake 1947.

the second Ashanti expedition in 1895–1896. His duties took him to Accra and Cape Coast, where he finally settled eight miles east of Elmina, employed as the chief clerk in the telegraph service (Kingslake 1947, 8–9).

He remained in government service until 1910, when he resigned his post and bought land near Egwanga, ten miles from Opobo, and set himself up as a trader in what became known as Mensah Town. He also started a Wesleyan mission in the area and built a congregation and a small day school. The mission soon numbered about 120 people, and a minister was sent from Logos to care for the group. The movement rapidly spread to other towns in the eastern part of the Niger Delta (Kingslake 1947, 9–11).

In 1915, at the age of forty, Mensah saw an advertisement for the works of Emanuel Swedenborg in an American journal. He was attracted by the claims of the advertisement and sent for a book containing extracts from Swedenborg's works. When it arrived he read it immediately; his reaction was no less than delight. He ordered copies of the same book to sell at his store, as well as volumes of the theological works themselves and other New Church literature. This material he read thoroughly, quickly becoming a believer in the teachings of the New Church, though he remained a member of the Methodist church (Kingslake 1947, 11–12).

World War I brought ruin to his business. He went back to Elmina and set up another store there, where he also displayed copies of Swedenborg's religious writings. At this time he became reacquainted with a man by the name of R.S.M. Akwonu, who had worshipped in the General Conference's Camden Road Church in London during the time he lived in Britain.[24] On his return to Gold Coast, Akwonu considered himself to be the official agent of the Swedenborg Society, a British organization devoted to publication and distribution of Swedenborg's works. Mensah learned from Akwonu about the organized New Church in Europe. The two men became good friends and dreamed of bringing the New Church to Gold Coast; but Akwonu's death in 1926 brought an end to their mutual plans (Kingslake 1947, 14).

During this same period, Mensah continued his endeavors on behalf of the Methodist church. Trouble developed when he presented New Church

---

24. Akwonu (died 1926) was the older brother of a schoolmate of Mensah's in Mount Pleasant. He became a wealthy gold trader and lived in Britain for a number of years. See Kingslake 1947, 13.

doctrines in his preaching and in 1929 sent New Church pamphlets to the
Methodist synod at Cape Coast. They were branded heretical and publicly
burned. By 1933 his avowed Swedenborgianism became a scandal in
Elmina, and he was tried and suspended by the Methodist church. He appealed the decision, but to no avail. At the age of sixty he was expelled
from the church with which he had been affiliated since his youth, an
event that meant as well the end of his employment (Kingslake 1947, 160).

Family obligations brought him to Port Harcourt, and he decided to
focus his energy on spreading the New Church there. He wrote to the
Overseas Mission Committee of the General Conference in Britain
about his decision and became a correspondence student in the New
Church Theological College. He also opened a book room in order to
sell New Church literature (Kingslake 1947, 17).

In 1934 a decision was made by the Overseas Mission to investigate
the possibilities of supporting a missionary effort in West Africa. Arthur
Clapham (1896–1964), a General Conference minister, was selected for
the task, and he arrived in Port Harcourt in November 1934. He held
worship services in Port Harcourt and then went on a lecture tour of
many of the large towns in Nigeria. He also traveled to Gold Coast and
lectured there. Mensah was his guide on the tour, and in Sekondi, Gold
Coast, he was baptized into the New Church (Kingslake 1947, 17–19).

Clapham returned to Britain in 1935 and gave a very affirmative report
about Mensah's work. "I have the greatest admiration," he wrote, "for
Mensah's work as a missioner and colporteur. He is untiring, zealous and
eminently successful. Where he goes the New Church becomes known"
(Kingslake 1947, 18). As a result of this report Mensah was appointed a lay
missionary and given an annual stipend (Kingslake 1947, 18).

b. Rapid Growth in Nigeria

In his initial communications to the Overseas Mission Committee, Mensah
often said he had nothing of interest to report, although he made some
converts in the Port Harcourt area. In 1936, however, his reports showed a
dramatic change. He was invited to preach in Owo, Nigeria, to a group
that had recently seceded from a church missionary society and that was
looking for another European missionary affiliation. The town itself is
about eighty miles north of Benin City; at that time it had about twenty-
five thousand inhabitants. On June 6, 1936, Mensah spoke about the
New Church to a large assembly of people in Owo. He was also inter-
viewed by the chief, or Olowo, and the European district officer. He was

invited by them to come and establish himself in the town. He agreed on the spot, and the next day conducted worship in a temporary building.[25]

He immediately sent this news by telegram to the annual gathering of the General Conference, which was being held in Glasgow, observing that "God moves in mysterious ways" (Kingslake 1947, 22). He described the wholesale conversion of about 700 people and reported preaching to a crowd of 1,000. He also informed the General Conference that he had been invited to become the supervisor of the converts and that he had consented. The inauguration service was to take place on July 5, 1936. He hurried back to the coast to settle his affairs and returned for the ceremony, which was attended by 2,300 people (Kingslake 1947, 23).

From this point the growth of the New Church in Owo in particular and in Nigeria in general was very rapid, although not always smooth. In 1937, a building was erected in Owo for a church and a school. It was dedicated to "the sole worship of the Lord Jesus Christ" on the anniversary of the founding of the society (Kingslake 1947, 24). The school was called the Swedenborg Memorial School, and opened on August 5 with 128 pupils and eight teachers. As other day schools were founded by the mission in Nigeria, they too were given the name Swedenborg Memorial School.

In 1938 two new societies were founded in Nigeria: one in Degema in the Niger Delta, and another in Ibo country in Umuana Ndume. They were both officially inaugurated in January of that year by Mensah, before he sailed to Britain to be ordained.

He spent two months overseas. First he was tutored for his ordination examination by Kingslake in Blackburn, Great Britain. After successfully writing his examination, he traveled to Camberwell, London, to be ordained at the annual General Conference meeting on June 22, 1938. Kingslake later wrote that he was particularly impressed by Mensah's deep mind and profound New Church spirit (Kingslake 1947, 31–32).

c. Problems with Polygamy

Mensah returned to Nigeria in July 1938, and in December of that year Arthur Clapham returned to West Africa. The purpose of the visit was to

---

25. It is worth observing that Owo is in the Yoruba-speaking area of Nigeria and that Mensah never learned that language or any Nigerian language. He always spoke in English, which was translated by an interpreter. See Kingslake 1947, 33.

oversee the developments in the region since Clapham's last visit and to attend to any issues that had arisen. One problem simmering in Owo was the status of the polygamists associated with Mensah's group.[26] They had provided most of the money for the church building and wanted a commensurate voice in the affairs of the organization; and thus they were at odds with Mensah, who would not allow them to predominate. The Claphams stayed in Owo for four months, and although they strengthened the ties between the people there and the New Church, they were not able to bring the problem with the polygamists to a satisfactory solution (Kingslake 1947, 33).

In March 1939 Clapham and Mensah took a brief tour of the other societies in the mission. Two new groups had recently formed in Egbolom and Buguma. They also visited Accra, in Gold Coast, and met with a study circle there. Then Clapham returned to Britain, and later that year, at the annual meeting of the General Conference, the New Church Mission in West Africa was officially established. Africanus Mensah became its first superintendent (Kingslake 1947, 34–35).

The official resolution of the General Conference adopting the mission in West Africa provided that a mission conference be held every January. In accordance with this resolution, the first conference was held in January 1940 in Owo. The constitution and rules excluded the polygamists from full membership in the mission. This led to a heated debate, and order was maintained only with difficulty. At this point there were now ten societies in Nigeria with a registered membership of 1,300 adults and 800 children. Many of the adults were practicing polygamists (Kingslake 1947, 42).

The problem of polygamy resurfaced in 1941. Mensah dismissed the headmaster of the school (who was not a member of the church) for immoral behavior, and a polygamist associated with the school countered by dismissing Mensah. The matter was taken to court and ultimately Mensah won; but for a time he felt unwelcome in Owo. While the dispute was cooling, he took the opportunity to make another tour of the mission, which lasted several months. The tour included the annual mission conference, which was held in Umuana Ndume in 1942. At that conference the mission was divided into four sections for organizational

---

26. Swedenborg expressly declared that it was not allowable for a Christian to have more than one wife (see, for example, *Secrets of Heaven* 3246:4). He did, however, believe that polygamy was not a sin for those whose religion allowed it (that is, non-Christians); see his 1768 work *Marriage Love* 348.

purposes. Each section had its own district boards and other administrative units (Kingslake 1947, 48).

When Mensah returned to Owo, the matter regarding the ownership of the church building was finally resolved, and a service of rejoicing was held on June 21, 1942. The adult members of the congregation now numbered only 110—60 men and 50 women—but all were solidly dedicated to the faith of the New Church and determined to create a strong and healthy society (Kingslake 1947, 51).

Mensah, however, was not in good health himself. In July he planned a trip to visit his family in Elmina, but was not strong enough to go. He died on Sunday, August 23, 1942; his last words were "I am in Jerusalem" (Kingslake 1947, 52).

At the time Africanus Mensah passed on, the mission included thirteen New Church societies, three day schools, seven women's leagues, and a young people's association. The membership included approximately one thousand adults, with one hundred associates and seven hundred children. Michael O. Ogundipe, a minister of the New Church in Nigeria, was appointed Mensah's successor in the post of superintendent. By 1946 the mission had nearly doubled in size.

Since that time, over fifty years ago, the mission has achieved its independence from the General Conference, though the Conference still has an interest in the activities of the church. For example, in 2000 it planned to assist the societies in Nigeria in the training of their student ministers (General Conference 1999–2000, 33). The Mission's independence has made actualizing such assistance more difficult, as is obtaining statistical information about the size of the New Church in Nigeria. In recent correspondence with the author, the Overseas Secretary of the General Conference, Norman Ryder, reported a figure for the Nigerian New Church membership of about three thousand, though this information must be used with caution, as the date it was collected is not clear. The latest (July 2004) report he had received concerning the societies put their number at thirty-one. Ryder also noted that he had been in contact with a young man who studied at the Theological College in Owo, in the state of Ondo, Nigeria, though he had not been ordained. Ryder's contact reported having established a society ten years ago in an area previously not served by the New Church in Nigeria. Such evidence suggests that the prognosis of the Church in Nigeria is mixed. It appears to have achieved modest growth since its founding, but is in need of international support both for its general finances and for its training of ministers.

III. Conclusion

From its international origins within Europe, the New Church has established a presence that, while not numerically large, has an extremely wide distribution. In Africa there are more members of the New Church than on any other continent. Development of New Church organizations the world over reflects the same pattern described here, in which inspired and dedicated individuals work in partnership with older New Church organizations to build lasting and dynamic Swedenborgian institutions to suit their own spiritual needs.

At the conclusion of his 1769 work *Soul-Body Interaction,* Swedenborg describes himself as a "spiritual fisher," which he defines as someone who at first investigates and teaches truths about nature, and then moves on to use rational powers to investigate truths about things spiritual. He connects this term to Christ's reference to his disciples as fishers of people, implying that his own investigations into truth were intended to be shared.[27] The narratives presented here demonstrate that such "fishers"— the ministers and organizers of the church—play a highly important role in its internationalization. In the examination of a church built on the charisma of written teachings, it is important to appreciate the power of human interaction and support.

---

27. See *Soul-Body Interaction* 20, as well as the Bible passages cited in Swedenborg's text: Matthew 4:18–19; Mark 1:16–17; and Luke 5:9–10.

An Alternative Approach to Studying Swedenborg's Impact

Swedenborg's Influence

The Power of Three Selected Ideas

ALICE B. SKINNER

Outline

I. Spiritual Reality
    a. Nature and Spirit: Worcester, Reed, Emerson, and Whitman
    b. Seeing the Spiritual: Borges and Frost
    c. Spiritual Architecture: Worcester, Brown, and Porter
    d. The Human as Representative of the Spiritual: Flaxman and Powers
    e. Themes of Spiritual Growth: Pyle, Inness, Keith, Tiffany, and Yardumian

II. Useful Living
    a. Forging Links for Community: Mussey, Child, and Chapman
    b. The Value of Appointed Work: Barrett Browning, Galli-Curci, and Jewett

III. Ways of Knowing
    a. Knowing as Loving Thought: Andrews
    b. Knowing as an Inner Process: Keller
    c. Mystical Ways of Knowing: Blake and Yeats

IV. Conclusion

THIS essay selects three powerful ideas found in Swedenborg's theological works: the spiritual essence of reality, useful living, and the nature of knowing. It examines how those ideas influenced a number of creative people, including thinkers writing in prose and poetry; artists in paint, stone, and glass; architects; a lawyer; and a composer.[1]

---

1. The challenges of documenting influence in other cultures restrict the examples presented here to British and American figures.

This approach may mislead the reader on two counts. First, the examination of just a few themes out of the many to be found in Swedenborg's works may suggest that those few sum up Swedenborg's theology. Even a modest familiarity with his works will correct this misimpression. Second, limiting the examples to a few creative individuals may imply that all possible examples have been cited. The field of Swedenborgian influence, however, is one in which examples multiply like stalks of grain rippling on and on to the horizon rather than one in which the crop is readily counted and exhausted.

Even the word *influence* may be misleading, implying a passive subject who receives and transmits another's thought. The alternative term *impact* at least carries the notion of something struck and reactive, righting itself after its worldview has sustained a resounding shock. However, to those who study Swedenborg's influence or impact, whichever you will, it is clear that neither the metaphor of inflowing nor that of striking is adequate. Elizabeth Barrett Browning—herself deeply influenced by Swedenborg, as will be shown below—describes the effect of influence on young poets as one in which "being acted on and acting seem the same." As she puts it, "In that first onrush of life's chariot-wheels,/We know not if the forests move or we" (Browning [1856] 1995, 1:968–970).

No one could argue that William Blake, for instance, was a passive receiver of Swedenborg's thought. In the first onrush of Swedenborg's new ideas into his mind, he both absorbed and rejected, wrestling with the new ways of thinking he had encountered. When he had writhed long enough in his old skin, now too small for him, he sloughed it off. This was no passive process.

Typically, studies of Swedenborg's influence focus on specific thinkers or artists and trace their ideas back to him.[2] In this essay that procedure is reversed: it follows specific ideas forward to thinkers and artists who made creative use of them. This reversal of the usual approach in studies of influence allows a glimpse of the enormous web of Swedenborg's influence in Western culture. It suggests a method for further study.

---

2. Among previous studies that describe Swedenborg's influence are two volumes published to celebrate the tricentennial of his birth in 1988, one a collection of articles broadly surveying things Swedenborgian (Larsen and others 1988), the other a volume of lectures given at a symposium in Bryn Athyn, Pennsylvania, specifically addressing the topic of influence (Brock and others 1988). See also Hallengren 1998b and Silver 1983, who each treat a variety of individuals influenced by Swedenborg.

As already noted, the ideas studied here are: (1) the spiritual essence
of reality, (2) the importance of usefulness, and (3) the nature of knowing. They have been selected to represent three separate categories of
Swedenborg's thought: his basic premises, his practical instruction for
living, and his philosophical theory of knowledge, respectively. I present
the examples as they group logically under various aspects of the ideas I
explore, rather than tracing them chronologically.

I. Spiritual Reality

One reader of Swedenborg has described his works as "a system for encountering the unknown through the known" (Promey 1994, 50); another has called them "golden keys to unlock the massive gates between
the external and spiritual worlds" (Karcher 1994, 14). Indeed, one of
Swedenborg's main themes is the notion that the spiritual is what is most
real. The spiritual is not some shadowy phantom of material reality, or
some distant or future realm; it is in fact so much more real than materiality that according to Swedenborg the material reality we see actually
draws its shape and being from the spiritual.

The result of this inflow of the spiritual into the material is a constant
connection and mutual relationship between spiritual and earthly things:

> Now since absolutely everything in the world and Nature emerges and
> remains in existence (or endures) from something prior to itself, it fol-
> lows that it emerges and endures from a realm above Nature called the
> spiritual world. With this realm it must have a constant connection in
> order to endure, or remain in existence. The conclusion follows, then,
> that the purer or deeper elements within Nature and therefore within a
> person come from that realm, and that they are substances capable of
> receiving spiritual inflow.[3]

Swedenborg terms the connections between the material and the spiritual "correspondences." He saw these correspondences as material symbols or natural representations of spiritual realities. "Nothing exists in the

---

3. *Secrets of Heaven* 4524. (It is customary to refer to passages in Swedenborg's works by section
numbers rather than page numbers, as the former are uniform in all editions.) Except where
noted, the translations from *Secrets of Heaven* quoted in this essay are those of Lisa Hyatt Cooper.

natural world and its three kingdoms," he notes, "that does not represent something in the spiritual world, or that does not have something in the spiritual world to which it corresponds" (*Secrets of Heaven* 2992).

The concept of the greater reality of the spiritual world, and of its complete *interconnectedness,* or correspondence, with the material world, can be traced through numerous thinkers beginning in the early 1800s, though the scope of this essay permits only a brief look at a few of them.

a. Nature and Spirit: Worcester, Reed, Emerson, and Whitman

One thread of the web of influence begins with Thomas Worcester (1795–1878). Worcester was born in New Hampshire in an extended family that included ministers in several generations. He became curious about Swedenborg while a student at Harvard University, but in the early 1800s Swedenborg's works were hard to obtain. The Harvard library had a few volumes donated possibly as early as 1794 by the British minister and Swedenborgian William Hill (1762–1804). Yet when Worcester looked for them in 1815, he was unable to find the books in their assigned places on the shelves. After a determined search, he and the librarian at length discovered the Latin edition of the multivolume *Secrets of Heaven* in a storeroom full of disused books and artifacts. He was given permission to take the volumes to his own room, which soon became a study center for students reading and discussing Swedenborg's ideas (Shaw 1992, iii).

Worcester's college roommate was one Sampson Reed (1800–1880). Under Worcester's influence, Reed too took up the study of Swedenborg. Like Worcester, who went on to become one of the founding members of the Swedenborgian community in Boston, Reed became what was then termed "a receiver of the doctrines," and his Swedenborgianism soon found expression in his academic work. Presumably the reason that Reed did not specifically ascribe his ideas to Swedenborg or even mention him is that at the time Swedenborg's teachings were frowned upon by Congregationalist and Unitarian churches prominent in Boston. However, his 1820 dissertation about the Bible as the source of truth, based on Swedenborgian principles, so impressed the Harvard faculty that he was chosen to give a speech to the students when he received his divinity degree at the graduation exercises in 1821. This "Oration on Genius," again based on Swedenborg's ideas but presented without reference to their source, asserts the connection between the spiritual and natural worlds, and describes correspondences as "a language of nature": "There is a unison of spirit and nature. . . . Thoughts fall to the earth with power, and make a language out of nature" (Reed 1992, 15). He foretells an age in which humans will be able to speak in this language again, as had Adam and Eve, whose language was "but their garden. . . . They had nothing to communicate by words. . . . The sun of the spiritual world shone bright on their hearts, and their senses were open with delight to natural objects" (Reed 1992, 15). Science, he predicts, will likewise be "full of life, as nature is full of God" (Reed 1992, 16). He speaks in highly mysterious, oracular terms of a time when humans will reconnect with the spiritual world and again portray truth in art, poetry, and other human endeavors.

In the audience of graduating seniors was eighteen-year-old Ralph Waldo Emerson (1803–1882). He was so stirred by Reed's oration that he asked to copy it. When Reed published his further work on aesthetics in 1826, Emerson obtained that as well, to read and reread it many times in subsequent years (Shaw 1992, viii). In this work, titled "Observations on the Growth of the Mind," Reed defined poetry as "all those illustrations of truth by natural imagery, which spring from the fact that this world is the mirror of Him who made it" (Reed 1992, 31). He further observed that "when we study the works of God as we should, we cannot disregard that inherent beauty and harmony in which [poetry and music] originate" (Reed 1992, 31). Here, reclothed in the language of nineteenth-century Romanticism, is Swedenborg's principle of the truer and more beautiful spiritual world acting upon the lesser material world that mirrors and corresponds to it.

Emerson knew of the source of these recast ideas and developed a strong interest in Swedenborg. He purchased copies of Swedenborg's works as they were translated and printed in Boston, and for many years he subscribed to the *New Jerusalem Magazine,* a Swedenborgian periodical edited by Reed. Swedenborg's ability to connect the natural and the spiritual particularly intrigued Emerson. Swedenborg, Emerson declared in his "American Scholar" address of 1837, was "the most imaginative of men; yet writing with the precision of a mathematician, he endeavored to engraft a purely philosophical Ethics on the popular Christianity of his time. . . . He saw and showed the connection between nature and the affections of the soul. He pierced the emblematic or spiritual character of the visible, audible, tangible world" (Emerson 1929, 1:35). Furthermore, in his 1844 essay "The Poet," Emerson expressed his admiration for what he called Swedenborg's capacity to translate "nature into thought," adding, "I do not know the man in history for whom things stood so uniformly for words. Before him the metamorphosis continually plays.

Everything on which his eye rests obeys the impulses of moral nature"
(Emerson 1929, 1:249).

Again and again Swedenborg's ideas of spiritual reality and correspondence can be traced in Emerson; for example, again in "The Poet":

> Nature offers all her creatures to [the poet] as a picture-language. . . .
> Things admit of being used as symbols, because nature is a symbol, in
> the whole, and in every part. . . . The Universe is the externalisation of
> the soul. . . . The world is a temple, whose walls are covered with em-
> blems, pictures, and commandments of the Deity. . . . We are symbols,
> and inhabit symbols; workman, work, and tools, words and things,
> birth and death, all are emblems. . . . The poet, [who is] but an ulterior
> intellectual perception, gives them a power which makes their old use
> forgotten, and puts eyes, and a tongue, into every dumb and inanimate
> object. (Emerson 1929, 1:242–243, 244)

In his work Reed gave specific instructions to poets to aspire to a
high moral function, to use the language of correspondences, and to dis-
pense with any artificial impediments, such as rhyme and meter, that in-
terfered with the representation of the truth (Shaw 1992, viii). Emerson
echoed these strictures in "The Poet"; but it was not until the work of
Walt Whitman (1819–1892), who had in turn carefully studied Emerson's
essay, that modern American poetry fully cast off the older conventions
in its striving to represent spiritual truths.[4]

This is not to gloss over Emerson's reservations about Swedenborg.
For example, in his essay "Swedenborg, or the Mystic" in *Representative
Men* (1850) he complained about Swedenborg's religious orientation:
"The vice of Swedenborg's mind is its theologic determination. Nothing
with him has the liberality of universal wisdom, but we are always in a
church."[5] Although impatient with many aspects of Swedenborg's theology, Emerson still chose him as a representative mystic, one of six great
men who improved the world. He concludes his essay with this qualified
encomium:

> Swedenborg has rendered a double service to mankind, which is now
> only beginning to be known. . . . He observed and published the laws

---

4. Shaw 1992, ix. For more on Swedenborg's influence on Whitman, see Hallengren 1991; Hallengren
1992; Hallengren 1998b, 95–100; Hallengren 2004, 45–59.

5. Emerson 1929, 1:367. In essence, the specifically Christian nature of Swedenborg's revelation of-
fended Emerson's transcendentalist yearning for universal truths. For a discussion of Emerson's
objection, see Johnson 2003, 64–66.

of nature; and ascending by just degrees from events to their summits and causes, he was fired with piety at the harmonies he felt, and abandoned himself to his joy and worship. . . . If the glory was too bright for his eyes to bear, if he staggered under the trance of delight, the more excellent is the spectacle he saw, the realities of being which beam and blaze through him. (Emerson 1929, 1:370)

b. Seeing the Spiritual: Borges and Frost

Particularly significant in Emerson's final assessment of Swedenborg is his emphasis on Swedenborg as a seer, or "see-er"; that is, on Swedenborg's ability to see the spiritual within the material. The thread of this idea can be traced well into the twentieth century. Commenting on Emerson's essay, Argentine author Jorge Luis Borges (1899–1986) reemphasizes Swedenborg's encounter with spiritual reality and questions Emerson's description of Swedenborg as a "mystic":

> The word ["mystic"], while it is extremely accurate, runs the risk of suggesting a man apart, a man who instinctively removes himself from the circumstances and urgencies we call, though I will never know why, reality. No one is further from that image than Emanuel Swedenborg, who journeyed, lucid and laborious, through this and all other worlds. No one accepted life more fully, no one investigated it with a passion so great, with the same intellectual love, or with such impatience to learn about it. (Borges 1988, 349)

Like Emerson, Borges admired Swedenborg's ability to see what the materially minded could not. He gave his essay on Swedenborg the title "Testimony to the Invisible," and concludes it with this sonnet:

> Taller than all others, walked
> that man, solitary among men;
> barely calling the angels
> by their secret names, he'd see
> what earthly eyes do not:
> the passionate geometry, the crystalline
> edifice of God and the sordid
> whirlwind of infernal delights.
> He knew that Heaven and Hell are in
> your soul, and so too their myths:
> he knew, like the Greeks, that
> time's days are Eternity's mirrors.

In arid Latin he went on recording
ultimate things without whys or wherefores.[6]

The influence of the idea of correspondence and the symbols of the natural world can also be tracked through the work of the American poet Robert Frost (1874–1963). Like Emerson, Frost distanced himself from any identification as a Swedenborgian. Asking himself the question "What's my philosophy?" he gives this somewhat evasive answer:

> That's hard to say. I was brought up a Swedenborgian. I am not a Swedenborgian now. But there's a good deal of it that's left with me. I am a mystic. I believe in symbols. I believe in change and in changing symbols. (Frost 1966a, 49)

An account by Frost's daughter, Lesley Frost (1899–1983), amplifies his statement:

> As a boy, Robert was steeped in the religion of a mother to whom he was strongly attached: a gallant, intelligent woman of Scotch descent with poetic leanings of her own. Isabel (Belle) Moodie Frost was a devout Swedenborgian, as her church in San Francisco can testify, and she was with her son during his adolescence and youth. . . . Thus the direct influence of Belle Moodie Frost on Robert should not be underestimated. . . . He had been read aloud to over those years from the books *she* chose . . . [including] the teachings of Swedenborg.[7]

The links in Frost's poetry to Swedenborg's concept of spiritual reality are subtle.[8] Here analysis plunges into debatable territory, because, as Emerson pointed out, the poet's business since time immemorial has been to give a new use to symbols and put "a tongue into every dumb and inanimate object." To say that Frost drew this understanding from Swedenborg is unprovable. But time and again the epiphany at the conclusion of Frost's early poems derives from an experience in which a natural object becomes a symbol for a spiritual quality.

---

6. Translation from the Spanish by Sylvia Shaw. The original can be found in Borges 1969, 153.

7. Frost 1984, xi–xii. Frost himself identified the ultimate origin of the Swedenborgian influence on him as Emerson's essay in *Representative Men,* because it was instrumental in his mother's adoption of Swedenborgianism (Frost 1966c, 112, quoted in Hall 1994, 11).

8. For a study of Frost in this light see Hall 1994. King 1999a, 48–58, offers a rich and balanced analysis of various aspects of Frost in the context of Swedenborgian thought.

For example, "The Tuft of Flowers" (Frost 1966b, 22–23) describes the poet at the task of turning new-mown hay in a field. The worker who cut the hay has already left, and the poet feels his loneliness, thinking that truly all humans are alone "whether they work together or apart" (line 10). However, a butterfly—an age-old symbol of the soul—draws his attention to a tuft of flowers spared by the mower. In his shared appreciation of the beauty of the flowers, the poet feels the mower possesses "a spirit kindred" to his own (line 33). At the spiritual level he can now converse with the other, even though he is absent, and can affirm the essential togetherness of humankind in spirit:

> And dreaming, as it were, [I] held brotherly speech
> With one whose thought I had not hoped to reach.

> "Men work together," I told him from the heart,
> "Whether they work together or apart."
>   (lines 37–40)

In Frost's treatment the tuft of flowers becomes a rich metaphor. In one sense, it is a clutch of poems spared in the great reaping of time, whose beauty is appreciated by later generations, and which affirms our common bond in spirit with those who have gone before. In another reading, the flowers are spiritual beauty in the abstract; in this case, the reaper may be God, to whom humans are seen to be still connected even when they "work apart" from him. Frost uses a symbol drawn from nature to demonstrate a bond with others at the spiritual level. The spiritual connection that the flowers symbolize is more real than the material appearance of human solitariness.

From this and the many other examples that could be adduced, as well as from what is known about Frost's upbringing, it seems likely that his encounters with Swedenborgian thought helped form his poetic vision.

c. Spiritual Architecture: Worcester, Brown, and Porter

From the fields of New England I turn to the West Coast and the architecture of Joseph Worcester (1836–1913), a Bostonian, son of Thomas Worcester, and Swedenborgian minister transplanted to San Francisco. Critic Kevin Starr links the architectural style Worcester initiated with the belief that spirit informs matter: "As a Swedenborgian and disciple of Ruskin,[9] Worcester believed that matter revealed spirit and vice versa;

---

9. John Ruskin (1819–1900), British writer and art critic.

hence each detail of one's living environment and lifestyle should be orchestrated into an harmonious whole, which included diet, furniture, and gardens" (Starr 1987, 96). Worcester's application of the principle of spiritual reality had significant architectural consequences: Starr sees the home that Worcester built for himself on a hilltop in the East Bay as "the first text, the founding archetype of the Bay Region shingle style flourishing at the turn of the century" (Starr 1987, 95).

Arthur Page Brown (1859–1896) was the architect for the Swedenborgian church built during Joseph Worcester's pastorate in San Francisco. This church draws on various stylistic models—an Italian hillside church that had been sketched in Italy by parishioner Bruce Porter (1865–1953), the Mission Revival style commemorating California's Franciscan heritage, and the walled gardens of Japan—and melds them with stained-glass windows designed by Porter and murals of the California seasons painted by William Keith (who will be discussed below). Starr comments that the church suggests

> interpenetrations of spirit and nature, the seen and the unseen. . . . In lieu of pews and conventional church appointments, there was an atmosphere of arts and crafts domesticity, [including] an off-center fireplace in the rear of the church and eighty handmade maple chairs, designed by Brown himself, with seats woven from tule reeds from the Sacramento Delta. Madrone tree trunks . . . arch overhead in support of the ceiling, an effect at once Gothic and Californian.[10]

d. The Human as Representative of the Spiritual: Flaxman and Powers

Artists in other fields who were influenced by Swedenborg tried to represent the reality of the spiritual in depictions of the human form. One of them was John Flaxman (1755–1826), a member of the British Royal Academy and its first professor of sculpture.[11] As a reader of Swedenborg, he applied the notion of spirituality to funerary art using symbolism that was then new but is now taken for granted.

---

10. Starr 1987, 97. The use of tree trunks to support the ceiling was very likely derived from a description of such construction in a temple in Swedenborg's *Secrets of Heaven* 10514, with parallels in *Other Planets* 151 and *Spiritual Experiences* (= Swedenborg 1998–2002) §2:1681.

11. Though best known as a sculptor, Flaxman also drew a series of sketches inspired by the accounts in *Secrets of Heaven* of Swedenborg's experiences in the spiritual world. One such sketch, for example, shows angels sitting by the head of a man who has not yet awakened from death, illustrating *Secrets of Heaven* 172–173. See Gyllenhaal 1996, 1–71.

This new trend in funerary depiction began in 1784, when Flaxman was commissioned to sculpt a memorial for a young woman who was buried at sea after dying in childbirth on her way home from India (see figure 1). He represented her holding up her child and rising from the waves toward the welcome of heavenly spirits. One critic comments:

> This, I think, is the first tomb based on the Swedenborgian conception of the human soul. . . . Not only does [Flaxman] define the fate of the soul, but he also says what the attributes of the soul are, in other words, what aspects of the living person belong to the soul rather than the body. He is the first to tell us, for instance, that all capacity for sense experience belongs to the soul rather than the body and therefore goes along with the soul when the body and soul separate at the moment of death.[12]

The work of the American sculptor Hiram Powers (1805–1873) was also deeply influenced by his reading of Swedenborg. After receiving training in sculpture from Frederick Eckstein (1775?–1852) in Cincinnati in the 1820s, Powers developed his reputation in Washington, D.C., by creating neoclassical sculptures of historic figures such as George Washington. In 1837 he went to Italy, then a mecca for sculptors; he worked in Florence, near Seravezza, the source of the purest Italian marble, and eventually became one of the most well-known American artists of his day (Tucker 1967, 32).

Powers was known for the sensitivity of his portraits in stone. An example is his bust of Thomas Worcester, whose early career has already been mentioned; he visited Powers in Florence in 1850. Another clergyman who sat for Powers, the Unitarian Henry W. Bellows (1814–1882), recorded the conversations he had with Powers during his sittings, in which he attempted to learn how Powers was able to create such close likenesses. During one sitting Bellows started a conversation on the ability of the human soul to shape the body. Powers commented:

> People think I am needlessly anxious and careful about the small and fine lines in human faces. It is because I know how much each line represents, and what great distinctions dwell in the smallest hiding-places. Let me rub out, for a moment, this little depression in this lip. Do you

---

12. Janson 1988, 118–119. In response to Janson, it could be argued that the assumption that angels have a bodily existence is not uncommon; see 1 Corinthians 15, particularly verse 44: "There is a natural body, and there is a spiritual body." Swedenborg himself notes: "When people see paintings or statues of angels [having a body], they believe that this is what they look like" (*Divine Providence* 274:7; translation by George F. Dole).

see how it robs the expression of the mouth? Now I put it in again, and you see it all back. (Bellows 1869, 2:55)

Implicit in Powers's remark is the assumption that the material is a representation of the spiritual ("I know *how much* each line represents"). The expression of the mouth is thus an expression of the soul. As a reader of Swedenborg, Powers was clearly aware of the identification Swedenborg makes between the inner person and the face, through which the soul shines.[13]

Powers went further than merely representing the soul in its material vessel. He sought to depict it without its veil of materiality, a goal that he described in a letter to Elizabeth Barrett Browning (concerning whom see below) as a "legitimate and spiritual aim of art."[14] For Powers, as for Swedenborg, the soul was not to be represented by a gauzy semblance of a human being, but by a form with full human characteristics and features. Therefore, in a program that might have seemed paradoxical to the non-Swedenborgian, he represented souls by depicting their *spiritual* bodies.

This attempt led him to sculpt idealized nude female figures inspired by spiritual concepts. In these works by Powers one can see the same Swedenborgian influence that led Emerson to declare, "We are symbols." Art historian Martha Gyllenhaal comments: "From his regular reading of Swedenborg's writings, [Powers] was convinced that the human body is in the image of heaven and that heaven is in the image of God, the Divine Human. His knowledge of these correspondences also gave him a profound respect for the female form."[15]

Powers's attempt to represent spiritual reality through the human form was immediately obvious to the contemporary art critic G. H. Calvert (1803–1889). Concerning the most famous of Powers's works, *The Greek Slave,* he writes:

> The two great sources of human interest, the human body, and shining through it, the human soul, are here. The artist has had the creative

---

13. See *Secrets of Heaven* 358, among many other instances.

14. From an unpublished letter by Powers, dated August 7, 1853; quoted in Reynolds 1977b, 394.

15. Gyllenhaal and others 1988, 11. Another critic has a slightly different judgment of the depth of Powers's understanding of Swedenborg: "In his ideal statues . . . , Powers fused Swedenborg's notion of the 'material covering' and the 'spiritual body' with his own, probably imperfect, understanding of those terms and his erotic conception of the earthly body (Swedenborg's 'material covering') in a unique combination of the erotic and the spiritual, the real and the ideal, which he called the 'unveiled soul'" (Reynolds 1977b, 399–400). For more on Powers, see Crane 1972 and Wunder 1991.

Figure 1. *Tomb of Sarah Morley.* Marble relief by John Flaxman, 1784. Courtesy of The Conway Library, Courtauld Institute of Art, London.

vigor to reproduce, in its indescribable symmetry, its matchless grace, its infinite beauty, that chief marvel of the earth, the human body, making transparent through these attributes, deep inward powers and emotion; and it is because he has had this inspired mastery, that, standing before his work, the beholder is not only spellbound by beauty, but awed by a solemn, ineffable feeling, and mysteriously drawn closer into the chastening presence of God.[16]

In its day this representation of a soul by means of characteristics typically considered material created enormous tension in viewers. *The Greek Slave* was a full portrait in white marble of a Greek woman being sold by her Turkish captors in a public market. White viewers of the statue in the antebellum United States suddenly found themselves in unexpected sympathy with a slave, a sympathy that challenged their assumptions about the spiritual nature—the essential human nature—of black slaves. For example, in one review written in 1851, an anonymous critic imagines the statue scornfully addressing a slave owner who is viewing the statue in St. Louis:

> I was fashioned by a hand whose every motion was the offspring of love for man in all his relations, with a sublime conception of the beautiful and the true, and it is *therefore* that he has sent me around the world to preach by this loveliness and nakedness, and by this cruel chain, joy to the forsaken, comfort to the destitute, and liberty to the captive. . . . Whatever claims of justice I may secure for me, and those like me, are due to those equally oppressed in your very midst. Think you that it was cruel to rob me of liberty, purity, and happiness? Though my skin were black as night, my soul would have the same aspirations, and need the same sympathies, my intellect would have the same laws and need the same development. Cease your sympathy for a slave in Constantinople, and go show kindness and justice to those over whom you have power.[17]

Thus in Powers's art the theological principle of the reality of the spiritual achieves not only artistic ends, but moves toward political and social reform as well.

---

16. Calvert 1847, 159–160. One of the many versions of the statue can be found in the Corcoran Gallery, Washington, D.C.

17. "Powers's Greek Slave in St. Louis" 1851, 10. Compare the poem by Elizabeth Barrett Browning mentioned in note 31 below.

e. Themes of Spiritual Growth: Pyle, Inness, Keith, Tiffany,
and Yardumian

Painters too have been fascinated by the Swedenborgian notion that the
things of this world are emblems for, or correspondences of, things in a
"more real" spiritual world. One well-known painter drawn to Swedenborg
for this reason was illustrator Howard Pyle (1853–1911). Pyle worked during
the golden age of American illustration, at a time when books and magazines were a primary source of home entertainment. His students included
Jessie Willcox Smith (1863–1935) and N. C. Wyeth (1882–1945), and a thread
of Swedenborgian influence can be traced through all three of these artists.

Pyle felt compelled to portray the reality of the spiritual world as a result of the death of his six-year-old son. In the aftermath of that loss Pyle
wrote and illustrated *The Garden behind the Moon: A Real Story of the Moon
Angel* (1903), a story that echoes Swedenborg's accounts of children in
heaven (see figure 2).[18] The young hero leaves his familiar home to journey
to a land in the sky where he meets the Man-in-the-Moon, an all-wise figure who answers his questions in a Swedenborgian vein: "Everything that
has an inside must have an outside as well, for there can be no inside unless
there is an outside. And this is true, little child: the more sad the outside,
the more beautiful almost always is the inside."[19] In Swedenborg's theology,
the interior is the spiritual part of humankind, connected with spiritual reality, and the exterior is the material part, connected with the material
world. Pyle hints that the process of spiritual regeneration, or achieving inner beauty, may well involve pain and sadness, or what Swedenborg termed
vastatio, a "devastating," "shattering," or "purging" experience.

The Swedenborgian concept of spiritual growth was also an implicit
concern of artists George Inness (1825–1894) and William Keith
(1838–1911); in their painting they tried to compel the viewer to grow in
knowledge of spiritual reality. As Richard Silver says of their painting,
"The viewer had to give the work meaning, and that meaning changed as
the viewer's own understanding and knowledge changed. . . . The great
inner truth that the artists sought to portray was the reality of the soul of
man" (Silver 1983, 270–271).

Inness learned of Swedenborg from fellow artist William Page
(1811–1885) when the two worked together in Eagleswood, New Jersey,

---

18. See, for example, *Heaven and Hell* 329–345.

19. Pyle [1903] 2002, 40. On the necessity that each "outside" must have an "inside," see, for example, *True Christianity* 785.

Figure 2. Headpiece illustration from the foreword to *The Garden behind the Moon: A Real Story of the Moon Angel* by Howard Pyle, 1903. Courtesy of the Delaware Art Museum, Wilmington, Delaware.

between 1863 and 1867.[20] He became so deeply involved in Swedenborgian thought that a group of his friends pledged ten thousand dollars for his use during 1867 "for the production of any sort of pictures to illustrate Swedenborgian theories."[21] The result was a series of three paintings entitled *The Triumph of the Cross,* the first (and only extant) of which is *The Valley of the Shadow of Death.*[22] Inness described its intention thus:

> I have endeavored to convey to the mind of the beholder an impression of the state into which the soul comes when it begins to advance toward a spiritual life, or toward any more perfected state in its journey, until it arrives to its sabbath or rest. Here the pilgrim is leaving the natural light whose warm rays still faintly illumine the foreground of the scene. Before him all is uncertainty. His light hereafter must be that of faith alone. This I have represented by the cross, giving it the place of the moon, which is the natural emblem of faith, reflecting light upon the sun its source, assuring us, that although the origin of life [the sun, which corresponds to the divine] is no longer visible, it still exists: but here, clouds may at any moment obscure even the light of faith, and the soul, left in ignorance of what may be its ultimate condition, can only lift its eyes in despair to Him who alone can save, and lead it out of disorder and confusion.[23]

Inness communicated his interest in Swedenborg to his student Louis Comfort Tiffany (1848–1933), whose name has now become nearly a byword for artwork in glass. Under his influence, Tiffany created a series of stained-glass memorial windows featuring Swedenborgian ideas. For one window, memorializing financier Russell Sage (1816–1906), he chose a group of trees as an emblem.[24] He was very likely aware that Swedenborg links the planting and growth of trees with the spiritual

---

20. Page, in turn, had learned of Swedenborg when he visited Powers in Italy. See Cikovsky 1977, 43, 203. For more on Page, see Taylor 1957.

21. Quoted in Promey 1994, 52, from Pattison 1913, no page given.

22. This painting is in the collection of the Francis Lehman Loeb Art Center, Vassar College, Poughkeepsie, New York.

23. As quoted in Promey 1994, 52–53, who cites an article in the *New York Evening Post* of May 11, 1867, which in turn cites, without further information, a circular that accompanied the exhibition of the paintings at Snedecor's Gallery on Broadway in New York. It is not clear whose parenthetical addition is indicated by the square brackets.

24. The window is in the First Presbyterian Church, Russell Sage Memorial Chapel, Far Rockaway, New York.

regeneration of the individual (*Secrets of Heaven* 8326). One critic theo-
rizes that the depiction of trees

> may therefore have been particularly appropriate for Russell Sage, whose
> reputation as a shrewd money-lender was not always flattering. . . . By
> explaining Russell Sage's character as a tree that grew and increased in
> spiritual goodness during its lifetime, the window acted as a kind of
> apologia for [Sage], and as an intercession, both with God and hu-
> mankind, on his behalf. (De Rosa 1995, 188)

Concern about spiritual regeneration is also powerfully present in the
work of composer Richard Yardumian (1917–1985).[25] Introduced to Swedenborgian thought in his adulthood, thereafter Yardumian made his
life's work a consistent attempt to portray what Swedenborg saw as the
true reality, the spiritual world. Drawing upon ancient chants and modes
as well as his own Middle Eastern heritage, Yardumian developed a
unique polymodal harmony, expressed in works for chorus, orchestra, and
solo instruments. In an explanation of the evolution of his style, he says:

> Of greatest importance, and from very early on, was an inspiration
> to formalize a kind of polyphony invoked by a passage from Emanuel
> Swedenborg's [*True Christianity* 625]: "I looked up and lo the whole
> heaven above me was resplendent with light, and from the east to the
> west I heard a long continued glorification by the angels of the eastern
> and western heavens[, and . . .] from the northern and southern heav-
> ens there was heard a gentle murmur."
> Striving to clothe such a beautiful image in valid musical form was
> and is a strong motivation for mastering the polyphonic art.[26]

The occasional notes Yardumian wrote to himself in the margins of
his works bear witness to the importance of the drive toward spiritual regeneration in his composition. One such note declares: "Only that music
has a future which has been inspired by a noble love to grow into the wisdom of the spiritual."[27]

II. Useful Living

The Swedenborgian principle of usefulness is highly developed; it operates
in Swedenborg's theology at every level of the chain of being that stretches

---

25. For a list of Yardumian's music and a discography to 1988, see Worden 1988, 77.

26. Yardumian n.d., quoted in Worden 1988, 76.

27. Yardumian 1986, as quoted in Worden 1988, 74.

from the lowliest stone to God himself. According to Swedenborg, everything has its useful function in the ordered system of the universe, from
minerals to plants to animals to human beings. Community itself is built
up of each individual's useful actions for others; usefulness is actually the
linkage that holds society together:

> People do not have wisdom or life for the sake of themselves alone, but
> for others as well. Society exists as a result; otherwise there would be no
> society. To live for others is to be of service to them. Acts of service are
> the glue that binds society together.[28]

Swedenborg certainly did not invent usefulness as a value; but tracing
usefulness as a Swedenborgian principle operative in a given individual's
life is in many respects less problematic than tracking the influence of
other Swedenborgian concepts. One need only document that the principle has been absorbed into the individual's belief system; its effect on
the individual's actions is unmistakable, even dramatic.

a. Forging Links for Community: Mussey, Child, and Chapman

Ellen Spencer Mussey (1850–1936) is the first case in point. Her contact
with Swedenborg's theology is clearly documented: she was a member
of a Swedenborgian church in Washington, D.C. The field of her usefulness was the law, a profession that in her lifetime was hostile to
women. Though law schools would not admit her for that reason, in
1876 she began unofficially practicing law with her husband, attorney
Reuben Delavan Mussey (1833–1892). After his death she passed the bar
examination, relying on self-study and her extensive experience, and began her own legal practice. She co-founded a law school for women, the
Washington College of Law, and became dean—the first woman in the
world to fill this role in a school of law. Her subsequent career is a long
train of hard work and successful efforts in social reform.

In a speech at the World's Parliament of Religions in 1893, Mussey
urged women to pursue the principle of usefulness to society despite possible opposition from men:

> Dear sisters, let us fit ourselves and our daughters for a life of active
> use. Let us not be led astray by personal ambition, or love of ease. Let
> us remember that every soul is accountable to God, and that we must

---

28. *True Christianity* 746:1; translation by Jonathan S. Rose.

form our [own] opinions, even though they differ from those we love
best. (Scammon and others 1895, 190–191)

A similar pattern of an encounter with Swedenborgian thought leading to a career in reform can be seen in the life of Lydia Maria Child
(1802–1880). She began reading Swedenborg at age eighteen, when she
was a teacher in Gardiner, Maine. She then moved to the Boston area
and became an active member of the Swedenborgian Church in Boston
in the 1820s. A meeting with abolitionist William Lloyd Garrison
(1805–1879) in 1831 marked the beginning of her devotion to the abolitionist cause.[29] Her first major attack on slavery was *An Appeal in Favor
of That Class of Americans Called Africans* (1833), which considerably
broadened the base of the abolitionist movement. She went on to edit an
abolitionist magazine and make her home a station on the Underground
Railroad. Her agitation for freedom for African Americans through authorship and letter writing was unrelenting. She also was an outspoken
advocate of women's rights, and her views on other social issues were far
ahead of her time.[30]

A third example is that of John Chapman (1774–1845), an orchardist
and reader of Swedenborg, better known as Johnny Appleseed. Chapman
is legendary for planting the apple trees prized by the first settlers moving
into Ohio and Indiana in the early 1800s. It is less well known that he
was an unofficial missionary of Swedenborg, distributing Swedenborgian
tracts throughout his travels. Though disentangling legend from fact can
be difficult in this case, Chapman's story does suggest the strong influence of the principle of usefulness. As Lydia Maria Child wrote in a children's poem on the topic:

> Poor Johnny was bended well-nigh double
> With tears of toil, and care, and trouble;
> But his large old heart still felt the need
> Of doing for others some kindly deed. . . .
>   (Child 2000, 35)

---

29. Her insistence on the equal rights of African Americans was in all likelihood also inspired by
passages in Swedenborg's theological works in which he describes Africans as excelling in spiritual
qualities. See page 202 note 18 above.

30. Child could also serve as an example of the idea of spiritual reality. In a reference to the conse-
quences of her study of Swedenborg, she wrote to a friend in a letter on December 8, 1842: "Now
I have lost the power of looking merely on the surface. Everything seems to me to come from the
Infinite, to be filled with the Infinite, to be tending toward the Infinite" (Child 1843).

b. The Value of Appointed Work: Barrett Browning, Galli-Curci, and Jewett

Usefulness, in Swedenborg's view, does not necessarily entail crusading for social reform. Even everyday work fulfills the principle of usefulness:

> While we are living in the world, the uses we can serve are to do our job well, each of us in our own position; to help our country, our communities, and our neighbor in the process; to deal honestly with acquaintances, and to perform services for others wisely, taking into account their individual character. These uses are the main ways we have of exercising neighborly love and also of worshiping the Lord. (*Secrets of Heaven* 7038)

Elizabeth Barrett Browning (1806–1861) was both a crusader and an upholder of the value of doing one's appointed work. According to Barrett Browning scholar Linda M. Lewis,

> Once she has positioned herself as spokesperson for God, or rather in fact as the image is evolving, Barrett Browning uses her pedestal to speak out on social issues (in "philanthropic poetry" as reviewers of her day were inclined to call it). Among her issues are child labor, prostitution, illegitimacy, slavery, injustice, poverty, and oppression. . . . She often formulates her views on both national and international politics by means of her faith. . . . Barrett Browning unabashedly employs her reputation for wisdom on behalf of society's weakest victims. . . . Thus the poet becomes Reformer.[31]

That was her crusader side; the other is attested in her poem *Aurora Leigh* (1856), which examines the meaning of useful work at length, including a confirmation of the value of simply performing one's everyday tasks:

> Be sure, no earnest work
> Of any honest creature, howbeit weak,
> Imperfect, ill-adapted, fails so much,
> It is not gathered as a grain of sand
> To enlarge the sum of human action used
> For carrying out God's end. No creature works

---

31. Lewis 1998, 173, 186. It is worth noting, as a further indication of the weblike nature of Swedenborgian connections in the 1800s, that Barrett Browning met Hiram Powers in Italy and wrote a poem on his statue *The Greek Slave* predicting that "Art's fiery finger" would break "the serfdom of this world" (Browning [1856] 1995, 375).

So ill, observe, that therefore he's cashiered.
The honest, earnest man must stand and work.
The woman also,—otherwise she drops
At once below the dignity of man,
Accepting serfdom. Free men freely work:

· · · · · · · · · · ·

   Let us be content, in work,
To do the thing we can, and not presume
To fret because it's little. . . .[32]

The same impulse to live up to the principle of usefulness is evident in the life of Amelita Galli-Curci (1889–1963), a twentieth-century coloratura soprano. Her early years in her native Italy were spent in luxury until her father lost his fortune; she was then only sixteen. As she later described it, "I then said, 'Here is my opportunity to help.' And from sixteen to twenty I carried the family with my music and teaching" (Barron 1926). She applied the same principle to her singing:

> I am not exhausted at all by my singing. Swedenborg shows the reason, and how life comes in as you pour it forth usefully to others. You don't have to try or worry or fret. You know it is not you but that it is just being done through you. (Barron 1926)

The American writer Sarah Orne Jewett (1849–1909) provides an interesting twist on the motif of usefulness. Jewett was for a time beset with guilt in the belief that writing was a selfish pursuit. Under the influence of the Swedenborgian concept of usefulness she overcame this obstacle, as Sylvia Shaw relates:

> The Swedenborgian concept that any vocation, high or lowly, is worthy if one strives to do it well and sincerely, gave Jewett a sense of high

---

32. Browning [1856] 1995, 8:705–715, 732–734. In a letter to her sister Arabella Barrett (1813–1868), dated December 10–18, 1856, just after the publication of *Aurora Leigh*, Barrett Browning wrote, "That there *is* an amount of spiritual truth in the book to which the public is unaccustomed, I know very well—only, I was helped to it—did not originate it—& was tempted much (by a natural feeling of honesty) to say so in the poem, & was withheld by nothing except a conviction that the naming of the name Swedenborg, that great Seer into the two worlds, would have utterly destroyed any hope of general acceptance & consequent utility. Instead of Mrs. Browning's 'gospel,' it wd. have been Mrs. Browning's rhodomantade! 'What! that imposter, Swedenborg! that madman, Swedenborg!' But that imposter & madman, such as he is, holds sublime truths in his right hand, & most humbly I have used them as I could. My desire is, that the weakness in *me,* may not hinder the influence" (quoted in Browning [1856] 1992, 339). For more on Swedenborg's influence on Elizabeth Barrett Browning, see Lines 2004, 23–43.

moral purpose in her writing, the ardent hope that she could fulfill her usefulness on earth through her honest efforts at writing. She could now see her love for writing as a gift that might help other people. Jewett also saw herself as a mentor for struggling women writers and took pleasure in helping and encouraging them. (Shaw 1998, 2)

III. Ways of Knowing

Swedenborg's epistemology is not only complex but quite distinctive. The facets I would like to examine here are knowing as an act necessarily bound up with love, knowing as a state originating in the inner self, and mystical knowing that sees what lies within material reality.

a. Knowing as Loving Thought: Andrews

Swedenborg depicts knowing as an individual enterprise derived from each person's experience, always based on a combination of love (emotion, pleasure) with wisdom (truth, knowledge). Thus from a Swedenborgian perspective knowing involves more than the rational accumulation of facts—it includes an emotional component and depends on the values associated with the subject:

> Rationality is born not of secular and religious knowledge, as people think it is, but of an emotion: the desire for knowledge. This can be seen simply from the fact that no one can possibly become rational without feeling some kind of pleasure in knowledge, or some desire for it. (*Secrets of Heaven* 1895:2)

The affective component of knowledge in Swedenborg's theology is described by the artist Joseph Andrews (1806–1873), who worked as an engraver of pictures in the 1800s. (His contact with Swedenborg was a result of his marriage with Tomazine Minot [?–1835], a daughter of one of the founders of the Swedenborgian church in Boston.) In order to appreciate the beauties of nature, Andrews says, we must approach them with "loving hearts and patient eyes." The result then

> is that [nature's] capacity to delight us excites our wonder. As we pursue the study, hidden charms open to us at each step, our pleasure is enhanced, our minds grow in the sense of its loveliness. . . . If we advance, the imagination comes to our aid, and leads us to higher and

more exquisite sources of pleasure. Untrammeled by space we can course in freedom the entire region of mind to seek and converse with the soul of nature. (Andrews 1868, 510–512)

b. Knowing as an Inner Process: Keller

One of the most remarkable examples of Swedenborg's influence can be seen in the life of Helen Keller (1880–1968), the twentieth-century author and social advocate for the handicapped (see figure 3). In Keller's case the example is particularly striking because it is one in which Swedenborg's writings seem to corroborate and clarify the experience of the reader just as much as they instill new ideas. Here I would like to examine only Swedenborg's corroborative effect on Keller's way of knowing.

Left blind and deaf by an illness in her childhood, in her early years Keller was virtually without knowledge:

> For nearly six years I had no concepts whatever of nature or mind or death or God. . . . I was like an unconscious clod of earth. There was nothing in me except the instinct to eat and drink and sleep. My days were a blank without past, present, or future, without hope or anticipation, without interest or joy. (Keller 2000, 5)

Keller's lifelong struggle to find knowledge and to assimilate it into her inner world is epic in proportions.[33] The particular story of how she initially learned to connect physical objects with words has been told many times on the printed page, and on stage and screen. As her teacher, Anne Sullivan (1866–1936), held Keller's hand under a gushing pump, she repeatedly spelled the word *water* into Keller's palm with her own fingers. Keller later wrote:

> Then suddenly, I knew not how or where or when, my brain felt the impact of another mind, and I awoke to language, to knowledge, to love, to the usual concepts of nature, good, and evil. I was actually lifted from nothingness to human life. (Keller 2000, 6)

At the age of sixteen, Keller met John Hitz (1828–1908), consul general for Switzerland and later superintendent of the Volta Bureau, an

---

33. For biographies of Keller see Herrmann 1998 and Lash 1980.

Figure 3. Helen Keller, renowned advocate for the deaf and blind. The Braille lettering is repeated in Keller's hand: "God is light . . . Helen Keller." Courtesy of the American Foundation for the Blind, Helen Keller Archives.

agency for the deaf in Washington, D.C. In her autobiography Keller recounts her introduction to Swedenborg through Hitz:

> In our many conversations, Mr. Hitz came to realize fully my hunger
> for literature on subjects that especially interested me. . . . He put into
> my hands a copy of Emanuel Swedenborg's *Heaven and Hell* in raised
> letters. He said he knew I would not understand much of it at first; but
> it was fine exercise for my mind, and it would satisfy me with a likeness
> of a God as lovable as the one in my heart. . . . (Keller 2000, 16–17)

Keller also describes how in the preface to the book Hitz had given
her, she came across the story of a blind reader of Swedenborg "whose
darkness was illumined with beautiful truths . . . that imparted a light to
her mind that more than compensated for her loss of earthly light"
(Keller 2000, 17). Her own encounter with Swedenborg essentially repli-
cated this experience.

Though Keller's autobiographical material details at length the influence of Swedenborg on her life, perhaps its most powerful effect can be
seen in a passage in which she explains how difficult it is for her not to
lapse into an isolated inner life, succumbing to what she calls the "mystic sense":

> My life is so complicated by a triple handicap of blindness, deafness, and
> imperfect speech that I cannot do the simplest thing without thought
> and effort to rationalize my experiences. If I employed this mystic sense
> constantly without trying to understand the outside world, my progress
> would be checked, and everything would fall about me in chaos. It is
> easy for me to mix up dreams and reality, the spiritual and the physical
> that I have not properly visualized; without discernment I could not
> keep them apart. So even if I commit errors in forming concepts of
> color, sound, light, and intangible phenomena, I must always try to pre-
> serve equilibrium between my outer and inner life. (Keller 2000, 130)

She then immediately adds that she has been "especially helped" by a
particular passage from Swedenborg, which she quotes:

> It appears as if the things which are in the world flow in through the
> sense toward the interiors, but this is a fallacy of sense. The influx is of
> interiors into exteriors, and by means of this influx man has percep-
> tion. . . . It is the interior man that sees and perceives what goes on out-
> side of him, and from this interior source the sense-experience has its
> life; for from no other than this subjective source is there any faculty of

feeling or sensation. But the fallacy that the sense comes from the outside is of such a nature and so common that the natural mind cannot rid itself of it, nor even the rational mind, until it can think abstractly apart from the senses.[34]

Keller seems to be saying that her progress from an "unconscious" life to one of conscious wisdom was made possible because she learned how to deliberately apply independent rational thought to the sensory data spilling chaotically into the three senses that remained to her. Swedenborg provided the explanation of why this process was necessary, and why it worked: in acquiring her way of knowing, Keller found the inner person who could perceive what was going on outside her.

c. Mystical Ways of Knowing: Blake and Yeats

For my final examples, I pick up the theme of mystical ways of knowing introduced by Keller and turn back to poet and artist William Blake (1757–1827), who was profoundly influenced by Swedenborg (see figure 4). Blake scholar Kathleen Raine (1908–2003) in particular sees the impact as definitive for Blake. "Wonderful as are Blake's poems, his visionary paintings, his aphorisms," she claims, "it is, in essence, the doctrines of Swedenborg that Blake's works embody and to which they lend poetry and eloquence" (Raine 1988, 79).

Raine describes Blake's fascination with Swedenborg's concept of the New Jerusalem or New Church, an era that Swedenborg reported as beginning in 1757, the year of Blake's birth. It was to bring in with it a return to mystical ways of knowing that had been lost in former times. In the context of her analysis of Blake, Raine goes so far as to assert that "it seems that such a change in the understanding of the nature of spiritual events did begin to manifest itself at that time, which has continued to grow like a plant from a small seed. Swedenborg's seed fell on fertile ground in the spirit of William Blake" (Raine 1988, 81).

In his poem *Jerusalem* (1804), Blake prayed to be able to open the eyes of the human race to this new way of knowing:

Trembling I sit day and night, my friends are astonish'd at me.
Yet they forgive my wanderings, I rest not from my great task!
To open the Eternal Worlds, to open the immortal Eyes

---

34. *Secrets of Heaven* 5119. The version quoted here is from Keller 2000, 130; she does not indicate the translator. It differs slightly from the standard version current in her time.

Figure 4. *Jacob's Ladder,* watercolor by William Blake, 1805. Copyright The Trustees of the British Museum. The biblical patriarch Jacob sleeps at the foot of a stairway to heaven as recounted in Genesis 28:11–22. Blake's choice of a spiral shape for the staircase echoes the importance of this form in Swedenborg's thought. In *Divine Love and Wisdom* 263, Swedenborg writes: "The state of the earthly mind before its reformation might be compared to a spiral twisted or twisting downward, while after its reformation it might be compared to a spiral twisted or twisting upward" (translation by George F. Dole). In *Secrets of Heaven* 3701, Swedenborg explains the angels ascending and descending on the staircase in Genesis as representing communication with the Divine.

Of Man inwards into the Worlds of Thought: into Eternity
Ever expanding in the Bosom of God, the Human Imagination[.]
O Saviour pour upon me thy Spirit of meekness & love:
Annihilate the Selfhood in me, be thou all my life!
Guide thou my hand which trembles exceedingly upon the rock of ages.[35]

Blake, in turn, bestowed his zeal for mystical knowing on generations of later artists, among them Irish poet and student of mysticism William Butler Yeats (1865–1939).[36] Yeats, like Raine, saw Blake as ushering in the new way of knowing that had been foretold by Swedenborg. In a study of Blake for which he served as coauthor, he explains:

> In the year 1757, according to Emanuel Swedenborg, a new age of the world began. The divine description of the kingdom of heaven as "within you" was to become more true than before by reason of a greater influx of spiritual light. . . . Swedenborg's prediction has undoubtedly received, and is still receiving, something of actuality from the general growth of that influence of mind over personality and conduct which is characteristic of the present century. . . . It is the fashion of to-day to attribute this to education. But behind education lies the great force of that flood of illumination foreseen by Swedenborg, and destined, as he declared, to break over and submerge the formalism of science and the materialism of the churches. Like a voice crying in the wilderness of half-awakened imagination, Swedenborg foretold the influence in exalting the standard of inner and of outer conduct which would be exercised by the visionary life, when a higher scholarship should have prepared the way. We can already see a beginning of this around us now. Society half recognises the utility of its dreamers. Mysticism, ceasing to be misunderstood, is ceasing to be disobeyed.
>
> William Blake, born in the year 1757, and brought up under the influence of Swedenborgian ideas, looked on himself as before all things the poet of the age that was to begin in that year. He saw in himself the chosen teacher of the Rule of Free Imagination. "A new

---

35. Blake [1804] 1970a, 146 (*Jerusalem,* chapter 1, plate 5, lines 16–23). For more on Blake and Swedenborg, see Bellin and Ruhl 1985 and Bellin 1988.

36. Yeats, unlike earlier poets, was quite frank about his debt to Swedenborg. For example, in one letter he wrote: "My chief mystical authorities have been Boehme, Blake, and Swedenborg" (Yeats 1954, 592).

heaven is begun," he writes in 1790, "and it is now thirty-three years since its advent."[37]

Following Blake and Swedenborg, Yeats applied mystic insight to his own poetic craft, employing symbolism in a way that made poetry a new language for the new way of knowing. As Yeats scholar Robert O'Driscoll points out, it was the poet's intent to "alter the substance, style, and form of poetry. Art would be created not for the sake of description of external things or for the presentation of moral opinions, . . . but that it might unfold the pictures in the artist's heart" (O'Driscoll 1975, 18).

IV. Conclusion

This essay has briefly sketched the influence of a few ideas from Swedenborg's theological system. It is my hope that it will leave the reader with some sense of the powerful impact these ideas had on the individuals who absorbed them.

In her analysis of the social movement known as the "Aquarian Conspiracy," Marilyn Ferguson traces its evolution over the centuries through the work of seers such as Meister Eckhart (about 1260–about 1327), Giovanni Pico della Mirandola (1463–1494), Jacob Boehme (1575–1624), and Swedenborg. These visionaries, according to Ferguson, maintained that "only through a new mind can humanity remake itself, and the potential for such a new mind is natural. . . . We are spiritually free, they said, the stewards of our own evolution. Humankind has a choice. We can awaken to our true nature. Drawing fully from our inner resources we can achieve a new dimension of mind; we can see more" (Ferguson 1980, 45–46).

It is primarily by making such a choice to awaken and change that the individuals here described accomplished their life work; and Swedenborg can be seen to have been instrumental in that choice.

---

37. Ellis and Yeats 1973, 1–2; compare the similar unpublished manuscript (Yeats n.d.) titled "The Works of William Blake" in the University of Reading library, as quoted in O'Driscoll 1975, 18. The Blake passage quoted here by Ellis and Yeats can be found in Blake 1970b, 34 (*The Marriage of Heaven and Hell*, plate 3); it continues: "And lo! Swedenborg is the Angel sitting at the tomb; his writings are the linen clothes folded up."

BIBLIOGRAPHIES
and
INDEX

Recommended Works

DAVID B. ELLER

Outline

    I. Reference Works (Including Collections, Compendiums, Indices, and Dictionaries)

    II. Major Biographical Treatments

    III. Works on Swedenborg's Influence
        a. General or Collected Studies
        b. Literature, Literary Culture, and Swedenborg
        c. Institutional Developments
        d. Philosophy
        e. Natural and Social Sciences
        f. Social History
        g. Spiritualism, Esotericism, and Other Religious Traditions

THE following list of works recommended for further reading or study is by no means exhaustive, but it includes most of the titles important to Swedenborgian studies. Its preparation has been significantly aided by Woofenden 2002 (see entry under reference works below).[1] The compiler also wishes to acknowledge recent bibliographical research by Anders Hallengren, Inge Jonsson, Robert H. Kirven, Jonathan S. Rose, and Jane Williams-Hogan.

I. Reference Works (Including Collections, Compendiums, Indices, and Dictionaries)

Acton, Alfred. 1927. *An Introduction to the Word Explained.* Bryn Athyn, Pa.: Academy of the New Church. A comprehensive study of Swedenborg's publications and unpublished manuscripts to 1749 by a careful New Church translator and researcher.

---

1. All author-date references in this bibliography refer to other entries herein, not to entries in the general list of works cited in this volume.

————, trans. 1939. *The Mechanical Inventions of Emanuel Swedenborg.* Philadelphia: Swedenborg Scientific Association. A fifty-page publication containing descriptions of all of Swedenborg's mechanical inventions.

————. 1948–1955. *The Letters and Memorials of Emanuel Swedenborg.* 2 vols. Bryn Athyn, Pa.: Swedenborg Scientific Association. A narrative account giving context for copious citations of Swedenborg's correspondence, memoranda, and travel notes.

————. 1963. "Depositories of Manuscripts by and Relating to Emanuel Swedenborg." Bryn Athyn, Pa.: Swedenborg Library. Typescript. A revision by B. G. Briscoe of the version compiled in 1920.

Beyer, Gabriel Anderson. 1779. *Index Initialis in Opera Swedenborgii Theologica Tripartita.* Amsterdam: Sellschop and Huart. This "first index to the theological works of Swedenborg, in three parts" was written by one of his earliest adherents.

Bogg, John Stuart. 1994. *A Glossary, or The Meaning of Specific Phrases Used by Swedenborg in his Theological Writings.* Bryn Athyn, Pa.: Swedenborg Association. Reprint of 1915 edition, London: Swedenborg Society.

Dole, George F., comp. and trans. 1995. *A Thoughtful Soul.* West Chester, Pa.: Chrysalis Books. Previously issued as *A View from Within,* New York: Swedenborg Foundation, 1985. A brief compendium of major ideas in Swedenborg's thought.

Eby, S. C. 1926. *The Story of the Swedenborg Manuscripts.* New York: New Church Press. A brief overview of the manuscripts of Swedenborg's published and unpublished writings.

Hyde, James. 1906. *A Bibliography of the Works of Emanuel Swedenborg, Original and Translated.* London: Swedenborg Society. An essential reference tool listing (as of 1906) translations, editions, and reprints of Swedenborg's complete writings, as well as compilation volumes, biographies, and even portraits. For additional material after 1906, see Wainscot 1967 (below).

Jonsson, Inge. 1961. *Swedenborgs skapelsedrama De cultu et amore Dei: En studie av motiv och intellektuell miljö.* Dissertation, Stockholm University. Stockholm: Natur och Kultur. The only major study to date on the prose poem and "creation drama" from Swedenborg's pretheological period, *Worship and Love of God.* In Swedish with a summary in English. English version: *A Drama of Creation: Sources and Influences in Swedenborg's "Worship and Love of God,"* translated by Matilda McCarthy, Swedenborg Foundation: West Chester, Pa., 2005.

————. 1969. *Swedenborgs korrespondenslära. Stockholm Studies in History of Literature* 10. Stockholm: Almqvist & Wiksell. A seminal work on Swedenborg's doctrine of correspondence; in Swedish with a summary in English.

Nicholson, George, comp. 1931. *A Dictionary of Correspondences, Representatives, and Significatives, Derived from the Word of the Lord, Extracted from the Writings of Emanuel Swedenborg.* 13th ed. Boston: Massachusetts New Church Union. Although the dictionary approach to correspondences is frowned upon by scholars as too simplistic, the popularity of this work led to numerous printings and revisions of the first edition of 1800 (London: J. Bonsor).

Potts, John F. 1888–1902. *The Swedenborg Concordance. A Complete Work of Reference to the Theological Writings of Emanuel Swedenborg; Based on the Original Latin Writings of the Author.* 6 vols. London: Swedenborg Society. Though this concordance is keyed to the Latinate translation of terms common in Potts's era, it is and will remain an essential reference for those interested in Swedenborg's theology. For additions, see Rose 1980 (below).

Rose, Donald L. 1980. *Additions to the Swedenborg Concordance.* Bryn Athyn, Pa.: General Church Press.

Searle, Arthur Hodson, ed. 1954. *General Index to Swedenborg's Scripture Quotations.* 2nd ed. London: Swedenborg Society.

Sechrist, Alice Spiers, comp. 1973. *A Dictionary of Bible Imagery.* New York: Swedenborg Foundation. Based on Nicholson's work (see Nicholson 1931 above).

Stroh, Alfred H. 1902. "Analysis and Review of the *Worship and Love of God." The New Philosophy* 5:33–75.

———. 1908. *Catalogus Bibliothecae Emanuelis Swedenborgii.* Bryn Athyn, Pa.: Swedenborg Scientific Association. Catalog of the library of Emanuel Swedenborg, many of the volumes of which are now held in the Swedenborg Library, Bryn Athyn, Pa.

Stroh, Alfred H., and Greta Ekelöf, comps. 1910. *An Abridged Chronological List of the Works of Emanuel Swedenborg, Including Manuscripts, Original Editions and Translations Prior to 1772.* Uppsala: Almqvist and Wiksell.

Tafel, R. L. 1875–1877. *Documents Concerning the Life and Character of Emanuel Swedenborg.* 2 vols. London: Swedenborg Society. A mainstay of Swedenborg scholarship, "Tafel's Docs" is the major English collection of biographical and bibliographical material related to Swedenborg. The first volume was issued in 1875; the second, issued in 1877, was bound as two volumes. The latest reprint, a print-on-demand edition issued by Elibron Classics, is bound in six volumes. Thus it is simpler to refer to the 1875 material and the 1877 material by publication date than by volume number. They are separately paginated.

Wainscot, A. S., comp. 1967. *List of Additions to the Bibliography [of the Works of Emanuel Swedenborg, Original and Translated, by the Rev. James Hyde] Since Its Publication in 1906.* London: [Swedenborg Society]. Mimeographed.

Warren, Samuel M., ed. 1979. *A Compendium of the Theological Writings of Emanuel Swedenborg.* New York: Swedenborg Foundation. Reprint of 1875 edition, London: James Speirs.

Woofenden, William Ross. 2002. *Swedenborg Explorer's Guidebook.* West Chester, Pa.: Swedenborg Foundation. An indispensable guide to the labyrinth. This is a second, revised edition of *Swedenborg Researcher's Manual,* Bryn Athyn, Pa.: Swedenborg Scientific Association, 1988.

Wunsch, William F. 1929. *The World within the Bible: A Handbook to Swedenborg's "Arcana Coelestia."* New York: New Church Press.

II. Major Biographical Treatments

Acton, Alfred. 1958. *The Life of Emanuel Swedenborg: A Study of the Documentary Sources of His Biography, Covering the Period of His Preparation, 1688–1744.* Edited by Beryl Briscoe. Foreword by Hugo Lj. Odhner. Bryn Athyn, Pa.: Academy of the New Church.

Antón Pacheco, José Antonio. 1991. *Un Libro sobre Swedenborg.* Seville, Spain: Publicaciones de la Universidad de Sevilla. English version: *Visionary Consciousness: Emanuel*

Swedenborg and the Immanence of Spiritual Reality, translated by Robert E. Shillenn, Charleston, S.C.: Arcana Books, 2000.

Benz, Ernst. 1948. *Emanuel Swedenborg: Naturforscher und Seher.* München: Hermann Rinn. A detailed and influential study by a European scholar on Swedenborg as a natural philosopher and seer.

————. 1969. *Emanuel Swedenborg: Naturforscher und Seher.* 2nd ed. Revised and edited by Friedemann Horn. Zürich: Swedenborg Verlag. A revision of Benz 1948 (above).

————. 2002. *Emanuel Swedenborg: Visionary Savant in the Age of Reason.* Translated by Nicholas Goodrick-Clarke. West Chester, Pa.: Swedenborg Foundation. An English translation of Benz 1969 (above).

Bergquist, Lars. 1999. *Swedenborgs hemlighet: Om Ordets betyldese, änglarnas liv och tjänsten hos Gud.* Stockholm: Natur och Kultur. English version: *Swedenborg's Secret: A Biography,* London: Swedenborg Society, forthcoming.

Hobart, Nathaniel. 1831. *Life of Swedenborg: With Some Accounts of His Writings.* Boston: Allen & Goddard. A classic account that went through numerous reprints.

Jonsson, Inge. 1999. *Visionary Scientist: The Effects of Science and Philosophy on Swedenborg's Cosmology.* Translated from Swedish by Catherine Djurklou. West Chester, Pa.: Swedenborg Foundation. Reprint of *Emanuel Swedenborg,* New York: Twayne Publishers, 1971.

Kingslake, Brian. 1986. *A Swedenborg Scrapbook.* London: Seminar Books.

Lamm, Martin. 1987. *Swedenborg: En studie över hans utveckling till mystiker och andeskådare.* With a new foreword by Olle Hjern and afterword by Inge Jonsson. Stockholm: Hammarström & Åberg. A seminal study of Swedenborg's thought by a nonchurch scholar. Reprint of 1915 edition, Stockholm: Hugo Gebers. Translated into German (1922), French (1936), and English (see Lamm 2000, below).

————. 2000. *Emanuel Swedenborg: The Development of His Thought.* Translated by Tomas Spiers and Anders Hallengren. West Chester, Pa.: Swedenborg Foundation.

Sigstedt, Cyriel Odhner. 1981. *The Swedenborg Epic: The Life and Works of Emanuel Swedenborg.* London: Swedenborg Society. Reprint of 1952 edition, New York: Bookman Associates. A highly readable, comprehensive, and thoroughly researched account by a devoted Swedenborgian.

Stroh, Alfred H. 1915–1916. "Swedenborg's Early Life, Scientific Works, and Philosophy." *The New-Church Magazine* 34:172–179, 204–210, 262–269, 354–359, 396–403, 440–445, 490–498, 540–547; 35:6–14.

Toksvig, Signe. 1983. *Emanuel Swedenborg: Scientist and Mystic.* New York: Swedenborg Foundation. Reprint of 1948 edition, New Haven: Yale University Press.

Trobridge, George. 1920. *A Life of Emanuel Swedenborg: With a Popular Exposition of His Philosophical and Theological Teachings.* London: Swedenborg Society. Often reprinted, Trobridge's biography is one of the standard Swedenborgian interpretations.

————. 1992. *Swedenborg: Life and Teachings.* 5th ed. Revised by Richard H. Tafel, Sr., and Richard H. Tafel, Jr. New York: Swedenborg Foundation. Extensive revision of Trobridge 1920.

White, William. 1866. *Emanuel Swedenborg: His Life and Writings.* Introduction by Benjamin F. Barrett. Philadelphia: J. B. Lippincott. This short but ably compiled biography should not be confused with the later, two-volume version (*Emanuel Swedenborg: His Life and Writings,* London: Simpkin, Marshall, 1867), which is notoriously hostile toward its subject.

Wilkinson, James John Garth. 1886. *Emanuel Swedenborg: A Biographical Sketch.* 2nd ed. London: James Speirs. Wilkinson, a member of the Royal College of Surgeons, was an expert on Swedenborg's scientific publications and translated many of them.

Worcester, Benjamin. 1883. *The Life and Mission of Emanuel Swedenborg.* Boston: Roberts Brothers.

III. Works on Swedenborg's Influence

a. General or Collected Studies

Bergmann, Horst, and Eberhard Zwink, eds. 1988. *Emanuel Swedenborg, 1688–1772: Naturforscher und Kundiger der Überwelt.* Stuttgart: Württembergische Landesbibliothek. Essays in honor of the tricentennial of Swedenborg's birth.

Bigelow, John. [1893] 1979. *The Bible That Was Lost and Is Found.* 4th ed. New York: Swedenborg Press. A classic defense of Swedenborg's method of Scripture interpretation.

Brock, Erland J., and others, eds. 1988. *Swedenborg and His Influence.* Bryn Athyn, Pa.: Academy of the New Church. Essays on various topics in honor of the tricentennial of Swedenborg's birth.

Eller, David B. 1999. *Illuminating the World of Spirit: A Sesquicentennial Record of the Swedenborg Foundation, 1850–2000.* West Chester, Pa.: Swedenborg Foundation. A historical overview and bibliography of the largest American publisher of Swedenborg and related literature.

Griffith, Freda G. 1960. *The Swedenborg Society, 1810–1960.* London: Swedenborg Society. A historical overview of the major British publisher of Swedenborg.

Hallengren, Anders. 1998. *Gallery of Mirrors: Reflections of Swedenborgian Thought.* West Chester, Pa.: Swedenborg Foundation.

Hite, Lewis F. 1928. *Swedenborg's Historical Position.* Boston: Massachusetts New Church Union. Contains testimonies from notable personages, most from the nineteenth century, favorable to Swedenborg.

James, Henry, Sr. 1983. *The Secret of Swedenborg: Being an Elucidation of His Doctrine of the Divine Natural Humanity.* New York: AMS Press. Reprint of 1869 edition, Boston: Fields, Osgood.

Larsen, Robin, and others, eds. 1988. *Emanuel Swedenborg: A Continuing Vision. A Pictorial Biography and Anthology of Essays and Poetry.* New York: Swedenborg Foundation. Richly illustrated, this anthology contains numerous essays by many writers exploring Swedenborg's impact on literature, art, religious ideas, and science. Issued in honor of the tricentennial of Swedenborg's birth.

Lawrence, James F., ed. 1995. *Testimony to the Invisible: Essays on Swedenborg.* West Chester, Pa.: Swedenborg Foundation. Includes essays by Jorge Luis Borges, D. T. Suzuki, Czeslaw Milosz, and Colin Wilson.

Swedenborg Society. 1910. *Transactions of the International Swedenborg Congress: Held in Connection with the Swedenborg Society's Centenary, July 4–9, 1910.* London: Swedenborg Society. Essays on Swedenborg's influence; republished in 1911 and 1912.

Taylor, Eugene. 1995. "Swedenborgianism." In *America's Alternative Religions,* edited by Timothy Miller. Albany, N.Y.: State University of New York Press.

b. Literature, Literary Culture, and Swedenborg

Barrett, Benjamin F. 1879. *Swedenborg and Channing: Showing Many Remarkable Agreements in the Beliefs and Teachings of These Writers.* Philadelphia: Claxton, Remsen.

Bellin, Harvey F., and Darrell Ruhl, eds. 1985. *Blake and Swedenborg: Opposition Is True Friendship.* New York: Swedenborg Foundation.

Bernheim, Pauline. 1914. *Balzac und Swedenborg: Einfluss der Mystik Swedenborgs und Saint Martin auf die Romandichtung Balzacs.* Berlin: Ebering.

Bush, George. 1857. *Reply to Ralph Waldo Emerson on Swedenborg.* New York: John Allen.

Cameron, Kenneth W. 1958. "Emerson's *Nature* and British Swedenborgianism." *Emerson Society Quarterly* 10:14–20.

Collins, Christopher. 1971. *The Uses of Observation: A Study of Correspondential Vision in the Writings of Emerson, Thoreau, and Whitman.* The Hague: Mouton.

Deck, Raymond Henry, Jr. 1978. *Blake and Swedenborg.* Dissertation, Brandeis University.

Edmisten, Leonard Martin. 1954. *Coleridge's Commentary on Swedenborg.* Dissertation, University of Missouri, Columbia.

Emerson, Ralph Waldo. 1850. *Representative Men: Seven Lectures.* Boston: Phillips Sampson.

Gladish, Robert W. 1964. *Elizabeth Barrett Browning and America, 1840–1861.* Dissertation, University of Chicago.

———. 1973. "Swedenborg Among the Nineteenth-Century Literati." *The New Philosophy* 76:498–510.

Hallengren, Anders. 1992. *Deciphering Reality: Swedenborg, Emerson, Whitman and the Search for the Language of Nature.* Minneapolis: University of Minnesota Press.

———. 1994. "The Code of Concord: Emerson's Search for Universal Laws." *Stockholm Studies in History of Literature* 34. Stockholm: Almqvist & Wiksell.

Hotson, Clarence Paul. 1929a. *Emerson and Swedenborg.* Dissertation, Harvard University.

———. 1929b. "Sampson Reed, A Teacher of Emerson." *New England Quarterly* 2:249–277.

Kurtz, Benjamin P. 1943. "Coleridge on Swedenborg: With Unpublished Marginalia on the 'Prodromus.'" *Essays and Studies* 44. Berkeley, Ca.: University of California Press.

Milosz, Czeslaw. 1995. "Dostoevsky and Swedenborg." Translated by Louis Iribarne. In *Testimony to the Invisible: Essays on Swedenborg,* edited by James F. Lawrence. West Chester, Pa.: Swedenborg Foundation. Previously published in 1975 in *Slavic Review* 34:203–318; in 1977 in *Emperor of the Earth: Modes of Eccentric Wisdom,* Berkeley, Ca.: University of California Press; and in 1988 in *Emanuel Swedenborg: A Continuing Vision,* edited by Robin Larsen and others, New York: Swedenborg Foundation.

Pasquale, Elisabetta Duina. 1992. *Blake/Swedenborg.* Dissertation, University of Milan.

Peebles, Waldo C. 1933. "Swedenborg's Influence upon Goethe." *The Germanic Review* 8:147–156.

Roos, Jacques. 1951. *Aspects littéraires du mysticisme philosophique et l'influence de Boehme et de Swedenborg au début du romantisme: William Blake, Novalis, Ballanche.* Strasbourg: P. H. Heitz.

Studebaker, William V. 1971. *Poetic Affinities of Emerson and Swedenborg.* M.A. thesis, Idaho State University.

Underwood, W. J. 1896. *Emerson and Swedenborg.* London: James Speirs.

Wilkinson, Lynn R. 1996. *The Dream of an Absolute Language: Emanuel Swedenborg and French Literary Culture.* Albany, N.Y.: State University of New York Press.

c. Institutional Developments

Academy of the New Church. 1910. *The Kramph Will Case: The Controversy in Regard to Swedenborg's Work on "Conjugial Love."* Bryn Athyn, Pa: Academy of the New Church. A report of the bitter legal case that stirred up differences in the New Jerusalem Church between the General Convention and the Academy movement (General Church).

Block, Marguerite Beck. 1984. *The New Church in the New World: A Study of Swedenborgianism in America.* New York: Swedenborg Publishing Association. Reprint of 1932 edition, New York: Holt, Rinehart & Winston. This is the standard treatment of the history of the Swedenborgian church in America. The 1984 edition includes an introduction and epilogue by Robert H. Kirven.

Field, George M. 1879. *The Early History of the New Church in the Western States and Canada.* New York: E. H. Swinney.

Häll, Jan. 1995. *I Swedenborgs labyrint: Studier i de gustavianska swedenborgarnas liv och tänkande.* Stockholm: Atlantis. A study of early Swedenborgianism in Sweden; includes a summary in English.

Heinrichs, Michael. 1979. *Emanuel Swedenborg in Deutschland: Eine kritische Darstellung der Rezeption des schwedischen Visionärs im 18. and 19. Jahrhundert.* Frankfurt am Main: Peter D. Lang. Surveys the introduction of Swedenborgian ideas in Germany.

Hindmarsh, Robert. 1861. *Rise and Progress of the New Jerusalem Church.* London: Hodson & Son. An important summary of early Swedenborgianism in England and elsewhere by an early reader and organizer of the New Jerusalem Church.

Lenhammar, Harry. 1966. *Tolerans och bekännelsetvång: Studier i den svenska swedenborgianismen 1765–1795.* Uppsala: Acta Universitatis Uppsaliensis. A study of early Swedenborgianism in Sweden, with a summary in English.

Mercer, L. P., ed. 1894. *The New Jerusalem in the World's Religious Congresses of 1893.* Chicago: Western New-Church Union.

Odhner, Carl Th. 1898. *Annals of the New Church, with a Chronological Account of the Life of Emanuel Swedenborg.* Vol. 1 (1688–1850). Bryn Athyn, Pa.: Academy of the New Church. This and its companion volume (Odhner and Whitehead 1976, below) cover the development of the Academy movement within the New Jerusalem Church.

Odhner, Carl Th., and William Whitehead. 1976. *Annals of the New Church.* Edited by Morley D. Rich. Vol. 2 (1851–1890). Bryn Athyn, Pa.: General Church of the New Jerusalem.

Silver, Ednah. 1920. *Sketches of the New Church in America, on a Background of Civic and Social Life; Drawn from Faded Manuscript, Printed Record and Living Reminiscence.* Boston: Massachusetts New Church Union. Descriptions and recollections of prominent Swedenborgian individuals.

Sjödén, Karl-Eric. 1985. *Swedenborg en France.* Stockholm: Almqvist & Wiksell. Surveys the early reception of Swedenborg in France.

Wilkins, John H. 1841. *Letters on Subjects Connected with the History and Transactions of the General Convention of the New Jerusalem in America.* Boston: Otis Clapp.

Williams-Hogan, Jane. 1985. *A New Church in a Disenchanted World: A Study of the Formation and Development of the General Conference of the New Church in Great Britain.* Dissertation, University of Pennsylvania, Philadelphia.

d. Philosophy

Arrhenius, Svante. 1908. "Emanuel Swedenborg as a Cosmologist." In *Opera Quaedam,* vol. 2. Stockholm: Aftonbladet. Arrhenius, a Swedish Nobel laureate, offers an overview of Swedenborg's understanding of the universe.

Barnitz, Harry W. 1969. *Existentialism and the New Christianity: A Comparative Study of Existentialism and Swedenborgianism.* New York: Philosophical Library.

Benz, Ernst. 1938. "Swedenborg und Lavater." *Zeitschrift für Kirchengeschichte* 57:153–216.

———. 1947. *Swedenborg in Deutschland: F. C. Oetingers und Immanuel Kants Auseinandersetzung mit der Person und Lehre Emanuel Swedenborgs.* Frankfurt am Main: Vittorio Klostermann.

Calatrello, Robert. 1966. *The Basic Philosophy of Emanuel Swedenborg, with Implications for Western Education.* Dissertation, University of Southern California.

Florschütz, Gottlieb. 1993. *Swedenborg and Kant: Emanuel Swedenborg's Mystical View of Humankind and the Dual Nature of Humankind in Immanuel Kant.* Translated by George F. Dole. West Chester, Pa.: Swedenborg Foundation.

———. 1993–1995. "Swedenborg's Hidden Influence on Kant." Translated by Kurt P. Nemitz and J. Durban Odhner. *The New Philosophy* 96:171–225, 277–307; 97:347–396, 461–498; 98:99–108, 229–258; 99:341–385.

Horn, Friedemann. 1954. *Schelling und Swedenborg: Ein Beitrag zur Problemgeschichte des deutschen Idealismus und zur Geschichte Swedenborgs in Deutschland, nebst einem Anhang über K.C.F. Krause und Swedenborg sowie Ergänzungen zu R. Schneiders Forschungen.* Zürich: Swedenborg-Verlag. This work on German Idealism and Swedenborg's influence in Germany, with an appendix on K.C.F. Krause, is translated in Horn 1997 (below).

———. 1997. *Schelling and Swedenborg: Mysticism and German Idealism.* Translated by George F. Dole. West Chester, Pa.: Swedenborg Foundation. See Horn 1954 (above).

Jaspers, Karl. [1947] 1977. *Strindberg and van Gogh: An Attempt at a Pathographic Analysis with Reference to Parallel Cases of Swedenborg and Hölderlin.* Translated by Oskar Grunow and David Woloshin. Tucson, Ariz.: University of Arizona Press. The noted psychiatrist considers Swedenborg a classic illustration of schizophrenia.

Johnson, Gregory R. 1996–1997. "Kant on Swedenborg in the *Lectures on Metaphysics.*" *Studia Swedenborgiana* 10(1):1–38; 10(2):11–39.

Kant, Immanuel. [1766] 2002. *Kant on Swedenborg: Dreams of a Spirit Seer and Other Writings.* Edited by Gregory R. Johnson and translated by Gregory R. Johnson and Glenn Alexander Magee. West Chester, Pa.: Swedenborg Foundation. Documents the attack on Swedenborg by the noted philosopher, protesting that his works were based on "sense data" rather than reason.

Kirven, Robert H. 1965. *Emanuel Swedenborg and the Revolt Against Deism.* Dissertation, Brandeis University.

Nemitz, Kurt P. 1991. "Leibniz and Swedenborg." *The New Philosophy* 94:445–488.

———. 1994. "The German Philosophers Leibniz and Wolff in Swedenborg's Philosophic Development." *The New Philosophy* 97:411–425.

Odhner, Carl Th. 1912. "Swedenborg and Ernesti." *New Church Life* 32:133–151, 197–209, and plates facing pages 133 and 197.

Odhner, Hugo Lj. 1951. "Christian Wolff and Swedenborg." *The New Philosophy* 54:237–251.

Schlieper, Hans. 1901. *Emanuel Swedenborgs System der Naturphilosophie, besonders in seiner Beziehung zu Goethe-Herderschen Anschauungen.* Dissertation, University of Berlin. Explores Swedenborg's system of natural philosophy as it appears in the work of Goethe and Herder.

Sewall, Frank. 1902. *Swedenborg and Modern Idealism: A Retrospect of Philosophy from Kant to the Present Time.* London: James Speirs.

Taylor, Eugene. 1986. "Peirce and Swedenborg." *Studia Swedenborgiana* 6(1):25–51.

Tobisch, Othmar. 1933. "Lavater and Swedenborg." *The New-Church Review* 40:210–233.

Woofenden, William Ross. 1969. *Swedenborg's Concept of Love in Action.* A.M. thesis, St. Louis University.

———. 1970. *Swedenborg's Philosophy of Causality.* Dissertation, St. Louis University. Ann Arbor: University Microfilms.

Wright, Theodore F. 1900. "Kant and the Spirit-Seer." *The New-Church Review* 7:428–432.

e. Natural and Social Sciences

de Charms, Richard. 1854. *A Defense of Homœopathy against Its New Church Assailants.* Philadelphia: New Jerusalem Press.

Ekström, Sören. 1972. *The Dreams of Emanuel Swedenborg: Psychological Study of a Dreambook from 1743–44.* Zürich: C. G. Jung Institut.

Mack, Charles S. 1890. *Philosophy in Homœopathy.* Chicago: Gross and Delbridge. Links homeopathy with Swedenborgian ideas.

Newton, Norman. 2000. *The Listening Threads: The Formal Cosmology of Emanuel Swedenborg.* Bryn Athyn, Pa.: Swedenborg Scientific Association.

Ramstrom, Martin. 1910. *Emanuel Swedenborg's Investigations in Natural Science and the Basis for His Statements Concerning the Functions of the Brain.* Uppsala: University of Uppsala.

Taylor, Eugene. 1991. "Jung in His Intellectual Context: The Swedenborgian Connection." *Studia Swedenborgiana* 7(2):47–69.

Van Dusen, Wilson. 2004. *The Presence of Other Worlds: The Psychological/Spiritual Findings of Emanuel Swedenborg.* Reprint of 1974 edition, New York: Harper and Row.

Very, Frank W. 1927. *An Epitome of Swedenborg's Science.* 2 vols. Boston: Four Seas.

f. Social History

Garrett, Clarke. 1984. "Swedenborg and the Mystical Enlightenment in Late Eighteenth-Century England." *Journal of the History of Ideas* 45:67–81.

Gladish, Robert W. 1983. *Swedenborg, Fourier, and the America of the 1840s.* Bryn Athyn, Pa.: Swedenborg Scientific Association.

Hempel, Charles Julius. 1848. *The True Organization of the New Church as Indicated in the Writings of Emanuel Swedenborg, and Demonstrated by Charles Fourier.* New York: William Radde.

Meyers, Mary Anna Dye. 1976. *Jerusalem on Pennypack Creek: A Dissertation in American Civilization.* Dissertation, University of Pennsylvania, Philadelphia.

Silver, Richard Kenneth. 1983. *The Spiritual Kingdom in America: The Influence of Emanuel Swedenborg on American Society and Culture, 1815–1860.* Dissertation, Stanford University.

g. Spiritualism, Esotericism, and Other Religious Traditions

Barrett, Benjamin F. 1845. *Open Intercourse with the Spiritual World: Its Dangers, and the Cautions Which They Naturally Suggest.* Boston: Otis Clapp. A strong criticism distancing the New Church from spiritualism and the use of mediums.

Bell, Reuben. 1995. "Swedenborg and the Kabbalah." *Arcana* 1(4):23–32.

Bush, George. 1847. *Mesmer and Swedenborg: or, The Relation of the Development of Mesmerism to the Doctrines and Disclosures of Swedenborg.* New York: John Allen.

Corbin, Henry. 1995. *Swedenborg and Esoteric Islam.* Translated by Leonard Fox. West Chester, Pa.: Swedenborg Foundation. This study finds parallels between Swedenborg and the mystic Sufi tradition.

Dresser, Horatio. 1961. *The Quimby Manuscripts: Showing the Discovery of Spiritual Healing and the Origin of Christian Science.* New York: Julian Press. Reprint of 1921 edition, New York: Thomas Y. Crowell. Explores links between Swedenborg, Phineas P. Quimby (1802–1866), and Swedenborgian minister Warren Felt Evans (1817–1889) in the development of Christian Science and the New Thought movement.

Harris, Thomas Lake. 1976. *The Arcana of Christianity: An Unfolding of the Celestial Sense of the Divine Word through T. L. Harris.* New York: AMS Press. Reprint of first edition, which was published as follows: vol. 1, parts 1 and 2, New York: New Church Publishing Association, 1858; vol. 1, part 3, New York: Brotherhood of the New Life, 1867. (No other volumes were published.) Thomas Lake Harris (1823–1906), a reader of Swedenborg, founded several communal societies combining Swedenborgian beliefs with spiritualism.

Judah, J. Stillson. 1967. *The History and Philosophy of the Metaphysical Movements in America.* Philadelphia: Westminster Press. Well researched and documented, this study demonstrates how Swedenborg's works were important in various metaphysical movements.

Podmore, Frank. 1902. *Modern Spiritualism.* London: Methuen.

Schuchard, Marsha Keith Manatt. 1975. *Freemasonry, Secret Societies, and the Continuity of the Occult Traditions in English Literature.* Dissertation, University of Texas at Austin. Suggests that Swedenborg was a Freemason in England.

————. 1998. "Leibniz, Benzelius, and Swedenborg: The Kabbalistic Roots of Swedish Illuminism." In *Leibniz, Mysticism, and Religion,* edited by Allison P. Coudert, Richard H. Popkin, and Gordon M. Weiner. Boston: Kluwer.

Suzuki, D. T. 1996. *Swedenborg: Buddha of the North.* Translated by Andrew Bernstein. West Chester, Pa.: Swedenborg Foundation. Two essays by a noted Zen scholar linking Swedenborgian thought to Buddhism.

Swank, Scott Trego. 1970. *The Unfettered Conscience: A Study of Sectarianism, Spiritualism, and Social Reform in the New Jerusalem Church, 1840–1870.* Dissertation, University of Pennsylvania, Philadelphia.

Whitehead, John. 1907. *The Illusions of Christian Science, with an Appendix on Swedenborg and the Mental Healers.* Boston: Garden Press.

Williams-Hogan, Jane. 1998. "The Place of Emanuel Swedenborg in Modern Western Esotericism." In *Western Esotericism and the Science of Religion,* edited by Antoine Faivre and Wouter J. Hanegraaff. Leuven: Peeters.

Annotated Bibliography of Swedenborg's Writings

JONATHAN S. ROSE

Outline

I. Description of the Scope and Particulars of the List
    a. Categories Included in the List
    b. Categories Excluded from the List
    c. The Nature of the Material Listed
    d. Access to the List
    e. Criteria for Determining Individual Works
    f. Information Supplied in the List

II. Index to Short Titles, Both Traditional and New

III. Category P: Works by Swedenborg, Published in His Lifetime (128)

IV. Category U: Documents by Swedenborg, Unpublished in His Lifetime (182)

V. Category X: Works of Uncertain Authorship, and Projected Works That Were Never Written (11)

VI. Chronological Synopsis of Published Works (Category P) and Unpublished Documents (Category U)

ONCE the student of Emanuel Swedenborg's writings ventures beyond the well-tended garden of the theologian's most popular works, a seemingly impenetrable thicket of bibliography looms ahead. The following list offers explanation and guidance through that thicket, in a more concise, complete, and synoptic fashion than can be found in other such bibliographies. Originally it was undertaken in response to a pressing need for appropriate and intelligible short titles (that is, short titles in the bibliographical sense, meaning a standardized title, regardless of length). These new short titles were required primarily to replace the varying systems of arcane abbreviations and inappropriate short titles used for Swedenborg's works in the older scholarship.

The traditional titles have many failings. In some cases they are not Swedenborg's; in others they are not accurate, or are actually misleading and misrepresentative of the contents; in still others they show no intelligible relation to Swedenborg's life work in its entirety. These shortcomings are not surprising, inasmuch as the old titles were assigned by different people, with varying purposes, at different times. As a result, traditional titles assigned to drafts of published works tend either to bear no resemblance to the final published title (see *De Praeceptis* and *The Doctrine of Life,* the first of which is a draft for the second) or to resemble each other too closely (see *Divine Love* and *Divine Wisdom,* which are drafts for *Divine Love and Wisdom*). In other instances, tradition has applied exactly the same titles to several different works. Many titles were either left in Latin or given new, independently fabricated Latin titles, and others were translated so literally as to be misleading (see the work traditionally titled *Animal Kingdom,* which is a work on human anatomy, not zoology).

In the preparation of this list, then, the traditional short titles have undergone close examination, and those that have been found inadequate have been changed. The old letter abbreviations keyed to the old titles have been abandoned altogether, though it was found necessary to supply reference numbers for internal use in this bibliography, as will be seen below. Neither the traditional titles nor their abbreviations were lightly dispensed with. The old titles have come to be revered in themselves, and the old abbreviations possess in many cases the potency of a charm for followers of Swedenborg.

Any reevaluation of tradition soon involves the reviser in unforeseen ramifications. The list, once undertaken, made certain organic demands of its own, and has become, it is hoped, more useful to the reader as those demands have been met. Increased usefulness has also brought increased complexity, however. Before turning to the list proper, therefore, it would be appropriate to explain its overall design.

I. Description of the Scope and Particulars of the List

This bibliography steps beyond previous lists of Swedenborg's works in the following ways: It breaks Swedenborg's output into published works and unpublished works, sorting the former by publication date and the latter by initial date of writing; avoids the misleading terms "posthumous" and "memorial"; treats articles and books differently; avoids the use of fabricated titles, masquerading as authorial, for documents to which Swedenborg gave no title; lists Swedenborg's articles in his own scientific journal individually; records the length of the items; indicates what was published anonymously; attempts to identify in the short titles themselves the nature of the work; heavily cross-references previous short titles and numbered lists; and includes six items not listed elsewhere,[1] as well as citing for the first time Swedenborg's annotations and underlinings in his van der Hooght Bible.[2] It should observed, however, that this list, despite its innovations, is not the list to end all lists. Much has yet to be learned about Swedenborg's corpus, and future lists will doubtless find new forms to convey that new knowledge.

a. Categories Included in the List

Three categories of works are set out below: 128 works that were published during Swedenborg's lifetime (1688–1772); 182 pieces that remained unpublished at his death; and 11 entities that do not belong in either of the above categories: 6 works whose former ascription to Swedenborg is now questioned, and 5 works that Swedenborg projected he would write but never did. The works in each category have been sorted chronologically as far as surviving information will allow.

Works in the first category are labeled P1 to P128 (meaning the 1st published work to the 128th published work). Works in the second category are labeled U1 to U182 (meaning the 1st unpublished piece to the 182nd unpublished piece). Works in the third category are labeled X1 to X11 (meaning the 1st disputed or projected work to the 11th disputed or projected work). An integrated chronology showing the approximate relationship in time of the first two categories appears in part VI below.

b. Categories Excluded from the List

Although this list is more complete than any previous such accounting of Swedenborg's works, it still does not (and cannot) represent all that Swedenborg wrote in his lifetime. There are two main categories of material it omits. First, all extant letters are absent from it, except those that were published during Swedenborg's lifetime either by Swedenborg or

---

1. See items P116–P117, U39, U143, X10, X11. (These letter-and-number references are fully explained below.)

2. See item U125.

by someone else.[3] Since Swedenborg seems routinely to have destroyed correspondence that was sent to him, and since letters from him to others were scattered far and wide, we have no idea how much correspondence originally existed, or even how much now survives.

Second, the rough copies and fair copies[4] of Swedenborg's published works are not represented here. Just as he destroyed letters sent to him, Swedenborg seems to have destroyed, as a matter of course, the rough copy of each work after it appeared in print; and either he himself or his printer destroyed the fair copies.[5] One notable exception is *Secrets of Heaven.* Though its fair copy was indeed destroyed, the rough copies of all but the first volume survive (see item U128 below).[6]

Even without the types of material just mentioned, this list represents 13,924 pages of published material and over 28,000 pages of manuscripts, for a total of over 42,000 extant pages.

---

3. Some of Swedenborg's unpublished letters are available in Acton 1948–1955, some in Swedenborg 1975e, and some in Tafel 1875 and Tafel 1877. Still more are available in Academy Documents. Omitted from the list below are Swedenborg's letters identified by Stroh and Ekelöf 1910 as items 29, 30, 37, 54, 56, 57, 59, 72, 73, 81, 82, 84–88, 91, 92, 94, 99–101, 107, 111, 112, 116–118, 127, 156, 163, 170, and 171. Also omitted is a piece just two paragraphs long, traditionally known as *Influx.* This originally untitled Latin piece, an English translation of which can be found in Swedenborg 1996s, 2:607, was written on the inside cover of a book that Swedenborg gave to a friend on April 10, 1760. The exquisitely careful handwriting suggests that it was written at the time of the presentation of the gift; yet its first paragraph quotes some otherwise unknown material that Swedenborg dates to 1750. Because it appears in no prior list, and fits reasonably well into the category of an unpublished letter, it has not been included in this list.

4. In producing a book, Swedenborg would write fewer drafts than we might nowadays. He would often first produce an outline or sketch of a work, and perhaps write out a draft of portions in prose form. (Such works have been referred to in this list as sketches and drafts.) He would then write out a complete work in a "rough copy," that is, a complete manuscript intended for publication but written in a rough form. Then he would copy the rough manuscript over more legibly as a "fair copy" to be handed to the printer.

5. Though none of the fair copies actually used in producing Swedenborg's *published* works survives, some fair copies of his *unpublished* works survive from instances in which he decided not to publish a work even though he had prepared most or all of it for publication. These items are included in the list (see U62–U65, U134, U136, U157).

6. In the case of all volumes of *Secrets of Heaven* except the first (that is, items P86–P96, P100), Swedenborg was not present at the time of printing. Instead he sent the fair copies (of all volumes but the first) to London from wherever he was at the time; presumably this is the reason that *rough* copies of these volumes are still extant (item U128). That is, he must have preserved the rough copies as a safeguard against the loss of the fair copies in transit. One of these rough copies (codex 80 = Swedenborg 1916a, 1:344–407; part of U128) is unusual in other respects as well: it begins as fair copy and then devolves into rough copy. Pages 344–367 carry instructions to the printer in the margins, but these instructions then disappear and the legibility decreases.

c. The Nature of the Material Listed

The works that were published during Swedenborg's lifetime (P1–P128) take a variety of forms. They include articles that were published by other editors; articles published in the first scientific journal in Sweden, *Daedalus Hyperboreus* (The Northern Daedalus), which Swedenborg himself initiated, edited, and funded; poems published in volumes by others; individual letters and poems published separately; and books and pamphlets in Swedish and Latin—most of them prose, but not all—ranging from single broadsides to multivolume works of thousands of pages.

Swedenborg did not, then, have equal control over all the published items on this list. For example, he had much more control over the articles (P15–P25, P27–P29, P31–P37, P39–P41, P45–P47) and poems (P14, P38) he published in *Daedalus Hyperboreus* and over the letters he published himself (P121, P127) than he had over the articles (P53, P60, P62, P63, P72, P106) and poems (P2, P3, P6, P9, P10, P73) he contributed to other publications or over the letters he allowed or encouraged others to publish (P116–P117, P122–P124, P128).

Although the works Swedenborg published were generally much better known in his lifetime than the documents he did not publish, even some of the latter were influential in his lifetime. The most influential unpublished works were his handwritten "memoranda" (official communications), addressed to members of the Swedish government, including the monarch; the combined houses of legislature (known as the Diet); the House of Nobles, of which he was a member; and the Board of Mines, on which he served for decades. These memoranda were often copied many times over by hand, sometimes by Swedenborg himself, for distribution. His personal letters, not included here, were also presumably influential to his correspondents, although obviously on a smaller scale than his political memoranda. The many other unpublished works listed here, however, had no direct effect on his own times, although the indexes to the Bible and to his own works, and the private documentation of his spiritual experiences, did supply abundant references and lengthy narrative accounts to his printed works.

d. Access to the List

To provide various points of access to this list, titles for Swedenborg's works both new and old are listed in an alphabetical index in part II below. Each title is linked with its letter-and-number reference (for example, *Heat Conservation* is linked to P60) or several letter-and-number references (for example, *Arcana Coelestia* is linked to P85–P96, P100, U128, U130). These letter-and-number references point to the complete listings in parts III, IV, and V below. In those complete listings the letter-and-number labels are printed in red boxes in the margins.

In the index, otherwise identical traditional titles that are only differentiated by a hyphen or a space, such as "Air Pump" and "Air-Pump," have been condensed into a single entry. In the sorting of the index, initial articles and prepositions have been ignored, with the exception of the Latin preposition *de* ("concerning").

e. Criteria for Determining Individual Works

In the list of published works (category P, part III below), separate entries are given to parts of a work that have their own title pages and pagination, as well as to subsequent editions published during Swedenborg's lifetime. By contrast, Hyde 1906, the largest of all Swedenborgian bibliographies, generally (but not always) groups multivolume and multiedition works under a single short title. Separate short titles are here given to Swedenborg's many articles in *Daedalus Hyperboreus,* whereas authors of other lists have presented these with but a single entry under the journal name.

Since the documents not published during Swedenborg's lifetime (category U, part IV below) often lack a clear beginning and almost always lack a clear end, identifying them and differentiating them from each other are more arbitrary. Here again is a divergence from Hyde's approach: Hyde groups the drafts on the brain together under one short title, whereas in some instances in this list they are itemized separately. Conversely, Hyde lists the various codices of *Spiritual Experiences* separately, whereas here they are grouped together.

f. Information Supplied in the List

The entries in parts III, IV, and V present the following information, as relevant, on each piece:

Short Title As has been suggested above, the short titles given in this list attempt to describe the pieces in question with greater accuracy than the traditional titles. Therefore with a few exceptions, unpublished material is labeled a draft, a sketch, a paper, or notes. Although such terminology is inevitably imprecise, a "sketch" here generally refers to an outline or series of points, whereas a "draft" is in more complete prose. In the most difficult area, titling Swedenborg's unpublished pieces, general direction was provided by Frank S. Rose's essay on Swedenborg's manuscripts (pages 117–148 in this volume).

The language or languages in which the work was written and its basic form (prose or poetry) These facts refer to the first volume of the first edition. If they are the same for later volumes or editions, they are not repeated. It is worth noting that quite often in the eighteenth century, works written in Swedish were given Latin titles.

The status of the original(s) of the work, if it was unpublished This status, unfortunately, cannot be taken for granted. A fair number of the original manuscripts have been lost, and in some cases not even copies survive.

The traditional title or titles of the work Sometimes the traditional titles listed next to a work represent that entire work; sometimes they represent just a piece of it, or even something of which that work is sometimes considered to be just a part.

The original title of the work At least enough of the original title is given to confirm identification, with a translation in English; or if it is in poem form and lacks a title, its first words are supplied.

Publication information If the work was published, its publication information is supplied, including place and date, if available, and its length in pages (of prose) or lines (of poetry); if it was unpublished, only its approximate length in pages is given. The pagination given may not represent the true size of a work to an English reader, since one page of Swedenborg's originals—densely set in Latin, an economical language—generally becomes three to four pages of English text, especially as set in the more open typography of modern times. The pagination for unpublished works is necessarily imprecise, as it sometimes includes blank areas of the manuscript, especially in the case of indexes.

The date of writing of the work, if it was unpublished The list of published works (category P, part III below) is arranged chronologically by the date of publication; that is, the work is placed in sequence by the date at which it was completed and presented to the public. However, the list of unpublished works (category U, part IV below) is arranged chronologically by the date when the piece was first begun, although information on when the writing ceased is also occasionally given. Therefore the two chronologies are somewhat incompatible with each other. Furthermore, neither sequence can be considered canonical, since even some published works cannot be placed accurately.

Notes concerning the work[7] Although in many cases multiple editions and translations of these works have appeared since Swedenborg's lifetime, the notes generally point the reader to a single source for a given work: a recent English translation; or, in the case of unpublished pieces, if there is no English translation, the latest edition in the original language or a facsimile of the original; or if all else fails, the location of the original itself, if extant.[8] The notes on the published works also indicate if the work was published anonymously. Fully 46 of the 128 published works listed here were anonymous: items P4, P8, P11, P42, P51, P52, P54–P56, P61, P65–P67, P74–P75, P85–P105, P107–P115, and P125. However, they are traceable to Swedenborg by evidence given in other volumes or in his letters.

The notes occasionally cite locations in which sources are kept. Most of the original manuscripts are housed in the library of the Swedish Royal Academy of Sciences *(Kungliga Vetenskapsakedemien)* in Stockholm. It is also appropriate, however, to give here the repositories in which the most complete collections of Swedenborg's published works and related literature may be found; they are, in alphabetical order:

Swedenborg Foundation, West Chester, Pennsylvania
Swedenborg Library, Bryn Athyn College of the New Church, Bryn Athyn, Pennsylvania
Swedenborg Library, Cambridge, Massachusetts
Swedenborg Library, Urbana University, Urbana, Ohio
Swedenborg Library and Inquiry Center, Roseville, New South Wales, Australia
Swedenborg Society, London, England
Swedenborg Verlag, Zurich, Switzerland
Swedenborgian House of Studies, Pacific School of Religion, Berkeley, California

---

7. David B. Eller supplied some of the material for these notes.

8. No English translation has been cited in the case of the works that comprise the New Century Edition—namely, the transitional work *Worship and Love of God,* and the theological works proper: *Secrets of Heaven, Heaven and Hell, New Jerusalem, Last Judgment, White Horse, Other Planets, The Lord, Sacred Scripture, Life, Faith, Supplements, Divine Love and Wisdom, Divine Providence, Revelation Unveiled, Marriage Love, Survey, Soul-Body Interaction,* and *True Christianity.*

The notes refer to certain individuals as well. Persons referred to in just a single entry in this list are identified in the note in that entry. People mentioned in more than one entry are identified by last name (or royal name) as follows:

Acton	Alfred Acton (1867–1956), American translator and scholar of Swedenborg
Benzelius	Erik Benzelius the younger (1675–1743), Swedish scholar, librarian, and eventually bishop
Brenner	Sophia Elisabeth Brenner (1659–1730), Swedish poet
Casaubon	Isaac Casaubon (1559–1614), French Huguenot scholar
Celsius	Anders Celsius (1701–1744), Swedish scientist, developer of the Celsius temperature scale
Charles XII	Charles XII (1682–1718), king of Sweden
Clemm	Heinrich Wilhelm Clemm (1725–1775), German theologian and son-in-law of Oetinger (see below)
Cuno	Johann Christian Cuno (1708–1796), Dutch merchant
Ernesti	Johann August Ernesti (1707–1781), German theologian
Frederick I	Frederick I (1676–1751), king of Sweden
Hartley	Thomas Hartley (1708–1784), Anglican cleric
Oetinger	Friedrich Christoph Oetinger (1702–1782), German theologian
Polhem	Christopher Polhem (1661–1751), Swedish inventor and engineer
Quensel	Conrad Quensel (1676–1732), Swedish professor
Schmidt	Sebastian Schmidt (1617–1696), German biblical scholar
Swedberg	Jesper Swedberg (1653–1735), Swedish bishop and father of Emanuel Swedenborg[9]
Vieussens	Raymond de Vieussens (1641–1715), French physician and anatomist
Winslow	Jacques-Bénigne[10] Winslow (1669–1760), Danish/French anatomist
Wolff	Christian Wolff (1679–1754), German philosopher

---

9. Although Emanuel Swedenborg's last name was Swedberg during the first thirty-one years of his life, before the family was ennobled in 1719, whenever the name "Swedberg" appears without further identification in this essay it refers to Bishop Jesper Swedberg, Emanuel's father.

10. Born Jacob B. Winslow, he later changed his name to Jacques-Bénigne Winslow.

References to further information on the work in previous lists of this kind Finally, a list of reference numbers points the reader to the designation of the work in question in one, several, or all of five prior lists of Swedenborg's works: Tafel 1877, 884–1023; Hyde 1906; Stroh and Ekelöf 1910; Whitehead 1914, 565–582; and Wainscot 1967.[11]

There are also heavily annotated lists of Swedenborg's works in Woofenden 1988, 4–116, and Woofenden 2002, 20–126, which have been profitably consulted in the building of this list. The latter two works are more difficult to reference, however, since they lack item numbers. The short titles used in these two bibliographies have nevertheless been included here, both in the index in part II and in the traditional titles listed for each entry in parts III, IV, and V.

Hyde 1906 gives each work by Swedenborg a roman numeral, and then lists various forms of that work in arabic numerals. Later lists and libraries of Swedenborgiana have largely followed Hyde's *roman* numerals, yet the running heads in Hyde 1906 only mention the *arabic* numerals. Therefore this list provides both. For ease of reading, Hyde's roman numerals have here been converted to arabic numerals. These are followed by a colon and Hyde's arabic numerals. For example Hyde 189:2593 refers to the item listed in Hyde 1906 as roman numeral CLXXXIX, arabic numeral 2593 (see Hyde 1906, 532). Wainscot (1967) adds items unknown to Hyde by putting a lowercase letter after the nearest Hyde roman numeral in sequence; Wainscot's roman numerals too have been converted to arabic numerals here. Wainscot's references have been included in this list only for works that Hyde either did not know of or did not list separately.

II. Index to Short Titles, Both Traditional and New

The following index shows 676 titles by which Swedenborg's works are or have been known,[12] with a key to the information in parts III, IV, and V. The key consists of a letter followed by a number. In the main sections of this bibliography, the information is organized on the pattern of P1–P128, U1–U182, and X1–X11. As indicated above, P refers to works that were

---

11. Complete bibliographic information on these lists themselves, as well as on other sources mentioned here, can be found in the general list of works cited in this volume.

12. Publishers of Swedenborg's works have often compiled several smaller works, or extracts from larger works, in a single volume under a new title. Such fabricated titles of compilations are omitted from this list.

published during Swedenborg's lifetime; U refers to documents that remained unpublished during Swedenborg's lifetime; and X refers either to disputed works, once thought to be by Swedenborg but now in question as to their authorship, or to projected works that were never written.

13. For a very small piece also called *Influx*, see note 3 on page 388 above.

III. Category P: Works by Swedenborg, Published in His Lifetime (128)

P1   *Verses for a Wedding*

Language and form: Swedish poetry

Traditional titles: *Kolmodin's Marriage; On Kolmodin's Marriage; Post Nubila Phoebus*

Original title: *Post Nubila Phoebus. . . . Korteligen besinnat. Tå . . . Johannes Kolmodinus . . . ingick ett . . . förbund med then . . . Beata Hesselia* [After Clouds the Sun. . . . Briefly Considered. When . . . Johannes Kolmodin . . . Married . . . Beata Hesselia]

Publication facts: N.p.: 1700. 4 pages.

Note: A ten-verse poem of forty lines, with an introductory quatrain in the dedication. For an English translation, see Swedenborg [1700] 1902.

Reference numbers: Hyde 1:1; Stroh and Ekelöf 1; Whitehead 1

P2 *Verses to Notman*
Language and form: Swedish poetry
Traditional title: *Verses to Notman*
Original title: "Til herr candidaten [To Mr. Candidate]"
Publication facts: In Christiernus Notman, *Auspicia Christianorum in Livonia* [Indications of Christians in Livonia].[14] Graduation essay. Uppsala: Keyser, [1700]. A poem of 4 lines.
Note: A dedicatory quatrain. No English translation exists. For a Swedish text, see Swedenborg 1910b, 3.
Reference numbers: Stroh and Ekelöf 2; Whitehead 2; Wainscot 1a

P3 *Verses to Bredberg*
Language and form: Latin poetry
Traditional title: *Verses to Bredberg*
Original title: "Doctissimo et Ornatissimo Juveni [To a Most Learned and Gifted Young Man]"
Publication facts: In Bengt Bredberg, *Astronomicum Argumentum de Asterismis* [Astronomical Disputation Concerning the Constellations]. Graduation essay. Uppsala: Werner, [1707]. A poem of 12 lines.
Note: A poem dedicated to Swedish scholar Bengt Bredberg (1686–1740). For a Latin text, English translation, and commentary, see Swedenborg [1707–1740] 1995b, 46–47, 142–143.
Reference numbers: Stroh and Ekelöf 3; Whitehead 3; Wainscot 1b

P4 *Elegy for Benzelius the Elder*
Language and form: Latin poetry
Traditional titles: *On the Death of Erik Benzelius the Elder; Patriae Planctus et Lacrimae; Verses to Benzelius; Verses to Eric Benzelius, Sr.*
Original title: *Patriae Planctus et Lacrimae, in Funere . . . Doct. Erici Benzelii . . .* [The Nation's Lamentations and Tears at the Funeral of . . . Doctor Erik Benzelius . . .]
Publication facts: Skara: Kiellberg, 1709. 4 pages.
Note: Published anonymously on the death of Erik Benzelius the elder (1632–1709), archbishop of Sweden. For a Latin text,

---

14. Livonia is a historical place-name for an area (also known as Livland) that is currently the southern part of Estonia and the northern part of Latvia; this area was under Swedish control from the 1620s until 1721.

English translation, and commentary, see Swedenborg [1707–1740] 1995b, 48–51, 143–147.

Reference numbers: Stroh and Ekelöf 4; Whitehead 4; Wainscot 1c

P5 *Graduation Essay on Maxims*

Languages and form: Latin and Greek prose

Traditional titles: *Select Sentences; Selectae Sententiae; Selected Sentences*

Original title: . . . *L. Annaei Senecae et Pub. Syri Mimi . . . Selectae Sententiae cum Annotatibus Erasmi, et Graeca Versione Jos. Scaligeri* . . . [. . . Choice Maxims from Lucius Annaeus Seneca, Publilius[15] Syrus the Mimographer . . . with Erasmus's Notes and Greek Translations by Joseph Scaliger . . .]

Publication facts: Uppsala: Werner, 1709. 70 pages.

Note: Swedenborg's graduation essay from Uppsala University. For an English translation, see Swedenborg [1709] 1967.

Reference numbers: Tafel 1; Hyde 2:4; Stroh and Ekelöf 5; Whitehead 5

P6 *Latin Verse Translation Accompanying Swedberg's "Rule of Youth"*

Language and form: Latin poetry

Traditional title: *Rule of Youth*

Original title: "Til then högwyrdige och högförtiente fadrens och biskopens . . . utferdade [Executed for the Most Reverend and Deserving Father and Bishop . . .]"

Publication facts: In Jesper Swedberg, *Ungdoms regel och ålderdoms spegel, af Salamos Predik. XII. kapitel, förestelt i ene wisa, med thess förklaring, i twå predikningar* . . . [Rule of Youth and Mirror of Old Age, from Solomon's Ecclesiastes, Chapter 12, Represented in Song with Its Interpretation in Two Sermons . . .]. Skara: 1709. A poem of 154 lines.

Note: An expanded Latin translation of a Swedish poem by Swedberg. This work was also published separately: see P7 just below.

Reference numbers: Tafel 2; Hyde 3:8; Stroh and Ekelöf 6; Whitehead 6

---

15. Until the mid-nineteenth century, this name sometimes appeared in the incorrect form "Publius."

P7 *Separately Printed Latin Verse Translation of Swedberg's "Rule of Youth"*

Language and form: Latin poetry

Traditional title: *Rule of Youth*

Original title: *Jesperi Swedbergii . . . Canticum Svecicum, "Ungdoms regel och ålderdoms spegel," ex Ecclesiast. C. XII Latino Carmine Exhibitum* [Jesper Swedberg's . . . Swedish Poem, "Rule of Youth and Mirror of Old Age," Based on Ecclesiastes 12, Presented as a Latin Poem]

Publication facts: Skara: Kiellberg, 1709. 8 pages.

Note: The Latin poem in P6 printed separately. For a Latin text, English translation, and commentary, see Swedenborg [1707–1740] 1995b, 52–63, 147–149.

Reference numbers: Tafel 2; Hyde 3:9; Stroh and Ekelöf 6; Whitehead 6

P8 *Verses on Stenbock's Victory*

Language and form: Latin poetry

Traditional title: *Stenbock's Victory*

Original title: *Festivus Applausus in Insignem Victoriam Quam . . . Magnus Stenbock . . . de Danis . . . Reportavit* [Joyous Accolade for the Significant Victory That . . . Magnus Stenbock . . . Has Reported . . . against the Danes]

Publication facts: Skara: Kiellberg, 1710. 4 pages.

Note: An anonymously published ode in honor of the victory over the Danes won by Swedish general Count Magnus Stenbock (1665–1717). For a Latin text, English translation, and commentary, see Swedenborg [1707–1740] 1995b, 84–89, 165–186.

Reference numbers: Hyde 4:12; Stroh and Ekelöf 7; Whitehead 7

P9 *Verses to Unge*

Language and form: Latin poetry

Traditional title: *Verses to Unge*

Original title: "Pl. Rev. . . . Dn. Andreae Amb. Unge [To the Right Honorable Mr. Andreas Amberni Unge . . .]"

Publication facts: In Andreas Unge, *De Consummatione Mundi* [On the End of the World]. Uppsala: Werner, [1710]. A poem of 22 lines.

Note: Verses in a master's thesis in theology at Uppsala University by Swedish cleric Andreas Unge (1662–1736) concerning large bone fragments unearthed near Skara. For a Latin text, English translation, and commentary, see Swedenborg [1707–1740] 1995b, 62–65, 149–151.

Reference numbers: Stroh and Ekelöf 8; Whitehead 8; Wainscot 4a

P10 *Verses to Brenner*

Language and form: Latin poetry

Traditional title: *To Sophia Brenner*

Original title: "Ad Sophiam Brenneriam, Unicam Aetatis Nostrae Camoenam Cum Carmina Sua de Novo Caneret [To Sophia Brenner, Sole Muse of Our Age, When She Sang Her Songs Anew]"

Publication facts: In Urban Hjärne, editor, *De Illustri Sveonum Poëtria, Sophia Elisabetha Brenner, Testimoniorum Fasciculus* [Collection of Testimonials Concerning the Famous Poetess of the Swedes, Sophia Elisabeth Brenner]. Stockholm: Werner, 1713.[16] A poem of 26 lines.

Note: See also U3. For a Latin text, English translation, and commentary, see Swedenborg [1707–1740] 1995b, 66–67, 152–154.

Reference numbers: Tafel 3; Hyde 5:21; Stroh and Ekelöf 10; Whitehead 10

P11 *Joyous Accolade*

Language and form: Latin prose

Traditional titles: *Festal Ode on Charles XII; Festivus Applausus*

Original title: *Festivus Applausus in Caroli XII . . . in Pomeraniam Suam Adventum* [Joyous Accolade for Charles XII's . . . Arrival in His Own Pomerania]

Publication facts: Greifswald: Daniel Benjamin Starck, [1714 or 1715]. 28 pages.

Note: An anonymous laudatory tribute to Charles XII on his return from exile. For a Latin text, English translation, and commentary, see Swedenborg [1714 or 1715] 1985.

Reference numbers: Hyde [20a]:3481; Stroh and Ekelöf 13; Whitehead 27; Wainscot 20a

P12 *Heliconian Pastime*

Language and form: Latin poetry

Traditional titles: *Heliconian Pastimes; Heliconian Sports; Heliconian Sports or Miscellaneous Poems; Ludus Heliconius*

---

16. The book is not paginated; Swedenborg's poem appears on what would be pages 27–28.

Original title: *Ludus Heliconius, sive Carmina Miscellanea, Quae Variis in Locis Cecinit Eman. Swedberg* [Heliconian Pastime, or Miscellaneous Poems That Emanuel Swedberg Composed for Various Occasions]

Publication facts: Greifswald: Daniel Benjamin Starck, [1714 or 1715]. 20 pages.

Note: For the second edition, see P26. For a Latin text, English translation, and commentary, see Swedenborg [1707–1740] 1995b.

Reference numbers: Hyde 20:38; Stroh and Ekelöf 12; Whitehead 26

P13 *Northern Muse*
Language and form: Latin prose
Traditional titles: *Camena Borea; Northern Muse*
Original title: *Camena Borea cum Heroum et Heroidum Factis Ludens* [The Northern Muse Amusing Herself with the Deeds of Heroes and Heroines]
Publication facts: Greifswald: Daniel Benjamin Starck, 1715. 95 pages.
Note: This is a collection of twenty-two fables. For a Latin text, English translation, and commentary, see Swedenborg [1715] 1988a.
Reference numbers: Tafel 4; Hyde 21:55; Stroh and Ekelöf 14; Whitehead 28

P14 *First Epigram for "Daedalus Hyperboreus"*
Language and form: Latin poetry
Traditional title: *Epigram on Northern Daedalus*
Original title: "Saecula vel redeunt . . . [Either the ages are returning . . .]"
Publication facts: In *Daedalus Hyperboreus* 1 ([January] 1716):title page. A poem of 4 lines.
Note: See also P38. For a Latin text, English translation, and commentary, see Swedenborg [1707–1740] 1995b, 134–135 (no. 50), 227–229.
Reference numbers: Hyde 22:58; Stroh and Ekelöf 16; Whitehead 30

P15 *Hearing Aid Invented by Polhem*
Language and form: Swedish prose
Original title: "Assessor Polhammars instrument at hielpa hörslen [Assessor Polhem's Instrument to Aid Hearing]"

Publication facts: In *Daedalus Hyperboreus* 1 ([January] 1716):1–4, and plate facing page 1.

Note: No English translation exists. For a reproduction of the original, see Swedenborg [1716–1717] 1910a.

Reference number: Hyde 22:58

P16 *Another Hearing Aid*

Language and form: Swedish prose

Original title: "Ett annat dylikt instrument [Another Similar Instrument]"

Publication facts: In *Daedalus Hyperboreus* 1 ([January] 1716):4–5.

Note: No English translation exists. For a reproduction of the original, see Swedenborg [1716–1717] 1910a.

Reference number: Hyde 22:58

P17 *British Hearing Aid*

Language and form: Swedish prose

Original title: "Om then lilla i England brukade örtuben [On the Little Ear-Trumpet Used in England]"

Publication facts: In *Daedalus Hyperboreus* 1 ([January] 1716):6.

Note: No English translation exists. For a reproduction of the original, see Swedenborg [1716–1717] 1910a.

Reference number: Hyde 22:58

P18 *Polhem's Experiments on Sound*

Language and form: Swedish prose

Original title: "Assessor Polhammars experimenter om liudts beskaffenhet [Assessor Polhem's Experiments on the Quality of Sound]"

Publication facts: In *Daedalus Hyperboreus* 1 ([January] 1716):6–10.

Note: No English translation exists. For a reproduction of the original, see Swedenborg [1716–1717] 1910a.

Reference number: Hyde 22:58

P19 *Future Possible Experiments on Sound*

Language and form: Swedish prose

Original title: "Experimenter som ännu åstertå i wårt land at giöra om liudet [Experiments That Yet Remain to Be Conducted in Our Country on Sound]"

Publication facts: In *Daedalus Hyperboreus* 1 ([January] 1716):10–12.

Note: No English translation exists. For a reproduction of the original, see Swedenborg [1716–1717] 1910a.

Reference number: Hyde 22:58

P20 *Speaking-Tube*
Language and form: Swedish prose
Original title: "Om en dåntub [On a Speaking-Tube]"
Publication facts: In *Daedalus Hyperboreus* 1 ([January] 1716):12–14, and plate facing page 12.
Note: No English translation exists. For a reproduction of the original, see Swedenborg [1716–1717] 1910a.
Reference number: Hyde 22:58

P21 *First Lifting Machine*
Language and form: Swedish prose
Original title: "Then första opfodrings och omwäxlings machinen [First Lifting and Reversing Machine]"
Publication facts: In *Daedalus Hyperboreus* 1 ([January] 1716):14–20, and plate facing page 14.
Note: For an English translation, see Swedenborg 1939, 37–41.
Reference number: Hyde 22:58

P22 *Second Lifting Device*
Language and form: Swedish prose
Original title: "Then andra opfodrings konsten [Second Lifting Device]"
Publication facts: In *Daedalus Hyperboreus* 1 ([January] 1716):20–23, and plate facing page 20.
Note: For an English translation, see Swedenborg 1939, 41–43.
Reference number: Hyde 22:58

P23 *Winter Experiments*
Language and form: Swedish prose
Original title: "Experimenter som kunna werkstellas i wintertiden . . . [Experiments That Can Be Conducted in Winter . . .]"
Publication facts: In *Daedalus Hyperboreus* 2 (April 1716):30–31.
Note: No English translation exists. For a reproduction of the original, see Swedenborg [1716–1717] 1910a.
Reference number: Hyde 22:59

P24 *Currency Conversion Tables*
Language and form: Swedish prose
Original title: "Tafla hwarmedelst Caroliners wärde i dal.kp:mt, silf:mt, och riksdaler uthräknas [Table for Converting Carolins to Copper Dalers, Silver Dalers, and Riksdalers]"
Publication facts: In *Daedalus Hyperboreus* 2 (April 1716):33–34.

Note: No English translation exists. For a reproduction of the original, see Swedenborg [1716–1717] 1910a.

Reference number: Hyde 22:59

P25 *Universal Conversion of Carolins*

Language and form: Swedish prose

Original title: "Ett annat behendigt maneer at bringa Carolin-tahlen . . . i hwad sort af penningar . . . [Another Handy Method for Converting Carolins . . . into Any Type of Currency . . .]"

Publication facts: In *Daedalus Hyperboreus* 2 (April 1716):34–39.

Note: No English translation exists. For a reproduction of the original, see Swedenborg [1716–1717] 1910a.

Reference number: Hyde 22:59

P26 *Heliconian Pastime,* **Second Edition**

Publication facts: Skara: [1716]. 32 pages.

Note: For the first edition, see P12. For a Latin text, English translation, and commentary, see Swedenborg [1707–1740] 1995b.

Reference numbers: Tafel 5; Hyde 20:39

P27 *Polhem's Division of Steelyards*

Language and form: Swedish prose

Original title: "Assessor Polhaimers betsmans-utdelning [Assessor Polhem's Division of a Steelyard]"

Publication facts: In *Daedalus Hyperboreus* 3 (July 1716):41–50, and plate facing page 41.

Note: No English translation exists. For a reproduction of the original, see Swedenborg [1716–1717] 1910a.

Reference number: Hyde 22:60

P28 *Air Pump*

Language and form: Swedish prose

Original title: "Om en wäderpump . . . [On an Air Pump . . .]"

Publication facts: In *Daedalus Hyperboreus* 3 (July 1716):50–57, and plate facing page 50.

Note: No complete English translation exists. For an abridged English paraphrase, see Swedenborg 1939, 13–15. For a reproduction of the original, see Swedenborg [1716–1717] 1910a.

Reference number: Hyde 22:60

P29 *Measuring Volume*
Language and form: Swedish prose
Original title: "Utrekning och afmätning för watnets och wädrets rymd och högd i sådana antlior [Calculation and Measurement of the Width and Height of Water and Air in Such Pumps]"
Publication facts: In *Daedalus Hyperboreus* 3 (July 1716):58–64, and plate facing page 58.
Note: No English translation exists. For a reproduction of the original, see Swedenborg [1716–1717] 1910a.
Reference number: Hyde 22:60

P30 *Sapphic Ode*
Language and form: Latin poetry
Traditional title: *Sapphic Ode*
Original title: *Cantus Sapphicus in Charissimi Parentis, Doct. Jesperi Swedbergii . . . Diem Natalem* [A Sapphic Ode for the Birthday of My Beloved Father, Doctor Jesper Swedberg . . .]
Publication facts: Skara: Kiellberg, 1716. 4 pages.
Note: For a Latin text, English translation, and commentary, see Swedenborg [1707–1740] 1995b, 68–71, 154–156.
Reference numbers: Tafel 6; Hyde 30:78; Stroh and Ekelöf 22; Whitehead 38

P31 *Polhem's Calculations of Air Resistance*
Language and form: Swedish prose
Original title: "Assessor Polheimers wissa anmerckningar om wädrets resistence mot fallande tyngder och areer [Assessor Polhem's Reliable Observations on the Air's Resistance to Falling Weights and Surfaces]"
Publication facts: In *Daedalus Hyperboreus* 4 (October–December 1716):65–70, and plate facing page 65.
Note: No English translation exists. For a reproduction of the original, see Swedenborg [1716–1717] 1910a.
Reference number: Hyde 22:61

P32 *Flying Machine*
Language and form: Swedish prose
Original title: "Utkast til en machine at flyga i wädret [Sketch of a Machine to Fly in the Air]"
Publication facts: In *Daedalus Hyperboreus* 4 (October–December 1716):80–83.

Note: See also U15, U22. For an English translation, see Swedenborg 1939, 24–27.
Reference number: Hyde 22:61

P33   *Experiment with Round Shot and Paper*
Language and form: Swedish prose
Original title: "Ett experiment med en kula och papper [An Ex-
periment with Round Shot and Paper]"
Publication facts: In *Daedalus Hyperboreus* 4 (October–December
1716):83–84.
Note: No English translation exists. For a reproduction of the
original, see Swedenborg [1716–1717] 1910a.
Reference number: Hyde 22:61

P34   *Experiment on the Resistance of Water and Snow*
Language and form: Swedish prose
Original title: "Ett experiment om watns och snös resistence mot
kulor [An Experiment on the Resistance of Water and Snow to
Round Shot]"
Publication facts: In *Daedalus Hyperboreus* 4 (October–December
1716):84–86.
Note: No English translation exists. For a reproduction of the
original, see Swedenborg [1716–1717] 1910a.
Reference number: Hyde 22:61

P35   *Method of Finding Longitudes*
Language and form: Swedish prose
Original title: "En ny och wiss method at finna östra och westra
lengden . . . igenom månan [A New and Reliable Method of
Finding East and West Longitudes . . . by Means of the Moon]"
Publication facts: In *Daedalus Hyperboreus* 4 (October–December
1716):86–89.
Note: See also P36–P37, P44, P56, P62, P67, P99, P115, U46. No
English translation of this article exists. For a reproduction of
the original, see Swedenborg [1716–1717] 1910a.
Reference number: Hyde 22:61

P36   *First Way to Find Longitude*
Language and form: Swedish prose
Original title: "Thet första och lettesta sett, at finna accurate här
igenom Longitudinem [The First and Easiest Way: Accurate
Location by Means of the Longitude Here]"

Publication facts: In *Daedalus Hyperboreus* 4 (October–December 1716):89–94.

Note: See also P35, P37, P44, P56, P62, P67, P99, P115, U46. No English translation of this article exists. For a reproduction of the original, see Swedenborg [1716–1717] 1910a.

Reference number: Hyde 22:61

P37   *Finding Longitudes by Stars*

Language and form: Swedish prose

Original title: "Thet andra settet, at finna Differentiam Meridianorum eller Longitudines Loci, genom the samma förbemelta stiernor [The Second Way: Find the Difference of Meridians or Longitudes of a Place by Means of the Aforementioned Stars]"

Publication facts: In *Daedalus Hyperboreus* 4 (October–December 1716):94–99.

Note: See also P35–P36, P44, P56, P62, P67, P99, P115, U46. No English translation of this article exists. For a reproduction of the original, see Swedenborg [1716–1717] 1910a.

Reference number: Hyde 22:61

P38   *Second Epigram for "Daedalus Hyperboreus"*

Language and form: Latin poetry

Traditional title: *Epigram on Northern Daedalus*

Original title: "Daedalus en auras carpit . . . [Behold, Daedalus takes to the air . . .]"

Publication facts: In *Daedalus Hyperboreus* 1–4 (1716):title page. A poem of 4 lines.

Note: See also P14. For a Latin text, English translation, and commentary, see Swedenborg [1707–1740] 1995b, 134–135 (no. 48), 227–229.

Reference numbers: Hyde 22:58; Stroh and Ekelöf 16; Whitehead 30

P39   *Polhem's Tap*

Languages and form: Swedish and Latin prose

Original title: " . . . Polheimers konstige tapp . . . /Polheimeri . . . Ingeniosa Fabrica Siphunculi . . . [. . . Polhem's Ingenious Tap . . .]"

Publication facts: In *Daedalus Hyperboreus* 5 (January–March 1717):100–114, and plate facing page 101.

Note: No English translation exists. For a reproduction of the original, see Swedenborg [1716–1717] 1910a.

Reference number: Hyde 22:62

Calculating Volumes

Languages and form: Swedish and Latin prose

Original title: "En tafla på cubers, cylindrers och sphaerers in-
nehåll, när man tager sidorna i wissa tum[17] [Table for Calculating the Volumes of Cubes, Cylinders, and Spheres When One
Knows the Surface Measurements in Inches]"

Publication facts: In *Daedalus Hyperboreus* 5 (January–March
1717):114–124.

Note: No English translation exists. For a reproduction of the
original, see Swedenborg [1716–1717] 1910a.

Reference number: Hyde 22:62

 Analytical Demonstration

Languages and form: Swedish and Latin prose

Original title: "Ett lett analytiskt sett at demonstrera så thet
föregående som annat dylikt Geometrice/Methodus Nova Alge-
braico Analytica Praecedentia et Insuper Alia Facillime Demon-
strandi [An Easy Analytical Method of Demonstrating Both the
Preceding and Other Points Geometrically]"

Publication facts: In *Daedalus Hyperboreus* 5 (January–March
1717):124–138, and plate facing page 138.

Note: No English translation exists. For a reproduction of the
original, see Swedenborg [1716–1717] 1910a.

Reference number: Hyde 22:62

 Tinwork

Language and form: Swedish prose

Traditional titles: *Tin-Work; Tin Work*

Original title: *Underrättelse om thet förtenta Stiernesunds arbete,
thess bruk, och förtening* [Information about the Tinwork of
Stiernsund, Its Use, and Tinning]

Publication facts: Stockholm: Johan Henrich Werner, 1717. 4 pages.

Note: Published anonymously. No English translation exists. For
a reproduction of the original, see Sahlin 1923 at the end.

Reference numbers: Tafel 8; Hyde 39:104; Stroh and Ekelöf 33;
Whitehead 48

---

17. This article appears in the fifth issue of *Daedalus Hyperboreus* (The Northern Daedalus) in
which, by order of the king, the Swedish articles were to be printed on facing pages with Latin
translations. Therefore in *Polhem's Tap* just above and *Analytical Demonstration* just below, the
Swedish title is followed by a slash and a Latin title. This article, however, has a Swedish title but
no corresponding Latin title on the facing page; instead there is a blank space in the text.

P43 *Algebra*
Language and form: Swedish prose
Traditional title: *Algebra*
Original title: *Regel-konsten* [Algebra]
Publication facts: Uppsala: Johan Henrich Werner, [1718]. 136 pages.
Note: This is the first work on algebra published in Swedish. No published English translation exists; a manuscript translation by E. R. Cronlund exists at the Swedenborg Library in Bryn Athyn, Pa., and at the Swedenborg Society in London.
Reference numbers: Tafel 15; Hyde 45:116; Stroh and Ekelöf 40; Whitehead 54

P44 *Attempt to Find the Longitude*
Language and form: Swedish prose
Traditional titles: *Finding Longitude; To Find the Longitude*
Original title: *Försök at finna östra och westra lengden igen, igenom månan* [Attempt to Find the East and West Longitude by the Moon]
Publication facts: Uppsala: Johan Henrich Werner, 1718. 42 pages.
Note: Uses the moon to determine longitude. No English translation of this edition exists. Preceded by three articles in Swedish (P35–P37), this is Swedenborg's only book on the subject in the Swedish language. After this he produced a Latin book on the subject that came out in four editions (P56, P67, P99, P115). See also P62, U46.
Reference numbers: Tafel 17; Hyde 46:117; Stroh and Ekelöf 41; Whitehead 55

P45 *Counting Round Shot*
Language and form: Swedish prose
Original title: "En lett uträkning på kulors samma leggningar uti triangel-stapel [An Easy Way of Counting Round Shot Stacked Together in a Triangular Pile]"
Publication facts: In *Daedalus Hyperboreus* 6 (April–June 1717):4–9.
Note: Although Swedenborg assigned this the bibliographical date of April to June 1717, it was not actually published until mid-September to early October 1718. No English translation exists. For a reproduction of the original, see Swedenborg [1716–1717] 1910a.
Reference number: Hyde 22:63

P46 *Small Vibrations*
Language and form: Swedish prose
Original title: "Bewis at wårt lefwander wesende består meren-
dels i små darringar thet är tremulationer [A Proof That Our
Vital Essence Consists for the Most Part of Small Vibrations,
That Is, of Tremulations]"
Publication facts: In *Daedalus Hyperboreus* 6 (April–June 1717):
10–14.
Note: See also U41–U42. Swedenborg's first anatomical treatise.
Although Swedenborg assigned this the bibliographical date of
April to June 1717, it was not actually published until mid-
September to early October 1718. For an English translation,
see Swedenborg [1717] 1976d, 1–7.
Reference number: Hyde 22:63

P47 *A Curve Whose Secants Form Equal Angles to It*
Language and form: Swedish prose
Original title: "Om en boglinia eller Curva, hwars skärlinier thet
är Secantes, giöra altid med boglinien lika wincklar [On a
Rounded Line or Curve Whose Dividing-Lines, That Is, Se-
cants, Always Form Equal Angles to the Curve]"
Publication facts: In *Daedalus Hyperboreus* 6 (April–June 1717):
14–16.
Note: Although Swedenborg assigned this the bibliographical
date of April to June 1717, it was not actually published until
mid-September to early October 1718. No published English
translation exists. For a reproduction of the original, see
Swedenborg [1716–1717] 1910a.
Reference number: Hyde 22:63

P48 *Rotation of the Earth*
Language and form: Swedish prose
Traditional title: *Earth's Revolution*
Original title: *Om jordenes och planeternas gång och stånd* [On the
Motion and Rest of the Earth and the Planets]
Publication facts: Skara: A. Kiellberg's Widow, [1719]. 40 pages.
Note: See also U33, U38. For an English translation, see Swedenborg
[1719] 1915.
Reference numbers: Tafel 18; Hyde 51:124; Stroh and Ekelöf 46;
Whitehead 60

P49 *Height of Water*
Language and form: Swedish prose
Traditional title: *Height of Water*
Original title: *Om wattnens högd, och förra werldens starcka ebb och flod* [On the Height of Water, and the Great Ebb and Flow of the Primeval World]
Publication facts: Uppsala: Johan Henrich Werner, 1719. 16 pages.
Note: A second, enlarged edition was published in Stockholm in the same year; see P50 just below. Suggests geological evidence in Sweden confirming the Genesis flood. No English translation of this edition exists.
Reference numbers: Tafel 19; Hyde 52:127; Stroh and Ekelöf 47; Whitehead 61

P50 *Height of Water*, **Second Edition**
Publication facts: Uppsala: Johan Henrich Werner, 1719. 40 pages.
Note: For the first edition, see P49 just above. For an English translation, see Swedenborg [1719] 1992a, 17–50.
Reference numbers: Tafel 19; Hyde 52:128; Stroh and Ekelöf 47

P51 *Proposed Change in Money and Measures*
Language and form: Swedish prose
Traditional title: *Money and Measures*
Original title: *Förslag til wårt mynts och måls indelning så at rekningen kan lettas och alt bråk afskaffas* [Proposal to Divide Our Money and Measures So That Calculation Would Be Easy and Fractions Eliminated]
Publication facts: Stockholm: [Johan Henrich Werner's] Royal Press, 1719. 8 pages.
Note: An anonymously published plan to divide Sweden's coinage on the decimal system. No English translation exists.
Reference numbers: Tafel 24; Hyde 55:138; Stroh and Ekelöf 50; Whitehead 64

P52 *Docks, Locks, and Saltworks*
Language and form: Swedish prose
Traditional titles: *Docks, Canal Locks, and Salt Works; Docks, Sluice- and Salt-Works; Docks, Sluice, and Salt Works*
Original title: *Underrettelse om docken, slysswercken, och saltwercket* [Information on Docks, Locks, and Saltworks]

Publication facts: [Stockholm: Johan Henrich Werner], 1719. 8 pages.

Note: Published anonymously. No English translation of this version exists. Much of this material, rewritten in Latin, became part of P56, under the heading "Nova Artificia . . ."

Reference numbers: Tafel 23; Hyde 57:142; Stroh and Ekelöf 52; Whitehead 66

P53 *Signs of Earth's Former Submersion*

Language and form: Latin prose

Traditional title: *Indications of the Deluge*

Original title: "Epistola Nobiliss. Emanuelis Svedenborgii ad Vir Celeberr. Jacobum a Melle [A Letter from Nobleman Emanuel Swedenborg to the Celebrated Jacob a Melle]"

Publication facts: In *Acta Literaria Sveciae* 1 (July–September 1721):192–196.

Note: For an English translation, see Swedenborg 1992c, 74–79.

Reference numbers: Tafel 27; Hyde 61:152; Stroh and Ekelöf 58; Whitehead 70

P54 *Chemistry and Physics*

Language and form: Latin prose

Traditional titles: *Chemistry; Principles of Chemistry; Principles of Natural Things*

Original title: *Prodromus Principiorum Rerum Naturalium, sive Novorum Tentaminum Chymiam et Physicam Experimentalem Geometrice Explicandi* [A Precursor to the Basic Principles of Nature or of New Attempts at a Geometrical Explanation of Chemistry and Experimental Physics]

Publication facts: Amsterdam: Johan Oosterwyk, 1721. 203 pages.

Note: Published anonymously, at the same time as P55 and P56. For the second and third editions, see P65 and P97. See also P68. For an English translation, see Swedenborg [1721] 1976f, 1–179.

Reference numbers: Tafel 28; Hyde 62:157; Stroh and Ekelöf 60; Whitehead 71

P55 *Iron and Fire*

Language and form: Latin prose

Traditional title: *Iron and Fire*

Original title: *Nova Observata et Inventa circa Ferrum et Ignem, et Praecipue circa Naturam Ignis Elementarem; Una cum Nova*

Camini Inventione [New Observations and Discoveries Regarding Iron and Fire, Especially the Elementary Nature of Fire; Also a New Furnace Design]

Publication facts: Amsterdam: Johan Oosterwyk, 1721. 56 pages.

Note: Published anonymously, at the same time as P54 and P56. For the second and third editions, see P66 and P98. For an English translation, see Swedenborg [1721] 1976f, 181–211.

Reference numbers: Tafel 29; Hyde 63:162; Stroh and Ekelöf 61; Whitehead 72

P56 | ***Finding Longitudes***
Language and form: Latin prose

Traditional title: *Finding Longitudes*

Original title: *Methodus Nova Inveniendi Longitudines Locorum Terra Marique Ope Lunae* [A New Method of Finding the Longitudes of Places on Land and at Sea with the Help of the Moon]

Publication facts: Amsterdam: Johan Oosterwyk, 1721. 55 pages.

Note: Published anonymously, at the same time as P54 and P55. Continues Swedenborg's idea for determining longitude using the moon. For Swedenborg's response to a critique of this publication, see P62. For the second, third, and fourth editions of this book, see P67, P99, and P115. See also P35–P37, P44, P52, U46. For an English translation, see Swedenborg [1721] 1976f, 213–241.

Reference numbers: Tafel 30, 31; Hyde 64:167; Stroh and Ekelöf 62, 63; Whitehead 73

P57 | ***Miscellaneous Observations*, Volume 1**
Language and form: Latin prose

Traditional title: *Miscellaneous Observations*

Original title: *Miscellanea Observata circa Res Naturales, et Praesertim circa Mineralia, Ignem, et Montium Strata* [Miscellaneous Observations of Phenomena in Nature, Especially Regarding Minerals, Fire, and the Strata of Mountains]

Publication facts: Parts 1–3, Leipzig: 1722. 179 pages.

Note: See also P58, U47–U48. For an English translation, see Swedenborg [1722] 1976c.

Reference numbers: Tafel 33; Hyde 65:175; Stroh and Ekelöf 65; Whitehead 75

P58 | ***Miscellaneous Observations*, Volume 2**
Original title: *Pars Quarta Miscellanearum Observationum circa Res Naturales, et Praecipue circa Mineralia, Ferrum, et Stallactitas*

in Cavernis Baumannianis [Miscellaneous Observations of Phenomena in Nature, Part Four, Especially Regarding Minerals, Iron, and the Stalactites in Baumann's Cave]

Publication facts: Part 4, Schiffbeck: Hermann Heinrich Holle, 1722. 56 pages.

Note: See also P57, U47–U48. For an English translation, see Swedenborg [1722] 1976c.

Reference numbers: Tafel 33; Hyde 65:176; Stroh and Ekelöf 65; Whitehead 75

P59   *Verses on Urania's Metamorphosis*

Language and form: Latin poetry

Traditional titles: *Love and Metamorphoses of Urania; Love and Metamorphosis of Urania; Ode to Count Wellingk*

Original title: *Ad . . . Comitem de Wellingk, Musarum Patronus* [To . . . Count Vellingk, Patron of the Muses]

Publication facts: Schiffbeck: Hermann Heinrich Holle, 1722. 8 pages.

Note: The author is identified as "E. S." Count Mauritz Vellingk (1651–1727) was a Swedish officer and diplomat. For a Latin text, English translation, and commentary, see Swedenborg [1707–1740] 1995b, 72–81, 158–162.

Reference numbers: Tafel 34; Hyde 66:185; Stroh and Ekelöf 66; Whitehead 76

P60   *Heat Conservation*

Language and form: Latin prose

Traditional title: *Conserving Heat*

Original title: "Novae Regulae de Caloris Conservatione in Conclavibus [New Principles Concerning the Conservation of Heat in Rooms]"

Publication facts: In *Acta Literaria Sveciae* 1 (April–June 1722): 282–285.

Note: For an English translation, see Swedenborg [1722] 1976c, 153–156.

Reference numbers: Tafel 32; Hyde 67:190; Stroh and Ekelöf 68; Whitehead 78

P61   *Deflation and Inflation*

Language and form: Swedish prose

Traditional titles: *Swedish Currency and Finance; Swedish Money*

Original title: *Oförgripelige tanckar om swenska myntetz förnedring och förhögning* [Modest Thoughts on the Deflation and Inflation of Swedish Currency]

Publication facts: Stockholm: Johan Henrich Werner, 1722. 20 pages.

Note: Published anonymously. A revised and expanded version of this pamphlet was published in 1771; see P125. No English translation exists.

Reference numbers: Tafel 36; Hyde 72:203; Stroh and Ekelöf 75; Whitehead 84

P62 *Reply to Quensel*

Language and form: Latin prose

Traditional titles: *Reply to Quensel; Reply to Quenzel*

Original title: "Amicum Responsum ad Objectionem Factam a Celeberr. Dn. Profess. C. Quensel contra Nobiliss. Dn. Assessor. E. Svedenborgii Novam Methodum Longitudinis Inveniendae . . . [Friendly Response to an Objection Raised by the Celebrated Professor Quensel to the Noble Assessor E. Swedenborg's New Method for Finding Longitude . . .]"

Publication facts: In *Acta Literaria Sveciae* 1 (July–September 1722):315–317.

Note: See also U52. A "friendly reply" to Quensel, who had criticized Swedenborg's data in *Finding Longitudes* (P56) above. For an English translation, see Swedenborg [1722] 1929.

Reference numbers: Hyde 70:201; Stroh and Ekelöf 71; Whitehead 81

P63 *Hydrostatics*

Language and form: Latin prose

Traditional title: *Hydrostatics*

Original title: "Expositio Legis Hydrostaticae, Qua Demonstrari Potest Effectus et Vis Aquae Diluvianae Altissimae in Saxa et Materias Fundi Sui [Explanation of a Hydrostatic Law That Proves the Effect and the Power That the Deepest Floodwaters Have on Rocks and Materials at the Bottom]"

Publication facts: In *Acta Literaria Sveciae* 1 (October–December 1722):353–356.

Note: For an English translation, see Swedenborg 1992c, 80–84.

Reference numbers: Tafel 35; Hyde 73:205; Stroh and Ekelöf 76; Whitehead 85

P64 *Prospectus of a Work on Metallurgy*
Language and form: Latin prose
Traditional title: *Genuine Treatment of Metals*
Original title: *De Genuina Metallorum Tractatione* [On the Best Way to Process Metals]
Publication facts: [n.p.], 1722. 4 pages.
Note: An advertisement to raise subscriptions for a proposed book of nineteen parts. Only four parts were later written (see U62–U65), and none of those were published. No English translation exists.
Reference numbers: Tafel 38; Stroh and Ekelöf 83; Whitehead 86; Wainscot 67a

P65 *Chemistry and Physics,* Second Edition
Publication facts: Amsterdam: Johan and Abraham Strander, 1727. 212 pages.
Note: Published anonymously, at the same time as P66 and P67. For the first and third editions, see P54 and P97.
Reference numbers: Tafel 28; Hyde 62:158; Stroh and Ekelöf 60

P66 *Iron and Fire,* Second Edition
Publication facts: Amsterdam: Johan and Abraham Strander, 1727. 56 pages.
Note: Published anonymously, at the same time as P65 and P67. For the first and third editions, see P55 and P98.
Reference numbers: Tafel 29; Hyde 63:163; Stroh and Ekelöf 61

P67 *Finding Longitudes,* Second Edition
Publication facts: Amsterdam: Johan and Abraham Strander, 1727. 55 pages.
Note: Published anonymously, at the same time as P65 and P66. For the first, third, and fourth editions, see P56, P99, and P115. See also P35–P37, P44, P62, U46.
Reference numbers: Tafel 30, 31; Hyde 64:168; Stroh and Ekelöf 62

P68 *Philosophical and Metallurgical Works I: Basic Principles of Nature*
Language and form: Latin prose
Traditional titles: *Basic Principles of Nature; Philosophical and Metallurgical Works; Philosophical and Mineralogical Works; Principia*

Original title: *Principia Rerum Naturalium sive Novorum Tentaminum Phaenomena Mundi Elementaris Philosophice Explicandi* [Basic Principles of Nature or of New Attempts to Explain Philosophically the Phenomena of the Natural World]

Publication facts: Dresden and Leipzig: Frederick Hekel, 1734. 468 pages.

Note: The first volume of a three-volume set; see P69–P70. See also U53, U66, U67, U75. For a facsimile of the first edition, see Swedenborg [1734] 1954. For an English translation, see Swedenborg [1734] 1912.

Reference numbers: Tafel 45; Hyde 86:228; Stroh and Ekelöf 95; Whitehead 102

P69 *Philosophical and Metallurgical Works II: Iron*

Original title: *Regnum Subterraneum sive Minerale: De Ferro . . .* [The Subterranean or Mineral Kingdom: On Iron . . .]

Publication facts: Dresden and Leipzig: Frederick Hekel, 1734. 400 pages.

Note: The second volume of a three-volume set; see P68, P70. See also U53. No English translation exists.

Reference numbers: Tafel 45; Hyde 86:229; Stroh and Ekelöf 95; Whitehead 102

P70 *Philosophical and Metallurgical Works III: Copper and Brass*

Original title: *Regnum Subterraneum sive Minerale: De Cupro et Orichalco . . .* [The Subterranean or Mineral Kingdom: On Copper and Brass . . .]

Publication facts: Dresden and Leipzig: Frederick Hekel, 1734. 550 pages.

Note: The third volume of a three-volume set; see P68–P69. See also U53, U61, U62, U64, U67. For an English translation, see Swedenborg [1734] 1938.

Reference numbers: Tafel 45; Hyde 86:230; Stroh and Ekelöf 95; Whitehead 102

P71 *The Infinite*

Language and form: Latin prose

Traditional titles: *The Infinite; The Infinite and the Final Cause of Creation*

Original title: *Prodromus Philosophiae Ratiocinantis de Infinito, et Causa Finali Creationis: Deque Mechanismo Operationis Animae et Corporis* [Precursor to a Philosophy Reasoning about the Infinite and about the Final Cause of Creation; Also about the Operative Mechanism between the Soul and the Body]

Publication facts: Dresden and Leipzig: Frederick Hekel, 1734. 270 pages.

Note: See also P120, U73. For an English translation, see Swedenborg [1734] 1965.

Reference numbers: Tafel 46; Hyde 87:244; Stroh and Ekelöf 96; Whitehead 103

 P72   *Memoir of Charles XII*

Language and form: Swedish prose

Traditional titles: *Letter to Nordberg; Memoir of Charles XII*

Original title: [Untitled essay]

Publication facts: In Göran Nordberg, *Carl den tolftes historia* [History of Charles XII]. Vol. 2. Stockholm: 1740, pages 599–602.

Note: This memoir of Charles XII by Swedenborg may have been written as early as 1732. For an English translation, see Tafel 1875, 558–565.

Reference numbers: Hyde 102:337; Stroh and Ekelöf 108; Whitehead 125

P73   *Verses in Celebration of Printing*

Language and form: Latin poetry

Traditional title: *In Celebration of Printing*

Original title: "Artis, Qvae Format Non Ore, sed Aere Loquelas . . . [Of the Art That Expresses Itself Not by Mouth but by Copper . . .]"

Publication facts: In *Gepriesenes Andencken von Erfindung der Buchdruckerey . . .* [Laudatory Remembrance of the Invention of Printing . . .]. Leipzig: 1740, page 93. A poem of 10 lines.

Note: A poem written to celebrate three hundred years of movable type. For a Latin text, English translation, and commentary, see Swedenborg [1707–1740] 1995b, 82–83, 164–165.

Reference numbers: Hyde 99:307; Stroh and Ekelöf 103; Whitehead 118

P74 *Dynamics of the Soul's Domain,* **Volume 1**
Language and form: Latin prose
Traditional title: *Economy of the Animal Kingdom*[18]
Original title: *Oeconomia Regni Animalis in Transactiones Divisa: Quarum Haec Prima, de Sanguine, Ejus Arteriis, Venis, et Corde Agit: Anatomice, Physice, et Philosophice Perlustrata. Cui Accedit Introductio ad Psychologiam Rationalem* [Dynamics of the Soul's Domain, Divided into Treatises, the First of Which Concerns the Blood, Its Arteries and Veins, and the Heart, Examined from the Point of View of Anatomy, of Physics, and of Philosophy; Which Also Includes an Introduction to Rational Psychology][19]
Publication facts: Amsterdam: François Changuion, 1740. 400 pages.
Note: For the second volume, see P75. The first edition was published anonymously. For the second and third editions, see P76–P77 and P83–P84. See also U93, U101. For an English translation, see Swedenborg [1740–1741] 1955.
Reference numbers: Tafel 52; Hyde 97:288; Stroh and Ekelöf 102; Whitehead 115

P75 *Dynamics of the Soul's Domain,* **Volume 2**
Original title: *Oeconomia Regni Animalis in Transactiones Divisa: Quarum Haec Secunda de Cerebri Motu et Cortice, et de Anima Humana Agit: Anatomice, Physice, et Philosophice Perlustrata* [Dynamics of the Soul's Domain, Divided into Treatises, the Second of Which Concerns the Motion and the Cortex of the Brain, and Also the Human Soul, Examined from the Point of View of Anatomy, of Physics, and of Philosophy]
Publication facts: Amsterdam: François Changuion, 1741. 198 pages.
Note: For the first volume, see P74. The first edition was published anonymously. For the second and third editions, see

---

18. Although the title *Economy of the Animal Kingdom* has been the sole title preferred for this work in the past, it is highly misleading. The Latin *animalis* does not here mean "animal" but "of the soul." This work has nothing to do with what we term in English "the animal kingdom," that is, animals as opposed to plants or minerals. It is a work on human anatomy as reflecting the soul.

19. The term "rational psychology" refers to a rational method of studying the soul or mind, that is, a method that relies on reason as the chief source and test of knowledge, as opposed to an empirical method, which would use experience as its chief source and test, or an esoteric method, which would rely on special experience or intuition.

426 BIBLIOGRAPHIES

P76–P77 and P83–P84. For an English translation, see Sweden-
borg [1740–1741] 1955.
Reference numbers: Tafel 52; Hyde 97:289; Stroh and Ekelöf 102;
Whitehead 115

P76 *Dynamics of the Soul's Domain,* **Volume 1, Second Edition**
Publication facts: Amsterdam: François Changuion, 1742. 402
pages.
Note: Although the first edition of 1740–1741 was published
anonymously, this edition was not. For the second volume, see
P77. For the first and third editions, see P74–P75 and P83–P84.
Reference numbers: Tafel 52; Hyde 97:290; Stroh and Ekelöf 102;
Whitehead 115

P77 *Dynamics of the Soul's Domain,* **Volume 2, Second Edition**
Publication facts: Amsterdam: François Changuion, 1742. 198
pages.
Note: Although the first edition of 1740–1741 was published
anonymously, this edition was not. For the first volume, see
P76. For the first and third editions, see P74–P75 and P83–P84.
Reference numbers: Tafel 52; Hyde 97:291; Stroh and Ekelöf 102;
Whitehead 115

P78 *The Soul's Domain,* **Volume 1**
Language and form: Latin prose
Traditional titles: *Animal Kingdom; The Animal Kingdom*[20]
Original title: *Regnum Animale, Anatomice, Physice, et Philosoph-
ice Perlustratum. Cujus Pars Prima, de Visceribus Abdominis seu
de Organis Regionis Inferioris Agit* [The Soul's Domain Thor-
oughly Examined by Means of Anatomy, Physics, and Philoso-
phy. Part 1: The Viscera of the Abdomen or Organs of the
Lower Region]
Publication facts: The Hague: Adrian Blyvenburg, 1744. 442
pages.
Note: For the second and third volumes, see P79–P80. For an
English translation, see Swedenborg [1744–1745] 1960, vol. 1.
Reference numbers: Tafel 71; Hyde 124:436; Stroh and Ekelöf 121;
Whitehead 153

20. On the meaning of the Latin phrase mistakenly translated "animal kingdom," see note 18 above.

P79 *The Soul's Domain,* Volume 2

Original title: *Regnum Animale, Anatomice, Physice, et Philosoph-ice Perlustratum. Cujus Pars Secunda, de Visceribus Thoracis seu de Organis Regionis Superioris Agit* [The Soul's Domain Thoroughly Examined by Means of Anatomy, Physics, and Philosophy. Part 2: The Viscera of the Thorax or Organs of the Higher Region]

Publication facts: The Hague: Adrian Blyvenburg, 1744. 290 pages.

Note: For the first and third volumes, see P78 and P80. For an English translation, see Swedenborg [1744–1745] 1960, vol. 2.

Reference numbers: Tafel 71; Hyde 124:437; Stroh and Ekelöf 121; Whitehead 153

P80 *The Soul's Domain,* Volume 3

Original title: *Regnum Animale, Anatomice, Physice, et Philosoph-ice Perlustratum; Cujus Pars Tertia, de Cute, Sensu Tactus, et Gus-tus; et de Formis Organis in Genere Agit* [The Soul's Domain Thoroughly Examined by Means of Anatomy, Physics, and Philosophy. Part 3: Skin, the Sense of Touch, and the Sense of Taste, As Well as the Forms of Organs in General]

Publication facts: London: 1745. 171 pages.

Note: For the first and second volumes, see P78–P79. For an English translation, see Swedenborg [1744–1745] 1960, vol. 2.

Reference numbers: Tafel 77; Hyde 124:438; Stroh and Ekelöf 121; Whitehead 153

P81 *Worship and Love of God,* Part 1

Language and form: Latin prose

Traditional title: *Worship and Love of God*

Original title: *Pars Prima de Cultu et Amore Dei; Ubi Agitur de Telluris Ortu, Paradiso, et Vivario, Tum de Primogeniti seu Adami Nativitate, Infantia, et Amore* [Part 1: Concerning the Worship and Love of God; In Which Is Discussed the Earth's Origin, Paradise, and the Garden, and Then the Birth of the Firstborn, or Adam, His Infancy, and Love]

Publication facts: London: 1745. 122 pages.

Note: A poetic creation drama that marks Swedenborg's transition from writing about the natural sciences to writing biblical studies and other religious works. This and part 2 (P82) were published; part 3 was not (see U113–U114).

Reference numbers: Tafel 78; Hyde 125:458; Stroh and Ekelöf 123; Whitehead 154

P82 *Worship and Love of God,* **Part 2**
Original title: *Pars Secunda de Cultu et Amore Dei; Ubi Agitur de Conjugio Primogeniti seu Adami, et Inibi de Anima, Mente Intellectuali, Statu Integritatis, et Imagine Dei* [Part 2: Concerning the Worship and Love of God; In Which Is Discussed the Marriage of the Firstborn, or Adam, and Therein the Soul, the Understanding Mind, the State of Wholeness, and the Image of God]
Publication facts: London: John Nourse and Richard Manby, 1745. 28 pages.
Note: For other parts, see P81, U113–U114.
Reference numbers: Tafel 78; Hyde 125:459; Stroh and Ekelöf 123; Whitehead 154

P83 *Dynamics of the Soul's Domain,* **Volume 1, Third Edition**
Publication facts: Amsterdam: Petrus Henrik Charlois, 1748. 400 pages.
Note: Although the first edition of 1740–1741 was published anonymously, this edition was not. For the second volume, see P84. For the first and second editions, see P74–P75 and P76–P77.
Reference numbers: Tafel 52; Hyde 97:292; Stroh and Ekelöf 102; Whitehead 115

P84 *Dynamics of the Soul's Domain,* **Volume 2, Third Edition**
Publication facts: Amsterdam: Petrus Henrik Charlois, 1748. 198 pages.
Note: Although the first edition of 1740–1741 was published anonymously, this edition was not. For the first volume, see P83. For the first and second editions, see P74–P75 and P76–P77.
Reference numbers: Tafel 52; Hyde 97:293; Stroh and Ekelöf 102; Whitehead 115

P85 *Secrets of Heaven, Genesis,* **Volume 1**
Language and form: Latin prose
Traditional titles: *Arcana Caelestia; Arcana Coelestia; Heavenly Mysteries; Heavenly Secrets*

Original title: *Arcana Coelestia, Quae in Scriptura Sacra, seu Verbo Domini Sunt, Detecta: Hic Primum Quae in Genesi, Una cum Mirabilibus Quae Visa Sunt in Mundo Spirituum, et in Coelo Angelorum* [A Disclosure of Secrets of Heaven Contained in Sacred Scripture, or the Word of the Lord; Here First Those in Genesis, Together with Amazing Things Seen in the World of Spirits and in the Heaven of Angels]

Publication facts: [London: John Lewis], 1749. 634 pages.

Note: Swedenborg's most exhaustive theological study, this anonymously published multivolume work is a verse-by-verse exposition of the inner or spiritual meaning of Genesis and Exodus. At the beginning and end of many of the chapters are essays on theological matters and accounts of Swedenborg's experiences in the spiritual world. For other volumes of this work, see P86–P96, P100. For indexes to this work, see U129, U134. For Swedenborg's rough copies of other volumes, see U128.

Reference numbers: Tafel 94; Hyde 138:565; Stroh and Ekelöf 129; Whitehead 169

P86 *Secrets of Heaven, Genesis Chapter 16*

Original title: *Arcana Coelestia, Quae in Scriptura Sacra, seu Verbo Domini Sunt, Detecta: Sequuntur Quae in Genesi: Hic Quae in Capite Decimo Sexto, Una cum Mirabilibus Quae Visa Sunt in Mundo Spirituum, et Coelo Angelorum* [A Disclosure of Secrets of Heaven Contained in Sacred Scripture, or the Word of the Lord; Continuation on Genesis, Here Chapter Sixteen; Together with Amazing Things Seen in the World of Spirits and the Heaven of Angels]

Publication facts: [London: John Lewis], 1750. 48 pages.

Note: Published anonymously. Although Swedenborg does not mention a volume number on the title page, he clearly intended this as the first chapter of volume 2 (of six chapters in all). Like the other chapters of volume 2 (P87–P91), this chapter was published separately with its own title page and pagination. For other volumes of this work, see P85, P92–P96, P100. For the rough copy, see U128. For indexes to this work, see U129, U134.

Reference numbers: Tafel 94; Hyde 138:566; Stroh and Ekelöf 129; Whitehead 169

P87 *Secrets of Heaven, Genesis Chapter 17*

Original title: *Arcana Coelestia, Quae in Scriptura Sacra, seu Verbo Domini Sunt, Detecta: Hic Quae in Genesi Capite Decimo Septimo, Una cum Mirabilibus Quae Visa et Audita Sunt in Mundo Spirituum, et Coelo Angelorum: Hic ad Finem, Quae de Ultimo Judicio* [A Disclosure of Secrets of Heaven Contained in Sacred Scripture, or the Word of the Lord; Here Those in Genesis Chapter Seventeen; Together with Amazing Things Seen and Heard in the World of Spirits and the Heaven of Angels—Here at the End, Things Relating to the Last Judgment]

Publication facts: [London: John Lewis], 1750. 64 pages.

Note: Published anonymously. Although Swedenborg does not mention a volume number on the title page, he clearly intended this as the second chapter of volume 2 (of six chapters in all). Like the other chapters of volume 2 (P86, P88–P91), this chapter was published separately with its own title page and pagination. For other volumes of this work, see P85, P92–P96, P100. For the rough copy, see U128. For indexes to this work, see U129, U134.

Reference numbers: Tafel 94; Hyde 138:567; Stroh and Ekelöf 129; Whitehead 169

P88 *Secrets of Heaven, Genesis Chapter 18*

Original title: *Arcana Coelestia, Quae in Scriptura Sacra, seu Verbo Domini Sunt, Detecta: Hic Quae in Genesi Capite Decimo Octavo, Una cum Mirabilibus Quae Visa et Audita Sunt in Mundo Spirituum, et Coelo Angelorum: Hic ad Finem, Quae de Statu Infantum in Altera Vita* [A Disclosure of Secrets of Heaven Contained in Sacred Scripture, or the Word of the Lord; Here Those in Genesis Chapter Eighteen; Together with Amazing Things Seen and Heard in the World of Spirits and the Heaven of Angels—Here at the End, Things Relating to the State of Little Children in the Other Life]

Publication facts: [London: John Lewis], 1750. 75 pages.

Note: Published anonymously. Although Swedenborg does not mention a volume number on the title page, he clearly intended this as the third chapter of volume 2 (of six chapters in all). Like the other chapters of volume 2 (P86–P87, P89–P91), this chapter was published separately with its own title page and pagination. For other volumes of this work, see P85,

P92–P96, P100. For the rough copy, see U128. For indexes to this work, see U129, U134.

Reference numbers: Tafel 94; Hyde 138:568; Stroh and Ekelöf 129; Whitehead 169

P89 *Secrets of Heaven, Genesis Chapter 19*

Original title: *Arcana Coelestia, Quae in Scriptura Sacra, seu Verbo Domini Sunt, Detecta: Hic Quae in Genesi Capite Decimo Nono, Una cum Mirabilibus Quae Visa et Audita Sunt in Mundo Spirituum, et Coelo Angelorum: Hic ad Finem, Quae de Memoria Remanente Hominis post Mortem, et Reminiscentia Eorum, Quae Egerat in Vita Corporis* [A Disclosure of Secrets of Heaven Contained in Sacred Scripture, or the Word of the Lord; Here Those in Genesis Chapter Nineteen; Together with Amazing Things Seen and Heard in the World of Spirits and the Heaven of Angels—Here at the End, Things Relating to Our Memory after Death and Recollection of What We Had Done during Our Physical Lives]

Publication facts: [London: John Lewis], 1750. 83 pages.

Note: Published anonymously. Although Swedenborg does not mention a volume number on the title page, he clearly intended this as the fourth chapter of volume 2 (of six chapters in all). Like the other chapters of volume 2 (P86–P88, P90–P91), this chapter was published separately with its own title page and pagination. For other volumes of this work, see P85, P90–P96, P100. For the rough copy, see U128. For indexes to this work, see U129, U134.

Reference numbers: Tafel 94; Hyde 138:569; Stroh and Ekelöf 129; Whitehead 169

P90 *Secrets of Heaven, Genesis Chapter 20*

Original title: *Arcana Coelestia, Quae in Scriptura Sacra, seu Verbo Domini Sunt, Detecta: Hic Quae in Genesi Capite Vigesimo, Una cum Mirabilibus Quae Visa et Audita Sunt in Mundo Spirituum, et Coelo Angelorum: Hic ad Finem, Quae de Gentium et Populorum, Qui extra Ecclesiam Nati Sunt, Statu et Sorte in Altera Vita* [A Disclosure of Secrets of Heaven Contained in Sacred Scripture, or the Word of the Lord; Here Those in Genesis Chapter Twenty; Together with Amazing Things Seen and Heard in the World of Spirits and the Heaven of Angels—Here at the End,

Things Relating to the State and the Situation in the Other Life
of Nations and Peoples Who Were Born outside the Church]

Publication facts: [London: John Lewis], 1750. 59 pages.

Note: Published anonymously. Although Swedenborg does not
mention a volume number on the title page, he clearly intended this as the fifth chapter of volume 2 (of six chapters in
all). Like the other chapters of volume 2 (P86–P89, P91), this
chapter was published separately with its own title page and
pagination. For other volumes of this work, see P85, P92–P96,
P100. For the rough copy, see U128. For indexes to this work,
see U129, U134.

Reference numbers: Tafel 94; Hyde 138:570; Stroh and Ekelöf
129; Whitehead 169

P91 *Secrets of Heaven, Genesis Chapter 21*

Original title: *Arcana Coelestia, Quae in Scriptura Sacra, seu Verbo
Domini Sunt, Detecta: Hic Quae in Genesi Capite Vigesimo
Primo, Una cum Mirabilibus Quae Visa et Audita Sunt in Mundo
Spirituum, et Coelo Angelorum: Hic ad Finem, de Conjugiis, Quo-
modo Considerantur in Coelo, et de Adulteriis* [A Disclosure of
Secrets of Heaven Contained in Sacred Scripture, or the Word
of the Lord; Here Those in Genesis Chapter Twenty-One; To-
gether with Amazing Things Seen and Heard in the World of
Spirits and the Heaven of Angels—Here at the End, Things Re-
lating to Heaven's Views on Marriage and on Adultery]

Publication facts: [London: John Lewis], 1750. 71 pages.

Note: Published anonymously. Although Swedenborg does not
mention a volume number on the title page, he clearly intended this as the sixth chapter of volume 2 (of six chapters in
all). Like the other chapters of volume 2 (P86–P90), this chapter was published separately with its own title page and pagination. For other volumes of this work, see P85, P92–P96, P100.
For the rough copy, see U128. For indexes to this work, see
U129, U134.

Reference numbers: Tafel 94; Hyde 138:571; Stroh and Ekelöf 129;
Whitehead 169

P92 *Secrets of Heaven, Genesis,* Volume 3

Original title: *Arcana Coelestia, Quae in Scriptura Sacra, seu Verbo
Domini Sunt, Detecta: Hic Quae in Genesi, Una cum Mirabilibus*

Quae Visa Sunt in Mundo Spirituum, et in Coelo Angelorum [A Disclosure of Secrets of Heaven Contained in Sacred Scripture, or the Word of the Lord; Here Those in Genesis, Together with Amazing Things Seen in the World of Spirits and in the Heaven of Angels]

Publication facts: [London: John Lewis], 1751. 643 pages.

Note: Published anonymously. For other volumes of this work, see P85–P91, P93–P96, P100. For a sketch of portions of this volume, see U130. For the rough copy, see U128. For indexes to this work, see U129, U134.

Reference numbers: Tafel 94; Hyde 138:572; Stroh and Ekelöf 129; Whitehead 169

P93 *Secrets of Heaven, Genesis,* Volume 4

Publication facts: [London: John Lewis], 1752. 559 pages.

Note: Published anonymously. For other volumes of this work, see P85–P92, P94–P96, P100. For a sketch of portions of this volume, see U130. For the rough copy, see U128. For indexes to this work, see U129, U134.

Reference numbers: Tafel 94; Hyde 138:573; Stroh and Ekelöf 129; Whitehead 169

P94 *Secrets of Heaven, Genesis,* Volume 5

Publication facts: [London: John Lewis], 1753. 537 pages.

Note: Published anonymously. For other volumes of this work, see P85–P93, P95–P96, P100. For a sketch of portions of this volume, see U130. For the rough copy, see U128. For indexes to this work, see U129, U134.

Reference numbers: Tafel 94; Hyde 138:574; Stroh and Ekelöf 129; Whitehead 169

P95 *Secrets of Heaven, Exodus,* Volume 1

Original title: *Arcana Coelestia, Quae in Scriptura Sacra, seu Verbo Domini Sunt, Detecta: Hic Quae in Exodo, Una cum Mirabilibus Quae Visa Sunt in Mundo Spirituum, et in Coelo Angelorum* [A Disclosure of Secrets of Heaven Contained in Sacred Scripture, or the Word of the Lord; Here Those in Exodus, Together with Amazing Things Seen in the World of Spirits and in the Heaven of Angels]

Publication facts: [London: John Lewis], 1753. 580 pages.

Note: Published anonymously. Although Swedenborg presents this as volume 1 because its exposition turns to another book of the Bible, he clearly intended it as a continuation of his five earlier volumes on Genesis (P85, P86–P91, P92, P93, P94); therefore in later Latin editions this is known as volume 6 of eight. For later volumes of this work, see P96, P100. For the rough copy, see U128. For indexes to this work, see U129, U134.

Reference numbers: Tafel 95; Hyde 138:575; Stroh and Ekelöf 129; Whitehead 169

P96 *Secrets of Heaven, Exodus,* **Volume 2**

Publication facts: [London: John Lewis], 1754. 521 pages.

Note: Published anonymously. Although Swedenborg presents this as volume 2, he clearly intended it as a continuation of his six earlier volumes on Genesis and Exodus (P85, P86–P91, P92, P93, P94, P95); therefore in later Latin editions this is known as volume 7 of eight. For the last volume of this work, see P100. For the rough copy, see U128. For indexes to this work, see U129, U134.

Reference numbers: Tafel 95; Hyde 138:576; Stroh and Ekelöf 129; Whitehead 169

P97 *Chemistry and Physics,* **Third Edition**

Publication facts: Hildburghausen: Johan Godofred Hanisch, 1754.[21] 212 pages.

Note: Published anonymously, at the same time as P98 and P99. For the first and second editions, see P54 and P65.

Reference numbers: Tafel 28; Hyde 62:159; Stroh and Ekelöf 60

P98 *Iron and Fire,* **Third Edition**

Publication facts: Hildburghausen: Johan Godofred Hanisch, 1754. 56 pages.

Note: Published anonymously, at the same time as P97 and P99. For the first and second editions, see P55 and P66.

Reference numbers: Tafel 29; Hyde 63:164; Stroh and Ekelöf 61

P99 *Finding Longitudes,* **Third Edition**

Publication facts: Hildburghausen: Johan Godofred Hanisch, 1754. 55 pages.

---

21. The exact timing of publication of P97–P99 in relation to P96 is not clear.

Note: Published anonymously, at the same time as P97 and P98. For the first, second, and fourth editions, see P56, P67, and P115. See also P35–P37, P44, P62, U46.

Reference numbers: Hyde 64:169; Stroh and Ekelöf 62

P100   *Secrets of Heaven, Exodus,* **Volume 3**

Publication facts: [London: John Lewis], 1756. 695 pages.

Note: Published anonymously. Although Swedenborg presents this as volume 3, he clearly intended it as a continuation of his seven earlier volumes of Genesis and Exodus (P85, P86–P91, P92, P93, P94, P95, P96); therefore in later Latin editions, this is known as volume 8 of eight. For the rough copy, see U128. For indexes to this work, see U129, U134.

Reference numbers: Tafel 95; Hyde 138:577; Stroh and Ekelöf 129; Whitehead 169

P101   *Heaven and Hell*

Language and form: Latin prose

Traditional title: *Heaven and Hell*

Original title: *De Coelo et Ejus Mirabilibus, et de Inferno, ex Auditis et Visis* [Heaven and Its Wonders and Hell: Drawn from Things Heard and Seen]

Publication facts: London: [John Lewis], 1758.[22] 275 pages.

Note: Published anonymously. By far Swedenborg's most familiar and popular work, this book has been translated into more than thirty languages. It describes heaven, the world of spirits, and hell. For a supplement, see P111.

Reference numbers: Tafel 101; Hyde 145:1002; Stroh and Ekelöf 132; Whitehead 176

P102   *New Jerusalem*

Language and form: Latin prose

Traditional titles: *Heavenly Doctrine; New Jerusalem and Its Heavenly Doctrine; The Heavenly City*

---

22. The works here labeled P101–P105 were all published in London in 1758. Although Hyde arrives at the sequence P105, P101, P103, P102, P104 for these five works published in 1758 by using cross-references to show the order in which they were *written,* Swedenborg himself on more than one occasion gives the sequence of *publication* that is presented here (see the last page of P118, and Acton 1948–1955, 745).

Original title: *De Nova Hierosolyma et Ejus Doctrina Coelesti: Ex Auditis e Coelo: Quibus Praemittitur Aliquid de Novo Coelo et Nova Terra* [The New Jerusalem and Its Heavenly Teaching: Drawn from Things Heard from Heaven: Preceded by a Discussion of the New Heaven and the New Earth]

Publication facts: London: [John Lewis], 1758. 157 pages.

Note: Published anonymously. A systematic summary of Swedenborg's theology.

Reference numbers: Tafel 103; Hyde 147:1210; Stroh and Ekelöf 134; Whitehead 178

 P103   *Last Judgment*

Language and form: Latin prose

Traditional titles: *Last Judgment; Last Judgment in Retrospect; The Last Judgment*

Original title: *De Ultimo Judicio, et de Babylonia Destructa: Ita Quod Omnia, Quae in Apocalypsi Praedicta Sunt, Hodie Impleta Sunt: Ex Auditis et Visis* [The Last Judgment and Babylon Destroyed, Showing That at This Day All the Predictions of the Book of Revelation Have Been Fulfilled: Drawn from Things Heard and Seen]

Publication facts: London: [John Lewis], 1758. 56 pages.

Note: Published anonymously. This small work makes the unique claim that the Last Judgment is not a future event, but something that has already taken place in the spiritual world. For a supplement, see P111. See also U150.

Reference numbers: Tafel 105; Hyde 146:1166; Stroh and Ekelöf 133; Whitehead 177

P104   *White Horse*

Language and form: Latin prose

Traditional titles: *The White Horse; White Horse*

Original title: *De Equo Albo, de Quo in Apocalypsi, Cap. XIX: Et Dein de Verbo et Ejus Sensu Spirituali seu Interno, ex Arcanis Coelestibus* [The White Horse in Revelation Chapter 19, and the Word and Its Spiritual or Inner Sense, from "Secrets of Heaven"]

Publication facts: London: [John Lewis], 1758. 23 pages.

Note: See also U171. Published anonymously. The imagery of the horse is from Revelation; the book concerns the inner meaning of Scripture.

Reference numbers: Tafel 102; Hyde 148:1313; Stroh and Ekelöf 135; Whitehead 179

P105 *Other Planets*
Language and form: Latin prose
Traditional titles: *Earths in the Universe; The Worlds in Space*
Original title: *De Telluribus in Mundo Nostro Solari, Quae Vocantur Planetae, et de Telluribus in Coelo Astrifero, deque Illarum Incolis, Tum de Spiritibus et Angelis Ibi: Ex Auditis et Visis* [Planets or Worlds in Our Solar System, and Worlds in the Starry Heavens, and Their Inhabitants, As Well as the Spirits and Angels There: Drawn from Things Heard and Seen]
Publication facts: London: [John Lewis], 1758. 73 pages.
Note: Published anonymously. One of Swedenborg's more controversial publications, this work recounts conversations with spirits who reported having lived on other planets in the solar system or on the earth's moon.
Reference numbers: Tafel 104; Hyde 144:956; Stroh and Ekelöf 131; Whitehead 175

P106 *Inlaying Marble*
Language and form: Swedish prose
Traditional titles: *Inlaying Marble; Inlaying Tables*
Original title: "Beskrifning huru inläggningar ske uti marmorskifvor, til bord eller annan hus-zirat [Description of the Mode in Which Marble Slabs Are Inlaid for Tables and Other Ornaments]"
Publication facts: In *Kongl. Vetenskaps Akademiens handlingar* 24 (April–June 1763):107–113.
Note: See also U146. For an English translation, see Tafel 1875, 586–590.
Reference numbers: Tafel 121; Hyde 166:1715; Stroh and Ekelöf 147; Whitehead 200

P107 *The Lord*
Language and form: Latin prose
Traditional titles: *Doctrine of the Lord; The Four Doctrines*
Original title: *Doctrina Novae Hierosolymae de Domino* [Teachings for the New Jerusalem on the Lord]
Publication facts: Amsterdam: 1763. 64 pages.
Note: Published anonymously. See also U137.

Reference numbers: Tafel 116; Hyde 167:1717; Stroh and Ekelöf 148; Whitehead 201

P108 *Sacred Scripture*
Language and form: Latin prose
Traditional titles: *Doctrine of Sacred Scripture; Doctrine of the Sacred Scripture; The Four Doctrines*
Original title: *Doctrina Novae Hierosolymae de Scriptura Sacra* [Teachings for the New Jerusalem on Sacred Scripture]
Publication facts: Amsterdam: 1763. 54 pages.
Note: Published anonymously. See also U148.
Reference numbers: Tafel 117; Hyde 168:1790; Stroh and Ekelöf 149; Whitehead 202

P109 *Life*
Language and form: Latin prose
Traditional titles: *Doctrine of Life; The Four Doctrines*
Original title: *Doctrina Vitae pro Nova Hierosolyma ex Praeceptis Decalogi* [Teachings about Life for the New Jerusalem: Drawn from the Ten Commandments]
Publication facts: Amsterdam: 1763. 36 pages.
Note: Published anonymously. See also U149.
Reference numbers: Tafel 118; Hyde 169:1856; Stroh and Ekelöf 150; Whitehead 203

P110 *Faith*
Language and form: Latin prose
Traditional titles: *Doctrine of Faith; Seeing's Believing; The Four Doctrines*
Original title: *Doctrina Novae Hierosolymae de Fide* [Teachings for the New Jerusalem on Faith]
Publication facts: Amsterdam: 1763. 23 pages.
Note: Published anonymously.
Reference numbers: Tafel 119; Hyde 170:1935; Stroh and Ekelöf 151; Whitehead 204

P111 *Supplements*
Language and form: Latin prose
Traditional titles: *Continuation Concerning the Last Judgment; Continuation of Last Judgment; Continuation of the Last Judgment*
Original title: *Continuatio de Ultimo Judicio: Et de Mundo Spirituali* [Supplements on the Last Judgment and the Spiritual World]

Publication facts: Amsterdam: 1763. 28 pages.

Note: Published anonymously. This work contains supplements to P103 and P101, in that order. See also U150.

Reference numbers: Tafel 120; Hyde 171:1988; Stroh and Ekelöf 152; Whitehead 205

P112 *Divine Love and Wisdom*

Language and form: Latin prose

Traditional title: *Divine Love and Wisdom*

Original title: *Sapientia Angelica de Divino Amore et de Divina Sapientia* [Angelic Wisdom about Divine Love and Wisdom]

Publication facts: Amsterdam: 1763. 151 pages.

Note: Published anonymously. This work surveys the nature of God, the universe, and the inner self. P113 forms a sequel to it. See also U151–U152.

Reference numbers: Tafel 124; Hyde 172:2035; Stroh and Ekelöf 153; Whitehead 206

P113 *Divine Providence*

Language and form: Latin prose

Traditional title: *Divine Providence*

Original title: *Sapientia Angelica de Divina Providentia* [Angelic Wisdom about Divine Providence]

Publication facts: Amsterdam: 1764. 214 pages.

Note: Published anonymously. This sequel to P112 addresses the problem of evil and describes spiritual laws by which God governs the world.

Reference numbers: Tafel 125; Hyde 173:2097; Stroh and Ekelöf 154; Whitehead 207

P114 *Revelation Unveiled*

Language and form: Latin prose

Traditional title: *Apocalypse Revealed*

Original title: *Apocalypsis Revelata, in Qua Deteguntur Arcana Quae Ibi Praedicta Sunt, et Hactenus Recondita Latuerunt* [The Book of Revelation Unveiled, Uncovering the Secrets That Were Foretold There and Have Lain Hidden until Now]

Publication facts: Amsterdam: 1766. 629 pages.

Note: Published anonymously. This book is a verse-by-verse exposition of the Book of Revelation. It is a completely new examination of the subject treated in Swedenborg's earlier unpublished work, *Revelation Explained* (U135–U136). For indexes to this work, see U156–U157. See also U153. Includes narrative accounts of his spiritual experiences.

Reference numbers: Tafel 127; Hyde 176:2195; Stroh and Ekelöf 155; Whitehead 211

P115 *Finding Longitudes,* **Fourth Edition**
Original title: *Methodus Nova Inveniendi Longitudines Locorum Terra Marique per Lunam* [A New Method of Finding the Longitudes of Places on Land and at Sea by the Moon]
Publication facts: [Amsterdam: 1766]. 9 pages.
Note: Published anonymously. For the first, second, and third editions, see P56, P67, and P99. See also P35–P37, P44, P62, U46.
Reference numbers: Tafel 128; Hyde 64:171; Stroh and Ekelöf 62

P116 *Reply to Oetinger*
Language and form: Latin prose
Original title: [Untitled letter]
Publication facts: In Heinrich Wilhelm Clemm, *Vollständige Einleitung in die Religion und gesamte Theologie.* Vol. 4. Tübingen: Johann Georg Cotta, 1767, pages 209–210.
Note: See also P117 just below. This brief reply dated September 23, 1766, to a letter dated October 13, 1765, from Oetinger was published by Clemm. For a Latin text and English translation, see Swedenborg 1975e, 282–285.
Reference numbers: [Not listed]

P117 *Answer to Oetinger's Reply*
Language and form: Latin prose
Original title: [Untitled letter]
Publication facts: In Heinrich Wilhelm Clemm, *Vollständige Einleitung in die Religion und gesamte Theologie.* Vol. 4. Tübingen: Johann Georg Cotta, 1767, pages 211–212.
Note: See also P116 just above. This brief response dated November 11, 1766, to Oetinger's reply of October 7, 1766, to P116 was also published by Clemm. For a Latin text and English translation, see Swedenborg 1975e, 286–289.
Reference numbers: [Not listed]

P118 *Marriage Love*
Language and form: Latin prose
Traditional titles: *Conjugial Love; Love in Marriage; Marital Love; Married Love*

Original title: *Delitiae Sapientiae de Amore Conjugiali: Post Quas Sequuntur Voluptates Insaniae de Amore Scortatorio* [Wisdom's Delight in Marriage Love: Followed by Insanity's Pleasure in Promiscuous Love]

Publication facts: Amsterdam: 1768. 328 pages.

Note: See also U154, U159, U163–U165. Swedenborg's controversial work on marriage, the first shipment of which was impounded on its arrival in Sweden. Includes narrative accounts of his spiritual experiences. The first of Swedenborg's theological works not published anonymously, it included a page at the back identifying him as the author of his previous theological works (P85–P96, P100–P105, P107–P109,[23] P111–P114).

Reference numbers: Tafel 135; Hyde 184:2400; Stroh and Ekelöf 159; Whitehead 219

P119 *Survey*

Language and form: Latin prose

Traditional titles: *Brief Exposition; Brief Exposition of the Doctrine of the New Church*

Original title: *Summaria Expositio Doctrinae Novae Ecclesiae, Quae per Novam Hierosolymam in Apocalypsi Intelligitur* [Survey of Teachings for the New Church Meant by the New Jerusalem in the Book of Revelation]

Publication facts: Amsterdam: 1769. 67 pages.

Note: A precursor to *True Christianity* (P126). See also U166–U169.

Reference numbers: Tafel 139; Hyde 186:2475; Stroh and Ekelöf 162; Whitehead 222

P120 *Soul-Body Interaction*

Language and form: Latin prose

Traditional titles: *Influx; Interaction of Soul and Body; Interaction of the Soul and Body; Intercourse between the Soul and Body; Intercourse of Soul and Body*

Original title: *De Commercio Animae et Corporis, Quod Creditur Fieri vel per Influxum Physicum, vel per Influxum Spiritualem, vel per Harmoniam Praestabilitam* [The Interaction between Soul and Body That Some Attribute to a Flow of Energy from

---

23. It seems quite clear that P110 should have been on this list and was omitted only in error.

the Body, Some to a Flow of Energy from the Spirit, and Some
to a Preestablished Harmony]

Publication facts: London: 1769. 23 pages.

Note: Swedenborg's final complete treatment of a topic that had
fascinated him for much of his life, and on which he had first
published in 1734 (P71).

Reference numbers: Tafel 140; Hyde 188:2536; Stroh and Ekelöf
166; Whitehead 225

P121 *Answer to a Friend*

Language and form: Latin prose

Traditional title: *Answer to a Letter*

Original title: *Responsum ad Epistolam ab Amico ad Me Scriptam*
[Answer to a Letter Written to Me by a Friend]

Publication facts: London: 1769. 3 pages.

Note: Swedenborg's reply to a letter from Hartley, giving various
biographical details of Swedenborg's life and work. It has appeared in dozens of publications since. For an English translation, see Acton 1948–1955, 676–679.

Reference numbers: Tafel 141; Hyde 189:2593; Stroh and Ekelöf
167; Whitehead 226

P122 *Letter to Beyer on the Swedish Church*

Language and form: Swedish prose

Traditional title: *Letter to Beyer*

Original title: *Utdrag af ett wälb. hr. assessor Swedenborgs bref,
dateradt Stockholm, den 30 october, 1769* [Extract of a Letter
from the Noble Assessor Swedenborg, Dated Stockholm, October 30, 1769]

Publication facts: Göteborg: Immanuel Smitt, 1769. 4 pages.

Note: Swedenborg gave permission to Gabriel Beyer (1720–1779),
Swedish professor of theology, to publish this letter; Beyer edited it lightly and did so. Its contents, describing local ecclesiastical leaders as infernal, caused an uproar in Göteborg. For a
translation of the original letter, see Acton 1948–1955, 691–695.

Reference numbers: Stroh and Ekelöf 164; Whitehead 223

P123 *The Word's Earthly and Spiritual Meanings*

Language and form: Latin prose

Traditional title: *Natural and Spiritual Sense of the Word*

Original title: "De Sensu Naturali et Spirituali Verbi [On the
Word's Earthly and Spiritual Meanings]"

Publication facts: In *Von den Erdcörpern der Planeten* [On the Planetary Bodies], translated by F. C. Oetinger. [N.p.]: 1770, pages 222–226.

Note: Swedenborg sent the original manuscript (which is now lost) as an attachment to a letter he wrote from Amsterdam on November 8, 1768, to Oetinger. Oetinger subsequently published the letter, and the attachment in Latin, at the end of his German translation of *Other Planets* (see P105). For the second and third editions, see P124 and P128. For a Latin text and English translation of both the letter and the attachment, see Swedenborg 1975e, 288–295.

Reference numbers: Tafel 136; Hyde 185:2455; Stroh and Ekelöf 160; Whitehead 220

P124 | *The Word's Earthly and Spiritual Meanings,* **Second Edition**

Original title: "De Sensu Naturali et Spirituali Verbi [On the Word's Earthly and Spiritual Meanings]"

Publication facts: In *Von den Erdkörpern der Planeten* [On the Planetary Bodies], translated by F. C. Oetinger. 2nd edition. Frankfurt and Leipzig: 1771, pages 215–218.

Note: For the first and third editions, see P123 and P128.

Reference numbers: Tafel 136; Hyde 185:2456; Stroh and Ekelöf 160; Whitehead 220

P125 | *Deflation and Inflation,* **Second Edition**

Original title: *Oförgripelige tanckar om myntets uphöjande och nedsättjande* [Modest Thoughts on the Deflation and Inflation of Currency]

Publication facts: Uppsala: Johan Edman, 1771. 68 pages.

Note: Published anonymously. Revised and expanded version of a pamphlet published in 1722 (see P61). No English translation exists.

Reference number: Hyde 72:204

P126 | *True Christianity*

Language and form: Latin prose

Traditional titles: *Theorema; True Christian Religion; Universal Theology*

Original title: *Vera Christiana Religio, Continens Universam Theologiam Novae Ecclesiae a Domino apud Danielem Cap. VII:13–14, et in Apocalypsi Cap. XXI:1, 2 Praedictae* [True Christianity: Containing the Whole Theology of the New Church Predicted by the Lord in Daniel 7:13–14 and Revelation 21:1, 2]

Publication facts: Amsterdam: 1771. 542 pages.

Note: This work is a sequel to and fulfillment of P119. Although it contains much that is new, it draws heavily on P107–P112, P114, and P118. See also U160, U170, U172–U174, U178–U179. Swedenborg's last major publication, this systematic and highly structured work addresses many aspects of Christian and even specifically Lutheran belief, including the Trinity, the Bible, and efficacious actions, beliefs, and rituals. Includes narrative accounts of his spiritual experiences.

Reference numbers: Tafel 145; Hyde 195:2725; Stroh and Ekelöf 173; Whitehead 232

P127   *Reply to Ernesti*

Language and form: Latin prose

Traditional title: *Reply to Ernesti*

Original title: [Untitled][24]

Publication facts: [Amsterdam: 1771.] 1 page.

Note: See also U177. Ernesti had severely criticized Swedenborg's approach to revealing the spiritual or hidden meaning of Scripture. Cuno did not comply with Swedenborg's request that he (Cuno) print and distribute the letter, so Swedenborg published it himself. For a Latin text and English translation, see Swedenborg 1975e, 198–199.

Reference numbers: Hyde 197:2900; Whitehead 234

P128   *The Word's Earthly and Spiritual Meanings,* **Third Edition**

Original title: "De Sensu Naturali et Spirituali Verbi [On the Word's Earthly and Spiritual Meanings]"

Publication facts: In *Von den Erdcörpern der Planeten* [On the Planetary Bodies], translated by F. C. Oetinger. 3rd edition. Anspach: 1771,[25] pages 199–202.

Note: For the first and second editions, see P123 and P124.

Reference numbers: Tafel 136; Hyde 185:2457; Stroh and Ekelöf 160; Whitehead 220

---

24. This broadside, although printed, has no title.

25. The exact timing of the appearance of this work in relation to the previous work is not known. The previous item was published shortly before July 2, 1771, according to Hyde 197:2900.

IV. Category U: Documents by Swedenborg, Unpublished in His Lifetime (182)

U1 *Draft of One Epigram to Casaubon*
Language and form: Latin poetry
Status: Original extant
Traditional title: *Verses to Casaubon*
First words: "Marmore cur ornas tumulum? [Why do you adorn the tomb with marble?]"
Length: 4 lines
Written before or during: October 1710
Note: The first of two quatrains in honor of Casaubon, written in a letter to Benzelius. See also U2 just below. For a Latin text, English translation, and commentary, see Swedenborg [1707–1740] 1995b, 64–65 (no. 5), 152.
Reference numbers: Stroh and Ekelöf 9; Whitehead 9; Wainscot 4b

U2 *Draft of Another Epigram to Casaubon*
Language and form: Latin poetry
Status: Original extant
Traditional title: *Verses to Casaubon*
First words: "Urna Tuos cineres . . . habet [Your ashes the urn . . . holds]"
Length: 4 lines
Written before or during: October 1710
Note: The second of two quatrains in honor of Casaubon; see U1 just above. For a Latin text, English translation, and commentary, see Swedenborg [1707–1740] 1995b, 64–65 (no. 6), 152.
Reference numbers: Stroh and Ekelöf 9; Whitehead 9; Wainscot 4b

U3 *Lost Draft of "Verses to Brenner"*
Language and form: Latin poetry
Status: Original not extant; no copies survive
Traditional title: *To Sophia Brenner*
Written before or during: October 1710
Note: This draft of P10 was sent to Benzelius with a letter dated October 1710.
Reference numbers: Hyde 5:21; Whitehead 10

U4 *Lost Draft Invention of a Submersible Ship*
Language and form: Swedish or Latin prose
Status: Original not extant; no copies survive

Traditional title: *Submarine Ship*
Written before or during: September 1714
Note: Swedenborg mentions this document in a letter to Benzelius
    dated September 8, 1714.
Reference numbers: Hyde 6:24; Whitehead 12

U5 ***Lost Draft Invention of a Siphon***
Language and form: Swedish or Latin prose
Status: Original not extant; no copies survive
Traditional title: *New Siphon*
Written before or during: September 1714
Note: Swedenborg mentions this document in a letter to Benzelius
    dated September 8, 1714.
Reference numbers: Hyde 7:25; Whitehead 13

U6 ***Lost Draft on Hoisting Heavy Objects***
Language and form: Swedish or Latin prose
Status: Original not extant; no copies survive
Traditional title: *Lifting Weights*
Written before or during: September 1714
Note: Swedenborg mentions this document in a letter to Benzelius
    dated September 8, 1714.
Reference numbers: Hyde 8:26; Whitehead 14

U7 ***Lost Draft on Constructing Sluices***
Language and form: Swedish or Latin prose
Status: Original not extant; no copies survive
Traditional title: *Constructing Sluices*
Written before or during: September 1714
Note: Swedenborg mentions this document in a letter to Benzelius
    dated September 8, 1714.
Reference numbers: Hyde 9:27; Whitehead 15

U8 ***Lost Draft Invention of a Massive Water Pump***
Language and form: Swedish or Latin prose
Status: Original not extant; no copies survive
Traditional title: *Machine for Throwing Water*
Written before or during: September 1714
Note: Swedenborg mentions this document in a letter to Benzelius
    dated September 8, 1714.
Reference numbers: Hyde 10:28; Whitehead 16

U9 *Lost Draft Invention of a Drawbridge*
Language and form: Swedish or Latin prose
Status: Original not extant; no copies survive
Traditional titles: *Drawbridge; Draw-Bridge*
Written before or during: September 1714
Note: Swedenborg mentions this document in a letter to Benzelius dated September 8, 1714.
Reference numbers: Hyde 11:29; Whitehead 17

U10 *Lost Draft Inventions of Air Pumps*
Language and form: Swedish or Latin prose
Status: Original not extant; no copies survive
Traditional titles: *Air-Pumps; Air Pumps*
Written before or during: September 1714
Note: Swedenborg mentions this document in a letter to Benzelius dated September 8, 1714.
Reference numbers: Hyde 12:30; Whitehead 18

U11 *Lost Draft Invention of Air Guns*
Language and form: Swedish or Latin prose
Status: Original not extant; no copies survive
Traditional titles: *Air-Guns; Air Guns*
Written before or during: September 1714
Note: Swedenborg mentions this document in a letter to Benzelius dated September 8, 1714. Although this text is not extant, a carefully labeled but unexplained set of engraved drawings by Swedenborg of a multibarreled, air-powered machine gun was inserted into some versions of *Daedalus Hyperboreus* 4 (October–December 1716) after page 100.
Reference numbers: Hyde 13:31; Whitehead 19

U12 *Lost Draft Invention of a Universal Musical Instrument*
Language and form: Swedish or Latin prose
Status: Original not extant; no copies survive
Traditional title: *Universal Musical Instrument*
Written before or during: September 1714
Note: Swedenborg mentions this document in a letter to Benzelius dated September 8, 1714.
Reference numbers: Hyde 14:32; Whitehead 20

U13 *Lost Draft Method of Creating Shading in Engravings*
Language and form: Swedish or Latin prose
Status: Original not extant; no copies survive
Traditional titles: *Art of Shade-Drawing; Art of Shade Drawing*
Written before or during: September 1714
Note: Swedenborg mentions this document in a letter to Benzelius
   dated September 8, 1714.
Reference numbers: Hyde 15:33; Whitehead 21

U14 *Lost Draft Invention of a Water Clock*
Language and form: Swedish or Latin prose
Status: Original not extant; no copies survive
Traditional titles: *Water-Clock; Water Clock*
Written before or during: September 1714
Note: Swedenborg mentions this document in a letter to Benzelius
   dated September 8, 1714.
Reference numbers: Hyde 16:34; Whitehead 22

U15 *Lost Draft Inventions of a Mechanical Carriage and a Flying
Carriage*
Language and form: Swedish or Latin prose
Status: Original not extant; no copies survive
Traditional title: *Mechanical Carriage*
Written before or during: September 1714
Note: Swedenborg mentions this document in a letter to Benzelius
   dated September 8, 1714. See also P32, U22.
Reference numbers: Hyde 17:35; Whitehead 23

U16 *Lost Draft Method of Analyzing Feelings*
Language and form: Swedish or Latin prose
Status: Original not extant; no copies survive
Traditional title: *Inclinations of the Mind*
Written before or during: September 1714
Note: Swedenborg mentions this document in a letter to Benzelius
   dated September 8, 1714.
Reference numbers: Hyde 18:36; Whitehead 24

U17 *Lost Draft on Cords and Springs*
Language and form: Swedish or Latin prose
Status: Original not extant; no copies survive
Traditional title: *Cords and Springs*
Written before or during: September 1714

Note: Swedenborg mentions this document in a letter to Benzelius
dated September 8, 1714.
Reference numbers: Hyde 19:37; Whitehead 25

U18 *Draft on Types of Soil and Mud*
Language and form: Swedish prose
Status: Original extant
Traditional title: *Soils and Muds*
Original title: *Om åtskillig slagz jordmohner och gyttior* [On Several Types of Soils and Muds]
Length: 1 page
Written during or after: April 1716
Note: For an English translation, see Swedenborg 1992c, 1–2.
Reference numbers: Hyde 26:70; Stroh and Ekelöf 18; Whitehead 34

U19 *Lost Draft Reflections on Perspective*
Language and form: Swedish or Latin prose
Status: Original not extant; no copies survive
Traditional title: *Reflections on Perspective*
Written before or during: June 1716
Note: Swedenborg refers to this document in letters to Benzelius
dated March 4 and June 12, 1716.
Reference numbers: Hyde 24:67; Whitehead 32

U20 *Draft Memorandum on a Society of Sciences*
Language and form: Swedish prose
Status: Original extant
Traditional titles: *Draft Memorial on Mechanical Laboratory; Society of Sciences*
Original title: [Untitled]
Length: 1 page
Written between: July and November 1716
Note: For an English translation, see Acton 1948–1955, 123.
Reference numbers: Hyde 25:68; Stroh and Ekelöf 17; Whitehead 33

U21 *Draft on Fossils*
Language and form: Swedish prose
Status: Original extant
Traditional titles: *Fossils; On Fossils*

Original title: *Anmärckningar om musslor, sneckor, m.m. i kacksten och om skifwer* [Remarks on Mussels, Snails, and So On in Limestone and on Slate]
Length: 1 page
Written during: 1716?[26]
Note: For an English translation, see Swedenborg 1992c, 3–4.
Reference numbers: Hyde 27:72; Stroh and Ekelöf 19; Whitehead 35

U22   *Draft Invention of a Flying Machine*
Language and form: Swedish prose
Status: Original extant
Traditional title: *Flying Machine*
Original title: *Descriptio Machinae Daedaleae sive Volatilis* [Description of a Daedalian or Flying Machine]
Length: 1 page
Written before or during: September 1716
Note: See also P32, U15. Includes an illustration. For an English translation, see Swedenborg 1939, 20–24.
Reference numbers: Hyde 28:74; Stroh and Ekelöf 20; Whitehead 36

U23   *Draft Invention of a Siphoning Machine*
Language and form: Swedish prose
Status: Original extant
Traditional title: *Siphon*
Original title: *Machina Siphonica* [A Siphoning Machine]
Length: 1 page
Written before or during: September 1716
Note: No English translation exists. For a reproduction of the original, see Swedenborg 1869b, 20.
Reference numbers: Hyde 29:76; Stroh and Ekelöf 21; Whitehead 37

U24   *Draft on Sailing Upstream*
Language and form: Swedish prose
Status: Original extant
Traditional titles: *Sailing Upstream; Sailing Up Stream*
Original title: *Nya sett at segla emot strömmen . . .* [New Ways to Sail against the Stream . . .]

---

26. In the absence of better dating information about this work, I have followed the placements in Hyde's and Stroh and Ekelöf's lists.

Length: 3 pages
Written toward the end of: 1716
Note: For an English translation, see Swedenborg 1939, 27–30.
Reference numbers: Hyde 31:85; Stroh and Ekelöf 23; Whitehead 39

U25 *Draft on Small Tests and Experiments*
Language and form: Swedish prose
Status: Original extant
Traditional title: *Experiments*
Original title: *Pro Memoria om några små prof och experimenter* [Notes on Some Small Tests and Experiments]
Length: 1 page
Written toward the end of: 1716
Note: No English translation exists. For a reproduction of the original, see Swedenborg 1869b, 92.
Reference numbers: Hyde 32:89; Stroh and Ekelöf 24; Whitehead 40

U26 *Draft of a Screw Jack*
Language and form: Swedish prose
Status: Original extant
Traditional titles: *Screw-Jack; Screw Jack*
Original title: [Untitled]
Length: 3 pages
Written toward the end of: 1716
Note: No English translation exists. For an illustration and commentary, see Swedenborg 1939, 32–33.
Reference numbers: Hyde 33:91; Stroh and Ekelöf 25; Whitehead 41

U27 *Draft on Stereometry*
Language and form: Swedish prose
Status: Original extant
Traditional title: *Stereometry*
Original title: *Proportiones Stereometricae, och några nya stereometriska reglor* [Stereometric Proportions and Some New Principles of Stereometry]
Length: 3 pages
Written toward the end of: 1716
Note: No English translation exists. For a reproduction of the original, see Swedenborg 1869b, 100–101.
Reference numbers: Hyde 34:93; Stroh and Ekelöf 26; Whitehead 42

U28 *Draft on Calculating Lead Amounts*
Language and form: Swedish prose
Status: Original extant
Traditional title: *Weights*
Original title: *Uträkning på watns medeljärns, blys caliber när tyng-den är lika; från ung. lika marck* [The Use of Water to Calculate the Amount of Lead in Medium Quality Iron of the Same Weight and Source]
Length: 2 pages
Written toward the end of: 1716
Note: No English translation or reproduction of the original exists. The handwritten original is number 16 in codex 14a of the Benzelius Collection in the Diocesan Library, Linköping, Sweden.
Reference numbers: Whitehead 43; Wainscot 34a

U29 *Draft of a Crane*
Language and form: Swedish prose
Status: Original extant
Traditional title: *Crane*
Original title: *Beskrifning öfwer en kran* [Description of a Crane]
Length: 3 pages
Written toward the end of: 1716
Note: For an English translation, see Swedenborg 1939, 34–35.
Reference numbers: Hyde 35:95; Stroh and Ekelöf 27; Whitehead 44

U30 *Draft on Echo*
Language and form: Swedish prose
Status: Original extant
Traditional title: *Echo*
Original title: *Experiment om echo* [Experiment with Echoes]
Length: 2 pages
Written toward the end of: 1716
Note: No English translation exists. For a reproduction of the original, see Swedenborg 1869b, 205–206.
Reference numbers: Hyde 36:97; Stroh and Ekelöf 28; Whitehead 45

U31 *Draft Memorandum on Improvements at Carlscrona*
Language and form: Swedish prose
Status: Original extant
Traditional titles: *Improvements at Carlscrona; Improvements at Karlscrona; Memorial on Improvements at Karlscrona*

Original title: *Memorial på de förbättringar som wid Carlzcrona stå att practiseras* [Memorandum on the Improvements That Await Being Made at Carlscrona]
Length: 4 pages
Written between: December 1716 and May 1717
Note: A plan to build a dry dock for use by the Swedish navy. For an English translation, see Acton 1948–1955, 132–134.
Reference numbers: Hyde 41:107; Stroh and Ekelöf 35; Whitehead 50

U32 *Draft Memorandum on Salt Boileries*
Language and form: Swedish prose
Status: Original extant
Traditional titles: *Memorial on Salt Making; Salt-Boileries; Salt Boileries*
Original title: *Memorial om salt-sjuderiets inrättning i Swerige* [Memorandum on the Institution of Salt Boileries in Sweden]
Length: 4 pages
Written between: Late January and March 1717
Note: For an English translation, see Acton 1948–1955, 140–143.
Reference numbers: Tafel 13; Hyde 38:102; Stroh and Ekelöf 32; Whitehead 47

U33 *Draft on Derotation of the Earth*
Language and form: Swedish prose
Status: Original extant
Traditional title: *Stoppage of the Earth*
Original title: *En ny theorie om jordens afstannande* [A New Theory Concerning the Stoppage of the Earth]
Length: 38 pages
Written during: April 1717
Note: See also P48, U38. For an English translation, see Swedenborg 1950.
Reference numbers: Tafel 11; Hyde 40:105; Stroh and Ekelöf 34; Whitehead 49

U34 *Draft on Instituting an Observatory*
Language and form: Swedish prose
Status: Original extant
Traditional title: *Instituting an Observatory*
Original title: [Untitled]
Length: 4 pages

Written during: June 1717

Note: No English translation exists. For a reproduction of the original, see Swedenborg 1869b, 3–6.

Reference numbers: Tafel 9; Hyde 42:110; Stroh and Ekelöf 36; Whitehead 51

 Memorandum on Commerce and Manufacture

Language and form: Swedish prose

Status: Original extant

Traditional titles: *Commerce and Manufacture; Commerce and Manufactures; Commerce and Manufacturing*

Original title: [Untitled]

Length: 6 pages

Written: Probably at the end of 1717

Note: A proposal to establish a public stock company to control the export of Swedish iron and tar. No English translation exists.[27] For a reproduction of the original, see Swedenborg 1869b, 68–73.

Reference numbers: Tafel 12; Hyde 43:112; Stroh and Ekelöf 38; Whitehead 52

U36 Draft on Fire and Colors

Language and form: Swedish prose

Status: Original extant

Traditional titles: *Fire and Colors; Fire and Colours*

Original title: [Untitled]

Length: 6 pages

Written: Probably at the end of 1717

Note: For an English translation, see Swedenborg 1992c, 9–16.

Reference numbers: Tafel 14; Hyde 44:114; Stroh and Ekelöf 39; Whitehead 53

U37 Draft on a New Arithmetic

Language and form: Swedish prose

Status: Original extant

Traditional title: *New Arithmetic*

---

27. This item should not be confused with a June 11, 1717, memorandum to the king that Acton labeled "Memorial on Manufactures" (Acton 1948–1955, 155–156). Acton does not include U35 in his volumes of letters and memoranda.

Original title: *En ny räkenkonst, som omwexlas wid 8 i stelle then wahnliga wid thalet 10, hwarigenom all ting angående mynt, wicht, mål, och mått, monga resor lettare än effter wahnligheten uträknas* [A New Arithmetic, in Which 8 Is Exchanged for the Usual Number 10, Whereby All Things Relating to Money, Weight, Measures, and Dimensions Are Calculated Much More Easily Than They Customarily Are]

Length: 28 pages

Written: October 1718

Note: This work proposes a form of practical calculation using base 8 rather than the customary base 10. For an English translation, see Swedenborg 1941.

Reference numbers: Hyde 47:118; Stroh and Ekelöf 42; Whitehead 56

U38 *Draft of "Rotation of the Earth"*

Language and form: Swedish prose

Status: Original extant

Traditional title: *Earth's Revolution*

Original title: *En ny mening om jordens och planeternas gång och stånd* . . . [A New Opinion on the Earth's and Planets' Moving and Halting . . .]

Length: 32 pages

Written: 1718

Note: A draft of P48. See also U33. No English translation of this draft exists. For a Swedish text, see Swedenborg 1907–1911, 3:283–298.

Reference numbers: Stroh and Ekelöf 46; Wainscot 50a

U39 *Memorandum Proposing Redemption of Token Currency*

Language and form: Swedish prose

Status: Original extant

Traditional titles: *Memorial on Redemption of Tokens; Proposal for Redemption of Token Currency*

Original title: *Förslag till myntetecknens och sedlarnas inlösen* [A Proposal for Redeeming the Tokens and Paper Currency]

Length: 10 pages

Written: February 26, 1719

Note: For an English translation, see Acton 1948–1955, 205–211.

Reference numbers: [Not listed]

U40 *Notes on Geometry, Algebra, and Science*
Language and form: Latin prose
Status: Original extant
Traditional title: *Geometry and Algebra*
Original title: *Geometrica et Algebraica* [Observations on Geometry and Algebra]
Length: 203 pages
Written between: 1718 and 1720
Note: No English translation exists. Part of this manuscript, containing notes on geometry, algebra, and motion, is reproduced in Swedenborg 1870b, 1–100; there is no reproduction of the rest. The original itself is codex 86 in the Swedish Royal Academy of Sciences.
Reference numbers: Tafel 16; Hyde 58:143; Stroh and Ekelöf 53; Whitehead 67

U41 *Lost Paper on Small Vibrations*
Language and form: Swedish prose
Status: Original not extant; no copies survive
Traditional titles: *Motive and Vital Essence; On Tremulation; Tremulations*
Written before: October 1719
Note: See also P46, U42. Swedenborg submitted this paper to the Board of Health in Stockholm.
Reference numbers: Tafel 21; Hyde 53:130

U42 *Another Draft on Small Vibrations*
Language and form: Swedish prose
Status: Original extant
Traditional titles: *Motive and Vital Essence; On Tremulation; Tremulations*
Original title: [Untitled]
Length: 50 pages
Written between: Summer 1719 and February 1720
Note: See also P46, U41. For an English translation, see Swedenborg [1717] 1976d, 9–76.
Reference numbers: Tafel 21; Hyde 53:130; Stroh and Ekelöf 48; Whitehead 62

U43 *Drafts on Swedish Blast Furnaces*
Language and form: Swedish prose
Status: Originals extant

Traditional titles: *Blast-Furnaces; Blast Furnaces*

Original title: *Beskrifning öfwer swänska masugnar och theras blås-ningar* [Description of Swedish Blast Furnaces and Their Methods of Blasting Air]

Length: 86 pages (Board of Mines copy); 138 pages (Swedish Royal Academy of Sciences copy); 32 pages (Stockholm Royal Library copy)

Written before or on: November 2, 1719

Note: No English translation or reproduction of the originals exists. For the locations of the originals themselves, see just above under "Length."

Reference numbers: Tafel 20; Hyde 54:133–135; Stroh and Ekelöf 49; Whitehead 63

 Draft on Discovering Mines

Language and form: Swedish prose

Status: Original extant

Traditional title: *Discovering Mines*

Original title: *Nya anledningar till grufwors igenfinnande . . .* [New Hints for the Discovery of Mines . . .]

Length: 14 pages

Written before or during: November 1719

Note: This piece suggests that veins of ores have properties in the earth that determine the type of vegetation on the surface. For an English translation, see Swedenborg 1992c, 51–64.

Reference numbers: Tafel 22; Hyde 56:140; Stroh and Ekelöf 51; Whitehead 65

U45 **Draft on the Fall and Rise of Lake Wenner**

Language and form: Swedish prose

Status: Original extant

Traditional titles: *Fall and Rise of Lake Wenner; Fall and Rise of Wenner*

Original title: *Om Wennerns fallande och stigande . . .* [On the Fall and Rise of Wenner . . .]

Length: 7 pages (Swedish Royal Academy of Sciences copy); 12 pages (another copy not in Swedenborg's handwriting)

Written before or during: July 1720

Note: For an English translation, see Swedenborg 1992c, 65–73.

Reference numbers: Tafel 25; Hyde 60:148–149; Stroh and Ekelöf 55; Whitehead 69

Paper on Finding Longitudes
Language and form: Latin prose
Status: Original extant
Traditional title: *Finding Longitudes*
Original title: *I[n] N[omine] D[omini]: Methodus Nova Inveniendi Longitudines Locorum Terra Marique Ope Lunae* [In the Name of the Lord: A New Method of Finding the Longitudes of Places on Land and at Sea with the Help of the Moon]
Length: 12 pages
Written before or during: June 1721
Note: See also P35–P37, P44, P56, P62, P67, P99, P115. No English translation exists. The handwritten original is number 108 in codex 14a of the Benzelius Collection in the Diocesan Library, Linköping, Sweden.
Reference numbers: Hyde 64:166; Stroh and Ekelöf 62

 Draft of "Miscellaneous Observations"
Language and form: Latin prose
Status: Original extant
Traditional title: *Miscellaneous Observations*
Original title: [Untitled]
Length: 18 pages
Written before or during: November and December 1721
Note: Draft of P57–P58. See also U48. No English translation or reproduction of the original exists. The handwritten original is number 148 in codex 14a of the Benzelius Collection in the Diocesan Library, Linköping, Sweden.
Reference numbers: Tafel 33; Hyde 65:173; Stroh and Ekelöf 65

 Postscript to "Miscellaneous Observations"
Language and form: Latin prose
Status: Original extant
Traditional titles: *Miscellaneous Observations; Postscript to Miscellaneous Observations*
Original title: [Untitled]
Length: 1 page
Written: December 15, 1721
Note: This was a letter attached to a draft of "Miscellaneous Observations" (see U47) sent to Benzelius. See also P57–P58. No English translation or reproduction of the original exists. The

handwritten original is number 148 in codex 14a of the Benzelius
Collection in the Diocesan Library, Linköping, Sweden.
Reference numbers: Hyde 65:173; Stroh and Ekelöf 64; White-
head 74

U49 *Draft Verses to Augustinus*
Language and form: Latin poetry
Status: Original extant
Traditional titles: *Augustinus; Verses Entitled Augustinus*
Original title: *Augustinus*
Length: 4 lines and a dedication on a piece of paper
Written during: 1722?
Note: No English translation exists. For a Latin text, see Stroh
and Ekelöf 1910, 23–24.
Reference numbers: Stroh and Ekelöf 67; Whitehead 77; Wain-
scot 66a

U50 *Letter to Frederick I on Working Copper*
Language and form: Swedish prose
Status: Originals extant
Traditional title: *Working Copper*
Original title: *Stormägstigste allernådigste konung* [Most Mighty
and Gracious King]
Length: 2 pages (Archives of Board of Mines copy); 2 pages
(Diocesan Library in Linköping copy)
Written: July 14, 1722
Note: For an English translation, see Acton 1948–1955, 263–265.
Reference numbers: Hyde 68:193–194; Stroh and Ekelöf 69;
Whitehead 79

U51 *Manuscript Ode to Frederick I*
Language and form: Latin poetry
Status: Original extant
Traditional titles: *Festal Ode to Fredrik I; Ode to Fredrik I*
Original title: *Festivitas ad Diem in Fastis Solennem Frederici . . .*
[A Celebration of the Name-Day of Frederick . . .]
Length: 14 lines
Written before or during: July 1722
Note: For a Latin text, English translation, and commentary, see
Swedenborg [1707–1740] 1995b, 82–83, 162–164.
Reference numbers: Hyde 69:197; Stroh and Ekelöf 70; White-
head 80

U52 *Paper in Reply to Quensel*
Language and form: Latin prose
Status: Original extant
Traditional titles: *Reply to Quensel; Reply to Quenzel*
Original title: *Amicum Responsum ad Objectionem Factam a Cele-
berr. Dn. Professore Quenzel contra Cel. Assess. Swedenborgii Novam
Methodum Longitudinis Inveniendae Datum in Absentia Auctoris
ab Amico* [Friendly Response to the Objection Raised by Profes-
sor Quensel to Assessor Swedenborg's New Method of Finding
the Longitude, Delivered in the Author's Absence by a Friend]
Length: 2 pages
Written before or during: August 1722
Note: This paper, read before the Swedish Royal Academy of Sciences on August 17, 1722, was soon published; see P62. No
English translation exists. For a reproduction of the original,
see Swedenborg 1869b, 203–204.
Reference numbers: Hyde 70:199; Stroh and Ekelöf 71; Whitehead 81

U53 *Draft on Magnets*
Language and form: Latin prose
Status: Original extant
Traditional titles: *On the Magnet; The Magnet*
Original title: *De Magnete et Diversis Ejus Qualitatibus* [On Mag-
nets, and Their Various Properties]
Length: 297 pages
Written before or during: 1722
Note: Contains thirty-four illustrations. Portions of the work
were later used in Swedenborg's three-volume work on philoso-
phy and metallurgy (see P68–P70). No English translation or
reproduction of the original exists. The handwritten original
is codex 81 in the Swedish Royal Academy of Sciences.
Reference numbers: Tafel 37; Hyde 71:202; Stroh and Ekelöf 74;
Whitehead 82

U54 *Draft Calculation of Currency*
Language and form: Swedish prose
Status: Original extant
Traditional titles: *Calculation Concerning Currency; Swedish Cur-
rency and Finance*

Original title: *Calculation öfwer 100rd. smt. silfwer . . .* [Calculation of 100 smt.[28] of silver . . .]

Length: 10 pages

Written before or during: 1722

Note: This document largely comprises mathematical sums. No English translation exists. For a reproduction, see Swedenborg 1934, 287–291.

Reference numbers: Whitehead 83; Wainscot 71a

U55 *Memorandum on Balance of Trade*

Language and form: Swedish prose

Status: Original extant

Traditional titles: *Memorial on Balance of Trade; Swedish Finance*

Original title: *Swedenborgs memorial angående balancen i handelen* [Swedenborg's Memorandum Concerning Balance of Trade]

Length: 12 pages

Written before or on: February 5, 1723

Note: For an English translation, see Acton 1948–1955, 289–296.

Reference numbers: Hyde 74:207; Stroh and Ekelöf 77; Whitehead 87

U56 *Memorandum against the Priority Given to Nobler Metals*

Language and form: Swedish prose

Status: Original extant

Traditional titles: *Discrimination against Iron; Memorial in Favor of Iron; Mining Copper and Iron*

Original title: *Swedenborgs memorial angående bearbetandet af jern och koppar i Sverige* [Swedenborg's Memorandum Concerning the Working of Iron and Copper in Sweden]

Length: 4 pages

Written before or on: February 18, 1723

Note: A proposal to eliminate the favored status of copper in mining areas and instead produce more iron for export. For an English translation, see Acton 1948–1955, 301–303.

Reference numbers: Hyde 75:209; Stroh and Ekelöf 78; Whitehead 88

U57 *First Memorandum against Excluding Foreign Traders*

Language and form: Swedish prose

Status: Original extant

---

28. "Smt." is an old Swedish abbreviation for *silvermynt,* a unit of currency.

Traditional title: *Memorial against Exclusion of Foreign Traders*
Original title: [Untitled]
Length: 1 page
Written before or on: April 2, 1723
Note: See also U59. For an English translation, see Acton 1948–1955, 305.
Reference numbers: Hyde 75:209; Stroh and Ekelöf 78; Whitehead 88

U58 *Memorandum on Establishing Ironworks*
Language and form: Swedish prose
Status: Original extant
Traditional titles: *Establishing Iron-Works; Establishing Iron Works*
Original title: *Swedenborgs memorial angående jernverks anläggande i Sverige* [Swedenborg's Memorandum Concerning Establishing Ironworks in Sweden]
Length: 8 pages
Written before or on: April 11, 1723
Note: For an English translation, see Acton 1948–1955, 306–309.
Reference numbers: Hyde 76:211; Stroh and Ekelöf 79; Whitehead 89

U59 *Second Memorandum against Excluding Foreign Traders*
Language and form: Swedish prose
Status: Original extant
Traditional titles: *Exclusion of Foreign Traders; Memorial against Exclusion of Foreign Traders; Memorial on Exclusion of Foreign Traders*
Original title: [Untitled]
Length: 9 pages
Written before or on: April 13, 1723
Note: See also U57. For an English translation, see Acton 1948–1955, 310–313.
Reference number: Wainscot 76a

U60 *Memorandum on Production of Iron*
Language and form: Swedish prose
Status: Original extant
Traditional titles: *Memorial in Favor of Iron; Production of Iron*
Original title: *Swedenborgs memorial angående jernproduktionen i Sverige* [Swedenborg's Memorandum Concerning the Production of Iron in Sweden]
Length: 3 pages

Written between: May 15 and 22, 1723
Note: For an English translation, see Acton 1948–1955, 315–318.
Reference numbers: Hyde 77:213; Stroh and Ekelöf 80; White-
head 90

U61 *Lost Draft on Copper*
Language and form: Latin prose
Status: Original not extant; no copies survive
Traditional title: *On Copper*
Written between: January and March 1724
Note: Hyde presumes that this material formed the basis for P70,
pages 105–109.
Reference numbers: Hyde 78:215; Whitehead 91

U62 *Fair Copy on Extracting Silver*
Language and form: Latin prose
Status: Original extant
Traditional title: *On Silver*
Original title: *De Secretione Argenti a Cupro* . . . [On the Extrac-
tion of Silver from Copper . . .]
Length: 367 pages
Written between: 1724 and 1733
Note: See P64, U63–U65. This material was used in the writing
of P70, part 1. No English translation exists. For a reproduction
of the original, see Swedenborg 1927b.
Reference numbers: Tafel 38:3; Hyde 79:216; Stroh and Ekelöf 83;
Whitehead 92

U63 *Fair Copy on Vitriol*
Language and form: Latin prose
Status: Original extant
Traditional title: *On Vitriol*
Original title: *De Victriolo deque Modis Victriolum Elixandi* . . .
[On Vitriol and on Methods of Boiling Vitriol . . .]
Length: 450 pages
Written between: 1724 and 1733
Note: See P64, U62, U64–U65. Contains three illustrations. No
English translation exists. For a reproduction of the original,
see Swedenborg 1927c.
Reference numbers: Tafel 38:4; Hyde 80:217; Stroh and Ekelöf 83;
Whitehead 93

U64 *Fair Copy on Sulfur and Pyrites*
Language and form: Latin prose
Status: Original extant
Traditional title: *On Sulphur and Pyrites*
Original title: *De Sulphure et Pyrite* [On Sulfur and Pyrites]
Length: 331 pages
Written between: 1724 and 1733
Note: See P64, U62–U63, U65. Contains three illustrations. Used in writing P70, part 2. No English translation exists. For a reproduction of the original, see Swedenborg 1927a.
Reference numbers: Tafel 38:1; Hyde 81:218; Stroh and Ekelöf 83; Whitehead 94

U65 *Fair Copy on Salt*
Language and form: Latin prose
Status: Original extant
Traditional titles: *On Common Salt; On Salt*
Original title: *De Sale Communi: H.E., de Sale Fossili vel Gemmeo, Marino, et Fontano* [On Common Salt: That Is, on Rock or Glittering Salt, Sea Salt, and Spring Salt]
Length: 329 pages
Written between: 1724 and 1733
Note: See P64, U62–U64. For an English translation, see Swedenborg 1983–1992.
Reference numbers: Tafel 38:2; Hyde 82:219; Stroh and Ekelöf 83; Whitehead 95

U66 *One Draft for "Basic Principles of Nature"*
Language and form: Latin prose
Status: Original extant
Traditional titles: *First Principles; Lesser Principia; Minor Principia*
Original title: *Sit Felix Faustumque!—Principia Rerum Naturalium ab Experimentis et Geometria sive ex Posteriori et Priori Educta* [May It Be Fortunate and Successful! The Basic Principles of Nature Derived through Both Experiments and Reasoning, That Is, Both Inductively and Deductively]
Length: 560 pages
Written before or during: November 1729
Note: See also P68, U67, U75. For an English translation, see Swedenborg [1734] 1912, 2:297–528. Tafel and Hyde originally

dated this work to 1720, but a letter from Swedenborg to Celsius of November 27, 1729 (see Acton 1948–1955, 436–437) convinced later scholars to move the date to 1729.

Reference numbers: Tafel 26; Hyde 59:145; Stroh and Ekelöf 89; Whitehead 96

U67 *Miscellaneous Drafts for "Philosophical and Metallurgical Works"*
Language and form: Latin prose
Status: Original extant
Traditional titles: *Addenda to "Principia"; Adversaria in Principia Rerum Naturalium*
Original titles: *In Praefatione Mea ad Principia* [In My Preface to "Basic Principles of Nature"]; *De Puncti Attributis* [On the Attributes of the Point]; *De Ordine Particularum* [On the Order of the Particles]; *Quod Natura Sit Simile Telae Araneae* [Nature Is like a Spider's Web]; *De Aqua Caementaria Hungariae* [On the Cement Liquid in Hungary]; *Processus Fusoris Cupri ad Cuttenberg, Bohemiae* [The Process for Smelting Copper Used in Cuttenberg, Bohemia]
Length: 27 pages
Written between: July 15, 1730, and August 21, 1733
Note: See also P68–P70, U66, U75. For an English translation, see Swedenborg 1992c, 94–114.
Reference numbers: Tafel 40; Hyde 86:226

U68 *Draft on the Motion of the Elements*
Language and form: Latin prose
Status: Original extant
Traditional title: *Motion of the Elements*
Original title: *Generaliter de Motu Elementorum* [On the Motion of the Elements in General]
Length: 5 pages
Written before or during: May 1733
Note: For an English translation, see Swedenborg 1992c, 85–93.
Reference numbers: Tafel 39; Hyde 83:220; Whitehead 99

U69 *Journal of 1733 to 1734*
Language and form: Latin prose
Status: Original extant

Traditional title: *Journal*
Original title: [Untitled]
Length: 110 pages
Written between: October 1733 and March 1734
Note: See also U80. For an English translation, see Tafel 1877, 6–74.
Reference numbers: Tafel 44; Hyde 88:250; Whitehead 105

U70 *Notes on Wolff's "Empirical Psychology"*
Language and form: Latin prose
Status: Original extant
Traditional title: *Wolff's Ontology and the Principia*
Original title: [Untitled]
Length: 48 pages
Written between: May 10, 1733, and March 4, 1734
Note: A comparison with the views of Wolff, whose work on empirical psychology was published in 1732. See also U71. For an English translation, see Swedenborg 1923b.
Reference numbers: Tafel 42; Hyde 84:222; Whitehead 100

U71 *Quotation from Wolff's "Empirical Psychology"*
Language and form: Latin prose
Status: Original not extant; copies survive
Traditional title: *Empirical Psychology*
Original title: [Untitled]
Length: 1 page
Written during or after: 1733
Note: See also U70. No English translation exists. The Swedenborg Library in Bryn Athyn, Pa., and the Swedenborg Society in London have unpublished copies of the original.
Reference numbers: Hyde 85:225; Whitehead 101

U72 *Extracts from Schurig and Translation of Richter*
Language and form: Latin prose
Status: Original extant
Traditional titles: *Human Body; Observations on the Human Body*
Original title: [Untitled]
Length: 53 pages
Written between: October 1733 and March 1734
Note: In this portion of his manuscripts Swedenborg penned forty-three pages of extracts from Schurig 1729, and made a ten-page Latin translation from German of selections of Richter 1722. Although Swedenborg was originally thought to have authored the

latter material, it is now clear that he translated it instead. No English translation, Latin edition, or reproduction of the extracts from Schurig 1729 exists; the original itself is found in codex 88, pages 131–152, 216–236, in the Swedish Royal Academy of Sciences. For an English translation of Swedenborg's translation of portions of Richter 1722, see Swedenborg 1992c, 147–156.

Reference numbers: Tafel 43; Hyde 89:255; Whitehead 106

U73 *Draft of "The Infinite" on the Soul-Body Mechanism*
Language and form: Latin prose
Status: Original extant
Traditional title: *Mechanism of the Soul and Body*
Original title: *De Mechanismo Animae et Corporis* [Mechanism of the Soul and Body]
Length: 16 pages
Written between: Late 1733 and early 1734
Note: See also P71. For an English translation, see Swedenborg 1992c, 123–146.
Reference numbers: Tafel 41; Hyde 87:242

U74 *Notes about Faith in Christ*
Language and form: Latin prose
Status: Original extant
Traditional title: *Faith in Christ*
Original title: *De Fide in Christum* [On Faith in Christ]
Length: 1 page
Written before or during: February 1734
Note: For a Latin edition and English translation, see Swedenborg 1923b, 158–161.
Reference numbers: Hyde 84:222; Wainscot 84a

U75 *Extracts from "Basic Principles of Nature"*
Language and form: Latin prose
Status: Original extant
Traditional titles: *Abstract of the Principia; Summary of the Principia*
Original title: *Ex "Principiis Rerum Naturalium" Meis* [Extracts from My "Basic Principles of Nature"]
Length: 37 pages
Written between: March 1734 and July 1736
Note: See also P68, U67. For an English translation, see Swedenborg 1904b.
Reference numbers: Tafel 47; Hyde 91:259; Whitehead 109

U76 *Draft Memorandum against War with Russia*
Language and form: Swedish prose
Status: Original extant
Traditional titles: *Declaring War against Russia; Project on War with Russia*
Original title: *Projekt* [Draft]
Length: 12 pages
Written during or after: July 1734
Note: A memorandum to the Secret Committee in the House of Nobles on the folly of war against Russia. For an English translation, see Acton 1948–1955, 468–475.
Reference numbers: Hyde 90:257; Stroh and Ekelöf 97; Whitehead 107

U77 *Quotations from Wolff on General Knowledge*
Language and form: Latin prose
Status: Original extant
Original title: *Ex Wolfio de Scientia Generali* [Extracts from Wolff on Knowledge in General]
Length: 93 pages
Written: July 21, 1736
Note: No English translation exists. For a reproduction of the original, see Swedenborg 1870a, 273–365.
Reference number: Hyde 84:222

U78 *Notes on the Infinite and the Finite*
Language and form: Latin prose
Status: Original extant
Traditional titles: *The Infinite and Finite; The Infinite and the Finite*
Original title: [Untitled]
Length: 8 pages
Written before or during: August 1738
Note: For an English translation, see Swedenborg 1992c, 115–122.
Reference numbers: Hyde 92:262; Whitehead 110

U79 *First Draft of Three Transactions on the Brain*
Language and form: Latin prose
Status: Original extant
Traditional titles: *The Brain; The Cerebrum*
Original title: [Untitled]
Length: 1,394 pages
Written before or during: August 1738

Note: See also U84, U88–U89, U111. This material is found in manuscript codex 65 in the Swedish Royal Academy of Sciences. Acton labeled this "the Venice work on the cerebrum." For an English translation, see Swedenborg 1976g, vol. 1.

Reference numbers: Tafel 48; Hyde 100:312; Stroh and Ekelöf 98; Whitehead 120

U80 *Draft Summary of Trips Abroad*
Language and form: Swedish prose
Status: Original extant
Traditional title: *Journeys*
Original title: *Mina resors beskrifning* [Description of My Journeys]
Length: 45 pages
Written before or during: March 1739
Note: See also U69. Includes travel sketches for the years 1710, 1721, 1733, 1736, 1737, 1738, and 1739. For an English translation, see Tafel 1877, 3–6, 75–130.
Reference numbers: Tafel 49; Hyde 93:264; Whitehead 111

U81 *Quotations from Other Authors Concerning Muscles*
Language and form: Latin prose
Status: Original extant
Traditional title: *Muscles in General*
Original title: *De Musculis in Genere* [Muscles in General]
Length: 22 pages
Written during or after: March 1739
Note: A manuscript fragment of anatomical quotations from noted Dutch physician Hermann Boerhaave (1668–1738), Vieussens, British physician and anatomist Thomas Willis (1621–1675), and Winslow. No English translation or reproduction of the original exists. For the original itself, see codex 65, pages 1913–1934, in the Swedish Royal Academy of Sciences.
Reference numbers: Hyde 94:274; Stroh and Ekelöf 98; Whitehead 112

U82 *Notes about a Pathway to Knowledge of the Soul*
Language and form: Latin prose
Status: Original extant
Traditional title: *Knowledge of the Soul*
Original title: *De Via ad Cognitionem Animae* [On the Pathway to a Knowledge of the Soul]
Length: 5 pages

Written during or after: March 1739

Note: For an English translation, see Swedenborg 1992c, 157–161.

Reference numbers: Tafel 50; Hyde 95:275; Stroh and Ekelöf 98; Whitehead 113

U83 *Notes about Faith and Good Works*

Language and form: Latin prose

Status: Original extant

Traditional title: *Faith and Good Works*

Original title: *De Fide et Bonis Operibus* [On Faith and Good Works]

Length: 21 pages

Written during or after: March 1739

Note: For an English translation, see Swedenborg 1984c, 11–18.

Reference numbers: Tafel 51; Hyde 96:280; Stroh and Ekelöf 98; Whitehead 114

U84 *Quotations from Others' Works on the Brain*

Language and form: Latin prose

Status: Original extant

Traditional title: *The Cerebrum*

Original title: [Untitled]

Length: 300 pages

Written toward the end of: 1739

Note: See also U79, U88–U89, U111. Contains anatomical excerpts from British anatomist Humphrey Ridley (1653–1708), Vieussens, and Winslow. This material is found in manuscript codex 88, pages 366–495, 544–713, in the Swedish Royal Academy of Sciences. No English translation or reproduction of the original exists.

Reference number: Hyde 100:314

U85 *Notes about the Skin and Tongue*

Language and form: Latin prose

Status: Original extant

Traditional title: *The Skin and the Tongue*

Original title: *De Cute, deque Lingua* [On the Skin and Tongue]

Length: 12 pages

Written around: 1740

Note: No English translation exists. For a reproduction of the original, see Swedenborg 1869a, 1–12.

Reference numbers: Hyde 98:305; Whitehead 117

Brief Notes on Corpuscular Philosophy
Language and form: Latin prose
Status: Original extant
Traditional title: *Corpuscular Philosophy in Brief*
Original title: *Philosophia Corpuscularis in Compendio* [Corpuscular Philosophy in Brief]
Length: 1 page
Written around: 1740
Note: For an English translation, see Swedenborg 1992c, 162–164.
Reference numbers: Tafel 55; Whitehead 123

 Notes Proposing an Algebraic Language for Philosophy
Language and form: Latin prose
Status: Original extant
Traditional titles: *Characteristic and Mathematical Philosophy of Universals; Philosophy of Universals*
Original title: *Philosophia Universalium Characteristica et Mathematica* [Philosophy of All Things Expressed in Characters and Mathematical Symbols]
Length: 5 pages
Written around: 1740
Note: For an English translation, see Swedenborg 1992c, 165–171.
Reference numbers: Tafel 53; Whitehead 126

 Additions to First Draft on the Brain
Language and form: Latin prose
Status: Original extant
Traditional title: *The Cerebrum*
Original title: [Untitled]
Length: 124 pages
Written before or during: January 1740
Note: See also U79, U84, U89, U111. This material is found in manuscript codex 57 in the Swedish Royal Academy of Sciences. Acton labeled this the "Amsterdam additions." For an English translation of all but the last forty pages of this material, see Swedenborg 1976g, 2:7–122.
Reference numbers: Tafel 54; Hyde 100:316

U89 *Second, Rearranged Draft on the Brain*
Language and form: Latin prose
Status: Original extant
Traditional title: *The Cerebrum*

Original title: [Untitled]

Length: 627 pages

Written before or during: 1740

Note: See also U79, U84, U88, U111. This material is found in manuscript codex 55 in the Swedish Royal Academy of Sciences. Acton labeled this the "Stockholm work." Albeit heavily rearranged, some of this material has been translated in Swedenborg 1882–1887.[29]

Reference numbers: Tafel 56a; Hyde 100:318

 Paper on the Declination at Uppsala

Language and form: Swedish prose

Status: Original extant

Traditional title: *Declination of the Needle*

Original title: *Uträkning af magnetens declination till Upsala meridian . . .* [Calculation of the Needle's Declination at the Uppsala Meridian . . .]

Length: 21 pages

Written before or during: December 1740

Note: A reply to Celsius, who had publicly challenged the accuracy of some of Swedenborg's astronomical observations. For an English translation, see Tafel 1875, 568–577.

Reference numbers: Tafel 58; Hyde 101:333; Stroh and Ekelöf 106; Whitehead 124

U91 *Notes on Mathematics and Physics*

Language and form: Latin prose

Status: Original extant

Traditional title: *Mathematics and Physics*

Original title: [Untitled]

Length: 10 pages

Written around: 1741

Note: No English translation exists. For a reproduction of the original, see Swedenborg 1870a, 175–179.

Reference numbers: Hyde 104:348; Whitehead 129

---

29. For a detailed correlation of Swedenborg 1882–1887 with these and other manuscripts on the brain, see Hyde 100:322–323.

U92 *Quotations on Various Philosophical and Theological Topics*
Language and form: Latin prose
Status: Original extant
Traditional titles: *A Philosopher's Note Book; Philosophical and Theological Notes*
Original title: [Untitled]
Length: 228 pages
Written around: 1741
Note: An extensive listing of notes and definitions of various philosophical and theological terms. For an English translation, see Swedenborg 1976e.
Reference numbers: Hyde 105:350; Whitehead 130

U93 *Draft Introduction to a Rational Psychology*
Language and form: Latin prose
Status: Original extant
Traditional titles: *Correspondences and Representations; Introduction to Rational Psychology*[30]
Original title: [Untitled]
Length: 26 pages
Written around: 1741[31]
Note: See also P74, U101. For an English translation, see Swedenborg 1984c, 217–262.
Reference numbers: Tafel 59; Hyde 106:352; Whitehead 131

U94 *Lost Draft on Divine Prudence*
Language and form: Latin prose
Status: Original not extant; no copies survive
Traditional title: *Divine Prudence*
Reported title: *De Prudentia Divina, Praedestinatione, Fato, Fortuna; et Prudentia Humana* [On Divine Prudence, Predestination, Fate, Fortune; and Human Prudence]

---

30. On the term "rational psychology," see note 19 on page 425 above.

31. Hyde dates this piece to 1741, because it occurs in three segments among the notes that comprise U92, which were written in 1741. Acton, however, takes the contents of this piece as indicating that it came after U106, which he reassigns to "the early or middle part of 1744." With some apparent hesitation—"it would indeed seem not improbable," he says of the dating—he places this piece in 1744 as well; see Swedenborg 1984c, xxvii–xxviii.

Written around: 1742[32]

Note: In P76, just after the title page, Swedenborg listed four books soon to be published, of which this is one; evidence in U101 suggests that the piece was in fact written, although it has since been lost; see Hyde 113:384 (= Hyde 1906, 86).

Reference numbers: Hyde 103:347; Whitehead 127

 Draft on the Soul and the Body
Language and form: Latin prose
Status: Original extant
Traditional title: *Soul and Body*
Original title: *Transactio Prima de Anima et Ejus et Corporis Harmonia in Genere* [First Treatise on the Soul and the Harmony between It and the Body in General]
Length: 45 pages
Written before or during: 1742
Note: For an English translation, see Swedenborg 1984c, 21–64.
Reference numbers: Tafel 61; Hyde 107:354; Whitehead 132

 Draft on Red Blood
Language and form: Latin prose
Status: Original extant
Traditional title: *Red Blood*
Original title: *De Sanguine Rubro* [On Red Blood]
Length: 24 pages
Written before or during: 1742[33]
Note: For an English translation, see Swedenborg 1984c, 95–114.
Reference numbers: Tafel 62; Hyde 109:364; Whitehead 134

U97 *Draft on the Soul's Fluid*
Language and form: Latin prose
Status: Original extant
Traditional titles: *Animal Spirit; Animal Spirits*

---

32. Hyde's evidence, but not his date, is accepted here. He dates the work to 1741, but his evidence points to 1742, since in that year the work is advertised as already written but not yet printed. See Hyde 103:347.

33. All bibliographers agree that this item and the four that follow it make a set. The order in which they should appear is up for debate. Tafel and I follow the sequence in which they appear in the handwritten original. Hyde presents them in the order U97, U96, U98, U100, U99. In Swedenborg 1984c, Acton presents them in the order U99, U97, U96, U100, U98.

Original title: *De Spiritu Animali* [The Soul's Fluid][34]
Length: 24 pages
Written before or during: 1742
Note: For an English translation, see Swedenborg 1984c, 75–92.
Reference numbers: Tafel 63; Hyde 108:359; Whitehead 133

U98 *Draft on Sensation*
Language and form: Latin prose
Status: Original extant
Traditional title: *Sensation*
Original title: *De Sensatione, seu de Corporis Passione* [On Sensation, or the Passive Organs of the Body]
Length: 13 pages
Written before or during: 1742
Note: For an English translation, see Swedenborg 1984c, 145–153.
Reference numbers: Tafel 64; Hyde 110:369; Whitehead 135

U99 *Draft on the Origin of the Soul*
Language and form: Latin prose
Status: Original extant
Traditional title: *Origin of the Soul*
Original title: *De Origine et Propagatione Animae* [On the Origin and the Propagation of the Soul]
Length: 8 pages
Written before or during: 1742
Note: For an English translation, see Swedenborg 1984c, 67–71.
Reference numbers: Tafel 65; Hyde 112:379; Whitehead 137

U100 *Draft on Action*
Language and form: Latin prose
Status: Original extant
Traditional title: *Action*
Original title: *De Actione* [On Action]
Length: 32 pages
Written before or during: 1742
Note: For an English translation, see Swedenborg 1984c, 117–142.
Reference numbers: Tafel 66; Hyde 111:374; Whitehead 136

---

34. On the fact that the Latin word *animalis* is sometimes not to be translated "animal" see note 18 on page 425 above.

U101   *Draft of a Rational Psychology*
Language and form: Latin prose
Status: Original extant
Traditional title: *Rational Psychology*[35]
Original title: [Untitled]
Length: 240 pages
Written before or during: 1742
Note: See also P74, U93. For an English translation, see Swedenborg 2001a.
Reference numbers: Tafel 67; Hyde 113:384; Whitehead 139

U102   *Draft on Ontology*
Language and form: Latin prose
Status: Original extant
Traditional title: *Ontology*
Original title: *Ontologia* [Ontology]
Length: 20 pages
Written before or during: 1742
Note: Quotations on various subjects from French philosopher Scipion Dupleix (1569–1661), Scottish philosopher and theologian Robert Baron (1593?–1639), and Wolff, with comments. For an English translation, see Swedenborg 1901.
Reference numbers: Tafel 68; Hyde 114:390; Whitehead 140

U103   *Commonplace Book*
Language and form: Latin prose
Status: Original extant
Traditional titles: *Common-Place Book; Common Place Book*
Original title: [Untitled]
Length: 226 pages
Written before or during: 1742
Note: No English translation exists. For a Latin edition in typescript form, see Swedenborg 1966.
Reference numbers: Hyde 115:394; Whitehead 141

U104   *Draft on the Fiber*
Language and form: Latin prose
Status: Original extant

---

35. On the term "rational psychology," see note 19 on page 425 above.

Traditional titles: *The Cerebrum; The Fiber*
Original title: [Untitled]
Length: 369 pages
Written around: 1742
Note: For an English translation, see Swedenborg 1976a.
Reference numbers: Tafel 57; Hyde 100:320

U105 *Draft on Metaphysics*
Language and form: Latin prose
Status: Original extant
Traditional title: *Metaphysics*
Original title: [Untitled]
Length: 38 pages
Written around: 1742
Note: No English translation exists. For a reproduction of the first portion of the work, see Swedenborg 1869a, 343–348. For the original itself, see codex 37, pages 218–255, in the Swedish Royal Academy of Sciences.
Reference numbers: Hyde 116:395; Whitehead 142

U106 *Draft of a Hieroglyphic Key*
Language and form: Latin prose
Status: Original extant
Traditional title: *Hieroglyphic Key*
Original title: *Clavis Hieroglyphica Arcanorum Naturalium et Spiritualium per Viam Representationum et Correspondentiarum* [A Hieroglyphic Key to the Secrets of Material and Spiritual Things by Way of Representations and Correspondences]
Length: 48 pages
Written around: 1742
Note: "Hieroglyphic" as used by Swedenborg here designates a method of representing something that is hidden or secret, not an ancient Egyptian form of writing. For an English translation, see Swedenborg 1984c, 157–194.
Reference numbers: Tafel 60; Hyde 117:397; Stroh and Ekelöf 115; Whitehead 143

U107 *Draft on the Reproductive Organs*
Language and form: Latin prose
Status: Original extant

Traditional titles: *Anatomy of the Body; Generation; The Reproductive Organs*

Original title: [Untitled]

Length: 272 pages

Written around: 1743

Note: For an English translation, see Swedenborg 1928.

Reference numbers: Tafel 69; Hyde 118:406; Whitehead 145

U108 *Notes on Swammerdam's "Book of Nature"*

Language and form: Latin prose

Status: Original extant

Traditional title: *Swammerdam's Book of Nature*

Original title: *Johannis Swammerdamii "Biblia Naturae"* [Jan Swammerdam's "Book of Nature"]

Length: 94 pages

Written around: 1743

Note: Swedenborg's notes on a book by Dutch naturalist Jan Swammerdam (1637–1680), published in Leiden in 1737, which described insects and small aquatic animals. For English translations of brief portions of these notes by Swedenborg, see Iungerich 1923 and Swedenborg 1923a.[36] For a reproduction of the original notes, see Swedenborg 1869a, 184–264.

Reference numbers: Tafel 70; Hyde 119:413; Whitehead 146

U109 *Journal of Dreams*

Language and form: Swedish prose

Status: Original extant

Traditional titles: *Dreams; Journal of Dreams*

Original title: [Untitled]

Length: 108 pages

Written between: July 1743 and December 1744

Note: A private diary kept by Swedenborg, 1743–1744, analyzing the symbolism in his dreams. For an English translation with commentary, see Swedenborg 2001b.

Reference numbers: Tafel 72; Hyde 123:428; Stroh and Ekelöf 120; Whitehead 152

---

36. Iungerich 1923 contains several lengthy passages from Swedenborg's notes on Swammerdam translated into English. Swedenborg 1923a is a translation of four pages of the photolithographed original (namely, Swedenborg 1869a, 231–234).

U110 *Draft on the Five Senses*
Language and form: Latin prose
Status: Original extant
Traditional titles: *Physical and Optical Experiments; Sense in General; The Five Senses*
Original title: [Untitled]
Length: 195 pages
Written before or during: July 1744
Note: For an English translation, see Swedenborg 1976b.
Reference numbers: Tafel 73, 75; Hyde 120:415; Whitehead 149

U111 *Further Notes on the Brain*
Language and form: Latin prose
Status: Original extant
Traditional titles: *The Brain; The Brain II*
Original title: [Untitled]
Length: 44 pages
Written before or during: July 1744
Note: See also U79, U84, U88–U89. Acton labeled this the "London additions." This material is found in manuscript codex 58 in the Swedish Royal Academy of Sciences. Albeit rearranged, all this material has been translated into English in Swedenborg 1882–1887.[37]
Reference numbers: Tafel 76; Hyde 121:423; Whitehead 150

U112 *Notes on the Muscles of the Face and Abdomen*
Language and form: Latin prose
Status: Original extant
Traditional title: *Muscles of the Face and Abdomen*
Original title: *De Musculis Faciei* [On the Muscles of the Face]
Length: 14 pages
Written before or during: July 1744
Note: No published English translation exists; a typescript translation by Eldred E. Iungerich in 1924 can be found at the Swedenborg Library in Bryn Athyn, Pa.
Reference numbers: Tafel 74; Hyde 122:426; Whitehead 151

---

37. For a detailed correlation of Swedenborg 1882–1887 with this manuscript on the brain, see Hyde 121:425.

U113　*Draft of "Worship and Love of God, Part 3"*
Language and form: Latin prose
Status: Original extant
Traditional title: *Worship and Love of God*
Original title: *Pars Tertia, de Vita Conjugii Paris Primogeniti* [Part 3: Concerning the Life of the Firstborn Married Couple]
Length: 26 pages
Written during: 1745
Note: See also P81–P82, U114. For an English translation, see Swedenborg 1996x, 247–278.
Reference numbers: Tafel 79; Hyde 125:461; Stroh and Ekelöf 123; Whitehead 154

U114　*Page Proofs of a Portion of "Worship and Love of God, Part 3"*
Language and form: Latin prose
Status: Original extant
Traditional title: *Worship and Love of God*
Original title: *Pars Tertia, de Vita Conjugii Paris Primogeniti* [Part 3: Concerning the Life of the Firstborn Married Couple]
Length: 16 pages
Written during: 1745
Note: For an English translation, see U113. See also P81–P82. For a reproduction of the first nine pages of these page proofs, see Swedenborg 1870c, 87–91.
Reference numbers: Tafel 79; Hyde 125:460; Stroh and Ekelöf 123; Whitehead 154

U115　*Notes on the Creation Story*
Language and form: Latin prose
Status: Original extant
Traditional title: *History of Creation*
Original title: *In Nomine Domini. Historia Creationis a Mose Tradita. Ex Smidio et ex Castellione* [In the Name of the Lord. The Creation Story Passed down by Moses. Based on Schmidt and Castellio]
Length: 16 pages
Written during: Summer 1745
Note: For an English translation, see Swedenborg 1927–1951a.
Reference numbers: Tafel 80; Hyde 126:479; Whitehead 156

U116 *Passages on the Coming Messiah*
Language and form: Latin prose
Status: Original extant
Traditional titles: *Messiah About to Come; The Messiah; The Messiah About to Come*
Original title: *De Messia Venturo in Mundum* [On the Messiah Who Is Going to Come into the World]
Length: 65 pages
Written before or during: November 1745
Note: For an English translation, see Swedenborg 1949.
Reference numbers: Tafel 81; Hyde 127:481; Whitehead 157

U117 *The Old Testament Explained*
Language and form: Latin prose
Status: Original extant
Traditional titles: *Adversaria; Explicatio; Historical Word; The Word Explained; The Word of the Old Testament Explained*
Original title: *Explicatio in Verbum Historicum Veteris Testamenti* [The Historical Word of the Old Testament Explained]
Length: 1,951 pages
Written during: November 1745 to February 1747
Note: Lengthy commentaries on the books of Genesis and Exodus, with briefer commentaries on the books of Joshua, Judges, Ruth, 1 and 2 Samuel, 1 and 2 Kings, 1 and 2 Chronicles, Leviticus, Numbers, and Deuteronomy. See also U122. The earliest form of a thread that would later become U120 began in this work as indented paragraphs between expository passages; these indented paragraphs were indexed in U131. For an English translation, see Swedenborg 1927–1951b, vols. 1–7.
Reference numbers: Tafel 82; Hyde 128:483–485; Stroh and Ekelöf 124; Whitehead 158

U118 *Concordance of Historical Books of the Old Testament*
Language and form: Latin prose
Status: Original extant
Traditional titles: *Bible Index; Bible Indexes; Index Biblicus*
Original title: [Untitled]
Length: 716 pages
Compiled during: 1746

Note: This material is found in manuscript codex 40 and its continuation, codex 41, in the Swedish Royal Academy of Sciences. For
a complete reproduction of these manuscripts, see Swedenborg
1916c, 1:1–174, 177–354. For Swedenborg's other Bible concordances, see U119, U123–U124, U126, U172. For the complex state
of Swedenborg's concordances to the Bible and their Latin editions and English translations in general, see Rose 2002.

Reference numbers: Tafel 83; Hyde 129:496; Stroh and Ekelöf 125;
Whitehead 160

 U119 *Concordance of Proper Nouns in the Bible*
Language and form: Latin prose
Status: Original extant
Traditional titles: *Bible Index; Bible Indexes; Index Biblicus*
Original title: *Nomina Virorum, Terrarum, Regnorum, Urbium*
[Names of People, Lands, Realms, and Cities]
Length: 278 pages
Compiled during: 1746 to 1748
Note: This material is found in manuscript codex 39 in the
Swedish Royal Academy of Sciences. For a complete reproduc-
tion of the manuscript, see Swedenborg 1916c, 3:511–646. For an
English translation rearranged into biblical order and inter-
woven with material from U124 and U125, see Swedenborg
1917. For Swedenborg's other Bible concordances, see U118,
U123–U124, U126, U172. For the complex state of Swedenborg's
concordances to the Bible and their Latin editions and English
translations in general, see Rose 2002.

Reference numbers: Tafel 90; Hyde 135:508; Stroh and Ekelöf 125;
Whitehead 163

U120 *Spiritual Experiences*
Language and form: Latin prose
Status: Original extant
Traditional titles: *Diarium Minus; Memorabilia; Smaller Diary;
Spiritual Diary; Spiritual Diary Minor; Spiritual Experiences*
Original title: *Experientiae Spirituales* [Spiritual Experiences]
Length: 1,201 pages
Written during: 1747 to 1765
Note: These personal notes document Swedenborg's spiritual ex-
periences over a number of years. Although this material was not

published during Swedenborg's lifetime, much of it was copied or recast in his later theological publications. For Swedenborg's index to this material, see U131. See also U117, U121. For an English translation see Swedenborg 1998–2002 and Swedenborg 1978c.[38]

Reference numbers: Tafel 87, 93, 96, 97, 99a; Hyde 137:513, 139:896, 140:915, 174:2163; Stroh and Ekelöf 128; Whitehead 168, 170, 208

U121 *Note on Gad and Asher*

Language and form: Latin prose

Status: Original extant

Traditional titles: *Gad and Asher; On Gad and Asher; The Bath Fragment*

Original title: [Untitled]

Length: 1 page

Written: February 8, 1747

Note: This is now generally believed to be a fragment from §§1–148, which are otherwise missing, from the beginning of *Spiritual Experiences* (U120). For an English translation, see Swedenborg 1998–2002, 1:196–197.

Reference numbers: Hyde 130:498; Whitehead 161

U122 *Isaiah and Jeremiah Explained*

Language and form: Latin prose

Status: Original extant

Traditional title: *Isaiah and Jeremiah Explained*

Original title: [Untitled]

Length: 107 pages

Written around: February 1747

Note: See also U117. For an English translation, see Swedenborg 1927–1951b, vol. 8.

Reference numbers: Tafel 84; Hyde 131:499; Whitehead 162

---

38. As of this writing, the more recent translation of the two cited here (Swedenborg 1998–2002), begun by J. Durban Odhner, has not been completed; thus it is necessary to cite the 1998–2002 translation for the first volumes and the 1978c translation for the later volumes. The reader should also be aware that the two translations break the volumes at different points of the text. This confusing situation will end when the final volumes of the translation begun by Odhner are issued.

U123 *First Draft Concordance of Prophetic Material in the Bible*
Language and form: Latin prose
Status: Original extant
Traditional titles: *Bible Index; Bible Indexes; Index Biblicus*
Original title: [Untitled]
Length: 362 pages
Compiled during: 1747
Note: This material is found in manuscript codex 6 in the Swedish Royal Academy of Sciences. Swedenborg copied most of it over into U124. For a reproduction of the manuscript, see Swedenborg 1916c, 1:356–719. For Swedenborg's other Bible concordances, see U118–U119, U124, U126, U172. For the complex state of Swedenborg's concordances to the Bible and their Latin editions and English translations in general, see Rose 2002.
Reference numbers: Tafel 86; Hyde 132:501; Stroh and Ekelöf 125; Whitehead 165

U124 *Second Draft Concordance of Prophetic Material in the Bible*
Language and form: Latin prose
Status: Original extant
Traditional titles: *Bible Index; Bible Indexes; Index Biblicus*
Original title: [Untitled]
Length: 673 pages
Compiled during: 1747 and early 1748
Note: This material is found in manuscript codex 4 in the Swedish Royal Academy of Sciences. Some of it was copied over from U123. For a complete reproduction of the manuscript, see Swedenborg 1916c, vol. 2. For an English translation rearranged into biblical order and interwoven with material from U119 and U125, see Swedenborg 1917. For Swedenborg's other Bible concordances, see U118–U119, U123, U126, U172. For the complex state of Swedenborg's concordances to the Bible and their Latin editions and English translations in general, see Rose 2002.
Reference numbers: Tafel 91; Hyde 134:505; Stroh and Ekelöf 125; Whitehead 166

U125 *Marginal Notes in the Schmidt and van der Hooght Bibles*
Language and form: Latin prose
Status: Originals extant

Traditional titles: *Marginal Notes; Marginalia; Schmidius Marginalia*
Original title: [Untitled]
Written during: Late 1747 to 1752
Note: Swedenborg made annotations in two of his Bibles: Schmidt 1696, a Latin translation of the Old and New Testaments, and van der Hooght 1740, an Old Testament with van der Hooght's Hebrew text and Schmidt's Latin translation in parallel columns. Swedenborg's van der Hooght Bible, sparsely annotated and occasionally underlined, is in the Swedish Royal Academy of Sciences; no reproduction, edition, or English translation exists. Swedenborg's Schmidt Bible, copiously annotated, is reproduced in Schmidt and Swedenborg 1872. For an English translation of Swedenborg's annotations to the Schmidt Bible, interwoven with material from U119 and U124, see Swedenborg 1917.
Reference numbers: Tafel 85, 88, 89; Hyde 133:502–503; Stroh and Ekelöf 126; Whitehead 164

U126 *Concordance of the Four Gospels*
Language and form: Latin prose
Status: Original extant
Traditional titles: *Bible Index; Bible Indexes; Index Biblicus*
Original title: [Untitled]
Length: 486 pages
Compiled during: 1748
Note: This material is found in manuscript codex 5 in the Swedish Royal Academy of Sciences. For a reproduction of the manuscript, see Swedenborg 1916c, 3:2–477. For Swedenborg's other Bible concordances, see U118–U119, U123–U124, U172. For the complex state of Swedenborg's concordances to the Bible and their Latin editions and English translations in general, see Rose 2002.
Reference numbers: Tafel 92; Hyde 136:511; Stroh and Ekelöf 125; Whitehead 167

U127 *Greek Orthodox Religion*
Language and form: Latin prose
Status: Original extant
Traditional title: *Greek Religion*
Original title: *Religio Graeca* [Greek Religion]
Length: 3 pages

Written during: 1748
Note: For an English translation, see Swedenborg 1922.
Reference numbers: Hyde 136:511; Stroh and Ekelöf 125

U128 *Rough Copy of "Secrets of Heaven"*
Language and form: Latin prose
Status: Original extant
Traditional titles: *Arcana Caelestia; Arcana Coelestia; Heavenly Mysteries; Miracles and Signs; On Miracles*
Original title: [Untitled][39]
Length: 5,759 pages
Written around: 1748 to 1756
Note: A surviving rough copy of P86–P96, P100, U130. Of most of this rough copy no English translation exists. For a reproduction of the original, see Swedenborg 1916a. A small portion on the topic of miracles, originally intended to come after Genesis 22 but later replaced, has been translated into English: see Swedenborg 1942, 400–411.
Reference numbers: Hyde 138:550–564; Stroh and Ekelöf 129

U129 *Rough Copy Index to "Secrets of Heaven"*
Language and form: Latin prose
Status: Original extant
Traditional titles: *Index to Arcana Coelestia; Index to Heavenly Mysteries*
Original title: *Index Verborum, Nominum, et Rerum in "Arcanis Coelestibus"* [Index of Words, Names, and Things Found in "Secrets of Heaven"]
Length: 529 pages
Written during: 1748 to 1756
Note: An index to P85–P96, P100. See also U134. No English translation of the rough copy of the index exists. For an English translation of the fair copy of the index, see information given in the note to U134 below.
Reference numbers: Tafel 100; Hyde 143:937; Whitehead 174

U130 *Sketch for Portions of "Secrets of Heaven"*
Language and form: Latin prose
Status: Original extant

39. Eleven of the fifteen sets of manuscripts that comprise the rough copy of *Secrets of Heaven* have no titles. The other four sets carry titles much like those of the finished works: compare the titles of Hyde 138:550 and P86, Hyde 138:554 and P93, Hyde 138:556 and P94, and Hyde 138:558 and P96.

Traditional titles: *Arcana Caelestia; Arcana Coelestia; Heavenly Mysteries*
Original title: [Untitled]
Length: 90 pages
Written around: 1750
Note: See also P85–P96, P100, U128. This is a sketch for or outline of portions of *Secrets of Heaven* that were published from 1751 to 1753 (see P92–P94). No English translation of this material exists. For a reproduction of the original, see Swedenborg 1916a, 1:2–99.
Reference numbers: Hyde 138:549; Stroh and Ekelöf 129

U131   *Index to "Spiritual Experiences"*
Language and form: Latin prose
Status: Original extant
Traditional titles: *Index to Spiritual Diary; Index of Spiritual Experiences*
Original title: [Untitled]
Length: 1,354 pages
Written around: 1751 and 1765
Note: An index to indented paragraphs in U117, and to U120 as a whole. No English translation exists. For a Latin text, see Swedenborg 1983–1997, vols. 5 and 6.
Reference numbers: Tafel 98, 99b; Hyde 141:926, 175:2193; Stroh and Ekelöf 128; Whitehead 172, 210.

U132   *Notes in an Almanac*
Language and form: Swedish prose
Status: Original extant
Traditional title: *Swedenborg's Almanac for 1752*
Original title: [Untitled]
Length: 24 pages
Written: 1752
Note: A draft of notes sent with the manuscript of *Secrets of Heaven* 4700–5993 to the printers; the manuscript also includes Swedenborg's notes on seeds, flowers, and vegetables for his garden. No published English translation exists;[40] for a Swedish edition, see Swedenborg 1904a. The original is in the Royal Library in Stockholm.
Reference number: Stroh and Ekelöf 129

---

40. The Swedenborg Library in Bryn Athyn, Pa., contains a handwritten translation by Marta Persson.

U133 *Draft Memorandum on the Swedish Liquor Trade*
Language and form: Swedish prose
Status: Original extant
Traditional titles: *Draft Memorial on Distillation of Spirits; Liquor Trade in Sweden*
Original title: [Untitled]
Length: 2 pages
Written: November 3, 1755
Note: For an English translation, see Acton 1948–1955, 519.
Reference numbers: Hyde 142:935; Stroh and Ekelöf 130; Whitehead 173

U134 *Fair Copy Index to "Secrets of Heaven"*
Language and form: Latin prose
Status: Original extant
Traditional titles: *Index to Arcana Coelestia; Index to Heavenly Mysteries*
Original title: *Index Verborum, Nominum, et Rerum in "Arcanis Coelestibus"* [Index of Words, Names, and Things Found in "Secrets of Heaven"]
Length: 452 pages
Written during: 1756 to 1757
Note: The author's own index to P85–P96, P100. For the rough copy of this index, see U129. For an English translation, see Swedenborg 1909.
Reference numbers: Tafel 100; Hyde 143:938–939; Whitehead 174

U135 *Rough Copy of "Revelation Explained"*
Language and form: Latin prose
Status: Original extant
Traditional titles: *Apocalypse Explained; Revelation Explained*
Original title: [Untitled]
Length: 2,590 pages
Written during: 1758 to 1759
Note: Because U153 concerns the Book of Revelation and is found in the same manuscript as U134, Hyde assigned the present manuscript a date of 1757, on the assumption that U153 was a precursor to it and that U134 and U153 were written at the same time. Both assumptions have since proven incorrect. All other indications are that this draft was begun late in 1758, since the manuscript refers back to the five works Swedenborg

published in mid- to late 1758. This rough copy and the fair copy (U136) were created almost simultaneously—both end abruptly in the middle of explaining Revelation 19:10, just three sections apart. In 1766 Swedenborg published a briefer exposition of the Book of Revelation from a somewhat different perspective (see P114). For an English translation, see Swedenborg 1994–1997a, vols. 1–5, and vol. 6, pages 1–408.
Reference numbers: Tafel 106; Hyde 149:1356–1364; Stroh and Ekelöf 136; Whitehead 180

 U136 *Fair Copy of "Revelation Explained"*
Language and form: Latin prose
Status: Original extant
Traditional titles: *Apocalypse Explained; Revelation Explained*
Original title: *Apocalypsis Explicata secundum Sensum Spiritualem, Ubi Revelantur Arcana, Quae Ibi Praedicta, et Hactenus Recondita Fuerunt* [The Book of Revelation Explained as to Its Spiritual Meaning, Which Reveals Secret Wonders That Were Predicted There and Have Been Hidden until Now]
Length: 1,985 pages
Written during: 1758 to 1759
Note: The rough copy of the work (U135) and this fair copy were created almost simultaneously—both end abruptly in the middle of explaining Revelation 19:10, just three sections apart. See also U153. For an English translation, see U135.
Reference numbers: Tafel 106; Hyde 149:1366–1369; Stroh and Ekelöf 136; Whitehead 180

U137 *Draft of "The Lord"*
Language and form: Latin prose
Status: Original not extant; copies survive
Traditional titles: *Concerning the Lord and the Holy Spirit; De Domino; The Lord*
Reported original title: *De Domino* [On the Lord]
Length: 12 pages
Written between: 1759 and 1760
Note: This is a draft for P107. For an English translation, see Swedenborg 1994–1997c, 6:639–647.
Reference numbers: Tafel 108; Hyde 151:1527; Stroh and Ekelöf 137; Whitehead 183

U138 *Commentary on the Athanasian Creed*
Language and form: Latin prose
Status: Original not extant; copies survive
Traditional titles: *Athanasian Creed; De Athanasii Symbolo*
Reported original title: *De Athanasii Symbolo* [On the Athanasian Creed]
Length: 84 pages
Written before or during: Early 1760
Note: An incomplete commentary. The so-called Athanasian creed dates from the early fifth century. It is improperly named after Athanasius of Alexandria (around 295–373 C.E.). It championed orthodoxy against Arian attacks on the nature of the Trinity. For an English translation of Swedenborg's commentary, see Swedenborg 1994–1997b, 6:577–634.
Reference numbers: Tafel 107; Hyde 150:1516; Stroh and Ekelöf 137; Whitehead 182

U139 *Memorandum on the Exchange Rate*
Language and form: Swedish prose
Status: Original extant
Traditional titles: *Memorial on the Course of Exchange; Metallic Currency; On the Metallic Currency*
Original title: *Ödmjukt memorial* [Humble Memorandum]
Length: 6 pages
Written: November 17, 1760
Note: For an English translation, see Acton 1948–1955, 537–544.
Reference numbers: Hyde 152:1537; Stroh and Ekelöf 138; Whitehead 184

U140 *Memorandum Recommending Doing Away with Paper Money*
Language and form: Swedish prose
Status: Original extant
Traditional titles: *Memorial on the Course of Exchange; Restoration of the Coinage*
Original title: [Untitled]
Length: 1 page
Written during: Early December 1760
Note: This is a brief warning of financial crisis for Sweden if paper currency is not replaced with coinage of actual value. For an English translation, see Acton 1948–1955, 546–547.

Reference numbers: Hyde 153:1540; Stroh and Ekelöf 139; White-head 185

 U141 *Additional Memorandum on the Exchange Rate*
Language and form: Swedish prose
Status: Original extant
Traditional titles: *Additional Considerations on Exchange; Appendix to Memorial on Exchange; Course of Exchange*
Original title: *Ödmjukt memorial* [Humble Memorandum]
Length: 5 pages
Written: December 13, 1760
Note: For an English translation, see Acton 1948–1955, 547–550.
Reference numbers: Hyde 154:1550; Stroh and Ekelöf 140; White-head 186

U142 *Memorandum against Exporting Copper*
Language and form: Swedish prose
Status: Original extant
Traditional titles: *Exportation of Copper; Memorial against Export of Copper*
Original title: *Underdånigt memorial* [Humble Memorandum]
Length: 2 pages
Written between: December 1760 and February 1761
Note: For an English translation, see Acton 1948–1955, 569–570.
Reference numbers: Hyde 155:1552; Stroh and Ekelöf 141; White-head 187

U143 *Memorandum Defending the Swedish Government*
Language and form: Swedish prose
Status: Original extant
Traditional title: *Memorial on Stora Deputation*
Original title: *Ödmiukt memorial* [Humble Memorandum]
Length: 4 pages
Written: January 12, 1761
Note: For an English translation, see Acton 1948–1955, 551–555.
Reference numbers: [Not listed]

U144 *Memorandum Criticizing Nordencrantz's Book*
Language and form: Swedish prose
Status: Original extant
Traditional titles: *Criticism of Nordencrantz's Book; Memorial Commenting on Nordencrantz's Book*

Original title: *Ödmjukt memorial* [Humble Memorandum]

Length: 4 pages

Written: Mid- to late January 1761

Note: A defense of the Swedish constitutional monarchy against criticisms circulated by Anders Nordencrantz (1697–1772), the head of the Commerce Council. For an English translation, see Acton 1948–1955, 559–566.

Reference numbers: Hyde 156:1554; Stroh and Ekelöf 142; Whitehead 188

U145 *Memorandum Defending Political Freedom*

Language and form: Swedish prose

Status: Original extant

Traditional titles: *Memorial on the Upholding and Strengthening of the Kingdom in Its Freedom; Preservation of Freedom*

Original title: *Oförgripaliga tanckar om rikets upprätthållande och befästande i sin frihet* [Modest Thoughts on the Upholding and Strengthening of the Kingdom in Its Freedom]

Length: 4 pages

Written between: March and July 1761

Note: For an English translation, see Acton 1948–1955, 591–595.

Reference numbers: Hyde 157:1571; Stroh and Ekelöf 143; Whitehead 189

U146 *Presentation Draft of "Inlaying Marble"*

Language and form: Swedish prose

Status: Original extant

Traditional title: *Inlaying Marble*

Original title: *Beskrifning, huru inleggningar af allahanda desseiner ske uti marmor, til bord eller annan husziratz* [Description of the Mode in Which Marble Slabs Are Inlaid for Tables and Other Ornaments to Compose All Sorts of Designs]

Length: 3 pages

Written before or on: June 10, 1761

Note: See also P106. This manuscript was presented as a paper to the Swedish Royal Academy of Sciences. No English translation of it exists. The original is part of the archives of the Swedish Royal Academy of Sciences.

Reference number: Stroh and Ekelöf 147

U147 *Draft on the Inner Meaning of Prophets and Psalms*

Language and form: Swedish prose

Status: Original extant

Traditional titles: *Prophets and Psalms; Summaries of the Internal Sense*
Original title: [Untitled]
Length: 24 pages
Written around: 1761
Note: For an English translation, see Swedenborg 1996s, 2:21–234.
Reference numbers: Tafel 109; Hyde 158:1581; Stroh and Ekelöf 144; Whitehead 190

U148 *Draft of "Sacred Scripture"*
Language and form: Latin prose
Status: Original extant
Traditional titles: *De Verbo; Sacred Scripture; The Word of the Lord from Experience; Word from Experience*
Original title: *De Scriptura Sacra seu Verbo Domini ab Experientia* [On Sacred Scripture, or the Word of the Lord, from Experience]
Length: 33 pages
Written around: 1762
Note: See P108. For an English translation, see Swedenborg 1997c, 5–51.
Reference numbers: Tafel 113; Hyde 161:1618; Whitehead 194

U149 *Draft of "Life"*
Language and form: Latin prose
Status: Original extant
Traditional titles: *De Praeceptis; Decalogue; Precepts of the Decalog; Precepts of the Decalogue*
Original title: *De Praeceptis Decalogi* [On the Precepts of the Decalog]
Length: 11 pages
Written around: 1762
Note: See P109. For an English translation, see Swedenborg 1997c, 207–215.
Reference numbers: Tafel 114; Hyde 162:1636; Whitehead 195

U150 *Draft of "Supplements"*
Language and form: Latin prose
Status: Original extant
Traditional titles: *Argument Concerning the Judgment; Last Judgment; Last Judgment (Posthumous); Sketch for Supplement to Last Judgment; The Spiritual World*

Original title: *De Ultimo Judicio* [On the Last Judgment]
Length: 88 pages
Written around: 1762 to early 1763
Note: This is a draft for P111, which contains supplements to P103 and P101. For an English translation, see Swedenborg 1997c, 57–202.
Reference numbers: Tafel 111, 112, 115; Hyde 163:1642; Whitehead 196

U151 ***Draft on Divine Love***
Language and form: Latin prose
Status: Original extant
Traditional titles: *Divine Love; Doctrine of Uses; On Divine Love; On Divine Love and Divine Wisdom; Sketch for Divine Love*
Original title: *De Divino Amore* [On Divine Love]
Length: 22 pages
Written around: Late 1762 to early 1763
Note: See also U152. This brief manuscript forms part of the basis for P112. For an English translation, see Swedenborg 1994–1997a, 6:413–452.
Reference numbers: Tafel 122; Hyde 164:1659; Stroh and Ekelöf 146; Whitehead 198

U152 ***Draft on Divine Wisdom***
Language and form: Latin prose
Status: Original extant
Traditional titles: *Angelic Idea of Creation; Divine Wisdom; Doctrine of Uses; On Divine Love and Divine Wisdom; On Divine Wisdom; Sketch for Divine Wisdom*
Original title: *De Divina Sapientia* [On Divine Wisdom]
Length: 51 pages
Written: Early 1763
Note: See also U151. This manuscript forms part of the basis for P112. For an English translation, see Swedenborg 1994–1997a, 6:453–537.
Reference numbers: Tafel 123; Hyde 165:1687; Stroh and Ekelöf 146; Whitehead 199

U153 ***Summaries Explaining the Book of Revelation***
Language and form: Latin prose
Status: Original extant
Traditional titles: *Summaries in Explanation of the Apocalypse; Summary in Explanation of the Apocalypse*

Original title: *Summaria in Explicatione Apocalypseos* [Summaries in Explanation of the Book of Revelation]
Length: 5 pages
Written around: 1764
Note: See also P114, U135–U136. For a Latin text and English translation, see Swedenborg 1975e, 86–97.
Reference numbers: Hyde 143:939; Wainscot 143a

U154 *First Sketch for "Marriage Love"*
Language and form: Latin prose
Status: Original extant
Traditional titles: *Articles on Marriage; De Conjugio I*
Original title: *De Conjugio* [On Marriage]
Length: 1 page
Written around: 1764 to 1765
Note: See also P118, U159, U163–U165. For a Latin text and English translation, see Swedenborg 1975e, 100–103.
Reference numbers: Hyde 143:939; Wainscot 143b

U155 *Swedenborg Family Genealogy*
Language and form: Swedish prose
Status: Originals extant
Traditional titles: *Genealogy; Genealogy of the Swedenborg Family*
Original title: *Genealogie utaf swedenborgiska familien* [Genealogy of the Swedenborg Family]
Length: 2 to 4 pages
Written around: 1765[41]
Note: Three copies in Swedenborg's own hand survive in the genealogical records kept in the Swedish House of Nobles. No English translation, Swedish edition, or facsimile of the original exists in print.
Reference numbers: Stroh and Ekelöf 158; Whitehead 209

U156 *Rough Copy Index to "Revelation Unveiled"*
Language and form: Latin prose
Status: Original extant
Traditional title: *Index to Apocalypse Revealed*
Original title: [Untitled]
Length: 425 pages

---

41. Stroh and Ekelöf originally assigned this work to 1767, but scholars since have assigned it to 1765.

Written around: 1766

Note: See also U157. This is an index to P114. For an English translation of the fair copy, see U157.

Reference numbers: Tafel 130; Hyde 177:2273; Stroh and Ekelöf 155

U157 *Fair Copy Index to "Revelation Unveiled"*
Language and form: Latin prose
Status: Original extant
Traditional title: *Index to Apocalypse Revealed*
Original title: *Index Rerum in "Apocalypsi Revelata"* [Index to Revelation Unveiled]
Length: 75 pages
Written around: 1766
Note: See also U156. This is an index to P114. For an English translation, see Swedenborg 1997a, 2:561–653.
Reference numbers: Tafel 130; Hyde 177:2274; Stroh and Ekelöf 155; Whitehead 212

U158 *Notes on Conversations with Angels*
Language and form: Latin prose
Status: Original extant
Traditional title: *Conversations with Angels*
Original title: *Colloquia cum Angelis* [Conversation with Angels]
Length: 3 pages
Written around: 1766
Note: For a Latin text and English translation, see Swedenborg 1975e, 182–189.
Reference numbers: Tafel 132; Hyde 178:2316; Stroh and Ekelöf 155; Whitehead 213

U159 *Second Sketch for "Marriage Love"*
Language and form: Latin prose
Status: Original extant
Traditional titles: *De Conjugio; De Conjugio II; Marriage*
Original title: *De Conjugio* [On Marriage]
Length: 19 pages
Written around: 1766
Note: See also P118, U154, U163–U165. For a Latin text and English translation, see Swedenborg 1975e, 102–157.
Reference numbers: Tafel 134; Hyde 181:2370; Stroh and Ekelöf 157; Whitehead 216

| U160 | *Sketch on Goodwill* |

Language and form: Latin prose
Status: Original extant
Traditional titles: *Charity; Doctrine of Charity*
Original title: *De Charitate* [On Charity]
Length: 37 pages
Written between: April and September 1766
Note: Swedenborg appears to have used this material later as the basis for the seventh chapter in P126. For an English translation, see Swedenborg 1995a.
Reference numbers: Tafel 126; Hyde 179:2323; Whitehead 214

| U161 | *Draft of Five Memorable Occurrences* |

Language and form: Latin prose
Status: Original not extant; copies survive
Traditional title: *Five Memorable Relations*
Reported original title: *Memorabilia* [Memorable Occurrences]
Length: 4 pages
Written around: 1766
Note: For a Latin text and English translation, see Swedenborg 1975e, 160–179.
Reference numbers: Tafel 131; Hyde 180:2364; Stroh and Ekelöf 137; Whitehead 215

| U162 | *Answers to Three Questions* |

Language and form: Swedish prose
Status: Original extant
Traditional title: *Answers to Three Questions*
Original title: *Pro Memoria* [Memorandum]
Length: 2 pages
Written: February 1767
Note: For an English translation, see Acton 1948–1955, 630–632.
Reference numbers: Hyde 182:2378; Whitehead 217

| U163 | *Lost Sketches for "Marriage Love"* |

Language and form: Latin prose
Status: Original not extant; no copies survive
Traditional title: *Lost Work on Marriage*
Written around: 1767
Note: See also P118, U154, U159, U164–U165. Two extant sets of indexes (U164–U165) point to the existence of lost documents

used in preparation for P118. One document was apparently a topical outline, with section numbers generously assigned to each topic—the numbering reached around 2,050. Another document was some ninety pages of memorable occurrences, in either full or abbreviated form. A third document was a draft that apparently stopped after the first eighty-three sections or so. All these have been lost, but their contents seem to have been closely parallel to what survives in P118. For a reconstruction in English based on the information in U164–U165, see Swedenborg 1956.

Reference numbers: Tafel 133; Hyde 183:2392

U164   *General Indexes to Lost Sketches for "Marriage Love"*
Language and form: Latin prose
Status: Originals extant
Traditional titles: *De Conjugio III; Index on Marriage; Index to Conjugial Love; Indexes to Marriage; Indexes to "Missing Treatise" on Marriage; Marriage Index 1*
Original title: [Untitled]
Length: 105 pages
Written around: 1767
Note: See also P118, U154, U159, U163, U165. These indexes are found in manuscript codex 46 in the Swedish Royal Academy of Sciences. They comprise several slightly rearranged tables of contents, an index to memorable occurrences in the ninety-page document mentioned in the note to U163, and a topical index to what was apparently an early outline for the work on marriage, given that most of the entries in this index point to a whole range of section numbers rather than to individual sections, as U165 does. For an English translation, see Swedenborg 1996s, 2:403–497.
Reference numbers: Hyde 183:2393; Whitehead 218

U165   *Detailed Index to Lost Sketches for "Marriage Love"*
Language and form: Latin prose
Status: Original extant
Traditional titles: *De Conjugio III; Index on Marriage; Index to Conjugial Love; Indexes to Marriage; Marriage Index 2*
Original title: [Untitled]
Length: 212 pages (roughly 80 percent of which are blank)
Written around: 1767

Note: See also P118, U154, U159, U163–U164. This index is found in manuscript codex 7 in the Swedish Royal Academy of Sciences. Mostly very detailed, it points to individual sections up to §83 of some lost document, with just a few entries that point beyond §83 to ranges of section numbers, more like the entries in the final index in U164. For an English translation, see Swedenborg 1996s, 2:499–514.

Reference numbers: Hyde 183:2392; Whitehead 218

 Brief Index of Catholic Teachings
Language and form: Latin prose
Status: Original extant
Traditional titles: *De Justificatione; Justification and Good Works; On Justification and Good Works; Various Theological Works*
Original title: [Untitled]
Length: 6 pages
Written around: 1769
Note: This brief index was written in preparation for P119. For an English translation, see Swedenborg 1996s, 2:539–549.
Reference numbers: Tafel 137; Hyde 186:2473; Stroh and Ekelöf 161; Whitehead 221

 Notes on a Conversation with Calvin
Language and form: Latin prose
Status: Original extant
Traditional titles: *Conversation with Calvin; Conversations with Calvin; Various Theological Works*
Original title: [Untitled]
Length: 2 pages
Written around: 1769
Note: These notes were written in preparation for P119. For an English translation, see Swedenborg 1996s, 2:551–556.
Reference numbers: Tafel 137; Hyde 186:2473; Stroh and Ekelöf 161; Whitehead 221

U168 **Outline about God the Savior**
Language and form: Latin prose
Status: Original extant
Traditional titles: *God the Savior Jesus Christ; On God the Savior Jesus Christ; Various Theological Works*
Original title: [Untitled]

Length: 1 page

Written around: 1769

Note: This outline was written in preparation for P119. For an English translation, see Swedenborg 1996s, 2:557–560.

Reference numbers: Tafel 137; Hyde 186:2473; Stroh and Ekelöf 161; Whitehead 221

 Summary of New Church Teachings

Language and form: Latin prose

Status: Original extant

Traditional titles: *Sciagraphia Doctrinae Novae Ecclesiae; Sketch of New Church Doctrine; Specimen and Sketch of the New Church; Various Theological Works*

Original title: [Untitled]

Length: 5 pages

Written around: 1769

Note: This brief summary was written in preparation for P119. For an English translation, see Swedenborg 1996s, 2:561–567.[42]

Reference numbers: Tafel 138; Hyde 186:2473; Stroh and Ekelöf 161; Whitehead 221

 Sketch for "True Christianity"

Language and form: Latin prose

Status: Original not extant; copies survive

Traditional title: *Canons of the New Church*

Reported original title: *Canones Novae Ecclesiae, seu Integra Theologia Novae Ecclesiae* . . . [Canons of the New Church, or the Entire Theology of the New Church . . .]

Length: 92 pages

Written around: 1769

Note: See also P126, U172–U174, U178–U179. There was another independent, and strikingly different, copy extant until at least 1885, but this too has now disappeared. For an English translation, see Swedenborg 1996s, 1:177–239.

Reference numbers: Tafel 143; Hyde 187:2513; Stroh and Ekelöf 165; Whitehead 224

---

42. For further details on this manuscript, which contains a few other tiny, fragmentary sketches for *Survey* not mentioned here, see Hyde 186:2473.

U171 *Draft Supplement to "White Horse"*
Language and form: Latin prose
Status: Original extant
Traditional titles: *Appendix to the White Horse; Appendix to White Horse; The Horse and the Hieroglyphics*
Original title: *Appendix ad Codicillum "De Equo Albo"* [Appendix to the Little Work "The White Horse"]
Length: 3 pages
Written: August 1769
Note: See also P104. Two copies of this document seem to have existed originally, both apparently in Swedenborg's handwriting. One of these, which Swedenborg sent to Hartley, is no longer extant. For an English translation, see Swedenborg 1996d, 419–423.
Reference numbers: Tafel 129; Hyde 190:2688; Stroh and Ekelöf 168; Whitehead 227

U172 *Bible Concordance for "True Christianity"*
Language and form: Latin prose
Status: Original extant
Traditional titles: *Confirmatory Passages; Dicta Probantia; Scriptural Confirmations; Scripture Confirmations*
Original title: [Untitled]
Length: 177 pages
Written after: September 1769
Note: For Swedenborg's other Bible concordances, see U118–U119, U123–U124, U126. For *True Christianity* and other related works, see P126, U170, U173–U174, U178–U179. Swedenborg apparently conducted this additional study of the Bible, including close examination of the book of Acts and the Epistles, in preparation for writing P126. For an English translation, see Swedenborg 1996s, 2:241–347.
Reference numbers: Tafel 144; Hyde 191:2711; Stroh and Ekelöf 169; Whitehead 228

U173 *Index to "The Book of Concord" for "True Christianity"*
Language and form: Latin prose
Status: Original extant
Traditional titles: *Formula Concordiae Index; Index to Formula Concordiae; Index to the Formula Concordiae*

Original title: [Untitled]

Length: 171 pages

Written around: Late 1769

Note: See also P126, U170, U172, U174, U178–U179. For some reason, Swedenborg consistently refers to *The Book of Concord* as *The Formula of Concord,* although in fact "the Formula of Concord" is just one part (see Kolb and Wengert 2000, 481–660) of the book that Swedenborg indexes here and refers to elsewhere. *The Book of Concord,* which first appeared in 1580, was (and still is) the major confessional statement of Lutheran orthodoxy. Swedenborg used an edition published in Leipzig in 1756. For a Latin text and English translation, see Swedenborg 1975e, 58–73.

Reference numbers: Hyde 192:2714; Stroh and Ekelöf 172; Whitehead 229

U174 *Draft Memorable Occurrences for "True Christianity"*

Language and form: Latin prose

Status: Original extant

Traditional titles: *Additions to True Christian Religion; Memorabilia in the True Christian Religion; Memorabilia in True Christian Religion*

Original title: [Untitled]

Length: 23 pages

Written during or after: July 1770

Note: See also P126, U170, U172–U173, U178–U179. Although this material has traditionally been referred to as "additions" to P126, it was in fact drafts for P126 that Swedenborg left on the ship on which he sailed from Stockholm to Amsterdam at the time. It differs little from material that is in P126. For an English translation, see Swedenborg 1996s, 1:157–172.

Reference numbers: Tafel 146; Hyde 193:2715; Whitehead 230

U175 *Sketch for a History of the New Church*

Language and form: Latin prose

Status: Original extant

Traditional titles: *Ecclesiastical History; Ecclesiastical History of the New Church; History of the New Church; Sketch of an Ecclesiastical History of the New Church*

Original title: *Historia Ecclesiastica Novae Ecclesiae* [An Ecclesias-
tical History of the New Church]
Length: 1 page
Written around: Late 1770
Note: For a Latin text and English translation, see Swedenborg
1975e, 192–195.
Reference numbers: Tafel 147; Hyde 194:2720; Stroh and Ekelöf
172; Whitehead 231

U176 *Answers to Nine Questions*
Language and form: Latin prose
Status: Original not extant; copies survive
Traditional title: *Nine Questions*
Reported original title: *Quaestiones Novem de Trinitate, etc. ad
Emanuelem Swedenborg Propositae a Thoma Hartley; Tum Illius
Responsa* [Nine Questions on the Trinity and So On, Proposed
to Emanuel Swedenborg by Thomas Hartley, and His Answers]
Length: 8 pages?
Written around: 1771
Note: Swedenborg's replies to questions posed to him by Thomas
Hartley. For an English translation, see Swedenborg 1997b,
127–132.
Reference numbers: Tafel 142; Hyde 196:2875; Stroh and Ekelöf
174; Whitehead 233

U177 *Draft of a Reply to Ernesti*
Language and form: Latin prose
Status: Original extant
Traditional title: *Reply to Ernesti*
Original title: [Untitled]
Length: 1 page
Written around: 1771
Note: This was sent to Cuno with the request that he print it.
When Cuno did not, Swedenborg printed it himself (see P127).
For an English translation of the published version, see P127.
Reference numbers: Hyde 197:2899; Whitehead 234

U178 *Sketch for "Coda to True Christianity"*
Language and form: Latin prose
Status: Original not extant; copies survive

Traditional titles: *Coronis; Crown;*[43] *Sketch of the Coronis; Summary of the Coronis*

Original title: *Coronis seu Appendix ad Veram Christianam Religionem*... [Coda or Appendix to "True Christianity"...]

Length: 5 pages

Written around: 1771

Note: See also P126, U170, U172–U174, U179. In §§15, 177, 343, 627, and 758 of P126, Swedenborg promised a coda or appendix to the work. For an English translation, see Swedenborg 1996s, 1:13–22.

Reference numbers: Tafel 148; Hyde 198:2918; Stroh and Ekelöf 161

U179 *Draft for "Coda to True Christianity"*

Language and form: Latin prose

Status: Original not extant; copies survive

Traditional titles: *Coronis; Crown*[44]

Original title: *Coronis seu Appendix ad Veram Christianam Religionem*... [Coda or Appendix to "True Christianity"...]

Length: 53 pages?

Written around: 1771

Note: See also P126, U170, U172–U174, U178. For an English translation, see Swedenborg 1996s, 1:23–106.

Reference numbers: Tafel 149; Hyde 198:2920; Stroh and Ekelöf 175; Whitehead 235

U180 *Sketch for "End of the Age"*

Language and form: Latin prose

Status: Original extant

Traditional title: *Consummation of the Age*

Original title: *De Consummatione Saeculi, de Adventu Secundo Domini, et de Nova Ecclesia* [On the End of the Age, the Second Coming of the Lord, and the New Church]

Length: 1 page

Written around: 1771

---

43. One of the most persistent fallacies in Swedenborgian scholarship is the notion that the Latin word *coronis* means a crown. Tafel, Hyde, and many other scholars of Swedenborg's works make this mistake. In the context of publishing, *coronis* means a coda or epilogue—a piece of text at the end of a work or supplemental to it that rounds it off without being essential to its integrity.

44. See note 43 just above.

Note: See also U181. For an English translation, see Swedenborg 1996s, 1:111–112.
Reference numbers: Hyde 199:2953; Whitehead 236

U181 *Outlines for "End of the Age"*
Language and form: Latin prose
Status: Original not extant; copies survive
Traditional titles: *Abominatio Desolationis; Abomination of Desolation; Consummation of the Age*
Original title: [Untitled]
Length: 4 pages
Written around: 1771
Note: See also U180. These brief outlines are generally assumed to be related to the *Coda to True Christianity* that Swedenborg planned but was unable to complete at the end of his life. For an English translation, see Swedenborg 1996s, 1:112–118.
Reference numbers: Tafel 150; Hyde 197:2955; Whitehead 236

U182 *Draft Invitation to the New Church*
Language and form: Latin prose
Status: Original not extant; copies survive
Traditional titles: *Consummation of the Age; Invitation to the New Church*
Original title: [Untitled]
Length: 12–16 pages
Written around: 1771
Note: This draft is generally assumed to be related to the work *Coda to True Christianity,* which Swedenborg planned at the end of his life but was unable to complete; see U178, U179. For an English translation, see Swedenborg 1996s, 1:125–150.
Reference numbers: Tafel 150; Hyde 197:2955, 2956; Whitehead 236

V. Category X: Works of Uncertain Authorship, and Projected Works That Were Never Written (11)

 Youth's Honor (**Authorship Uncertain**)
Language and form: Swedish prose
Traditional title: *Youth's Honor*
Original title: *Ungdoms heder, mandoms nytta, ålderdoms nöje*
  [Youth's Honor, Adulthood's Usefulness, Old Age's Satisfaction]

Written around: February 1716

Note: Hyde believed this to be a work by Swedenborg; later evidence suggests that it was written by Polhem and edited by Swedenborg. It is no longer extant.

Reference numbers: Hyde 23:66; Whitehead 31

 Causes of Things (**Authorship Uncertain**)

Language and form: Swedish prose

Traditional title: *Causes of Things*

Original title: *De Causis Rerum* [On the Causes of Things]

Length: 4 pages

Written around: 1717

Note: Stroh and Ekelöf discovered that this work, earlier believed to be by Swedenborg, was probably written by Polhem and copied by Swedenborg. For an English translation, see Swedenborg 1992c, 5–8.

Reference numbers: Tafel 10; Hyde 37:99; Stroh and Ekelöf 31; Whitehead 46

 Dialog on the Essence of Nature (**Authorship Uncertain**)

Language and form: Swedish prose

Traditional title: *Essence of Nature*

Original title: *Discours emellan mechaniquen och chymien om naturens wäsende* [Dialog between "Mechanica" and "Chemistra" on the Essence of Nature]

Length: 25 pages

Written around: 1718

Note: Although a version of this work in Swedenborg's handwriting survives, there is also a copy in Polhem's handwriting, and the work is filed in the Swedish Royal Library as a work by Polhem. It is likely, then, to have been written by Polhem and copied by Swedenborg. No English translation exists.

Reference numbers: Hyde 50:123; Stroh and Ekelöf 45; Whitehead 59

Welfare of a Country (**Authorship Uncertain**)

Language and form: Swedish prose

Traditional title: *Welfare of a Country*

Original title: *Copia af en instruction och fullmacht . . .* [Copy of an Instruction and Mandate . . .]

Length: 12 pages

Written around: December 1718

Note: This treatise on the economic welfare of Sweden is now thought to be a draft of an article by Polhem intended for *Daedalus Hyperboreus,* and copied by Swedenborg. No English translation exists.

Reference numbers: Hyde 49:121; Stroh and Ekelöf 44; White-head 58

X5 *Aims of a Literary Society* **(Authorship Uncertain)**
Language and form: Swedish prose
Traditional title: *Literary Society*
Original title: *Petenda Societatis Literariae* [Aims of a Literary Society]
Length: 1 page
Written before: November 1719
Note: Benzelius is now thought to be the author of this brief manuscript. No English translation exists.
Reference numbers: Hyde 48:119; Stroh and Ekelöf 43; White-head 57

X6 *Verses to Julin* **(Authorship Uncertain)**
Language and form: Latin poetry
Traditional title: *Verses to Julin*
Original title: *De Democratia Literaria . . . Petro Julin, Westmanno* [Literary Democracy . . . by Peter Julin from Westmannland]
Length: 9 lines
Written before: October 29, 1735
Note: The only evidence to suggest that Swedenborg authored this poem is the initials "E. S." at the end. Acton did not believe it to be genuine. For a transcript of the poem, see Academy Documents 5:580.
Reference number: Whitehead 108

X7 *Projected Work on Divine Qualities*
Language and form: Latin prose
Traditional title: *Omnipotence, Omnipresence, etc.*
Projected title: *Sapientia Angelica de Divina Omnipotentia, Omnipraesentia, Omniscientia, Infinitate, et Aeternitate* [Angelic Wisdom on Divine Omnipotence, Omnipresence, Omniscience, Infinity, and Eternity]
Projected to be written after: 1763

Note: In the preface to P107 Swedenborg lists this among works that will be published in the future. He later explained to a friend why he had not written the work (see Tafel 1877, 261).
Reference numbers: Hyde 159:1616; Whitehead 191

X8 *Projected Work on Life*
Language and form: Latin prose
Traditional title: *Concerning Life*
Projected title: *Sapientia Angelica de Vita* [Angelic Wisdom on Life]
Projected to be written after: 1763
Note: In the preface to P107 Swedenborg lists this among works that will be published in the future.
Reference numbers: Hyde 160:1617; Whitehead 192

X9 *Possible Projected Work on Miracles*
Language and form: Latin prose
Traditional title: *Miracles*
Projected title: *De Miraculis Divinis et de Miraculis Magicis* [Divine Versus Magical Miracles]
Projected to be written after: Mid-1771
Note: Some have taken the words *de* MIRACULIS DIVINIS, *& de* MIRACULIS MAGICIS (on DIVINE MIRACLES and on MAGICAL MIRACLES) in *True Christianity* 91 as the title of a forthcoming work by Swedenborg, because they are set partially in small capital letters, which are generally an indication of title citation in Swedenborg's works. Assuming he did plan such a work, a brief sketch of it can perhaps be seen in U178, which ends with five numbered points on miracles of both kinds (see Swedenborg 1996s, 1:21–22). However, whether Swedenborg was planning a whole separate title (or two) on this topic or a mere chapter (or two) in the appendix to *True Christianity* is moot.
Reference numbers: Hyde 200:2972; Whitehead 237

X10 *Projected Work on the Human Mind*
Language and form: Latin prose
Traditional title: *On the Human Mind*
Projected title: *De Mente Humana* [The Human Mind]
Projected to be written after: August 24, 1771
Note: In a letter to the Landgrave of Hesse-Darmstadt, Swedenborg listed this as a work soon to be printed (see Acton 1948–1955, 756).
Reference numbers: [Not listed]

XII *Projected Work on Egyptian Hieroglyphics*
Language and form: Latin prose
Traditional title: *Egyptian Hieroglyphics*
Projected title: *Hieroglyphica Aegyptiaca per Correspondentias Enucleata* [Egyptian Hieroglyphics Expounded through Correspondences]
Projected to be written after: August 24, 1771
Note: In a letter to the Landgrave of Hesse-Darmstadt, Swedenborg listed this as a work soon to be printed (see Acton 1948–1955, 756).
Reference numbers: [Not listed]

VI. Chronological Synopsis of Published Works (Category P) and Unpublished Documents (Category U)

The following synopsis presents a chronological overview of Swedenborg's writing and publishing. In it, unpublished works (represented in black) appear at the time of their commencement, whereas published works (represented in red) appear at the time of their final publication. This distinction in treatment, combined with the lack of exact dating for some of the works, renders this chronology approximate rather than exact. (Further information on dating is available in the list above and in the sources mentioned there.) This chronology does serve in general, however, to show that Swedenborg tended to alternate between periods of writing much but publishing little and periods of publishing much but writing little. Since short titles alone might mislead readers into thinking of each title as being of approximately the same size, information on the length of his published works is added here to highlight their variety.

1700 (2 published pieces, totaling 5 pages)
P1 *Verses for a Wedding* (4 pages)
P2 *Verses to Notman* (1 page)

1707 (1 published piece, totaling 1 page)
P3 *Verses to Bredberg* (1 page)

1709 (4 published pieces, totaling 90 pages)
P4 *Elegy for Benzelius the Elder* (4 pages)
P5 *Graduation Essay on Maxims* (70 pages)
P6 *Latin Verse Translation Accompanying Swedberg's "Rule of Youth"* (8 pages)

P7   *Separately Printed Latin Verse Translation of Swedberg's "Rule of Youth"* (8 pages)

1710 (2 published pieces, totaling 5 pages)
P8   *Verses on Stenbock's Victory* (4 pages)
P9   *Verses to Unge* (1 page)
U1   *Draft of One Epigram to Casaubon*
U2   *Draft of Another Epigram to Casaubon*
U3   *Lost Draft of "Verses to Brenner"*

1713 (1 published piece, totaling 1 page)
P10   *Verses to Brenner* (1 page)

1714 (2 published pieces, totaling 48 pages)
U4   *Lost Draft Invention of a Submersible Ship*
U5   *Lost Draft Invention of a Siphon*
U6   *Lost Draft on Hoisting Heavy Objects*
U7   *Lost Draft on Constructing Sluices*
U8   *Lost Draft Invention of a Massive Water Pump*
U9   *Lost Draft Invention of a Drawbridge*
U10   *Lost Draft Inventions of Air Pumps*
U11   *Lost Draft Invention of Air Guns*
U12   *Lost Draft Invention of a Universal Musical Instrument*
U13   *Lost Draft Method of Creating Shading in Engravings*
U14   *Lost Draft Invention of a Water Clock*
U15   *Lost Draft Inventions of a Mechanical Carriage and a Flying Carriage*
U16   *Lost Draft Method of Analyzing Feelings*
U17   *Lost Draft on Cords and Springs*
P11   *Joyous Accolade* (28 pages)
P12   *Heliconian Pastime* (20 pages)

1715 (1 published piece, totaling 95 pages)
P13   *Northern Muse* (95 pages)

1716 (25 published pieces, totaling 128 pages)
P14   *First Epigram for "Daedalus Hyperboreus"* (1 page)
P15   *Hearing Aid Invented by Polhem* (5 pages)
P16   *Another Hearing Aid* (1 page)
P17   *British Hearing Aid* (1 page)
P18   *Polhem's Experiments on Sound* (4 pages)
P19   *Future Possible Experiments on Sound* (2 pages)

P20	*Speaking-Tube* (3 pages)
P21	*First Lifting Machine* (7 pages)
P22	*Second Lifting Device* (4 pages)
P23	*Winter Experiments* (2 pages)
P24	*Currency Conversion Tables* (2 pages)
P25	*Universal Conversion of Carolins* (5 pages)
P26	*Heliconian Pastime,* Second Edition (32 pages)
U18	*Draft on Types of Soil and Mud*
U19	*Lost Draft Reflections on Perspective*
U20	*Draft Memorandum on a Society of Sciences*
U21	*Draft on Fossils*
P27	*Polhem's Division of Steelyards* (11 pages)
P28	*Air Pump* (8 pages)
P29	*Measuring Volume* (8 pages)
P30	*Sapphic Ode* (4 pages)
U22	*Draft Invention of a Flying Machine*
U23	*Draft Invention of a Siphoning Machine*
P31	*Polhem's Calculations of Air Resistance* (7 pages)
P32	*Flying Machine* (4 pages)
P33	*Experiment with Round Shot and Paper* (1 page)
P34	*Experiment on the Resistance of Water and Snow* (2 pages)
P35	*Method of Finding Longitudes* (3 pages)
P36	*First Way to Find Longitude* (5 pages)
P37	*Finding Longitudes by Stars* (5 pages)
U24	*Draft on Sailing Upstream*
U25	*Draft on Small Tests and Experiments*
U26	*Draft of a Screw Jack*
U27	*Draft on Stereometry*
U28	*Draft on Calculating Lead Amounts*
U29	*Draft of a Crane*
U30	*Draft on Echo*
U31	*Draft Memorandum on Improvements at Carlscrona*
P38	*Second Epigram for "Daedalus Hyperboreus"* (1 page)
	1717 (4 published pieces, totaling 45 pages)
P39	*Polhem's Tap* (16 pages)
P40	*Calculating Volumes* (10 pages)
P41	*Analytical Demonstration* (15 pages)
U32	*Draft Memorandum on Salt Boileries*
P42	*Tinwork* (4 pages)

U33   *Draft on Derotation of the Earth*
U34   *Draft on Instituting an Observatory*
U35   *Memorandum on Commerce and Manufacture*
U36   *Draft on Fire and Colors*

1718 (5 published pieces, totaling 191 pages)
P43   *Algebra* (136 pages)
P44   *Attempt to Find the Longitude* (42 pages)
P45   *Counting Round Shot* (6 pages)
P46   *Small Vibrations* (5 pages)
P47   *A Curve Whose Secants Form Equal Angles to It* (2 pages)
U37   *Draft on a New Arithmetic*
U38   *Draft of "Rotation of the Earth"*

1719 (5 published pieces, totaling 112 pages)
U39   *Memorandum Proposing Redemption of Token Currency*
P48   *Rotation of the Earth* (40 pages)
P49   *Height of Water* (16 pages)
U40   *Notes on Geometry, Algebra, and Science*
U41   *Lost Paper on Small Vibrations*
U42   *Another Draft on Small Vibrations*
U43   *Drafts on Swedish Blast Furnaces*
U44   *Draft on Discovering Mines*
P50   *Height of Water,* Second Edition (40 pages)
P51   *Proposed Change in Money and Measures* (8 pages)
P52   *Docks, Locks, and Saltworks* (8 pages)

1720
U45   *Draft on the Fall and Rise of Lake Wenner*

1721 (4 published pieces, totaling 319 pages)
U46   *Paper on Finding Longitudes*
P53   *Signs of Earth's Former Submersion* (5 pages)
P54   *Chemistry and Physics* (203 pages)
P55   *Iron and Fire* (56 pages)
P56   *Finding Longitudes* (55 pages)
U47   *Draft of "Miscellaneous Observations"*
U48   *Postscript to "Miscellaneous Observations"*

1722 (8 published pieces, totaling 278 pages)
P57   *Miscellaneous Observations,* Volume 1 (179 pages)
P58   *Miscellaneous Observations,* Volume 2 (56 pages)

P59   *Verses on Urania's Metamorphosis* (8 pages)
U49   *Draft Verses to Augustinus*
P60   *Heat Conservation* (4 pages)
U50   *Letter to Frederick I on Working Copper*
U51   *Manuscript Ode to Frederick I*
U52   *Paper in Reply to Quensel*
P61   *Deflation and Inflation* (20 pages)
P62   *Reply to Quensel* (3 pages)
U53   *Draft on Magnets*
U54   *Draft Calculation of Currency*
P63   *Hydrostatics* (4 pages)
P64   *Prospectus of a Work on Metallurgy* (4 pages)

1723
U55   *Memorandum on Balance of Trade*
U56   *Memorandum against the Priority Given to Nobler Metals*
U57   *First Memorandum against Excluding Foreign Traders*
U58   *Memorandum on Establishing Ironworks*
U59   *Second Memorandum against Excluding Foreign Traders*
U60   *Memorandum on Production of Iron*

1724–1733
U61   *Lost Draft on Copper*
U62   *Fair Copy on Extracting Silver*
U63   *Fair Copy on Vitriol*
U64   *Fair Copy on Sulfur and Pyrites*
U65   *Fair Copy on Salt*

1727 (3 published pieces, totaling 323 pages)
P65   *Chemistry and Physics,* Second Edition (212 pages)
P66   *Iron and Fire,* Second Edition (56 pages)
P67   *Finding Longitudes,* Second Edition (55 pages)

1729
U66   *One Draft for "Basic Principles of Nature"*

1730
U67   *Miscellaneous Drafts for "Basic Principles of Nature"*

1733
U68   *Draft on the Motion of the Elements*
U69   *Journal of 1733 to 1734*

U70   *Notes on Wolff's "Empirical Psychology"*
U71   *Quotation from Wolff's "Empirical Psychology"*
U72   *Extracts from Schurig and Translation of Richter*
U73   *Draft of "The Infinite" on the Soul-Body Mechanism*

1734 (4 published pieces, totaling 1,688 pages)
P68   *Philosophical and Metallurgical Works I: Basic Principles of Nature*
       (468 pages)
P69   *Philosophical and Metallurgical Works II: Iron* (400 pages)
P70   *Philosophical and Metallurgical Works III: Copper and Brass* (550
       pages)
P71   *The Infinite* (270 pages)
U74   *Notes about Faith in Christ*
U75   *Extracts from "Basic Principles of Nature"*
U76   *Draft Memorandum against War with Russia*

1736
U77   *Quotations from Wolff on General Knowledge*

1738
U78   *Notes on the Infinite and the Finite*
U79   *First Draft of Three Transactions on the Brain*

1739
U80   *Draft Summary of Trips Abroad*
U81   *Quotations from Other Authors Concerning Muscles*
U82   *Notes about a Pathway to Knowledge of the Soul*
U83   *Notes about Faith and Good Works*
U84   *Quotations from Others' Works on the Brain*

1740 (3 published pieces, totaling 405 pages)
U85   *Notes about the Skin and Tongue*
U86   *Brief Notes on Corpuscular Philosophy*
U87   *Notes Proposing an Algebraic Language for Philosophy*
U88   *Additions to First Draft on the Brain*
U89   *Second, Rearranged Draft on the Brain*
P72   *Memoir of Charles XII* (4 pages)
P73   *Verses in Celebration of Printing* (1 page)
P74   *Dynamics of the Soul's Domain,* Volume 1 (400 pages)
U90   *Paper on the Declination at Uppsala*

1741 (1 published piece, totaling 198 pages)

P75   *Dynamics of the Soul's Domain,* Volume 2 (198 pages)
U91   *Notes on Mathematics and Physics*
U92   *Quotations on Various Philosophical and Theological Topics*
U93   *Draft Introduction to a Rational Psychology*

1742 (2 published pieces, totaling 600 pages)

P76   *Dynamics of the Soul's Domain,* Volume 1, Second Edition (402 pages)
P77   *Dynamics of the Soul's Domain,* Volume 2, Second Edition (198 pages)
U94   *Lost Draft on Divine Prudence*
U95   *Draft on the Soul and the Body*
U96   *Draft on Red Blood*
U97   *Draft on the Soul's Fluid*
U98   *Draft on Sensation*
U99   *Draft on the Origin of the Soul*
U100 *Draft on Action*
U101 *Draft of a Rational Psychology*
U102 *Draft on Ontology*
U103 *Commonplace Book*
U104 *Draft on the Fiber*
U105 *Draft on Metaphysics*
U106 *Draft of a Hieroglyphic Key*

1743

U107 *Draft on the Reproductive Organs*
U108 *Notes on Swammerdam's "Book of Nature"*
U109 *Journal of Dreams*

1744 (2 published pieces, totaling 732 pages)

U110 *Draft on the Five Senses*
U111 *Further Notes on the Brain*
U112 *Notes on the Muscles of the Face and Abdomen*
P78   *The Soul's Domain,* Volume 1 (442 pages)
P79   *The Soul's Domain,* Volume 2 (290 pages)

1745 (3 published pieces, totaling 321 pages)

P80   *The Soul's Domain,* Volume 3 (171 pages)
P81   *Worship and Love of God,* Part 1 (122 pages)

1752 (1 published piece, totaling 559 pages)
P93 *Secrets of Heaven, Genesis,* Volume 4 (559 pages)
U132 *Notes in an Almanac*

1753 (2 published pieces, totaling 1,117 pages)
P94 *Secrets of Heaven, Genesis,* Volume 5 (537 pages)
P95 *Secrets of Heaven, Exodus,* Volume 1 (580 pages)

1754 (4 published pieces, totaling 844 pages)
P96 *Secrets of Heaven, Exodus,* Volume 2 (521 pages)
P97 *Chemistry and Physics,* Third Edition (212 pages)
P98 *Iron and Fire,* Third Edition (56 pages)
P99 *Finding Longitudes,* Third Edition (55 pages)

1755
U133 *Draft Memorandum on the Swedish Liquor Trade*

1756 (1 published piece, totaling 695 pages)
P100 *Secrets of Heaven, Exodus,* Volume 3 (695 pages)
U134 *Fair Copy Index to "Secrets of Heaven"*

1758 (5 published pieces, totaling 584 pages)
P101 *Heaven and Hell* (275 pages)
P102 *New Jerusalem* (157 pages)
P103 *Last Judgment* (56 pages)
P104 *White Horse* (23 pages)
P105 *Other Planets* (73 pages)
U135 *Rough Copy of "Revelation Explained"*
U136 *Fair Copy of "Revelation Explained"*

1759
U137 *Draft of "The Lord"*

1760
U138 *Commentary on the Athanasian Creed*
U139 *Memorandum on the Exchange Rate*
U140 *Memorandum Recommending Doing Away with Paper Money*
U141 *Additional Memorandum on the Exchange Rate*
U142 *Memorandum against Exporting Copper*

1761
U143 *Memorandum Defending the Swedish Government*
U144 *Memorandum Criticizing Nordencrantz's Book*
U145 *Memorandum Defending Political Freedom*

U146   *Presentation Draft of "Inlaying Marble"*
U147   *Draft on the Inner Meaning of Prophets and Psalms*

1762
U148   *Draft of "Sacred Scripture"*
U149   *Draft of "Life"*
U150   *Draft of "Supplements"*
U151   *Draft on Divine Love*

1763 (7 published pieces, totaling 363 pages)
U152   *Draft on Divine Wisdom*
P106   *Inlaying Marble* (7 pages)
P107   *The Lord* (64 pages)
P108   *Sacred Scripture* (54 pages)
P109   *Life* (36 pages)
P110   *Faith* (23 pages)
P111   *Supplements* (28 pages)
P112   *Divine Love and Wisdom* (151 pages)

1764 (1 published piece, totaling 214 pages)
P113   *Divine Providence* (214 pages)
U153   *Summaries Explaining the Book of Revelation*
U154   *First Sketch for "Marriage Love"*

1765
U155   *Swedenborg Family Genealogy*

1766 (2 published pieces, totaling 638 pages)
P114   *Revelation Unveiled* (629 pages)
P115   *Finding Longitudes,* Fourth Edition (9 pages)
U156   *Rough Copy Index to "Revelation Unveiled"*
U157   *Fair Copy Index to "Revelation Unveiled"*
U158   *Notes on Conversations with Angels*
U159   *Second Sketch for "Marriage Love"*
U160   *Sketch on Goodwill*
U161   *Draft of Five Memorable Occurrences*

1767 (2 published pieces, totaling 4 pages)
U162   *Answers to Three Questions*
P116   *Reply to Oetinger* (2 pages)
P117   *Answer to Oetinger's Reply* (2 pages)

U163 *Lost Sketches for "Marriage Love"*
U164 *General Indexes to Lost Sketches for "Marriage Love"*
U165 *Detailed Index to Lost Sketches for "Marriage Love"*

1768 (1 published piece, totaling 328 pages)
P118 *Marriage Love* (328 pages)

1769 (4 published pieces, totaling 97 pages)
U166 *Brief Index of Catholic Teachings*
U167 *Notes on a Conversation with Calvin*
U168 *Outline about God the Savior*
U169 *Summary of New Church Teachings*
P119 *Survey* (67 pages)
U170 *Sketch for "True Christianity"*
P120 *Soul-Body Interaction* (23 pages)
P121 *Answer to a Friend* (3 pages)
U171 *Draft Supplement to "White Horse"*
U172 *Bible Concordance for "True Christianity"*
P122 *Letter to Beyer on the Swedish Church* (4 pages)
U173 *Index to "The Book of Concord" for "True Christianity"*

1770 (1 published piece, totaling 4 pages)
P123 *The Word's Earthly and Spiritual Meanings* (4 pages)
U174 *Draft Memorable Occurrences for "True Christianity"*
U175 *Sketch for a History of the New Church*

1771 (5 published pieces, totaling 617 pages)
P124 *The Word's Earthly and Spiritual Meanings,* Second Edition (3 pages)
P125 *Deflation and Inflation,* Second Edition (68 pages)
P126 *True Christianity* (542 pages)
U176 *Answers to Nine Questions*
U177 *Draft of a Reply to Ernesti*
P127 *Reply to Ernesti* (1 page)
U178 *Sketch for "Coda to True Christianity"*
U179 *Draft for "Coda to True Christianity"*
U180 *Sketch for "End of the Age"*
U181 *Outlines for "End of the Age"*
U182 *Draft Invitation to the New Church*
P128 *The Word's Earthly and Spiritual Meanings,* Third Edition (3 pages)

Works Cited

The entries in the following list correspond to the author-date references in the text of this volume. The list is organized by the following criteria:

- First, on the basis of word-by-word alphabetization of the author's last name, or of the title if the author's name is lacking. Thus "Frost, Lesley" appears before "Frost, Robert," and "Harrity, Richard" appears before *Hawkstone Inn: The Report*."
- Second, in order of publication date. Thus "Tafel, R. L. 1875" appears before "Tafel, R. L. 1877."
- Third, within years, by word-by-word alphabetization of the title. A letter is appended to the publication date to reflect this alphabetic organization (and only this alphabetic organization—it does not indicate relative order of publication within a given year, which would be difficult for the bibliographer to discover, or relative order of appearance in the volume). Thus "Frost, Robert. 1966a. *Interviews with Robert Frost*" appears before "Frost, Robert. 1966b. *The Poetry of Robert Frost.*"

Some 160 of the approximately 800 entries are works by Swedenborg. They present challenges to the bibliographer for several reasons too complex to discuss here, but one significant distinction that can be made among them is that some were first published during his lifetime (1688–1772) and some were first published only posthumously. In this list, those that were published during his lifetime are marked by original publication dates in square brackets; or, to state the inverse, a work by Swedenborg that does not have a bracketed date can be understood to have been published only after his death. For example, the reader will know from the citation "Swedenborg [1722] 1929" that it refers to the 1929 version, in whatever form or language, of a work originally published in 1722; and may safely infer from the lack of a bracketed date in the author-date citation "Swedenborg 1901" that the work in question was never published during Swedenborg's lifetime. (In examples such as the latter, the version may or may not be the latest or most readily available, as the historical essays in the volume sometimes cite editions that have been superseded.)

In using the list, a reader will find it critical to know that *original publication dates in brackets are disregarded in organizing the entries.* Thus the entry corresponding to the author-date citation "Swedenborg 1956" appears before the entry for the author-date citation "Swedenborg [1734] 1965," just as the entry corresponding to the author-date citation "Swedenborg 1975a" appears before the entry for the author-date citation "Swedenborg [1771] 1975d" among the five works by Swedenborg that are listed as published in 1975.

In the citation of the works of other writers, the publication dates given are generally those of the original printing; but where this is not the case, the original dates are sometimes additionally supplied in brackets, especially when it has been judged potentially useful for the reader to have that information during the actual reading of the essay texts.

A. J. MacDonald Collection of Utopian Materials. Beinecke Rare Book and Manuscript Library. Yale University.

Academy Documents (Academy Collection of Swedenborg Documents). Swedenborg Library, Academy of the New Church. Bryn Athyn, Pa.

The Academy Journal. 1999–2000. Vol. 41. Bryn Athyn, Pa.: Academy of the New Church.

Academy of the New Church. 1910. *The Kramph Will Case: The Controversy in Regard to Swedenborg's Work on "Conjugial Love."* Bryn Athyn, Pa.: Academy of the New Church.

Acton, Alfred. 1922. "Two New Writings by Swedenborg." *New Church Life* 42:568–578.

———. 1926. "The Theological School: Its Origin, Establishment and Progress." In *The Academy of the New Church 1876–1926: An Anniversary Record.* Bryn Athyn, Pa.: Academy of the New Church.

———. 1927. *An Introduction to the Word Explained.* Bryn Athyn, Pa.: Academy of the New Church.

———. 1942. "Unpublished Parts of the *Arcana Coelestia.*" *New Church Life* 62: 396–400.

———. 1948–1955. *The Letters and Memorials of Emanuel Swedenborg.* 2 vols. Bryn Athyn, Pa.: Swedenborg Scientific Association.

———. 1956. *Angelic Wisdom Concerning Marriage, Being Two Indices by Emanuel Swedenborg to His Missing Draft on Marriage Arranged in the Order of the Paragraph Numbers.* Bryn Athyn, Pa.: Academy of the New Church.

———. 1957. "The History of the *Coronis.*" *New Church Life* 77:372–378.

Ad C. Herennium de Ratione Dicendi. 1954. Translated by Harry Caplan. Cambridge: Harvard University Press.

Adam, Max. 1986. "Anton v. Webern und Swedenborg." *Offene Tore* 30:237–246.

Aerthayil, James. 2001. *The Spiritual Heritage of the St. Thomas Christians.* Bangalore, India: Dharmaram Publications.

Afzelius, Arvid August. 1901. *Minnen.* Stockholm: Norstedt.

Afzelius, Arvid August, and Eric Gustav Geijer. 1814–1816. *Svenska folkvisor.* 3 vols. Stockholm.

Ager, John C. 1907. "New York Association." *Journal of the General Convention* 130–132.

Agrippa, Henry Cornelius. 1993. *Three Books of Occult Philosophy.* Edited by Donald Tyson. St. Paul, Minn.: Llewellyn.

Alcott, Bronson. 1836–1837. *Conversations with Children on the Gospels.* Boston: J. Monroe.

Almqvist, Carl Jonas Love. 1926. *Samlade Skrifter.* Edited by Fredrik Böök. Vol. 2. Stockholm: Albert Bonniers.

American National Biography. 1999. 24 vols. Edited by John A. Garraty and Mark C. Carnes. New York: Oxford University Press.

Anders, Tisa. 2002. *Religion and Advocacy Politics in the Career of L. Maria Child.* Dissertation, Iliff School of Theology and University of Denver, Colorado.

Anderson, C. Alan. 1993. *Healing Hypotheses.* New York: Garland Publishing.

———. 1996. "Horatio Dresser: Swedenborgian, New Thoughter, Free Spirit." Paper presented at the annual meeting of the American Academy of Religion, New Orleans.

Anderson, C. Alan, and Deborah G. Whitehouse. 1995. *New Thought: A Practical American Spirituality.* New York: Crossroad.

Andersson, Lars Gustaf. 1999. "Förälskelsemomentet." In *Den största lyckan: En bok till Vilhelm Ekelund,* edited by Per Erik Ljung and Helena Nilsson. Lund: Ellerström.

Andrews, Joseph. 1868. "Nature as a Means of Culture." *New Jerusalem Magazine* 37:508–515.

Antrobus, Derek. 1997. *A Guiltless Feast: The Salford Bible Christian Church and the Rise of the Modern Vegetarian Movement.* Salford: Salford City Council.

Arcana: Inner Dimensions of Spirituality. 2001. *Homeopathy Issue.* Vol. 6, no. 1.

Aristotle. 1952. *Nichomachean Ethics.* Translated by W. D. Ross. In vol. 9 of *Great Books of the Western World.* Chicago: Encyclopedia Britannica.

Atterbom, P.D.A. 1814. "Recensioner." *Litteraturtidningen* 19: columns 290–295.

———. 1862–1863. *Svenska siare och skalder.* 7 vols. Örebro: N. M. Lindh.

"B." 1888. "The New Church Not a Sect." *The Dawn: A New Church Home Journal* 6:573–574.

Baltimore New Church. 1792. *Liturgy of the New Church, also Hymns and Spiritual Songs by Joseph Proud.* Baltimore: Sam'l and Jno. Adams.

Balzac, Honoré de. [1832–1835] 1900. *Honoré de Balzac.* Vol. 25. New York: Peter Fenelon Collier & Son.

———. [1835] 1970. *Seraphita.* Freeport, N.Y.: Books for Libraries Press.

Barrett, Benjamin F. 1845. "Open Intercourse with the Spiritual World—Its Dangers and the Cautions Which They Naturally Suggest." *New Jerusalem Magazine* 19:13–28, 50–64, 89–104.

[———]. 1848. "Fourierism and the New Church." *New Church Repository* 1:529–543, 596–610.

———. 1908. *Benjamin Fisk Barrett: An Autobiography.* Revised and supplemented by Gertrude A. Barrett. Germantown, Pa.: Swedenborg Publishing Association.

Barron, Clarence W. 1906. "A Census of the New Church: Extracts from a Paper Read March 4 before the New-Church Club in Boston." *New-Church Messenger* 90:234–235.

———. 1924. "Reading Swedenborg—A Help for Every Man and Woman." *The New-Church Review* 31:178–179. Reprint, [Boston: New-Church Review], 1924.

———. 1926. "Galli-Curci Swayed by Swedish Mystic." *The Dearborn Independent,* April 3, 1926.

Barruel, Augustin de. 1798. *Mémoires pour servir à l'histoire du Jacobinisme.* Vol. 4. London: Le Boussonnier.

Bayley, Jonathan. 1867. *Dr. Bayley's Observations Made during a Tour through Norway, Sweden, Finland, and Russia, in the Summer of 1866.* London: C. P. Alvey.

———. 1884. *New Church Worthies, or Early but Little-Known Disciples of the Lord in Diffusing the Truths of the New Church.* London: James Speirs.

Bays, Gwendolyn, trans. 1983. *The Voice of the Buddha: The Beauty of Compassion.* Berkeley, Ca.: Dharma Publishing.

Beaumont, G. 1824. *The Anti-Swedenborg: or A Declaration of the Principal Errors and Anti-Scriptural Doctrines Contained in the Theological Writings of Emanuel Swedenborg: Being the Substance of a Lecture Delivered at Ebenezer Chapel, Ber Street, Norwich, on Sunday, August 24th, 1823, with Considerable Additions.* London: Richard Baynes.

Beecher, Jonathan, and Richard Bienvenu, trans. and eds. 1983. *The Utopian Vision of Charles Fourier: Selected Texts on Work, Love, and Passionate Attraction.* Columbia, Mo.: University of Missouri Press.

Bellin, Harvey F. 1988. "Opposition is True Friendship: Swedenborg's Influences on William Blake." In *Emanuel Swedenborg: A Continuing Vision,* edited by Robin Larsen and others. New York: Swedenborg Foundation.

Bellin, Harvey F., and Darrell Ruhl, eds. 1985. *Blake and Swedenborg: Opposition Is True Friendship.* New York: Swedenborg Foundation.

Bellows, Henry W. 1869. "Seven Sittings with Powers, the Sculptor." *Appleton's Journal of Literature, Science, and Art* 1:342–343, 359–361, 402–404, 470–471, 595–597; 2:54–55, 106–108.

Benner, Margaret, and Emin Tengstrom. 1977. *On the Interpretation of Learned Neo-Latin: An Explorative Study Based on Some Texts from Sweden (1611–1716).* Göteborg: University of Göteborg.

Benz, Ernst. 1947. *Swedenborg in Deutschland: F. C. Oetingers und Immanuel Kants Auseinandersetzung mit der Person und Lehre Emanuel Swedenborgs.* Frankfurt am Main: Vittorio Klostermann.

———. 1969. *Emanuel Swedenborg: Naturforscher und Seher.* 2nd ed. Revised and edited by Friedemann Horn. Zürich: Swedenborg Verlag.

———. 1979. *Vision und Offenbarung: Gesammelte Swedenborg-Aufsätze.* Zürich: Swedenborg Verlag.

———. 2002. *Emanuel Swedenborg: Visionary Savant in the Age of Reason.* Translated by Nicholas Goodrick-Clarke. West Chester, Pa.: Swedenborg Foundation.

Berendsohn, Walter A. 1948. *Strindbergs sista levnadsår.* Stockholm: Saxon & Lindström.

Berg, Wilhelm. 1891. *Göteborgs Stift under 1700-talet.* Göteborg: Wettergren & Kerber.

Bergquist, Lars. 1993. "Tillvarons hemlighet finns hos törnrosen." In *Parnass* 1993:2. Reprinted in *Väldarnas möte: Nya Kyrkans tidning* 4–5:15–20.

———. 1997. "Linnaeus and Swedenborg." *Arcana* 3(3):23–39.

———. 1999a. "Swedenborg-Ekelund: porträtt med dubbelexponering." In *Den största lyckan: En bok till Vilhelm Ekelund,* edited by Per Erik Ljung and Helena Nilsson. Lund: Ellerström.

———. 1999b. *Swedenborgs hemlighet: Om Ordets betyldese, änglarnas liv och tjänsten hos Gud.* Stockholm: Natur och Kultur.

———. 2001. Introduction to *Swedenborg's Dream Diary*, edited by Lars Bergquist and translated by Anders Hallengren. West Chester, Pa.: Swedenborg Foundation.

Bergquist, Olle. 1995. *Om "Frälsarens dyra blod" och tidningsläsning hos Gud*. Skellefteå: Artos.

Bestor, Arthur. 1970. *Backwoods Utopias: The Sectarian and the Owenite Phase of Communalism in America*. 2nd ed. Philadelphia: University of Pennsylvania Press.

[Beyer, Gabriel]. 1767. *Nya försök til upbyggelig förklaring öfwer evangliska sön- och högtidsdags texterne*. Göteborg: Lange.

Bigelow, John. 1880. *Resist Beginnings, or The Blinding Influences of Sin*. New York: New-Church Board of Publication.

———. 1895. *The Life of Samuel J. Tilden*. New York: Harper & Brothers.

———. 1905. *The Useful Life: A Crown to the Simple Life as Taught by Emanuel Swedenborg*. New York: Charles Scribner's Sons.

———. 1907. *The Proprium, and Other Essays and Studies, Posthumous*. New York: New-Church Board of Publication.

———. 1924. *The Mystery of Sleep*. New York: New-Church Press.

———. 1927. *Toleration, or What of Man Is Not His Own*. New York: New-Church Press.

———. [1893] 1979. *The Bible That Was Lost and Is Found*. 4th ed. New York: Swedenborg Press.

Björck, Albert. 1898. "Kongressens uppkomst." In *Religionsvetenskapliga kongressen i Stockholm 1897*, edited by S. A Fries. N.p.

———. 1900. *Swedenborg, Strindberg, och det ondas problem*. Stockholm.

Blake, William. 1907. Marginal Notes to Swedenborg's *Divine Love and Wisdom*. In *The Real Blake, A Portrait Biography*, by Edwin John Ellis. London: Chatto & Windus.

———. [1825–1827] 1927. *The Marriage of Heaven and Hell*. London: J. M. Dent & Sons.

———. 1966. Marginal Notes to Swedenborg's *Divine Providence*. In *The Theology of William Blake*, by J. G. Davies. Hamden, Conn.: Archon Books.

———. [1804] 1970a. *Jerusalem*. In *The Poetry and Prose of William Blake*, edited by David V. Erdman. Garden City, N. Y.: Doubleday.

———. [1790] 1970b. *The Marriage of Heaven and Hell*. In *The Poetry and Prose of William Blake*, edited by David V. Erdman. Garden City, N. Y.: Doubleday.

Blin, George. 1939. *Baudelaire*. Paris: Gallimard.

Block, Marguerite Beck. 1984. *The New Church in the New World: A Study of Swedenborgianism in America*. Enlarged edition. New York: Swedenborg Publishing Association.

Bohlin, Torsten. 1925. *Kierkegaards domatiska åskådning i dess historiska sammanhang*. Stockholm: Svenska Kyrkans Diakonistryrelses Bokförlag.

Böök, Fredrik. 1919. *Erik Johan Stagnelius*. Stockholm: Bonnier.

Borges, Jorge Luis. 1969. *El Otro, El Mismo*. Buenos Aires: Emecé.

———. 1988. "Testimony to the Invisible." In *Emanuel Swedenborg: A Continuing Vision*, edited by Robin Larsen and others. New York: Swedenborg Foundation.

Borowy, Wacław. 1999. *O poezji Mickiewicza*. 2nd rev. ed. Lublin: Towarzystwo Naukowe.

Bradford, Thomas. 1895. *Life and Letters of Samuel Hahnemann*. Philadelphia: Boericke & Tafel.

Brisbane, Albert. 1968. *Social Destiny of Man*. New York: B. Franklin. First edition: 1840, Philadelphia: C. F. Stollmeyer.

Broberg, Gunnar. 1988. "Swedenborg and Uppsala." Translated by Gunilla Stenman Gado. In *Emanuel Swedenborg: A Continuing Vision,* edited by Robin Larsen and others. New York: Swedenborg Foundation.

Brock, Erland J., and others, eds. 1988. *Swedenborg and His Influence.* Bryn Athyn, Pa.: Academy of the New Church.

Brody de Lamotte, Edouard. 1938. "Le culte de la Nouvelle Jérusalem à Saint-Amand-Montrond (1837–1937)." *Mémoires de la Société des Antiquaires du Centre* (Bourges) 47:133–173.

Brooks, Van Wyck. 1956. *Helen Keller: Sketch for a Portrait.* New York: E. P. Dutton.

Browning, Elizabeth Barrett. 1900. *The Complete Poetical Works of Mrs. Browning.* Edited by Harriet Waters Preston. Boston: Houghton Mifflin.

———. [1856] 1992. *Aurora Leigh.* Edited by Margaret Reynolds. Athens: Ohio University Press.

———. [1856] 1995. *Aurora Leigh.* Edited by John Robert Glorney Bolton and Julia Bolton Holloway. New York: Penguin Books.

Browning, Robert, and Elizabeth Barrett Browning. 1958. *Letters of the Brownings to George Barrett.* Edited by Paul Landis and Ronald Freeman. Urbana, Ill.: University of Illinois Press.

Bush, George. 1847. *Mesmer and Swedenborg; or The Relation of the Development of Mesmerism to the Doctrines and Disclosures of Swedenborg.* New York: John Allen.

———. 1857a. *Priesthood and Clergy Unknown to Christianity; or The Church a Community of Co-equal Brethren.* Philadelphia: J. B. Lippincott.

———. 1857b. *Reply to Ralph Waldo Emerson on Swedenborg.* New York: John Allen.

———. 1860. *Memoirs and Reminiscences of the Late George Bush.* Edited and arranged by Woodbury M. Fernald. Boston: Otis Clapp.

Buss, James F. 1924. *The Romantic Story of the South African Mission.* London: General Conference of the New Church.

———. 1927. *The Romantic Story of the South African Mission.* 2nd ed. London: General Conference of the New Church.

Buteux, Sarah. 1998. *The History of the Reverend Samuel Weems and the North Cambridge Community Church.* Senior Thesis, Swedenborg School of Religion.

[C.F.K.]. 1892. "Annals of the New Church in Washington. V." *New-Church Messenger* 63:26.

Calvert, G. H. 1847. "The Process of Sculpture." *The Literary World* 1:159–160.

Cameron, Kenneth Walter. 1984. *Emerson's Transcendentalism and British Swedenborgianism.* Hartford, Conn.: Transcendental Books.

Campbell, Dan. 1998. "The Poughkeepsie Seer." *Studia Swedenborgiana* 11(1):31–43.

Carlson, Maria. 1993. *"No Religion Higher than Truth": A History of the Theosophical Movement in Russia, 1875–1922.* Princeton: Princeton University Press.

Carroll, Bret E. 1997. *Spiritualism in Antebellum America.* Bloomington, Ind.: Indiana University Press.

Carter, Carrie Giles, ed. and comp. 1920. *The Life of Chauncey Giles: As Told in His Diary and Correspondence.* Boston: Massachusetts New-Church Union.

Carter, Robert. Collection of Letters. Swedenborgian House of Studies, Swedenborgian Library and Archives at the Pacific School of Religion, Berkeley, Ca.

Castellion, Sébastien. 1551. *Biblia Interprete Sebastiano Castalione: Una cum Eiusdem Annotationibus.* Basel: Iohannes Operinus.

[Chastanier, Bénédict]. 1786. *Tableau analytique et raisonné de la Doctrine céleste de l'Église de la Nouvelle Jérusalem.* London.

Chastanier, Bénédict. 1787. "Préface du Traducteur." In *Traité de la Vie,* by Emanuel Swedenborg, translated by Bénédict Chastanier. London: T. Spilsbury.

[Chevrier, Edmond]. 1879. *Histoire sommaire de la Nouvelle Eglise chrétienne fondée sur les doctrines de Swedenborg.* Paris: Librairie.

Child, Lydia Maria. 1833. *An Appeal in Favor of That Class of Americans Called Africans.* Boston: Allen & Ticknor.

———. 1843. *Letters from New York.* 1st ser. New York: Francis.

———. 2000. "Appleseed John." In *Johnny Appleseed: A Voice in the Wilderness,* edited by William Ellery Jones. West Chester, Pa.: Swedenborg Foundation.

Childs, Brevard S. 1977. "The *Sensus Literalis* of Scripture: An Ancient and Modern Problem." In *Beiträge zur alttestamentlichen Theologie: Festschrift für Walther Zimmerli zum 70. Geburtstag,* edited by W. H. Zimmerli and others. Göttingen: Vandenhoeck und Ruprecht.

Childs, Cephas P. 1827–1830. *Views in Philadelphia.* Philadelphia: Library Company of Philadelphia.

Childs, Walter C., comp. 1999. *The Life and Times of John Pitcairn.* Bryn Athyn, Pa.: Academy of the New Church.

"Church News: Washington, D.C." 1896. *New-Church Messenger* 71:250.

Cikovsky, Nicolai. 1977. *The Life and Works of George Inness.* New York: Garland Publishing.

Čiževskij, Dmitrij. 1956. "Svedenborg bei den Slaven." Chapter 17 in *Aus Zwei Welten: Beiträge zur Geschichte der slavish-westlichen literarischen Beziehungen.* 's Gravenhage: Mouton.

———. [1956] 2002. "Swedenborg among the Slavs." Translated by George F. Dole. *Studia Swedenborgiana* 12(3):1–30.

Clapp, Margaret. 1947. *Forgotten First Citizen: John Bigelow.* Boston: Little, Brown.

Clapp, Otis. 1845. "The Family Sphere." *The Harbinger, Devoted to Social and Political Progress* 1:70.

Clowes, John. 1787. *A Summary View of the Heavenly Doctrines.* Philadelphia: Francis Bailey.

———. 1874. *The Memoirs of John Clowes.* Edited by Theodore Compton. London: Longmans, Green.

Cole, Wertha Pendleton. 1933. "Swedenborg's Work on Longitude." *The New Philosophy* 36:169–178.

Collinson, Patrick. 1982. *The Religion of Protestants: The Church in English Society.* Oxford: Clarendon Press.

Compton, Theodore. 1895. *William Cookworthy.* London: E. Hicks, Jr.

Crane, Sylvia E. 1972. *White Silence: Greenough, Powers, and Crawford, American Sculptors in Nineteenth-Century Italy.* Coral Gables, Fla.: University of Miami Press.

Crasta, Maria Francesca. 1999. *La filosofia della natura di Emanuel Swedenborg.* Milano: Edizioni Franco Angeli.

Croce, Ann Jerome. 1996a. "Similars and Correspondences, Healing and Heaven: Swedenborg and the Philosophy of Homeopathy." Paper presented at the annual meeting of the American Academy of Religion, New Orleans.

Croce, Paul Jerome. 1988. "A Scientific Spiritualism: The Elder Henry James's Adaptation of Emanuel Swedenborg." In *Swedenborg and His Influence,* edited by Erland J. Brock and others. Bryn Athyn, Pa.: Academy of the New Church.

———. 1995. *Science and Religion in the Era of William James.* Vol. 1, *Eclipse of Certainty, 1820–1880.* Chapel Hill, N.C.: University of North Carolina Press.

———. 1996b. "Between Swedenborgianism and Science: William James on Religion and Human Nature." Paper presented at the annual meeting of the American Academy of Religion, New Orleans.

Cuno, J. C. 1947. *J. C. Cuno's Memoirs on Swedenborg.* Translated by Claire E. Berninger. Bryn Athyn, Pa.: Academy Book Room.

Dahlgren, Erik Wilhelm. 1915. "Carl Bernhard Wadström: hans verksamhet för slafhandelns bekämpande och de samtida kolonisationsplanerna i Västafrika. Bibliografisk sammanställning." *Nordisk tidskrift för Bok- och Biblioteksväsen* 2.

Dahlstrand, Frederick C. 1982. *Amos Bronson Alcott: An Intellectual Biography.* Rutherford, N.J.: Fairleigh Dickinson University Press.

Dakeyne, James. 1888. *History of the Bolton New Church.* London: James Speirs.

Dante Alighieri. 1964. "Letter to Can Grande della Scala." Translated by Nancy Howe. In *Essays on Dante,* edited by Mark Musa. Bloomington: Indiana University Press.

Davies, J. G. 1966. *The Theology of William Blake.* Hamden, Conn.: Archon Books.

Davis, Andrew Jackson. 1847. *Principles of Nature—Her Divine Revelations and a Voice of Mankind.* New York: S. S. Lyon and W. Fishbough.

———. 1857. *The Magic Staff: An Autobiography.* New York: J. S. Brown.

de Charms, Richard. 1850a. *Discourse on the True Nature of Slavery and Freedom.* Philadelphia: E. Ferrett.

———. 1850b. "Have the Principles of Homoeopathy an Affinity with the Doctrines of the New Church?" *New Church Repository* 3:501–508. Reprinted as "Hahnemann and Swedenborg" in *Arcana* 2001 6(1):80–90.

———. 1851. *Some Views of Freedom and Slavery in the Light of the New Jerusalem.* Philadelphia: George Chandler.

———. 1853. *Three Sermons Presented to the New York Society of the New Jerusalem Against the Pseudo-Spiritualism of Modern Times.* Philadelphia: New Jerusalem Press.

De Quincey, Thomas. 1824. "Abstract of Swedenborgianism: by Immanuel Kant." *London Magazine* 9(May):489–492. Reprinted in *The Works of Thomas De Quincey,* edited by Frederick Burwick, London: Pickering & Chatto, 2000, 4:160–166.

———. 1837. "Autobiography of an English Opium-Eater. Literary Connexions or Acquaintances." *Tait's Edinburgh Magazine,* n.s., 4:65–68. Reprinted as "A Manchester Swedenborgian and a Liverpool Literary Coterie" in *The Collected Writings of Thomas De Quincey,* edited by David Masson, Edinburgh: Adam & Charles Black, 1897, 2:113. Reprint of Masson's edition: New York: AMS Press, 1968.

De Rosa, Elizabeth Johnston. 1995. *Louis Comfort Tiffany and the Development of Religious Landscape Memorial Windows.* Dissertation, Columbia University.

Deck, Raymond Henry, Jr. 1978. *Blake and Swedenborg.* Dissertation, Brandeis University.

Deghaye, Pierre. 1969. *La doctrine ésotérique de Zinzendorf (1700–1760).* Paris: Éditions Klincksieck.

Delano, Sterling F. 1983. *The Harbinger and New England Transcendentalism: A Portrait of Associationism in America.* Rutherford, N.J.: Fairleigh Dickinson University Press.

Diaconoff, Andre. 1966. "She Envisioned the Wayfarers Chapel." *New-Church Messenger* 186:76.

Doering, Charles E. 1932. *A History of the Swedenborg Scientific Association.* Philadelphia: Swedenborg Scientific Association. Reprinted from *The New Philosophy* 35:82–97.

Dole, George F. 1988a. "An Image of God in a Mirror." In *Emanuel Swedenborg: A Continuing Vision,* edited by Robin Larsen and others. New York: Swedenborg Foundation.

———. 1988b. "A Rationale for Swedenborg's Writing Sequence, 1745–1771." In *Emanuel Swedenborg: A Continuing Vision,* edited by Robin Larsen and others. New York: Swedenborg Foundation.

———. 1988c. "*True Christian Religion* as Apologetic Theology." In *Swedenborg and His Influence,* edited by Erland J. Brock and others. Bryn Athyn, Pa.: Academy of the New Church.

———. 1990. "Philosemitism in the Seventeenth Century." *Studia Swedenborgiana* 7(1):5–17.

———. 1993. *With Absolute Respect: The Swedenborgian Theology of Charles Carroll Bonney.* West Chester, Pa.: Swedenborg Foundation.

———. 2000. Translator's preface to *Heaven and Hell,* by Emanuel Swedenborg, translated by George F. Dole. West Chester, Pa.: Swedenborg Foundation.

———. 2003. Translator's preface to *Divine Love and Wisdom,* by Emanuel Swedenborg, translated by George F. Dole. West Chester, Pa.: Swedenborg Foundation.

Dole, George F., and Robert H. Kirven. 1992. *A Scientist Explores Spirit.* New York City and West Chester, Pa.: Swedenborg Foundation.

Dombrowski, Daniel A. 1984. *The Philosophy of Vegetarianism.* Amherst, Mass.: University of Massachusetts Press.

Dress, Walter. 1979. *Johann Friedrich Immanuel Tafel, 1796–1863: Ein Lebensbericht.* Zürich: Swedenborg Verlag.

Dresser, Annetta Gertrude. 1895. *The Philosophy of P. P. Quimby.* Boston: Ellis.

Dresser, Horatio W. 1911. "Swedenborg" [Part 3]. *Practical Ideals* 23:1–6.

———. 1919. *A History of the New Thought Movement.* New York: Thomas Crowell.

———. [1921] 1961. *The Quimby Manuscripts: Showing the Discovery of Spiritual Healing and the Origin of Christian Science.* New York: Julian Press. First edition: New York: Thomas Y. Crowell.

Dresser, Julius A. 1899. *The True History of Mental Science: The Facts Concerning the Discovery of Mental Healing.* Revised edition with notes and additions by Horatio W. Dresser. Boston: Ellis.

Duckworth, Dennis. 1998. *A Branching Tree: A Narrative History of the General Conference of the New Church.* London: General Conference of the New Church.

Eby, S. C. 1926. *The Story of the Swedenborg Manuscripts.* New York: New-Church Press.

"Editorial Items: Swedenborg and Fourier." 1848. *New Church Repository* 1:186–187.

Edmisten, Leonard Martin. 1954. *Coleridge's Commentary on Swedenborg.* Dissertation, University of Missouri, Columbia.

Ekelöf, Gunnar. 1960. *En Mölna-Elegi.* Stockholm: Albert Bonniers.

———. 1984. *A Mölna Elegy.* Translated by Leif Sjöberg. Greensboro, N.C.: Unicorn Press.

Ekelund, Vilhelm. 1922. *På hafsstranden.* Stockholm: Bonnier.

Ekman, Hedda. 1924. *Tva släkter.* Stockholm.

Eller, David B. 1999. *Illuminating the World of Spirit: A Sesquicentennial Record of the Swedenborg Foundation, 1850–2000.* West Chester, Pa.: Swedenborg Foundation.

Ellis, Edwin John, and William Butler Yeats. 1973. "Memoir [of William Blake]." In vol. 1 of *The Works of William Blake: Poetic, Symbolic, and Critical,* by William Blake, edited by Edwin John Ellis and William Butler Yeats. New York: AMS Press. First edition: 1893, London: B. Quarich.

Ellwood, Robert S. 1991. "Swedenborg, Andrew Jackson Davis, and Spiritualism." Paper presented at the annual meeting of the American Academy of Religion, Kansas City, Mo.

Emerson, Ralph Waldo. 1850. *Representative Men: Seven Lectures.* Boston: Phillips Sampson.

———. [1849] 1884. *Nature, Addresses, and Lectures.* Boston: Houghton, Mifflin Co.

———. 1929. *The Complete Writings of Ralph Waldo Emerson.* 2 vols. New York: Wm. H. Wise.

———. 1959–1972. "The Poet." In vol. 3 of *The Early Lectures of Ralph Waldo Emerson,* edited by S. E. Whicher, R. E. Spiller, and W. E. Williams. Cambridge: Harvard University Press.

Ens, Adolf, and Leonard Doell. 1992. "Mennonite Swedenborgians." *Journal of Mennonite Studies* 10:101-111.

Erikson, Alvar. 1973. "Some Observations on the Style of Swedenborg." *Classica et Mediaevalia* 9:622–628.

Ernesti, Johann August. 1760. Review of *Secrets of Heaven,* by Emanuel Swedenborg. *Neue Theologische Bibliothek* 1:515–527.

———. 1768. Review of *Apocalypse Revealed,* by Emanuel Swedenborg. Translated into Swedish and annotated by Johan Rosén. *Preste-Tidningar* (April):97–109.

Evans, F[rederick] W. 1869. *Autobiography of a Shaker, and Revelation of the Apocalypse.* Mt. Lebanon, N.Y.: United Society of Believers.

Evans, Jean. [1994?]. *A History of the New Church in Southern Africa, 1909–1991, and a Tribute to the Late Reverend Obed S. D. Mooki.* Privately printed in South Africa.

Evans, Warren Felt. 1864. *The New Age and Its Messenger.* Boston: T. H. Carter.

———. 1869. *The Mental-Cure, Illustrating the Influence of the Mind on the Body, Both in Health and Disease, and the Psychological Method of Treatment.* Boston: H. H. and T. W. Carter.

F. P. 1841. "La littérature s'occupe de Swedenborg." *La Nouvelle Jérusalem: Revue religieuse et scientifique* 4:38–45.

Fairfax, Thomas. Papers. University of Virginia Library.

Faivre, Antoine. 2000. *Theosophy, Imagination, Tradition.* Translated by Christine Rhone. Albany: State University of New York Press.

Faivre, Antoine, and Jacob Needleman, eds. 1992. *Modern Esoteric Spirituality.* New York: Crossroad.

Falck-Odhner Correspondence. Swedenborg Library, Bryn Athyn, Pa.

Ferguson, Marilyn. 1980. *The Aquarian Conspiracy: Personal and Social Transformation in the 1980s.* Los Angeles: J. P. Tarcher.

Field, George. 1879. *Memoirs, Incidents, & Reminiscences.* New York: E. H. Swinney.

Florschütz, Gottlieb. 1992. *Swedenborgs verborgene Wirkung auf Kant: Swedenborg und die okkulten Phänomene aus der Sicht von Kant und Schopenhauer.* Würzburg: Königshausen & Neumann.

[Ford], A. E. 1869. "News and Correspondence from Italy." *New Jerusalem Messenger* 17:25.

Forster, Margaret. 1988. *Elizabeth Barrett Browning: A Biography.* New York: Doubleday.

The Founders. 1933. *Statement of the Urbana Movement.* Swedenborgian House of Studies Library, Pacific School of Religion, Berkeley, Ca.

Freeman, Arthur J. 1998. *An Ecumenical Theology of the Heart: The Theology of Count Nicholas Ludwig von Zinzendorf.* Bethlehem, Pa.: Moravian Church in America.

Frost, Lesley. 1984. Introduction to *Robert Frost: Contours of Belief,* by Dorothy Judd Hall. Athens, Ohio: Ohio University Press.

Frost, Robert. 1966a. *Interviews with Robert Frost.* Edited by Edward Connery Lathem. New York: Holt, Rinehart and Winston.

———. 1966b. *The Poetry of Robert Frost.* Edited by Edward Connery Lathem. New York: Holt, Rinehart and Winston.

———. 1966c. *Selected Prose of Robert Frost.* Edited by Hyde Cox and Edward Connery Lathem. New York: Collier Books.

Garrett, Clarke. 1987. *Origins of the Shakers from the Old World to the New.* Baltimore: John Hopkins University Press.

Garrett, Martin, ed. 2000. *Elizabeth Barrett Browning and Robert Browning: Interviews and Recollections.* New York: St. Martin's Press.

Gauvey, Ralph. 1958. "Implementing a Philosophy of Education." *The Messenger* 178:273–275.

Geijer, Erik Gustaf. 1820. *Thorild: Tillika en philosophisk eller ophilosophisk bekännelse.* Uppsala: Palmblad.

———. 1873. *Svenska folkets historia.* In vol. 5 of *Samlade Skrifter.* Stockholm: P. A. Norstedt & Söner.

General Church. 1908. *A Liturgy for the General Church of the New Jerusalem.* Bryn Athyn, Pa.: Academy Book Room.

———. 1922. *A Liturgy for the General Church of the New Jerusalem.* Rev. ed. Bryn Athyn, Pa.: Academy of the New Church Book Room.

General Conference. 1885. *Minutes of the First Seven Sessions of the General Conference of the New Church.* London: James Speirs.

———. 1902. *Minutes of the Ninety-Fifth Session of the General Conference.* London: General Conference of the New Church.

———. 1999–2000. *General Conference of the New Church Year Book, 1999–2000.* London: General Conference of the New Church.

General Convention. 1836. *Book of Public Worship.* Boston: Otis Clapp.

———. 1854. *Liturgy, or Book of Worship, for the Use of the New Church Signified by the New Jerusalem.* Rev. ed. Boston: Otis Clapp.

———. 1857. *Book of Worship, for the Use of the New Church Signified by the New Jerusalem.* Rev. ed. New York: General Convention Board of Publications.

———. 1888. *Reprint of Early Journals of the General Convention of the New Jerusalem.* Part 1, *Journals One to Eight, 1817–1826.* Boston: General Convention of the New Jerusalem.

———. 1902–1912. Board of Missions, Correspondence Files. Swedenborgian Church of North America, Newtonville, Mass.

———. 1907. *Book of Public Worship*. New York: New-Church Board of Publication.

———. 1910a. *Book of Public Worship*. New York: New-Church Board of Publication.

———. 1910b. *The Magnificat*. New York: New-Church Press.

———. 1913. *Book of Public Worship*. New York: New-Church Board of Publication.

———. 1950. *Book of Worship: Containing Services, Chants, Sacraments, Rites, Prayers, and Hymns*. New York: New-Church Board of Publication.

"George Field." 1884. *New-Church Magazine* 8:60.

Gill, Gillian. 1998. *Mary Baker Eddy*. Cambridge, Mass.: Perseus Books.

Gill, Robert A., and Helen Laidlaw. [2000]. *The New Jerusalem Church in Scotland 1798–1998*. [Scottish Association of the New Church].

Gladish, Richard R. 1968–1973. *A History of New Church Education*. 4 vols. Bryn Athyn, Pa. Mimeographed for the author.

———. 1984. *Bishop William Henry Benade: Founder and Reformer*. Bryn Athyn, Pa.: Academy of the New Church.

———. 1988. *Richard de Charms, Senior: New Church Champion*. Bryn Athyn, Pa. Self-published.

———. 1989. *John Pitcairn, Uncommon Entrepreneur*. Bryn Athyn, Pa.: Academy of the New Church.

———. 1991. "Retrospective of the New Church Theological School, 1866–1966." *Studia Swedenborgiana* 7(3):21–49. An edited version of material in Gladish 1968–1973.

Gladish, Robert W. 1965. "Elizabeth Barrett Browning and Swedenborg." *New Church Life* 85:506–513, 559–570.

———. 1983. *Swedenborg, Fourier and the America of the 1840's*. Bryn Athyn, Pa.: Swedenborg Scientific Association.

Gleason, Philip. 1961. "From Free-Love to Catholicism: Dr. and Mrs. Thomas L. Nichols at Yellow Springs." *Ohio Historical Quarterly* 70:283–307.

Glen, James. 1813. "On the Negro Character." *Intellectual Repository* 1:338–341.

Glenn, E. Bruce. 1971. *Bryn Athyn Cathedral: The Building of a Church*. Bryn Athyn, Pa.: Bryn Athyn Church of the New Jerusalem.

Glover, Mary Baker. 1875. *Science and Health*. Boston: Christian Scientist Publishing.

Goerwitz, Feodor. 1894. "The New Church on the Continent of Europe." In *The New Jerusalem in the World's Religious Congresses of 1893*, edited by L. P. Mercer. Chicago: Western New-Church Union.

Goldschmidt, Meir. 1862. *Swedenborgs ungdom*. Copenhagen: Høst.

Götrek, Per. 1854. *Swedenborgs lära, kort, enkelt och tydligt fram ställd*. Carlshamn: E. R. Hööks.

Goyder, Thomas. 1833. *Christianity and Colonial Slavery Contrasted*. London. Privately printed.

Grattan, C. Hartley. 1932. *The Three Jameses: A Family of Minds*. London: Longmans, Green.

[Green, Calvin, and Seth Wells]. 1848. *A Summary View of the Millennial Church, or The United Society of Believers*. 2nd rev. ed. Albany, N.Y.: C. van Benthuysen.

Greenall, R. L. 2000. *The Making of Victorian Salford*. Lancaster: Carnegie Publishing Ltd.

Griffith, Freda G. 1960. *The Swedenborg Society, 1810–1960.* London: Swedenborg Society.

Groth, Friedhelm. 1995. "Peter Eberhard Müllensiefen, Iserlohner Landrat von 1818 bis 1836, in seinen Beziehungen zum Tübinger Swedenborgianer Immanuel Tafel." *Blätter zur Deilinghofer Kirchengeschichte* 3a. Iserlohn: Zeitungsverlag Iserlohn.

Gutfeldt, Horan. 1994. "Encountering Saint Emanuel." *The Messenger* 215:145–147.

[Gyllenborg, Elisabet Stierncrona]. 1756–1760. *Marie bäste del eller Thet ena nödwändiga.* Vol. 1, Stockholm: Lorentz Ludwig Grefing. Vol. 2, Stockholm: Lars Salvius.

Gyllenhaal, Martha. 1996. "John Flaxman's Illustrations to Emanuel Swedenborg's *Arcana Coelestia.*" *Studia Swedenborgiana* 9(4):1–71.

Gyllenhaal, Martha, and others. 1988. *New Light: Ten Artists Inspired by Emanuel Swedenborg.* Bryn Athyn, Pa.: Glencairn Museum.

Habegger, Alfred. 1994. *The Father: A Life of Henry James, Sr.* New York: Farrar, Straus and Giroux.

Hahnemann, Samuel. [1836] 1982. *Organon.* Los Angeles: Tarcher.

Halcyon Luminary and Theological Repository. 1812–1813 (vols. 1–2). New York: Samuel Woodworth & Co. and E. Riley; Boston: J. W. Burdett & Co.; Baltimore: Anthony Miltenberger.

Hall, Dorothy Judd. 1994. "The Mystic Lens of Robert Frost." *Studia Swedenborgiana* 9(1):1–26.

Häll, Jan. 1995. *I Swedenborgs labyrint: Studier i de gustavianska swedenborgarnas liv och tänkande.* Stockholm: Atlantis.

Hall, Manly P. 1972. *Man: Grand Symbol of the Mysteries.* 3rd ed. Los Angeles: Philosophical Research Society.

Hallengren, Anders. 1989. *Carl Robsahm: Anteckningar om Swedenborg, med en inledande sjalvbiografisk text av Emanuel Swedenborg Svar pa brev fron en van.* Stockholm: ABA Cad/Copy & Tryck.

———. 1991. "Hermeneutics, Transcendence, and Modernity: The Swedenborg-Whitman Connection." Paper presented at the annual meeting of the American Academy of Religion, Kansas City, Mo.

———. 1992. *Deciphering Reality: Swedenborg, Emerson, Whitman and the Search for the Language of Nature.* Minneapolis: University of Minnesota Press.

———. 1994a. *Code of Concord: Emerson's Search for Universal Laws.* Stockholm: Almqvist & Wiksell.

———. 1994b. "Västindien, swedenborgianismen och slavieriet." *Väldarnas möte: Nya Kyrkans tidning* 4:128–142. English version: "The New Church in the West Indies," translated by George F. Dole, in *Gallery of Mirrors: Reflections of Swedenborgian Thought,* West Chester, Pa.: Swedenborg Foundation, 1998.

———. 1998a. *Gallery of Mirrors: Reflections of Swedenborgian Thought.* West Chester, Pa.: Swedenborg Foundation.

———. 1998b. "Swedenborgs wäg till Boston." *Väldarnas möte: Nya Kyrkans tidning* 3:34–37.

———. 2004. "A Hermeneutic Key to the Title *Leaves of Grass.*" In *In Search of the Absolute: Essays on Swedenborg and Literature,* edited by Stephen McNeilly. London: Swedenborg Society.

Hamilton, J. Taylor, and Kenneth G. Hamilton. 1967. *History of the Moravian Church: The Renewed Unitas Fratrum, 1722–1857.* Bethlehem, Pa.: Interprovincial Board of Christian Education, Moravian Church in America.

Hamilton, Malcolm B. 1995. *The Sociology of Religion: Theoretical and Comparative Perspectives.* London: Routledge.

Hammarsköld, Lorenzo. 1821. *Historiska anteckningar rörande fortgången och utvecklingen af det Philosophiska Studium i Sverige.* Stockholm: Haeggström.

Hanegraaff, Wouter J. 1998. *New Age Religion and Western Culture: Esotericism in the Mirror of Secular Thought.* Albany: State University of New York Press.

The Harbinger: Devoted to Social and Political Progress. 1845–1849. New York: Burgess, Stringer & Co.; Boston: Redding & Co.

Harding, Brian. 1974. "Swedenborgian Spirit and Thoreautic Sense." *Journal of American Studies* 7:64–79.

Harner, Michael. 1990. *The Way of the Shaman.* San Francisco: Harper SanFrancisco.

Harris, Thomas Lake. [1858–1867] 1976. *Arcana of Christianity: An Unfolding of the Celestial Sense of the Divine Word through T. L. Harris.* New York: AMS Press. First edition: vol. 1, parts 1 and 2, New York: New Church Publishing Association, 1858; vol. 1, part 3, New York: Brotherhood of the New Life, 1867. (No other volumes were published.)

Harrison, J.F.C. 1969. *Quest for the New Moral World: Robert Owen and the Owenites in America.* New York: Scribner.

Harrity, Richard, and Ralph G. Martin. 1962. *The Three Lives of Helen Keller.* New York: Doubleday.

Hawkstone Inn: The Report. 1806. Minutes of the annual meeting of the New Church Nonseparatists. Liverpool: Wright and Cruickshank.

Hawley, Charles A. 1935. "A Communistic Swedenborgian Society in Iowa." *Iowa Journal of History and Politics* 33:3–26.

———. 1936. "The Historical Background of the Attitude of the Jasper Colony toward Slavery and the Civil War." *Iowa Journal of History and Politics* 34:172–197.

Hayward, T. B. 1829. *Book of Public Worship.* Boston: Hilliard, Gray, Little and Wilkins.

Heinrichs, Michael. 1979. *Emanuel Swedenborg in Deutschland: Eine kritische Darstellung der Rezeption des schwedischen Visionärs im 18. and 19. Jahrhundert.* Frankfurt am Main: Peter D. Lang.

Helander, Hans. 1993. "Swedenborg's Latin." *Studia Swedenborgiana* 8(1):21–48.

———. 1995. Introduction to *Ludus Heliconius and Other Latin Poems,* by Emanuel Swedenborg, edited and translated by Hans Helander. Uppsala: University of Uppsala.

De Hemelsche Leer. January 1930 (no. 1)–February 1939 (no. 11). The Hague: Swedenborg Genootschap.

Hempel, Charles Julius. 1843. "The Phalanx." *Newchurchman* 2:369–370.

———. 1848. *The True Organization of the New Church as Indicated in the Writings of Emanuel Swedenborg and Demonstrated by Charles Fourier.* New York: William Radde.

[———]. 1848–1849. "A Reply to the *Repository.*" *The Harbinger: Devoted to Social and Political Progress* 8(1848):69; 8(1849):85–86; 8(1849):100–101; 8(1849):108–109.

Herrmann, Dorothy. 1998. *Helen Keller: A Life.* New York: Knopf.

[Hibbard, J. R.]. 1884. "Reminiscences of a Pioneer." *New Jerusalem Messenger* 46:81.

Hiebert, Clarence. 1973. *The Holdeman People, The Church of God in Christ, Mennonite, 1859–1969.* South Pasadena, Ca.: William Carey Library.

Higgins, Frank. 1977. *"The Will to Survive": Urbana College, 1850–1975.* Urbana, Ohio: Urbana College.

Higham, Charles. 1914. "Some Phases of the Swedenborg 'Insanity' Myth." Part 1. *New-Church Magazine* 33:32–38.

[Hinckley, Willard H.]. 1892. "Contributed: An Historical Address by the Rev. Willard Hall Hinckley . . . at the Centennial Celebration of the First Proclamation of the Doctrines of the New Church in Baltimore, April 1st, 1892." *New-Church Messenger* 62:249–252.

Hindmarsh, James. 1794. *A New Dictionary of Correspondences.* London: R. Hindmarsh.

Hindmarsh, Robert. 1793. [Note on the *Coronis.*] In *Minutes of a General Conference of the Members of the New Church.* London: General Conference.

———. 1861. *Rise and Progress of the New Jerusalem Church.* London: Hodson & Son.

Hines, Thomas S. 1974. *Burnham of Chicago, Architect and Planner.* Oxford: Oxford University Press. Reprint, Chicago: University of Chicago Press, 1979.

Hirst, Désirée. 1964. *Hidden Riches: Traditional Symbolism from the Renaissance to Blake.* London: Eyre & Spottiswoode.

Hite, Lewis F. 1939. *Urbana University and Higher Education.* Urbana, Ohio: Urbana University.

Hjern, Olle. 1963a. "Runeberg om Swedenborg." *Nya Kyrkans tidning* 88:107.

———. 1963b. "Swedenborg i Paris." *Nya Kyrkans tidning* 88:12.

———. 1964. "A. A. Afzelius och Nya Kyrkan." *Nya Kyrkans tidning* 89:11–12.

———. 1988a. "Carl Jonas Love Almqvist—Great Poet and Swedenborgian Heretic." In *Swedenborg and His Influence,* edited by Erland J. Brock and others. Bryn Athyn, Pa.: Academy of the New Church.

———. 1988b. "Swedenborg in Stockholm." In *Emanuel Swedenborg: A Continuing Vision,* edited by Robin Larsen and others. New York: Swedenborg Foundation.

———. 1999a. "Love Almqvist och Nya Kyrkan i Pennsylvania." *Väldarnas möte: Nya Kyrkans tidning* 4–5:42–45.

———. 1999b. "Religiositet och andlighet hos Vilhelm Ekelund." In *Den största lyckan: En bok till Vilhelm Ekelund,* edited by Per Erik Ljung and Helena Nilsson. Lund: Ellerström.

[Hobart, William N.]. 1911. *Outline History of the New Jerusalem Church of Cincinnati.* Cincinnati: New Jerusalem Church.

Holcombe, William H. 1881. *The End of the World: With New Interpretations of History.* Philadelphia: J. B. Lippincott.

"The Holy League." 1817. *New Jerusalem Church Repository* 1:58–61.

Hoover, Dwight. 1969. *Henry James, Senior, and the Religion of Community.* Grand Rapids, Mich.: William B. Eerdmans.

———. 1988. "The Influence of Swedenborg on the Religious Ideas of Henry James, Senior." In *Swedenborg and His Influence,* edited by Erland J. Brock and others. Bryn Athyn, Pa.: Academy of the New Church.

Horn, Friedemann. 1997. *Schelling and Swedenborg: Mysticism and German Idealism.* Translated by George F. Dole. West Chester, Pa.: Swedenborg Foundation.

———. 1999. "Swedenborgs verborgerner Einfluss auf die Literatur." *Offene Tore* 43:188–204.

Horn, Vivi. 1921. *De små Knösarna.* Stockholm: Geber.

Hotson, Clarence Paul. 1929a. *Emerson and Swedenborg.* Dissertation, Harvard University.

———. 1929b. "Sampson Reed, A Teacher of Emerson." *New England Quarterly* 2:249–277.

Hübener, Anja. 1988. "Carolus Linnaeus." In *Emanuel Swedenborg: A Continuing Vision,* edited by Robin Larsen and others. New York: Swedenborg Foundation.

Hunt, Harriot K. 1856. *Glances and Glimpses; Or Fifty Years Social, Including Twenty Years Professional Life.* Boston: John P. Jewett.

Hyatt, Lisa. [1978?]. *Latin Editions of Theological Works Not Published by Swedenborg.* Bryn Athyn, Pa. Unpublished manuscript.

Hyde, James. 1906. *A Bibliography of the Works of Emanuel Swedenborg, Original and Translated.* London: Swedenborg Society.

IJsewijn, Jozef. 1990. *Companion to Neo-Latin Studies. Part I: History and Diffusion of Neo-Latin Literature.* 2nd ed. Leuven: Leuven University Press.

Iungerich, Eldred E. 1923. "The Propagation of Bees." *The New Philosophy* 26:122–135.

James, Henry, Sr. 1863. *Substance and Shadow, or Morality and Religion in Their Relation to Life: An Essay upon the Physics of Creation.* Boston: Ticknor and Fields.

———. 1869. *The Secret of Swedenborg: Being an Elucidation of His Doctrine of the Divine Natural Humanity.* Boston: Fields, Osgood.

———. 1879. *Society the Redeemed Form of Man, and the Earnest of God's Omnipotence in Human Nature.* Boston: Houghton, Osborn.

———. [1854] 1983. *The Church of Christ Not an Ecclesiasticism: A Letter to a Sectarian.* New York: AMS Press. First edition: New York: Redfield.

James, William. 1902. *The Varieties of Religious Experience.* New York: Modern Library.

———. 1910. *The Varieties of Religious Experience.* New York: Longmans, Green & Co.

———. 1920. *Letters of William James.* Vol. 1. Edited by Henry James, Jr. Boston: Atlantic Monthly Press.

———. 1978. "A Pluralistic Mystic." In *Essays in Philosophy: The Works of William James,* edited by Frederick H. Burkhardt and others. Cambridge: Harvard University Press.

James Archives. Swedenborgian House of Studies Library, Pacific School of Religion, Berkeley, Ca.

Janecek, Jaroslav I. 1949–1950. "The Search for and the Finding of God." Translated by Lillian V. Novak. *The Swedenborg Student* 30, no. 6:91–96; no. 7:106–110; no. 8:125–127; no. 9:139–140; no. 10:158–160; no. 11:171–173; no. 12:187–189; vol. 31, no. 1:203–207; no. 2:221–224; no. 3:44–47.

Janson, H. W. 1988. "Psyche in Stone: The Influence of Swedenborg on Funerary Art." In *Emanuel Swedenborg: A Continuing Vision,* edited by Robin Larsen and others. New York: Swedenborg Foundation.

Johnson, Gregory R. 1996–1997. "Kant on Swedenborg in the *Lectures on Metaphysics.*" *Studia Swedenborgiana* 10(1):1–38; 10(2):11–39.

———. 2003. "William James on Swedenborg: A Newly Discovered Letter." *Studia Swedenborgiana* 13(1):61–67.

Johnson, P. H. 1949. Preface to *Arcana Caelestia.* 3rd ed. Vol. 1. Edited by P. H. Johnson and E. C. Mongredien. London: Swedenborg Society.

Jones, William Ellery, ed. 2000. *Johnny Appleseed: A Voice in the Wilderness.* West Chester, Pa.: Swedenborg Foundation.

Jonsson, Inge. 1961. *Swedenborgs skapelsedrama De Cultu et Amore Dei: En studie av motiv och intellektuell miljö.* Dissertation, Stockholm University. Stockholm: Natur och Kultur.

Jørgensen, Johannes. 1916. *Mit livs legende.* Vol. 2. Copenhagen: Gyldendalkse Boghandel.

Josefson, Ruben. 1937. *Andreas Knös' teologiska åskådning.* Dissertation, University of Uppsala.

Judah, J. Stillson. 1967. *The History and Philosophy of the Metaphysical Movements in America.* Philadelphia: Westminster Press.

[Kahl, Achatius]. 1847–1864. *Den Nya Kyrkan och dess inflytande på theologiens studium i Swerige.* 4 vols. Lund: Berling.

Kallenbach, Jozef. 1926. *Adam Mickiewicz.* Lvov, Warsaw, and Cracow: Wydawnictwo Zakładu Narodowego im. Ossolińskich.

Kant, Immanuel. [1766] 1902. *Träume eines Geistersehers.* In vol. 2 of *Kants Gesammelte Schriften.* Königsberg: Königlich Preussischen Akademie der Wissenschaften.

———. [1781] 1929. *Critique of Pure Reason.* Translated by Norman Kemp Smith. New York: St. Martin's Press.

———. [1766] 2002. *Kant on Swedenborg: Dreams of a Spirit Seer and Other Writings.* Edited by Gregory R. Johnson and translated by Gregory R. Johnson and Glenn Alexander Magee. West Chester, Pa.: Swedenborg Foundation.

Kaplan, Justin. 1980. *Walt Whitman: A Life.* New York: Simon and Schuster.

Karcher, Carolyn L. 1994. *The First Woman in the Republic: A Cultural Biography of Lydia Maria Child.* Durham, N.C.: Duke University Press.

Keller, Helen. 1927. *My Religion.* Garden City, N.Y.: Doubleday, Page.

———. 2000. *Light in My Darkness.* 2nd ed. Edited by Ray Silverman. West Chester, Pa.: Swedenborg Foundation. Revision of 1927 edition of *My Religion,* with added material, Garden City, N. Y.: Doubleday, Page.

———. 2003. *The Story of My Life.* Restored ed. Edited by James Berger. New York: Modern Library.

Kellow, Margaret M. R. 1991. "Swedenborg's Influence on Antebellum Reform: The Case of Lydia Maria Child." Paper presented at the annual meeting of the American Academy of Religion, Kansas City, Mo.

Kern, Hermann. 2000. *Through the Labyrinth: Designs and Meanings over 5,000 Years.* Munich: Prestel.

Kienitz, Gail. 1991. "Efficacies and Ambiguities: Swedenborg, Browning, and a Religious Culture in Crisis." Paper presented at the annual meeting of the American Academy of Religion, Kansas City, Mo.

King, Kristin. 1999a. "The Power and Limitations of Language in Swedenborg, Shakespeare, and Frost." *Studia Swedenborgiana* 11(3):1–63.

———. 1999b. "Reading What Swedenborg's Writings Say They Cannot Say." *New Church Life* 119:344–359, 392–410.

Kingslake, Brian. 1947. *Africanus Mensah and the New Church in Nigeria.* London: General Conference of the New Church.

———. 1986. *A Swedenborg Scrapbook.* London: Seminar Books.

Kirmmse, Bruce H. 1996. *Encounters with Kierkegaard: A Life as Seen by His Contemporaries.* Translated by Bruce H. Kirmmse and Virginia R. Laursen. Princeton: Princeton University Press.

Kirven, Robert H. 1965. *Emanuel Swedenborg and the Revolt against Deism.* Dissertation, Brandeis University.

———. 1984. "The Church since 1932." Epilogue to *The New Church in the New World,* by Marguerite Beck Block. New York: Swedenborg Publishing Association.

————. 1988. "Swedenborg and Kant Revisited: The Long Shadow of Kant's Attack and a New Response." In *Swedenborg and His Influence,* edited by Erland J. Brock and others. Bryn Athyn, Pa.: Academy of the New Church.

Kirven, Robert H., and Robin Larsen. 1988. "Emanuel Swedenborg: A Pictorial Biography." In *Emanuel Swedenborg: A Continuing Vision,* edited by Robin Larsen and others. New York: Swedenborg Foundation.

[Knös, Gustaf]. 1827. *Samtal med mig sjelf om werlden, Menniskan och Gud.* 2nd ed. 2 vols. Uppsala: Palmblad.

Koke, Steve. 1995. "Swedenborg's Long Sunrise: An Analytic Look at His Theological Years." *Studia Swedenborgiana* 9(2):21–58; 9(3):23–58.

————. 1998. "Further Thoughts on Three Famous Statements by John Lewis, Emanuel Swedenborg, and Carl Robsahm." *Studia Swedenborgiana* 11(1):11–29.

Kolb, Robert, and Timothy J. Wengert, eds. 2000. *The Book of Concord.* Minneapolis: Fortress Press.

Kylén, Hjalmar. 1910. "Some Indications of Swedenborg's Influence on Swedish and German Thought." In *Transactions of the International Swedenborg Congress.* London: Swedenborg Society.

Lagercrantz, Olof. 1996. *Dikten om livet på den andra sidan: En bok om Emanuel Swedenborg.* Stockholm: Wahlström & Widstrand.

————. 2002. *Epic of the Afterlife: A Literary Approach to Swedenborg.* Translated by Anders Hallengren. West Chester, Pa.: Swedenborg Foundation.

Lamartine, Alphonse de. 1847. *Histoire des Girondins.* 8 vols. Paris.

Lamm, Martin. 1936. *Strindberg och makterna.* Stockholm: Svenska Kyrkans Diakonistyrelses.

————. 1987. *Swedenborg: En studie över hans utveckling till mystiker och andeskådare.* With a new foreword by Olle Hjern and an afterword by Inge Jonsson. Stockholm: Hammarström & Åberg. First edition: 1915, Stockholm: Hugo Gebers. (For the English translation, see Lamm 2000.)

————. 2000. *Emanuel Swedenborg: The Development of His Thought.* Translated by Tomas Spiers and Anders Hallengren. West Chester, Pa.: Swedenborg Foundation.

Larsen, Robin, and others, eds. 1988. *Emanuel Swedenborg: A Continuing Vision. A Pictorial Biography and Anthology of Essays and Poetry.* New York: Swedenborg Foundation.

Lash, Joseph P. 1980. *Helen and Teacher: The Story of Helen Keller and Anne Sullivan Macy.* New York: Delacorte Press.

Lavater, Johann Kaspar. 1775–1778. *Physiognomische Fragmente zur Beförderung der Menschenkenntnis und Menschenliebe.* Leipzig.

Lawrence, James. 2001. "Editorial Notes." *Studia Swedenborgiana* 12(2):iv–vi.

Le Boys des Guays, Jean-François-Étienne. 1865. *Collection de Mélanges concernant la Nouvelle Jérusalem.* Vol. 4. Saint-Amand: Librairie de la Nouvelle Jérusalem.

Le Forestier, René. 1987. *La Franc-Maçonnerie occultiste et templière aux XVIIIe et XIXe siècles.* 2nd ed. Paris: La Table d'Emeraude.

Lenhammar, Harry. 1966. *Tolerans och bekännelsetvång: Studier i den svenska swedenborgianismen 1765–1795.* Uppsala: Acta Universitatis Uppsaliensis.

Levy, Andrew. 2002. "The Anti-Jefferson." In *Best American Essays,* edited by Stephen Jay Gould. New York and Boston: Houghton Mifflin.

Lewis, John. [1750] 1790. Advertisement for *Arcana Coelestia*. *The New Magazine of Knowledge* 1:395–401.

Lewis, Linda M. 1998. *Elizabeth Barrett Browning's Spiritual Progress: Face to Face with God*. Columbia, Mo.: University of Missouri Press.

Lindh, F. G. 1927–1930. "Swedenborgs ekonomi." *Nya Kyrkans tidning* 52(1927):57–59, 77–79, 97–101, 117–121; 53(1928):113–116; 54(1929):1–5, 25–28, 41–45, 65–69, 85–91, 113–118; 55(1930):16–19, 26–31.

Lindqvist, Svante. 1984. *Technology on Trial: The Introduction of Steam Power Technology into Sweden, 1715–1736*. Stockholm: Almqvist & Wiksell.

Lineham, Peter J. 1978. *The English Swedenborgians 1770–1840: A Study in the Social Dimensions of Religious Sectarianism*. Dissertation, University of Sussex.

———. 1988. "The Origins of the New Jerusalem Church in the 1780s." *Bulletin of the John Rylands University Library of Manchester* 70:109–122.

Lines, Richard. 2004. "Swedenborgian Ideas in the Poetry of Elizabeth Barrett Browning and Robert Browning." In *In Search of the Absolute: Essays on Swedenborg and Literature*, edited by Stephen McNeilly. London: Swedenborg Society.

London Committee for the World Assembly. [1972]. *New Church World Assembly*. London: [London Committee for the World Assembly].

London Conference, No. 2. 1815. *Minutes*. London: General Conference of the New Church.

The Lord's New Church. 1985. *Handbook of the Lord's New Church Which Is Nova Hierosolyma*. Bryn Athyn, Pa.: The Lord's New Church.

Lowrie, Walter. 1938. *Kierkegaard*. London: Oxford University Press.

Lundblad, Sven. 1825. *Christna religionens hufwud-läror*. Uppsala: Palmblad.

Lysell, Roland. 1993. *Erik Johan Stagnelius*. Stockholm/Stehag: B. Östling.

———. 1999. "Almqvist och Swedenborg." *Väldarnas möte: Nya Kyrkans tidning* 4–5:4–10.

[The Madness Hypothesis]. 1998. *The New Philosophy*, vol. 101, nos. 1 and 2. Bryn Athyn, Pa.: Swedenborg Scientific Association.

Maintenance Committee. 1922. *History of the Philadelphia Bible-Christian Church for the First Century of Its Existence, from 1817 to 1917*. Philadelphia: J. B. Lippincott.

Mansén, Elisabeth. 1993. *Konsten att förgylla vardagen: Thekla Knös och romantikens*. Dissertation, University of Lund.

Martin, Ernest O. 1985. "Swedenborgian Growth Centers." *The Messenger* 205:13–14.

———. 1986. "The Philadelphia Story." *The Messenger* 206:199–202.

———. 1987. "Temenos at Broad Run: A Vision Taking Shape." *The Messenger* 207:114–115.

Mason, Martha. 1911. "Benj. Worcester and the Waltham New-Church School." *New-Church Messenger* 100:366.

Mayer, Jean-François. 1984. *La Nouvelle Église de Lausanne et le mouvement swedenborgien en Suisse romande, des origines à 1948*. Zürich: Swedenborg Verlag.

McDannell, Colleen, and Bernhard Lang. 2001. *Heaven: A History*. 2nd ed. New Haven: Yale University Press.

Meillassoux-Le Cerf, M. 1992. *Dom Pernety et les Illuminés d'Avignon, suivi de la transcription intégrale de la Sainte Parole*. Milan: Archè.

Mercer, L. P., ed. 1894. *The New Jerusalem in the World's Religious Congresses of 1893.* Chicago: Western New-Church Union.

The Messenger. See *New-Church Messenger.*

Metcalfe, William. 1872. *Out of the Clouds: Into the Light. Seventeen Discourses on the Leading Doctrines of the Day in the Light of Bible Christianity.* Philadelphia: J. B. Lippincott.

Meyers, Mary Ann. 1983. *A New World Jerusalem: The Swedenborgian Experience in Community Construction.* Westport, Conn.: Greenwood Press.

Milosz, Czeslaw. 1988. "Dostoevsky and Swedenborg." Translated by Louis Iribarne. In *Emanuel Swedenborg: A Continuing Vision,* edited by Robin Larsen and others. New York: Swedenborg Foundation. Previously published in 1975 in *Slavic Review* 34:203–318, and again in 1977 in *Emperor of the Earth: Modes of Eccentric Wisdom,* Berkeley, Ca.: University of California Press.

"Minute Book of the New Church at Great East-Cheap, London." 1885. In *Minutes of the First Seven Sessions of the General Conference of the New Church Signified by the New Jerusalem in the Revelation, Together with Those of Other Contemporary Assemblies of a Similar Character.* London: James Speirs.

"Miscellanea—Germany." 1846. *The New Church Advocate and Examiner* 1:107–108.

"Miscellaneous Information: France." 1836. *The Intellectual Repository for the New Church* 4:214–219.

"Miscellaneous Intelligence." 1824. *The Intellectual Repository for the New Church,* n.s. 3:244–246.

"Miscellaneous Intelligence." 1825. *The Intellectual Repository for the New Church,* n.s. 8:693–697.

"Miscellaneous Intelligence: Manchester Report." 1817. *Intellectual Repository* 3:188–189.

Morris, H. N. 1915. *Flaxman, Blake, Coleridge, and Other Men of Genius Influenced by Swedenborg.* London: New-Church Press.

Morton, Louis. 1969. *Robert Carter of Nomini Hall, a Virginia Tobacco Planter of the Eighteenth Century.* Charlottesville, Va.: Dominion Books, a division of the University Press of Virginia.

Moskowitz, Richard. 1988. "What is Homeopathy?" In *Emanuel Swedenborg: A Continuing Vision,* edited by Robin Larsen and others. New York: Swedenborg Foundation.

Murdock, Florence. 1945. "Summary of the Manuscript Recollections of Milo G. Williams." *Ohio State Archaeological and Historical Quarterly* 54:113–126.

Murray, Walter B. 1927. "Report of the New-Church Lecture and Publicity Bureau." *Journal of the General Convention* 128–131.

Mussey, Ellen Spencer. 1932. "The First African Church of the New Jerusalem." Archives of the Swedenborgian Church of North America, Newton, Mass. Typed ms.

New Church Collection. Royal Library, Stockholm.

New Church Life. This publication of the General Church of the New Jerusalem has appeared as *New Church Life: A Monthly Journal for the Young People of the New Church,* 1881–1884 (vols. 1–4); *New Church Life: A Monthly Journal,* 1885–1889 (vols. 5–19); *New Church Life: A Monthly Magazine Devoted to the Teachings Revealed through Emanuel Swedenborg,* 1900– (vol. 20–). Its place of publication shifted from Philadelphia to Huntingdon Valley, Pa., in 1898, and from there to Bryn Athyn, Pa., in 1903.

New-Church Messenger. The history of this publication is too complex to catalog here in full, but briefly it can be said that it has appeared as *New Jerusalem Messenger,*

1855–1884 (vols. 1–47), New York: General Convention of the New Jerusalem; as *New-Church Messenger,* 1885–June, 1966 (vols. 48–186[6]), New York: New-Church Board of Publication; and as *The Messenger,* July, 1966– (vol. 186[7]–), Newtonville, Mass.: Swedenborgian Church of North America.

"New-Church Settlement House, Lynn, Mass." 1906. *New-Church Messenger* 91:346.

New Jerusalem Messenger. See *New-Church Messenger.*

New-Jerusalem Missionary. 1823–1824 (vols. 1–2). New York: New York Society for the Dissemination of the Heavenly Doctrines of the New Jerusalem, As Contained in the Writings of E. Swedenborg.

The New Philosophy. 1889– (vols. 1–). Urbana, Ill./Philadelphia: Swedenborg Scientific Association.

"News Gleanings." 1886. *New Church Life* 6:175.

Nicholson, George, comp. [1800] 1931. *A Dictionary of Correspondences, Representatives, and Significatives, Derived from the Word of the Lord, Extracted from the Writings of Emanuel Swedenborg.* 13th ed. Boston: Massachusetts New-Church Union. First edition: London: J. Bonsor.

Nilsson, Albert. 1916. *Svensk Romantik.* Lund.

Noyes, John Humphrey. [1870] 1961. *History of American Socialisms.* New York: Hillary House. First edition: Philadelphia: J. B. Lippincott.

Nya Kyrkans tidning. This publication of the Swedish New Church has had several different names: *Skandinavisk Nykyrk-tidning* (1876–1891), *Nya Kyrkans tidning* (1891–1983), and *Väldernas möte: Nya Kyrkans tidning* (1989–1998).

"Obituary [for James Glen]." 1815. *Intellectual Repository* 2:445–446.

Odhner, Carl Th. 1895. *Robert Hindmarsh: A Biography.* Philadelphia: Academy Book Room.

———. 1904a. *Annals of the New Church.* Vol. 1 (1688–1850). Bryn Athyn, Pa.: Academy of the New Church.

[———]. 1904b. "The Russian Nation." *New Church Life* 24:268–270.

Odhner, Hugo Lj. 1943. *The Writings of the Lord's Second Advent: A Brief Bibliographical Study Tracing the Sequence and Connection of the Various Theological Works of Emanuel Swedenborg.* Bryn Athyn, Pa. Mimeographed.

Odhner, J. Durban. 1998. Translator's preface to *Emanuel Swedenborg's Diary Recounting Spiritual Experiences.* Vol. 1. Bryn Athyn, Pa.: General Church of the New Jerusalem.

[Odhner, Sanfrid]. 1976. *Toward a New Church University.* Bryn Athyn, Pa.: Academy of the New Church.

Odhner Translation Manuscript. Archives of the Swedenborg Society. London.

O'Driscoll, Robert. 1975. *Symbolism and Some Implications of the Symbolic Approach: W. B. Yeats during the Eighteen-Nineties.* Dublin: Dolmen Press.

Oetinger, Friedrich Christoph. 1767. *Fragen und Antworten zur Prüfung der Schwedenborgischen Lehren.* Murrhardt.

———. [1765] 1855. *Swedenborgs und anderer irdische und himmlische Philosophie.* Edited by Karl C. E. Ehmann. Reutlingen: Rupp & Baur.

"Open Intercourse with the Spiritual World." 1846a. *New Jerusalem Magazine* 19:280.

"Open Intercourse with the Spiritual World." 1846b. *New Jerusalem Magazine* 19:364.

Oppenheim, Janet. 1985. *The Other World: Spiritual and Psychical Research in England, 1850–1914.* Cambridge: Cambridge University Press.

Origen. 1966. *On First Principles.* Translated by G. W. Butterworth. New York: Harper & Row.

Parker, Gail T. 1973. *Mind Cure in New England: From the Civil War to World War I.* Hanover, N.H.: University Press of New England.

Pattison, James William. 1913. "George Inness, N.A." *Catalogue of the Loan Exhibition of Important Works by George Inness, Alexander Wyant, Ralph Blakelock.* Chicago Galleries of Moulton and Ricketts, March 10–March 22.

Peebles, Elinore. 1988. "Homeopathy and the New Church." In *Emanuel Swedenborg: A Continuing Vision,* edited by Robin Larsen and others. New York: Swedenborg Foundation. Reprinted in *Arcana* 6(1):46–56.

Pendleton, Willard. 1957. *Foundations of New Church Education.* Bryn Athyn, Pa.: Academy of the New Church.

Pendleton, William F. 1915. *The Science of Exposition.* Bryn Athyn, Pa.: Academy of the New Church.

Pernety, Antoine Joseph. 1758a. *Dictionnaire mytho-hermétique, dans lequel on trouve les allégories fabuleuses des poètes, les métaphores, les énigmes et les termes barbares des philosophes hermétiques expliqués.* Paris: Bauche.

———. 1758b. *Les fables égyptiennes et grecques: dévoilées & réduites au même principe, avec une explication des hiéroglyphes, et de la guerre de Troye.* Paris: Bauche.

———. 1782. "Observations ou notes sur Swédenborg." In vol. 1 of *Les Merveilles du Ciel et de l'Enfer,* by Emanuel Swedenborg, translated by Antoine Joseph Pernety. Berlin: G. J. Decker.

Perry, Ralph Barton. 1935. *The Thought and Character of William James.* Boston: Little, Brown.

Photolithographs [*Emanuelis Swedenborgii Editio Photolithographica* (Photolithographic Edition [of Selected Manuscripts] of Emanuel Swedenborg)]. 1869–1870. 10 vols. Stockholm: Photolithographic Society. These reproductions of various works of Emanuel Swedenborg were created under the direction of R. L. Tafel by order of a committee of the New Church in North America and England. For a description and list of contents, see Eby 1926, 44–47, and Hyde 1906, entries 3029–3038.

Photostats [*Emanuelis Swedenborgii Autographa Editio Photostata* (Photostatic Autograph Edition [of Selected Manuscripts] of Emanuel Swedenborg)]. 1926–1930. 21 vols. These reproductions of various autograph manuscripts of Emanuel Swedenborg were created under the direction of Alfred Acton. For a list of contents, see Wainscot 1967, entries 3038/22–3038/42 (pages 174–175).

Phototypes [*Emanuelis Swedenborgii Autographa Editio Phototypica* (Phototyped Autograph Edition [of Selected Manuscripts] of Emanuel Swedenborg)]. 1901–1916. 18 vols. Stockholm: Warner Silfversparre (vol. 1) and Lagrelius & Westphal (vol. 2–18). These reproductions of various autograph manuscripts of Emanuel Swedenborg were created under the direction of J. E. Boyesen and Alfred H. Stroh with the support of the Swedenborg Society, the General Convention of the New Jerusalem, the Academy of the New Church, the Rotch Trustees, and the American Swedenborg Printing and Publishing Society. For a description and list of contents, see Eby 1926, 47–57, and Wainscot 1967, entries 3038/1–3038/19 (pages 172–173). The latter list includes a nineteenth volume.

Pigoń, Stanisław. 1922. "Przypuszczalny ślad Swedenborga w III. części 'Dziadów.'" In *Z epoki Mickiewicza, studja i szkice.* Lvov: Wydawn. Zakładu Narodowego im. Ossolińskich.

Pitcairn, Theodore. 1967. *My Lord and My God: Essays on Modern Religion, the Bible, and Emanuel Swedenborg.* New York: Exposition Press.

Plato. 1952. *The Republic.* Translated by Benjamin Jowett. In vol. 7 of *Great Books of the Western World.* Chicago: Encyclopedia Britannica.

Podmore, Frank. 1902. *Modern Spiritualism.* London: Methuen.

———. 1963. *From Mesmer to Christian Science: A Short History of Mental Healing.* Hyde Park, N.Y.: University Books.

"Eine polnische Ausgabe der Schriften der neuen Kirche in Aussicht." 1874. *Wochenschrift für die Neue Kirche* 3:238.

Poole, Susan. 1999. *Lost Legacy: Inspiring Women of Nineteenth-Century America.* West Chester, Pa.: Chrysalis Books.

Potts, John F. 1888–1902. *The Swedenborg Concordance. A Complete Work of Reference to the Theological Writings of Emanuel Swedenborg; Based on the Original Latin Writings of the Author.* 6 vols. London: Swedenborg Society.

The Precursor. 1836–1842 (vols. 1–12). Cincinnati: The Book Committee of the Western Convention.

Price, Robert. 1944. *A Bibliography of "Johnny Appleseed" in American History, Literature and Folklore.* Paterson, N.J.: Swedenborg Press.

———. 1967. *Johnny Appleseed: Man and Myth.* Gloucester, Mass.: Peter Smith. First edition: 1954, Bloomington, Ind.: Indiana University Press.

Priestley, Joseph. [1791] 1989. *Letters to Members: Bound with the Farewell Sermon.* Oxford: Woodstock Books. First edition: Birmingham: J. Thompson.

"Professor Bush and Mesmerism." 1848. *New Jerusalem Magazine* 21:509–515.

Promey, Sally M. 1994. "The Ribband of Faith: George Inness, Color Theory, and the Swedenborgian Church." *The American Art Journal* 26:45–65.

"Prüfungsversuch, ob es wol ausgemacht sei, daß Swedenborg zu den Schwärmern gehöre." 1786. In *Revision der bisherigen Theologie* (German translation of *Survey*), by Emanuel Swedenborg. Breslau: Gottlieb Löwe.

Pyle, Howard. [1903] 2002. *The Garden Behind the Moon: A Real Story of the Moon Angel.* New York: Tom Doherty Associates.

[R. A.]. 1849. "Obituary [for Thomas Goyder]." *Intellectual Repository* 120:474–476.

Raine, Kathleen. 1979. *William Blake and the New Age.* Boston: G. Allen & Urwin.

———. 1988. "The Human Face of God." In *Emanuel Swedenborg: A Continuing Vision,* edited by Robin Larsen and others. New York: Swedenborg Foundation.

Rama, Swami, and others. 1979. *Science of Breath: A Practical Guide.* Honesdale, Pa.: Himalayan International Institute of Yoga Science and Philosophy.

[Reed, Caleb]. 1848. Review of *The True Organization of the New Church as Indicated in the Writings of Emanuel Swedenborg and Demonstrated by Charles Fourier,* by Charles Julius Hempel. *New Jerusalem Magazine* 21:298–304.

Reed, James. 1908. "Massachusetts Association." *Journal of the General Convention* 142–144.

———. 1909. "Massachusetts Association." *Journal of the General Convention* 129–131.

Reed, Sampson. 1880. *A Biographical Sketch of Thomas Worcester.* Boston: Massachusetts New-Church Union.

———. 1992. *Sampson Reed: Primary Source Material for Emerson Studies.* Compiled by George F. Dole. New York and West Chester, Pa.: Swedenborg Foundation.

Regamey, Alfred G. 1935. *Swedenborg au Travail.* Lausanne: Agence des Publications de la Nouvelle Église.

Review of *Letters from England: by Don Manuel Alvarez Espriella,* by Robert Southey. 1808. *Edinburgh Review* 11:370–390.

Reynolds, Donald M. 1977a. *Hiram Powers and His Ideal Sculpture.* New York: Garland Publishing, Inc.

———. 1977b. "The 'Unveiled Soul': Hiram Powers's Embodiment of the Ideal." *The Art Bulletin* 59:394–415.

Rich, Morley D. 1956. *"The Messiah About to Come." New Church Life* 76:63–76.

Richter, Christian Friedrich. 1722. *Höchst-nöthige Erkenntniss des Menschen.* Leipzig: Johan Friedrich Gleditsch.

Ripley, George. 1845. "Association Not Sectarian." *The Harbinger, Devoted to Social and Political Progress* 2:92–94.

Robinson, I. A., ed. 1980. *A History of the New Church in Australia, 1832–1980.* Melbourne: The New Church in Australia.

"Roll of Ministers." 2000. *Journal of the Swedenborgian Church* 178:14–26.

Roos, Jacques. 1951. *Aspects littéraires du mysticisme philosophique et l'influence de Boehme et de Swedenborg au début du romantisme: William Blake, Novalis, Ballanche.* Strasbourg: P. H. Heitz.

Rose, Alanna. 2002. *"Index Biblicus:* Swedenborg's Indexes to the Bible." *The New Philosophy* 105:301–315.

Rose, Donald L., and Frank S. Rose. 1970. *That All May Know.* Bryn Athyn, Pa.: General Church Publication Committee. Pamphlet.

Rose, Frank S. 1964. "The Crucial Years: 1743–1748." *New Church Life* 84:6–17.

Rose, Jonathan S. 1994a. "Boundaries, Looks, and Style: Overlooked Aspects of Faithful Translation." *Studia Swedenborgiana* 8(4):49–64.

———. 1994b. "Similes in Emanuel Swedenborg's *Vera Christiana Religio* (1771)." In *Acta Conventus Neo-Latini Hafniensis.* Binghamton: Medieval & Renaissance Texts & Studies.

———. 1998a. "Latin Styles of Swedenborg and His Contemporaries: Early Spadework." *The New Philosophy* 101:247–302.

———. 1998b. "The Ornaments in Swedenborg's Theological First Editions." *Covenant: A Journal Devoted to the Study of the Five Churches* 1:293–362.

Rubow, Paul V. 1952. *Goldschmidt og Kierkegaard.* Copenhagen: Gyldendalkse Boghandel Nordisk Forlag.

Sahlin, Carl. 1923. *Vår järnindustris äldsta reklamtryck.* Örebro: Örebro Dagblads Tryckeri.

Sanchez Walsh, Arlene. 1997. "Warren F. Evans, Emanuel Swedenborg, and the Creation of New Thought." *Studia Swedenborgiana* 10(3):13–35.

Scammon, A. E., and others, eds. 1895. *Round-Table Talks.* Chicago: Western New-Church Union.

Schmidt, Sebastian. 1696. *Biblia Sacra sive Testamentum Vetus et Novum ex Linguis Originalibus in Linguam Latinam Translatum.* Strasbourg: J. F. Spoor.

Schmidt, Sebastian, trans., and Emanuel Swedenborg, annotator. 1872. *Biblia Sacra sive Testamentum Vetus et Novum ex Linguis Originalibus in Linguam Latinam*

Translatum . . . Annotationibus Emanuelis Svedenborgii Manu Scriptis Locupletati. . . . Edited by R. L. Tafel. Stockholm: Photolithographic Society.

Schneider, Herbert W., and George Lawton. 1942. *A Prophet and a Pilgrim: Being the Incredible History of Thomas Lake Harris and Laurence Oliphant.* New York: Columbia University Press.

Schoeps, Hans-Joachim. 1965. *Barocke Juden, Christen, Judenchristen.* Bern: Francke Verlag.

Schuchard, Marsha Keith Manatt. 1975. *Freemasonry, Secret Societies, and the Continuity of the Occult Traditions in English Literature.* Dissertation, University of Texas at Austin.

———. 1988. "Swedenborg, Jacobitism, and Freemasonry." In *Swedenborg and His Influence,* edited by Erland J. Brock and others. Bryn Athyn, Pa.: Academy of the New Church.

Schurig, Martin. 1729. *Muliebria Historico-medica; Hoc Est, Partium Genitalium Muliebrium Consideratio Physico-medico-forensis. . . .* Dresden and Leipzig: Christopher Hekel.

Science and Spirituality. 1989. *Chrysalis* vol. 4, no. 1. New York: Swedenborg Foundation.

Scott, Franklin D. 1988. *Sweden: The Nation's History.* Rev. ed. Carbondale, Ill.: Southern Illinois University Press.

Sechrist, Alice Spiers. 1973. *A Dictionary of Bible Imagery.* New York: Swedenborg Foundation.

Séguy, Jean. 1980. *Christianisme et Société: Introduction à la sociologie de Ernst Troeltsch.* Paris: Cerf.

Shaw, Sylvia. 1992. Preface to *Sampson Reed: Primary Source Material for Emerson Studies,* by Sampson Reed, compiled by George F. Dole. New York and West Chester, Pa.: Swedenborg Foundation.

———. 1998. "Sarah Orne Jewett and Swedenborgian Beliefs." Unpublished paper.

Shirigian, John. 1961. *Lucius Lyon: His Place in Michigan History.* Dissertation, University of Michigan.

Sigstedt, Cyriel Odhner. 1981. *The Swedenborg Epic: The Life and Works of Emanuel Swedenborg.* London: Swedenborg Society. First edition: 1952, New York: Bookman Associates.

Silver, Ednah. 1920. *Sketches of the New Church in America, on a Background of Civic and Social Life; Drawn from Faded Manuscript, Printed Record and Living Reminiscence.* Boston: Massachusetts New-Church Union.

Silver, Richard Kenneth. 1983. *The Spiritual Kingdom in America: The Influence of Emanuel Swedenborg on American Society and Culture, 1815–1860.* Dissertation, Stanford University.

Silver-Isenstadt, Jean. 2002. *Shameless: The Visionary Life of Mary Gove Nichols.* Baltimore: Johns Hopkins University Press.

———. 2003. "Passions and Perversions: The Radical Ambition of Dr. Thomas Low Nichols." In *Right Living: An Anglo-American Tradition of Self-Help Medicine and Hygiene,* edited by Charles E. Rosenberg. Baltimore: Johns Hopkins University Press.

Simmons, Jack. 1951. Introduction to *Letters from England: by Don Manuel Alvarez Espriella,* by Robert Southey. London: Cresset Press.

Sjödén, Karl-Erik. 1966. "Remarques sur le 'Swedenborgisme' balzacien." In *L'Année balzacienne 1966.* Paris: Garnier.

———. 1985. *Swedenborg en France.* Stockholm: Almqvist & Wiksell.

Skinner, Alice B. 2001. "Stay by Me, Roses: A Biography of Alice Archer Sewall James." Unpublished manuscript.

Skytte, Göran. 1986. *Det kungliga svenska slaveriet.* Stockholm: Askelin & Hägglund.

Słowacki, Juliusz. [1834] 1996. *Kordian.* Translated by Jacques Donguy and Michel Maslowski. Lausanne: L'Age d'Homme.

Smith, A. Tolman. 1903. *The African New Church Mission.* Swedenborgian House of Studies Library, Pacific School of Religion, Berkeley, Ca. Pamphlet.

Smith, Ophia D. 1952–1953. "The Beginnings of the New Jerusalem Church in Ohio." *Ohio State Archeological and Historical Quarterly* 61:384–385.

———. 1955. "The New Jerusalem Church in Missouri." *Bulletin of the Missouri Historical Society* 11:228–248.

Smith, William E., and Ophia D. Smith. 1953. *Buckeye Titan.* Cincinnati: Historical and Philosophical Society of Ohio.

Smoley, Richard. 2002. *Inner Christianity: A Guide to the Esoteric Tradition.* Boston: Shambhala.

Smoley, Richard, and Jay Kinney. 1999. *Hidden Wisdom: A Guide to the Western Inner Traditions.* New York: Penguin Arkana.

Sobel, Dava. 1995. *Longitude: The True Story of a Lone Genius Who Solved the Greatest Scientific Problem of His Time.* New York: Walker & Co.

Soloviev, Vladimir. 1900. "Swedenborg." In *Brockhaus-Ephron Encyclopedia.* St. Petersburg.

Solovyov, Vladimir. [1900] 2001. "Swedenborg." Translated by George F. Dole. *Studia Swedenborgiana* 12(2):39–73.

Southey, Robert. [1807] 1951. *Letters from England: by Don Manuel Alvarez Espriella.* Edited by Jack Simmons. London: Cresset Press. First edition: London: Longman, Hurst, Rees, Orme.

Spencer, Colin. 1993. *Heretic's Feast: A History of Vegetarianism.* London: Fourth Estate.

The Spiritual Herald. 1856 (vol. 1, nos. 1–6). London and New York: H. Bailliere.

Starkie, Enid. 1958. *Baudelaire.* Norfolk, Conn.: New Directions.

Starr, Kevin. 1987. "Beginnings of the California Style." *Chrysalis* 2:93–98.

Stein, Stephen J. 1992. *The Shaker Experience in America: A History of the United Society of Believers.* New Haven: Yale University Press.

Stockenström, Goran. 1972. *Strindberg som mystiker.* Dissertation, University of Uppsala.

———. 1988. "Strindberg and Swedenborg." In *Emanuel Swedenborg: A Continuing Vision,* edited by Robin Larsen and others. New York: Swedenborg Foundation.

Strindberg, August. 1897. *Inferno.* Stockholm: Gernandt.

———. 1898. *Legender.* Stockholm: Beijer.

———. 1901. *Dödsdansen.* Stockholm: Gernandt.

———. 1907–1912. *En blå bok.* 4 vols. Stockholm: Björck & Börjesson.

Stroh, Alfred H. 1911. "The Sources of Swedenborg's Early Philosophy of Nature." Introduction to *Opera Quaedam aut Inedita aut Obsoleta de Rebus Naturalibus,* by Emanuel Swedenborg, edited by Alfred H. Stroh. Stockholm: Aftonbladet.

Stroh, Alfred H., and Greta Ekelöf. 1910. *Abridged Chronological List of the Works of Emanuel Swedenborg, Including Manuscripts, Original Editions and Translations Prior to 1772.* Uppsala: Almqvist and Wiksell.

Studia Swedenborgiana. 1974–2002, vols. 1–12, Newton, Mass.: Swedenborg School of Religion; 2003–, vols. 13–, Berkeley, Ca.: Swedenborgian House of Studies, Pacific School of Religion.

Sugden, Emily Robbins. 1910. "Swedenborg in English Literature III: Thomas De Quincey." *The New-Church Review* 33:70–82.

Sundelin, Robert. 1886. *Svedenborgianismens historia i Sverige under förra århundradet.* Uppsala: W. Schultz.

Sundgren, Nils Petter. 1998. "I mästarens grepp." *Månadsjournalen* 3.

Suzuki, D. T. 1996. *Swedenborg: Buddha of the North.* Translated by Andrew Bernstein. West Chester, Pa.: Swedenborg Foundation.

Swank, Scott Trego. 1970. *The Unfettered Conscience: A Study of Sectarianism, Spiritualism, and Social Reform in the New Jerusalem Church, 1840–1870.* Dissertation, University of Pennsylvania, Philadelphia.

Swedenborg Society. 1910. *Transactions of the International Swedenborg Congress.* London: Swedenborg Society.

—————. 1968. *Catalog of Publications.* London: Swedenborg Society.

Swedenborg, Emanuel. 1716–1718. *Daedalus Hyperboreus: eller mathematiske och physicaliske försök.* Uppsala: J. H. Werner.

—————. 1718. *Försök at finna östra och westra lengden igen, igenom månan, som til the lårdas omprófwande framstelles.* Uppsala: J. H. Werner.

—————. 1721. *Methodus Nova Inveniendi Longitudines Locorum Terra Marique Ope Lunae.* Amsterdam: Johan Oosterwyk.

—————. 1734. *Opera Philosophica et Mineralia.* 3 vols. Dresden and Leipzig: Frederick Hekel.

—————. 1766. *Methodus Nova Inveniendi Longitudines Locorum Terra Marique per Lunam.* 2nd ed. Amsterdam.

—————. 1768. *Delitiae Sapientiae de Amore Conjugiali.* Amsterdam.

—————. [1758] 1770. *Von den Erdcörpern der Planeten* (Other Planets). Translated by Friedrich Christoph Oetinger. N.p.

—————. 1771. *Oförgripelige tankar om myntets uphöjande och nedsättjande.* Uppsala: Joh. Edman.

—————. [1763] 1772. *The Doctrine of Life for the New Jerusalem.* Translated by William Cookworthy. London: Robert Weatherby.

—————. [1758] 1778. *A Treatise Concerning Heaven and Hell.* Translated by William Cookworthy and Thomas Hartley. London: James Phillips.

—————. [1758] 1782. *Les Merveilles du Ciel et de l'Enfer.* Translated by Antoine Joseph Pernety. Berlin: G. J. Decker.

—————. [1758] 1787. *Om Nya Jerusalem och dess himmelska lära.* Translated by Carl Friedrich Nordenskjöld, with an introduction by Carl Bernhard Wadström. In vol. 4 of *Samlingar för philantroper.* Stockholm: Exegetical and Philanthropical Society.

—————. 1788. *Abrégé des Ouvrages d'Ém. Swédenborg.* Prepared by D'Aillant de la Touche. Stockholm [Strasbourg]: Exegetical and Philanthropical Society.

—————. [1771] 1789–1792. *True Christian Religion.* 2 vols. Philadelphia: Francis Bailey.

—————. [1763] 1821. *Doctrine de la Vie pour la Nouvelle Jérusalem.* Translated by J. P. Moët. Paris: "Un Ami de la Vérité."

—————. 1844–1846. *Diarii Spiritualis.* 4 vols. Edited by J. F. Immanuel Tafel. London: William Newbery.

—————. 1847–1854. *Adversaria in Libros Veteris Testamenti.* 4 vols. Edited by J. F. Immanuel Tafel. Tübingen: Verlagsexpedition.

———. 1859–1873. *Index Biblicus.* Vols. 1–3 edited by J. F. Immanuel Tafel, vol. 4 edited by Achatius Kahl, and vol. 5 edited by R. L. Tafel. London: Swedenborg Society.

———. 1869a. *Emanuelis Swedenborgii . . . Miscellanea Anatomica et Philosophica, sive Supplementum Regni Animalis . . .* Edited by R. L. Tafel. Stockholm: Photolithographic Society. [= Photolithographs, vol. 6]

———. 1869b. *Emanuelis Swedenborgii . . . Miscellanea Physica et Mineralogica ex Annis 1715 ad 1722 . . .* Edited by R. L. Tafel. Stockholm: Photolithographic Society. [= Photolithographs, vol. 1]

———. 1870a. *Emanuelis Swedenborgii . . . Itineraria et Philosophica . . .* Edited by R. L. Tafel. Stockholm: Photolithographic Society. [= Photolithographs, vol. 3]

———. 1870b. *Emanuelis Swedenborgii . . . Mathematica et Principia Rerum Naturalium . . .* Edited by R. L. Tafel. Stockholm: Photolithographic Society. [= Photolithographs, vol. 2]

———. 1870c. *Emanuelis Swedenborgii . . . Opusculum de Cultu et Amore Dei.* Edited by R. L. Tafel. Stockholm: Photolithographic Society. [= Photolithographs, vol. 7]

———. 1882–1887. *The Brain.* Translated and edited by R. L. Tafel. Vol. 1, London: Swedenborg Society. Vol. 2, London: James Speirs.

———. [1734] 1886. *Prodromus Philosophiae Ratiocinantis de Infinito, et Causa Finali Creationis.* 2nd ed. Edited by Thomas Murray Gorman. London: Kegan Paul, Trench.

———. 1889. *The Spiritual Diary of Emanuel Swedenborg.* Vol. 4. Translated by George Bush and revised and edited by James F. Buss. London: James Speirs.

———. 1890. *Index Verborum, Nominum, et Rerum in* Arcanis Coelestibus. 4 vols. Edited by R. L. Tafel. London: Swedenborg Society.

———. 1896. *God, Providence, and Creation.* Edited by John C. Ager. New York: American Swedenborg Printing and Publishing Society.

———. 1901. *Ontology, or the Significance of Philosophical Terms.* Translated by Alfred Acton. Boston: Massachusetts New-Church Union.

———. 1901–1905. *Swedenborgii Memorabilia, seu Diarium Spirituale.* Stockholm: Warner Silversparre.

———. [1700] 1902. "Swedenborg's Earliest Writing." *Morning Light* 25:182–183.

———. [1771] 1903. *Den sanna kristna religionen som innehåller hela läran om Gud för den Nya Kyrkan.* Translated by Adolph Theodor Boyesen. Stockholm: Nykyrkliga Bokförlag.

———. 1904a. *Anteckningar i Swedenborgs almanacka för år 1752.* Edited by Alfred H. Stroh. Stockholm: Systrarna Lundberg.

———. 1904b. *Summary of the Principia.* Translated by Alfred H. Stroh. Bryn Athyn, Pa.: Swedenborg Scientific Association.

———. 1907–1911. *Opera Quaedam aut Inedita aut Obsoleta de Rebus Naturalibus.* 3 vols. Edited by Alfred H. Stroh. Stockholm: Aftonbladet.

———. 1909. *Arcana Coelestia: Index of Words, Names and Subjects in the Heavenly Arcana.* Translated by James Hyde. London: Swedenborg Society.

———. [1716–1717] 1910a. *Daedalus Hyperboreus.* A complete facsimile in *Kungliga Vetenskaps Societetens i Upsala tvåhundraårsminne.* Uppsala: Academic Press.

———. 1910b. *Emanuelis Swedenborgii Opera Poetica.* [Edited by Alfred H. Stroh.] Uppsala: Uppsala University Press.

———. [1758] 1910c. *La Nueva Jerusalem*. Valencia.

———. [1758] 1911a. *El Cielo y sus Maravillas y el Infierno*. Translated by J. H. Andersen and revised by Alice Worcester. New York: American Swedenborg Printing and Publishing Society.

———. [1771] 1911b. *La Verdadera Religion Cristiana*. Abbreviated. Valencia: Viva Mores.

———. [1734] 1912. *The Principia, or the First Principles of Natural Things, to Which Are Added the Minor Principia*. 2 vols. Translated by James R. Rendell and Isaiah Tansley. London: Swedenborg Society.

———. [1719] 1915. *The Motion and Position of the Earth and Planets*. [Translated by L. P. Ford.] London: Swedenborg Society.

———. 1916a. *Emanuelis Swedenborgii Arcana Coelestia*. 5 vols. Stockholm: Lagrelius and Westphal.

———. 1916b. *Emanuelis Swedenborgii Explicationes in Verbum seu Adversaria*. Stockholm: Lagrelius and Westphal.

———. 1916c. *Emanuelis Swedenborgii Index Biblicus*. 3 vols. Stockholm: Lagrelius and Westphal.

———. 1916d. *Emanuelis Swedenborgii Index Verborum, Nominum, et Rerum in "Arcanis Coelestibus."* Stockholm: Lagrelius and Westphal.

———. 1917. *The Schmidius Marginalia Together with the Expository Material of the Index Biblicus*. Translated by Eldred E. Iungerich. Bryn Athyn, Pa.: Academy of the New Church.

———. 1921. *Debess un elle: Pēc redzētā un dzirdētā*. Translated by R. Grava. Liepāja: Jaunā Baznīca.

———. 1922. "The Greek Religion." Translated by Alfred Acton. *The New Philosophy* 25:165–178.

———. 1923a. "The Government of Bees." Translated by E. E. Iungerich. *The New Philosophy* 26:141–146.

———. 1923b. *Psychologica, Being Notes and Observations on Christian Wolf's Psychologia Empirica*. Latin-English edition by Alfred Acton. Bryn Athyn, Pa.: Swedenborg Scientific Association.

———. 1927a. *Emanuelis Swedenborgii Autographa Editio Photostata. Codex 82. De Sulphure et Pyrite*. [N.p.]

———. 1927b. *Emanuelis Swedenborgii Autographa Editio Photostata. Codex 84. De Secretione Argenti a Cupro*. [N.p.]

———. 1927c. *Emanuelis Swedenborgii Autographa Editio Photostata. Codex 85. De Victriolo*. [N.p.]

———. 1927–1951a. *The History of Creation as Given by Moses*. In vol. 1 of *The Word of the Old Testament Explained*, translated by Alfred Acton. Bryn Athyn, Pa.: Academy of the New Church. First edition: 1911, Bryn Athyn, Pa.: Academy of the New Church.

———. 1927–1951b. *The Word of the Old Testament Explained*. 10 vols. Translated and edited by Alfred Acton. Bryn Athyn, Pa.: Academy of the New Church.

———. 1928. *The Animal Kingdom, Considered Anatomically, Physically, and Philosophically, Parts 4 and 5: The Organs of Generation*. Translated and edited by Alfred Acton. Bryn Athyn, Pa.: Academy of the New Church. First edition of this translation: 1912, Philadelphia: Boericke & Tafel.

————. [1722] 1929. "Answer to Quensel." *The New Philosophy* 32:118–120.

————. 1931. *The Coronis or Appendix to the True Christian Religion.* Edited and revised by James Buss. London: Swedenborg Society.

————. 1934. *Epistolae et Autographa.* Edited by Alfred Acton. Vol. 2. Bryn Athyn, Pa: Academy of the New Church Library.

————. [1734] 1938. *Swedenborg's Treatise on Copper.* 3 vols. Translated by Alfred Hodson Searle. London: Swedenborg Society and British Non-Ferrous Metals Research Association.

————. 1939. *The Mechanical Inventions of Emanuel Swedenborg.* Translated and edited by Alfred Acton. Bryn Athyn, Pa.: Swedenborg Scientific Association.

————. 1941. *A New System of Reckoning Which Turns at 8.* Translated by Alfred Acton. Philadelphia: Swedenborg Scientific Association.

————. 1942. *On Miracles.* Translated by Alfred Acton. *New Church Life* 62:400–411.

————. 1947. *De Miraculis.* Rev. ed. In Latin, with an English translation by P. Johnson. London: Swedenborg Society.

————. 1949. *Concerning the Messiah About to Come and Concerning the Kingdom of God and the Last Judgment.* Translated by Alfred Acton. Bryn Athyn, Pa.: Academy of the New Church.

————. 1950. "A New Theory about the Retardation of the Earth." Translated by Hugo Lj. Odhner. *The New Philosophy* 53:43–56.

————. [1734] 1954. *Principia Rerum Naturalium sive Novorum Tentaminum Phaenomena Mundi Elementaris Philosophice Explicandi.* Basel: Swedenborg Institut. Facsimile of first volume of 1734 edition, Dresden and Leipzig: Frederick Hekel.

————. [1740–1741] 1955. *The Economy of the Animal Kingdom, Considered Anatomically, Physically, and Philosophically.* 2 vols. Translated by Augustus Clissold. Bryn Athyn, Pa.: Swedenborg Scientific Association. First edition of this translation: 1845–1846, London: W. Newbery, H. Bailliere, and Boston: Otis Clapp.

————. 1956. *Angelic Wisdom Concerning Marriage, Being Two Indices by Emanuel Swedenborg to His Missing Draft on Marriage, Arranged in the Order of the Paragraph Numbers.* Translated and edited by Alfred Acton. Bryn Athyn, Pa.: Academy of the New Church.

————. [1744–1745] 1960. *The Animal Kingdom, Considered Anatomically, Physically, and Philosophically.* 2 vols. Translated by James John Garth Wilkinson. [Bryn Athyn, Pa.]: Swedenborg Scientific Association. First edition of this translation: 1843–1844, London: W. Newbery.

————. 1962a. *Scripture Confirmations of New Church Doctrine* (Dicta Probantia): *Being Proof Passages from the Scriptures, from the Latin of Emanuel Swedenborg, Servant of the Lord Jesus Christ.* Translated by John Whitehead. London: Swedenborg Society.

————. 1962b. *The Spiritual Diary.* Translated by W. H. Acton, A. W. Acton, and F. F. Coulson. London: Swedenborg Society. Only the first of five projected volumes has been completed.

————. [1734] 1965. *Forerunner of a Reasoned Philosophy Concerning the Infinite, the Final Cause of Creation; Also the Mechanism of the Operation of the Soul and Body.* 3rd ed. Translated by James John Garth Wilkinson, with an introduction by Lewis F. Hite. London: Swedenborg Society. Revision of the 1847 edition, London: William Newbery.

————. 1966. *Emanuelis Swedenborgii Varia in Mineralogia, Anatomia, Chymia, Psychologia, Pathologia, etc.* Typescript. Edited by Beryl G. Briscoe. Bryn Athyn, Pa.: [Academy of the New Church].

————. [1709] 1967. *Selected Sentences from L. Annaeus Seneca and Publius [Publilius] Syrus the Mime.* Translated by Alfred Acton, revised and edited by Beryl Briscoe. Bryn Athyn, Pa.: Swedenborg Scientific Association.

————. [1758] 1971. *Om himlen og dens undere og om helvede.* 3rd ed. Revised by Gudmund Boolsen. London: Swedenborg Society.

————. 1975a. *Ecclesiastical History of the New Church.* In *Small Theological Works and Letters of Emanuel Swedenborg,* translated and edited by John E. Elliot. London: Swedenborg Society.

————. 1975b. *The Formula of Concord.* In *Small Theological Works and Letters of Emanuel Swedenborg,* translated and edited by John E. Elliott. London: Swedenborg Society.

————. 1975c. *On Marriage I.* In *Small Theological Works and Letters of Emanuel Swedenborg,* translated and edited by John E. Elliott. London: Swedenborg Society.

————. [1771] 1975d. *Reply to Dr. Ernesti.* In *Small Theological Works and Letters of Emanuel Swedenborg,* translated and edited by John E. Elliott. London: Swedenborg Society.

————. 1975e. *Small Theological Works and Letters of Emanuel Swedenborg.* Translated and edited by John E. Elliott. London: Swedenborg Society.

————. 1976a. *The Economy of the Animal Kingdom, Considered Anatomically, Physically, and Philosophically, Transaction III.* Translated by Alfred Acton. Bryn Athyn, Pa.: Swedenborg Scientific Association. First edition: 1918, Philadelphia: Swedenborg Scientific Association.

————. 1976b. *The Five Senses.* Translated by Enoch S. Price. Bryn Athyn, Pa.: Swedenborg Scientific Association. First edition of this translation: 1914, Philadelphia: Swedenborg Scientific Association.

————. [1722] 1976c. *Miscellaneous Observations Connected with the Physical Sciences.* Translated by Charles E. Strutt. Bryn Athyn, Pa.: Swedenborg Scientific Association. First edition of this translation: 1847, London: William Newbery.

————. [1717] 1976d. *On Tremulation.* Translated by Carl Th. Odhner. Bryn Athyn, Pa.: Swedenborg Scientific Association. First edition of this translation: 1899, Boston: Massachusetts New-Church Union.

————. 1976e. *A Philosopher's Note Book.* Translated by Alfred Acton. Bryn Athyn, Pa.: Swedenborg Scientific Association. First edition: 1931, Philadelphia: Swedenborg Scientific Association.

————. [1721] 1976f. *Some Specimens of a Work on the Principles of Chemistry.* Translated by Charles Edward Strutt. Bryn Athyn, Pa.: Swedenborg Scientific Association. First edition of this translation: 1847, London: William Newbery, and Boston: Otis Clapp.

————. 1976g. *Three Transactions on the Cerebrum.* 2 vols. Translated by Alfred Acton. Bryn Athyn, Pa.: Swedenborg Scientific Association. First edition: 1938, Philadelphia: Swedenborg Scientific Association.

————. [1758] 1978a. *Om klodene i vort solsystem, som kaldes planeter.* Translated by Gudmund Boolsen. Copenhagen: Nykirkeligt Tidsskrift.

———. 1978b. *The Spiritual Diary.* 5 vols. Translated by George Bush, John H. Smithson, and James F. Buss. New York: Swedenborg Foundation. First edition of this translation: 1889–1902, London: J. Speirs.

———. 1978c. *The Spiritual Diary of Emanuel Swedenborg.* Vol. 4, pages 91–494, and vol. 5. Translated by James F. Buss. New York: Swedenborg Foundation. First edition: 1889, London: J. Speirs.

———. 1983–1992. "On Common Salt." Translated by Michael V. David and J. Durban Odhner. *The New Philosophy* 86:150–165; 87:397–411; 88:542–554, 595–606; 90:256–280; 91:650–653, 698–701; 92:47–49, 94–97; 94:599–637; 95:133–151.

———. 1983–1995. *Den åndelige dagbog.* 8 vols. Translated by Gudmund Boolsen. Copenhagen: Nykirkeligt Tidsskrift.

———. 1983–1997. *Experientiae Spirituales.* 6 vols. Edited by J. Durban Odhner. Bryn Athyn, Pa.: Academy of the New Church.

———. [1749–1756] 1983–1999. *Arcana Caelestia.* Translated by John Elliott. London: Swedenborg Society.

———. 1984a. *Emanuel Swedenborg: The Universal Human and Soul-Body Interaction.* Translated by George F. Dole. New York: Paulist Press.

———. 1984b. "Hieroglyphic Key to Spiritual and Natural Arcana." In *Psychological Transactions and Other Posthumous Tracts 1734–1744.* Translated by Alfred Acton. 2nd ed. Bryn Athyn, Pa.: Swedenborg Scientific Association.

———. 1984c. *Psychological Transactions and Other Posthumous Tracts 1734–1744.* Translated by Alfred Acton. 2nd ed. Bryn Athyn, Pa.: Swedenborg Scientific Association.

———. [1714 or 1715] 1985. *Festivus Applausus in Caroli XII in Pomeraniam Suam Adventum.* Translated and edited by Hans Helander. Uppsala: University of Uppsala.

———. [1722] 1987. "Modest Thoughts on the Deflation and Inflation of Swedish Coinage." Translated by Bjorn Boyeson and Alfred Acton and edited by George F. Dole. *Studia Swedenborgiana* 6(2):5–21.

———. [1715] 1988a. *Camena Borea.* Translated and edited by Hans Helander. Uppsala: University of Uppsala.

———. [1734] 1988b. *The Principia; or, The First Principles of Natural Things.* 2 vols. Translated by Augustus Clissold. Bryn Athyn, Pa.: Swedenborg Scientific Association. First edition of this translation: 1846, London: W. Newbery.

———. [1771] 1988c. *True Christian Religion.* Translated by John Chadwick. London: Swedenborg Society.

———. [1758] 1990. *The New Jerusalem and Heaven's Teaching for It.* Translated by John Chadwick. London: Swedenborg Society.

———. [1719] 1992a. *Height of Water.* Translated by Joseph E. Rosenquist. In *Scientific and Philosophical Treatises,* edited by Alfred H. Stroh. 2nd edition edited and rearranged by William Ross Woofenden. Bryn Athyn, Pa.: Swedenborg Scientific Association.

———. [1758] 1992b. *The Last Judgment.* Translated by John Chadwick. London: Swedenborg Society.

———. 1994–1997a. *Apocalypse Explained.* 6 vols. Translated by John C. Ager, revised by John Whitehead, and edited by William Ross Woofenden. West Chester, Pa.: Swedenborg Foundation.

———. 1994–1997b. *The Athanasian Creed.* Translated by Samuel Worcester, revised by John C. Ager, and edited by William Ross Woofenden. In vol. 6 of *Apocalypse*

Explained, translated by John C. Ager, revised by John Whitehead, and edited by William Ross Woofenden. West Chester, Pa.: Swedenborg Foundation.

———. 1994–1997c. *Concerning the Lord and Concerning the Holy Spirit.* Translated by Samuel Worcester, revised by John C. Ager, and edited by William Ross Woofenden. In vol. 6 of *Apocalypse Explained,* translated by John C. Ager, revised by John Whitehead, and edited by William Ross Woofenden. West Chester, Pa.: Swedenborg Foundation.

———. 1995a. *Charity: The Practice of Neighborliness.* 2nd ed. Translated by William F. Wunsch and edited by William Ross Woofenden. West Chester, Pa.: Swedenborg Foundation. First edition: 1931, Philadelphia: J. B. Lippincott.

———. [1707–1740] 1995b. *Ludus Heliconius and Other Latin Poems.* Translated and edited by Hans Helander. Uppsala: University of Uppsala.

———. [1758] 1995c. *Om dommedag og om det ødelagte Babylon.* Translated by Gudmund Boolsen. Copenhagen: Nykirkeligt Tidsskrift.

———. [1768] 1995d. *Visdommens glæder om den aegteskabelige kaerlighed.* Translated by Gudmund Boolsen. Copenhagen: Nykirkeligt Tidsskrift.

———. 1996a. *Additions to True Christian Religion.* In vol. 1 of *Posthumous Theological Works,* translated by John Whitehead and edited by William Ross Woofenden. West Chester, Pa.: Swedenborg Foundation.

———. [1769] 1996b. *Answer to a Letter Written to Me by a Friend.* In vol. 1 of *Posthumous Theological Works,* translated by John Whitehead and edited by William Ross Woofenden. West Chester, Pa.: Swedenborg Foundation.

———. 1996c. *Answers to Three Questions.* In vol. 2 of *Posthumous Theological Works,* translated by John Whitehead and edited by William Ross Woofenden. West Chester, Pa.: Swedenborg Foundation.

———. 1996d. *Appendix to "The White Horse."* In *Miscellaneous Theological Works,* translated by John Whitehead and edited by William Ross Woofenden. West Chester, Pa.: Swedenborg Foundation.

———. 1996e. *Argument Concerning Judgment.* In vol. 1 of *Posthumous Theological Works,* translated by John Whitehead and edited by William Ross Woofenden. West Chester, Pa.: Swedenborg Foundation.

———. 1996f. *Concerning the Sacred Scripture or the Word of the Lord from Experience.* In vol. 1 of *Posthumous Theological Works,* translated by John Whitehead and edited by William Ross Woofenden. West Chester, Pa.: Swedenborg Foundation.

———. [1768] 1996g. *Conjugial Love.* Translated by John Chadwick. London: Swedenborg Society.

———. 1996h. *The Consummation of the Age, the Lord's Second Coming, and the New Church.* In vol. 1 of *Posthumous Theological Works,* translated by John Whitehead and edited by William Ross Woofenden. West Chester, Pa.: Swedenborg Foundation.

———. 1996i. *A Conversation with Calvin and Fifty of His Followers Concerning the Athanasian Creed.* In vol. 2 of *Posthumous Theological Works,* translated by John Whitehead and edited by William Ross Woofenden. West Chester, Pa.: Swedenborg Foundation.

———. 1996j. *Coronis or Appendix to "True Christian Religion."* In vol. 1 of *Posthumous Theological Works,* translated by John Whitehead and edited by William Ross Woofenden. West Chester, Pa.: Swedenborg Foundation.

————. 1996k. *God the Savior, Jesus Christ.* In vol. 2 of *Posthumous Theological Works,* translated by John Whitehead and edited by William Ross Woofenden. West Chester, Pa.: Swedenborg Foundation.

————. 1996l. *Indexes to the "Missing Treatise"* Angelic Wisdom concerning Marriage. In vol. 2 of *Posthumous Theological Works,* translated by John Whitehead and edited by William Ross Woofenden. West Chester, Pa.: Swedenborg Foundation.

————. 1996m. *Invitation to the New Church.* In vol. 1 of *Posthumous Theological Works,* translated by John Whitehead and edited by William Ross Woofenden. West Chester, Pa.: Swedenborg Foundation.

————. 1996n. *Justification and Good Works.* In vol. 2 of *Posthumous Theological Works,* translated by John Whitehead and edited by William Ross Woofenden. West Chester, Pa.: Swedenborg Foundation.

————. 1996o. *Last Judgment (Posthumous) [and the Spiritual World].* In vol. 1 of *Posthumous Theological Works,* translated by John Whitehead and edited by William Ross Woofenden. West Chester, Pa.: Swedenborg Foundation.

————. 1996p. *On Marriage* (De Conjugio). In vol. 2 of *Posthumous Theological Works,* translated by John Whitehead and edited by William Ross Woofenden. West Chester, Pa.: Swedenborg Foundation.

————. 1996q. *Miscellaneous Theological Works.* Translated by John Whitehead and edited by William Ross Woofenden. West Chester, Pa.: Swedenborg Foundation.

————. [1770] 1996r. *The Natural and Spiritual Sense of the Word.* In vol. 2 of *Posthumous Theological Works,* translated by John Whitehead and edited by William Ross Woofenden. West Chester, Pa.: Swedenborg Foundation.

————. 1996s. *Posthumous Theological Works.* 2 vols. Translated by John Whitehead and edited by William Ross Woofenden. West Chester, Pa.: Swedenborg Foundation.

————. 1996t. *The Precepts of the Decalogue.* In vol. 1 of *Posthumous Theological Works,* translated by John Whitehead and edited by William Ross Woofenden. West Chester, Pa.: Swedenborg Foundation.

————. 1996u. *Scripture Confirmations of New Church Doctrine.* In vol. 2 of *Posthumous Theological Works,* translated by John Whitehead and edited by William Ross Woofenden. West Chester, Pa.: Swedenborg Foundation.

————. 1996v. *Specimen and Sketch of the Doctrine of the New Church in a Summary.* In vol. 2 of *Posthumous Theological Works,* translated by John Whitehead and edited by William Ross Woofenden. West Chester, Pa.: Swedenborg Foundation.

————. 1996w. *Summaries of the Internal Sense of the Prophetical Books, the Psalms of David, and the Historical Parts of the Word.* In vol. 2 of *Posthumous Theological Works,* translated by John Whitehead and edited by William Ross Woofenden. West Chester, Pa.: Swedenborg Foundation.

————. 1996x. *The Worship and Love of God.* Translated by Alfred H. Stroh and Frank Sewall. West Chester, Pa., and London: Swedenborg Foundation and Swedenborg Society. First edition: 1914, Boston: Massachusetts New-Church Union.

————. 1997a. *Apocalypse Revealed.* 2 vols. Translated by John Whitehead. West Chester, Pa.: Swedenborg Foundation. First edition: 1912, New York: American Swedenborg Printing and Publishing Society.

———. 1997b. *Nine Questions.* In *Four Doctrines, with the Nine Questions,* translated by John Faulkner Potts and edited by William Ross Woofenden. West Chester, Pa.: Swedenborg Foundation.

———. 1997c. *Three Short Works.* Translated by N. Bruce Rogers. Bryn Athyn, Pa.: General Church of the New Jerusalem.

———. [1758] 1997d. *The Worlds in Space.* Translated by John Chadwick. London: Swedenborg Society.

———. [1763] 1998a. *Englenes visdom om den guddommelig kaerlighed og den guddommelige visdom.* Translated by Gudmund Boolsen. Copenhagen: Nykirkeligt Tidsskrift.

———. [1763] 1998b. *Laeren om livet og Laeren om troen.* Translated by Gudmund Boolsen. Copenhagen: Nykirkeligt Tidsskrift.

———. 1998–2002. *Emanuel Swedenborg's Diary, Recounting Spiritual Experiences during the Years 1745 to 1765.* 3 vols. Translated by J. Durban Odhner. Bryn Athyn, Pa.: General Church of the New Jerusalem. The first three volumes, in English, of the six volumes of Swedenborg's Latin work *Experientiae Spirituales,* edited by J. Durban Odhner (Bryn Athyn, Pa.: Academy of the New Church, 1983–1997). Further volumes forthcoming.

———. 2001a. *Rational Psychology.* Translated by Norbert H. Rogers and Alfred Acton. Bryn Athyn, Pa.: Swedenborg Scientific Association. Revision of 1950 edition, Philadelphia: Swedenborg Scientific Association.

———. 2001b. *Swedenborg's Dream Diary.* Edited by Lars Bergquist and translated by Anders Hallengren. West Chester, Pa.: Swedenborg Foundation.

———. 2003. *Angelic Wisdom about Divine Love and about Divine Wisdom.* Translated by George F. Dole. West Chester, Pa.: Swedenborg Foundation.

———. 2004. *Arcana Coelestia Indexes.* Edited by John Elliott. London: Swedenborg Society.

"The Swedenborgian Church—Statistics as of December 31, 1999." 2000. *Journal of the Swedenborgian Church* 178:116.

Szymanis, Eligiusz. 1992. *Adam Mickiewicz Kreacja Autolegendy.* Wrocław, Warsaw, and Cracow: Zakład Narodowy im. Ossolińskich—Wydawnictwo Polskiej Akademii Nauk.

Tafel, J. F. Immanuel. 1845. Letter to Kramph, May 4. Archives of the Academy of the New Church, Bryn Athyn, Pa.

———. 1847. Transcript of a letter to the Central Convention of the New Church in America, August 20. Archives of the Academy of the New Church, Bryn Athyn, Pa.

Tafel, R. L. 1875. *Documents Concerning the Life and Character of Emanuel Swedenborg.* Vol. 1. London: Swedenborg Society.

———. 1877. *Documents Concerning the Life and Character of Emanuel Swedenborg.* Vol. 2, parts 1 and 2. London: Swedenborg Society.

———. 1890. *Index Verborum, Nominum, et Rerum in "Arcanis Coelestibus."* London: Swedenborg Society.

Talbot, Michael. 1988. "The Holographic Paradigm." In *Emanuel Swedenborg: A Continuing Vision,* edited by Robin Larsen and others. New York: Swedenborg Foundation.

Taylor, Eugene. 1988. "The Appearance of Swedenborg in the History of American Psychology." In *Swedenborg and His Influence,* edited by Erland J. Brock and others. Bryn Athyn, Pa.: Academy of the New Church.

———. 1995. "Swedenborgianism." In *America's Alternative Religions,* edited by Timothy Miller. Albany, N.Y.: State University of New York Press.

Taylor, Joshua C. 1957. *William Page: The American Titian.* Chicago: University of Chicago Press.

Tegnér, Esajas. [1827] 1921. Letter to C. G. von Brinkman, March 27. In vol. 5 of *Samlade Skrifter.* Stockholm: Norstedt.

The Temperance Advocate and Journal of the Times. 1832–1835. West Chester, Pa.: Simeon Siegfried.

The Temple of Truth, or A Vindication of Various Passages and Doctrines of the Holy Scriptures [by John Hargrove]. 1801 (vols. 1–13). Baltimore: Warner & Hanna.

Tessin, Carl Gustaf. 1760. Academy Collection of Swedenborg Documents. Vol. 6, no. 793.12. Swedenborg Library, Academy of the New Church, Bryn Athyn, Pa.

Theological Dictionary of the Old Testament. 1986. Edited by G. Johannes Botterweck and Helmer Ringgren, translated by John T. Willis. Vol. 5. Grand Rapids, Mich.: William B. Eerdmans.

Thoreau, Henry David. 1854. *Walden, or Life in the Woods.* Boston: Ticknor and Fields.

Thorild, Thomas. 1790. *True Heavenly Religion Restored.* London. To be reprinted in Thomas Thorild, *Samlada Skrifter,* edited by Stellan Arvidson, Stockholm: Svenska Vitterhetssamf, forthcoming.

Thurman, Robert A., trans. 1994. *The Tibetan Book of the Dead.* New York: Bantam Doubleday Dell.

Ticknor, Caroline. 1969. *Hawthorne and His Publisher.* Port Washington, N.Y.: Kennikat Press. First edition: 1913, Boston: Houghton Mifflin.

Treuherz, Francis. 2001. "The Origins of Kent's Homeopathy: The Influence of Swedenborg." *Arcana* 2001 6(1):10–38. Reprinted from *Journal of the American Institute of Homeopathy* 77:130–149.

Trobridge, George. 1992. *Swedenborg: Life and Teaching.* 5th ed. Revised by Richard H. Tafel, Sr., and Richard H. Tafel, Jr. New York: Swedenborg Foundation.

Troeltsch, Ernst. 1960. *Social Teaching of the Christian Churches.* 2 vols. Translated by Olive Wyon. New York: Harper & Row.

Tucker, Louis Leonard. 1967. "Hiram Powers and Cincinnati." *Bulletin of the Cincinnati Historical Society* 25:21–49.

Tyler, Alice Felt. 1962. *Freedom's Ferment: Phases of American Social History from the Colonial Period to the Outbreak of the Civil War.* New York: Harper Torchbooks.

van der Hooght, Everardus. 1740. *Biblia Hebraica secundum Editionem Belgicam Everardi van der Hooght, Collatis Aliis Bonae Notae Codicibus, Una cum Versione Latina Sebastiani Schmidii.* Leipzig: Wolfgang Deer.

Van Dusen, Wilson. 1975. "Another Key to Swedenborg's Development." *New Church Life* 95:316–319.

———. 1992. "Uses: A Way of Personal and Spiritual Growth." In *The Country of Spirit: Selected Writings.* San Francisco and Boston: J. Appleseed.

———. 1994. "Saint Emanuel Swedenborg." *The Messenger* 215:148–150.

———. 1999. *Beauty, Wonder, and the Mystical Mind.* West Chester, Pa.: Swedenborg Foundation.

———. 2004. *The Presence of Other Worlds: The Psychological/Spiritual Findings of Emanuel Swedenborg.* 2nd ed. West Chester, Pa.: Swedenborg Foundation. First edition: 1974, New York: Harper & Row.

Van Dyke, Henry. 1924. "Address Delivered at a Memorial Meeting before the Century Association, New York, March 9, 1912." In *The Mystery of Sleep*, by John Bigelow. New York: New-Church Press.

Viatte, Auguste. 1931. "Les Swedenborgiens en France de 1820 à 1830." *Revue de Littérature comparée* 11:417–450.

———. 1969. *Les Sources occultes du Romantisme: Illuminisme-Théosophie, 1770–1820.* Vol. 1. Paris: Librairie Honoré Champion.

von Beskow, Bernhard. 1860. *Minne öfver assessoren i Bergskollegium Emanuel Swedenborg.* Stockholm: P. A. Norstedt & Söner.

[W.B.H.]. 1848. "A Few Words about Shakerism and the Shakers." *New Church Repository and Monthly Review* 1:573–578.

Wadström, Carl Bernhard. 1790. "Letter I" and "Letter II." *New-Jerusalem Magazine* 1:70–73, 126–132.

Wainscot, A. Stanley, comp. 1967. *List of Additions to the Bibliography [of the Works of Emanuel Swedenborg, Original and Translated, by the Rev. James Hyde] Since Its Publication in 1906.* London: [Swedenborg Society]. Mimeographed.

Wallin, Johan Olof. 1819. *Psalmbok.* Stockholm: Olof Grahn.

"Waltham School to Observe Centennial." 1960. *New-Church Messenger* 180:175.

[Wayfarers]. 1974. *The Messenger* 194:98–112.

Weinlick, John R. 1984. *Count Zinzendorf: The Story of His Life and Leadership in the Renewed Moravian Church.* Bethlehem, Pa.: The Moravian Church in America.

Weintraub, Wiktor. 1954. *The Poetry of Adam Mickiewicz.* The Hague: Mouton.

Weisenberger, Francis P. [1950]. *A Brief History of Urbana University.* Urbana, Ohio: Urbana College.

Wetterbergh, Carl Anton. 1848. *Altartaflan.* N.p.

Wheaton, Ola-Mae, and Margaret W. Briggs. 1980. *O Jerusalem: A New Church on Earth, A New Church in Fryeburg.* Fryeburg, Maine: Church of the New Jerusalem.

White, Helen C. 1964. *The Mysticism of William Blake.* New York: Russell & Russell. First edition: 1927, University of Wisconsin Studies in Language and Literature 23, Madison: University of Wisconsin.

Whitehead, John. 1914. "A Brief Bibliography of Swedenborg's Works." In vol. 2 of *Posthumous Theological Works of Emanuel Swedenborg.* New York: Swedenborg Foundation.

Whitman, B. M. 1922. "Lynn Neighborhood House." *New-Church Messenger* 123:116.

Whitman, Walt. 1921. *The Uncollected Poetry and Prose of Walt Whitman.* Edited by Emory Holloway. Garden City, N.Y.: Doubleday.

Whitmont, Edward C. 1988. "Homeopathy and Archetypal Meaning." In *Emanuel Swedenborg: A Continuing Vision,* edited by Robin Larsen and others. New York: Swedenborg Foundation.

Wilkinson, Clement John. 1911. *James John Garth Wilkinson: A Memoir of His Life, with a Selection from His Letters.* London: Kegan Paul, Trench, & Trubner.

Wilkinson, James John Garth. 1849. *Emanuel Swedenborg: A Biography.* London: W. Newbery.

———. 1857. *Improvisations from the Spirit.* London: William White; Manchester: Dunnill and Palmer.

[Williams, Rudolph]. 1906. *The New Church and Chicago: A History.* Chicago: Western New-Church Union.

Williams-Hogan, Jane. 1985. *A New Church in a Disenchanted World: A Study of the Formation and Development of the General Conference of the New Church in Great Britain.* Dissertation, University of Pennsylvania, Philadelphia.

———. 1997. "Moving Beyond Weber's Concept of Charisma: The Role of Written Text in the Founding of the Swedenborgian Church." Paper presented at the Swedenborg Seminar of the annual meeting of the American Academy of Religion, San Francisco, Ca.

———. 2003. "Field Notes: The Swedenborgian Church in South Africa." *Novo Religio* 7:90–97.

———. Forthcoming. "Charisma of the Book: Weber's Concept Modernized."

Wirmark, Margareta. 1999. "Det går an—en sju dagar lång skapelseakt." *Väldarnas möte: Nya Kyrkans tidning* 4–5:27–34.

Woofenden, William Ross. 1974. "Period of Transition in Swedenborg's Life." *Studia Swedenborgiana* 1(1):3–10.

———. 1988. *Swedenborg Researcher's Manual: A Research Reference Manual for Writers of Academic Dissertations, and for Other Scholars.* Bryn Athyn, Pa.: Swedenborg Scientific Association.

———. 2002. *Swedenborg Explorer's Guidebook: A Research Manual for Inquiring New Readers, Seekers of Spiritual Ideas, and Writers of Swedenborgian Treatises.* 2nd ed. (of Woofenden 1988). West Chester, Pa.: Swedenborg Foundation.

Worcester, J. R. 1923. "Waltham History." *New-Church Messenger* 124:139–140.

Worcester, John. 1987. *Physiological Correspondences.* Bryn Athyn, Pa.: Swedenborg Scientific Association. First edition: 1889, Boston: Massachusetts New-Church Union.

Worcester, Samuel. 1843. "No. XXXIV. Letter from S. W. to D. L. Boston, February 25th, 1822." *The Newchurchman-Extra* 1:105–108.

Worden, Ethelwyn. 1988. "The Influence of Swedenborg on the Music of Richard Yardumian." In *Emanuel Swedenborg: A Continuing Vision,* edited by Robin Larsen and others. New York: Swedenborg Foundation.

Wörner, Karl H., and Friedemann Horn. 1994. "Von Swedenborg über Balzac zu Schönberg." *Offene Tore* 38:239–248.

Wunder, Richard P. 1991. *Hiram Powers: Vermont Sculptor, 1805–1873.* Newark, Del.: University of Delaware Press. First edition: 1974, Taftville, Vt.: Countryman Press.

Yardumian, Richard. [n.d]. "Essay on the Musical Idiom, Style, and Method of Composition of Richard Yardumian." Unpublished manuscript.

Yardumian, Ruth. 1986. Paper presented at the New Church Music Festival, Bryn Athyn, Pa.

Yeats, William Butler. 1954. *The Letters of W. B. Yeats.* Edited by Allan Wade. London: R. Hart-Davis.

———. n.d. "The Works of William Blake." Unpublished manuscript. University of Reading Library.

Young, Frederic H. 1951. *The Philosophy of Henry James, Sr.* New York: Bookman Associates.

Zwink, Eberhard. 1988. "Johann Gottlieb Mittnacht and Gustav Werner: Forms of Open and Hidden Swedenborgianism in 19th-Century German Southwest." In *Swedenborg and His Influence,* edited by Erland J. Brock and others. Bryn Athyn, Pa.: The Academy of the New Church.

———. 1993. "Die Neue Kirche im deutschsprachigen Südwesten des 19. Jahrhunderts." *Forum Freies Christentum: Arbeitstexte des Bundes für Freies Christentum* 26.

Index

Readers using this index should be aware that the annotated bibliography of Swedenborg's works in this volume has its own separate index on pages 394–402. A brief list of Swedenborg's theological works can be found on page 98 above. A list of New Church (Swedenborgian) societies in the United States and Canada during the period 1790–2003 can be found on pages 311–316; the listings on those pages are not further referenced in the index below.

For the sake of simplicity this index occasionally employs the current title "the Swedenborgian Church of North America" in references to the Swedenborgian church organization formerly known as "the General Convention of the New Jerusalem," despite the anachronism that obtains in some historical contexts. The term "new church" appears in two forms: in lowercase, in which it refers to the general theological concept advanced by Swedenborg (see pages 70–71 above); and in uppercase, in which it refers to the church organizations developed by adherents of Swedenborg's theology.

Monogamy, 80
   spiritual, restoration of in the new church, 71
     note 45
Monophysite Syrian Orthodox Church, 296
Moody, Raymond, 253
Mooki, David W., 254, 319, 321–324, 326, 328
Mooki, Obed S. D., 324–325, 328
Morals
   Marriage Love a work on, 110–111
   training in, 39
Moravian Brethren, 20, 22, 287 note 76
Moses, "books of," 67 note 32. *See also* The Pentateuch
"Mother" Ann Lee, 226 and note 80
Mouravieff, Alexander, 186–187
Müllensiefen, Peter Eberhard, 177, 178
Music. *See also* "Universal musical instrument"
   work of composer Richard Yardumian, 358
Mussey, Ellen Spencer, 275 and note 59
   on forging links for community, 359–360
Mussey, Reuben Delavan, 275–276, 359
My Religion, 240, 253 and note 16
Mysteries, revealed by Swedenborg, 97 note 97
The mystic sense, of Helen Keller, 367–368
Mystical experiences, 22–24
   associated with breath regulation, 6
Mystical ways of knowing, in Blake and Yeats, 368–372
Mysticism
   in the Swedenborgian tradition, 154
   utility of, 371
Mythological allusions, in Swedenborg's earliest works, 91

N
Napoleon, 181
National Council of Churches, 304–305
Nature, a "representative theater" of the spiritual world, 158
Nature, Addresses, and Lectures, 209
Nature and spirit, in Worcester, Reed, Emerson, and Whitman, 342–345
Neo-Latin, 7 note 8
   contemporary scholarship in, 92 and notes 89 and 90
   and Swedenborg's earlier writings, 90–91
Nerval, Gérard de, 183
Nerve fascicles, truths have a structure like, 95
The Netherlands, 17, 20, 42, 131
   censorship in, 96
The New Age and Its Messenger, 235
New Age movement, 77, 236
New Attempts at Explaining the Texts for Sundays and Holidays, 44
New church, era referred to by Swedenborg, 41, 70–71, 168 note 2, 246 note 2. *See also* New Church
   affiliation and communion with heaven, 71 note 45

doctrine of, 40
   possibility of revealed, 33
   Swedenborg's invitation to, 48
   Swedenborg's prediction regarding, 71 note 44
New Church, organization established by readers of Swedenborg, 202. *See also* New church
   formation of, in Great Britain by separatists, 257–258
   havoc wreaked by spiritualism within, 221
   terminology for, 248
New Church College, 263 note 38
New Church in Africa, 317–335
   in Nigeria, 329–334
   in South Africa, 319–329
New Church in America, 265–294
   early societies, 265–271
   ethnic churches, 274–277
   the West and Canada, 271–274
New Church in Southern Africa, 254, 328–329
New Church Life, 233, 288
New Church Review, 217
New Church societies in the United States and Canada, 1790–2003, 311–316
   the General Church of the New Jerusalem, 315–316
   the Lord's New Church Which Is Nova Hierosolyma, 316
   the Swedenborgian Church of North America, 311–315
New Church Theological School, 240 note 114, 276, 301
"New Era movement," 269
New Harmony, Indiana, 227
New Jerusalem, doctrine of, 40, 71
New Jerusalem, 32, 105, 114, 133
   Italian translation of, 184
   on the sacraments, 75 note 52
   Spanish translation of, 185
New Jerusalem Church. *See* General Church of the New Jerusalem; General Convention of the New Jerusalem; New Church
New Jerusalem Free School, London, 297
New Jerusalem Magazine, 220, 231, 281, 343
New Jerusalem Messenger, 184
The New Philosophy, 306
New South Wales, Australia, Swedenborg Library and Inquiry Center in, 392
New Thought movement, Swedenborg's influence on, 234–236
New York City, 205
   Swedenborgian Church of North America in, 268–269, 277, 280
New York Evening Post, 214, 357 note 23
New York Tribune, 228
The New-Jerusalem Missionary, 269
NewSearch, 122 note 14